Aboriginal
Self-Government
in Canada

Aboriginal Self-Government in Canada

Current trends and issues
3rd edition

edited by Yale D. Belanger

Purich Publishing Limited,
Saskatoon, Saskatchewan, Canada

PURICH

Purich Publishing Ltd.
Box 23032, Market Mall Post Office, Saskatoon, SK, Canada, S7J 5H3
Phone: (306) 373-5311 Fax: (306) 373-5315 Email: purich@sasktel.net
Website: www.purichpublishing.com

Library and Archives Canada Cataloguing in Publication

Aboriginal self-government in Canada : current trends and issues / edited by Yale D. Belanger. — 3rd ed.

(Purich's aboriginal issues series)
Previous eds. edited by John H. Hylton.
Includes bibliographical references and index.
ISBN 978-1-895830-32-3

1. Native peoples—Canada—Politics and government.
2. Native peoples—Canada—Government relations.
3. Native peoples—Legal status, laws, etc.—Canada.
1. Belanger, Yale Deron, 1968- II. Series.
E92.A266 2008   323.1197'071   C2008-900416-7

Cover design, book design, and layout by Duncan Campbell.
Editing and index by Ursula Acton.
Printed in Canada by Houghton Boston Printers & Lithographers.

URLS for websites contained in this book are accurate to the time of writing, to the best of the authors' knowledge.

The publishers gratefully acknowledge the assistance of the Government of Canada through the Book Publishing Industry Development Program and the Government of Saskatchewan through the Cultural Industries Development Fund in the production of this book.

This book is printed on 100% post-consumer recycled and ancient forest friendly paper.

CONTENTS

Acknowledgements

A RARE OPPORTUNITY

I t is rare for any editor to adopt a successful series such as that developed by John Hylton, and his winning model made this project a joy to pursue. This book is the third edition of a series initiated by John back in 1994, and its continued success owes much to his painstaking efforts to elaborate upon the academic and practical aspects of Aboriginal self-government. I would also like to thank John personally for his support and expressed confidence upon being informed of my editorial appointment for this book.

I am equally grateful for the assistance and support I have once again received from Don Purich and Karen Bolstad. Thank you for recruiting me as editor and for providing the resources needed to keep the second edition in print and to reanimate this series for a third volume. Once again, your critical commentary and optimism enabled the completion of this project and your scheduling flexibility will not be soon forgotten. I hope that the book in published form meets all expectations.

I must also thank Ursula Acton for her meticulous copy-editing and fine suggestions which improved the text in several places. The assistance of Natasha Fairweather and Maria Berlando, in particular their efforts reformatting citations and resolving several critical copy-editing issues, cannot be overstated. This compilation could not have been completed without a study leave granted by the University of Lethbridge. I also owe gratitude to the 31 authors whose contributions appear in this book for their fine work and, above all else, their patience with a neophyte editor who at times missed the occasional procedural step in his excitement to put this project to bed. I do hope that we will work together in the future.

Finally, special thanks to Tammie-Jai who has remained incredibly supportive of my work. During the time period devoted to this project she managed to not only curb my frustrations by her constant encouragement, she also successfully completed her own graduate studies in accounting while taking on a new and demanding career. Through this process she has remained a source of inspiration, and her encouragement and support enabled the completion of this work. I am grateful to have her in my life.

Yale Belanger
January 2008
Lethbridge, Alberta

Foreword

Aboriginal Self-Government in Canada, 3rd Edition:
FROM THEORY TO PRACTICE TO BEST PRACTICES

So much appears in popular media about the social ills experienced by Aboriginal people that it is all too easy for many Canadians to lose sight of the pathways to a better future. At the same time, for Aboriginal people who frequently confront these social ills first hand, slow progress in addressing even the most basic community concerns often leads to frustration and discouragement. When it comes to relations between Aboriginal peoples and Canadian governments, time and again the reality has been: "one step forward—two steps back." Generally, there has been far more attention paid to the failures of Aboriginal policy than to the successes Aboriginal people have achieved.

Aboriginal people have a vision of a better future. It is a vision of self-reliance, independence, and self-determination. Aboriginal people want to live together with other Canadians as equals, enjoying the gifts of the Creator. Aboriginal people also seek a Canada where differences in languages and cultures are celebrated and where rights are respected. This is a future that all Canadians should heartily embrace, because it is a vision of a more progressive and prosperous Canada.

Realizing a better future depends in no small part on supporting the development of self-governing Aboriginal programs and institutions that are effective, transparent, and accountable. This is the kind of governance that Aboriginal people enjoyed for tens of thousands of years before settlers arrived. However, successive colonial regimes severely disrupted the natural evolution of these governance practices and prevented them from adapting to changing circumstances over time. Instead, foreign systems of control were imposed from the outside—with devastating consequences.

Since the 1970s, modern forms of Aboriginal self-government that are responsive to the contemporary needs and aspirations of Aboriginal people have begun to emerge. These forms of self-government are still in their infancy and they are not without controversy. Much more experience will be required to firmly establish these new arrangements within Canadian society and, in particular, much more experimentation will be needed to determine how these arrangements can best be adjusted and adapted so that they reflect the wide diversity of cultures and circumstances that constitute the Aboriginal reality in Canada. At the same time, as this volume attests, much has been, and is being, accomplished. These success stories mark an exciting new chapter in the history of Aboriginal-Canadian relations.

The publication of the first edition of *Aboriginal Self-Government in Canada* in 1994 was itself an experiment. Spurred on by the groundbreaking work of the Royal Commission on Aboriginal Peoples, it was an early attempt to capture emergent new thinking about self-government. By the time the second edition was published in 1999, it was possible to go far beyond discussions about the meaning of self-government and what it could or should become, to catalogue the emerging practice of self-government, including how self-governing arrangements were taking hold in different sectors and regions across the country.

Remarkably, this third edition demonstrates that experience and expertise are accumulating at such a rapid pace that it is now possible, perhaps for the first time, to meaningfully discuss self-government best practices. Thus, in little more than a decade, scrutiny and commentary have moved from an emphasis on theory to an emphasis on practice to an emphasis on best practices. This is a noteworthy achievement and indicates that self-government is not only being supported, it is becoming self-sustaining.

In many ways, the history of the three editions of *Aboriginal Self-Government in Canada* parallels the history of its chief proponent—Purich Publishing. In the early 1990s there were very few avenues to publish research and thoughtful analyses of important Aboriginal issues. When Don Purich left the Native Law Centre at the University of Saskatchewan, it was with a bold agenda to establish a new Canadian publishing house that would specialize in this emerging new area of systematic study. The first edition of *Aboriginal Self-Government in Canada* was one of Purich's initial projects. Fortunately, it met with considerable success; both the first and second editions were widely acclaimed by scholars and practitioners and they were adopted as standard texts in many undergraduate and graduate university courses throughout Canada and in several other countries. The rest is, as they say, history. As the success of *Aboriginal Self-Government in Canada* combined with numerous other successes, Don and his partner, Karen Bolstad, succeeded in developing an ambitious, credible, and widely recognized publishing program that continues to expand and flourish to this day.

I was delighted to learn that Professor Yale Belanger had accepted Purich Publishing's invitation to prepare a third edition of *Aboriginal Self-Government in Canada*. Professor Belanger is a widely respected researcher and scholar studying Aboriginal issues. In addition to his own considerable expertise, he has assembled an impressive roster of distinguished contributors who together present a detailed and comprehensive analysis of the current issues that self-government practitioners most often face. These include, for example: how the theory of self-government is evolving and how conflicting ideologies are influencing its directions; how different forms and models of self-government are being implemented, including emerging regional and cultural variations; how self-government is being adapted to new circumstances; the practical aspects of implementation, including how obstacles are being overcome; the new challenges to self-government that are now being addressed; and the future prospects for self-government in Canada.

Canada is a wealthy country and Canada's citizens enjoy opportunities that are the envy of the world. Yet the living conditions for Aboriginal people in Canada continue to attract national and international attention because they remain far below the standards that other Canadians have come to expect. This is a serious concern. Health status, educational attainment, crime, the pervasiveness of poverty, participation in the labour force, as well as many other social and economic realities, point to the fact that Aboriginal people are not yet full and equal participants in Canadian society.

Achieving comparable living conditions and offering comparable opportunities so that Aboriginal people can achieve their aspirations is surely the ultimate test of the policies and programs enacted by Canadian and Aboriginal governments.

Self-government is helping to address inequity and Aboriginal aspirations, but the continuing differential in living standards indicates that the promise of Aboriginal self-government is not yet being fully realized. Therefore, a continuing commitment to support self-government will be required. This is not only a concrete and practical strategy for improving conditions for Aboriginal people, it is also an important pathway for Canada in realizing its potential as a fair, just, and equitable society.

John H. Hylton
Ottawa, December 2007

Introduction

From the early 1970s, Aboriginal peoples have been agitating for increased capacities of self-determination. Largely the result of a federal policy initiative colloquially known as the White Paper, the Liberal government faced surprising resistance to what the plan's architects envisioned as a progressive policy essential to improving Native socio-economic conditions across Canada. The policy's tabling acted as a catalyst galvanizing Native leaders to unprecedented levels of political opposition and activism, and led to a subsequent period of organizing calculated to ensure the protection of what were now being described as Aboriginal rights. And so the modern-day self-government movement was born. Over the next three decades, the desire to see Aboriginal self-government acknowledged as an inherent right and operationalized according to traditional political ideologies would be articulated in a series of papers and policy proposals prepared by Aboriginal leaders, their political organizations, and grassroots groups. Add to this mix the growing academic literature to surface since the 1980s and you have a detailed, albeit necessarily incomplete, record of some of the central themes and issues that confronted Aboriginal leaders and public policy makers striving to clarify the essence of Aboriginal self-government.

This difficult and oftentimes contentious process has for the better part of a quarter century dominated several political agendas while advancing incrementally. Most people involved would agree that Aboriginal self-government has developed slowly, at times almost painfully so. Somewhat curiously, despite the impressive attention paid to the concept of self-government, a clear-cut definition eludes us as does transparency concerning self-government's fit with Canada's varied political processes. Nor are we sure how Aboriginal political ideologies will continue to drive self-government's operations once implemented or facilitate its ongoing evolution.[1] From the initial rumblings of discontent found in the Indian Chiefs of Alberta's official response to the White Paper known as the Red Paper, to contemporary critiques characterizing Aboriginal self-government as a restrictive, federally delegated authority, self-government has faced turbulent times. In particular, demonstrated public resistance of the late 1980s to improving collective understanding of what self-government meant to Canada resulted in the Charlottetown Accord's failure by national referendum in 1992. This was a significant political blow and, in the end, undermined major attempts to constitutionally entrench the inherent right of self-government. Current negotiations and several finalized self-government agreements have resulted in the wake of Charlottetown. Even when self-government is realized, as in the case of the Nisga'a in British Columbia in the late 1990s, those battles have been hard won. Of the fact that self-government is an imperfect solution to our myriad political needs there is no doubt. Yet we cannot ignore changes that are arguably traceable to self-government becoming a national policy issue.

A world of difference exists between 1969's tabling of the White Paper and today's political milieu. In the space of approximately one generation, Canada's official policy aimed at terminating the special legal status for Indian people has given way to a policy of recognition of Aboriginal self-government as an inherent right contained within Canada's Constitution. And notwithstanding the popular belief that Canada controls the self-government agenda, we often lose sight of the fact that Aboriginal self-government began in the communities, sparked by leaders seeking to create healthy and stable governments to foster community well being.[2] Many of these ideas continue to inform our understanding of a movement Aboriginal leaders consistently promote as necessary and integrative. Emphasizing the need to work in unison with Canadian officials to strengthen community resolve will reinvigorate traditional governing philosophies, many suggest, leading to political stability, economic development, and capacity-building. Unfortunately, despite the media attention paid to explaining self-government to the general public, the widespread belief that self-government is a separatist movement remains problematic.

So too does the impression of constant change associated with self-government. Specifically, the constant change in how we understand self-government reflects Aboriginal and government response to a continuously changing political environment. The fact that self-government is apt to change is impressive, for it demonstrates that those involved in formulating new models and self-government processes are not above recurrently incorporating new ideas and theories into their work. This is required if self-government is to remain relevant. A brief review of the some significant reports released in the last 25 years demonstrates the diversity of ideas as they relate to self-government and as such the need to remain aware of recent developments in the field and academic writings. Beginning in 1983 with the Penner Report recommending affirmation of the inherent right to Aboriginal self-government, *Denedeh Public Government* and the Union of British Columbia Indian Chiefs' *Aboriginal Title and Rights Position Paper* argue for greater power of self-determination.

Three additional yet often overlooked reports released in 1992 convey a similarly unique Aboriginal perspective concerning the meaning of self-government. The First Peoples Constitutional Review Commission released *Aboriginal Directions for Coexistence in Canada: Native Council of Canada Constitutional Review Commission Working Paper no. 1* in 1992, that sought a renewed Canada-First Nations relationship; and the final report of the National Treaty Conference held that year in Edmonton entitled *Indigenous Treaties and Self-Determination: Past-Present-Future*, demonstrated that Aboriginal consensus on potentially divisive issues could be generated. In particular, those in attendance agreed to pursue the implementation of inherent treaty rights as agreed upon by treaty commissioners and First Nations signatories. It was also agreed that individual First Nations should negotiate with Canada on a nation-to-nation basis to preserve the bilateral nature of the treaty relationship. The Assembly of First Nations (AFN) followed with *First Nations Circle on the Constitution: Commissioners' Report*, which distilled the findings generated at 80 meetings held throughout Canada with elders, youth, women, and off-reserve residents. This grassroots response revealed a deep-seated desire for self-government. Report recommendations ranged from speeding up the existing claims process to establishing cost-sharing agreements to ensuring each agreement made provision for the constitutional protection of the inherent right to self-government.

Finalizing this list is the Royal Commission on Aboriginal Peoples (RCAP), established in 1991 by Prime Minister Brian Mulroney. By the time its findings were published in 1996 it was the most expensive Royal Commission in history, its total cost estimated to be close to $60 million. The final report was unprecedented in terms of the depth of its proposals, including a multiplicity of new arrangements to foster self-government. Suggesting that the right of Aboriginal peoples to govern themselves is recognized in both international and domestic law, the RCAP commissioners stated that the four principles of mutual recognition, mutual respect, sharing, and mutual responsibility helped define "a process that can provide the solutions to many of the difficulties afflicting relations among Aboriginal and non-Aboriginal people." When taken in sequence, it was anticipated that "the four principles form a complete whole, each playing an equal role in developing a balanced societal relationship. Relations that embody these principles are, in the broadest sense of the word, partnerships."[3] Finally, the RCAP envisaged a new Canadian partnership based on mutual recognition in which Aboriginal and non-Aboriginal people would "acknowledge and relate to one another as equals, coexisting side by side and governing themselves according to their own laws and institutions."[4] Embraced by Aboriginal leaders, the RCAP represents the most comprehensive telling of the post-contact experience in Canada, something that troubled many politicians who found some of the conclusions and recommendations problematic. In all, the final report commissioned by the Progressive Conservatives in 1991 to help educate Canadians about Aboriginal issues was, literally upon its release, shelved by the sitting Liberal government.

Their limited impact notwithstanding, this impressive catalogue of reports was and continues to be utilized to better define self-government. Yet there is still considerable discrepancy as to what self-government represents to the various parties involved. Countless Aboriginal leaders equate self-government with self-determination. In support, a growing cadre of academics promote unilateral assertion of sovereignty over people, lands, and resources while others dispute the existence of the inherent right of self-government outright. More recent events suggest that frustration with Canada's lackadaisical approach to advancing the cause of improving community capacity is in part a symptom of Aboriginal dissatisfaction with the unfolding self-government agenda. The recent Kelowna Accord debacle is a case in point. In November 2005, the Liberal government proposed a five-year, $5-billion plan to improve the lives of First Nations, Métis, and Inuit by improving education, housing, economic development, health, and water services. The Accord would compel officials to detail specifically how and where the money would be spent in addition to assigning responsibility for service delivery. Within days the Liberal government fell to Stephen Harper's Conservatives, and despite Harper's obscure claims of support, by January 2006, the proposal was dead. The Accord was, all the same, a double-edged sword. In one sense, the money earmarked for community capacity-building would have improved Aboriginal self-governance in Canada. Perhaps more importantly, however, this episode demonstrates Canada's reluctance to engage Aboriginal leaders as contemporaries; instead, Aboriginal people are considered a population in need of ministering through federally proscribed programming, a process Aboriginal leaders consider antithetical to supporting self-government efforts.

As John Hylton eloquently identified in the second edition of this book, "Ignoring the problems or tinkering with solutions, approaches that have characterized Canadian Aboriginal policy for the past one hundred years, cannot possibly bring about the wholesale changes that are needed to recognize the legitimate aspirations of Aboriginal people to govern their own affairs." Maintaining allegiance to such tried and true approaches will, in Hylton's opinion, only "breed further contempt."[5] What precisely are the obstacles to progress? And once identified, how are they overcome? This volume endeavours to articulate several of these issues and to identify the strategies Aboriginal leaders utilized to overcome these challenges. With that said, I am also in agreement with Hylton, who, in 1999 wrote, "The implementation of Aboriginal self-government should be a national priority. It should be pursued, both through the constitutional process when it again becomes available, and also within the existing constitutional framework," while adding that such an approach would require "an overarching framework for proceeding, as well as a strong commitment from government."[6] The self-government movement is at this point self-sustaining, suggesting that ideas will continue to develop, thereby fostering new and unique approaches to existing and anticipated challenges. The goal is to sustain this momentum while promoting the advancement of Aboriginal self-government, something countless individuals vigorously pursue as evidenced by the reality of self-government.

Continued Interest in Self-Government

What began as a handful of reactionary reports produced in response to the White Paper of 1969 soon took on its own momentum. By the late 1970s, Aboriginal organizations had adopted a leadership role producing the majority of the work related to the fledgling self-government movement. They were also establishing the foundational principles that continue to animate both the practical and ideological aspects of what Aboriginal self-government represents. Native community leaders argued for the development of a contemporary form of self-government that was rooted in traditional philosophies. As the agenda developed, grassroots leaders found themselves overwhelmed by local priorities, and responsibility for pursuing Aboriginal self-government was delegated to many Aboriginal political organizations. Progress was made, so much so that the federal government appropriated the self-government agenda in the early 1980s, ostensibly to control its evolution while squeezing out Aboriginal leaders still interested in guiding its development.[7]

In the 1980s, academic writing about self-government led to scholars probing Aboriginal self-government's varied exigencies. Output increased in the 1990s, a period of numerous self-government agreements adding to the growing literature base. Dissecting these agreements offered new dimensions to the study of self-government, and not only improved Canada-First Nations relations, but also the creation of new dispute-resolution techniques. Further, the agreements themselves offered what could be described as a best practices inventory for those interested in implementing self-government talks with the federal government or further intellectualising the idea. Aboriginal people at that point began "challenging Canada to rationalize its exercise of power over them. In so doing, they are also arguing that this status allows—indeed requires—them to participate in the design of those institutions which exercise political power in Canada."[8]

A tremendous amount of time and effort has been spent examining and critiquing the mechanics of self-government, the rights of Aboriginal women and self-government, policy issues, health and healing, and justice. Additional work highlights the anticipated impact of Aboriginal self-government on federal, provincial, and municipal jurisdictions and at the community level. There has even been a fair amount of comparative literature generated focusing on American and Canadian contexts, although as Jim Frideres points out in chapter six of this volume, little in the way of national comparative self-government examinations have been conducted. The exigencies of Métis self-government have become an increasingly popular academic field, as has evaluating the current Nunavut governance process. Finally, a wealth of material pertaining to self-government available in the RCAP case-study section examines a multitude of issues; it also requires further academic reflection. Over time, federal officials came to acknowledge the role First Nations played in self-government's development and many of the leaders from the 1970s remained proactive in determining what steps were required prior to establishing the structural forms of self-government. Ideas such as federal recognition of Aboriginal self-governing authority, the creation and recognition of rights at the self-governing level, and an economic base were considered not only essential components of self-government; they soon became statements of belief. These ideas drove further research and ways of conceptualising self-government, as did a process of consistently revisiting these ideas.

The need to constantly return and reflect also reaffirmed to Aboriginal leaders that self-government was not only evolving, but that their efforts resulted in the slow integration of Aboriginal knowledge into this vision.[9] This influence led to unique policy frameworks and an ever-evolving self-government concept, something this volume explores.

The Purpose of this Book

Remaining true to the original two volumes expertly crafted by John Hylton, this book seeks to make a practical contribution to the self-government field. As will be seen, it is not about, nor is it possible to provide, a definition of self-government or to supply a definitive analysis of the meaning or merits of self-government. Self-government is a reality in Canada, and the need to develop new self-governing institutions mounts, even if in recent years the regular change in federal governments hobbled by minority status has challenged this momentum. As such, this book seeks to provide a practical guide for students and practitioners who are both interested in designing and implementing self-government arrangements and understanding the evolutionary scope of self-government and its ideological drivers.

The first edition of this book was published in 1994. It contained thirteen chapters. The second edition, published in 1999, contained 21 chapters: 13 new and eight revised. As Hylton highlighted in the second volume, the goal from the beginning was to select materials to provide a holistic, interdisciplinary perspective on self-government. The result: contributions were included "from individuals with quite different perspectives—academics, policy analysts, consultants, and practitioners."[10] This third edition builds on the first two volumes in several important respects. With an emphasis on articulating the evolution of self-government during the past three decades, the current volume provides insight into the continuing challenge of conflicting Aboriginal and Canadian political ideologies. Different forms/models have emerged, and an effort has been made to provide detailed descriptions and analyses of many existing and proposed self-government arrangements. Several chapters were commissioned to further illustrate how the process has evolved in Canada, demonstrating how both regional and cultural variances influence implementation trends while they impact on how self-government is understood.

Similar to the second edition, by demonstrating how self-government is already working, and by pointing out the opportunities that lie ahead, this volume seeks to challenge policy makers determined to fit Aboriginal self-government into federal and provincial governing templates. Self-government is a policy option not only worth supporting, it is an inherent right demanding proper consideration to its design, structure, operations, and, perhaps most important, its ideological foundation. The promise of self-government is found in this common foundation, something that should be probed. As indicated in the previous edition, this volume will succeed if it encourages and emboldens those involved in negotiating and implementing self-government arrangements, and if it helps to promote public acceptance and support of those efforts.

An Overview of the Contents

The four chapters in part I are introductory in nature, and are intended to provide a framework for the discussion of self-government trends and issues presented in parts II, III, and IV. The focus is not definition. Rather, these chapters point out why self-government is a just, appropriate, feasible, and necessary policy direction for Canada.

The general uncertainty surrounding self-government and what it represents to various factions is the focus of chapter one by Native Studies Professors David Newhouse and Yale Belanger. Critically examining what they describe as the Aboriginal self-government ideal, their review of eight reports, starting with the 1966 release of the Hawthorn-Tremblay Report, found thematic consistencies in all of the documents produced by Aboriginal political organizations and grassroots groups in the 1970s. Each report was cumulative in that the best ideas relating to self-determination informed the evolving base of principles that would later be acknowledged as the Native perspective. Striking similarities are evident in how non-Native writers also chose to frame Aboriginal self-government: as a nebulous concept in need of defined operating parameters. The self-government ideal discussed in this chapter is a hybrid, a manifestation of assorted ideas from the Native and non-Native perspectives variously combined to create an ever-shifting, evolutionary formula we identify as the Aboriginal self-government ideal that is neither exclusively Aboriginal nor Canadian in origin or ideology.

In chapter two, Professor James [Sákéj] Youngblood Henderson, Research Director of the University of Saskatchewan's Native Law Centre of Canada and an internationally respected legal scholar, provocatively suggests that modern Aboriginal self-government agreements are little more than neo-colonial policies that tend to overshadow the important fact that Aboriginal governance exists, and that we need to alter the existing paradigm by returning to the treaty-order principles recognizing Aboriginal governance. The treaties with the British Crown represent colonial acknowledgement of the inherent sovereignty of the tribes, their system of law and rights, and their right to choose their destiny and relationships, and their way of life: "It seeks not to be either utopian or trivial by adhering to the existing treaty rights and the proper interpretation of treaties, but is relatively distant from the operational policy of the Canadian governments. It remains the source that enables Treaty First Nations to implement their right to Treaty governance." Henderson's lucid argument has yet to stir Canadian officials or convince the courts that treaty federalism is a viable option, but it challenges our popular notions of how self-government ought to look and operate while further fuelling its development.

In chapter three, Law Professor Bradford Morse discusses the inherent right of Aboriginal self-government and the work currently underway to reaffirm the First

Nations, Inuit, and Métis right of self-determination. Employing case law associated with the Aboriginal self-government movement as his lens, Morse offers the reader a glimpse into the various legal arguments emphasizing that Aboriginal governance is an inherent right and how this legal position informs Aboriginal leaders' efforts to obtain domestic recognition of the constitutional space by which to govern their own affairs within Canada. Particularly critical of the federal and provincial grip on the self-government negotiations process that ultimately results in "a context in which federal and provincial laws will prevail in case of conflict in many important fields," Morse argues that reconciliation is the key to improving existing Aboriginal-Canada relations. The result of this approach would be the simultaneous expansion of the definition of self-government and its elevation to a more egalitarian political plane in Canadian politics.

Chapter four is especially timely considering the September 2007 refusal of Canada, the United States, Australia, and New Zealand to sign the United Nations' Declaration on the Rights of Indigenous Peoples. Professors Roger Maaka and Augie Fleras provide a discussion of colonial politics in Canada and New Zealand structured to explain why the politics of self-determination are at times so vociferously contested. To one side of the divide sit the transformative dynamics implicit within Indigenous models of self-determining autonomy; on the other side exists the hegemonic statism of state-centric determination models. Arguing that Indigenous self-determining models endorse a politically charged social contract for relations-repair resulting in a new sense of belonging based on power sharing, partnership, and participation, Maaka and Fleras promote adopting a co-sovereignty model that acknowledges Indigenous peoples as political communities who share in the sovereignty of society at large, yet at the same time are sovereign communities in their own right due to their inherent and collective rights. This chapter concludes on an optimistic note: the authors' constructive-engagement model could well provide a blueprint for negotiating post-colonial Indigenous governance without being forced to embrace the foundational principles of a colonial constitutional order.

The four chapters in part II expand on the more theoretical explorations contained in part I. Examining the practical issues challenging our definition of Aboriginal self-government and its operations forces critical analyses of the relationship between treaties and self-government, how self-government is conceptualised, common trends in implementation and operations, financing self-government, as well as how different Aboriginal groups envision growing self-government powers.

In chapter five, Professors Ken Coates and William Morrison warn that self-government's promise has yet to be fully realized and that community leaders and academics should spend additional time poring over negotiated agreements to best discern precisely what self-government looks like, how it operates, and, perhaps most importantly, the ideologies driving its structure. In its evolution from panacea, or the perceived solution to socio-economic and political realities facing

Aboriginal communities, to reality, which is a negotiated ideal that simply provides a starting point for leaders who must take the reins and guide community development, Aboriginal self-government has in many ways challenged paternalistic federal assumptions concerning the placement of Aboriginal people and their communities in Canada. Now the discussion is rooted in constitutional politics, economic development, education, and health care management, to name a few fields of interest. In essence, self-government is presented as a promising and important stage in the revitalization and cultural renaissance of Aboriginal peoples and their communities across Canada.

Chapter six offers a critical review of the Royal Commission on Aboriginal Peoples (RCAP) framed by Professor Jim Frideres' question: Was the RCAP a waste of time and money? Acknowledging the complexity of self-government, Frideres argues that the Canadian government has attempted to circumvent development of principled frameworks to discuss the issue and good-faith negotiation and implementation self-government. This is a disturbing trend aggravated further by the Canadian courts' refusal to engage the issue or pronounce on the validity of the inherent right to self-government. Frideres does note, however, that the RCAP served several functions not the least of which was to empower Aboriginal people by providing a public forum to voice their concerns in a way that engaged non-Aboriginal people in a dialogue about philosophical issues pertaining to self-government. Frideres concludes by hinting at the missed opportunity to employ a unique model that promoted cultural interface. Instead officials paid lip service to the need to expansively define Aboriginal self-government all the while maintaining allegiance to tried and true, *Indian Act*-proscribed methods of implementing governance in First Nations communities.

In chapter seven, Larry Chartrand innovatively traces the antecedents of existing Métis governance structures to the 'Rules of the Hunt' developed in the nineteenth century to govern large numbers of prairie Métis buffalo hunters. Well-structured and site-specific, the rules embraced a fluid governing structure that was adaptable to fit each context as it arose. Chartrand contends that the ideas that once governed thousands on the open grasslands offered an appropriate choice for the Métis, who, by the 1870s were facing uncertain times. The importance of this system cannot be over-emphasized, especially during the late nineteenth century, a period characterized by the Métis diaspora into Western Canada and the emergence of multiple prairie Métis settlements—it was incredibly important to quickly establish democratically elected governments and the attendant rules of governance. The 'Rules of the Hunt' provided a foundation from which these processes were developed. Over time, this approach to governance took on a life of its own, eventually developing into specific political philosophies that, Chartrand argues, continue to animate modern-day Métis governing ideologies and processes and that the existing legal right to self-government continues today.

Professors Frances Abele and Michael Prince discuss the financing of Aboriginal self-government in chapter eight. They examine four pathways to self-determination models currently under discussion or development and the separate funding regimes needed to finance operations, and they present various options available from generating funding independently to transferring funds from the Canadian government to Aboriginal communities. Abele and Prince point out that an independent source of revenue is necessary, and that establishing financial regimes is no easy task. With that said, administrative and policy considerations in managing financial arrangements are crucial elements in the success of self-government.

The six chapters in part III explore recent trends in the implementation of self-government in Canada while expanding on some of the more theoretical explorations contained in part I and the more practical considerations associated with the idea of self-government in part II. This section endeavours to shed light on the question raised in chapter one: What does self-government look like? These chapters detail the diversity of self-governing arrangements that have emerged in Canada.

Beginning with chapter nine, Josée Lavoie, John O'Neil, Jeff Reading, and Yvon Allard examine Aboriginal self-government in the health field. They trace the history of Aboriginal health service development and provide a contemporary analysis of current federal policies. They also discuss the impact of this on what are lower health standards among Aboriginal people nationally, and that incremental gains are offset by the excessive burden of illness and social problems. The authors suggest that the current self-government agenda, while helping to bring about some improvements, is impotent to facilitate the required change. Greater powers of self-government and jurisdiction over health in communities and urban centres are needed to improve community well-being, which will in turn support the healing process now underway. The empowerment that comes of self-government will have a positive health benefit beyond mere service improvement.

In chapter ten, Gabrielle Slowey considers the ways in which the promises of self-government made and encapsulated in the *James Bay and Northern Quebec Agreement* signed in 1975 have not yet been fulfilled. Slowey examines the ways in which Cree self-government has been challenged by the agenda of the state and the consequences for political and economic development. Concerned also that the Cree remain vulnerable to outside interests that in turn influence internal decision-making processes, she connects the Cree and Canadian self-government desires to the larger forces of globalization, the need to promote development of local resources, and neo-liberal ideology. The author discusses the need for increased intergovernmental co-operation to fulfill the promise of Cree self-government and suggests that many of the struggles currently confronting the Cree, from implementing self-governance to delivering programs to managing economic development, are experiences common to other First Nations in Canada.

In chapter eleven, Ailsa Henderson assesses the Nunavut self-government model to determine whether public expectations associated with the claim have been met. In many ways, social indicators suggest that little has changed since the

Agreement's implementation contract was signed in July 1993, and in some cases the situation seems even worse. There are various reasons for this statistical lack of development. Henderson suggests the problem lies in the negotiated pact and its inability to foster de facto government, a term coined by the Harvard Project on American Indian Economic Development to describe tribal governments that guide the real-life decisions. Since genuine self-governance requires that the people affected be willing and able to assert their decision-making in practice, those tribes that have successfully broken the cycle of dependency to become economically independent carry the primary responsibility for economic conditions on reserves. Concluding that the lack of de facto sovereignty has handicapped Nunavut officials, who are effectively unable to make their own decisions as they relate to various issues from resource use to educational matters, Henderson promotes the constructive aspects of a de facto sovereignty model for rehabilitating territorial governance.

In chapter twelve, Professor Rob Innes and former Cowessess Chief and Treaty Land Entitlement (TLE) coordinator Terrence Pelletier provide a case study of the TLE process in Saskatchewan, focusing on the efforts of the Cowessess First Nation to develop a nation-building strategy that would act as an internal guide for community negotiators. Highlighting the fact that there was also a desire on the part of community members to aggressively influence negotiations resulting in an improved settlement, greed did not drive this behaviour. The additional funds were needed to promote local economic development activities to nurture First Nations capacity-building. The authors also identify the potential benefits, difficulties, and challenges that have been associated with the process.

The eight Métis settlements in central and northern Alberta are home to approximately seven thousand Métis, and are Canada's only legislated, land-based Métis government. In chapter thirteen, Professor Catherine Bell and Harold Robinson, Executive Coordinator for the Métis Settlements General Council, outline the structure of Métis settlement government, describing the changes the settlements and their administrations have experienced since their inception. This includes recent legislative reforms arising from the Métis Settlement Appeals Tribunal (MSAT) Task Force Report. The authors also reflect on practical issues of governance and complicated questions about Métis Aboriginal rights. Following intense lobbying by Métis in the 1930s, the government of Alberta created farm colonies (later known as settlements). Issues arising in administration of settlement lands led to litigation against the province over natural resource revenues and creation of a joint committee to make recommendations for reform. In 1990, the Federation of Métis Settlements and the Government of Alberta signed the Métis Settlements Accord. New legislation negotiated reflects four primary goals: protection of settlement lands, local autonomy, economic self-sufficiency, and protection of Métis culture.

In chapter fourteen, Joe Garcea examines the evolution of new reserves, often labelled urban or satellite reserves, in Saskatchewan to promote new and innovative economic development opportunities to help finance self-government. Cognizant of the irony associated with promoting what was, and in many ways still is, considered a stark reminder of colonial injustice intended to subdue and prepare Aboriginal peoples for their inevitable integration into the urban centers of settler society, the creation of such reserves has nevertheless been endorsed by First Nations leaders. Adapting what was a negative colonial legacy into a positive means of fostering self-government is innovative and an act of self-government in and of itself. As a result, many different models have emerged among the 32 designated urban and satellite reserves in Saskatchewan. The factors influencing this trend are also examined with an emphasis on highlighting their key characteristics and the barriers that exist for First Nations leaders seeking to implement urban economic development *vis-à-vis* satellite reserves.

The four chapters in part IV highlight current issues confronting Aboriginal leaders and policy makers. In chapter fifteen, Professor Jo-Anne Fiske draws on primary research to consider how identity and citizenship interact within the self-government realm. She identifies how the passing of *Indian Act* amendments in 1985 led to new categories of 'status'. Bill C-31 attempted to right a previous wrong by granting Aboriginal women and children Indian status lost due to *Indian Act* provisions structured to legislatively eliminate Indians. This brought with it new gender markings of identity and belonging, stigmatization of C-31 urban women, and the politicization of C-31 individuals as a distinct category of citizens. These complex ideas are a product of self-government in need of resolution through the mechanisms of self-government.

In chapter sixteen, Brian Calliou, Program Director for the Banff Centre's Aboriginal Leadership and Management, challenges Aboriginal leaders to develop needed leadership skills in what has become an increasingly technologically based and competitive domestic commercial environment and global economy. In recent years much attention has been directed to the interdependent nature of economic development and self-government. Originating with the Harvard Project, the RCAP utilized these ideas to develop a policy framework suggesting that self-government was unattainable without a strong economic foundation. The key to sustainable economic development is strong leadership, and Calliou tackles this contentious issue by urging community leaders to begin developing competencies such as knowledge, skills, and attitudes—in sum, the beliefs and values that help people perform in their roles. Adopting such an approach would enable leaders to blend tradition and modernity, ideas that, once applied, would lead their organizations and communities to achieve their own vision of self-government.

In chapter seventeen, Professors Val Napoleon and Angela Cameron and Native Studies students Colette Arcand and Dahti Scott conclude that local law still motivates people in First Nations communities even if they are unconscious of its influence. Employing a broad legal framework, the authors discern and describe the parameters and functions of local law that, they argue, is derived from the social interactions of groups in particular geographic areas. Whether specific restorative justice models could be useful as expressions or forms of local law are considered, and if applicable, the authors debate the implications associated with this practice. Specifically, examples from the Alexis First Nation in Alberta are utilized to discuss how local law has been integrated into existing operational justice models. These are employed to explore how our perceptions change when we shift from portraying restorative justice from a programmatic approach to considering it an expression of local law. Further to this, the authors suggest that restorative justice as an expression of local law is in fact a critical aspect of on-the-ground self-government, and discuss self-government's implications by personalizing the experiences and trends associated with the implementation of local law.

In the section's final chapter, Professor Jean Paul Restoule evaluates an assortment of strategies employed by Canadian Aboriginal leaders intent on establishing control and restoring local jurisdiction for education. The National Indian Brotherhood's 1972 report, *Indian Control of Indian Education*, initiated a protracted effort to regain control of education at the community level. Restoule goes on to evaluate numerous national education agreements, identifying a cross-section of strategies that range from extended negotiations highlighting education jurisdiction issues to grassroots organizations adopting a 'just do it' approach and taking unilateral action. As Restoule argues, Aboriginal education in Canada is at a crossroads. In many ways, even though Canada has made significant concessions to enable the integration of Aboriginal perspectives into provincial curricula, the fact that Aboriginal leaders have a limited say in not only curriculum development but also in what aspects of Aboriginal culture will become representative artifacts is problematic. To Restoule this is little more than the vestige of a colonial mentality that 'Indian control over Indian education' was intended to mitigate if not outright eliminate. The question he seeks to answer: How well is this strategy working?

Final Thoughts

During the last three decades, various models have been employed to foster community economic development and capacity-building. Aboriginal communities are still suffering from many of the same problems, making it clear that none of these models has effectively promoted the foundation needed to improve either local conditions or the Aboriginal-Crown relationship. Aboriginal leaders have made it known that fitting their governing philosophies into existing legislative regimes is unacceptable. And Canada refuses to fully acknowledge the inherent right to self-government, instead using the Inherent Rights Policy (IRP) as a guide in its dealings with Aboriginal leaders. So, with both sides refusing to acquiesce, we are seemingly left at an impasse. Yet the evidence exists demonstrating that self-government "would result in improved relations between Aboriginal people and the Canadian state, and make more efficient and effective the use of scarce resources for social support and economic development."[11] The goal then is to make use of resources such as this volume to further expand the idea of Aboriginal self-government. A number of common themes identified in the previous two volumes are reinforced by the discussions about self-government and its various arrangements in this book, which speaks volumes to the potential mechanisms that could be employed to cultivate self-government:

- The importance of a bottom-up, community-based approach to designing programs;
- The problems of implementing programs in a top-down manner, especially when the programs are not based on Aboriginal values and belief systems;
- The importance of adapting programs to local community circumstances so that they are not simply transplanted from other communities, even other Aboriginal communities;
- The value of examining how traditional Aboriginal practices and customs can be adapted to address the contemporary realities in Aboriginal communities;
- The danger that existing approaches that have not worked very well in the dominant society will simply be replicated in Aboriginal communities, especially if time and resources available for planning are restricted;
- The importance of integrative, holistic approaches to meeting individual and community needs—approaches that break down the artificial barriers that often exist in current segmented programs;
- The need to invest in and develop human and other capital in Aboriginal communities so that their capacity to be self-governing can be enhanced; and,
- The need to develop policy, legislative, and funding frameworks for self-government initiatives so that programs are not vulnerable to the changing priorities and directions of Canadian governments.

Much has transpired in the last 35 years. As will be seen, the path to modern self-government was often murky, clearing from time to time to offer a solution to an obstacle to progress. As stated above, self-government and Canada's general acceptance of the principle of the inherent right to Aboriginal self-government is in stark contrast to the policy of termination tabled in 1969. Deferring once again to Hylton: "If our governments are prepared to meet Aboriginal peoples halfway, there is every reason to believe that they may yet take up their just and proper place as full partners in Canada."[12] Well stated.

1 Sally Weaver, "Indian Government: A Concept in Need of a Definition," in *Pathways to Self-Determination: Canadian Indians and the Canadian State*, eds. Leroy Little Bear, Menno Boldt, & J. Anthony Long (Toronto: University of Toronto Press, 1984), 65-8.

2 For this discussion, see Yale D. Belanger & David R. Newhouse, "Emerging from the Shadows: The Pursuit of Aboriginal Self-Government to Promote Aboriginal Well-Being," *Canadian Journal of Native Studies* 24, no. 1 (2004): 129-222; and David R. Newhouse & Yale D. Belanger, *Aboriginal Self-Government in Canada: A Review of Literature Since 1960* (Queen's University, Kingston: Institute of Intergovernmental Relations, 2001).

3 Royal Commission on Aboriginal Peoples, *Looking Forward, Looking Back*, Vol. 1. (Ottawa: Canada Communications Group, 1996), 677-8.

4 *Ibid.*, 678.

5 John H. Hylton, *Aboriginal Self-Government in Canada: Current Trends and Issues*, 2nd ed. (Saskatoon: Purich Publishing Ltd. 1999), 2.

6 *Ibid.*, 3.

7 For this argument, see Belanger & Newhouse, "Emerging from the Shadows."

8 Quoted in Belanger & Newhouse, "Emerging from the Shadows," 132.

9 Thomas Isaac, "Authority, Rights and an Economic Base: The Reality of Aboriginal Self-Government," *Native Studies Review* 7, no. 2 (1991): 69-74.

10 Hylton, *Aboriginal Self-Government in Canada*, 5.

11 *Ibid.*, 10.

12 *Ibid.*, 11.

Part I:

An Introduction to Aboriginal Self-Government

RECONCILING SOLITUDES:

A Critical Analysis of the Self-government Ideal

Yale D. Belanger, University of Lethbridge
& David R. Newhouse, Trent University [1]

While the exercise of power may have its source in the inherent right to self-government, the exercise of the power transpires in a fashion that is completely new to the people employing it. The exercise is neither adopted nor traditional, but is an amalgamation of the two perspectives. [2]

Introduction

Aboriginal self-government as a political ideal and political goal has been accepted and gaining operational definition since 1984. What we mean by political ideal is it is an idea that animates much of contemporary Aboriginal political activity. It represents a state of affairs that many Aboriginal people wish to achieve. It is an attempt to reconcile the presence and sovereignty of Canada with the continuing nationhood of Aboriginal peoples. Some argue that self-government is a federally delegated authority similar or coincidental with self-determination, and that available municipal models make it impossible to reconcile traditional Aboriginal political cultures with those of Canada. Others suggest that the only game in town is to negotiate and find ways of fitting into the current federal-provincial constitutional order. In an attempt to acquire augmented jurisdictional authority many First Nation leaders reluctantly acquiesce to negotiating with the federal government for legally recognized self-governing powers while others aggressively promote the benefits of this form of self-government to their communities. Consensus concerning self-government's benefits has not yet developed; neither has a formal and agreed upon definition of Aboriginal self-government. [3] With that being said, Aboriginal self-government has been realized first with the *Cree-Naskapi Act* of 1984, and more formally in the *Sechelt Act* of 1986, both of which were followed by two decades of negotiations between various First Nations and the federal officials. So negotiations forge ahead in the face of limited consensus as to what Aboriginal self-government represents, forcing the questions, "What are the antecedents of Aboriginal self-government?" and, "How do these ideas influence our current conceptualisation of Aboriginal self-government?"

To answer these questions, we examine eight particular documents to provide a short history of the ideas that have come to dominate the self-government discussion, ideas that are now considered foundational. This chapter focuses on political documents that we consider seminal to advancing the debate and that show evidence of indigenous intellectual influence. The central document, in our opinion, is the 1977 Federation of Saskatchewan Indians (FSI) paper on Indian government.[4] It contains the ideas that have become accepted by Aboriginal peoples as fundamental to the self-government conversation. We also identify major themes in Aboriginal political thought while synthesizing the issues that require further examination and discussion for public policy makers. In thinking about the last four decades of self-government discussions, we divide the period since 1960 into two stages: pre-Penner Report, to 1983, and post-Penner, after 1984. Prior to the Penner Report the discussion focused on articulating principles and a rationale for self-government most often developed by Aboriginal and grassroots organizations. Arguably, the nature of the self-government debate changed significantly following the tabling of the Report, when the focus shifted to the details concerning how self-government will work within the Canadian federation. The reports examined briefly in this chapter are:

- The 1966 Hawthorn-Tremblay Report
- The 1969 White Paper
- The 1972 Red Paper
- The 1973 Council of Yukon Indians land claim proposal
- The 1977 FSI Indian Government Paper
- The 1983 Report of the Special Committee on Indian Self-government (Penner)
- The 1995 Federal Policy Statement on Indian self-government
- The 1996 Report of the Royal Commission on Aboriginal Peoples.

In this sense, this chapter attempts to capture Aboriginal thought about Aboriginal government as it evolved over the last three decades. It also considers why these innovative approaches were ignored or accepted piecemeal by a federal government with little inspiration of its own concerning how to respond to Aboriginal desires for inclusion.

Pre-Penner (1960-1983)

For Native people in Canada, 1960 was a promising year. First, the *Canadian Bill of Rights* was introduced, prohibiting discrimination on the basis of race, colour, and creed, legislation that protected Native interests; also, the federal fran-chise and full citizenship rights were both extended to Native people permitting them to vote in federal or provincial elections without compromising status or making participation "conditional upon complete assimilation into Canadian society."[5] A special joint parliamentary investigative committee established in 1959 to develop recommendations "to meet the varying stages of development of the Indians during the transition period" reported in this pivotal year. The commis-sioners were brief: they believed that the time was right for Native people to "assume the responsibility and accept the benefit of full participation as Canadian citizens".[6] For many it appeared as though federal officials had dedicated them-selves to improving the social, political, and economic standing of Indians in Canada. Responsibility for Indian Affairs, originally vested with the Department of Immigration and Citizenship in 1950, remained centred in Ottawa, and little thought was given to devolving any authority or jurisdiction to Indian Band Councils.

In 1961, largely due to the efforts of prairie Native leaders, the National Indian Council (NIC) was established with federal government funding to represent three of the four major groups of Native people in Canada: treaty and status Indians, non-status Indians, and the Métis (the Inuit were not involved). The NIC's goal was to promote "unity among all Indian people," although the organization's lead-ers soon discovered the immense difficulty in reconciling the interests of all of the various Native groups on a national scale. NIC lobbying efforts helped generate awareness of what could be described as the federal government's benign neglect of Native peoples. In particular media reports of poor reserve socio-economic and living conditions became commonplace and provincial and federal politicians were pressured to improve the situation. The Minister of the Department of Citizenship and Immigration responded in 1963 by commissioning a number of studies to review the situation. University of British Columbia sociologist Harry Hawthorn and Université Laval anthropologist Marc-Adélard Tremblay were asked to examine Native socio-economic conditions and provide recommenda-tions for change. In what David Newhouse suggests laid "the foundation for mod-ern Indian policy" by presenting "the radical idea that Indians ought to be 'citizens plus'," the Hawthorn-Tremblay report was presented in two volumes: part one in 1966, and part two in 1967.[7] The first part focused on reserve conditions and fed-eral programs that were economic, political, and administrative in nature.

The Hawthorn-Tremblay report rejected assimilation as a policy goal, propos-ing instead that Indians should be regarded as "citizens plus" benefiting from Canadian citizenship while also maintaining those rights guaranteed as a result of Indian status and treaty arrangements. Indians were now to be included as "char-ter members of the Canadian community" as commissioners stressed "a common citizenship as well as the reinforcement of difference."[8] As evidenced by recom-mendations 67 and 68, Hawthorn and Tremblay were mindful of the need for Indians to govern themselves: "Continuing encouragement should be given to the development of Indian local government" and "the problem of developing Indian local government should not be treated in the either/or terms of the *Indian Act* or the provincial framework of local government. A partial blending of the two frameworks within the context of an experimental approach which will provide an opportunity for knowledge to be gained by experience is desirable." The idea was that Indian governments would still be *Indian Act*-proscribed albeit integrated with provincial municipal frameworks, in essence becoming a federal-provincial-Indian hybrid. Recommendation 72, for instance, reads, "The partial ad hoc integration of Indian communities into the provincial municipal framework should be deliberately and aggressively pursued while leaving the organization, legal and political structure of Indian communities rooted in the *Indian Act*." How this was to be achieved was not described, nor were there any details given of this proposal for Indian government. In these recommendations, we have a notion that Indians could govern themselves in some fashion within the constitutional structure of Canada.

As Native leaders considered the various proposals in anticipation of a formal government response, a new Liberal government led by Pierre Trudeau and his promise of a 'Just Society' took office in 1968. One scholar has commented that the new Trudeau government "was imbued with a strong liberal ideology that stressed individualism and the protection of individual rights ... that emphasized individual equality and de-emphasized collective ethnic survival."[9] This philosophy of individual rights would guide Prime Minister Trudeau and his Minister of Indian Affairs, Jean Chrétien, in the creation of a new Indian policy that, in 1969, was tabled in the House of Commons. Entitled *A Statement of the Government of Canada on Indian Policy*, the Government of Canada rejected the Hawthorn-Tremblay idea of Indians as citizens plus. Instead the Statement positioned Indians as Canadian citizens with neither special status nor valid claims to special administrative provisions or unique legal standing. The Statement's key proposition was to ensure citizen equality and equity, and that Indians, by virtue of their treaties, for instance, were more than equal to mainstream, read non-Native, citizens. As expected, the Statement said little about Indian governance although one could infer from its proposals concerning the transfer of land to Indian control and for transfer of responsibility for Indians to the provinces that Trudeau and Chrétien envisioned a municipal style of government. Since the policy promoted repealing the *Indian Act*, we assume that Indian governments would be treated as something akin to municipalities under provincial legislation.

Articulated within the document was the notion that innovative legislation would result enabling "Indian people to be free to develop Indian cultures in an environment of legal, social and economic equality with other Canadians." The Liberal government argued that it was this status and the resulting policies that "kept the Indian people apart from and behind other Canadians" and that this "separate road cannot lead to full participation, to better equality in practice as well as theory." All references to Indian special and separate status were to be removed from Canada's Constitution to promote equality among all citizens. The government however recognized the unique status of land and title that resulted from treaty negotiations (i.e. reserves); accordingly, provisions would be made enabling Indian individuals to gain control and acquire title to these lands in addition to determining who would share in ownership. Finally, driving this policy approach was the federal government's desire to offload its responsibilities by devolving bureaucratic control over social programs to the provinces, in particular health care, an agenda it had begun aggressively promoting at the Dominion-Provincial Conference on Indian Affairs in 1964.[10]

Responding aggressively to the White Paper proposals, Indian leaders responded that they had rights emanating from the treaties in addition to having rights as Canadians – they were in fact citizens plus. The Statement's two primary architects, Trudeau and Chrétien, were ill-prepared for the fallout their White Paper proposal generated. Promoting a policy of legislative termination of Indians was unacceptable, and the late Harold Cardinal took the lead censuring the Trudeau government's lack of political and cultural sensitivity. The Indian Chiefs of Alberta responded with *Citizens Plus* (known colloquially as the Red Paper), which represents the first written response to the White Paper by a Native organization.[11] In it the authors chastised the government for its lack of vision and its use of the Hawthorn-Tremblay Report's recommendations to reject Indian concerns. The report also presented an Indian political vision of the nature of the Indian/Ottawa relationship.[12] Intense lobbying pressure combined with public disregard for the enfranchisement package eventually led to a meeting between Indian leaders and Prime Minister Trudeau, at which time *Citizens Plus* was proclaimed the official Indian response. In reply, the Liberal government formally withdrew the White Paper in 1971, albeit still convinced of the suitability of their policy proposal. The consistent federal dismissal of their nationhood claims left Indian leaders feeling anxious as Ottawa continued to promote Indians as one of several multi-cultural ethnic groups in need of federal assistance to enhance their political participation. That 'Indians' represented diversity within one unified nation was problematic, and the fear that their historic role and potential contributions to Canadian society might go ignored was palpable. The new multicultural policy also transformed ethnic groups such as Indians into 'political clientele' while at the same time promoting their participation in Canadian society in a highly structured manner. It was a way of managing Indian cultural expressions without the need to change the federal political system in any significant way.[13]

This desire for increased levels of Native participation in Canadian society was echoed by Native leaders, although their idea of participation differed from the Canadian vision. The concerted resistance to the 1969 White Paper proposal to rescind the unique legal relationship represented on the part of Indian leaders a reiteration of their time-honoured treaty message rooted in a nation-to-nation union of equal coexistence with the Crown. This unfortunately contrasted sharply with the federal view of Indians as one multi-cultural ethnic group among many, all in need of federal assistance if they were to participate in and contribute to Canadian society. Simply put, the official Canadian view was that Indians were no different from other minorities albeit uniquely impoverished and politically disorganized. Native peoples constituted "an ethnic group in the functional sense but they have not reached the level of organizational structure (European style) which would make it possible for government to deal with them through the same approach as would be effective with other ethnic groups."[14]

As a result of the fallout of the White Paper proposal and the resistance generated by the 'disorganized' Native political organizations, the Canadian government struggled throughout the 1970s to establish a cogent Indian policy. Exacerbating Indian ill-will was Ottawa's systematic disregard of Indian claims to Aboriginal rights and federal maintenance of the elective band council model on reserves, a policy that ignored the newly articulated notion of Aboriginal self-government reflected in the technical reports and position papers being produced at a prolific rate by Native organizations.[15] The withdrawal of the White Paper in 1971 was followed two years later by the Supreme Court of Canada's *Calder* v. *The Attorney General of British Columbia*[16] decision recognizing the existence of Aboriginal rights. In the wake of this decision and ongoing Native political mobilization, most observers concluded that federal officials needed to prepare themselves to deal with Native political, social, and economic issues. The Indian Claims Commission was established in 1974 and the first modern treaty with the James Bay Cree was signed in 1975. The federal government initiated the devolution of social control to Native people by transferring administrative responsibility for programs such as education to many respective organizations and communities.[17] Native organizations grew increasingly influential during this period resulting in the National Indian Brotherhood, the Native Council of Canada, and the Inuit Committee on National Issues being invited in 1978 to participate in the constitutional discussions. Eleven additional Native organizations initiated an influential lobby effort and were granted observer status at the talks.[18] During this period Native groups such as the Federation of Saskatchewan Indians started to formally develop the foundational ideas that would eventually become known as Aboriginal self-government.

Also at this time, Native leaders nationally adopted the term 'self-government' into their legal and political lexicon. Many leaders and organizations began to articulate its meaning in position papers and proposals. In 1973, the Council of Yukon Indians (CYI), for instance, presented a plan for regaining control over lands and resources that included a comprehensive approach to development in its land claims statement. Their position represented a significant shift in how self-determination and self-government was now being understood by Native leaders as the CYI asserted the importance of retaining a land base prior to becoming self-governing. Arguing that the Indian people must own the land, and that land is required to be self-governing, for the first time we see the importance of land elucidated in the context of self-government, for "without land Indian people have no soul—no life—no identity—no purpose. Control of our own land is necessary for our cultural and economic survival."[19] Aboriginal self-government was also promoted as a political ideal that would improve existing relationships with Canada while fostering new ones and generating forms of government that were both accountable and indigenous to the land-base Canada asserted sovereignty over. It would, in the parlance of the late 20th century, improve the social capital of the country. The CYI argued that to achieve its objective of obtaining "a settlement in place of a treaty that will help us and our children learn to live in a changing world" and taking "part in the development of the Yukon and Canada," the Native people of the Yukon must own the land. This would require compensation by Canada for past and future forfeiture of surface and subsurface rights and Native representation on all land and water development agencies. The link between land and self-government was clearly made.

In 1977, the Federation of Saskatchewan Indians became the first Indian organization to formally articulate the principles of Aboriginal self-government in their position paper entitled *Indian Government*. We view this paper as the seminal document to emerge during the 1970s. It articulately, clearly, and firmly conveyed what Native leaders believed Aboriginal self-government to represent. The FSI document started with a strong assertion: "No one can change the Indian belief. We are Nations; we have Governments. Within the spirit and meaning of the Treaties, all Indians across Canada have the same fundamental and basic principles upon which to continue to build their Governments ever stronger." The 'fundamental and basic principles' are:

- that Indian nations historically are self-governing;
- that section 91(24) gives the federal government the authority to regulate relations with Indian nations but not regulate their internal affairs;
- that Indian government powers have been suppressed and eroded by legislative and administrative actions of Canada;
- that Indian government is greater than what is recognized or now exercised and cannot be delegated;
- that treaties reserve a complete set of rights, including the right to be self-governing and to control Indian lands and resources without federal interference;
- that treaties take precedence over provincial and federal laws;
- that the trust relationship imposes fiduciary obligations on the trustee, but the federal government has mismanaged this relationship; and,
- that Indians have inalienable rights, including the "inherent sovereignty of Indian Nations, the right to self-government, jurisdiction over their lands and citizens and the power to enforce the terms of the Treaties."[20]

The FSI defined sovereignty as "the right to self-government. It is inherited and it comes from the people. We have never surrendered this right and we were never defeated militarily." Sovereignty, for the FSI, was "inherent and absolute," and its authors argued further that Indian governments traditionally exercised the powers of sovereign nations and the most fundamental right of a sovereign nation is the right to govern its people and territory under its own laws and customs. "Inherent" here suggested that the right of self-government was not granted by Parliament or any other branch of any foreign government. Simply put, Indians always had that right, a belief they considered to be supported by the treaty process and the treaties themselves.

The Indian position initiated with *Indian Government* soon became quite familiar to public policy makers in Canada as the political discussion regarding what self-government was began in earnest. It was a new idea that had at that time no effective definition. The FSI contributed greatly to this discussion by outlining the areas, both theoretical and practical, that would need to be addressed. These involved how Native governments would exercise their powers; the extent of Native sovereignty within the Canadian federation; what exactly the fundamental features of Native government were; how the existing relationship between Native people and the government was going to be redefined; and how negotiations ought to proceed. The FSI set out the major areas that would require joint discussion among Canada's Native groups prior to the restoration/establishment of Indian government becoming a reality. Ever aware that the federal government would play an important role, contingencies were built into the FSI structure to accommodate future developments in Indian policy as handed down by Ottawa. It was clear to the FSI that, prior to any significant negotiations taking place, Native groups and their leaders would need to fully develop the elemental principles from which Aboriginal self-government could evolve.

Complementing this discussion was the FSI's 1979 release, *Indian Treaty Rights: The Spirit and Intent of Treaty*. In it, the FSI asserted that between 1817 and 1929, over 20 major international treaties were signed between the Crown and the Indian Nations. The primary objective of this report was to define treaty rights and provide a contemporary interpretation of their meaning. In return for these treaty rights, the Indian Nations agreed to cede certain lands for use and settlement by Canada. The FSI claimed that during treaty negotiations, Native leaders were guaranteed all powers of Indian Nationhood. Native leaders also articulated the right to self-government was bound by international law resulting from the treaty relationship with the Crown.[21] As the 1970s came to a close, Native peoples were moving from being "wards of the state" unable to speak for themselves and relying primarily upon federal largesse to political players focused on educating the Canadian public and federal politicians about Canada's treaty obligations.[22] They were determined to create a seat at the table of Canadian Confederation. A mountain of published reports by this point provided the foundation for the right to self-government, which would come to dominate self-government discussions in the late 1980s and throughout the 1990s.

Even as Native organizational influence grew, band councils nonetheless remained under the watchful eyes of the Department of Indian Affairs, and their operations continued to be *Indian Act*-proscribed. The previous decade's struggle for federal recognition of Aboriginal rights was exhausting, and Native leaders by 1979 were once again engaged in a battle to secure Constitutional recognition of self-government during the Constitutional repatriation efforts. The impressive work of the 1970s did not go unnoticed, and the succession of reports resulted in the formation of common ideas that would coalesce into what we today understand as Aboriginal self-government. Prime Minister Pierre Trudeau seemed to accept the inevitability of self-government when he stated that "we are not here to consider whether there should be institutions of self-government, but how these institutions should be brought into being ... [and] how they fit into the interlocking system of jurisdictions by which Canada is governed."[23] To determine this fit, in December 1982 Prime Minister Trudeau established the Parliamentary Task Force on Indian Self-Government chaired by Ontario Member of Parliament (MP) Keith Penner to define the parameters of Aboriginal self-government and to "partially reverse hundreds of years of oppressive government policies and neglect, and to improve their intolerable socio-economic condition."[24] The special committee was "mandated to review all legal and related institutional factors affecting status, development, and responsibilities of band councils on Indian reserves, and to make recommendations in respect to establishing, empowering and funding Indian self-government."[25] Arguably, the Task Force was struck in response to the expressed reluctance of Canada's First Ministers to constitutionally entrench a right to Aboriginal self-government that was antithetical to the historic legal and political methods associated with promoting 'Indian assimilation' in Canada.[26]

Travelling across Canada, the committee obtained first-hand testimony from Native people and presented its findings in October 1983. The Penner Report urged federal officials to forge a new relationship with Native peoples based once more on Trudeau's commentary at the initial First Ministers' Conference on Native Constitutional Matters: "Clearly, our Aboriginal peoples each occupied a special place in history. To my way of thinking, this entitles them to special recognition in the Constitution and to their own place in Canadian society, distinct from each other and distinct from other groups who, together with them, comprise the Canadian citizenry."[27] Specifically, the committee advanced a view of Aboriginal government that was keeping with its intellectual precursors: an enhanced municipal-style government within a federal legislative framework but with three important differences:

1. The report envisaged Indian government as a 'distinct order' of government within Canada with a set of negotiated jurisdictions and fiscal arrangements;

2. The report recommended that the right of Indian self-government be constitutionally entrenched with enabling legislation to recognize Indian governments;

3. The report defined areas of authority for Indian governments as education, child welfare, heath care, membership, social and cultural development, land and resource use, revenue-raising, economic and commercial development, justice and law enforcement, and intergovernment relations.

The report also recommended that "the federal government establish a new relationship with Indians and that an essential element of this relationship be recognition of Indian self-government."[28] Further, "the right of Indian peoples to self-government [should] be explicitly stated and entrenched in the Constitution of Canada. The surest way to achieve permanent and fundamental change in the relationship between Indian peoples and the federal government is by means of a constitutional amendment. Indian Natives would form a distinct order of government in Canada, with their jurisdiction defined." The report further indicated that "virtually the entire range of law-making, policy, program delivery, law enforcement and adjudication powers would be available to an Indian Native government within its territory."[29]

What makes the Penner Report important in the history of the development of Aboriginal government is that it accepts and reinforces the FSI argument that Indian nations have always been self-governing and presented historical evidence for it. The acceptance of the report in the House of Commons and the detailing of a plan for recognition of Indian self-government in our view represent the end of a phase in the debate about Aboriginal self-government. The first phase of the debate focused on the question: do Aboriginal peoples have the right to govern themselves? In 1984, the federal government responded: Yes, but within the Canadian federation.

Post-Penner (1984-2008)

The Penner Report, in addition to articulating the need to both acknowledge and implement Aboriginal self-government, is notable as it represents a fundamental turning point in the debate: it accepts the idea that Aboriginal people ought to be self-governing; that this recognition should be within a federal legislative framework as a distinct order of government; and that it ought to be entrenched in the constitution. The House of Commons acceptance of the report followed by a detailed plan that would ultimately result in the formal recognition of Aboriginal self-government represented the end of this phase in the self-government debate. Perhaps most importantly, for the first time not only were Native leaders embracing the concept of a right to self-government but so too was the Canadian government. What, specifically, they were embracing would be the subject of further discussion and debate.

The Government of Canada officially responded to the Penner Report in March 1984: "The Committee's recommendations have a special importance because they were unanimously supported by Committee members of all Parties.

It agreed with the need to establish a new relationship with Indian peoples." In all, "the effect ... is to call for the Government and Indian Natives to enter into a new relationship ... many of the details of the restructured relationship will have to be worked out after careful consideration and full consultation with Indian people." Furthermore, "the Government agrees with the argument put forth by the Committee that Indian communities were historically self-governing and that the graduate erosion of self-government over time has resulted in a situation which benefits neither Indian people nor Canadians in general."[30] However, the 1984 government did not accept the idea of Aboriginal self-government's constitutional entrenchment, although within a decade government officials would reluctantly read the constitution in such a way as to acknowledge this right. As one writer stated, the "realities expressed by Indian peoples have been considered in the formulation of Indian policy, at least at a philosophical level. Reflecting these realities to the exclusion of the more traditional Euro-Canadian views, the Penner Report recommended a paradigm shift to Indian self-government."[31] Several of Penner's recommendations were rejected, although the idea of Aboriginal self-government, "as a component in the existing paradigm,"[32] was accepted. Despite this optimistic pronouncement, the implementation issues that followed from the recommendations were not addressed.[33] The result of the Penner Report's recommendations had they been implemented: "Indian people would determine their own form of government, establish criteria for the self-identification of membership in Indian communities, and exercise jurisdiction in such fields as resources, social services, taxation, and education."[34] Many Native leaders in particular interpreted this to mean that jurisdiction for economic development, the key ingredient to any successful administration, had been effectively transferred to Native interests.[35]

The acceptance of the Penner Report notwithstanding, the complexity of Aboriginal self-government was by now clearly evident. The 1984 *Cree-Naskapi Act* was considered the first Aboriginal self-government model in Canada. In return for ceding vast tracts of territory and voluntarily extinguishing their Aboriginal title, the Cree and Naskapi of northern Quebec were recognized as possessing unique title and interests in addition to descending degrees of access to, and control over, resources, and varied powers of self-government. These powers included, but were not limited to, the administration of band affairs and internal management, public order, taxation for local purposes, and local services, including fire protection.[36] The momentum built in the 1970s and early 1980s would however take a significant blow following the Brian Mulroney-led Progressive Conservative Party's ascension to power in 1985. Primarily concerned with reanimating the dormant US-Canada relationship, Aboriginal issues quickly fell by the wayside during his tenure, forcing Native leaders to lead the continued evolution of self-government. Unfazed by this lack of interest, something the previous Liberal government was also guilty of, in 1981 the Dene Nation and Métis Association of the Northwest Territories released *Public Government for the People of the North* describing a form of government that would protect and respect all people and their respective cultures under its jurisdiction according to a system of 'consociation', democratically based on majority rule to ensure that the rights of minority cultural communities would be protected.[37] The Union of British Columbia Indian Chiefs followed with *Aboriginal Title and Rights Position Paper* that promoted a theme of coexistence. Its authors argued that Canada and the First Nations (a term that had recently come into public consciousness) forged a bond predicated on the basis of mutual co-operation that in turn recognized the validity of, and promoted the need to maintain, cultural institutions thereby ensuring the continued survival and political and economic success of all people in Canada.[38]

By the end of the 1980s, Aboriginal leaders declared their status as a third foundational nation of Canada, alongside the English and French, and academics began to help clarify the increasingly murky and complex self-government concept.[39] A number of important conclusions concerning self-government developed during this period. Provincial governments for the first time became major players in the unfolding self-government movement. Specifically, jurisdictional overlap in the *British North America Act*'s (1867) sections 91/92 meant that the provinces were influential players in the lives of Aboriginal people, and that reconciling this pattern of involvement was required prior to executing Aboriginal self-government.[40] The federal government remained the primary guardian of Aboriginal collective rights, the provinces guardians of their individual rights.[41] An obvious tension developed as the provinces were required to treat Aboriginal people as full citizens while the federal government maintained a guardian-ward relationship while also retaining responsibility for their special Aboriginal nature.[42] Accordingly, there was a provincial role to be played for Aboriginal peoples in the area of programs, and that provincial involvement in negotiations *vis-à-vis* a tripartite model became requisite in any self-government negotiations.

Not specifically related to the provincial role but influential nonetheless was the proposition that the "drive for constitutionally-based aboriginal self-government at the national level, and the provision of meaningful programs and services to aboriginal peoples at the community level, ought to be viewed as complementary rather than contending objectives."[43] Emerging from this line of argumentation was the recognition that a secure fiscal base was required prior to establishing successful Aboriginal self-government.[44] Perhaps more importantly, two key questions were posited that still steer the self-government debate: (1) should Aboriginal self-government be considered a third level of government?; and, (2) what is the source of power for Aboriginal governments, and is the source of power more of a barrier to agreement than the range of such powers?[45] The latter issue remains a major stumbling block despite formal federal acknowledgement of the inherent right to Aboriginal self-government. But what exactly *was* Aboriginal self-government? As one issue was dealt with, additional questions would arise, highlighting self-government's evolutionary quality thus making it difficult to develop a formal definition within the Canadian context. These questions aside, by the end of the 1980s the push for self-government appeared stalled, a situation that was exacerbated by the threat of violent response to Canadian colonialism as occurred at Oka in 1990. Two failed constitutional conferences followed, Meech Lake and the Charlottetown Accord. Some have suggested that Native people tended not to view the demise of the Meech Lake Accord as a failure, but note the educational value of the exercise and the openness of the process;[46] however, the Charlottetown Accord's demise in 1992, specifically the Canadian public's rejection of a distinct order of Aboriginal government, was not as easily forgotten.

The Oka crisis propelled Mulroney to establish in 1991 the Royal Commission on Aboriginal Peoples (RCAP), initiating an intensive period of increased academic participation in the clarification of the self-government idea. Costing close to $60 million, the final report of the RCAP is a five-volume report consisting of 3,536 pages that deals with a myriad of issues including, but not limited to justice issues, suicide, and self-government. In all "the Commission met 100 times, had 178 days of hearings, recorded 76,000 pages of transcripts, generated 356 research studies, published four special reports, and two commentaries on self-government."[47] Despite an impressive mandate to examine issues as diverse as land claims, relocation of the Inuit, and health, the RCAP was viewed first and foremost as an unparalleled means of renewing Canada's relationship with Aboriginal peoples. Published in 1996, the RCAP's final report envisaged a new Canadian partnership based on mutual recognition, one in which Aboriginal and non-Aboriginal people would "acknowledge and relate to one another as equals, coexisting side by side and governing themselves according to their own laws and institutions."[48]

The RCAP also commissioned a series of 17 case studies of contemporary Aboriginal governments to inform its discussions. These case studies present an interesting picture of the challenges facing developing Aboriginal governments. The RCAP defined self-government as a right to be vested in 'people' and "whatever the more general meaning of that term, we consider that it refers to what we will call Aboriginal nations . . . [meaning], a sizeable body of Aboriginal people with a shared sense of national identity, that constitutes the predominant population of a certain territory or collection of territories."[49] Delineating self-government as a right dependent upon an Aboriginal peoples' claim to nationhood, some academics and politicians considered the RCAP vision a "pooling of existing sovereignties" compelling the formation of unified entities from these varied groups who could then exercise their right to self-government. Unlike the grassroots vision of self-government which views each independent nation as capable of negotiating their own self-government provisions with Canada, the Royal Commission suggested that only once Aboriginal nations are reconstituted and recognized as nations can they exercise their right to self-government and the "sphere of jurisdiction implicit in section 35 of the *Constitution Act, 1982*."[50] The jurisdiction of Aboriginal nations was further separated into two co-dependent parts: (1) core jurisdiction; and (2) periphery. In short, the RCAP viewed the right of self-government as being vested in nations or peoples rather than in the bands defined by the *Indian Act* of 1876.[51]

Critiques of the RCAP self-government model vary, the most forceful suggesting that the Royal Commission failed to endorse an Aboriginal vision of self-government and that it ignored diversity in lieu of promoting the idea that "Aboriginal nations can be reconstituted, created and imagined regardless of historical differences and colonial legacies."[52] The concept of negotiated inferiority was fashioned to describe the RCAP model, although it has been argued that despite what could be portrayed as a dangerously naïve strategy, consideration must be given to the practicalities involved with the exercise of self-governing powers.[53] What we see emerging from the Royal Commission, specifically the case studies, are local Aboriginal governments tackling issues within their own communities as best they can within the current legislative and regulatory framework and demonstrating that Aboriginal self-governments are developing and are making a difference in people's lives.

In advance of the RCAP tabling its final report, the newly elected Liberal government under the leadership of former Indian Affairs minister Jean Chrétien tabled its Inherent Rights Policy (IRP) in 1995. Fulfilling a Liberal government election promise previously outlined in its Red Book of 1993, the Liberals acknowledged in the IRP that Aboriginal peoples have an inherent right to self-government and that it is an existing right within section 35 of the *Constitution Act, 1982*, in matters "internal to their communities, integral to their unique cultures, identities, traditions, languages and institutions and with respect to their special relationship to their land and their resources."[54] The 1995 federal statement on the inherent right to self-government is an affirmation of the original FSI position even if there is now much debate about the effect of the term 'inherent' as well as the range of powers and jurisdictions that would be available to Aboriginal governments.

This debate is perhaps the most politically-charged and challenging issue confronting the continued evolution of the self-government ideal. It has been suggested that the IRP is little more than a policy on rights as opposed to a legal definition of those rights, reflecting Canada's negotiating position. It also indicates what federal negotiators are willing to negotiate in a self-government package and that sovereignty issues will not be considered, necessitating the harmonization of Aboriginal jurisdiction with municipal, provincial, and federal jurisdictions. Others argue that even if this is the federal position the "right of Aboriginal self-government, exercised by Aboriginal peoples with diverse historical experiences, and acknowledged by the Crown in the Royal Proclamation of 1763 and elsewhere, has never been relinquished."[55] Critics challenge the federal government's conception of inherent rights, especially when a First Nation is forced to extinguish their Aboriginal title as a prerequisite to obtaining self-government. As a result, First Nations in their attempts to achieve self-government must give up the very rights they argue are inherent in order to gain the one primary right (self-government) that in turn will protect the rights of the collective. Suspicion of the IRP may be warranted, but the recognition of inherent rights to self-government in this case is a policy guideline and, unlike constitutional provisions, is with little difficulty open to alteration at a later date. If anything, Aboriginal self-government is clearly an evolutionary idea apt to change.

Conclusion

Apparent in the examination of eight major reports and associated policy directives to emerge since 1969 is the evolution of the idea of Aboriginal self-government from a localized political objective to one appropriated by the federal government and the Aboriginal political elite, which invariably altered its development and our interpretation of the concept. The threads of the initial discourse regarding Aboriginal self-government are nevertheless woven into contemporary notions of what Aboriginal self-government represents. From a policy of termination to a policy of affirmation of the inherent right of self-government, significant changes are evident that are traceable to the ever-evolving self-government discourse driven by indigenous political philosophies and grounded in traditional Aboriginal ideas about political relationships. But what began as community statements and concern with community well-being has moved away from these important sites. The conversation about Aboriginal governance has become a conversation of elites—Aboriginal, government, and academic—a trend that we to a degree perpetuate. To bring the discussion back to the communities for their input, we suggest that the critical ideas contained in the eight reports supply a template describing the original self-governance idea as it emerged from the shadows beginning in 1969. In sum:

1. The idea of self-government has broadened considerably over the last three decades. It has grown from an initial concept of local municipal-style government rooted in the *Indian Act* to a concept of a constitutionally protected inherent right finding its most recent expression in the idea of 'Aboriginal national government' as a distinct order of government within the Canadian federation.

2. The scope of people affected by the discussions has grown considerably. The initial focus of self-government was on status Indians residing on reserves. This has now broadened to include Métis, Inuit, and urban Aboriginal peoples.

3. The basis of self-government has fundamentally changed. We no longer conceive of Aboriginal self-government as rooted in the *Indian Act* but see it as an inherent right, rooted in history and treaties.

4. The scope of authority and jurisdiction for self-government has also enlarged considerably. Aboriginal governments are now seen as more than municipalities, also encompassing federal, provincial, and municipal authorities as well as some unique Aboriginal authorities.

5. The debate about self-government has fundamentally changed, from how rather than why. There are now multiple sites for the debate: among lawyers, Aboriginal leaders and academics, the literature focuses on broad issues and still has an element of why; but among local Aboriginal community leaders and politicians and consultants, it is about how to govern on a day-to-day basis.

The central question surrounding Aboriginal self-government is no longer why but how. This next phase of the debate and discussion is one that will continue as long as there is an entity called Canada. Aboriginal leaders have consistently attempted to encourage federal officials to revisit the foundations of the original relationship that preceded Canada as a country by some 250 years for the purposes of strengthening an already existing bond. This could ultimately result in the Canadian government acknowledging and building upon this relationship. At the same time, despite historical precedent situating Aboriginal people as one of Canada's three founding people, using history to sort out where Aboriginal people fit into the Canadian federation is not likely to have much effect. It will only generate more debate. There are groups that will argue that they are in fact a part of Canada and that creating an Aboriginal place within the federation is unwarranted. Others argue that the process of Confederation needs to continue and see the self-government discussions in this fashion, as bringing Aboriginal people into confederation as full partners. Achieving self-government will occur as localized acts of negotiation and compromise. Legal scholar John Borrows warns, however, that Canada's First Nations cannot ignore the world they live in and that in the process of "reconstructing our world we cannot just do what we want."[56]

At present, Canada sets the table for the self-government discussion, with a little help from the courts. The models that it proposes are similar to those that it is familiar with: provinces, territories, and municipalities. These are, in the view of most people, the building blocks of the nation. The self-government idea of 'Aboriginal nation' doesn't fit within this Anglo-Saxon political schema. The challenge will be to create formal Constitutional space for Aboriginal self-government in Canada that extends beyond fitting available self-government models into existing federal and provincial jurisdictional structures. Until this happens, indigenous thought remains peripheral to the self-government movement, as a latent idea to be engaged only after the governance structures are firmly in place. The creation and recognition of Aboriginal governments is Canada's great, unfinished, nation-building project. It entails dealing with our history and the recognition of fundamental rights and resolving how the self-determination project of Aboriginal people will be expressed within the Canadian constitutional context.

NOTES

1   Research and writing of this article was equally shared by the authors. The listing of names is alphabetical.
2   John Borrows, "Contemporary Traditional Equality: The Effect of the *Charter* on First Nation Politics," *University of New Brunswick Law Journal* 43 (1994), 19.
3   Sally M. Weaver, "Indian Government: A Concept in Need of a Definition," in *Pathways to Self-Determination: Canadian Indians and the Canadian State*, eds. Leroy Little Bear, Menno Boldt & J. Anthony Long (Toronto: University of Toronto Press, 1984), 65-8.
4   A reorganization effort in the early 1980s resulted in the FSI evolving from a long-time provincial non-profit governing body into the FSIN, described as a true federation of nations. On April 16, 1982, following an agreement to form Canada's first Indian legislative assembly, the chiefs gained formal control of the executive and administrative functions of Saskatchewan First Nations government at the band, tribal council, and provincial levels. A resolution known as the Provisional Charter of the Federation of Saskatchewan Indian Nations (Convention Act) was adopted, outlining the FSIN's governing structure. The first Chiefs' legislative assembly was held one year later, on October 19, 1983.
5   J. Rick Ponting, "Historical Overview and Background, Part II: 1970-96," in *First Nations in Canada: Perspectives on Opportunity, Empowerment, and Self-Determination*, ed. J. Rick Ponting (Toronto: McGraw-Hill Ryerson, 1997), 29.
6   Canada, Joint Committee of the Senate and the House of Commons on Indian Affairs, Minutes of Proceeding (Ottawa: 1961), 605.
7   David R. Newhouse, "Hidden in Plain Sight: Aboriginal Contributions to Canada and Canadian Identity: Creating a New Indian Problem." Presentation First Nations, First Thoughts 5 May 2005. Edinburgh, Scotland.
8   Alan Cairns, *Citizens Plus: Aboriginal Peoples and the Canadian State* (Vancouver: UBC Press. 2000), 8.
9   Ponting, "Historical Overview and Background, Part II: 1970-96," 31.
10   Canada, *Statement of the Government of Canada on Indian Policy* (Ottawa: 1969) 3.
11   Noel Dyck, "Representation and Leadership of a Provincial Indian Association," in *The Politics of Indianness: Case Studies and Ethnopolitics in Canada*, ed. Adrian Tanner (St. John's, Newfoundland: Institute of Social and Economic Research, Memorial University of Newfoundland, 1983), 197-305.
12   Indian Chiefs of Alberta, *Citizens Plus* (Edmonton: Indian Association of Alberta, 1970), 4.
13   For this discussion, see David Newhouse, Kevin Fitzmaurice & Yale D. Belanger, *Creating a Seat at the Table: Aboriginal Programming at Canadian Heritage* (Ottawa: Canadian Heritage, 2005).
14   *Ibid.*, 5.
15   Yale D. Belanger & David R. Newhouse, "Emerging from the Shadows: The Pursuit of Aboriginal Self-government to Promote Aboriginal Well-Being," *Canadian Journal of Native Studies* 24, no. 1 (2004): 129-222.
16   [1973] S.C.R. 313, 7 C.N.L.C. 91.
17   Yvonne Pompana, "Devolution to Indigenization: The Final Path to Assimilation of First Nations" (M.A. thesis, University of Manitoba, 1997).
18   D.E. Sanders, "The Indian Lobby," in *And No One Cheered: Federalism, Democracy and the Constitution Act*, eds. K. Banting and R. Simeon. (Toronto: Methuen, 1983).
19   Council for Yukon Indians (CYI), *Together Today for Our Children Tomorrow: A Statement of Grievances and an Approach to Settlement by the Yukon Indian People* (Whitehorse: 1973), 31.
20   Federation of Saskatchewan Indians, *Indian Government* (Saskatchewan: 1977).
21   See for example Russel L. Barsh & James Youngblood Henderson, "Aboriginal Rights, Treaty Rights and Human Rights: Indian Tribes and Constitutional Renewal, *Journal of Canadian Studies* 17, no. 2 (1982), 80-1; The Royal Commission on Aboriginal Peoples (RCAP), *For Seven Generations: An Information Legacy of the Royal Commission on Aboriginal Peoples* (6 Vol.) (Ottawa: Queen's Printer, 1996); Kiera Ladner, "Unequal Partners in Confederation: RCAP's Plan for a Renewed Relationship," *Revista Mexicana de Estudios Canadienses* 2, no. 3 (September 2000): 81-106.
22   Newhouse, Fitzmaurice & Belanger, *Creating a Seat at the Table*, 9.
23   Olive Patricia Dickason, *Canada's First Nations: A History of Founding Peoples from Earliest Times* (Toronto: McClelland and Stewart, 1992), 408.
24   David C. Hawkes, *The Search for Accommodation* (Kingston: Institute of Intergovernmental Relations, 1987), 1.

25 Menno Boldt, *Surviving as Indians: The Challenge of Self-Government* (Toronto: University of Toronto Press, 1993), 88.

26 J. Anthony Long, Leroy Little Bear & Menno Boldt, "Federal Indian Policy and Indian Self-Government in Canada: An Analysis of a Current Proposal," *Canadian Public Policy* 8, no. 2 (1982): 192-4.

27 Canada, *Special Committee on Indian Self-Government* (Task Force) (Ottawa: Queen's Printer, 1983), 39.

28 Keith Penner, "Their Own Place: The Case for a Distinct Order of Indian First Nation Government in Canada," in *Governments in Conflict? Provinces and Indian Nations in Canada,* eds. J. Anthony Long & Menno Boldt (Toronto: University of Toronto Press, 1988), 141.

29 Canada, *Special Committee on Indian Self-Government,* 39-40.

30 Quoted in Belanger & Newhouse, "Emerging from the Shadows."

31 A.M. Mawhiney, *Toward Aboriginal Self-Government: Relations Between Status Indian Peoples and the Government of Canada, 1969-1984* (New York: Garland Publishing, Inc., 1994), 125-6.

32 *Ibid.*

33 Evelyn J. Peters, *Aboriginal Self-Government in Canada: A Bibliography, 1986* (Kingston: Institute of Intergovernmental Relations, Queen's University, 1986), 23.

34 David Hawkes, Negotiating *Aboriginal Self-Government: Developments Surrounding the* 1985 *First Ministers' Conference* (Kingston: Institute of Intergovernmental Relations, Queen's University, 1985), 10.

35 David R. Newhouse, "The Invisible Infrastructure: Urban Aboriginal Institutions and Organizations," in *Strangers in These Parts: Urban Aboriginal Peoples,* eds. David R. Newhouse & Evelyn J. Peters (Ottawa: Policy Research Initiative, 2004), 243-53.

36 Thomas Isaac, *Aboriginal Law in Canada: Cases, Material and Commentary,* 2nd Ed. (Saskatoon: Purich Publishing, 1999), 507.

37 Dene Nation and Métis Association of the Northwest Territories, *Public Government of the People of the North,* Discussion Paper (Yellowknife: November 9, 1981).

38 J.R. Miller, *Skyscrapers Hide the Heavens: A History of Indian-White Relations in Canada* (Toronto: University of Toronto Press, 1997).

39 See, for example, John Ralston Saul, *Reflections of a Siamese Twin: Canada at the End of the Twentieth Century* (Toronto: Penguin Books, 1997), in particular Chapter 5, "A Triangular Reality."

40 Frances Abele & Katherine Graham, "High Politics is Not Enough: Policies and Programs for Aboriginal Peoples in Alberta and Ontario," in *Aboriginal Peoples and Government Responsibility,* ed. David C. Hawkes (Ottawa: Carleton University Press, 1989); and, Evelyn J. Peters, "Federal and Provincial Responsibilities for the Cree, Naskapi, and Inuit Under the *James Bay* and *Northern Quebec, and Northeastern Quebec Agreements,"* in Aboriginal Peoples and Government Responsibility, ed. David C. Hawkes (Ottawa: Carleton University Press, 1989), 173-242.

41 A. Pratt, "Federalism in the Era of Aboriginal Self-Government," in *Aboriginal Peoples and Government Responsibility,* ed. David C. Hawkes (Ottawa: Carleton University Press, 1989), 19-58.

42 I.G. Scott, "Respective Roles and Responsibilities of Federal and Provincial Governments Regarding the Aboriginal Peoples of Canada," in *Aboriginal Peoples and Government Responsibility,* ed. David C. Hawkes (Ottawa: Carleton University Press, 1989), 351-8.

43 David C. Hawkes, *Aboriginal Peoples and Government Responsibility: Exploring Federal and Provincial Roles* (Ottawa: Carleton University Press, 1989), 363.

44 David C. Hawkes & Allan Maslove, "Fiscal Arrangements for Aboriginal Self-Government," in *Aboriginal Peoples and Government Responsibility,* ed. David C. Hawkes (Ottawa: Carleton University Press, 1989), 93-138.

45 Hawkes, *Aboriginal Peoples and Government Responsibility,* 365.

46 David C. Hawkes, *Aboriginal Peoples and Constitutional Reform: What Have We Learned?* (Kingston: Institute of Intergovernmental Relations, Queen's University, 1989), 61.

47 In Cairns, *Citizen's Plus,* 116.

48 Royal Commission on Aboriginal Peoples (RCAP), *Looking Forward, Looking Back,* Vol. 1. (Ottawa: Queen's Printer, 1996), 678.

49 RCAP, *Restructuring the Relationship,* Vol. 2, (Ottawa: Queen's Printer, 1996), 177-8.

50 Ladner, "Unequal Partners in Confederation," 85.

51 Marlene Brant Castellano, "Renewing the Relationship: A Perspective on the Impact of the Royal Commission on Aboriginal Peoples," in *Aboriginal Self-Government in Canada: Current Trends and Issues,* 2nd Ed., ed. John H. Hylton (Saskatoon: Purich Publishing Ltd., 1999), 98.

52 Ladner, "Unequal Partners in Confederation," 101.

53 Kiera Ladner, "Negotiated Inferiority: RCAP's Vision of Renewed Relationship," *The American Review of Canadian Studies* 31, no. 1 (Spring 2001): 241; see also Fred Wien, "Economic Development and Aboriginal Self-Government: A Review of the Implementation of the Report of the Royal Commission on Aboriginal Peoples," in *Aboriginal Self-Government in Canada: Current Trends and Issues,* 2nd Ed., ed. John H. Hylton (Saskatoon: Purich Publishing Ltd., 1999), 257; R. McDonnell & R. Depew, "Aboriginal Self-Government

and Self-Determination in Canada," in *Aboriginal Self-Government in Canada: Current Trends and Issues,* 2nd Ed., ed. John H. Hylton (Saskatoon: Purich Publishing Ltd., 1999), 357.

54 Canada, *Aboriginal Self-Government: The Government of Canada's Approach to Implementation of the Inherent Right and the Negotiation of Aboriginal Self-Government* (Hull, Quebec: Department of Indian Affairs and Northern Development, 1995) http://www.ainc-inac.gc.ca/pr/pub/sg/plcy_e.html (accessed 13 September 2007).

55 Bradford Morse, "The Inherent Right of Self-Government," in *Aboriginal Self-Government in Canada: Current Trends and Issues,* 2nd Ed., ed. John H. Hylton (Saskatoon: Purich Publishing Ltd., 1999), 17; cf Bruce Clark, *Native Liberty, Crown Sovereignty: The Existing Aboriginal Right of Self-Government in Canada* (Montreal-Kingston: McGill-Queen's University Press, 1990).

56 John Borrows, "Contemporary Traditional Equality: The Effect of the Charter on First Nation Politics," 23.

TREATY GOVERNANCE

James [Sákéj] Youngblood Henderson,
University of Saskatchewan

Treaties serve to reconcile pre-existing Aboriginal sovereignty with
assumed Crown sovereignty and to define Aboriginal rights guaranteed by
s. 35 of the Constitution Act, 1982.—Chief Justice McLachlin [1]

Aboriginal governance is an ancient concept with numerous expressions and practices in Aboriginal law. This chapter is concerned with the affirmation and vesting of Aboriginal governance in imperial treaties with the British Crown's consent. The context, spirit, and intent of the more than 400 treaties were an attempt to conciliate pre-existing Aboriginal sovereignty with assumed Crown sovereignty that established an innovative transnational covenant that conversed both.

The existing and specific conciliations between First Nations and the imperial Crown in the written treaties arise from and are structured by the pre-existing Aboriginal sovereignty.[2] Aboriginal sovereignty and governance exist because First Nations had their own confederated civilization with distinct governance, law, and economies prior to the imperial treaties. These treaties, derived from the mutual consent of the First Nations sovereigns and the British sovereign, were independent, *sui generis* sources of transnational law.[3] The various discussions and written terms of these treaties vested Treaty governance, derived from pre-existing Aboriginal governance, in imperial constitutional law, and now as constitutionally protected treaty rights, in s. 35 and 52 of the *Constitution Act, 1982*.[4]

The shared purpose of the treaties was translated into the fundamental concepts of treaty federalism[5] and governance. Treaty federalism produced the shared relationship between the Aboriginal sovereignty of the confederations of First Nations and the imperial sovereign. Treaty governance, which was one of the fundamental and foundational promises of treaty federalism, guaranteed the continuation of Aboriginal sovereignty in the imperial treaty order in North America. The acceptance of these principles by the imperial sovereign created a constitutional covenant and forestalled military conquest of First Nations in British North America. The distinct sovereigns became allies by consensual treaties.

The treaty powers of the British sovereign in foreign jurisdictions with First Nations are distinct from the history of prerogative law and governance of Great Britain or its colonial institutions.[6] The treaty relationship is part of foreign relations. The treaty rights, obligations, and promises, as well as their underlying principles, acknowledge the inherent sovereignty of the tribes of the confederated nations, their system of law and rights, their right to chose their destiny and relationships, and their way of life as Treaty governance.[7]

Treaties Transform Aboriginal Governance into Vested Treaty Governance

For First Nations, maintaining Aboriginal sovereignty and governance over their shared territory and peoples was the indispensable purpose and internal architecture of the imperial treaties. These ancient concepts were the assumptions and rules of recognition that guided the negotiations of most of these treaties. Both interrelated concepts exist as either implicit or explicit principles of the shared interpretative framework of the treaty parties, the implicit structure of the treaties, and are illustrated in the text of the many written treaties. The imperial treaties extended Aboriginal governance, they did not reduce it.

One of the underlying principles behind the imperial treaties with the First Nations and confederacies was the acknowledgement of pre-existing *sui generis* Aboriginal sovereignty.[8] The Supreme Court of Canada has affirmed that Aboriginal sovereignty and governance pre-existed and continued regardless of an imperial claim to Crown jurisdiction or sovereignty over their territory.[9] These *sui generis* sovereigns are the ancient law of the land, and they are embedded in Aboriginal heritages, languages, and laws. They were distinct from the European traditions of aristocracy and sovereignty. They reflect a distinct vision of how to live well with the land and with other peoples by consent and collaboration.[10] The diversity within Aboriginal sovereignty reveals a generation of holistic orders that were designed to be consensual, interactive, dynamic, and cumulative. They are intimately embedded in Aboriginal worldviews, ceremonies, and stories, as expressed by the structure and media of Aboriginal languages and art. They reveal who First Nations are, what they believe, what their experiences have been, and how they act. In short, they reveal Aboriginal humanity's belief in freedom and order.

Sui generis Aboriginal sovereignty and governance operate by their Aboriginal law and jurisprudence. The realm of Aboriginal sovereignty is implicit, inherent, and unwritten. The courts have noted that all these manifestations of Aboriginal rights are constitutionally valid, even if they have never been positively affirmed by British or Canadian legislation.[11] Canadian courts have a duty to extend constitutional supremacy and equality before and under the law to these *sui generis* Aboriginal sovereignties, and these sovereignties and their rights modify the rules of evidence of the Canadian legal code.[12] The Supreme Court has affirmed Aboriginal nationhood.[13] Madame Justice L'Heureux-Dubé, in *Van der Peet,* said directly: "[I]t is fair to say that prior to the first contact with the Europeans, the Native people of North America were independent nations, occupying and controlling their own territories, with a distinctive culture and their own practices, traditions and customs."[14] Also in *Van der Peet*, Madame Justice McLachlin argued that the "golden thread" of British legal history was "the recognition by the common law of the ancestral laws and customs of the Aboriginal peoples who occupied the land prior to European settlement."[15] The Lamer Court held that if Aboriginal people were "present in some form" on the land when the Crown asserted sovereignty, their pre-existing right to the land in Aboriginal law "crystallized" in British law as a *sui generis* Aboriginal title to the land itself.[16]

Sui generis Aboriginal sovereignty and governance exist independently of British constitutional law, proclamation, or sovereign recognition, and independently of British common law.[17] They do not depend for their existence or legitimacy on consistency with alien British law. Since these rights arise independent of European legal theory of rights, they do not require recognition by European laws to be constitutionally valid.[18]

The Supreme Court has acknowledged that *sui generis* Aboriginal sovereignty and governance must be understood and interpreted as distinctive and integral to Aboriginal law and societies, rather than as part of European law and societies.[19] Not only are the Aboriginal concepts of sovereignty and law distinct from the political concepts of Europe or the traditions of civil or common law, they are distinct from the liberal principles and abstract rights used in *Charter* interpretations of personal rights.[20] The Supreme Court is aware that neither the British nor the French legal tradition can adequately describe Aboriginal sovereignty, laws, or rights.[21]

Against the background of *sui generis* Aboriginal sovereignty, written treaties with the Crown create consensual reconciliations, delegations, obligations, and rights for the treaty parties. Typically, First Nations in the treaties retained Aboriginal governance as a vested Treaty governance under the protection of the imperial constitutional law of Great Britain (or the emerging United Kingdom). Treaty governance rights are not delegated rights from the Crown; they are not executive or legislative power derived from the Crown. Treaty governance is not an artificial structure developed by colonial bureaucratic visions of band administration. It is not a gift of a cunning political party of reluctant nations. Consequently, Treaty governance does not depend on the British or Canadian constitution or British or Canadian law for its existence; it is a reflection of Aboriginal sovereignty and governance.

Treaty governance provisions are foundational parts of the "inviolable" compacts.[22] They are explicit exchanges of solemn promises between the Crown and Treaty chiefs, the nature of which the Supreme Court of Canada has characterized as sacred.[23] The Court has held that Crown's honour requires the governments and courts to always assume that the imperial Crown intended to fulfill its Treaty governance.[24]

The British sovereign in the Georgian treaties affirmed inherent and existing First Nations governance in the reserved treaty tenure, while most of the Victorian treaties vested it as treaty governance in the surrendered territory.[25] As the President of the Union of Nova Scotia Indians declared to the Royal Commission on Aboriginal Peoples about the Georgian treaties with the Mi'kmaq:

> We see our right of self-government as an inherent right, which does not come from other governments. It does not originate in our Treaties. The right of self-government and self-determination comes from the Mi'kmaq people—it is through their authority that we govern. The Treaties reflect the Crown's recognition that we were, and would remain, self-governing, but they did not create our Nationhood ... In this light, the treaties should be effective vehicles for the implementation of our constitutionally protected right to exercise jurisdiction and authority as governments. Self-government can start with a process of interpreting and fully implementing the 1752 Treaty, to build on it to an understanding of the political relationship between the Mi'kmaq people and the Crown.[26]

Treaty governance in these consensual treaties replaced the general protective jurisdiction over First Nations assumed unilaterally by the imperial Crown against other European or American sovereigns and colonial authorities. The written terms of the Victorian treaties in the nineteenth century expressly vested governance over the shared territories, travellers, and inhabitants in the Treaty Chiefs and Headmen of the First Nations in imperial constitutional law,[27] and now in Canadian constitutional law.[28]

They consciously used the imperial treaties to affirm Aboriginal governance and jurisdiction over the shared or transferred territory and peoples.[29] The treaty negotiations and the written terms of the Victorian treaties recognized that constitutional responsibility for Treaty governance existed in the treaty Chiefs and Headmen:

> Whereas all the Indians inhabiting the said country ... made certain Chiefs and Headmen who should be authorized on their behalf to conduct [treaty] negotiations and to sign any treaty [with Her Most Gracious Majesty, the Queen of Great Britain and Ireland] to be found thereon, and to become responsible to Her Majesty for the faithful performance by their respective bands and such obligations as should be assumed by them.[30]

The Treaty commissioners repeatedly assured the First Nations that the Crown had no intention of interfering with their worldview, their languages, their way of life, or their livelihood, in the treaties.[31] The importance of the central obligation of the Chiefs and Headmen to provide treaty government to the treaty beneficiaries is illustrated by various "peace and good order" clauses that comprise interrelated models.

Model 1: Treaty 1 (1871)

And the undersigned Chiefs do hereby bind and pledge themselves and their people strictly to observe this treaty and to maintain perpetual peace between themselves and Her Majesty's white subjects, and not to interfere with the property or in any way molest the person of Her Majesty's white or other subjects.[32]

Model 2.1: Treaty 2 (1871), Treaty 3 (1873), Treaty 4 (1874), Treaty 5 (1875), Treaty 6 (1876), and Treaty 7 (1877)[33]

And the undersigned Chiefs,[34] on their own behalf and on behalf of all other Indians inhabiting the tract within ceded, do hereby solemnly promise and engage to strictly observe this treaty, and to conduct and behave themselves as good and loyal subjects of Her Majesty the Queen.[35] They promise and engage that they will in all respect obey and abide by the law[36]; that they will maintain peace and good order[37] between each other, and also between themselves and other tribes of Indians,[38] and between themselves and other of Her Majesty's subjects, whether Indian or whites,[39] now inhabiting or hereafter inhabit any part of the said ceded tract, and they will not molest the person or property of any inhabitants[40] of such ceded tract or the property of Her majesty the Queen, or interfere with or trouble any person passing or travelling through the said tract, or any part thereof,[41] and they will aid and assist[42] the officers of Her Majesty[43] in bringing to justice[44] and punishment[45] any Indian offending against the stipulation of this treaty, or infringing the laws in force in the country so ceded.

Model 2.2: Treaty 8 (1899), Treaty 9 (1905), Treaty 10 (1906), and Treaty 11(1921)[46]

And[47] the undersigned Cree, Beaver, Chipewyan and other Indian Chiefs and Headmen, on their own behalf and on behalf of all other Indians inhabiting the tract within ceded, DO HEREBY SOLEMNLY PROMISE[48] and engage to strictly observe this treaty, and to conduct and behave themselves as good and loyal subjects of Her Majesty the Queen.

THEY[49] PROMISE AND ENGAGE[50] that they will in all respect obey and abide by the law; that they will maintain peace and good order between each other, and also between themselves and other tribes of Indians, and between themselves and other of Her Majesty's subjects, whether Indian or whites,[51] now inhabiting or hereafter inhabit any part of the said ceded tract, and they will not molest the person or property of any inhabitants of such ceded tract or the property of Her majesty the Queen, or interfere with or trouble any person passing or travelling through the said tract, or any part thereof, and they will assist the officers of Her Majesty in bringing to justice and punishment any Indian offending against the stipulation of this treaty, or infringing the laws in force in the country so ceded.

Model 3: Treaties of 1923 with Chippewa Indians of Christian Island, Georgia Island, and Rama, and Mississauga Indians of Rice Lake, Mud Lake, Scugog Lake and Alderville:[52]

AND THE UNDERSIGNED chiefs and headmen, on their own behalf and on behalf of all other Indians whom they represent, do hereby solemnly covenant, promise, and agree to strictly observe this treaty in all respects and they will not, nor will any of them, nor will any of the Indians whom they represent, molest or interfere with the person or property of anyone who now inhabits or shall hereafter inhabit any portion of the lands covered by this treaty, or interfere with, trouble, or molest any person passing or travelling through the said lands, or any part thereof, and they will assist the officers of Her Majesty in bringing to justice and punishment any Indian, party to this treaty, who may hereafter offend against the stipulation hereof or infringing the laws in force in the lands covered hereby.

Each of the peace and good order clauses of the Victorian treaties affirms the inherent right of Aboriginal sovereignty and governance for each ratifying tribe and people. This transformation to a vested Treaty governance right acknowledges the equal brotherhood between the peoples under the Great Spirit. As Treaty Commissioner Laird stated in Treaty 7 to the Blackfoot: "It is by the Great Spirit that the Queen rules over this great country and other great countries. The Great Spirit has made the white man and the red man brothers, and we should take each other by the hand."[53]

These clauses were embedded in every Victorian treaty. The importance of reaffirming these clauses in each treaty was viewed as so essential and integral to the purpose and operation of the treaties that little discussion of them by the treaty parties exists. Treaty governance is a constitutional expression of the right of self-determination, in the structure, spirit, intent, and terms of these treaties.

The Terms of the Treaties create
a Permanent Covenant with the Chiefs and Headmen

In each of the treaties, the treaty itself is structured to govern the relations of Treaty First Nations with the imperial Crown. The terms of a Victorian treaty itself establish the constitutional law for the Chief and Headmen. No provisions in the treaties provide for control of the Chiefs by any other executive or legislative power or governmental entity, such as Parliament or a Legislative Assembly.

The spirit and intent of the treaty is the controlling law for the Chiefs and the treaty people and supplements the existing First Nation jurisprudence. The Chiefs promised and engaged to "strictly observe" the treaty. Additionally, the Chiefs were explicit partners in the enforcement of the treaty; they promised the Crown that they would "aid and assist" the officers of Her Majesty in bringing to justice and punishment any Indian offending against the stipulation of a treaty.

The prerogative treaty order among the Treaty First Nations and the imperial Crown was a separate and distinct constitutional realm from the imperial

Parliament and its conventions. It was also a separate realm from the colonial assemblies that were created by the Crown-in-Parliament,[54] which ended prerogative authority over the British subjects.[55] These derivative governmental bodies had no constitutional capacity to extinguish or modify vested prerogative rights in the treaty order, since these rights continued as a distinct part of the imperial constitutional law.[56] Dickson C.J. acknowledged the separation of prerogative treaty federalism from provincial federalism:

> [T]he Indians' relationship with the Crown or sovereign has never depended on the particular representatives of the Crown involved. From the Aboriginal perspective, any federal-provincial divisions that the Crown has imposed on itself are internal to itself and do not alter the basic structure of Sovereign-Indian relations. This is not to suggest that aboriginal peoples are outside the sovereignty of the Crown, nor does it call into question the divisions of jurisdiction in relation to aboriginal peoples in federal Canada.[57]

The first thing to notice about interpreting these operative clauses of Treaty governance is that they simply assume the existing Aboriginal governance structures, the Chief and Headmen, will "maintain perpetual peace between themselves and Her Majesty's white subjects" or "maintain peace and good order."[58] The wording reveals that the source of this governance authority is not derived from the Crown, it is inherent in the Chief and Headmen by First Nations sovereignty and jurisprudence. The wording illustrates that the undivided imperial Crown affirmed that pre-existing First Nation authority would continue under the written treaties. It constitutes an imperial recognition and affirmation of all the general powers of governance in the Chiefs and Headmen.

The treaties provided the Chiefs' and Headmen's role is to maintain governance as a valid legitimate exercise of power in the shared territory recognized under imperial constitutional law against all other interests. It is an affirmative commitment to Treaty governance and First Nations law into the indefinite future—the haunting and endless—"forever." This wording is peremptory direction to law-making and law-enforcing officials of the United Kingdom and Canada that should not be denied or disparaged under any rule of law. Future governments and courts have to take the language of Treaty governance as expressed by the treaty commissioner in the treaty negotiations and as understood by the treaty Indians as vesting this governance power in imperial law.

The peace and good order clause in the treaties is analogous to the *Magna Carta*[59] and similar constitutional compacts that created the House of Lords, English Parliament, now the United Kingdom Parliament, and the model for the federal Parliament of Canada. This clause is of no less constitutional authority in North America than the original grants of the King's prerogative authority to the courts, the House of Lords, and the House of Commons in England.[60] Both the treaty article and the Crown grants are exercised in different contexts and territories but have the same constitutional significance. The treaty article is similar to the "Peace, Order, and good Government" clause in section 91 of the *Constitution Act, 1867*,[61] which gives residual authority to the federal government. The authority that Chiefs and Headmen had initially exercised by Aboriginal right over the protected territory is now exercised by the treaties throughout the shared land at the request of the Crown.[62] Treaty authority to govern the shared territory and people is an inviolable and a vested prerogative right.[63] Similar clauses are found in imperial British treaties in Africa and the Pacific.[64]

In 1909, Mr. Justice Davies explained the Supreme Court of Canada's decision in the dispute between the Dominion of Canada and the Province of Ontario over the issue of who owned the resources on reserve lands.[65] He acknowledged the fact that the two levels of government were constantly arguing over which had the proper authority over the title to the Indian territories, but noted that the jurisdictional obligation of the Treaty governance has been ignored:

> . . . the last clause of the treaty wherein the Indians agree "to obey and abide by the law" and "to maintain peace and good order between each other" and other people, and not "molest person or property in the ceded districts or interfere with any person passing or travelling through it," etc. from which I would be justified in concluding that the considerations of the treaty had been agreed to for other purposes than those of extinguishing Indian title.[66]

The Chiefs' authority in Treaty governance was distinct, pre-emptive, and paramount from the existing imperial delegations to the federal government.[67] The existing imperial delegation was not mentioned in the treaties. The wording of the treaties describe Treaty governance as a distinct order in British North America, in other words, Treaty governance was to be seen as sovereign in its own sphere in the land transferred to, but shared with, the imperial Crown. The spirit and intent of the treaty chiefs was to continue the Aboriginal order as vested imperial power. The treaties suggest annual treaty meetings with the Chiefs to work out problems of Treaty governance based on consensual reconciliations of conflicts and tensions. This comprehensive structure was the truly innovative feature of treaty federalism.

In 1973, the Queen and the federal government attempted to restore a constitutional balance to treaty federalism in Canada. The Queen formally conceded to First Nations that her government in Canada "recognizes the importance of full compliance with the spirit and terms of your Treaties."[68] This included the spirit and term of Treaty governance.

In fewer than ten years, treaty rights were affirmed and protection afforded to the vested right to Treaty governance by British imperial constitutional law when they were transferred to Canadian constitutional law by virtue of sections 35(1) and 52 of the *Constitution Act, 1982*.[69] The patriated constitution of Canada affirms

Treaty governance as an existing treaty right as part of the supreme law of Canada. It required that all federal and provincial laws had to be consistent with Treaty governance.[70]

The Crown, in all its manifestations, is judicially required to act in a trust-like and non-adversarial manner to fulfill its fiduciary obligations toward First Nations.[71] These constitutional obligations regulate and supervise the actions of Canadian governments and subjects toward constitutional rights of Aboriginal peoples,[72] including Treaty governance. They ensure the integrity and honour of the Crown,[73] and they are consistent with the "sacred" nature of treaty rights.[74] These protective obligations are always involved when governments or their administrations take any action, including judicial interpretation, which affects Treaty governance.[75]

These treaties are the highest form of constitutional covenants with the Crown or public contracts.[76] They are not controlled by either British or First Nation jurisprudence or private commercial or contractual law.[77] Courts cannot interpret consensual treaty rights as if they were expressions of statutory law, local common law rights, or customary law.[78] They are transnational law comprised of many different legal systems and complex conflict of law provisions.

The federal Crown, in its policy guide, has recognized that the inherent right of self-government is found within s. 35.[79] It recognizes that the inherent right may find expression in treaties, and in the context of the Crown's relationship with treaty First Nations. This recognition of the inherent right is based on the view that the Aboriginal peoples of Canada have the right to govern themselves in relation to matters that are internal to their communities, integral to their unique cultures, identities, traditions, languages, and institutions, and with respect to their special relationship to their land and their resources.[80]

Consistent with the expressed obligations of the Chiefs and Headmen to protect the terms of the imperial treaties, the Supreme Court has generated a number of impressive constitutional interpretative principles for the purpose of full compliance with the spirit and terms of the treaties.[81] A central part of these principles is the requirement that *sui generis* Aboriginal governance and Treaty governance clauses informed by constitutional rights must be interpreted in a large, liberal, and generous way.[82] The words of the peace and good order clause and the scope of Treaty governance must be given the sense they would naturally have held for the parties at the time the treaty was negotiated.[83] Subsequent technical or contractual interpretation of treaty wording is to be avoided.[84] Their interpretation cannot limit or alter the terms of the Treaty governance by either ignoring or exceeding what "is possible on the language."[85] The Supreme Court's interpretative principles are expansive and designed to sustain fair dealing and justice between Aboriginal peoples and the Crown.[86] They include implied and express intents,[87] and contextual,[88] textual,[89] implied,[90] and reasonably incidental rights.[91]

The wording of the peace and good order clauses have a primary place when it comes to determining constitutional obligations and rights of Treaty governance, however, the Supreme Court has found that treaty texts are not exhaustive. The Court has realized that every English word in the peace and good order clause has embedded in it a distinct First Nation jurisprudence and perspective that cannot be displaced by the English text.[92] The written text on Treaty governance provides an ancient, historical and political context and a structural foundation in interpreting the peace and good order clause that stretches back through the ages and encompasses both First Nations and British legal traditions and governance. These traditions function in symbiosis with the Treaty governance text. An analysis of these shared traditions aids the courts in their consideration of the underlying constitutional principles and their constitutional structure of Treaty governance.[93] These underlying meanings and principles are the vital, unstated assumptions upon which the Treaty governance clauses are based, and as such, they inform and sustain the promises of the Treaty governance.[94]

The purpose of any interpretation of a Treaty governance clause is determined by the perspectives of both parties at the time the treaty was negotiated and signed. This is important because the negotiations themselves would have incorporated certain constitutional principles and promises to Treaty governance that would not necessarily appear in the treaty text.[95] A *sui generis* analysis of the negotiations of a treaty and affirming Treaty governance invites the courts to turn those implicit principles and promises into specific constitutional premises that fill in gaps and clear up doubts about the express terms of the Treaty governance.

If a reviewing court is faced with many possible interpretations of the common intent of the treaty parties on Treaty governance, it must choose the mutual intent that best reconciles the shared interests of the parties.[96] In determining the treaty signatories' respective understandings and intents, the court must be sensitive to the unique cultural and linguistic differences between the parties regarding Aboriginal sovereignty, Treaty federalism, and Treaty governance.[97] In searching for the shared intent of the parties, the court must assume the integrity and honour of the Crown to fulfill its promises of Treaty governance, either during negotiations or in the text of the treaty.[98] The constitutional limitation of the honour of the Crown operates as an independent source of obligations as well as an interpretative principle.[99] It operates independently of the intent of the treaty parties. The courts cannot validate any hidden intents of the Crown, or any deceit, fraud, or sharp practices by the Crown's treaty agents, in its conceptualization of Treaty governance.

If, when the courts are using these interpretative principles on the peace and good order clauses and Treaty governance, any ambiguities or doubtful expressions arise about the language or meanings in the negotiations, the reviewing court should resolve the issue in favour of the Aboriginal signatories rather than in favour of the Crown.[100] Any treaty limitations that restrict the Treaty governance rights of Aboriginal signatories must be narrowly construed.[101] The interpretation of Treaty governance includes modern practices that are reasonably incidental to traditional Aboriginal practices.[102] Moreover, Treaty governance rights, obligations, and remedies are not frozen at the time of treaty signing; they can develop to meet new challenges and needs faced by the treaty signatories.[103]

Through either interpretative approach, the underlying principles and the treaty texts affirm Treaty governance as a distinct constitutional division of powers among the treaty parties. The express wording of the peace and good order clause recognizes, maintains, and extends the pre-existing sphere of jurisdiction and governance in the surrendered territory, and affirms and validates the scope of governing law, rights, and obligations of First Nations in the territory. Some Georgian treaty texts provide independent sources for the judicial review of controversies.[104]

The Terms of the Victorian Treaties Extended
Treaty Governance to Newcomers in the Shared Territory.

The Treaty governance authority covers not only internal governance of the confederating tribes and bands but also external governance in the shared territory. As stated in the Georgian treaty negotiations with the Mi'kmaw chiefs by the Lieutenant Governor: "In behalf of us, now your Fellow Subjects, I must demand, that you Build a Wall to secure our [English] Rights from being troden [*sic*] down by the feet of your people."[105] The purpose of the Victorian treaties was maintaining peace and good order by protecting the newcomers, rather than only within the confederated tribes.

The Chiefs and Headmen promised the Crown in both the Georgian and Victorian treaties that Treaty governance would be governed by the rule of law. Distinct from imperial delegation to the colonial governments, no long list of delegation of power or authority from the Sovereign to the Chiefs is enumerated in the Treaty governance clauses. Instead, the purposes of Treaty governance was directed at internal relationships with First Nations signing the treaty as well as the external relationships among other tribes of Indians[106] and other of Her Majesty's subjects, whether Indian or white, now inhabiting or hereafter inhabiting any part of the shared territory. The Chiefs promised they would not molest the person or property of any inhabitants of the shared territory or the property of the Queen. They promised not to interfere with or trouble any person passing or travelling through the territory, or any part thereof. They also promised to bring to justice any Indian infringing the laws in force in the shared territory.

These clauses extended Treaty governance to all of Her Majesty's subjects in the shared territory. They created the immigrants' bill of rights in Treaty governance. They created private or civil duties on the Chiefs toward the inhabitants and travellers through their jurisdiction, which is part of the rule of law inherent in the treaties. The treaty rule of law clauses sought to protect any person against violation of those boundaries of rightful possessions, against violations of the natural boundaries of the self, as well as mobility rights. It recognizes the inherent rights of individuals in their persons, in their labour, and in some specific interests in the shared territory in Treaty governance.

Supremacy of Treaty Governance in Canada

The *Final Report* of the Royal Commission of Aboriginal Peoples described how the Federal government ignored, failed to fulfill, and replaced Treaty governance with false assumptions and abuse of power and law.[107] The first false assumption that created federal law and policy asserted Aboriginal people to be inherently inferior and incapable of governing themselves. The second was that treaties and other agreements were, by and large, not covenants of trust and obligation but devices of statecraft, less expensive and more acceptable than armed conflict. Treaties were seen as a form of bureaucratic memorandum of understanding, to be acknowledged formally but ignored frequently. The third false assumption was that federal wardship was appropriate for all First Nations, so that actions deemed to be for their benefit could be taken without their consent or their involvement in design or implementation.[108]

Under these false premises, the Federal government, by federal law, created territorial governments and provincial governments for the non-Aboriginal people in the transferred land, which ruthlessly restricted the Treaty governance.[109] It enacted a distinct and oppressive regime of federal agency in the *Indian Act* and later created band administration on the family reserves independent from the treaty promises and rights.[110]

Treaty governance is a constitutional remedy to this oppressive regime. It builds upon fundamental promises and covenants that are now part of constitutional supremacy. The existing right to Treaty governance is fundamental to the special relationship between Treaty First Nations and the Crown. It is distinct from the neo-colonial idea of Indian self-government. The Federal government acknowledges that it does not have authority to re-open, change, or displace existing treaties.[111] For Treaty First Nations that so desire, the federal Crown has stated it is prepared to negotiate agreements on self-government that build on treaty federalism and governance already established by their treaties.[112] Twenty-five years after constitutionalizing treaty rights in 1982, both the federal and provincial Crowns continue to ignore implementing Treaty governance and persist in maintaining their own colonized version of self-administration and self-government.

Under the supremacy clause of s. 52(1), the honour of the Crown, and Treaty First Nation choice, however, the constitutional right of Treaty governance, as a vested constitutional right, will someday displace all inconsistent or infringing federal law and regulations. It will displace any inconsistent provisions of the federal *Indian Act* and its band system. Treaty governance will "displace" all inconsistent provincial laws of general application operating as federal law under s. 88 of the *Indian Act*.[113]

In Canadian constitutional analysis, Treaty governance of First Nations must be read together with other imperial acts of the United Kingdom Parliament, now constitutional acts and principles.[114] These historical acts cannot extinguish treaty rights,[115] without breaching the treaties, as they exist in the separate consensual transnational realm. However, the Supreme Court has held that if the Crown can prove a clear intent of an imperial act to modifying or extending treaty delegations, they may be valid.[116] Such modifications will be narrowly interpreted.[117] Since 1982, modern interpretation and federal or provincial legislation cannot extinguish treaty rights.[118]

Constitutional analysis requires the courts to create new analytical techniques to reconcile *sui generis* Treaty governance with purposes of creating a just Canada. Each individual element of the Canadian Constitution is linked to all the other elements in the Constitution and must be interpreted by reference to the structure of the Constitution as a whole.[119] This constitutional convergence breathes continuing vitality into Treaty governance within the Constitution of Canada.[120]

In such constitutional convergences, different and distinct legal systems combine to generate a theory of constitutional supremacy. Under said theory, Treaty governance did not have to surrender its unique visions and vitality to the immigrant theory of majority rule. Treaty governance is protected in its own right, as well as the underlying constitutional principles of the protection of minorities.[121] It is the constitutional right to create an effective governance system to provide real support for maintaining and exemplifying First Nations traditions, culture and language, and an enriched livelihood.

In any convergence of constitutional powers and the constitutional right of Treaty governance, the Supreme Court has asserted Crown or government actions must be consistent with treaty rights.[122] They must be read purposively with Treaty governance to accomplish the national goals of a just, post-colonial legal order. The convergence theory requires courts to acknowledge and affirm the "noble and prospective" purposes behind explicitly including Aboriginal and treaty rights in the patriated constitutional order. The Crown's actions can no longer arbitrarily ignore the constitutional rights of Treaty governance.[123]

Law professors Peter Hogg and Mary Ellen Turpel have suggested that constitutional analysis should reflect the central role of treaties and treaty-based government for Treaty First Nations. They suggest this could be accomplished by recognizing Treaty governance, which for Treaty First Nations will mean the articulation of rights and responsibilities flowing from existing treaties, which should be fully honoured and implemented by Canadian governments as a central part of inherent self-government implementation.[124]

Treaty governance presents as an existing set of connected values, ideas, and proposals, tentative in spirit and adaptable to diversity. It seeks not to be either utopian or trivial by adhering to the existing treaty rights and the proper interpretation of treaties, but is relatively distant from the operational policy of the Canadian governments. It remains the source that enables Treaty First Nations to implement their right to Treaty governance for the 21st century. It builds on the animating belief in alternative pluralisms rather than a singular sovereignty, to establish a culturally defined theory of government around the idea of ordered freedoms and shared values within a specific treaty boundary as well as relations with other treaties.

The implementation of constitutionally protected Treaty governance seeks to re-energize the treaty vision of self-determination and empowerment of family and human responsibilities by displacing the constraints of colonialism—the raw intrusiveness of its structural and institutional fetishism, its contaminated colonial methodologies, its racism, its separation of First Nation membership, and its institutional arrogance and inertia. Treaty governance will replace the dishonourable band administration regime under the *Indian Act* and its scandalous context of scarcity and poverty among First Nations along with the drudgeries and infirmities of their meaningless existence.

NOTES

1 *Haida Nation v. British Columbia* (Minister of Forests), [2004] 3 S.C.R. 511 at para. 20 [*Haida Nation*].

2 *Halsbury's Laws of England*, 4th ed., (London: Butterworths, 1991) states that the boundaries of constitutional law of the United Kingdom have never been satisfactorily defined (*ibid.*, vol. 8 at para. 801), but as part of the imperial constitutional law, treaties are included in the royal prerogatives (*ibid.*, at para. 985-86) and the United Nations (*ibid.*, at para. 988).

3 *R. v. Badger*, [1996] 1 S.C.R. 771 at paras. 76-79 [*Badger*]; see generally, in the context and the nature of Georgian treaties in imperial law, *R. v. Sioui*, [1990] 1 S.C.R. 1025 at 1053-56 [*Sioui*].

4 *Constitution Act, 1982*, being Schedule B to the *Canada Act 1982* (U.K.), 1982, c. 11 at Part II and VI.

5 For discussion of Treaty federalism, see "Empowering Treaty Federalism," 58 Sask. L. Rev. (1994): 243.

6 A.V. Dicey, *Introduction to the Study of the Law of the Constitution*, 8th ed. (London: Macmillan, 1915), 460 ("A treaty made by the Crown is valid without the authority or sanction of Parliament."); A.B. Keith, *Responsible Government in the Dominions* (Oxford: Clarendon press, 1912), 1102 ("There is no real doubt that treaties made by the Crown are binding on the Colonies whether or not the colonial governments consent to such treaties."); J.Y. Henderson, "Constitutional Power and Treaty Rights," 63 Sask. L. Rev. (2002): 719 [Constitutional Power].

7 *R. v. Sundown*, [1999] 1 S.C.R. 393 at paras. 6, 11, 25, 33, 35-36 [*Sundown*]; *Badger*, *supra* note 3 at paras. 76, 82; *R. v. Van der Peet*, [1996] 2 S.C.R. 507 at para. 31 [*Van der Peet*].

8 *Haida Nation*, *supra* note 1 at para. 20; *Van der Peet*, *supra* note 7 at paras. 31 and 60; *Sioui*, *supra* note 3 at 1053-56.

9 *Delgamuukw v. British Columbia*, [1997] 3 S.C.R. 1010 at paras. 15, 140-45, 172-81 [*Delgamuukw*].

10 McLachlin J., (as she was then), dissenting in *Van der Peet*, describes the majority's constitutional framework as "reasoning from first principles" rather than following imperial British common law and its historical and judicial methodology to the *sui generis* sovereignty, *supra* note 7 at para. 262.

11 *R. v. Côté*, [1996] 3 S.C.R. 139 at para. 48, Lamer C.J. [*Côté*] ("Although the doctrine [of Aboriginal rights] was a species of unwritten British law, it was not part of English common law in the narrow sense, and its application to a colony did not depend on whether or not English common law was introduced there."); *Van der Peet*, *supra* note 7 at para. 247 ("Aboriginal rights find their source not in a magic moment of European contact, but in the traditional laws and customs of the aboriginal people in question."), McLachlin, J., (as she then was) dissenting.

12 *Van der Peet, ibid.*

13 *Côté*, *supra* note 11 at para. 48, Lamer C.J.; *Van der Peet*, *supra* note 7 at para. 37, relying on *Worcester* v. *Georgia*, 31 U.S. (6 Pet.) 515 (1832) Marshall C.J.; *Sioui*, *supra* note 3 at 1053-55, Lamer J. (as he then was). Aboriginal nationality should not be confused with the federally created Indian Bands, which are entities of federal law, or the Liberal party's "inherent self-government" policies for these bands. See *R. v. Pamajewon*, [1996] 2 S.C.R. 821, where the Supreme Court assumed that the right of self-government is part of s. 35(1), but in the absence of evidence that it was an Aboriginal right attached to regulating gambling activities the Supreme Court did not have to determine the issue. A treaty argument may have given a different result. Compare with *Delgamuukw*, *supra* note 9, comment on Aboriginal system of governance at para. 159.

14 *Van der Peet*, *supra* note 7 at para. 106; *Calder v. Attorney General of British Columbia*, [1973] S.C.R. 313 at 328, Hall J.

15 *Van der Peet, ibid.*, at para. 263.

16 *Delgamuukw*, *supra* note 9 at para. 145. Also see *Delgamuukw v. British Columbia*, [1993] 5 C.N.L.R. 1 (B.C.C.A.) at para. 46, citing Brennon J. in *Mabo* v. *Queensland*, [1992] 5 C.N.L.R. 1 (H. C. Aus.) at 51; *Côté*, *supra* note 11 at para. 49.

17 *Côté, supra* note 11 at paras. 49, 52; *Van der Peet, supra* note 7 at para. 247, McLachlin J., dissenting (as she then was).

18 *Ibid.*

19 *Van der Peet, supra* note 7 at paras. 17, 20, 42.

20 *Ibid.*, at para. 19 (Aboriginal rights cannot be defined on the basis of the philosophical precepts of the liberal enlightenment.)

21 *Delgamuukw, supra* note 9 at paras. 130, 189; *St. Mary's Indian Band* v. *Cranbrook (City)*, [1997] 2 S.C.R. 657, at para. 14; *Canadian Pacific Ltd.* v. *Paul*, [1988] 2 S.C.R. 654 at 678; *Guerin* v. *The Queen*, [1984] 2 S.C.R. 335 at 382.

22 *Campbell* v. *Hall*, (1774) 1 Cowp. 204 (aff'd in *R.* v. *Secretary of State*, [1981] 4 C.N.L.R. 86 at 99, 127 (Eng. C.A.)); *Badger, supra* note 3 at paras. 41, 47; *Sundown, supra* note 7 at paras. 24, 46.

23 *Badger, ibid.*, at paras. 41 and 47, *Sioui, supra* note 3 at 1063; *Simon* v. *The Queen*, [1985] 2 S.C.R. 387 at 401; *Campbell, ibid.* By comparison, in British common law the most sacred principles appear to be the sovereignty of the King and the rule of law, while the sacred principles of British positive law was parliamentary supremacy. In the Canadian constitutional order, the most sacred principles are federalism, democracy, constitutional supremacy and the rule of law, and the protection of minorities, see *Re Reference by the Governor General in Council Concerning Certain Questions Relating to the Secession of Quebec*, [1998] 2 S.C.R. 217 at paras. 32, 49-82 [*Quebec Secession Reference*].

24 *Sundown, supra* note 7 at para. 46; *R.* v. *Marshall*, [1999] 3 S.C.R. 456 at para. 49 [*Marshall*]; *Badger, supra* note 3 at para. 47.

25 Canada, *Report of the Royal Commission on Aboriginal Peoples*, vol. 2 (Ottawa: Minister of Supply and Services, 1996) [RCAP] esp. at 139, 166-9, and 186-213. The Royal Commission had announced its support for the inherent right in *Partners in Confederation: Aboriginal Peoples, Self-Government and the Constitution* (Ottawa, Minister of Supply and Services, 1993), 29-45.

26 Union of Nova Scotia Indians, 1992. Alex Christmas (Address to the Royal Commission on Aboriginal Peoples, *ibid.* 6 May 1993 at Eskasoni, Nova Scotia).

27 Prerogative treaties and acts are protected in the imperial acts of parliament of the United Kingdom that establish responsible government, see sections 9, 12, 129, and 132 of *Constitution Act, 1867* (U.K.), 30 & 31 Vict., c. 3 (formerly *The British North America Act, 1867*) R.S.C. 1985, App. 1, No. 5; *Foreign Jurisdiction Act* (U.K.), 53 and 54 Vict., c. 37: *An Act to remove Doubts as to the Validity of Colonial Laws, 1863* (U.K.), 28 and 29 Vict., c. 63, and s. 35(1) and 52(1) of *Constitution Act, 1982, supra* note 4.

28 See sections 35(1) and 52(1) of *Constitution Act, 1982, ibid.*

29 *Delgamuukw, supra* note 9 at paras. 145, 166-9, 174, 176, 178.

30 R.A. Reiter, *The Law of Canadian Indian Treaties* (Edmonton: Juris Analytical) at Part III at 30 (Treaty 1, 1871); 38 (Treaty 2, 1871); 43 (Treaty 3, 1873); 55 (Treaty 4, 1874); 66 (Treaty 5, 1875); 87 (Treaty 6, 1876); 120 (Treaty 7, 1877); 138 (Treaty 8, 1899); 170 (Treaty 9, 1905 with the King); 195 (Treaty 10, 1906 with the King); 206 (Treaty 11, 1921 with the King); 214 Treaty of 1923 [*Canadian Treaties*].

31 A. Morris, *The Treaties of Canada with the Aboriginals of Manitoba and the Northwest Territories: Including the Negotiations on which they were Based, and Other Information Relating Thereto* (Toronto: Belfords, Clark, 1880), 28-9, 58, 96, 124, 184, 193, 211, 218, 221, 231-3, 241, 257, 269-70, 272.

32 Treaty 1, *Canadian Treaties, supra* note 30 at 32.

33 *Canadian Treaties, ibid.*, 39-40 (Treaty 2), 46 (Treaty 3), 57-58 (Treaty 4), 69 (Treaty 5), 89-90 (Treaty 6), and 122-23 (Treaty 7).

34 *Canadian Treaties, ibid.*, Treaty 7 at 122 includes Head Chiefs and Minor Chiefs, and Councillors.

35 In Treaties 6, 8-11 creates a new paragraph, *ibid.*, at 89-90 (Treaty 6), 140 (Treaty 8), 172 (Treaty 9), 197 (Treaty 10), and 207-08 (Treaty 11).

36 *Ibid.*, Treaty 7 capitalizes law.

37 Compare to section 91 (Legislative Authority of Parliament of Canada) of the *Constitution Act, 1867, supra* note 27: "It shall be lawful for the Queen, by and with the Advice and Consent of the Senate and House of Commons, to make Laws for the Peace, Order and good Government of Canada, in relation to all Matters not coming within the Classes of Subject by this Act assigned exclusively to the Legislatures of the Provinces."

38 Compare to section 132 of the *Constitution Act, 1867, ibid.*: "The Parliament and Government of Canada shall have all Powers necessary or proper for performing the Obligations of Canada or of any Province thereof, as Part of the British Empire, toward Foreign Countries, arising under Treaties between the Empire and Foreign Countries."

39 *Canadian Treaties, supra* note 30, Treaty 7 adds Half Breeds to the list. Compare to section 91 of the *Constitution Act, 1867, supra* note 37.

40 This clause creates private or civil duties on the Chiefs, which is part of tort law.

41 This clause creates mobility rights of the immigrants. Compare to section 6 (mobility rights) of *Canadian Charter of Rights and Freedoms*, being Schedule A to the *Canada Act 1982* (U.K.), 1982, c. 11 at Part II and VI.

Section 25 of the *Charter,* however, states "The guarantee in this *Charter* of certain rights and freedoms shall not be construed so as to abrogate or derogate from any aboriginal, treaty, or other rights or freedoms that pertain to the aboriginal peoples of Canada including (a) any rights or freedoms that have been recognized by the Royal Proclamation of October 7, 1763; and (b) any rights or freedoms that now exist by way of land claims agreements or may be so acquired."

42   *Canadian Treaties, supra* note 30, wording in Treaties 4 and 7 state "assist," rather than aid and assist.

43   Officers or servants of the Crown has been interpreted as service or employment with the Government in connection with some aspect of governmental administration or activity, *McAuthor* v. *R.,* [1943] 3 D.L.R. 225 at 266, [1943] Ex. C.R. 77, Thorson J. An Attorney General is an officer of the Crown, *Re Brown* [1994] 1 D.L.R. 365 at 367, Coady J.

44   Compare to section 92(14) of the *Constitution Act, 1867, supra* note 27: "In each Province the Legislature may exclusively make Laws in relation to Matters coming within the Classes of Subjects next hereinafter enumerated; that is to say. - [. . .] 14. The Administration of Justice in the Province, including the Constitution, Maintenance, and Organization of Provincial Courts, both of Civil and Criminal Jurisdiction, and including Procedure in Civil Matters in those Courts." Compare also to section 91(27), *supra* note 27, which delegates to the Parliament of Canada "27. The Criminal Law, except the Constitution of Courts of Criminal Jurisdiction, but including the Procedure in Criminal Matters."

45   Compare to section 92(15) of *Constitution Act, 1867, supra* note 27: "In each Province the Legislature may exclusively make Laws in relation to Matters coming within the Classes of Subjects next hereinafter enumerated; that is to say. - [. . .] 15. The Imposition of Punishment by Fine, Penalty or Imprisonment for enforcing any Law of the Province made in relation to any Matter coming within any of the Classes of Subjects enumerated in this Section," and "6. The Establishment, Maintenance, and Management of Public and Reformatory Prisons in and for the Province." Compare also to section 91(28), *supra,* which delegates the Parliament of Canada "28. The Establishment, Maintenance, and Management of Penitentiaries."

46   *Canadian Treaties, supra* note 30 at 140 (Treaty 8), 172 (Treaty 9), 197 (Treaty 10), and 207-08 (Treaty 11).

47   *Canadian Treaties, ibid.,* capitalized in Treaties 8 and 11, no capitalization in Treaties 9 and 10.

48   *Ibid.,* capitalized in Treaties 8 and 11, no capitalization in Treaties 9 and 10.

49   *Ibid.,* capitalized in Treaties 8 and 11, no capitalization in Treaties 9 and 10.

50   *Ibid.,* capitalized in Treaties 8 and 11, no capitalization in Treaties 9 and 10.

51   *Ibid.,* Treaties 9 and 10 provides for half-breeds.

52   *Canadian Treaties, ibid.,* at 216. This treaty corrects prior treaties that provide for governance of the Chippewa.

53   *Ibid.,* at 267. Also see Treaty 6, *ibid.,* at 199.

54   See *Foreign Jurisdiction Act, 1890, supra* note 27; and P.W. Hogg, *Constitutional Law of Canada,* 3d ed. (Toronto: Carswell, 1992), 13-17.

55   *Hogg, ibid.,* at 27-36. Also, from the middle of the nineteenth century, there was a convention against Parliament legislating for self-governing colonies without consent (*Halsbury's,* vol. 6, *supra* note 2 at para. 988).

56   *Halsbury's, ibid.,* vol. 8, at paras. 807-17 and 889-1082.

57   *Mitchell* v. *Peguis Indian Band,* [1990] 2 S.C.R. 85 at 109 (dissenting opinion on other points).

58   This term was used in the Haudenosaunee Belt of the Covenant Chain with 15 Rows (Treaty of Stanwix) where they promised "we will direct our thoughts to the maintenance of peace and good order." National Archives of Canada, Record Group 10, vol. 1826 (22 October and 5 November 1768) and in Treaty entered into with the Mi'kmaw Indians from Cape Tormentine to the Bay De Chaleurs, 22 September 1779 (restore peace and good order), Public Archives of Nova Scotia, Colonial Office 217/54 at 1252-57.

59   25 Edw. 1 (1215). J. C. Holt, *Magna Carta* (Cambridge: Cambridge University Press, 1965), 317.

60   *Halsbury's,* vol. 8, *supra* note 2 at para. 808-17. Originally, the whole of English government was the prerogative authority. This authority was gradually delegated to the courts and then to Parliament, becoming a limitation on prerogative authority in England. In the course of centuries, Parliamentary power strictly limited the prerogative powers and introduced a distinction between the Sovereign's power when acting in association with Parliament and when not acting in association with Parliament. The prerogative power remained valid authority in foreign affairs.

61   Hogg, *supra* note 54 at 435-39.

62   By the principle of legality in English constitutional law, the existence of a power or duty is a matter of law and not fact and so must be determined by reference to some prerogative or statutory enactment or reported case. See *Halsbury's,* vol. 8, *supra* note 2 at para. 828.

63   *Campbell* v. *Hall, supra* note 22 at 281. See also A. Chitty, *Treatise of the Law of the Prerogatives of the Crown: And the Relative Duties and Rights of the Subject* (London: Joseph Butterworths and Son, 1820), 29.

64   See the English version of the imperial Treaty of Waitangi with the Maori (1840) (Her Majesty Victoria Queen of the United Kingdom of Great Britain and Ireland regarding her Royal Favour the Native Chiefs and Tribes of New Zealand and anxious to protect their just Rights and Property and to secure to them the enjoyment of Peace and Good Order); Kingdom of Hawaiian Islands and Austro-Hungarian Treaty (1875) (Police

Regulations established for the preservation of peace and good order shall be duly respected). See generally, A. Anghie, "Finding the Peripheries: Sovereignty and Colonialism in Nineteenth-Century International Law," (1999) 40:1 Harv. Int'l L. J. 1; C.H. Alexandrowicz, *The European-African Confrontation: A Study In Treaty Making* (Leiden: Sijthoff, 1973).

65 Canada, Session Paper no. 50, 12 February 1909.

66 *Ibid.*

67 Section 91(24) of the *Constitution Act, 1867, supra* note 27: the imperial Parliament delegated to the Dominion "exclusive power to legislate with respect to Indians and Lands reserved for the Indians." It also provided authority to implement the obligations of imperial treaties, in s. 132, *ibid.* ("The Parliament and Government of Canada shall have all Powers necessary or proper for performing the Obligations of Canada or of any Province thereof, as Part of the British Empire, toward Foreign Countries, arising under Treaties between the Empire and such Foreign Countries.")

68 Queen Elizabeth II, as quoted in J. Chrétien, "Statement Made by the Honourable Jean Chrétien, Minister of Indian Affairs and Northern Development on Claims of Indian and Inuit People" (8 August 1973).

69 *R. v. Secretary of State, supra* note 22 at 99; *R. v. Sparrow,* [1990] 1 S.C.R. 1075 at 1091, 1101-12. In 1983, a special committee of the House of Commons had recommended federal legislative recognition and constitutional entrenchment of a form of First Nations self-government: see Canada, H.C., Special Committee on Indian Self-government, *Indian Self-Government in Canada* (Ottawa: Minister of Supply and Services, 20 October 1983) esp. 43-6.

70 Section 52(1) of *Constitution Act, 1982, supra* note 4 provides: "The Constitution of Canada is the supreme law of Canada, and any law that is inconsistent with the provisions of the Constitution is, to the extent of the inconsistency, of no force or effect."

71 *Sparrow, supra* note 69 at 1109.

72 *Ibid.*

73 *Ibid.*, at 1107-8 and 1110; *Badger, supra* note 3 at paras. 41 and 78; *Sundown, supra* note 7 at para. 24; *Marshall, supra* note 24 at paras. 4, 49-52; *Mikisew Cree First Nation,* [2005] 3 S.C.R. 388 at paras. 33, 47-59 [*Mikisew Nation*].

74 *Badger, ibid.*, at para. 41. Also see, *Campbell, supra* note 22.

75 *Quebec Secession Reference, supra* note 23 at paras. 70-72.

76 *Badger, supra* note 3 at para. 76 (treaties are analogous to contracts, albeit of a very solemn and special, public nature); *R. v. Keepness,* [2000] 2 C.N.L.R. 195 at para. 2, Smith J. ("[a] treaty is the most powerful of contracts").

77 *Sundown, supra* note 7 at para. 24; *Marshall, supra* note 24 at para. 10 (rules of interpretation in contract law are in general more strict than those applicable to treaties): *Badger, ibid.*, at para. 76. The rules of international law do not apply to extinguishment of Georgian treaties, *Simon, supra* note 23 at 404 and *Sioui, supra* note 3 at 1037-38. Some of the fundamental principles of promise and obligation in private law and First Nations law have some influence in the constitutional interpretation of sui generis treaties, *Marshall, supra* note 24 at para. 43, 52; *Badger, supra* note 3 at paras. 41, 47, 54-58, 72.

78 *Sundown, ibid.*, at para. 35.

79 Federal Policy Guide, Aboriginal Self-Government, The Government of Canada's Approach to Implementation of the Inherent Right and the Negotiation of Aboriginal Self-Government, 1995, http://www.ainc-inac.gc.ca/pr/pub/sg/plcy_e.html#PartI. [Inherent Rights Policy]. This follows the constitutional convention of the Charlottetown Accord (1992), reprinted in K. McRoberts and P. Monahan, *The Charlottetown Accord, the Referendum and the Future of Canada* (Toronto: University of Toronto Press, 1993).

80 This phrase implements the constitutional convention of section 41 of the Consensus Report on the Constitution, *The Charlottetown Accord, ibid.*, at 301.

81 *Sundown, supra* note 7 at para. 24; *Badger, supra* note 3 at para. 78; *Sioui, supra* note 3 at 1043; *Simon, supra* note 23 at 404. See also, J.Y. Henderson, "Interpreting *Sui generis* Treaties," (1997) 36 Alta. L. Rev. 46; L.I. Rotman, "Defining Parameters: Aboriginal Rights, Treaty Rights, and the Sparrow Justificatory Test," (1997) 36 Alta. L. Rev. 149; G. Christie, "Justifying Principles of Treaty Interpretation," (2000) 26 Queen's L. J. 143.

82 *Sparrow, supra* note 69 at 1106; *Simon, ibid.*, at 402; *Sioui, ibid.*, at 1035-36.

83 *Badger, supra* note 3 at para. 53; *Nowegijick v. The Queen,* [1983] 1 S.C.R. 29 at 36.

84 *Badger, ibid.*; *R. v. Horseman,* [1990] 1 S.C.R. 901 [*Horseman*]; *Nowegijick, ibid.*

85 *Marshall, supra* note 24 at para. 78, McLachlin J. (as she then was), relying on *Badger, ibid.*, at para. 76; *Sioui, supra* note 3 at 1069.

86 *Sundown, supra* note 7 at para. 24.

87 *Badger, supra* note 3 at paras. 51, 97; *Marshall, supra* note 24 at para. 44.

88 *Horseman, supra* note 84, Wilson J. dissent at para. 6; *Badger, supra* note 3 at para. 52; *Sundown, supra* note 7 at para. 24, *Marshall, supra* note 24, McLachlin J., (as she then was) dissenting at paras. 80-81.

89 *Badger, supra* note 3 at para. 52; *Sundown, supra* note 7 at para. 25, *Marshall, supra* note 24, Binnie J. at para. 5; McLachlin J. (as she then was), dissenting at para. 82.

90 *Sundown, supra* note 7 at para. 41 (employed the concept of implied rights to support the meaningful exercise of express rights granted to the First Nations in circumstances where no such implication might necessarily have been made absent the *sui generis* nature of the Crown's relationship to Aboriginal people).

91 In treaty interpretation, *Simon, supra* note 23 at 401; *Marshall, supra* note 24 at paras. 70, 78; and *Sundown, supra* note 7 at paras. 26-33. Similar rights have not been recognized in Aboriginal rights, *Van der Peet, supra* note 7 at para. 70. But see, *Côté, supra* note 11 at paras. 27, 31, and 56 at para. 56 ("to ensure the continuity of Aboriginal customs and traditions, a substantive Aboriginal right will normally include the incidental right to teach such a practice, custom and tradition to a younger generation."), Lamer C. J.

92 Aboriginal perspectives stand outside the English language and its dictionaries, *supra* notes 20-21. In any *sui generis* analysis, it is rare to find that a single meaning to any word exists for different treaty parties. It is more usual to find that infinite meanings exist, and that few of these meanings were ever shared.

93 *Quebec Secession Reference, supra* note 23 at para. 49-50 in *OPSEU* v. *Ontario (Attorney General)*, [1987] 2 S.C.R. 2 at 57.

94 RCAP, *supra* note 25 vol. 2(1) at 53-57 has identified some of the underlying principles of treaties; they include mutual recognition, mutual respect, sharing, and mutual responsibilities.

95 *Marshall, supra* 24 at para. 41. This operation is similar to how the preamble to the *Constitution Act, 1867, supra* note 27, operates in imperial legal traditions. *Quebec Secession Reference, supra* note 23 at para. 53.

96 Marshall, *supra* note 24 at para. 82, McLachlin J. (as she then was), dissenting on other grounds; *Sioui, supra* note 3 at 1068 and 1069.

97 *Badger, supra* note 3 at paras. 52-54; *Horseman, supra* note 84 at 907.

98 *Badger, ibid.,* at para. 41; *Marshall, supra* note 24 at paras. 49-52.

99 *Mikisew Nation, supra* note 73 at paras. 33, 51-52, 54, 56-57, 59; *Marshall, ibid.,* at paras. 4, 44.

100 *Simon, supra* note 23 at 402; *Sioui, supra* note 3 at 1035; *Badger, supra* note 3 at para. 52.

101 *Badger, supra* note 3 at para. 52.

102 *Marshall, supra* note 24 at paras. 70, 78; and *Sundown, supra* note 7 at paras. 26-33.

103 *Marshall, ibid.,* at para. 78, McLachlin J. (as she then was), relying on *Sundown, ibid.,* at para. 32; *Simon, supra* note 23 at 402.

104 For example, see Mi'kmaw treaties, in Constitutional Power, *supra* note 6 at 719, 720-29.

105 United Kingdom [UK], Colonial Office [CO] 217/8 at 276, "Ceremonials at Concluding Peace with the several Districts of the general Mickmack Nation of Indians in His Majesty's Province of Nova Scotia, and a Copy of the Treaty" (25 June 1761); R.H. Whitehead, *The Old Man Told Us: Excerpts from Micmac History 1500-1950* (Halifax: Nimbus, 1991), 159.

106 Compare to section 132 of the *Constitution Act, 1867, supra* note 27: "The Parliament and Government of Canada shall have all Powers necessary or proper for performing the Obligations of Canada or of any Province thereof, as Part of the British Empire, toward Foreign Countries, arising under Treaties between the Empire and such Foreign Countries."

107 RCAP, *supra* note 25 at vol. 1, at 245 -54, vol. 2(1), at 9-58.

108 RCAP, *ibid.,* at 248-9.

109 *Alberta Act,* S.C. 1905, c. 3, reprinted in R.S.C. 1970, App. II, no. 19, and *Saskatchewan Act,* S.C. 1905, c. 42, reprinted in R.S.C. 1970, App. II, No. 20. These federal acts were constitutionalized in *Constitution Act, 1982* in 52(2), *supra* note 4.

110 RCAP, *supra* note 25 at vol. 1 at 274-332.

111 Inherent Rights Policy, *supra* note 79.

112 *Ibid.*

113 *Indian Act,* R.S. 1985, c. I-5.

114 *Badger, supra* note 3 at paras. 47, 72, 83-85, Cory J, at paras. 1, 2, 12, Lamer C.J. and Sopinka J. dissent; *Quebec Secession Reference, supra* note 23 at para. 3.

115 Under s. 88 of the *Indian Act, supra* note 113, before the constitutionalizing of treaty rights, the Supreme Court held treaty rights may be unilaterally abridged by an imperial act, the *Constitution Act, 1930,* 20-21 George V, c. 26 (UK), modernized to the Constitution of Canada in Appendix II, Schedule to the *Constitutional Act, 1982, supra* note 4, item 16 by s. 52(2)(b). See *Horseman, supra* note 84 at 936; *R.* v. *Sikyea,* [1964] 2 C.C.C. 325 (N.W.T.C.A.), at 330, aff'd [1964] S.C.R. 642; and *Moosehunter* v. *The Queen,* [1981] 1 S.C.R. 282 at p. 293; discussed in *Badger, ibid.,* at para. 74; *Marshall, supra* note 24 at para. 46, *Sundown, supra* note 7 at para. 8. The cases deal with specific treaty delegations to the federal government to regulate treaty hunting avocations in a treaty, not with treaty rights. The continuing validity of these decisions is questionable under the theory of constitutional convergences. Moreover, since these rights were connected to the land cession granted to Indians by treaties and usually formed an integral part of the consideration for the surrender of their lands, *Badger, ibid.,* at para. 82, the Supreme Court noted it is unlikely it would proceed in that manner today, *ibid.,* at para. 84. The Supreme Court noted that any contemporary limitation on treaty rights requires justification, *ibid.,* at para. 85.

116 *Horseman, supra* note 84 at 932-34; *Badger, supra* note 3 at para. 84. See also *Halfway River First Nation* v. *B.C.* (Minister of Forest), [1999] 4 C.N.L.R. 1 (B.C.C.A.) at paras. 131-144, especially para. 136.

117 *Badger* and *Halfway River, ibid.*

118 *See Van der Peet, supra* note 7 at para. 28; *Delgammukw, supra* note 11 at paras. 173-74; *R.* v. *Mitchell,* [2001] 1 S.C.R. 911 at para. 11.

119 *Quebec Secession Reference, supra* note 23 at para. 50.

120 *Ibid.,* at paras. 49-54.

121 *Ibid.,* at para. 80.

122 *Marshall, supra* note 24 at para. 67.

123 *Ibid.,* at para. 64.

124 P. Hogg and M.E. Turpel, "Implementing Aboriginal Self-Government: Constitutional and Jurisdictional Issues," 74 Can. Bar Rev. (1995), 187.

REGAINING RECOGNITION OF THE INHERENT RIGHT OF ABORIGINAL GOVERNANCE

Bradford W. Morse, University of Ottawa

First Nations, Inuit, and Métis peoples' four centuries of experience with Europeans have encompassed many overwhelmingly horrific events. Canada's history is filled with stories of the suffering of Aboriginal peoples resulting from territorial dispossession, outright theft of traditional lands, various forms of exploitation, acts of direct and indirect violence often amounting to genocide, oppression of cultural practices and religious beliefs, wholesale removal of generations of children to church-run residential schools, the gross over-representation of Aboriginal people in Canadian prisons and child welfare systems, solemn treaties that regularly failed to capture the true nature of oral negotiations within their written terms, statutory and treaty obligations on the Crown that lay unfulfilled, and the blanket denial of legitimate sovereignty held by their governments. The Aboriginal peoples who live in what is now called Canada endure shorter life spans, poorer health circumstances, higher unemployment, lower educational levels, and generally far weaker socio-economic conditions than the Canadian average. Their distinct communities have far inferior infrastructure and receive significantly less expansive social and health care services.

One mere chapter cannot explore the history of the past four centuries, from the eras of peace and friendship treaty-making between sovereign nations based upon mutual respect and military alliances through the decades of racism and oppression or the more recent and sporadic attempts at rebuilding a sense of partnership. These few pages can merely offer a glimpse into the various efforts currently underway to reaffirm the First Nations, Inuit, and Métis right of self-determination through domestic recognition of the constitutional space to govern their own affairs within Canada.

Impact of the Constitution

The *Constitution Act, 1982,*[1] has fundamentally transformed the legal and political relationship between all Aboriginal peoples[2] and the rest of Canada. Not only does section 25 of the *Canadian Charter of Rights and Freedoms* protect "aboriginal, treaty or other rights or freedoms" of the Aboriginal peoples from being abrogated or derogated from by the balance of the Charter, but section 35 confirms the "existing aboriginal and treaty rights" as being "recognized and affirmed" so as to be part of the "supreme law of Canada" (section 52(1)). The term "aboriginal peoples" is also clearly defined in section 35(2) to include "the Indian, Inuit, and Métis peoples." The unique Aboriginal and treaty rights have been guaranteed equally among female and male Aboriginal persons through the 1984 amendments adding section 35(4), which also made certain that prior and future land claims settlements will receive the same constitutional status as historic treaties (through sections 25(b) and 35(3)). These latter amendments were intended to encompass the two settlements reached in Quebec in the late 1970s as well as all subsequent land claims agreements. The *Constitution Act, 1982*, was further altered in 1984 to ensure that no future amendments to any existing constitutional provisions that explicitly apply to Aboriginal peoples (including section 91(24) of the *Constitution Act, 1867*) can proceed before the Prime Minister has previously convened a First Ministers' Conference to which Aboriginal representatives have been invited (section 35.1). This latter provision at least guarantees the input of Aboriginal leaders into the discussion of any such proposed future constitutional change; however, Aboriginal consent is not required.

These provisions have had a profound effect upon Canadian judicial thinking in addition to significantly raising the political stature and public profile of Aboriginal peoples in Canada. It is beyond the scope of this chapter to explore the changes in the case law that have occurred over the past twenty-five years. It must be noted though that our perceptions of what constitutes a 'treaty' have been broadened considerably by the Supreme Court of Canada's decision in the *Sioui*[3] case. It is also now recognized that both Aboriginal and treaty rights can render federal and provincial laws inapplicable to Aboriginal peoples in appropriate situations as a result of this Court's decision in *R. v. Sparrow*.[4] The Supreme Court in 1990, also recognized in *Sioui* that Aboriginal peoples once constituted independent, sovereign nations (without commenting upon their current status) who could enter into treaties as such with the Crown and its representatives.

The new constitutional provisions may have also subtly affected judicial thinking even in matters that were formally before the court without reference to the new sections as the events arose prior to 1982. Our highest court applied a private law concept of fiduciary relationships and obligations to the Crown in *Guerin v. The Queen*[5] and stated that this relationship can apply to restrain the behaviour of both federal and provincial governments in the manner in which they deal with Indian, Inuit, and Métis peoples. The breach of specific obligations in that case warranted a remedy of $10 million in damages against the Government of Canada for the improper actions of the Department of Indians Affairs and Northern Development.

> [T]he nature of Indian title and the framework of the statutory scheme established for disposing of Indian land places upon the Crown an equitable obligation, enforceable by the courts, to deal with the land for the benefit of the Indians. This obligation does not amount to a trust in a private law sense. It is rather a fiduciary duty. If however, the Crown breaches this fiduciary duty it will be liable to the Indians in the same way and to the same extent as if such a trust were in effect.[6]

The Supreme Court in the *Simon*[7] case also made it clear, without relying upon the section 35(1) recognition of treaties, that treaty rights are not limited to status Indians but can potentially apply to any descendant of the treaty beneficiaries. The Court further elaborated a test and an approach to interpreting treaties that requires that they be given a liberal interpretation from the perspective of the First Nation party in light of all the evidence surrounding the negotiations of the treaty concerned. This position in *Simon* has been repeated on a number of subsequent occasions including the *Sioui, Badger*[8] and *Marshall*[9] decisions in which section 35(1) was influential.[10] A similar liberal approach to interpreting statutory provisions that may benefit Aboriginal peoples was declared to apply in the *Nowegijick*[11] case that arose prior to the 1982 constitutional changes. Chief Justice Dickson stated a general proposition in these terms: "It seems to me, however, that treaties and statutes relating to Indians should be liberally construed and doubtful expressions resolved in favour of the Indians."[12]

The Supreme Court of Canada issued a number of other critical pronouncements in the 1990s. The judges declared that Aboriginal rights exist across a spectrum from Aboriginal title granting exclusive possession at one end, to rights exercised within traditional territory, to practices or customs that are "integral to the distinctive cultures of aboriginal peoples" but are not site-specific rights at the other in two cases arising from Quebec (*Adams*[13] and *Coté*[14]). The Supreme Court jettisoned any lingering questions concerning the continuing relevance of Aboriginal title in the modern era in *Delgamuukw*[15] while suggesting that the test for Aboriginal title may have to be modified to accommodate the post-contact reality of the Métis. On the other hand, the Court declared that Aboriginal rights must be grounded in the specific factual context of a particular Aboriginal Nation, thereby effectively requiring each First Nation to persuade a court concerning the scope of its Aboriginal rights and title individually. The specific First Nation must prove that the rights in question were, at the time the Crown asserted sovereignty over its territory, and remain today, integral or fundamental to their distinct identity in order to be recognized as part of Canada's version of the common law that has become entrenched through section 35 (in *Van der Peet*,[16] *Gladstone*,[17] *Pamajewon*,[18] and others).

In 1999, the Supreme Court had its first opportunity to grapple with the inter-relationship between section 15, the equality rights provision of the *Charter of Rights and Freedoms*, and Aboriginal legal issues articulated in *Corbiere* v. *Canada*.[19] The Court accepted that "aboriginality-residence" was an analogous ground to those specified in section 15(1) such that election provisions excluding off-reserve members from voting under the *Indian Act* were discriminatory and unconstitutional. On the other hand, the Court subsequently made clear in *Lovelace* v. *Ontario*[20] that a provincial government scheme to share profits from an on-reserve casino among all *Indian Act* recognized First Nations, thereby excluding Métis and unrecognized Indian communities, was not a violation of section 15. In the Court's opinion, favouring one somewhat similarly situated disadvantaged group over another through an ameliorative initiative was not discriminatory. More than mere economic prejudice was required since the more restrictive accommodation did not truly exclude the Plaintiffs from "access to a fundamental social institution" or "a basic aspect of full membership in Canadian society (e.g. voting, mobility)." The Court did, however, determine that section 15 applied not merely to "laws" but to government programs as well.

More recently, our highest court has determined that both federal and provincial governments owe a legally enforceable duty to consult with Aboriginal communities whenever either government is considering a policy, program, or law that could infringe upon Aboriginal or treaty rights, regardless of whether such Aboriginal or treaty rights have previously been proven to exist.[21] The magnitude of the potential infringement will be seen as impacting upon the extent to which the consultation duty requires active interaction and the degree to which the Crown must negotiate to resolve the concerns of the effected Aboriginal communities. Where the section 35 rights that could be impacted upon have already been recognized, then the Aboriginal Nation concerned may possess a veto over Crown plans in appropriate circumstances. While the duties to consult, negotiate, and accommodate rest solely upon the Crown, third parties can clearly be involved as it is often their plans to exploit natural resources with governmental permission that initiate the process.

The Revival of the Self-government Debate

As Belanger and Newhouse discuss in detail in Chapter One,[22] the federal government's dramatic and draconian plan contained in the White Paper of 1969, to repeal the *Indian Act* and effectively abolish the unique legal and political position of "Indian bands" in Canada, provoked an immediate negative response from First Nations across the country. This reaction itself generated increased public attention to First Nations' assertions that they were not just Canadian citizens living on a separate land base. The development of federally funded national and regional organizations to represent those communities, as well as separate Inuit and off-reserve Indian and Métis associations, created a climate in which Aboriginal leaders had a much greater capacity to speak directly to governments, the media, and Canadians at large in a coordinated fashion about who they are and what they wanted for the future.

While these new organizations clearly were in the forefront of sparking a broad dialogue that had, in some senses, never previously occurred in Canada, the courts also had a profound role in legitimizing in the eyes of the dominant society what the chiefs and others were saying. The Supreme Court's reversal in 1973 of two lower court judgments in *Calder* v. *Attorney General of British Columbia*[23] regarding the continuing legal importance of Aboriginal title had a massive impact in shaking the comfortable assumptions of federal and provincial governments that Crown and private ownership of Canada's lands was secure. Not only did Prime Minister Trudeau have to abandon the White Paper, but he also had to withdraw his assertions that treaties were anachronisms that would not be repeated. Within months, the federal government announced its willingness to resume treaty-making with First Nations after a 40-year hiatus. The government also accepted the need to negotiate Aboriginal title claims with the Inuit for the first time in Canadian history.

The *Calder* case is also directly relevant to the subject of this chapter. Even while rejecting the Aboriginal title arguments of the Nisga'a as unextinguished, Justice Judson (writing for 3 of the 7 justices) felt compelled to recognize that "Indians were there, organized in societies, occupying the land as their forefathers had for centuries."[24] By doing so, he recognized not only a possessory interest in land as a proprietary right that could be accepted and enforced by the common law, but he also indirectly acknowledged that First Nations were self-governing prior to the arrival of Europeans. Justice Hall, writing in dissent for another 3 of the justices on the continued existence of title for the Nisga'a, was even clearer in this regard when he quoted US Supreme Court Chief Justice Marshall from a century and a half earlier in saying "America, separated from Europe by a wide ocean, was inhabited by a distinct people, divided into separate nations, independent of the rest of the world, *having institutions of their own, and governing themselves by their own laws* [emphasis added]."[25]

Although the Court did not have to address issues of continuing Aboriginal sovereignty and self-determination in *Calder*, it planted the seed for this ensuing debate. Far greater attention was paid in subsequent years to the existence of self-governing American Indian tribes exercising broad legislative jurisdiction encompassing most aspects of daily life in reference to all persons (both members and non-members alike) within reservation boundaries as a matter of their retained, residual sovereignty that had been affirmed by the American courts. The reality that Indian Nations—just across the invisible border—had their own courts, police, motor vehicle license plates, and legislatures enacting a broad array of laws (e.g. family, inheritance, property, child welfare, crime, taxation, corporations, traffic, and natural resources laws, amongst many others) demonstrated that a fundamental shift from the status quo was readily feasible, provided sufficient political will existed to break with the past century of assimilation to return to peaceful coexistence.

Belanger and Newhouse again have outlined the competing visions articulated through the following decades, while I have previously summarized the largely unsuccessful constitutional negotiations of the 1980s and 1990s, as well as the Chrétien government's Inherent Right Policy of 1995, in an earlier edition.[26] My objective here is to explore the two main domestic arenas in which some constitutional space has been accepted as permitting more extensive jurisdiction for Aboriginal self-government to develop, namely, under federal legislative auspices and through negotiating new treaties. This limited landscape is not intended to underestimate the growing import of international law developments in this regard (e.g. the International Labour Organization's Convention 169 *Concerning Indigenous and Tribal Peoples in Independent Countries* of 1989, or through the Declaration on the Rights of Indigenous Peoples adopted by the United Nations General Assembly on 13 September 2007); nor is it to suggest that First Nations cannot unilaterally exercise their inherent sovereignty. The focus is merely on what existing Canadian law already recognizes unquestionably as being authorized.

Acquiring an Economic Base in Traditional Territory

In many regions First Nations and Inuit peoples are clearly recognized as possessing an enforceable legal interest in traditional lands. As a result, a number of comprehensive land claims settlements have been achieved over the past three decades, or are under active negotiation. While these modern treaties fare well in comparison with the position of Indigenous peoples in many other nations, Canada is a huge country that the majority population has been reluctant to share with the original inhabitants. To add further insult, the Métis have no distinct land base beyond their remaining settlements in Alberta and currently are excluded from land claims negotiations except in the NWT. A land claim has been filed by the Labrador Métis Nation and is under review by the federal Justice Department. As of 2007, the federal government still does not accept the Labrador Métis Nation as possessing Aboriginal title or other Aboriginal rights,[27] while non-status Indians (except in the northern territories and the Innu in Labrador) are likewise left out. From the perspective of southern Métis and non-status Indians, the Canadian policy appears to be one based on aspects of segregation and inequality tied to federal recognition solely of certain *Indian Act* First Nations and Inuit communities. The colonialist inspiration for the *Indian Act* still plays a significant role in 2007, defining the nature and content of federal, and most provincial, policies on land claims and on recognized Aboriginal governments.

Quebec was the first province in Canada to accept the continued existence of Aboriginal title under Canadian law due to the decision of Justice Malouf in the *Kanatewat* case of 1973. The pressure to proceed with a massive hydroelectric project induced the province to quickly respond positively to the substance of this decision rather than rely upon the vacation of the original injunction granted by Justice Malouf one week later by the Court of Appeal.[28]

The *James Bay and Northern Quebec Agreement* (JBNQA) of 1975, followed by the *Northeastern Quebec Agreement* three years later, presented an historic breakthrough in the relations between Aboriginal peoples and other levels of government in Canada. Although both Agreements have been criticized over the years for a broad range of reasons, it must be appreciated how significant they were for their time and how they represented a dramatic change from prior policy. Their significance remains as profound today, over 30 years later.

Another historic entente was reached between the Government of Quebec and the Grand Council of the Crees on 7 February 2002, when then-Premier Bernard Landry and Grand Chief Ted Moses signed a fifty-year, multi-billion-dollar agreement. This final document was developed rather rapidly as the agreement-in-principle was only reached on 23 October 2001, and then was ratified by the Cree communities. The two parties committed to a "nation-to-nation" foundation for their relationship. The Cree agreed to withdraw a number of lawsuits challenging proposed hydroelectric projects for breaching the environmental assessment requirements of JBNQA, to bring no further lawsuits during the lifetime of the agreement, and not to seek redress for past violations. The agreement includes the transfer of all provincial responsibility for economic and community development under the JBNQA directly to the Cree. The Cree received $139 million from fiscal years 2002-03 to 2004-05, with subsequent years indexing a $70-million base payment to a formula reflecting "the evolution of activity in the James Bay territory in the hydroelectricity, forestry and mining sectors." The parties also agreed to adapt the provincial forestry management regime to involve the Cree more extensively in management processes so as to better reflect their traditional way of life and concern for sustainable development.

Neither the original JBNQA nor its many subsequent additional agreements are free from controversy. The financial resources that these arrangements have generated at least provide a significant financial basis on which the communities can build an economic future, albeit subject to the impacts of so many major hydroelectric projects upon their traditional territory, as well as provide a level of autonomy for their governments. They have also set a standard by which other First Nations and Inuit communities will look to negotiating new resource development arrangements with provincial governments in their regions.

Federal Legislative Initiatives

Federal legislation has been used on occasion in recent years to advance the Aboriginal agenda promoting greater community control beyond the incredibly confining straightjacket of the colonial-era *Indian Act*. The first very modest 'breakthrough' in this regard occurred in the form of the *Cree-Naskapi (of Quebec) Act*,[29] which was passed in 1984 in order to fulfill a commitment made by the Government of Canada in the first modern post-*Calder* land claim treaty: the *James Bay and Northern Quebec Agreement* of 1975 and its companion *Northeastern Quebec Agreement* of 1978. While marking a new page in local First Nations governance by enacting a statute only for specific communities, and possessing a link to a land claim agreement that was itself constitutionally protected by section 35(3), the jurisdictions that it recognizes and frames as delegated powers are exceedingly narrow in scope, albeit broader than those available under the *Indian Act*. The nine communities involved may enact bylaws generally free from the veto power of the federal Minister of Indian and Northern Affairs and regarding a longer list of subjects. It also established an independent three-member tribunal (the Cree-Naskapi Commission) to hear complaints about federal government non-compliance and to investigate the allegations in an ombudsman-type function. While this statute fell short of meeting First Nations governance goals, it was as far as the Trudeau government was willing to go.

The second federal venture at delegating more extensive law-making powers to a First Nation occurred two years later with the passage of the *Sechelt Indian Band Self-Government Act*.[30] This legislation was spearheaded by Brian Mulroney's Progressive Conservative government and reflected its preference for municipal-style forms of local government. The Sechelt First Nation was in a unique position—it possessed over 30 reserves scattered amongst non-Indian private and public properties on the Sunshine Coast just north of Vancouver. The reserve lands were so effectively interconnected with adjacent lands under municipal jurisdiction that a completely autonomous Sechelt government was difficult to envision. The legislation authorized the chief and council to enact laws on a broader range of issues than other *Indian Act* bands while also giving the Sechelt a guaranteed role in a new public government established for the region through complementary provincial legislation. The federal law at the time was widely condemned by many First Nations' leaders who feared that it would become a federal template for the community-based self-government program then being promoted by INAC.[31] It also stood in stark contrast to the inherent right of self-government position simultaneously being vigorously advocated by the leaders of all four national Aboriginal political organizations negotiating proposed constitutional amendments with the provincial Premiers, territorial leaders, and the Prime Minister during the First Ministers' Conference process that occurred during the 1980s.

Federal legislation ceased being used as a vehicle to increase powers through delegation to particular Aboriginal communities for the next seven years as negotiations on both sectoral initiatives and individual self-government arrangements did not achieve agreements until 1993.

Aboriginal Self-Government in Northern Canada

Although the First Nations, Inuit, and Métis peoples of the North have had significant influence in, if not control over, the development of the Yukon Territorial Government (YTG) and the Government of the Northwest Territories (GNWT) during the last three decades, they have also sought to obtain recognition for traditional Aboriginal governments or to re-establish local control under new forms of governance. First Nations in particular have watched with great interest as the debates raged across southern Canada concerning the termination of Indian status under the White Paper of 1969, through the government pressure for municipal-style Indian governments in the 1970s, and then through to the push for the inherent right of self-government that began to gain momentum in 1983.

Yukon

The First Nations in the Yukon, who represent approximately 25 per cent of the total territorial population, have placed considerable emphasis upon the negotiation of self-government agreements with the Government of Canada and the YTG. Their goal: to displace the federal *Indian Act* while reflecting the unique history, political status, and objectives of the First Nations in the Yukon Territory. The Council of Yukon First Nations (CYFN), formerly known as the Council of Yukon Indians, represents 14 First Nations in the Yukon with 16 communities: Beaver Creek, Burwash Landing, Carcross, Carmacks, Dawson, Faro, Haines Junction, Mayo, Old Crow, Pelly Crossing, Ross River, Stewart Crossing, Tagish, Teslin, Watson Lake, and Whitehorse. The CYFN sought to achieve a modern land claim settlement in keeping with their original submission presented to the Government of Canada in 1972 entitled, "Together Today for Our Children Tomorrow." CYFN demanded more than a land-surrender form of treaty, as reflected by the numbered treaties of an earlier era. Rather they pressed for an economic base to guarantee their future prosperity, along with retaining significant portions of their traditional territory so as to ensure that current and future needs would be met. They also sought to confirm their legitimate right to determine their own futures.

Although the negotiations were extremely long, frequently very frustrating, and extraordinarily expensive, an Umbrella Final Agreement (UFA) was reached on 29 May 1993, among CYFN, the YTG, and the federal government. The UFA established common key components that were intended to apply to all of the First Nations within the Yukon; however, each individual First Nation was required to negotiate its own land-selection and self-government agreements. The overall settlement lands encompassed 41,595 square kilometres, which included mines and minerals. The total payment to all Yukon First Nations was $242,673,000; however, significant loans previously advanced were deducted from this amount. The agreement also included the right to manage national parks and wildlife areas, the right to fish for certain species of fish, and increased employment opportunities.[32]

Four of the member First Nations were in the forefront and had negotiated the implementation of the umbrella agreement for their communities during the latter stages of negotiating the UFA. The Vuntut Gwitchin First Nation of Old Crow in the far north signed the *Vuntut Gwitchin First Nation Self-Government Agreement* also on 29 May 1993, with the Government of Canada and YTG. Very similar agreements were negotiated and signed by the First Nation of Nacho Nyak Dun, the Champagne and Aishihik First Nations, and the Teslin Tlingit Council on the same date with the other two governments. All four agreements were brought into force through the complementary enactment by the Yukon Territorial Legislature in 1993 of the *Yukon Final Land Claims Agreements Act*[33] and the *First Nations (Yukon) Self-Government Act*,[34] then subsequently by the Parliament of Canada in 1994.[35] These two federal statutes were formally proclaimed in February of 1996, after the *Yukon Surface Rights Act* was passed. It should be noted that all of these negotiations preceded the announcement by the Government of Canada in August of 1995 of its new policy that recognized the inherent right of self-government and undertook to negotiate the terms of its implementation with Aboriginal communities that so desired.

In 1997, final land and self-government agreements were signed with Little Salmon/Carmacks and Selkirk First Nations. The following year, similar agreements were signed with Tr'ondëk Hwëch'in in Dawson City. Land and self-government agreements were signed with the Ta'an Kwacha'n Council in Whitehorse in 2002, and similar agreements with the Kluane First Nation in 2003. Final land and self-government agreements were signed by the Kwanlin Dun First Nation and by the Carcross/Tagish First Nation in 2005 with YTG and Canada.

All of these self-government agreements are designed to clarify the powers of the three respective orders of government that are signatory to each agreement. For ease of review, the *Selkirk First Nation Self-Government Agreement* will be used as the template for consideration. Certain powers were identified as being within the exclusive authority of the Selkirk First Nation (SFN) (section 13.1). These exclusive powers included matters affecting the administration, operation and internal management of the SFN (section 13.1.1) as well as the management and administration of those rights and benefits that were conferred upon individual members of SFN who registered as beneficiaries under the land claim agreement (section 13.1.2). The SFN also possessed exclusive power to make laws ancillary to the foregoing matters (section 13.1.3). SFN's Self-Government Agreement further set out the following list of legislative spheres of jurisdiction (section 13.2):

1) Spiritual and cultural beliefs;
2) Aboriginal language spoken by the community;
3) Health care and services except off settlement land;
4) Social and welfare services except off settlement land;
5) Training programs subject to any Government requirement;
6) Adoption by and of citizens;
7) Guardianship, custody, care and placement of children except off settlement land;
8) Education programs and services except off settlement land;
9) Inheritance, wills, intestacy, and estates;
10) Determination of mental incompetency of citizens pursuant to procedures consistent with fundamental justice;

11) Alternative dispute resolution;
12) Solemnization of marriage;
13) Licences issued in relation to their other powers in order to raise revenue;
14) Necessary matters to fulfil the responsibilities under the Final Agreement; and
15) Ancillary matters to the foregoing.

Furthermore, this First Nation also had law-making powers of a more "local or private nature" concerning the following fields (section 13.3):

1) Use, management, control, and protection of settlement land;
2) Allocation of rights and interests;
3) Use, management, control, and protection of natural resources;
4) Hunting and fishing and the protection of fish and wildlife and habitat;
5) Control over posters, advertising, etc.;
6) Licensing and regulation of persons or entities carrying on business, trade, etc;
7) Control of gaming;
8) Control of construction, maintenance, repair, and demolition of buildings;
9) Prevention of overcrowding in residences, buildings, etc.;
10) Control of sanitary conditions of buildings or property;
11) Planning, zoning, and land development;
12) Curfews, and prevention of disorderly conduct, etc.;
13) Control over the use of vehicles;
14) Control over intoxicants;
15) Control over local services and facilities;
16) Control over livestock, poultry, pets, birds, and animals;
17) Administration of justice;
18) Control over actions that threaten or may threaten the public order, peace, or safety;
19) Control over actions that endanger or may endanger public health;
20) Control over the environment;
21) Control over firearms, weapons and explosives;
22) Control over the transport of dangerous substances; and
23) Matters coming within the good government of citizens on settlement land.

One of the challenges before the three levels of government in negotiating this agreement was the recognition that citizens of the SFN might live anywhere while other Canadian citizens, permanent residents, and visitors might choose to come within the territory of this First Nation. The Agreement also sought to address the fact that emergency situations might arise in which normal relationships and division of authorities among governments might need to be set aside to deal with the crisis at hand. With this in mind, the Agreement contained a separate section (section 13.4) to address these types of circumstances through outlining a core of basic principles that would authorize the federal or Yukon governments to exercise laws of general application upon a SFN citizen outside their Settlement Land while the SFN's authority might apply in the case of non-SFN citizens within the Settlement Land.

The Agreement established initial rules of paramountcy to apply in the case of laws of general application enacted by Canada or the Yukon (section 13.5). The basic principles that were negotiated dictated that territorial laws of general application were inoperative to the extent that they provided for matters that were also covered under laws passed by SFN. The territorial commissioner, when sitting in Executive Council, was further empowered to declare that a Yukon law of general application had ceased to apply in a situation where a SFN law would otherwise have rendered it only partially inoperative (section 13.5.6). The Agreement required Canada and SFN to engage in further negotiations in the future to identify those areas in which SFN laws should prevail over federal laws of general application to the extent of any inconsistency or conflict. The Agreement further outlined detailed provisions to guide negotiations between the three governments in order to achieve a more specific agreement through which SFN might exercise its legislative jurisdiction regarding the administration of justice. A fail-safe mechanism was described whereby SFN was assured that it would acquire significant authority in the justice field no later than 27 July 2002, or earlier if an agreement was reached prior to that date. In the meantime, an interim scheme was set out in section 13.6.4.

Negotiations have been underway since 1995 among these three governments, along with CYFN and the other individual First Nations governments in the Yukon, to achieve revisions to their self-government agreements so as to take advantage of the federal inherent right policy. These First Nations are seeking the same level of formal constitutional protection for the rights contained within their self-government agreements as already exist for their land claims settlements through section 35(3) of the *Constitution Act, 1982*. No success has been achieved in this regard to date despite the passage of 12 years since this process began and the initial expectation that the matter could be resolved expeditiously.

Nunavut

The settlement of Aboriginal title over 1.9 million square kilometres in Nunavut represents Canada's largest comprehensive land claim settlement to date and in all likelihood will never be surpassed.[36] The population of the 28 communities involved (Arctic Bay, Arviat, Baker Lake, Bathurst Inlet, Cambridge Bay, Cape Dorset, Chesterfield Inlet, Clyde River, Gjoa Haven, Grise Fiord, Hall Beach, Igloolik, Iqaluit, Kimmirut, Kugluktuk, Nanisivik, Pangnirtung, Pelly Bay, Pond Inlet, Povungnituk, Qikiqtarjuaq, Rankin Inlet, Repulse Bay, Resolute, Sanikiluaq, Taloyoak, Umingmaktok and Whale Cove) totaled 17,500 people in 1992. The representative of the Inuit beneficiaries (now called Nunavut Tungavik Inc.) received collective freehold title to 352,240 square km with 10 per cent of this land including subsurface resources. The financial portion of the agreement provided the Inuit with $580 million plus interest over 14 years and a share of the royalties from the future development of natural resources. In addition, the settlement confirmed Inuit hunting rights, and guaranteed involvement in decision-making bodies on wildlife issues, land-use planning, environmental impact assessment of potential development projects, parks, social and cultural policies, and the regulation of water use. All archaeological objects in Nunavut are declared to be jointly owned.

A political accord was signed by the parties in 1992, as a separate document outside the land claim agreement outlining the federal commitment to create the Nunavut Territorial Government. The *Nunavut Land Claims Agreement Act* (Bill C-133) and an *Act to Divide the NWT and Create the Territory of Nunavut* (Bill C-132) were passed in 1993. A tripartite Nunavut Implementation Commission was established in 1994 to work through the many practical issues arising in the creation of a new territory. The Commission determined the infrastructure needs of the planned new government, established its initial operations plan, developed a flag, addressed the objective of Inuit employment in the public service on a level equivalent to their percentage of the population, and resolved many other matters. A referendum was conducted resulting in the selection of Iqaluit as the capital; however, a plan for guaranteed gender equality in the election of legislators was rejected. An Interim Territorial Commissioner was later appointed and a secretariat established to begin to create a new government bureaucracy.

On 1 April 1999, the map of Canada changed to include the territory of Nunavut. The Nunavut Territorial Government's 19 legislators are publicly elected by all adult residents of Nunavut, of which approximately 85 per cent are Inuit. It operates without political parties, as the NWT Legislative Assembly does, with the elected legislators choosing the Premier and Cabinet. The Premier then assigns the Cabinet portfolios.

As a territorial government, its official legal basis for existing and its specific law-making powers are subject to control by the Government of Canada. Due to its heavy reliance upon transfer payments for the vast majority of its budget, it is especially vulnerable to federal budgetary decisions. Section 23 of the *Nunavut Act* grants the same basic powers that provinces possess under sections 92 and 95 of the *Constitution Act, 1867*; however, this is subject to "any other Act of Parliament" as well as a federal power to disallow any territorial law within one year of its passage.

Although its jurisdiction is controlled by the Parliament of Canada as a territory and it does not yet possess full control over its lands and waters the way that all provincial governments do so as to obtain revenue from any development of natural resources, the Government of Nunavut (GN) has sought to utilize its authority to operate uniquely. It has chosen to heavily decentralize governmental operations with many departments and functions headquartered in communities other than Iqaluit. It also seeks to incorporate Inuit traditional law, philosophy, values, and language wherever possible.

With an already-young population growing at a rate of over four per cent a year, there are major educational, social, and unemployment challenges that have undercut the GN's capacity to be as successful as hoped. The interplay between the public government that is dominated by non-Inuit public servants in key positions, an overwhelmingly Inuit legislature, and the distinct objectives of the Inuit land claim body creates an unusual and sometimes uncomfortable mix.

Northwest Territories

The remainder of the NWT, following the departure of Nunavut, presents a very different picture with approximately equivalent numbers of non-Aboriginal and Aboriginal residents, the latter comprised of the Inuvialuit in the Beaufort region and a variety of First Nations and Métis peoples in the rest of the territory.

The Inuvialuit (of Aklavik, Ulukhaktok (Holman), Inuvik, Paulatuk, Sachs Harbour, and Tuktoyaktuk) reached a final land claim agreement confirming their title to 91,000 out of 423,000 square kilometres of land in 1984.[37] Mineral rights were included on only 13,000 square kilometres of the total settlement land area. The financial settlement was for $95 million. Rights to hunting, socio-economic development, and participation in the economic and environmental development of the area were included in the agreement; however, there was no direct governmental component.

The Gwich'in (living in Aklavik, Fort McPherson, Unuvik and Tsiigetchic), who are the southern neighbours of the Inuvialuit, retained 16,264 square kilometres including mineral rights, and 1,554 square kilometres of Tetlit Gwich'in land in the Yukon, of their 57,000 square kilometres of traditional territory through a settlement reached in 1992.[38] This was the first comprehensive land claim agreement reached by a Dene and Métis group after the breakdown of the Dene-Métis Process in the Northwest Territories in 1990. The Gwich'in people received $75 million to be paid over 15 years; a share of the royalties from the Mackenzie Valley; hunting rights; and the right to participate in decisions regarding renewable resources, land use planning, environmental impact reviews, and land and water use regulation. Their land claim settlement, however, contained no governance component: they and the Inuvialuit have been pursuing various forms of negotiating the creation of a regional public government over the last 15 years.

The Sahtu Dene and Métis, representing the five communities of Colville Lake, Deline, Fort Good Hope, Norman Wells, and Tulita, in the Mackenzie Valley and Great Bear Lake region concluded their Agreement in 1994.[39] The agreement included money, land, a share of the royalties from the Mackenzie Valley, hunting rights, and participation in decisions about renewable resources, land use planning, environmental impact assessment, and land and water use regulation. This agreement also included a commitment to pursue negotiations of self-government agreements in the future. The community of Deline is in the final stages of concluding such an agreement, Tulita has begun, and other negotiations can be expected in the future with a possible regional model also developed.

The last settlement reached in the NWT to date applies to 210,000 square kilometres of traditional area of the Monfwi Gogha De Niitlee in the North Slave region.[40] The population of over 3,500 from the Tlicho (formerly known by outsiders as the Dogrib) communities of Rae-Edzo, Rae Lakes, Wha Ti and Wekweti agreed to create the Tlicho Government. They also abolished the Dogrib Treaty 11 Council, the Dogrib Rae Band, the Wha Ti First Nation, Gameti First Nation and Dechi Laot'i First Nation bands and replaced them with public governments in each community in the affected area. The Tlicho will receive $152 million over the span of 15 years, and a part of the royalties from any future development of the Mackenzie Valley. The Tlicho people retained the right to govern 39,000 square kilometres of their traditional land that has been confirmed for their exclusive use. The agreement reached in 2003 became effective in 2005, and also covers the rights to control their water, heritage, land, subsurface activities, and the Mackenzie Valley resources within their remaining lands. The Tlicho people possess the only Aboriginal government recognized by the federal and NWT governments outside the *Indian Act* structure, which is also protected under section 35(3) of the *Constitution Act, 1982*.

Aboriginal Self-government within the Provinces

Nisga'a Nation Treaty

After over a century of direct lobbying, litigation (as they were the sponsors of *Calder* v. *A.-G. of B.C.*[41]), and many years of negotiations, the Nisga'a Nation finally achieved the first modern treaty in British Columbia with the federal and provincial governments in 1998.[42] The 252-page agreement, concluded and signed by all three parties, constitutes a comprehensive land claim settlement as well as a self-government agreement, which was the first treaty in Canada explicitly to state that it recognizes the section 35 rights to both land *and* self-government. In the latter realm, the treaty recognizes the authority of both a regional Nisga'a Lisims Government and local governments for each of the four Nisga'a villages operating under the overall auspices of the Nisga'a Nation. Collectively, these governments function in accordance with the Nisga'a Constitution and possess primary legislative jurisdiction over matters concerning Nisga'a culture, citizenship, language, governmental structures, lands, assets, public works, solemnization of marriages, traffic and transportation, social services, health care, child welfare, adoption, education (from pre-school through grade 12 and post-secondary institutions), intoxicants, devolution of cultural property (chapter 11), policing and court services (chapter 12), and taxation (chapter 16). Certain other spheres of governmental responsibility are identified as subjects for a new form of co-management such that jurisdiction will be shared among all three levels of government, including the Nisga'a Lisims Government. It must be noted that some sectors of governance will only be subject to valid Nisga'a law if they are equivalent to, or impose higher standards than, applicable provincial or federal laws. Certain Nisga'a jurisdictions can also only be exercised in a manner that does not conflict with general federal or provincial legislation.[43]

Labrador Inuit Agreement

Over 6000 people of Inuit and mixed Inuit-European ancestry from the coast line, interior, and offshore of northern Labrador reached an agreement with the Governments of Canada and of Newfoundland and Labrador that came into effect in 2005.[44] After negotiations languished for years, the communities of Hopedale, Makkovik, Nain, Postville, and Rigolet had their agreement fast-tracked following discovery of a major deposit of nickel, copper, and cobalt at Voisey's Bay. This settlement provides for the creation of an Inuit-dominated regional government for northern Labrador, a sizeable exclusive land base, a significant cash payment, and entitlement to share in natural resource development within the area. The final agreement also sets the foundation for the establishment of the Nunatsiavut Assembly, which will exercise legislative authority, confirmed under the Agreement and by the Constitution, authorized by the Labrador Inuit. The Constitution provides for the regional Nunatsiavut Government and five Inuit Community Governments. The chief executive officer and mayor of the community government (AngajukKâk) must be an Inuk, although all residents will vote and may serve in other elected offices.[45]

A Transitional Government, consisting of the board of directors of the former Labrador Inuit Association (LIA), passed necessary laws, restructured the old LIA institutions as the new Nunatsiavut civil service, managed the investment of settlement funds and completed a transitional work plan until the new assembly was elected in October of 2006, following upon the election of the five AngajukKâk and community councillors in September. The first sitting of the Nunatsiavut Legislative Assembly was convened in Nain on 16 Ocotber 2006.[46] The Government is preparing for construction of the official legislative capital facilities in Hopedale and the infrastructure for the administrative headquarters in Nain.[47] The election for President is scheduled for 7 October 2008; as this office will have a four-year term, as do the members of the legislature, there will be staggered terms of office to promote a level of consistency across electoral periods. The Nunatsiavut Assembly and government have now been functioning for over one year with Cabinet Ministers, sittings in Hopedale, four governmental departments operating, and the passing of legislation; however, this is still somewhat of a transitional stage until the presidential position is filled.

Nunavik Regional Government

An agreement-in-principle, that is suggested to be very close to what the final agreement will ultimately look like, has recently been reached by the Inuit of northern Quebec with the federal and provincial governments and approved by both Cabinets.[48] Following upon the detailed work and active public consultation of a tripartite commission and several years of active negotiation, the outlines of a new public government to be created in the northern part of the province (now called Nunavik) is taking shape for the communities who were covered by the JBNQA of 30 years ago. The far more limited provincial legislative regime in place during the intervening years will have the institutions it created (the Kativik Regional Government, the Kativik School Board, and the Nunavik Regional Board of Health and Social Services) merged and placed under an elected assembly for the region. The Inuit of Nunavik have opted for a governance model that will be publicly elected by all residents, however, the concern over the potential future loss of their demographic dominance of the local population has led to the negotiation of a number of "safeguards" in the sense of protections for Inuktitut and an advisory council of Inuit elders whose involvement will be essential to enact laws in certain fields. Although following the non-partisan parliamentary approach that emphasizes consensual decision-making, as Nunavut and Nunatsiavut have done, Nunavik also proposes a distinct variation through the direct election by all residents of the five-member Executive Council. The other legislators will be elected on a riding-by-riding scheme. The distinct responsibilities of the individual Executive Council members [like Ministers] have also been determined. One unique aspect of this model is that it will be a regional public government formally established by the provincial government.

Thus, the Inuit in Nunavut, Nunavik, and Labrador have all chosen somewhat different models of governance. They all have, however, chosen to keep their land claim rights distinct from governance and retain a separate corporate entity to manage the benefits of those settlements.

The Return to Federal Legislative Measures

The federal government returned in the late 1990s to using regular legislation as a mechanism for advancing self-government objectives distinct from the enactment of statutes intended to implement or enable comprehensive claims and self-government agreements. The pattern of negotiating the terms of the actual Bills before their introduction established by the Cree-Naskapi and Sechelt statutes in the 1980s was maintained.

The Parliament of Canada enacted the *Mi'kmaq Education Act*[49] in 1998, to confirm authority over on-reserve primary and secondary education for the 13 Mi'kmaq First Nations of Nova Scotia. A jointly drafted *First Nations Land Management Act*[50] was passed in 1999, based upon a Canada-First Nations Framework Agreement signed three years earlier. This latter statute confirms full power for those participating First Nations to establish their own land codes and detailed land laws that will apply on their reserve lands in substitution for parts of the *Indian Act*. Not only does this cover many matters not available under the *Indian Act* (such as matrimonial property laws), but it also completely removes the control of INAC and the Crown so that the First Nation can deal with its own land in accordance with the community's wishes and the foundational code passed by community vote. The same arrangement is open to other First Nations who choose to pursue this more limited option for enhanced local control over reserve lands.

The *Kanesatake Interim Land Base Governance Act*[51] was passed and received Royal Assent on 15 June 2001, to implement an agreement reached between the Mohawk Council and the government that recognizes certain lands as falling within federal jurisdiction in relation to "Indians, and Lands reserved for Indians" within section 91(24) of the *Constitution Act, 1867*, although not being reserve lands under the *Indian Act*. It also provides statutory assurance that the Kanesatake Council has a legal foundation on which to adopt its own laws and regulations over land-related matters on that portion of its territory, as well as the necessary authority to enforce those laws. In addition, the Kanesatake *Act* sets out a framework intended to foster a constructive dialogue on harmonization between Kanesatake and the Municipality of Oka.

More recently, the Parliament of Canada has enacted the *First Nations Goods and Services Tax Act* in 2003,[52] the *First Nations Commercial and Industrial Development Act*,[53] the *First Nations Fiscal and Statistical Management Act*,[54] the *First Nations Oil and Gas and Moneys Management Act*,[55] and the *First Nations Jurisdiction over Education in British Columbia Act*[56] while continuing to pass a large number of individual land claim settlement implementation statutes concerning First Nations in Yukon, Northwest Territories, Manitoba, Saskatchewan, and Nova Scotia.[57]

Comprehensive Land Claims

As with JBNQA, comprehensive land claims based on the common law's recognition of continuing Aboriginal title can provide a land base to govern, some natural resources to enjoy, and some cash compensation on which to build an economy. The following is a complete list of Final Agreements regarding comprehensive land claims achieved to date:

2006 – *Nunavik Inuit Land Claims Agreement*
2005 – *Labrador Inuit Land Claims Agreement*
2003 – *Kluane First Nation - Final Agreement*
2003 – *Tlicho Agreement* (signed 25 August 2003)
2002 – *Ta'an Kwach'an Council Final Agreement*
1999 – *Nisga'a Final Agreement*
1998 – *Tr'ondëk Hwëch'in Final Agreement*
1997 – *Little Salmon/Carmacks Final Agreement*
1997 – *Selkirk First Nation Final Agreement*
1993 – *Sahtu Dene and Métis Comprehensive Land Claim Agreement* (effective date 1994)
1993 – *Umbrella Final Agreement between the Government of Canada, the Council for Yukon Indians and the Government of the Yukon*
1993 – *Vuntut Gwitchin First Nation Final Agreement* (effective date 1995)
1993 – *Champagne and Aishihik First Nations Final Agreement* (effective date 1995)

1993 – *Teslin Tlingit Council Final Agreement* (effective date 1995)
1993 – *Nacho Nyak Dun First Nation Final Agreement* (effective date 1995)
1993 – *Nunavut Land Claims Agreement*
1992 – *The Gwich'in Comprehensive Land Claim Agreement*
1984 – *The Western Arctic Claim: The Inuvialuit Final Agreement*
1978 – *The Northeastern Quebec Agreement*
1975 – *James Bay and Northern Quebec Agreement* and *Complementary Agreements* (effective date 1977).[58]

While each set of negotiations is unique, as local circumstances and Aboriginal community aspirations differ, all previous agreements reached were influenced by the precedents of prior ones and by the presence of a common denominator—the Government of Canada—which seeks to sustain the pattern previously negotiated so as to avoid prior settlements unravelling. All negotiations are also inevitably influenced by the relative bargaining strength of the parties, the quality of the leadership involved, national politics that determine the party in power, the presence of major economic development projects that may pressure governments for speedy action, the overall natural resource and property value of the territory in question, its proximity to urban centres, the evolution in regional negotiations and changes in the legal environment.

One third of Canada's First Nations are located in British Columbia and 171,200 Aboriginal people live in BC, comprising 4.4 per cent of the total provincial population of 3.8 million. Most First Nations communities in British Columbia have not signed treaties although 57 First Nations, or 70 per cent of the provincial First Nations communities in BC, which represent 116 of the 197 eligible First Nations in BC (or approximately 77,000 out of an estimated 120,000 total First Nations members in the province) had submitted Statements of Intent to the BC Treaty Commission (BCTC) indicating their intent to negotiate a treaty by January 2007.[59] The BCTC is an arm's-length, neutral organization that determines when the parties are ready to begin negotiating. It then facilitates negotiations, allocates funding for negotiations to First Nations, resolves disputes when asked, and provides information on negotiations in British Columbia. The BCTC receives Statements of Intent from First Nations who want to negotiate.

The 116 participating First Nations have formed 47 separate negotiation tables. Nine of these tables are in the early negotiating stage, and 39 have achieved agreements-in-principle. The McLeod First Nation, which signed an adhesion to Treaty 8 and received its treaty reserve land entitlements only a few years ago, has more recently signed a Statement of Intent to negotiate a self-government agreement that is independent of the BCTC process.

A Sechelt agreement-in-principle was signed in 1999, but the negotiation for a final agreement has since become inactive. In 2006, three final agreements were initialed, allowing the communities to conduct internal votes. The three agreements involved Lheidli T'enneh, Maa-Nulth, and Tsawwassen First Nations, although voters in the first of these turned down the agreement. Final agreements are still being negotiated with the In-SHUCK-ch, Sliammon, Yekooche, and Yale First Nations.

On the other hand, many First Nations adamantly refuse to participate in these land claims and self-government negotiations as they believe the federal and provincial governments insist upon the extinguishment of Aboriginal title as a key condition for agreement. They also dispute the genuineness of governmental declarations of their recognition of the inherent right of self-government. Some of these opponents of the BCTC process also argue that the provincial government has no business being involved in treaty negotiations.

Specific Land Claims

Specific land claims relate to unfulfilled treaty promises, the maladministration of reserve lands or band trust funds and other assets. These types of land claims can also be negotiated or litigated. As of the end of 2007, there are 75 specific land claims disputes before the courts across Canada.[60] Specific claims are the avenue through which First Nations have challenged the mismanagement and fraud of their assets by the federal government, such as the illegal sale of their land. From 1927 to 1951, First Nations were prohibited from raising money or hiring lawyers to deal with their specific claims issues, under the *Indian Act*.[61]

Since 1973, there have been 1,279 specific land claims filed with the federal government.[62] From 2006-2007, the federal share of the specific claims cases that were settled was $15,785,881. At present, 489 of these claims have been concluded and 790 are outstanding. Of the concluded claims, 282 were settled through negotiations and 207 were 'resolved' alternatively, by an administrative remedy or file closure. The proportion of claims that have been found to be valid is telling. As the Senate Standing Committee on Aboriginal Peoples declared:

> Canada has breached its fiduciary duty. There was outright theft of land, improper and illegal surrender of land. In spite of the unfair process that currently exists, over 300 claims have been validated and approximately 280 claims have been resolved in the last number of years. There is clear validity to our position on claims.[63]

There are currently 123 specific claims in negotiations across the country and 34 claims with the Indian Specific Claims Commission.[64] Negotiated settlements have ranged in financial payment by Canada from $15,000 to $125 million, with an average settlement value of $6.5 million. According to the Standing Committee, it will take 90 years to settle the outstanding specific land claims at the current pace, if only 70 per cent of them are valid.[65] To date, approximately 900 of the 1,300 claims are still in the system and have yet to be concluded.[66] For First Nations, the process is time-consuming and expensive.

The following statement of principle appears in the foreword of the federal government's specific claims policy booklet of 1982 entitled, "Outstanding Business":

The claims referred to in this booklet deal with specific actions and omissions of government as they relate to obligations undertaken under treaty, requirements spelled out in legislation and responsibilities regarding the management of Indian assets. They have represented, over a long period of our history, outstanding business between Indians and government which *for the sake of justice, equity and prosperity* now must be settled without further delay [emphasis added].[67]

To date, only 275 of the specific land claims that have been filed have been truly resolved.[68] Seventy percent of the First Nations in Canada have specific land claims that need to be settled. One must hope for better in the near future.

The issue of outstanding specific claims is one of the causes of the dire socio-economic position of Aboriginal peoples in Canada. According to the United Nations Special Rapporteur on the situation of human rights and fundamental freedoms of Indigenous peoples, Dr. Rodolfo Stavenhagen:

> Aboriginal people are justifiably concerned about continuing inequalities in the attainment of economic and social rights, as well as the slow pace of effective recognition of their constitutional Aboriginal and treaty rights, and the concomitant redistribution of lands and resources that will be required to bring about sustainable economies and socio-political development.[69]

In June of 2007, the Canadian government made a commitment to resolve the outstanding specific claims quickly. "Instead of letting disputes over land and compensation drag on forever, fuelling frustration and uncertainty, they will be solved once and for all by impartial judges on a new Specific Claims Tribunal," concluded Prime Minister Stephen Harper.[70] Canada's Specific Claims Action Plan proposes four key initiatives that would:

- Create a new tribunal staffed with impartial judges who would make final decisions on claims when negotiations fail;
- Make arrangements for financial compensation more transparent through dedicated funding for settlements in the amount of $250 million a year for 10 years;
- Speed up processing of small claims and improve flexibility in the handling of large claims; and
- Refocus the existing Indian Specific Claims Commission to concentrate on dispute resolution.[71]

Unresolved claims create a potential multi-billion dollar liability for the Canadian government that must eventually be paid.[72] Their resolution contains the potential of significantly augmenting the land base of First Nations as well as providing desperately necessary capital to spark the economic activity that is so indispensable to effective governance.

Regaining an Element of Self-Determination

For decades First Nations, Inuit, and Métis peoples' calls for action in both domestic and international arenas have been in reference to their core desire to regain full control over their lives. No non-Aboriginal government or court in Canada has been prepared to countenance complete decolonization and the full restoration of sovereign, independent, Indigenous governments in Canada. Instead, offers have been made from time to time by federal or provincial governments to negotiate various forms of domestic, internal self-government arrangements. Self-determination in the terms envisioned by the United Nations Charter of 1945, the International Covenant on Civil and Political Rights as well as the International Covenant on Economic, Social and Cultural Rights of 1966, amongst other international instruments, has not been welcomed in Canada.

The right to self-government in section 35 of the *Constitution Act, 1982*, was recognized as inherent by the federal government in 1995. The official policy of the then-Liberal government was that self-government negotiations should be based on certain key principles:

- The federal government accepts that the Aboriginal peoples have the right to govern themselves, decide on matters that affect their communities, and exercise the responsibility that is required to achieve true self-government.[73]

- The federal government recognizes the inherent right to self-government as an existing Aboriginal right under subsection 35(1) of the *Constitution Act, 1982*.[74]

- The federal government recognizes that all Aboriginal governments will not be the same—they will naturally possess varying degrees of authority in areas of federal and provincial jurisdiction reflecting the presence of separate negotiations and the impact of differing local circumstances and community objectives.[75]

- The costs of Aboriginal self-government should be shared among federal, provincial, territorial, and Aboriginal governments and institutions.[76]

The position of the federal government in this regard has received criticism from both poles of the political spectrum.[77] Whether the Government of Canada will even continue to recognize self-government as an inherent right is uncertain at this stage.

Final self-government agreements have been reached with certain First Nations communities on the following dates.[78]

2005 – *The Carcross/Tagish First Nation Self-Government Agreement*
2005 – *The Kwanlin Dun First Nation Self-Government Agreement*
2004 – *Anishnaabe Government Agreement*
2003 – *Westbank First Nation Self-Government Agreement*
2003 – *Kluane First Nation - Self-Government Agreement*
2003 – *Tlicho Agreement* (signed August 25, 2003)
2002 – *Ta'an Kwach'an Council Self-Government Agreement*
1999 – *Nisga'a Final Agreement*
1998 – *Tr'ondëk Hwëch'in Self-Government Agreement*
1997 – *Little Salmon/Carmacks Self-Government Agreement*
1997 – *Selkirk First Nation Self-Government Agreement*
1993 – *Vuntut Gwitchin First Nation Self-Government Agreement* (effective date 1995)
1993 – *Champagne and Aishihik First Nations Self-Government Agreement* (effective date 1995)
1993 – *Teslin Tlingit Council Self-Government Agreement* (effective date 1995)
1993 – *Nacho Nyak Dun First Nation Self-Government Agreement* (effective date 1995)

As indicated above, self-government agreements have been reached with 11 Yukon First Nations (Vuntut Gwitchin, Nacho Nyak Dun, Champagne and Aishihik, Teslin Tlingit, Selkirk, Little Salmon/Carmacks, Tr'ondëk Hwëch'in, Ta'an Kwach'an, Kluane, and Carcross/Tagish) in addition to their aforementioned comprehensive land claims settlements.[79] The *Nisga'a Nation Treaty* of 1999, the *Tlicho Agreement* of 2003 and the *Labrador Inuit Agreement* of 2005 are the only comprehensive claims agreements reached to date to include detailed self-government regimes within the same document as the land claims component.

The *Westbank First Nation Self-Government Agreement* was signed in 2003. This agreement confirms the First Nation's power to govern their language, land management, culture, and resources outside of the confines of the *Indian Act*. The agreement gave the 8,000 non-Westbank members who reside on reserve land the ability to deal with the Westbank government about issues that affect them.[80]

The *Anishnaabe Government Agreement* was reached in December 2004.[81] It was the first self-government agreement to be concluded in Ontario, and took 20 years to finalize.[82] It was the first agreement to recognize a regional group (approximately 4,200 members of the Chippewa Nation of Beausoleil, the Mississauga Nations of Curve Lake and Hiawatha, and the Pottawatomi Nation of Moose Deer Point) as a government outside of the comprehensive land claims process. The agreement would have replaced most of the *Indian Act* for the affected four First Nations; however, it has been rejected by the communities.

Indian and Northern Affairs Canada (INAC) indicates that it is currently at 72 self-government negotiating tables representing 445 Aboriginal communities (includes 427 First Nations, 18 Inuit communities, and some Métis locals) across Canada.

Current Legal Context

The Canadian courts have had relatively few occasions when compelled to address Indigenous governance issues, beyond the longstanding recognition of traditional law as part of the common law for various specific purposes.[83] More recently in the *Delgamuukw* decision,[84] our highest court not only reiterated that Aboriginal title is part of Canadian law but also indicated that the substantive content of the property law that is reflected within the common law's acceptance, and the allocation of its benefits, is determined by the traditional laws of the Aboriginal Nation concerned rather than by Canadian law. This view was reiterated four years later in *Mitchell* v. *M.N.R.*[85] Acknowledging the legitimacy of customary law and providing it legal force within the mainstream court system implicitly recognizes the authority of these communities and their systems of governance to establish and revise their law.

We have not, however, seen our courts clearly acknowledge that First Nations, Inuit, and Métis peoples are still part of sovereign nations, as the United States Supreme Court has been declaring for almost two centuries.[86] The Supreme Court of Canada did expressly declare in 1990 in *Regina* v. *Sioui*[87] that the Huron Nation in that case and First Nations generally, were fully independent sovereign nations when entering into treaty relationships with the British Crown. On the other hand, the judgment of Chief Justice Lamer did not comment on the current legal status of First Nations governments.

The Supreme Court returned to this topic in 1996 in the *Pamajewon*[88] decision dealing with high stakes gaming in the context of an assertion of the inherent right of self-government. After assuming for the purposes of the case that such an inherent right did exist, the Court elected to apply the *Van der Peet*[89] test for Aboriginal rights in this very different context. The Court concluded that the evidence was insufficient to prove that any form of gaming amongst Ojibway peoples was a practice that was "integral to the distinctive culture" and of "central significance" to their society prior to contact with the Crown. The outcome creates a requirement for a level of proof for *each* Aboriginal nation across the country on *each* subject matter of governance through a multitude of lawsuits that is almost unimaginable at an expense that is almost incalculable.[90]

The Supreme Court of Canada had a further opportunity to consider the inherent right in the context of an asserted historic Aboriginal right of the Mohawk Nation to cross the Canada-US border as a trading and mobility right in the *Mitchell* case in 2001.[91] The majority felt no need to address the self-government or autonomy aspect within the case based upon their view of the evidence as falling short of meeting the *Van der Peet* test. The concurring judgment of Justice Binnie (in which Major J. concurred) did consider the American jurisprudence on "domestic dependent nations" as well as the position of the Royal Commission on Aboriginal Peoples favouring a concept of "shared" or "merged" sovereignty. He concluded that neither interpretation was applicable in the unique circumstances of controlling access for people and goods to cross an international border that was an essential aspect of a modern state's sovereignty. Further, the border did not exist as such prior to contact such that a right to cross the border could not have been integral to the Mohawk society prior to contact.

The only clear acceptance of an inherent right of self-government to date has been by Justice Williamson of the BC Supreme Court in *Campbell et al.* v. *AG BC*.[92] In the course of rejecting the challenge to the Nisga'a Treaty brought by the current Premier when serving as Opposition Leader, the Court expressly recognized the pre-existing sovereignty of the Nisga'a Nation. He further accepted that elements of this sovereignty continued after the Crown's assertion of overarching sovereignty. On the other hand, his interpretation of prevailing case law was that the Crown's assertion was unchallengeable. As a result, Aboriginal peoples had their right to govern themselves diminished and made vulnerable to being extinguished up until the advent of section 35(1). Confederation and its allocation of powers between federal and provincial levels did not on its own serve to terminate this continued right of self-government. Justice Williamson declared that this right is an Aboriginal right now protected by section 35(1) that is subject to infringement that complies with the *Sparrow* test or is given "content" by a treaty such as the one he upheld in his decision. In doing so, he seemed to regard the self-government right as somewhat limited and internal, including at least jurisdiction over "social self-regulation," powers essential for the protection of their distinct culture, continuance of family laws, methods for the selection of governmental leaders, and the control of land usage. Justice Williamson thus characterized the right as constitutionally guaranteed by section 35(1) as "the limited form of self-government which remained with the Nisga'a Nation after the assertion of [Crown] sovereignty,"[93] which is then protected and elaborated upon (and perhaps expanded) by the Nisga'a Treaty.

The lack of strong judicial recognition for a domestic right of self-government beyond *Campbell*, let alone a right of self-determination in an international context, does not create the measure of impetus that federal and provincial governments always seem to require before being eager to move forward actively in addressing any Aboriginal issue. It also must be acknowledged that this lone judgment is from a single provincial supreme court so can hardly be defined as reflecting a widespread judicial sentiment. On the other hand, the decision was not appealed and no other Canadian court in recent years has directly rejected self-government as an Aboriginal or treaty right. The landscape is still open for further litigation; however, few First Nations indeed would be willing to empower the Canadian judiciary to determine a question so fundamental to their current and future identity, especially in light of recent decisions from our final court of appeal. Thus, the emphasis remains on efforts to build further support and leverage for achieving negotiated solutions.

Conclusions

Despite the federal government allocating $100s of millions to the costs of negotiating some form of self-government arrangements since 1985, relatively few agreements have been achieved. The lack of success does not mean that Aboriginal communities prefer the status quo. What then is the explanation? Part of this is a reflection of deep-seated distrust of both federal and provincial government motives. Not only are these governments viewed as continuing to sponsor the active exploitation of the natural resources within traditional Aboriginal lands, but they are also refusing to accept the legitimacy of Indigenous governments simply exercising the inherent right of self-determination. Express recognition of the right of all peoples to determine their own future under the International Covenant on Civil and Political Rights, which Canada ratified in 1976, amongst many other international instruments, carry no domestic weight with Canadian governments. Opposition to the UN Declaration on the Rights of Indigenous Peoples by the Harper government does not suggest that any sudden change in this regard is imminent. Instead, the federal government, along with those provincial ones who are even willing to discuss jurisdictional realignment, effectively insist on negotiating the scope, structure, and powers of Aboriginal governments in a context in which federal and provincial laws will prevail in case of conflict in many important fields.

It also must be realized that having extensive or even complete sovereignty is not a recipe for immediate success. The vast majority of American Indian tribes are sovereign with extensive criminal jurisdiction concerning Indian people (both tribal and non-tribal members) and almost complete law-making authority in civil (non-criminal) matters regarding all people, companies, and actions occurring within their reservations. Nevertheless, there are many tribes who are poor and some wracked by internal political and social conflict. Likewise, many nations around the world are sovereign yet are poverty-stricken or dictatorships. Thus, the nature of the governmental structure, the level of popular support, the attitudes of neighbouring nations and world powers, as well as the economic opportunities and human expertise available all influence the prospects for success. Being sovereign and having self-determination do not automatically guarantee a better future. There is a natural hesitancy within communities over the potential move from *Indian Act* band governments—with their limited powers and largely functioning as agents of the federal government carrying out its objectives—to something radically new. This can be a source of fear, especially within communities suffering from severe social problems or with ineffective governments.

The level of interaction and interconnectedness between non-Aboriginal and Aboriginal peoples and lands also means that a full exercise of the inherent right could not proceed simply or smoothly. Sorting out the relationship between any conflicting provisions in laws would be inevitable. Determining what forum or court system would have authority to resolve such conflicts would be essential.

Similarly, clarifying to whom, where, and in what contexts the laws of Aboriginal governments would apply would be preferable to leaving this as a matter of dispute arising on a case-by-case basis at great expense for both the individuals and corporations involved. Great uncertainty would reign in the minds of non-Aboriginal people and legal entities, as well as perhaps among off-reserve members of First Nations, about how they are affected by First Nations laws, if at all, unless principles of scope of legislation and conflicts of laws clearly exist so that they can know what the law is and properly plan their affairs in advance of taking any actions. How can this occur unless arrangements are negotiated among the relevant governments? In the US experience, absence of such agreed upon principles has meant a veritable flood of litigation in tribal, state, and federal courts over many decades. This American reality has, in recent years, sparked the frequent negotiation of tribal-state compacts to foster positive working relationships and resolve potential conflicts in their respective legislative provisions and administrative policies in specific fields. Negotiated agreements are necessary in Canada, too, however, the starting point for those discussions can be on the basis of a genuine acceptance of the inherent right, rather than a contingent right approach in which the status quo remains until an agreement is reached and implemented.

Canada today is a nation that was colonized illegally, as it was already occupied by Indigenous peoples with their own sovereign governments. While the First Nations of the east coast welcomed the newcomers as trading partners, they did not consent to be overwhelmed and have their governments effectively overthrown. Canada also was not regarded as a continuing European colony in the 20th Century, as so many lands in Africa and Asia were, such that it was not included within United Nations demands for decolonization. Over 95 per cent of our population traces their ancestry to various corners of the globe and they have no intention of returning to places they have come from—let alone to nations to which many Canadians have only the most distant ancestral links. We must all find a way to get along together—in one of the most wonderful countries in the world—but this does not and cannot mean that the legitimate calls by First Nations, Inuit and Métis peoples should go unheard. They merely seek the recognition of their rightful place in this magnificent part of Mother Earth that they and their ancestors have so willingly shared for generations with waves of newcomers. They wish to regain control of their lives and a significant portion of their traditional territories so as to refurbish their spiritual link and to resume their responsibilities as stewards of this land. Settling land claims can be, and for some has been, a major step along the road toward the reconciliation that is so needed. But far more is required.

These modest demands should be reciprocated by demonstrating the same spirit of generosity by non-Aboriginal Canadians that Aboriginal peoples have showed for so long.

1   The *Constitution Act, 1982,* being Schedule B to the *Canada Act 1982* (U.K.), 1982, c.11 [hereinafter *Constitution Act, 1982*].

2   The term "Aboriginal peoples" will be used herein when generally referring to First Nations, Inuit, and Métis peoples collectively, unless the context requires otherwise. It must be realized that there are well over 600 First Nations in Canada that represent individual communities from many different original nations with 11 different languages and over 50 distinct dialects. Similarly, there are dialect differences amongst the Inuit peoples across the far north of Canada as well as among the Métis peoples.

3   *R.* v. *Sioui,* [1990] 1 S.C.R. 1025.

4   *R.* v. *Sparrow,* [1990] 1 S.C.R. 1075.

5   *Guerin* v. *The Queen,* [1984] 2 S.C.R. 335.

6   *Ibid.*

7   *Simon* v. *The Queen,* [1985] 2 S.C.R. 387.

8   *R.* v. *Badger,* [1996] 1 S.C.R. 771.

9   *R.* v. *Marshall* (No. 1), [1999] 3 S.C.R. 456.

10 Although writing in dissent, Justice McLachlin, as she then was, in *R.* v. *Marshall* (No. 1), *ibid.*, summarized the prior case law regarding the principles governing treaty interpretation as including the following:

    1. Aboriginal treaties constitute a unique type of agreement and attract special principles of interpretation.

    2. Treaties should be liberally construed and ambiguities or doubtful expressions should be resolved in favour of the Aboriginal signatories.

    3. The goal of treaty interpretation is to choose from among the various possible interpretations of common intention the one which best reconciles the interests of both parties at the time the treaty was signed.

    4. In searching for the common intention of the parties, the integrity and honour of the Crown is presumed.

    5. In determining the signatories' respective understanding and intentions, the court must be sensitive to the unique cultural and linguistic differences between the parties.

    6. The words of the treaty must be given the sense which they would naturally have held for the parties at the time.

    7. A technical or contractual interpretation of treaty wording should be avoided.

    8. While construing the language generously, courts cannot alter the terms of the treaty by exceeding what "is possible on the language" or realistic.

    9. Treaty rights of Aboriginal peoples must not be interpreted in a static or rigid way. They are not frozen at the date of signature. The interpreting court must update treaty rights to provide for their modern exercise. This involves determining what modern practices are reasonably incidental to the core treaty right in its modern context.

11 *Nowegijick* v. *The Queen,* [1983] 1 S.C.R. 29.

12 *Ibid.,* 36.

13 *R.* v. *Adams,* [1996] 3 S.C.R. 101.

14 *R.* v. *Côté,* [1996] S.C.J. No. 93.

15 *Delgamuukw* v. *British Columbia,* [1997] 3 S.C.R. 1010.

16 *R.* v. *Van der Peet,* [1996] S.C.J. No.77.

17 *R.* v. *Gladstone,* [1996] 2 S.C.R. 723.

18 *R* v. *Pamajewon* [1996] S.C.J. No. 20.

19 *Corbiere* v. *Canada (Minister of Indian and Northern Affairs)* [1996] S.C.C.A. No. 625.

20 *Lovelace* v. *Ontario,* [2000] 1 S.C.R. 950, 188 D.L.R. (4th) 193.

21 See, for example, *Haida Nation* v. *British Columbia (Minister of Forests),* [2004] SCC 73; and *Taku River Tlingit First Nation* v. *B.C. (Project Assessment Director),* [2004] 3 S.C.R. 550 regarding alleged Aboriginal rights being affected and *Mikisew Cree First Nation* v. *Canada (Minister of Canadian Heritage),* [2005] 3 S.C.R. 388 concerning rights under Treaty No. 8.

22 Yale D. Belanger & David R. Newhouse, "The Self-Government Ideal," in this volume.

23 [1973] S.C.R. 313.

24 *Ibid.,* 328.

25 *Ibid.,* 383.

26 See Bradford Morse, "The Inherent Right of Self-Government," in *Aboriginal Self-Government in Canada: Current Trends and Issues,* 2nd Ed., ed. J. H. Hylton, (Saskatoon: Purich Publishing Ltd., 1999), 16-44.

27 Indian and Northern Affairs Canada, "Frequently Asked Questions About the Labrador Inuit Land Claims Agreement," 2 June 2007.

28 The Quebec Court of Appeal judgment suspending the interlocutory judgment was released on November 22, 1973 and is unreported. That decision was upheld by a 3-2 majority of the Supreme Court of Canada,

released on December 21, 1973, [1975] I S.C.R. 48. The Quebec Court of Appeal later formally reversed the original judgment of Justice Malouf, [1974] Q.J. No. 14 (November 21, 1974). Leave to appeal this latter decision was granted by the Supreme Court of Canada, [1975] I S.C.C.A. No.1 on January 28, 1975 but the appeal did not proceed when *James Bay and Northern Quebec Agreement* was achieved.

29   *Cree-Naskapi (of Quebec) Act,* S.C. 1984.

30   *Sechelt Indian Band Self-Government Act,* S.C. 1986, c. 27.

31   See, e.g., Carol E. Etkin, "The Sechelt Indian Band: An Analysis of a New Form of Native Self Government," http://www.brandonu.ca/Library/cjns/8.1/etkin.pdf at 85.

32   Indian and Northern Affairs Canada, "Comprehensive Land Claims Policy," http://www.ainc-inac.gc.ca/ps/clm/gbn/index1_e.html.

33   R.S.Y. 1993, c.19.

34   R.S.Y. 1993, c.5.

35   *Yukon First Nations Land Claim Settlement Act,* S.C. 1994, c. 34; *Yukon First Nations Self-Government Act,* S.C. 1994, c. 35.

36   Indian and Northern Affairs Canada, "Agreements," http://www.ainc-inac.gc.ca/pr/agr/index_e.html#Self-GovernmentAgreements, at 10.

37   *Ibid.,* at 7.

38   *Ibid.,* at 8.

39   *Ibid.,* at 9.

40   Indian and Northern Affairs Canada, "Backgrounder: Tlicho Agreement Highlights," http://www.ainc-inac.gc.ca/nr/prs/j-a2004/02462bbk_e.html.

41   [1973] S.C.R. 313.

42   The Nisga'a Treaty was finally confirmed by the passage of the *Nisga'a Final Agreement Act,* S.C. 2000, c. 7.

43   For judicial consideration of this regime, see, *Campbell* v. *Attorney General of British Columbia* (2000), 189 D.L.R. (4th) 333 (B.C.S.C.).

44   Indian and Northern Affairs Canada, "Agreements," 12.

45   http://www.nunatsiavut.com/en/governmentstructure.php.

46   http://www.nunatsiavut.com/pdfs/mediareleases/mediarelease_Oct6_issue1.pdf.

47   http://www.nunatsiavut.com/en/nunatsiavutgov.php.

48   http://www.nunavikgovernment.ca/en/documents/AIP_english.pdf.

49   *Mi'kmaq Education Act,* S.C. 1998, c. 24.

50   *First Nations Land Management Act,* S.C. 1999, c. 24.

51   *Kanesatake Interim Land Base Governance Act,* S.C. 2001, c. 8.

52   *First Nations Goods and Services Tax Act,* S.C. 2003, c. 15.

53   *First Nations Commercial and Industrial Development Act,* S.C. 2005, c. 53.

54   *First Nations Fiscal and Statistical Management Act,* S.C. 2005, c. 9.

55   *First Nations Oil and Gas and Moneys Management Act,* S.C. 2005, c. 48.

56   *First Nations Jurisdiction over Education in British Columbia Act,* S.C. 2006, c. 10.

57   Such as the *Gwich'in Land Claim Settlement Act,* S.C. 1992, c. 53; the *Nisga'a Final Agreement Act,* S.C. 2000, c. 7; the *Labrador Inuit Land Claims Agreement Act,* S.C. 2005, c. 27; and the *Tlicho Land Claims and Self-Government Act,* S.C. 2005, c. 1.

58   Indian and Northern Affairs Canada, "Agreements."

59   *Ibid.,* 32.

60   Indian and Northern Affairs, "Specific Claims: A Statistical Snapshot," http://www.ainc-inac.gc.ca/ps/clm/fct2-eng.asp.

61   "Negotiation or Confrontation: It's Canada's Choice," December 2006, Final Report of the Standing Senate Committee on Aboriginal Peoples Special Study on the Federal Specific Claims Process, at page 3.

62   Indian and Northern Affairs, "Specific Claims."

63   "Negotiation or Confrontation," 2.

64   *Ibid.*

65   *Ibid.,* v.

66   *Ibid.,* 9.

67   *Ibid.,* 1.

68   *Ibid.*

69   *Ibid.,* 2.

70   "Prime Minister Harper announces major reforms to address the backlog of Aboriginal treaty claims," 12 June 2007, http://pm.gc.ca/eng/media.asp?id=1695.

71   *Ibid.*

72   *Ibid.,* 3.

73   Canada, "Aboriginal Self-Government: Federal Policy Guide", (Ottawa: Supply and Services Canada, 1995) at 3.

74 *Ibid.*
75 *Ibid.*, 7.
76 *Ibid.*, 14.
77 For a debate on how different political theories have been used to suppress Aboriginal self-government, see Robert A. Williams, Jr., *The American Indian in Western Legal Thought: The Discourses of Conquest* (New York: Oxford University Press, 1990).
78 Indian and Northern Affairs Canada, "Agreements." The following is a list of Agreements-in-Principle that have been made to date:
   · 2005 - Yekooche First Nation Agreement-in-Principle
   · 2003 - Déline Self-Government Agreement-In-Principle for the Sahtu Dene / Métis of Déline
   · 2003 - Blood Tribe Governance and Child Welfare Agreement-In-Principle
   · 2003 - Sliammon Agreement-in-Principle
   · 2003 - Maa-Nulth First Nations Treaty Negotiations: Agreement-in-Principle
   · 2003 - Draft Tsawwassen First Nation Agreement-in-Principle
   · 2003 - Summary of Tsawwassen First Nation Agreement-in-Principle
   · 2003 - Lheidli T'enneh Agreement-in-Principle
   · 2003 - Sliammon Treaty Negotiations Summary of Draft Agreement-in-Principle
   · 2003 - Gwich'in and Inuvialuit Self-Government Agreement-in-Principle for the Beaufort-Delta Region
   · 2001 - Meadow Lake First Nations Comprehensive Agreement-In-Principle
   · 2001 - Meadow Lake First Nations Tripartite Agreement-In-Principle
   · 2001 - Sioux Valley Dakota Nation Comprehensive Agreement-In-Principle
   · 2001 - Sioux Valley Dakota Nation Tripartite Agreement-In-Principle
   · 2000 - Dogrib Agreement-In-Principle
   · 1998 - Anishnaabe Government Agreement-In-Principle
79 *Yukon First Nations Self-Government Act* (s.c. 1994, c. 35).
80 Indian and Northern Affairs Canada, "Westbank First Nation and Canada Sign Historic Self-Government Agreement," 3 October 2003, http://www.ainc-inac.gc.ca/nr/prs/s-d2003/2-02390_e.html.
81 Indian and Northern Affairs Canada, "Anishnaabe Government Agreement," December 2004, http://www.ainc-inac.gc.ca/pr/agr/ont/aga_e.pdf.
82 Indian and Northern Affairs Canada, "United Anishnaabe Councils Set to Vote on Landmark Self-Government Agreement," 8 December 2004, http://www.ainc-inac.gc.ca/nr/prs/s-d2004/2-02551_e.html.
83 For a dated, but largely still reflective of current jurisprudence, overview of the treatment of customary law by Canadian courts, see Bradford W. Morse, "Indian and Inuit Family Law and the Canadian Legal System," 8 American Indian Law Review (1980): 199-257.
84 *Delgamuukw v. British Columbia,* [1997] 3 s.c.r. 1010.
85 *Mitchell* v. *M.N.R.,* [2001] 1 s.c.r. 911.
86 See. e.g., *Johnson* v. *M'Intosh* (1823), 21 u.s. (8 Wheat.) 543.
87 *R.* v. *Sioui,* [1990] 1 s.c.r. 1025.
88 *R.* v. *Pamajewon,* [1996] 2 s.c.r. 821.
89 *R.* v. *Van der Peet,* [1996] 2 s.c.r. 507.
90 For a detailed critique of this decision see, "Permafrost Rights: Aboriginal Self-Government and the Supreme Court in *R.* v. *Pamajewon"* (1997) 47 McGill Law Journal, 1011-42.
91 *Mitchell* v. *M.N.R.,* [2001] 1 s.c.r. 911.
92 (2000) 79 b.c.l.r. (3d) 122.
93 *Ibid.*, at para 181.

CONTESTING INDIGENOUS PEOPLES GOVERNANCE:

The Politics of State-Determination vs. Self-Determining Autonomy

Roger Maaka, University of Saskatchewan
& Augie Fleras, University of Waterloo

Introduction: Paradoxes in 'Determinations'

The relational status of Indigenous peoples remains a paradox. To one side, the politics of indigeneity are moving toward centre stage as Indigenous peoples increasingly challenge the legitimacy and absolute sovereignty of the nation-state. To the other side, nation-states have generally fumbled this challenge, in part by misreading the transformational dynamics implicit within Indigenous models of self-determining autonomy, in part by miscalculating the foundational demands of a new post-colonial social contract. The end result is an emerging bottleneck as competing notions of state- versus self-determination intensify those polarized discourses that tend to inflame rather than inform.

There is yet another paradox at play over the politics of self- versus state-determination. After nearly 25 years of protracted negotiations, the finalization of the UN Declaration on the (self-determining) Rights of Indigenous Peoples in 2006 should have proven cause for celebration. But the negative reaction of pivotal settler societies put a damper on the festivities that eventually proved irrelevant because of UN politics. The betrayal by Canada[1] and New Zealand concealed more than it revealed. The flip-flop ripped the scab off those politely worded fictions that mask the contradictions inherent within a neo-colonial context. The gap between ideals and reality remains unbridgeable to date. Whereas widespread support for Indigenous people's rights to self-determining autonomy is unmistakable, there is less political enthusiasm for implementing those principles that challenge the status quo. The end result is a struggle between the old and the new. The new may be emerging but the old refuses to capitulate, in effect condemning settler societies to a vicious cycle of domination-resistance-domination.[2]

In looking to unlock the paradoxes that provoke debates over 'self-determination', a counter-hegemonic perspective is proposed. This chapter provides such a perspective by theorizing the politics of state- versus self-determination in advancing a post-colonial social contract for living together differently. The politicization of Indigenous models of self-determining autonomy is shown to be multidimensional, with a focus on relations repair rather than only borders and jurisdictions. The chapter also argues that, notwithstanding the emergence of Indigenous peoples' movements, even enlightened countries balk at dislodging a state-centric version of self-determination for fear of unleashing new uncertainties. This conflict of interest is not without consequences. In trying to squeeze 21st century political realities into 19th century ideological frameworks, state-determination models underestimate the magnitude and scope of indigeneity politics.[3] The implications of this challenge make it doubly important to reassess the debate over state- versus self-determination within the context of international dynamics and global interdependence.[4]

The chapter begins by exploring the politics of self- versus state-determination as refracted through the prism of established UN protocols. It continues by:

1. deconstructing the concept of self-determination;

2. contrasting Indigenous models of self-determining autonomy with state-determination models; and,

3. demonstrating the challenges of putting post-colonial principles into practice.

To put this theorizing to the test, the chapter discusses how these politics are played out by way of self-determining models of governance in Canada (The Nisga'a settlement as a prototype for the future) and New Zealand (The Ngai Tahu settlement as a template for the present). The conclusion seems inescapable: insofar as much of the debate over state- vs. self-determination often embraces a rigid choice between all or nothing—between outright secession or total denial—a middle way must be explored. To the extent that the principles of constructive engagement provide a working compromise for unblocking this constitutional impasse, the possibility of crafting a new post-colonial contract for living together differently is immeasurably enhanced.

Theorizing Self- vs. State-Determination

To say that the politics of self-determination are disrupting national destinies and global orders is surely an understatement. But repeated references to self-determination have had the unintended effect of absorbing a melange of meanings and messages that confuse and complicate rather than expose and enlighten. Not surprisingly, despite its popularity and importance, the concept of self-determination remains a highly contentious item on the political agenda. Indigenous peoples demand the broadest interpretation of self-determination on the grounds that all other rights flow from it. By contrast, central authorities want to limit this discursive framework for precisely the same reason, namely, a fear that too-expansive recognition of such rights may prove destabilizing.[5] In response to questions of "what is going on?" and "'why?" a theorizing of self- versus state-determination is critical in clarifying competing principles, opposing practices, and contrasting agendas.

UN Protocols on Self-Determination

References to self-determination first appeared on the international scene after World War I when the American president, Woodrow Wilson, articulated the principle of (but not necessarily the right to) national (i.e. state) determination.[6] This principle was later converted into a legal right and a moral imperative based on demands for independence by "salt-water" (overseas) colonies. Article 1 of International Covenant on Civil and Political Rights declares "All peoples have the right to self-determination. By virtue of that right they freely determine their political status in pursuit of economic, social, and cultural development." Indigenous peoples also possess the right to self-determination, according to Article 3 of the UN Declaration, with rights to: (a) shape public affairs; (b) pre-serve identity; (c) promote development; and, (d) manage their own affairs through self-governing autonomy.

This lofty ideal is widely praised and endorsed. Yet reference to self-determination has proven deceptive and misleading—deceptive, because there is no agreement over its meanings; misleading, because of another imperative in international law, namely, the principle of territorial integrity. According to UN protocols, each state has the right to protect and preserve its sovereignty, suggesting that the self-determining rights of Indigenous peoples rarely extend to secession, except under exceptional circumstances such as duress because of gross human rights violation. The United Nations Friendly Nations Declaration Act confirmed how the so-called right to self-determination

> ... shall not be constructed as authorizing or encouraging any action which would dismember or impair, totally or in part, the territorial integrity of sovereign or independent states conducting themselves in accordance with the principle of self-determination of peoples.

To the extent that an Indigenous self-determination is tolerated under a state-proclaimed sovereignty, restrictions apply. As long as central authorities act responsibility, are representative and freely elected, and comply with internation-ally recognised human rights standards, Indigenous claims to territorial independ-ence are inadmissible. Admittedly, secession is a possibility under specific circumstances; nevertheless, its reality reflects internal political developments rather than a principled application of international law. And interference by one state in the internal affairs of another state is disallowed except in cases of egre-gious violations to Indigenous peoples' rights.

In short, the right to self-determination under international law embraces a cardinal principle of global governance. Only nation-states can be sovereign in the sense of a final, exclusive, and undivided authority, in the process exposing the two-pronged nature of UN protocols. Yes, the UN offers a platform for the promotion of Indigenous peoples' rights, but it then occludes them within the narrow political parameters of sovereign statism.[7] Moreover, the UN is reluctant to recognize any further extension of these self-determining rights beyond the context of decolonizing overseas (salt-water) colonies.[8] Predictably then, the principle of state sovereignty and territorial integrity supersedes Indigenous rights to self-determination, even though settler colonies are themselves doubly articulated colonies: namely, salt water colonies of European powers, as well as sites of internal colonialism involving Indigenous peoples.

A double standard underscores the paradoxes of living together differently within colonial contexts. On the one hand, overseas colonies in Asia and Africa possess the right to independent statehood; on the other hand, internally colonized Indigenous peoples lack this right, despite comparable colonial experiences. This glaring inconsistency points to a profoundly unsettling question: By what right and on what grounds can the UN declare the right to territorial self-determination for overseas colonies, but not for internal colonies—especially when New Zealand and Canada were once overseas colonies that forcibly colonized the original occupants and their descendents? Efforts to justify this double standard have proven awkwardly self-serving, yet responses are necessary in sorting through the politics of self- versus state-determination.

The Politics of Determination: Self vs. State

Moves to un-gridlock the demands of Indigenous nationhood with those of hegemonic statehood are bottlenecked around conflicting discourses. At the core of this impasse are competing models of determination: state versus self.[9] State-centred models define self-determination in ways that reflect, reinforce, and advance state interests over those of Indigenous peoples. Conversely, Indigenous models of self-determining autonomy challenge this arrangement by proposing a radical alternative. Given that settler societies were founded on a lengthy colonial process whose values and structures continue to prevail, the consequences are profoundly hegemonic. State determination models not only define the terms of Indigenous peoples' participation in society, they also secure the primacy of settler priorities.[10]

State-Determination Models

Models of state determination cannot be trusted in advancing an Indigenous people's rights. A statist agenda promotes the self-sufficiency of Indigenous peoples within an existing institutional framework. But such an agenda cannot allow any self-determining arrangement that challenges the principles of territorial integrity and the final authority of the state as having supreme sovereignty over the land. Central authorities prefer to operate within the socio-economic confines that typically frame Indigenous peoples' rights around the micro-management of state-defined programmes.[11] Sham consultations and cosmetic reform are established for reducing social and economic disparities, if only to paper over those colonial paradoxes with potentially undermining overtones.[12] Not surprisingly, as Stephen Cornell reminds us, state-determination discourses—from capacity-building to "closing the gaps"—tend to conflate the politicized concerns of Indigenous peoples with the integrative worries of immigrant populations through standardized policies and programs.

The logic behind state determination is driven by national interests. For the state, a one-size-fits-all approach to governance is thought to ensure bureaucratic control, managerial efficiency, or administrative convenience.[13] Not surprisingly, Indigenous peoples' concerns and aspirations are either ignored or suppressed; or, alternatively, they are refracted though the prism of a Eurocentric lens, thus negating how Indigenous peoples' rights constitute a *sui generis* realm of political rights. Their voices and philosophical perspectives are dismissed as well, despite distinctive ways of understanding and responding to reality.[14] As a result of this dismissal, Indigenous peoples' demands for self determining autonomy must be articulated within a dominant discursive framework that often reinforces those very colonialist discourses under attack.[15] This hegemonic exercise in depoliticization is unmistakable:[16]

> From a state-centric point of view, the politics of pluralism is intended to devolve indigenous claims to national politics whereby indigenous 'difference' is pulverized into customs, usages, and traditions ... and ultimately subsumed into the national community. Not only are indigenous identities reduced to a mere behavior without history, but also historical alterity is hidden in the pluralist ethos. With that, indigenous resources are once again made available for taking ... In short, the sovereign power that determines the parameters within which indigeneity can "be" remains fundamentally modern statist in imagination and praxis. Left unchallenged, this power is poised to confine Indigenous Peoples within the juridico-political order of a state-centric geography.[17]

Admittedly, a commitment to state determination models is not without benefit. Moves to decolonize the foundational principles of Indigenous peoples-state relations ensured the removal of the most egregious expressions of colonialism. The illusion of change was conveyed by replacing mainstream elites with Indigenous elites in positions of administrative authority. But while lip service toward Indigenous peoples' rights is widely voiced, support is compromised by an unquestioned commitment to the absolute authority of the state. The end result? Not only do the fundamental structures and systemic Eurocentrisms remain intact, the colonialist mentality of "We know what is best for you" continues to infuse and impose. The central challenge in living together differently within a post-colonial framework is also glossed over, namely, a repairing of the relationship by reconciling competing claims: inherent Indigenous self-determining rights and those of unilateral Crown assertions of sovereign authority over the land and its inhabitants.[18]

Indigenous Models of Self-Determining Autonomy

Opposing state-centric models of self-determination are Indigenous models of self-determining autonomy. Indigenous peoples' experiences continue to be distorted by their forcible confinement in a colonialist framework. To circumvent this confinement, a commitment to Indigenous self-determining models is proposed, with their trifecta of post-colonial rationales:

1. recognition of Indigenous peoples as possessing distinctive ways of looking at the world;

2. taking this distinctiveness seriously through its incorporation into the new partnership; and,

3. that Indigenous peoples alone possess the right to decide for themselves what is best.

The challenge is inescapable. Their claim to constitutional status as original occupants and sovereign political communities secures a corresponding right to shape the political order of which Indigenous peoples are part, as well as the right to control land and resources that sets them apart.[19]

References to Indigenous models of self-determining autonomy reflect their constitutional status as the "nations within."[20] Indigenous peoples represent nations or peoples with inherent rights to self-determination based on their status as political communities who happen to be descendents of original occupants.[21] To be sure, problems of definition and scope persist; for example, what exactly is meant by the 'self' in self-determination? Conversely, what falls under the 'determination' in self-determination? Where does 'state' in state-determination end and the 'self' in self-determining autonomy begin? However vague and contested these concepts are, reality is unforgiving. Failure to attain Indigenous models of self-determining autonomy remains the root cause of those social, cultural, political, and economic woes that hinder and hurt, as explained by a prominent First Australian activist, Mick Dodson:

Time and again Indigenous Peoples express the view that the right to self-determination is the pillar on which all other rights rests. It is of such a profound nature that the integrity of all other rights depends on its observance. We hold that it is a right that has operated since time immemorial amongst our people, but it is the right that is at the centre of the abuses we have suffered in the face of invasion and colonization. The dominant theme of our lives since colonization has been that we have been deprived of the very basic right to determine with our future, to choose how we would live, to follow our own laws. When you understand that, you understand why the right to the right to self-determination is at the heart of our aspirations.[22]

The politicization of Indigenous self-determination is proving contestable.[23] Indigenous self-determining models go beyond a commitment to moving over and making space. Emphasis is focused on challenging those foundational principles that initially created the problem; first, by resisting the centralizing tendencies of both the state and capitalism; second, by transforming a settler/colonial constitutional order around a new social contract for post-colonial engagement. A commitment to Indigenous rights agendas challenges the central principle of liberal democracies, namely, a belief that rights are enjoyed by individuals who are equal before the law, although temporary special 'rights' may be assigned when required. In other words, models of Indigenous self-determining autonomy transcend the discursive framework of decolonization. Proposed instead is a post-colonial recognition of an alternative citizenship arrangement based on belonging to the state through membership in the Indigenous nation.[24]

A conceptual divide complicates the politics of state- versus self-determination. To one side of the divide is the state's right to territorial sovereignty; to the other side, the right of Indigenous peoples to freely determine their constitutional status in society. Central authorities worry of a pending disaster if the genie of self-determination is allowed to escape; after all, too much determination may prove disastrous if the centre collapses or cohesiveness erodes.[25] Yet the politics of Indigenous self-determination endorse a political and politicised discourse for:

1. challenging foundational arrangements that continue to exclude, exploit, or control;
2. curtailing state jurisdictions in domains that rightfully belong to Indigenous communities;
3. realigning Indigenous peoples-state relations along treaty-based lines; and,
4. acknowledging different levels of Indigenous self-governance for jurisdictional control over land, identity, and political voice.[26]

Put bluntly, the politics of indigeneity are about power. Although a plea for social equality or cultural space may be true in some cases, the politics of power focus on challenging the foundational principles of a settler constitutional order. That is, too much of what passes for settler governance, including policies, laws, and agendas, reflect structures and mindsets inconsistent with 21st century realities. In asserting a counter-hegemonic vision for living together differently, one that challenges and transforms by renegotiating the terms of 'staying in' by 'getting out', Indigenous self-determining models reflect the reality of political communities in search of new governance arrangements.

Self-Determination: Self-Governance vs. Self-Government

The politics of self-determination are often inseparable from debates over self-governance and self-government. The latter two are not synonymous. Consider governance, a term that has progressed from obscurity to widespread usage in less than a decade: a commitment to good governance is seen as pivotal in eradicating poverty, promoting development, and enhancing power-sharing. Or as Cornell and Kalt put it, economic growth is first and foremost a political problem because, in the final analysis, good governance provides the tools to address poverty and powerlessness.[27]

The concept of self-governance is largely prescriptive. It prescribes a framework that establishes a relationship between ruler and ruled with respect to how:

1. authority is divided;

2. power is distributed;

3. valued resources are allocated in a given jurisdiction;

4. priorities and agendas are set;

5. decisions are made; and

6. accountability is rendered.[28]

In that it involves procedures and protocols through which decisions are made and authority is exercised by those most intimately concerned and locally connected,[29] the concept of governance appears more consistent with Indigenous models of self-determining autonomy.[30] By contrast, reference to government entails the institutional expression of governance, namely, the specific forms of this relationship between ruler(s) and ruled in allocating power among constituent units.

In the case of Canada's Aboriginal peoples, the politics of (self) governance remain pivotal. Modern treaties since the mid 1970s have incorporated a significant component of governance/government into the compensation/settlement package—a largely unprecedented move since few countries believe they can address the principle of Indigenous self-rule without imploding in the process.[31] For example, treaty settlements in New Zealand rarely incorporate a governance component. Emphasis, instead, is geared toward financial restitution, a formal apology, and return of confiscated land still under Crown control. To be sure, governance structures must be in place for Maori tribes to qualify for, collect, and distribute government reparations (see Ngai Tahu case study below). But governance issues appear to be secondary to settlement concerns within the restitutional package.

Different levels of Indigenous self-determining governance can be discerned, namely, that of state, nation, community, and institution, each of which reflects varying levels of jurisdiction and scope.[32] At one end of this admittedly ideal continuum are models of absolute self-determination (statehood) with formal independence and control over internal and external jurisdictions. At the opposite pole are sovereignties in name only (nominal sovereignties), that is, a fictive self-determination option with residual decision-making powers within existing institutional frameworks. In between are self-determining models of de facto sovereignty, including nationhood, in addition to 'functional' sovereignty such as community-hood. Claims to nationhood embrace the notion of self-rule over internal affairs but without the authority over matters of (inter)national interests (sovereignty without secession). By contrast, the functional sovereignties of community-hood offer local autonomy, although these rights are limited by the legitimate concerns of similar subunits.[33] The table below provides an overview of different models of Indigenous self-determining governance—keeping in mind that distinctions should be approached as contextual rather than categorical.[34]

Models of Indigenous Self-Determining Governance

STATEHOOD	NATIONHOOD
• absolute (*de jure*) sovereignty • internal and external autonomy • complete independence with no external interference	• de facto sovereignty • control over multiple yet interlocking jurisdictions within framework of a secessionless sovereignty • toward a "nations within"
COMMUNITY-HOOD	**INSTITUTIONAL**
• functional sovereignty • community-based autonomy • internal jurisdictions, limited only by interaction with similar bodies and higher political authorities	• nominal sovereignty • decision-making power through institutional inclusion • create parallel structures

Consider the reactions of Indigenous peoples to these political possibilities. For some, a robust level of Indigenous self-determination entails a relatively high degree of separation, up to and including statehood. Others are less overtly political, but appear content to participate within existing institutions in ways that affirm the principle of their sovereignty in both processes and outcomes. In between are hybrids involving a combination of self- versus state-determination. With few exceptions, Indigenous peoples are not seeking independent statehood or political independence with ultimate authority over all matters within a bounded territory. The intent is not to demolish the society in general, but to dismantle that part of the structure that denies them their rightful place as original occupants and contemporary co-owners.[35] This excerpt from Canada's Royal Commission on Aboriginal Peoples is typical and should allay alarmist fears about "death by dismemberment":

To say that Aboriginal Peoples are nations is not to say that they are nation-states seeking independence from Canada. They are collectivities with a long shared history, a right to govern themselves and, in general, a strong desire to do it in partnership with Canada.[36]

In other words, inherent self-governance is not the same as secession or absolute sovereignty. A de facto (or functional) sovereignty is advocated instead where Indigenous peoples are treated as if they were sovereign for purposes of entitlement and engagement. Or as Henry Reynolds once explained, sovereign statehood may not be essential for Indigenous survival in the modern world,[37] but a commitment to nationhood autonomy most certainly is, especially if Indigenous communities expect to flourish as living and lived-in realities.

Aboriginal Self-Determining Autonomy in Canada: Self-Governance through Self-Government

Canada's Aboriginal peoples are in the midst of a drive to regain control over their lives and life chances. Central to this reconstruction process are the politics of aboriginality in severing the cycle of poverty, powerlessness, and dependency. The concept of Aboriginal self-determination rejects as a framework for co-operative coexistence the legitimacy of existing political relations and mainstream institutions. Also rejected is the moral authority of those structures that once colonized Aboriginal peoples. Proposed instead is the restoration of Aboriginal models of self-determining autonomy that sharply curtail state jurisdiction while bolstering Aboriginal control over land and resources. Key elements of this self-determination project include control over local governance, the attainment of cultural sovereignty, and a realignment of political relations around formal self-governing arrangements in key jurisdictional areas related to power, privilege, and resources.[38]

Of particular salience in advancing a new agenda is the right to Aboriginal self-governance, consistent with their status as the 'nations within'.[39] Few should be surprised that the politics of aboriginality revolve around debates over self-governance.[40] Canada itself is a territoriality-based polity involving an intricate allocation of separate but overlapping jurisdictions, and this division of jurisdictions between Ottawa and the provinces is expressed at the level of Aboriginal self-governance. Since 1995, the Canadian government has recognized Aboriginal peoples as having an inherent right to self-government. In the words of the former Minister of Indian Affairs, Ronald Irwin, in acknowledging an inherent right to self government as an existing Aboriginal right in section 35 of the *Constitution Act, 1982* :

The federal government is committed to building a new partnership with Aboriginal people, a partnership based on mutual respect and trust. Working steadily toward the implementation of *the inherent right of self-government* is the cornerstone of that relation [emphasis added].[41]

Such recognition signifies a departure from the past when governments resolutely opposed any self-determining concessions for fear of eroding the Canada-building project. And yet this shift in recognition is not without statist overtones. Inherent self-government draws on contingent rather than sovereign rights so that Aboriginal self-governments must (co)operate within the Canadian federal system, cannot declare independence or compromise Canada's territorial sovereignty, must be in harmony with other governments, cannot violate the principles of the *Canadian Charter of Rights and Freedoms,* and must enhance the participation of Aboriginal peoples in Canadian society. This commitment to renew Aboriginal peoples-state relations by strengthening Aboriginal governance was further reinforced through government policy initiatives such as "Gathering Strength" and a parallel document, *An Agenda for Action with First Nations.*[42] But it took the Nisga'a *Final Agreement* to clarify the reality of Aboriginal governance as Canada's third order of government.

Case Study

Nisga'a Self-Determination as Self-Governance

References to the "Indian problem" may be a misnomer, but public perception of Aboriginal peoples as having problems or creating problems will not be easily discarded. Proposed solutions are no less puzzling and provocative. To one side are those state determinists who believe that assimilation (or normalization) is key to solving the "Indian problem". According to the assimilationists, the Indian problem originates in their physical and social isolation from society because of reserves, special status, treaties, and welfare handouts. If only they would become "more like us"—that is, competitive, materialistic, individualistic—all their problems would disappear.[43] To the other side are those self-determinists who believe that less is more, and that solving the Indian's 'Canada problem' lies in becoming less like "us" because "we are not you."[44] For autonomists, relations-repair is key: any meaningful solution to the Indian problem must entail a new post-colonial social contract for co-operative coexistence. Any restructuring of this relationship must acknowledge Aboriginal peoples as a political community, with a corresponding right to Aboriginal models of self-determining autonomy over land, identity, and political voice.[45]

These polarized positions catapulted to the political forefront with ratification of the Nisga'a *Final Agreement* in May 2000—the first treaty settlement in British Columbia since 1859 and the first of 50 outstanding land claims across the province. The *Final Agreement* (the federal government prefers not to use the term treaty) did not materialize overnight.

Since 1885, the Nisga'a First Nation of central BC has sought compensation over the unlawful surrender of their land to the Crown. They petitioned the British Privy Council in 1913, and in 1968, took their case to court where a Supreme Court ruling in 1973 ruled against the Nisga'a (on a technicality rather than substance). Nonetheless, the *Calder* decision (as it came to be known) conceded the possibility of something called aboriginal title to unextinguished land.[46] The historic 2000 agreement proved the culmination.

Actual terms of the agreement are clearly specified but subject to diverse interpretation. The Nisga'a *Final Agreement* provides the 5,500-member band 800 kilometres north of Vancouver with a land base of 1,900 kilometres (a fraction of the amount originally proposed); control over forest and fishery resources; $200 million in cash; release from *Indian Act* provisions without loss of Indian status; a supra-municipal level of government including control over policing, education, community services, and taxes; and eventually elimination of on-reserve tax exemptions. To underwrite this infrastructure, the Nisga'a received regional forest and timber cutting rights, oil and mineral resources, and fishery-conservation trust as well as 26 percent of the salmon fishery plus $21.5 million for purchase of boats and equipment. This transfer in wealth and jurisdiction is expected to alleviate community dysfunctions, including high levels of unemployment, criminal activity, and crowded homes. The settlement is not without major significance: the Nisga'a have come a long way from the days when the late Pierre Elliott Trudeau denied the existence of Aboriginal rights by declaring that no country could be built on "historical might have beens."

How potent are the powers and authority of the Nisga'a nation? Critics tend to overestimate the aura attributed to the Nisga'a. True, Nisga'a self-governing powers may be constitutionally protected—a status that no municipality has. Nor are Nisga'a laws subject to override except by federal, provincial, and Nisga'a agreement. The Nisga'a government will have exclusive jurisdiction in matters related to language and culture in addition to control over citizenship and property, even when these conflict with federal/provincial laws. Yet Nisga'a powers are circumscribed and considerably less than those implied by federal recognition of Canada's First Nations as "peoples" with an "inherent right to self-government." Nisga'a self-government is firmly occluded within the framework of Canadian society, the *Constitution Act*, and the *Charter of Rights and Freedoms*. Health, education, and child welfare services must meet provincial standards, while the federal Criminal Code will remain in effect. Under the terms of the agreement, moreover, Nisga'a governments will reflect a "concurrent jurisdiction"—that is, shared and overlapping jurisdictions rather than watertight compartments whereby both Nisga'a laws and federal and provincial jurisdiction will continue to apply.[47]

Still, the political significance cannot be underestimated. Not only does the Nisga'a Nation constitute a third order of government alongside the federal and provincial, it also possesses control over jurisdictions that transcend certain federal and provincial laws without ever straying from the context of Canada's Constitutional framework. Nisga'a constitutes a hybrid of state- and self-determination: Nisga'a nationhood is embodied in provincial-like powers, but governance structures remain firmly embedded within the framework of Canadian society. A self-determining autonomy of such magnitude is not intended to be divisive or racial. The objective is to find some common grounds for a constructive re-engagement between founding peoples.

Of course, not everyone concurs with the government's endorsement of what some call an "Aboriginal orthodoxy" (the assumption that Aboriginal peoples are nations with rights to self-determination, and that governments must act accordingly).[48] Non-Aboriginal opinion is often confused, generally unenthused, and frequently resentful. Concerns are raised over costs, feasibility, effectiveness, degree of legitimacy, and belief that such devolutionary powers are more a problem than a solution.[49] Aboriginal leaders may be no less conflicted. Conventional forms of self-government are dismissed as a sell out or sell off. No matter how seemingly progressive the concept of state determination, any placement into Canada on its terms is largely an exercise in applying cosmetic changes to an outward face of power.[50] In rejecting state institutions of governance as extensions of white power and settler state interest, an Indigenous self-determining autonomy must begin by acknowledging the centrality of self-sufficiency on Indigenous peoples' terms and in their own way, in part through cultural and spiritual renewal, in part by overcoming internalized fears, in part by reclaiming what rightfully belongs to them.[51]

To sum up: Colonialism vs. Indigeneity

As always, there is a hitch because theory is one thing, reality is another. Indigenous peoples may be insisting on their right to self-determination as set out in international protocols—at least in principle if not always in practice—but the implementation of Indigenous self-determination rights is proving problematic. Non-Indigenous citizens are increasingly rebelling against the steady rise of Indigenous peoples' rights, especially when recognition involves costs or inconvenience. Both public and political enthusiasm for the idea of Indigenous peoples' rights draws more support than their actual exercise.[52] The disjunction is unmistakable: When Indigenous rights were a theoretical possibility, Ken Coates says, political support was palpable.[53] But now that these once-abstract rights are impacting on people's very real lives, support is shrivelling, in the process generating a looming backlash that could erupt or erode.

A conflict of interest infuses the political dynamics of Indigenous peoples-state relations.[54] To one side is pervasiveness of a Eurocentric and colonial constitutional order associated with state models of determination. To the other side are the transformational politics of indigeneity, including an embrace of Indigenous rights to self-determining autonomy as a framework for restoring relationships.[55] With state determination, the parameters of self-rule often amount to little more than an offloading of the state's administrative responsibilities. By contrast, the concept of self-determination reflects Indigenous realities, reinforces their political rights, and advances their status as the nations within. Indigenous self-determination is not about destroying society, but about crafting a new post-colonial social contract whose foundational principles acknowledge 'the nations within'. In challenging the state to move over and create constitutional space, Indigenous claims to self-determining autonomy are redefining the very contractual basis for living together differently.

Self-Determining Autonomy vs.
State-Determination: Aotearoa, New Zealand

Canada's Aboriginal peoples are not the only Indigenous peoples torn between the conflicting demands of self- versus state-determination. The Indigenous peoples of New Zealand are no less entrapped because of this conflict of interest. Consisting of the different tribes ("iwi" and "hapu") of varying sizes, Maori constitute about 16 percent of New Zealand's population of 4 million, with the vast majority (about 83 percent) living in larger urban centres, but often continuing to maintain close ties with their rural and tribal origins. Unlike those Aboriginal peoples in Canada whose ancestors signed treaties and whose descendents are registered in Ottawa with a corresponding entitlement to reserve residence and benefits, Maori neither entered into treaties in the conventional Canadian sense nor experienced the imposition of an isolationist reserve system. Like Aboriginal peoples in Canada, however, Maori endure comparable patterns of poverty and powerlessness because of structural constraints within a colonial constitutional order.[56]

Competing notions of self-determination infuse the politics of Maori-state relations. On the one hand are state models of self-determination (*kawanatanga*) with their dual focus on disparity reduction, capacity-building, and historical reparations over violations to the Treaty of Waitangi. On the other hand are Maori-driven models of self-determination (*rangatiratanga*), with a priority on constructing a new post-colonial social contract around the principles of power sharing, partnership, meaningful participation, and property-return. Unlike state-determination models with their Eurocentric assumptions and colonialist frameworks, Maori models reflect patterns of self-determining autonomy based on

Maori intellectual traditions and philosophical perspectives.[57] To the extent that the foundational principles of state- versus self-determination clash—as they do in Canada—the prospects for relations-repair are sharply reduced. Nevertheless, the principles for living together differently by balancing the demands of duelling determinations are under review by the Waitangi Tribunal.

Rangatiratanga (Self-Determining Autonomy) vs. Kawanatanga (State-Determination)

The new millennium is proving both the best of times and the worst of times for Maori-Crown relations. Nowhere is this more evident than in the politics over the Treaty of Waitangi. A political covenant between Maori and the Crown established with the Treaty of Waitangi in 1840 remains in effect. Many acknowledge the Treaty as a constitutional blueprint, despite a dearth of consensus regarding its importance or scope, except that Crown actions cannot be inconsistent with Treaty principles.[58] Moreover, although the Treaty of Waitangi approximates a foundational document, it remains unenforceable unless explicitly incorporated into national or local law.[59] Finally, thanks to interpretative difficulties because of differences in the English and Maori versions, the politics of self- versus state-determination are animated by competing Treaty discourses.

Signed in 1840 by representatives of the Crown and nearly 500 Maori chiefs, the Treaty of Waitangi may have transferred sovereignty to the Crown as set out in Article 1 of the English text.[60] But Article 2 of the Maori version also guaranteed unqualified chieftainship (te tino rangatiratanga) over land, resources, and taonga (treasured possessions). According to both versions, the transaction was cemented by the conferral of Article 3 citizenship rights to all Maori as British subjects. A conflict of interest prevails because of divergent translations. To one side of the interpretive divide is a Maori determination to expand their self-determining autonomy (rangatiratanga). To the other side is a Crown inclination to preserve its authority (kawanatanga) by blocking competing claims to state sovereignty. Maori struggles to preserve rangatiratanga from the clutches of governance (kawanatanga) are countered by equally determined Crown pre-emptions to protect kawanatanga from the transformational politics of rangatiratanga. For Maori, Article 2 may have reaffirmed the possibility of two coexisting sovereignties around a partnership arrangement, but the history of Maori-Crown relations demonstrates the displacement of rangatiratanga by a form of kawanatanga that has usurped all authority over people and lands.[61]

Not surprisingly, if there is a single theme that informs Maori-Crown relations, paramount is the historical struggle between competing constitutional accords. At one level is a colonial constitutional order with a few bicultural bits to offset a fundamental monoculturalism. At another level is a post-colonial constitutional blueprint that acknowledges the bi-nationality of New Zealand as two peoples ("nations") within the framework of a single state. The struggle between these ostensibly incompatible constitutional visions—self-determining autonomy (inclusion) or state-determination (integration)—strikes at the tension in Maori-Crown relations as articulated by the Taranaki Report:

> For Maori, their struggle for autonomy, as evidenced in the New Zealand wars, is not past history. It is part of a continuum that has endured to this day ... in the policies of the Kingitanga, Ringatu, the Repudiation Movement, Te Whiti, Tohu, the Kotahitanga, Rua, Ratana, Maori parliamentarians, iwi runanga, the Maori Congress, and others. It is a record matched only by the Government's opposition and its determination to impose instead an ascendancy, though cloaked under other names such as amalgamation, assimilation, majoritarian democracy, or one nation. [62]

The ongoing tension between the pull of kawanatanga and the push of tino rangatiratanga remains as taut as ever. Efforts to find a sustainable compromise between each of these constitutional principles—that of partnership, power-sharing, protection, and participation versus that of compliance and control—have proven both elusive and infuriating as neither partner can afford to capitulate to the other. It is within this scenario of challenge and opposition, as well as compromise and conflict, that the politics of self- versus state-determination are formed, reformulated, and transformed.

State-Determination: Kawanatanga in Principle and Practice

New Zealand governments have long endorsed state-determination models for solving the so-called "Maori problem." Orthodox government policy and programs depicted Maori as little more than social problems who could be saved by promoting Maori self-sufficiency through socio-economic improvements. [63] Government initiatives were predicated on the assumption that Maori constituted a troublesome constituent—a problem people—whose "needs" could be met by improving "outcomes" within the existing political/bureaucratic framework. Not surprisingly, any notion of Maori as constitutional partners was quickly quelled by references to Maori as minorities with needs rather than peoples with rights. This framing of Maori around disparity gaps and developmental discourses is politically driven. The threat to national unity and state legitimacy is defused by depoliticizing Maori demands for self-determination—itself a complex phenomena best envisaged as lying along a self-determining continuum from 'soft' to 'hard' autonomy. [64] In that references to state-determination tended to (dis)empower Maori around corporate development models, this commitment says more about power politics than social justice

To be sure, governments in recent years have discarded a traditional clientship approach in exchange for developmental models that foster self-sufficiency, disparities reduction, treaty settlements, and capacity building. [65] Deficit policy models have yielded ground to 'potential' (or 'investment') policy models encapsulated in the catch phrase "Maori succeeding as Maori." [66] And yet these capacity-building initiatives continue to miss the mark. Even well-intentioned developmental overtures are flawed since they reinforce state control in the design and delivery of Maori programs, tend to absorb Maori perspectives under existing goals and structures, and fail to build capacity for Maori-determined development.[67] Maori underperformance continues to be assessed by reference to non-Maori standards while ignoring Maori measures for defining success or evaluating performance.[68] Worse still, policy initiatives such as "Closing the Gap" (and its successor "Reducing Inequities") gloss over the structural bases of Maori disadvantage, from land confiscation to systemic racism.[69] The end result? Maori continue to be blamed for their problems rather than laying blame at declining opportunity structures and discriminatory barriers, in effect reinforcing the very colonialism that initially created the problem.[70]

Maori Self-Determination: Tino Rangatiratanga

In contrast to state-determination models are Maori self-determining alternatives. According to the canon of self-determining autonomy, Maori are not a historically disadvantaged minority with needs or problems. As articulated in Article 2 of the Treaty, they are Indigenous peoples, with collective and inherent rights to self-determining autonomy over jurisdictions pertaining to land, identity, and political voice. Admittedly, this "rights" discourse is not oblivious to Maori shortcomings and disadvantages. But problems and needs must be situated within the discursive framework of tino rangatiratanga rights, and then dealt with on the basis of nation-to-nation relationship. A rights-driven discourse assumes Maori ownership of policy formulation—from design to implementation to feedback—through initiatives that promote Maori intellectual and philosophical perspectives as inherently worthwhile, deserving of respect, and a blueprint for renewal and reform. In short, the colonial arrangements and Eurocentric mindsets that once swindled or suppressed are no longer applicable. Proposed instead are iwi-based models of self-determining autonomy that sharply curtail state jurisdictions while bolstering claims for a new constitutional order.

Clearly, then, the politics of tino rangatiratanga have catapulted to the forefront of Maori self-determination politics.[71] References to tino rangatiratanga go beyond the redress of historical grievances or the protection of customary property rights. Tino rangatiratanga is ultimately a discourse about the politics of power. Tino rangatiratanga entails a host of Maori aspirations for constitutional recognition as the "sovereigns within" with a corresponding right to a nation-to-nation (government-to-government) relationship. A discursive framework is constituted that justifies Maori models of self-determining autonomy over culture and identity, control and development of land and resources, and improvement in Maori lives and life-chances.[72] By contesting constitutional space, tino rangatiratanga is implicitly transformational. The absolute authority of the Crown is challenged by restoring Maori as constitutional partners in jointly exercising sovereign authority over New Zealand. With tino rangatiratanga, in other words, Maori are justified in claiming to constitute a relatively autonomous political community that is independently sourced because of status as "tangata whenua" (peoples of the land). But theory is one thing: its implementation can be something else without a principled framework to guide and assess.

Waitangi Tribunal: Reconciling State vs. Self-Determination

A restitutional process is currently in place to compensate Indigenous Maori peoples for Crown breaches to Treaty provisions. In securing a basis for resolving long-standing Maori grievances in a principled way, the Labour government institutionalized the Waitangi Tribunal in 1975 as a Commission of Inquiry to (a) make recommendations on claims to past and present breaches to Treaty principles, (b) consider whether any Crown action or proposed legislation was inconsistent with Treaty principles, and (c) determine the "meaning and effect" of the Treaty by negotiating the differences between the English and Maori language versions.[73] Of particular value is the work of the Tribunal in unsettling settler-Maori relations in New Zealand. By exposing Crown duplicity when not complying with Treaty principles, the cumulative impact of Tribunal reports in "radicalising history" is underscored. Not surprisingly, despite an underfunding that generates a backlog of claims,[74] the Tribunal has evolved into the "engine room"[75] of contemporary politics in advocating a new New Zealand.

Bicultural in mandate as well as process and composition (about half of the 16 members are Maori while procedures are conducted in accordance with Maori custom), the Waitangi Tribunal represents an institutional forum in which oppositional readings of the Treaty reappraise Maori Indigenous rights in light of emergent realities.[76] The Waitangi Tribunal can be likened to a "truth and reconciliation" in forum and function.[77] A permanent commission of inquiry is in place that registers Maori claims or grievances over Crown breaches to the Treaty of Waitangi, airs them through a public forum that tests these claims for legitimacy, and publishes reports on the accuracy of the claims. The reports provide a balanced assessment of what the Crown could and should have done in meeting its Treaty obligations, whether the claimant communities suffered harm because of Crown in/actions in breaching the Treaty, and makes recommendations for removing the harm, remedying the grievance, and repairing the relationship. Tribunal recommendations are neither binding (except in rare cases) nor do they have any standing in ruling on points of law over the return of land. Nevertheless, these recommendations may establish input for subsequent government negotiations.

Treaty settlements revolve around Crown reparations for breaches to the principles of the Treaty of Waitangi.[78] Settlements usually involve Maori grievances over land and resources that were unlawfully stolen or confiscated by Crown agents. In addition, grievances may include the following: broken Crown promises in creating Maori reserves; illegal Crown purchases of Maori land; and failure to protect traditional Maori food sources or sacred areas such as burial grounds.

Once negotiators agree on a settlement (usually involving the Office of Treaty Settlements), the claimant group votes on whether to accept or reject the Crown offer. Critics argue that in recent years the Crown has exerted pressure on tribes to bypass the Tribunal by proceeding directly into negotiations with OTS, resulting in a process perceived to be over controlled and unfair.[79] Most settlements include four components: (1) an apology to the claimant group, (2) commercial redress (a combination of Crown property and cash) for righting Crown wrongs, (3) some degree of cultural redress ranging from access to traditional food sources to a say in the management of sacred sites on Crown land, and (4) an agreement that the settlement is fair and final.

Key assumptions underpin the settlement process. Crown actions are predicated on the premise that it's impossible to fully compensate claimants for grievance. Rather, redress focuses on a symbolic recognition of the claimants' grievances, restoration of the relationship of claimant group to Crown, and contributions to the claimants' groups' economic development.[80] To ensure the management and distribution of settlement property and cash, the claimant group must establish an organization that the Crown believes is representative, transparent, and accountable to its members. Between 1992 and mid 2005, a total of 18 settlements of historical Treaty claims were finalized, amounting to a total value of $718 million. One of the more notable Treaty settlements involved the Ngai Tahu peoples of the South Island.

Case Study

Ngai Tahu Settlement: State-Determination as Self-Determination?

Ngai Tahu are the largest Maori tribe (iwi) of the southern region of New Zealand, consisting of individuals descended from five sub-tribes (hapu) who settled in the South Island around a thousand years ago. Their takiwa (ancestral land) as defined by the *Te Runanga Ngai Tahu Act* of 1996, encompasses much of the South Island (except for the northern sections and islands to the south). The Ngai Tahu may have signed the Treaty of Waitangi in 1840, but by 1848 claimed they had been victimized by Crown violations of Treaty promises. The Crown's settlement with Ngai Tahu in 1998 acknowledged the Crown's failure to honour Treaty obligations. In contrast to the Nisga'a *Final Settlement*, which constituted a modern day treaty involving a land base and self-governance package, the *Ngai Tahu Claims Settlement Act* is primarily a restitutional package. Terms of the settlement sought to restore the mana of Ngai Tahu by settling historical grievances, providing a redress package of cash ($170 million) and land (including right of first refusal for Crown assets within its takiwa), and included an apology from the Crown for its wrongdoings.

The infrastructure put in place by the Ngai Tahu reveals different levels of organization. Te Runanga o Ngai Tahu is the umbrella organization that services the tribe's statutory obligations, thereby ensuring that the long-term benefits of the *Settlement Act* enhance future generations.[81] Established by the 1996 *Act* to assume direct responsibility for the overall governance of the Ngai Tahu, the objective of the Te Runanga is create a stronger economic, political, social, and cultural base by managing tribal collective assets through the sustainable use of resources, sound environmental outcomes, and building relations to ensure an active role in the wider community. Te Runanga itself consists of 18 local runanga (local councils) with an elected representative from each local runanga making up the larger tribal council that oversees the groups assets and developments. The Te Runanga governance structure reflects a commitment to decentralization that allows a degree of relative autonomy within an overarching framework. Constituents include: the Ngai Tahu Development Corporation for administrative duties and provision of social and cultural programs; Charitable Trust; Communications; Finance; and Holdings Group that manages commercial and investment activities, including Equities, Property, Seafood, Tourism, and Tribal Services.

As of 2002, the Holding company was the largest private property owner in the South Island, with significant investments in the seafood industry and tourism ventures. Tribal equity leapt from $170 million to $270 million resulting in total tribal assets of $372 million. Returns on this investment allow the Ngai Tahu to build for the future by investing in health, education, social and economic well-being, and culture and identity.[82]

In addition to ruling on specific Maori claims such as Ngai Tahu, the Tribunal has been charged with promulgating the principles for interpreting the Treaty. Its mandate rests in looking beyond strict legalities for determining Treaty meaning and effects in hopes of reconciling and harmonizing the differences raised by the English version (with its kawanatanga commitment to state determination) and Maori version (with its rangatiratanga focus on self-determination).[83] Consider the contrasts: The English text claims to transfer sovereignty over to the Crown in exchange for the protection of Maori property until duly sold. With Crown sovereignty firmly established, Pax Britannica could be imposed with impunity. Maori law and customs would prevail only until they could be replaced with British laws, values, and institutions. By contrast, the Maori text claims to have transferred kawanatanga (governance) over to the Crown, while retaining sovereignty (rangatiratanga) rights over land, resources, and other treasures.[84] In doing so, the Treaty secured their tino rangatiratanga right to remain equal but separate.[85]

To date, a reading of both texts has culminated in the establishment of four principles that serve as a basis for determining which Crown actions were/are inconsistent with the spirit of the Treaty. They include the overarching principle, the partnership principle, the active protection principle, and the principle of autonomy.

The Overarching Principle

Of paramount importance is the overarching or reciprocity-exchange principle. According to the overarching principle, Maori ceded governorship/governance (kawanatanga) in exchange for reciprocal Crown protection of Maori sovereignty (tino rangatiratanga).[86] Stakeholders in the Treaty process must acknowledge the Crown's sovereign right to govern under Article 1. However, stakeholders must also accept the equally unassailable guarantees of rangatiratanga under Article 2 which qualifies the Crown's power to absolute governance. (Similarly, the *Delgamuukw* ruling in 1997 affirmed that Crown assertion of absolute sovereignty in Canada did not displace existing Aboriginal orders, lands, and rights, but put the onus on protecting them.)[87] The Crown may be sovereign, in other words, but its absolute authority is offset by rangatiratanga guarantees. By the same token, article 2 rights are more than simple customary rights but entail proprietary rights to property that imply a degree of self-determining autonomy. Moreover, Crown exercise of sovereignty is conditional on protecting Maori article 2 rights, based on the assumption that Maori "gifted" kawanatanga to the Crown in return for continued sovereignty (rangatiratanga) over land and resources.[88] To be sure, the Crown possesses overriding rights to exercise kawanatanga authority over rangatiratanga guarantees; nevertheless, it can only do so as a last resort or when national interests are at stake.[89]

The Principle of Partnership

According to the partnership principles, Maori and Pakeha (non-Indigenous New Zealanders) must be seen as partners—that is, co-signatories to a political covenant—whose partnership is constructed around the sharing of power, resources, and privileges. Reference to the Treaty as a "dialogue between sovereigns" establishes a partnership that requires both Maori and Pakeha to act toward each other reasonably, in mutual co-operation and trust, and in good faith. The Treaty is not a unilateral declaration involving closure, but entails the Crown duty to meaningfully and bilaterally consult across mutually relevant domains.[90]

The Principle of Active Protection

The Crown has a duty to actively protect rangatiratanga rights as set out in Article 2. A trust relationship of protection applies when one side is weaker and more vulnerable than the other. Two kinds of protection prevail: reactive protection entails the removal of laws, barriers, and constraints that inhibit Maori self-determination. Proactive protection includes measures to preserve and enhance Maori resources and taonga[91]—especially in those cases where developments may imperil Maori taonga.

The Principle of Autonomy

The concept of autonomy is justified on historical and principled grounds. When two people meet, the Tribunal has argued, their joint differences must be worked through in a manner that engages both as equals, invokes the validity of difference, and allows for the mediation of differences between them.[92] Autonomy cannot be vested in only one of the partners; after all, each partner is expected to recognise, respect, and be reconciled with the autonomy of the other.[93] As the Taranaki Claims Report concluded, Maori autonomy is pivotal in establishing a working partnership with the Crown; without it, they cannot possibly exercise their right to meaningful self-determination. Reference to autonomy by way of tino rangatiratanga secures the ground for taking control of domestic affairs though political arrangements that sharply curtail the jurisdiction of the state while expanding Maori control over land, identity, and political voice.[94]

In sum, in articulating the grounds for living together justly, the Waitangi Tribunal has fulfilled its mandate for righting historical wrongs. In doing so it has established a principled framework for framing Maori grievances to Crown breaches of Treaty principles. Tribunal rulings also appear to have initiated a dialogue for rethinking the concept of cooperative coexistence in a deeply divided Aotearoa. Whether intended or not, these rulings imply the possibility of a new social contract for Maori-Crown relations, including a comprehensive package that emphasises constitutionalism over contestation, contract over combativeness, relationships over legalism, interdependence over opposition, co-operation over competition, reconciliation over restitution, and listening over litigation.[95] A contract-based focus on claims-making is now sharing space with a "constitutionalisms" discourse that increasingly endorses a bi-national constitutional arrangement involving Maori rangatiratanga rights and Crown kawanatanga rights.[96] Inasmuch as Tribunal discourses are repositioning Maori-Crown relations from that of contractual obligations to one of a political compact between co-sovereign partners, its potential for constructive engagement deserves consideration.

Unblocking the Gridlock: Toward a Constructive Engagement Model

Aboriginal peoples are faced with the daunting task of trying to work themselves out of the absolute devastation of cultural instability wrought be colonialism. Even *beginning* to think about how to 'decolonize' is a daunting task [authors' emphasis].[97]

Indigenous peoples' struggles to sever the bonds of dependency and underdevelopment are gathering momentum. Several innovative routes have been explored for improving Indigenous peoples–state relations, including indigenization of policy and administration, devolution of power, and decentralization of service-delivery structures. Admittedly, many of the initiatives are little more that a bureaucratic/managerial exercise in off-loading government responsibility to Indigenous communities with minimal transfer of power or authority. Still, the shift toward a more decentralized arrangement is not without promise, especially in creating the basis for more power to the peoples.

Centrally important is a commitment to righting historical wrongs by way of reparations.[98] Few would deny the importance of settlements in compensating Indigenous peoples for past wrongs, providing a land base with which to regain self-sufficiency, and regaining the pride and culture to overcome marginalization.[99] But on its own and divorced from the bigger picture of rethinking the relationships, a preoccupation with restitution is fraught with hidden agendas and paralyzing contradictions.[100] Reliance on confrontational models for allocating power and resources may prove self-defeating if the debate over "who controls what" is without a unifying and overarching vision for fostering partnership, power-sharing, and participation. The attendant competition typically engenders confrontational dynamics that may inadvertently reinforce the very colonialisms that Indigenous peoples want to escape.[101] And settlements in the absence of clear principles may be counterproductive, little more than an administrative quick fix for 'solving' deep-rooted problems, thereby accentuating power-conflict models at odds with co-operative coexistence.

However unintended, the consequences of restitutional politics breed an adversarial mentality. New Zealand's Treaty claims process draws both tribal and urban Maori into a competitive struggle over valued resources with both the state and with each other (thus exposing class based rifts within Indigenous communities).[102] A zero-sum game of winners and losers locks disputants into a protracted struggle that concedes as little as possible while complicating the process of securing a compromise without losing face. Without a corresponding commitment to restore the relationship in a generous and unquibbling fashion, grievances remain grievances no matter how much money is being exchanged.[103] Contesting claims to the exclusion of engagement also glosses over the central element in any productive relationship, namely, the managing of a partnership in the spirit of constructive engagement.[104]

Pressure is mounting to discard an adversarial framework for Indigenous peoples-state relations. A more flexible and principled approach is proposed that privileges the process of engagement over the principle of entitlement.[105] Emergence of a constructive engagement model to replace confrontational models may provide a respite from the interminable bickering over "who owns what," while brokering a post-colonial social contract for living together differently. Of those key attributes at the core of a constructive engagement model, the following principles are central.

1. **De facto Sovereignty:** Indigenous peoples do not aspire to sovereignty *per se*. Strictly speaking, they already have sovereignty (or are sovereign) by virtue of original occupancy, having never surrendered by explicit agreement their sovereignty as politically autonomous peoples. The fact that Indigenous peoples are sovereign for purposes of entitlement or engagement reinforces the need for appropriate structures for putting this principle into practice.

2. Relations Repair/Partnership: Indigenous peoples are not looking to separate or become independent. Except for a few ideologues, appeals to sovereignty are largely about establishing relationships of relative yet relational autonomy.[106] Nor should Indigenous peoples be considered as competitors to be jousted and diminished, but as constitutional partners sharing the same land as co equals. In acknowledging that "let's face it, we are all here to stay," as former Canadian Chief Justice Antonio Lamer once observed, is there any other option except to nurture the primacy of relations between partners.

3. Peoples with Rights: Indigenous peoples are neither a problem for solution nor a need to be capped. They are a peoples (or nations) with collective and inherent rights that are derived from their status as political communities, descendents of the original inhabitants, and from a body of common and international law. These rights must be accepted as being independently sourced rather than delegated and shaped for majority convenience or subject to unilateral override.[107]

4. Political Nations not Ethnic Minorities: Indigenous peoples are not ethnic minorities but constitute fundamentally autonomous political communities. Unlike ethnic and immigrant minorities who are looking to settle down and fit in within the existing social and political framework, Indigenous peoples want to 'get out' of political arrangements that deny, exclude, or oppress. Proposed are arrangements that bolster their inherent right to Indigenous models of self-determining autonomy and self-governance.

5. Constitutional Space/Post-Colonial Social Contract: The politics of indigeneity transcend the concept of institutional reform to improve socioeconomic status. Indigenous peoples' politics are about power. They are focused on carving out constitutional space by challenging the foundational principles of the existing social contract in exchange for a post-colonial social contract based on the principles of partnership, participation, and power sharing.

6. Power-Sharing: In advancing co-operative engagement and co-sovereign coexistence, power sharing is critical. Deeply divided societies that have attained some degree of stability endorse a level of governance involving a sharing of constitutionally entrenched power.[108] Precise arrangements for rearranging power distributions are varied, of course, but predicated on the principle of justice rather than technicalities or points of law.

7. Jurisdictions as Relations: Concerns over jurisdiction cannot be taken lightly: Control and power must be allocated along clear lines by carefully calibrating what is mine, what is yours, and what is ours. Parties must enter into negotiations over jurisdictions not on the basis of jurisprudence but on the grounds of justice, not by cutting deals but by formulating a clear vision, and not by litigating but by listening. The objective in defining jurisdiction is not to create boundaries but to foster relations repair.

8. Meaningful Participation: In that Indigenous peoples are sovereign yet share sovereignty, a commitment to meaningful participation is critical. An adherence to bilateral consultations over issues of relevance goes without saying. No less critical to a participatory model is the establishment of venues and mindsets that facilitate the expression of meaningful participation.

9. Belonging as Citizenship: Innovative patterns of belonging are critical when two peoples share the same political and territorial space but neither is willing to be dominated by the other.[109] Indigenous proposals for belonging to society are anchored in primary affiliation with the group rather than as individual citizens, thus implying that peoples can differently belong without necessarily rejecting citizenship or loyalty to the whole.[110]

10. Indigenous Difference: Indigenous peoples are fundamentally different because of their constitutional and political status. These differences must be taken seriously and must be taken into account as basis for recognition, reward, and relationships.[111]

11. Conciliation/Restoration: An expression of regret for the deplorable acts of a colonial past is not meant to humiliate, embarrass, or extract reparations. A commitment to reconciliation is meant to exorcise the pain and humiliation endured by Indigenous peoples. The atonement is intended to create the basis for healing and restoration of Indigenous pride and dignity.[112] Restoration of land and resources that rightfully belong to Indigenous peoples is no less critical in establishing an economic basis for self-determining autonomy.

An adherence to constructive engagement transcends the legalistic (abstract rights) or restitutional (reparations)—however important these concerns are in fostering identity-building and resource mobilization. Increasing reliance on contractual relations for sorting out ownership may have elevated litigation to a preferred level in resolving differences.[113] But this reliance on the legalities of rights and reparations tends to emphasize continuities with the past at the expense of the situational and evolving.[114] By contrast, a new social contract based on the constitutional principles of constructive engagement goes beyond restitution or brokering deals. Emphasis is focused on advancing a relationship on a principled basis by taking into account shifting social realities in sorting out who controls what in a spirit of give and take. In that policy outcomes based on a post-colonial social contract cannot be viewed as final or authoritative, any more than they can be preoccupied with "taking" or "finalizing" but must be situated in the context of "sharing" and "extending," wisdom and justice must precede power, rather than vice versa.[115]

Toward Indigenous Self-Determining Autonomy: Two Steps Forward...

In June of 2006, the UN Human Rights Council passed a motion endorsing a draft Declaration on the Rights of Indigenous Peoples. Compiled by UN Permanent Forum on Indigenous Issues, after 25 years of protracted negotiations, the draft Declaration incorporated the efforts of many contributors, including the Working Group on Indigenous Populations, different governments, Indigenous peoples' representatives, and many non-governmental organizations.[116] Briefly compressed, the text read:

> ... Indigenous Peoples have the right to the full enjoyment, as a collective or as individuals, of all human rights and fundamental freedoms as recognized in the Charter of the United Nations, the Universal Declaration of Human Rights, and international human rights law. Indigenous Peoples and individuals are free and equal to all other peoples and individuals, and have the right to be free from any kind of discrimination, in the exercise of their rights, in particular that based on their indigenous origin or identity. Indigenous Peoples have the right of self-determination. By virtue of that right, they freely determine their political status and freely pursue their economic, social, and cultural development. Indigenous Peoples have the right to maintain and strengthen their distinct political, legal, economic, social, and cultural institutions, while retaining their rights to participate freely, if they so choose, in the political, economic, social, and cultural life of the State.

The intent of the draft Declaration could hardly be faulted: In an effort to curb massive human rights abuses that had engulfed Indigenous peoples for centuries, the draft Declaration calls on governments to recognize Indigenous peoples' rights to self-determination, including the right to autonomy and that of self-government "in exercising their right to self-determination." Or, as put in Article 4 of the draft Declaration: "Indigenous peoples, in exercising their right to self-determination, have the right to autonomy or self-government in matters relating to their internal and local affairs...." Additional rights were also articulated, including the right to (a) maintain and strengthen their institutions, culture, and traditions; (b) pursue development in accordance with their aspirations, realities, and needs; (c) confirm the principle of prior and informed consent over development on Indigenous peoples' land; (d) take measures to combat racism and racial discrimination; and (e) participate in the political and economic life of the state if they so choose.

But opposition to the draft Declaration proved painfully dismaying, especially since much of this rebuke originated with erstwhile supporters of Indigenous peoples' rights. Particularly galling was the abrupt reversal of Canada's position. Its stunning rejection of the draft Declaration contrasted sharply with this country's much ballyhooed reputation as a pacesetter in advancing an Indigenous rights agenda. In opposing passage of the Declaration, Stephen Harper's Conservative Government came under fire. With the government's seeming indifference to Aboriginal peoples' concerns and issues, the neo-conservative instincts of Harper instructed Canada's UN delegates to oppose the draft Declaration, thereby reversing its involvement in formulating the document.[117] To add insult to injury, another pacesetter in restructuring Indigenous people-state relations also voiced disapproval. New Zealand's decision to oppose the draft Declaration by way of a joint communiqué with Australia and the United States proved nearly as demoralizing.[118]

The irony is improbable: in looking to unlock the diplomatic impasse that had gridlocked the draft Declaration for years, both Canada and New Zealand had proven stalwart supporters. Many of their concerns and opinions were incorporated in annual negotiations since inception of talks in 1986.[119] And yet both countries balked at supporting the draft Declaration, in effect insisting on escape clauses to protect national and vested interests over Indigenous peoples' rights.[120] A fundamental shift in the balance of power proved too risky, suggesting the reversal reflected fundamental philosophical differences rather than semantics in the wording:[121]

> State compliance with many of the articles requires consultation with, participation by, and prior informed consent of Indigenous Peoples before decisions are taken. And many of the rights in the declaration require rethinking approaches to many global issues, such as national development, decentralization, free trade, and multicultural democracy. Rights recognition now hinges not only on who suffers but also who benefits... The declaration also thus requires communication and negotiation among all more equal partners. This not only changes the rules but also expands the playing field on which negotiations between Indigenous Peoples and states are played. Under the declaration all states must employ a participatory approach to their interactions with indigenous peoples...[122]

Clearly, then, a paradox is at play. On the one hand, a global jurisprudence is emerging that acknowledges Indigenous peoples' rights to self-determining autonomy. As noted by the UN Secretary General in sympathizing with the plight of 350 million Indigenous peoples in 70 countries,[123] such recognition is long overdue:

> For far too long, indigenous peoples' lands have been taken away, their cultures denigrated or directly attacked, their languages and customs suppressed, their wisdom and traditional knowledge overlooked or exploited, and their sustainable ways of developing natural resources dismissed. Some have even faced the threat of extinction.

On the other hand, those settler states that were expected to endorse such a progressive agenda rejected the draft's position. In going against the grain of international opinion on the rights of Indigenous peoples to self-determination, both

Canada and New Zealand are thought to have betrayed the cause by reversing their status from proponent to opponent.

Debate, disagreement, and disappointment over the draft Declaration has made it abundantly clear: despite promising starts, the concept of Indigenous self-determination remains an ideal rather than reality. A UN committee's decision to defer action on the draft Declaration, which left the much-delayed document in yet another limbo,[124] spoke of the gulf in question. Finally, in September of 2007, the UN General Assembly overwhelming voted to recognize the Universal Declaration of Indigenous Peoples Rights, with 143 countries accepting it, twelve abstentions, and four rejections—including Australia, the United States, New Zealand and Canada—prompting this stinging rebuke from Chief Stewart Phillip of the Union of B.C. Grand Chiefs in the October 2007 issue of *Windspeaker:* "It is truly ironic that four first world countries that have become prosperous through the exploitation of lands and resources of the Indigenous peoples, including Canada, chose to oppose the adoption of the declaration." Despite the dismay, a sense of perspective is useful. Settler societies are struggling to recast their relationship with Indigenous peoples. Growing awareness of massive disparities has combined with mounting resentment and emergent political realities to improve the outcomes for Indigenous peoples. Insofar as settler societies have become more respectful, reflective, and responsive to Indigenous peoples' realities and expectations, a process of decolonization is underway. The need for additional structural change is broadly acknowledged by Indigenous and non-Indigenous leaders alike. Nevertheless, opinions vary on how to hasten this transformation of Indigenous peoples from colonized subjects to self-determining nations in ways workable, necessary, and just.

While the rhetoric of transformation may be compelling, it may also be premature. Elimination of the most egregious colonialist structures notwithstanding, moves to decolonize Indigenous peoples-state relations are fraught with ambiguity because of competing paradigms, hidden agendas, and entrenched interests. In that the foundational principles of a settler constitutional order remain unmistakably Eurocentric with only a few Indigenous faces to replace the incumbents, a neo-colonialism continues to define the constitutional contract. The ideals of a nation-state continue to inform settler foundational principles, including the concept of one legal and sovereign political authority in a given territory with a single nationality and universal citizenship that acknowledges differences as having equal weight and equal status.[125] Not surprisingly, political authorities continue to call the shots in defining who gets what, while Indigenous peoples' self-determination aspirations are overwhelmed by majority priorities and structural constraints.[126] The fundamental objective of settler societies' agendas—to eliminate the Indigenous "problem" by fostering Eurocentric-style self-sufficiency—has barely budged with the passage of time.[127] Only the means have changed, with crude assimilationist strategies conceding ground to more sophisticated channels that co-opt Indigenous peoples discourses for self-serving purposes.[128]

A proposed paradigm shift is gathering momentum, partly in response to escalating pressure from Indigenous peoples, partly to deflect a growing crisis in state legitimacy. The politics of indigeneity secured a spot on the political agenda when central authorities shelved the idea of solving the "Native problem" through absorption into society proposing, instead, their recognition as ongoing political communities with distinctive status and rights.[129] But rather than a paradigm shift, a paradigm muddle persists instead. To one side of the muddle is the old social contract whose rules appear to be drawing to a close, but not without a struggle.[130] To the other, a new post-colonial social contract is emerging but lacks the critical mass of support to take hold. Proposals for change are imbued with an air of dissonance as colonialist paradigms grind up against post-colonizing realities, as the old collides with the new without quite knowing what's next. Neither state nor self models of determination are robust enough to dislodge the other, resulting in politics pervaded by discordant amalgams of the progressive with the hegemonic. This state of tension and conflict is likely to persist until such time as conventional thinking accepts as a basis for living together differently a constructive engagement model involving a partnership of two founding peoples—each self-determining in its own right yet sharing in the sovereignty of a post-colonial society.

NOTES

1   In that the Declaration is an aspirational and non-binding document, why did Canada risk international opprobrium by opposing Indigenous peoples' rights to be free of discrimination and the right to their difference? See John Ivison, "Canada Risks its Nice Image," Globe and Mail (27 September 2006). Supporters of the draft Declaration claim Canada's and New Zealand's fears are groundless. In international law, the right to self-determination as secession can only take place under limited circumstances, namely, the decolonization process, disintegration of federative states, and military occupation of one state by another. Since neither Canada nor New Zealand fit the UN criteria for lawful secession in regard to Indigenous peoples, fears of territorial dismemberment are unfounded. See Metiria Turei, NZ Parliamentary Debates, 12 October 2006. Similarly with the draft Declaration on Indigenous Peoples rights: once approved by the UN General Assembly, the draft becomes an international approved yardstick for assessing state actions that impact on Indigenous peoples. See Claire Charters, Report on the Working Group on the UN Draft Declaration on the Rights of Indigenous People Meeting, 5-16 December 2005. As it stands, the Declaration can only apply pressure for government compliance with universal principles related to rights of Indigenous peoples to their lands and resources, to live as they wish, be protected from forced assimilation and destruction of cultures, and to establish new working relations. See Haider Rizvi, "U.N. Faces Test on Native Rights," IPS News Service (2006). And unless incorporated into domestic law, provisions of the Declaration will remain subject to binding international law that safeguards both territorial integrity and the rights of individuals, with the result that political embarrassment may be the only sanction that can be applied for violation of the Declaration. See Pita Sharples, "Self-Determination: It Takes Two," http://www.scoop.co.nz/stories/2006 (accessed 15 September 2007); "A Sea Change at the United Nations," Cultural Survival Quarterly (Summer 2006).
2   Stuart Bradfield, "Separatism or Status Quo?: Indigenous Affairs from the Birth of Land Rights to the Death of ATSIC," Australian Journal of Politics and History 52, no. 1 (2006): 80-97; and, Tanya Korovkin, "Indigenous Movements in the Central Andes," Latin American and Carribean Ethnic Studies 1, no. 2 (2006): 143-63.
3   Roger Maaka & Augie Fleras, The Politics of Indigeneity: Challenging the State in Canada and Aotearoa New Zealand (Dundin NZ: University of Otago Press, 2005).
4   Roger Maaka & Chris Andersen, eds., The Indigenous Experience: Global Perspectives (Toronto: Canadian Scholars Press, 2006). Also Marisol de al Cadena and Orin Starn, eds. Indigenous Experience Today (New York: Berg Publishing, 2007); Andrea Muehlebach, "What Self in Self-Determination: Notes From the Frontiers of Transnational Indigenous Activism," Identities: Global Studies in Culture and Power, 10 (2003): 241-268. Any insights into Indigenous peoples' politics and the politics of self-determination cannot be divorced from a global and comparative perspective. Rather than focus on particular Indigenous communities in isolation

from others, or, alternatively, around a mechanically comparative study, Indigenous peoples should be framed as a collective constituting a global mosaic of diverse peoples who share a common experience of colonization, reflect a status not as minorities but as peoples with unique cultures and citizenship rights, insist on indigenous difference as basis for claims to collective and inherent rights, and demand a decolonization so they can escape the margins and participate fully in society without having to assimilate. See Daiva Stasiulis and Nira Yuval-Davis, *Unsettling Settler Societies* (Thousand Oaks, CA: Sage, 1995); Ronald Niezen, *The Origins of Indigenism: Human Rights and the Politics of Identity* (Berkeley: University of California Press, 2003); Maaka & Fleras, *The Politics of Indigeneity.* Of particular note is the pursuit and politics of self-determination which is increasingly global in ambition but reflective of reforms at the level of international organizations, national constitutions and laws, and organization and values of Indigenous peoples' communities. International networks are also important as Indigenous peoples look to each other's struggles and progress for inspiration in articulating their own concerns. As a result, the internationalization of Indigenous peoples' politics has generated both a global ideology (indigenism) and a global social movement (indigeneity-being indigenous) that affirms national Indigenous rights to self-determination while concomitantly globalizing them. See Maaka & Andersen, *The Indigenous Experience.*

5   Claire Charters, "Developments in Indigenous Peoples Rights under International Law and Their Domestic Implications." *New Zealand Universities Law Review* 21 (2005): 511-53. Also Muehlebach, "What Self in Self-Determination."

6   John B Henrickson, "Implementation of the Right to Self-Determination of Indigenous People with the Framework of Human Security," paper presented at the International Conference on Indigenous Peoples Self Determination and the Nation State in Asia, Baguio, Philippines, 18-21 April 1999.

7   Nezvat Soguk, "Indigenous People and Radical Futures of Global Politics," *New Political Science* 29, no. 1 (2007): 1-22.

8   Henrickson, "Implementation."

9   Louise Humpage, " 'Liabilities' and 'Assets:' The Maori Affairs Balance Sheet," in *Tangata Tangata: The Changing Ethnic Contours of New Zealand*, eds. Paul Spoonley & David George Pearson (Southbank Victoria: Thomson Dunmore, 2004), 25-42; Dominic O'Sullivan, *Beyond Biculturalism. The Politics of an Indigenous Minority* (Wellington, NZ., Huia Publishers, 2006).

10   Taiaiake Alfred, *Wasáse: Indigenous Pathways to Action and Freedom* (Peterborough ON: Broadview Press, 2005).

11   Humpage, "Liabilities and Assets"; Stephen Cornell, "Indigenous Peoples, Poverty, and Self-Determination," in *Indigenous Peoples and Poverty*, eds. Robyn Eversole, John-Andrew McNeish & Alberto Cimadamore (New York: Zed Books, 2005), 201-23.

12   H. Wooten, "Self Determination After ATSIC," *Academy of the Social Sciences* 24, no. 2 (2004): 16-25.

13   Stephen Cornell, "Indigenous Peoples, Poverty, and Self-Determination."

14   Maaka & Andersen, *The Indigenous Experience.*

15   Dale Turner, *This is Not a Peace Pipe: Toward a Critical Indigenous Philosophy* (Toronto: University of Toronto Press, 2006).

16   See also Stewart Bradfield, "Separatism or Status Quo?"

17   Nevzat Soguk, "Indigenous Peoples and Radical Futures of Global Politics," 19.

18   See also Turner, *This is Not a Peace Pipe.*

19   Jennifer Dalton, "International Law and the Right of Indigenous Self-Determination: Should International Norms Be Replicated in the Canadian Context" Working Paper. IIGR (Institute of Intergovernmental Relations), Kingston, Queen's University, 2005). As Dalton notes, there is no firm consensus over the concepts of Indigenous self-determination, but generally entails the right of Indigenous peoples to choose how they live their shared lives, structure their communities around their own values and laws, and control their own destiny. Also Cornell, "Indigenous Peoples, Poverty, and Self-Determination."

20   Augie Fleras & Jean Leonard Elliott, *The Nations Within: A Comparative Perspective in Indigenous-State Relations* (Toronto: Oxford University Press, 1992).

21   Turner, *This is Not a Peace Pipe.*

22   Mick Dodson, "The Human Rights Situation of Indigenous Peoples of Australia: A Paper Presented to the Intergovernmental Work Group on Indigenous Affairs," *Indigenous Affairs* (1999): 30-45.

23   Niezen, 2003. Also, Mark F.N. Franke, "Self-Determination Versus Determination of Self: A Critical Reading of the Colonial Ethics Inherent to the United Nations Declaration on the Rights of Indigenous Peoples," *Journal of Global Ethics* 3, no 3 (2007): 359-379.

24   John Andrew McNeish & Robyn Eversole, "Overview: The Right to Self-Determination," in *Indigenous Peoples and Poverty*, eds. Robyn Eversole, John-Andrew McNeish & Alberto Cimadamore (New York: Zed Books, 2005), 97-107.

25   Paul Havemann, *Indigenous Peoples Rights in Canada, Australia, and New Zealand* (Auckland, Oxford University Press, 1999); Duncan Ivison, Paul Patton & Will Sanders, *Political Theory and the Rights of Indigenous Peoples* (Oakleigh VIC, Cambridge University Press, 2000).

26 McNeish & Eversole, "Overview."

27 Stephen Cornell & Joseph Kalt, "Sovereignty and Nation-Building: The Development Challenge in Indian Country Today," *Harvard Project on American Indian Economic Development* (2001).

28 John Graham, Bruce Amos & Tim Plumptre, "Principles for Good Governance in the 21st Century," *Institute on Governance Policy* Brief No. 15 (August 2003).

29 Ghislain Otis, "Aboriginal Governance with or without the Canadian Charter?" in *Aboriginality and Governance,* ed. Gordon Christie (Penticton: Theytus Press, 2006), 265-312.

30 Gladys Jimeno Santoyo, "Indigenous Governance and Territory," FOCAL: Canadian Foundation for the Americas, (2006), www.focal.ca/pdf/gobernabilidad_indigena_e.pdf (accessed 15 September 2007).

31 "Aboriginal Governance," Institute on Governance (2006), www.iog.ca (accessed 15 September 2007).

32 Augie Fleras & Paul Spoonley, *Recalling Aotearoa* (Melbourne: Oxford University Press, 1999); Tipene O'Regan, *Indigenous Governance - Country Study, New Zealand,* Study Prepared for the Royal Commission on Aboriginal Peoples, Ottawa, 1994.

33 Donald Clark & Robert Williams, *Self-Determination in International Perspective* (Basinstoke, Macmillan, 1996).

34 From Maaka & Fleras, *The Politics of Indigeneity.*

35 John Borrows & Leonard Rotman, "The *Sui Generis* Nature of Aboriginal Rights: Does it Make a Difference?" *Alberta Law Review* 36 (1997): 9-45; Yale Belanger, "The Six Nations of the Grand River Territory's Attempts at Renewing International Political Relationships, 1921-1924," *Canadian Foreign Policy* 13 (2007): 29-43.

36 Royal Commission on Aboriginal Peoples, *Looking Forward, Looking Backward,* Vol 1 (Ottawa: Ministry of Supplies and Services, 1996), xi.

37 Henry Reynolds, *Aboriginal Sovereignty. Three Nations, One Australia?* (Sydney: Allen and Unwin, 1996). Also Michael F.Brown, "Sovereignty's Betrayals," in *Indigenous Experience Today,* eds. Marisol de la Cadena and Orin Starn (New York: Berg Publishing, 2007).

38 Ovide Mercredi & Mary Ellen Turpel, *In the Rapids: Navigating the Future of First Nations* (Toronto: Penguin Books, 1993).

39 Michael Murphy, "Culture and Courts; a New Direction in Canadian Jurisprudence on Aboriginal Rights," *Canadian Journal of Political Science* 34, no. 1 (2001): 109-29; Fleras & Elliot, *The Nations Within.*

40 Augie Fleras, "The Politics of Jurisdiction," in *Visions of the Heart,* eds. David Alan Long & Olive Patricia Dickenson (Toronto: Harcourt Brace, 2000).

41 Government of Canada, "Federal Government Begins Discussions on Aboriginal Self-Government" News Release 1-9354 (1995).

42 James Frideres, "Indigenous Peoples of Canada and the United States: Entering the 21st Century," *Images of Canadianness,* ed. L. d'Haenens (Ottawa, University of Ottawa Press, 1998).

43 Tom Flanagan, *First Nations? Second Thoughts* (Montreal/Kingston: McGill-Queens University Press, 1999); Tanis Fiss, *Apartheid: Canada's Ugly Secret* (Canadian Taxpayer Federation: Calgary, 2004).

44 Claude Denis, *We are Not You: First Nations and Canadian Modernity* (Peterborough: Broadview Press, 1997).

45 Maaka & Fleras, *The Politics of Indigeneity.*

46 *Calder* v *A.G. (B.C.),* [1973] S.C.R. 313.

47 Joseph Gosnell, "Nisga'a Treaty Options Open Economic Doors For Everyone" (Speech to the Canadian Club, May 15, Reprinted in Canadian Speeches, 14, no. 4 (2000): 10-14.

48 Flanagan, *First Nations? Second Thoughts.*

49 Fiss, *Apartheid.*

50 Alfred, *Wasáse.*

51 Jim Silver, *In Their Own Voices* (Halifax: Fernwood Publishing, 2006).

52 Ken Coates & Greg Polzer, "Caledonia's ominous message," *Toronto Star* 19 August 2006.

53 Ken Coates, "Reaching the boiling point" *National Post* 17 October 2006.

54 Niezen, *The Origins of Indigenism.*

55 John Eckstedt, "International Perspectives in Aboriginal Self-Government," in *Aboriginal Self-Government in Canada* 2nd ed., ed. John H. Hylton (Saskatoon: Purich Publishing, 1999), 45-60; Humpage, "Liabilities and Assets."

56 Maaka & Fleras, *The Politics of Indigeneity.*

57 See Turner, *This is Not a Peace Pipe.*

58 Sir Geoffrey Palmer, "The Treaty of Waitangi-Where to Go from Here? Looking Back to Move Forward," presentation to the Te Papa Treaty of Waitangi Debate Series, 2 February 2006.

59 Part of the problem in advancing indigenous Maori rights is the structure of New Zealand's political system. Since Parliament maintains absolute sovereignty, legislation inconsistent with human rights cannot be overturned while a simple majority in Parliament can override both domestic and international protocols on human and Indigenous peoples rights. See Claire Charters, "An Imbalance of Powers: Maori Land Claims and an Unchecked Parliament," *Cultural Survival Quarterly* (Spring 2006). As well, New Zealand does not have a

written constitution but several constitutional sources such as the Treaty of Waitangi, resulting in a fluid and easily changed framework for sharing power.

60 The Treaty should also be situated within a broader historical context: The Declaration of Independence that was signed at Waitangi in 1835 by the United Tribes of New Zealand, a loose confederation of northern Maori tribes, signalled recognition of Maori political autonomy. See "Declaration of Independence," *Waitangi Associates* (2006), http://waitangi.co.nz (accessed 15 September 2007).

61 Pita Sharples, "Self-Determination: It Takes Two."

62 Waitangi Tribunal (Wai) 143, *Taranaki Report: Kaupapa Tuatahi* (1996).

63 Maaka & Fleras, *The Politics of Indigeneity.*

64 Humpage, "Liabilities and Assets."

65 Mason Durie, "Indigeneity and the Promotion of Positive Mental Health," paper presented to the 2004 Third World Conference for the Promotion of Mental Health and the Prevention of Mental and Behavioural Disorders, University of Auckland, NZ, 1998. Available at http://mindset.org.nz; Loomis (2000).

66 Roger Maaka, "Maori and the State: Diversity Models and Debates in New Zealand," in *The Art of the State* III *Belonging? Diversity, Recognition, and Shared Citizenship in Canada,* eds. Keith Banting, Thomas J. Courchene, & F. Leslie Seidle (Montreal: Institute for Public Policy, 2006).

67 T. Loomis, S. Morrison & T. Nicholas, "Capacity-Building for Self-Determined Maori Economic Development" (Working Paper No 2, Department of Developmental Studies, Hamilton NZ, University of Waikato, 1998).

68 Humpage, "Liabilities and Assets."

69 Evan Poata-Smith, "Ka Tika a Mua: Maori Protest Activities and the Treaty of Waitangi Settlement Process," in *Tangata Tangata: The Changing Ethnic Contours of New Zealand* eds. Paul Spoonley & David George Pearson (Southbank Victoria: Thomson Dunmore, 2004), 59-88.

70 Louise Humpage & Augie Fleras, "Intersecting Discourses: Closing the Gaps, Social Justice, and the Treaty of Waitangi," *Social Policy* 14 (2002): 37-53.

71 Sharples, "Self-Determination."

72 Whatarangi Winiata, "The Reconciliation of Kawanatanga and Tino Rangatiratanga," The Rua Rautau Lecture, Rangiatea Church, Otaki New Zealand, January 30, 2005. Also Fleras & Spoonley, *Recalling Aotearoa.*

73 Eddie Durie, "Background Paper: The Tribunal and the Treaty," *Victoria University of Wellington Law Review* 25 (1995): 97-105.

74 Charters, *Report on the Working Group on the UN Draft Declaration on the Rights of Indigenous Peoples.*

75 Barry Rigby, "The Origins of the Modern Treaty Industry in New Zealand." Paper presented to the Waitangi Tribunal Members Conference, Wellington, 25 September 1998.

76 William Renwick, *Sovereignty and Indigenous Rights: The Treaty of Waitangi in International Contexts* (Wellington, Victoria University Press, 1991); Richard Boast, "The Waitangi Tribunal: Conscience of the Nation or Just Another Court," *University of New South Wales Law Journal* 16, no. 1 (1993): 223-44.

77 Waitangi Tribunal (2006) "Treaty Settlements. What Does the Waitangi Tribunal Do?" http://www.treaty-ofwaitangi.govt.nz (accessed 15 September 2007).

78 Waitangi Tribunal (2006) "Treaty Settlements. What is a Settlement?" http://www.treatyofwaitangi.govt.nz.

79 Rawiri Taonui, "Deadline spells the end of justice for Maori," *NZ Herald* (15 December 2006); and "A year of contrasts," *Sunday Star Times* 28 December 2006.

80 Charters, *Report on the Working Group.*

81 Te Runanga o Ngai Tahu, http://www.ngaitahu.iwi.nz (accessed 15 September 2007).

82 Mark Solomon, "Collaboration for Economic Growth Speech notes to the Regional Conference," Sept 24-26, 2003, http://www.regdev.govt.nz (accessed 15 September 2007).

83 Wai 6, *Motonui-Waitara Report* 6 (1983),47; Wai 27, *Ngai Tahu Report* (1991), 222.

84 Charters, *Report on the Working Group.*

85 Wai 38, *Te Roroa Report* (1992), 27.

86 Wai 55, *Te Whanganui-o-Otoku Report* (1995), 201.

87 James Youngblood Henderson, "Aboriginal Jurisprudence and Rights," in *Advancing Aboriginal Claims,* ed. Kerry Wilkins (Saskatoon: Purich Publishing 2004), 67-90.

88 Wai 350 (1993), 31.

89 Wai 84, *Turangi Township Report* (1995).

90 Wai 32, *Ngati Rangiteaorere Report* (1990), 31.

91 Wai 304, *Ngawha Geothermal Resources Report* (1993), 100.

92 Wai 55, *Te Whanganui-o-Otoku Report.*

93 Wai 143, *Taranaki Report.*

94 *Ibid.*

95 Maaka & Fleras, *The Politics of Indigeneity.*

96 Augie Fleras, "Working Through Differences: The Politics of Ism and Posts in New Zealand," *New Zealand Sociology* 13 no. 1 (1998): 62-96.

97 Gordon Christie, ed. *Aboriginality and Governance: A Multidisciplinary Perspective from Quebec* (Penticton: Theytus Press, 2006), xiv.

98 Kerry Wilkins, *Advancing Aboriginal Claims* (Saskatoon: Purich Publishing, 2004).

99 Frances Widdowson & Albert Howard, "The Aboriginal Industry's New Clothes," *Policy Options* (March 2002): 30-5.

100 Leonard Rotman, "Creating a Still Life out of Dynamic Objects: Rights Reduction at the Supreme Court in Canada," *Alberta Law Review* 36 (1997): 1-8.

101 Fleras, "The Politics of Jurisdiction."

102 Evan Poata Smith, "Maori Protest Activities and the Treaty of Waitangi Settlement Process," in *Tangata Tangata,* eds. Spoonley et al. (Southbank Vic: Thomson Dunmore, 2004), 59-88.

103 Stephanie Milroy, "Maori Issues," *New Zealand Law Review* Pt. 2 (1997): 247-73; Paul McHugh, "Aboriginal Identity and Relations—Models of State Practice and Law in North American and Australasia." Paper Presented to the Ministry of Justice, Wellington, 1998.

104 Maaka & Fleras, *The Politics of Indigeneity.*

105 *Ibid.*

106 Craig Scott, "Indigenous Self-Determination and Decolonization of the International Imagination," *Human Rights Quarterly* 18 (1996): 815-28; Iris Young, *Justice and the Politics of Difference* (Princeton University Press, 1990).

107 Michael Asch, *Aboriginal and Treaty Rights in Canada: Essays on Law, Equity, and Respect for Difference* (Vancouver: UBC Press, 1997)

108 W. Linden, *Swiss Democracy* (New York: St. Martins Press, 1994)

109 Anthony Oberschall, "Social Movements and the Transition to Democracy," *Democratization* 7, no. 3 (2000): 25-45.

110 McNeish & Eversole, "Overview."

111 Patrick Macklem, *Indigenous Difference and the Constitution in Canada* (Toronto: University of Toronto Press, 2002).

112 Maaka & Fleras, *The Politics of Indigeneity.*

113 Fleras & Spoonley, *Recalling Aotearoa.*

114 Richard Mulgan, *Maori, Pakeha, and Democracy* (Auckland: University of Auckland Press, 1989).

115 Frank Cassidy, "British Columbia and Aboriginal Peoples: The Prospects for the Treaty Process," *Policy Options* (March 1994): 10-13.

116 Haider Rizvi, "UN faces test on Native rights," *IPS News Service* (2006).

117 Peter H Russell, "Consensus or More Colonialism?" *Literary Review of Canada* (October 2006): 5-8; "So that's how it's going to be," *Windspeaker* (2007): 5.

118 Claire Charters, "An Imbalance of Powers": 32-35; also K. Horn, "UN Rip-off: Declaration of Indigenous Rights," http:www.mohawknationnews.com, 2006.

119 R. Brain Howe, "What's Behind Stephen Harper's Anti Aboriginal Agenda?" *Canadian Dimension,* Sept/Oct., 2006.

120 Mark Cherrington, "Declaration on the Verge of Independence," *Cultural Survival Quarterly* (Spring 2006): 5-6.

121 *Ibid.*

122 Theodore MacDonald, "New U.N. Human Rights Council Approves Declaration of the Rights of Indigenous Peoples," *Cultural Survival Quarterly* (Fall 2006): 5-8.

123 Cited by Hone Harawira, *NZ Parliamentary Debates* (12 October 2006); also James S. Anaya, "International Human Rights and Indigenous Peoples: the Move toward the Multicultural State," in *Indigenous Peoples in International Law,* ed., James S. Anaya (Oxford: Oxford University Press, 2004).

124 Olivia Ward, "UN Action on Native Rights Deferred," *Toronto Star* 29 November 2006.

125 Kenneth McRoberts, "Managing Cultural Differences in Multinational Democracies" in *The Conditions of Diversity in Multinational Democracies,* eds. A.G. Gagnon, et al. (Montreal: IRRP, 2003); S, Harty and M. Murphy, *In Defence of Multinational Citizenship* (Vancouver, UBC Press, 2005); Turner, *This is Not a Peace Pipe.*

126 Denis, *We are Not You.*

127 J. Rick Ponting, ed., *Arduous Journey: Canadian Indians and Decolonization* (Toronto: McClelland and Stewart, 1986).

128 Alfred, *Wasáse.*

129 Russell, "Consensus or More Colonialism?"

130 Borrows & Rotman, "The *Sui Generis* Nature of Aboriginal Rights," 31.

Part II:

Understanding Aboriginal Self-Government

FROM PANACEA TO REALITY:

The Practicalities of Canadian Aboriginal Self-Government Agreements

Ken S. Coates, University of Waterloo
& W.R. Morrison, University of Northern British Columbia

Almost since the beginning of contact, and increasingly since they realized that the First Peoples were not going to simply die off, governments have imposed on Aboriginal people in Canada a variety of mostly well-meant solutions to what were perceived as their social, cultural, economic, and political problems. From segregated reserves, the encouragement of assimilation, legal enfranchisement to residential schools, Aboriginal peoples and communities have been promised that some government program or other would end their isolation from the Canadian mainstream and provide them with the ability to prosper within Canada. As is well known, none of these initiatives worked as they were supposed to. Instead, they left bitter and negative legacies in Aboriginal communities across the country. Aboriginal leaders complained that the colonial mentality inherent in government-directed initiatives, and the Christian and capitalist assumptions that underlay the various programs, ignored Aboriginal needs, culture, and input. They warned that without paying proper attention to Aboriginal society, and without ensuring that Aboriginal people played a critical role in shaping and implementing any new initiatives, government attempts to address Aboriginal needs were sure to fail.

The idea of Aboriginal self-government that emerged in the 1970s and 1980s as a solution to the Aboriginal dilemma was, however, markedly different. In this instance, the concept had widespread support among the Aboriginal political leadership, as well as strong encouragement from some non-Aboriginal quarters. While the negotiations over the specifics of the self-government agreements took many years, a significant number of self-government arrangements were eventually signed and implemented.[1] Although it is far too early to provide a definitive assessment of either individual accords or the broader self-government movement, the experience with Aboriginal self-government provides important insights into the process, structures, and optimism surrounding the latest Aboriginal panacea in Canada.[2]

The self-government movement emerged out of the deep flaws in the *Indian Act* and Canadian government policy for Aboriginal peoples. By the early 1970s, Aboriginal leaders had mounted a vigorous protest against planned federal changes to the *Indian Act* and voiced their displeasure with the political and administrative status quo. The isolation of Indian reserves and the social and economic crises that dogged Aboriginal people created a strong consensus around the need to reform the governance system in Canada. There was little initial consensus, however, as how to best accomplish this. The federal government favoured a new mix of federal policies, most of them targeted at improving education and health conditions, with a strong emphasis on local economic development. Provincial governments rejected the idea of the political empowerment of Aboriginal communities and organizations, and argued that provincial programs could be modified to meet Aboriginal needs, provided the federal government put up more money. In the north, the Government of the Yukon resisted early steps toward land claims settlements, while the rapidly evolving government of the Northwest Territories took more positive steps toward incorporating Aboriginal concerns into the territorial system of governance. Municipal and other local governments in the provinces—often facing the most intense interactions with Aboriginal peoples—offered few concessions, and often found the task of dealing with assertive First Nations communities to be difficult. The provincial governments were disturbed by the concept of a third level of government and the seemingly inevitable erosion of provincial authority that would follow the establishment of Aboriginal governments. In the 1970s, such aspirations on behalf of Aboriginal people were dismissed as fanciful by critics who knew little of the potential for Aboriginal innovation and empowerment. By 1980, Aboriginal self-government seemed dead in the water, if only because of the opposition of provincial governments.[3]

Within a surprisingly short period of time, however, the idea of Aboriginal self-government gained political, legal, and constitutional strength. For Aboriginal organizations, self-government emerged as a minimum requirement in their discussions with the Government of Canada. Many Aboriginal politicians, supported by their communities, saw this as the only means of wresting control from the Department of Indian Affairs. For the federal and provincial governments, self-government provided the only widely-supported alternative to an admittedly flawed and unsuccessful system of Aboriginal administration. Even most of those who questioned the utility of empowering small and unprepared Aboriginal governments could not come up with another viable and saleable model for changing the way Canada manages Aboriginal affairs. In the Charlottetown Accord, designed primarily to bring Quebec into the constitution, Aboriginal leaders negotiated the inclusion of self-government for duly constituted Aboriginal governments. In British Columbia, in particular, but also in other parts of rural Canada, this element became a rallying point for opposition to the Accord. Opposition to the entrenchment of Aboriginal self-government in the constitution, ironically, coincided with Aboriginal criticism that the proposed constitutional amendment did not go far enough in entrenching power of Aboriginal governments. The failure of the referendum, therefore, was applauded by many on both sides of the debate, though for contradictory reasons.

From the ashes of Charlottetown came a revised and powerful approach to the assertion of Aboriginal governance. Section 35 of the Constitution guaranteed the protection of "existing aboriginal and treaty rights." Aboriginal and government officials reasoned that a self-government agreement between the Government of Canada (and potentially the provinces and territories) and an Aboriginal group could legitimately be described as a treaty. Thus, self-government agreements imbedded in land claims settlements, of which there were a significant number after the mid-1980s, or separate self-government agreements could be considered to have the same authority as a treaty. As governments increasingly recognized and accepted the idea of self-government and as deals were struck, self-government moved from being the focus of political debate to an administrative and legal reality within the Canadian federal system. Even British Columbia, for many years the leading opponent of Aboriginal treaty and self-government rights, came around under the Premiership of Gordon Campbell, moving quickly to support land claims settlements with substantial self-government elements.

The Nature of Aboriginal Self-Government

Canada now has an extensive set of Aboriginal self-government models in operation.[4] They are imbedded in land claims agreements, self-government accords, and agreements-in-principle. In each case, the agreements set out a framework for governance, outlining powers and responsibilities that a specific Aboriginal government may "take down," as the process is typically described. The agreements are wide-ranging and outline a long list of powers available to the Aboriginal group. There is no requirement, however, that the Aboriginal authority assumes any or all of the government powers, and no timetables are imposed on the transfer of federal and/or provincial responsibilities to the Aboriginal government.[5]

In typical Canadian fashion, and unlike American models, these self-government agreements suffer from a complete absence of poetry. Like our Constitution, they are highly legalistic and formal documents, with no ringing phrases for schoolchildren to memorize, and few beyond the narrow circle of negotiators understand the complex legal and administrative concepts imbedded in the various sections and clauses. The Aboriginal groups, for their part, generally prepare more accessible summaries of the self-government agreements, often in their own languages, for distribution within their communities. The agreements themselves are best understood as providing a framework within which future discussions with federal, provincial, and municipal/local authorities might take place and an aspirational guideline for evolving Aboriginal governments. The agreements follow a fairly standard approach—as with all Government of Canada-

Aboriginal negotiations, there is an understanding that only minimal variation can be tolerated between the different accords.

The Government of Canada has, however, recognized that a single model will not suit the very different Aboriginal groups across the country.[6] Within a general framework of acknowledging the "inherent right" of Aboriginal people to be self-governing, the federal government identified in the mid-1990s a series of basic models for self-government agreements:[7]

First Nations: The standard First Nations self-government model seeks to replace the *Indian Act*, protect federal government-Aboriginal relationships, and provide for culture-specific government structures and processes. The agreements typically focus on a specific First Nation and settlement area. For those with treaties, the self-government system must be consistent with the treaty rights and privileges and should not limit or undermine treaty powers. These agreements are also intended to incorporate the rights and needs of First Nations living off the reserve, although this is a contentious requirement in many parts of the country. Many of the First Nations agreements are community-specific, and do not attempt to draw together a number of Aboriginal communities into a single governance system.

Inuit Communities: Where the First Nations generally prefer a more focused approach to self-government, the Inuit sought broader public government approaches, of which Nunavut is the most obvious model.[8] Rather than being community or region-specific, the Inuit self-government approach sought economies of scale, by including many different settlements across very large areas, and by being inclusive of all Inuit people in a region. The evolution of self-government in the Western Arctic, through the Inuvialuit Regional Corporation, similarly demonstrated the Inuit commitment to the incorporation of multiple communities into a single governance structure.

Métis and First Nations Groups without a Land Base: With a growing number of Aboriginal people living off-reserve or operating without an official land base, it is not surprising that different approaches to self-government have been developed. For groups without a land base, greater flexibility is required. The Government of Canada has declared themselves open to working with various forms of public governments. This has required the development of new administrative structures and the transfer of government powers where Aboriginal governance systems have been put into place.

Métis with a Land Base: Governments in Canada have undertaken negotiations with Métis communities. In Alberta Métis communities reached agreements with provincial authorities and secured land bases much like

First Nations with treaty-based reserves. This provides a measure of local Aboriginal self-government. Provisions have been and will be made to extend voting rights and government privileges to Métis living off the land base.[9] The federal government's interest in this area has been shown by the creation of the office of the Federal Interlocutor for Métis and Non-Status Indians, established under the Liberal government.

Northwest Territories and Yukon: The negotiation of comprehensive land claims agreements in the Northwest Territories and Yukon created an unparalleled opportunity for the federal and territorial governments to incorporate self-government agreements in broader accords. The empowerment of Aboriginal groups through these settlements combined land, resource, and administrative power, and provided a foundation and road map for a revolutionary transformation of the governance of Aboriginal affairs in the North. The Government of Canada was initially skeptical about establishing separate self-governing Aboriginal communities, in large part because of the mixed population in most northern settlements. The successful negotiation of regional accords, covering several culturally-related communities, provided the basis for self-government in the North.

Generic descriptions of the models of self-government that have been established in Canada do not provide deep insights into the nature and extent of Aboriginal control envisaged under self-governing systems. It is important to note that the establishment of self-government is a process, not a single event. Even the highly technical self-government agreements that accompany northern land claims settlements only describe the powers and responsibilities that First Nations or other Aboriginal communities may assume, not a list of governmental duties that an Aboriginal community must provide. Communities, therefore, accept those powers that they are ready to manage, at the time when they choose, and only once agreements are in place to provide the required training for staff and financial resources. They can, as has happened with several northern communities in the area of child welfare, accept responsibilities and then turn them back to the territorial or federal government. The processes of Aboriginal self-government are more fluid, flexible, and multi-directional than public understanding would suggest. So, too, is the range of powers available to Aboriginal governments and communities.[10] A brief overview of several representative self-governing arrangements illustrates the variety of structures and models already being implemented in Canada.

Nisga'a Government: The Nisga'a treaty, implemented in 2000, was perhaps the most widely discussed modern agreement between the Government of Canada and a First Nation.[11] Under the terms of the Nisga'a land claim settlement, the Nisga'a received recognition of traditional forms of governance and the right to assume a variety of administrative responsibilities. The establishment of the Nisga'a Lisims government, which includes four village authorities and urban locals to represent the interests of Nisga'a living outside the Nass River valley, created an administrative and political framework for the First Nation. As with other self-government agreements, the Nisga'a arrangements are expected to function under the authority of the Canadian Constitution and *Charter of Rights and Freedoms*, although some First Nations leaders challenge the over-riding authority of these national acts. Any powers granted to and exercised by the Nisga'a authorities had to operate within the appropriate federal and provincial laws as well and had to provide comparable or better levels of service in areas assumed from other levels of government.[12]

With these caveats, the range of authority granted to the Nisga'a was quite sweeping. They could establish their own government, adopting Nisga'a traditional authority, provided that the basic tenants of Canadian law were recognized. The Nisga'a managed their own membership lists and established principles of membership in the First Nation. The Nisga'a Lisims had the right to manage its resources, lands, and other assets, a marked departure from the original *Indian Act* systems which placed all such valuable items under federal control. The Nisga'a could pass laws and regulations governing language and culture and other matters relating to the oversight of their communities. In addition, and very importantly, the Nisga'a were authorized to assume responsibilities in such diverse areas as resource management, marriage, emergency protection, health, transportation, child welfare, and education.[13]

The first Aboriginal self-government agreements, like those governing the Sechelt on British Columbia's southern coast, were typically described as representing municipal-type authorities.[14] The Nisga'a arrangements include a wide range of municipal, regional, provincial, and federal responsibilities, while stopping short of any power to engage in international affairs. The Nisga'a have the authority to operate Nisga'a courts and a Nisga'a policing system, and are required to raise the funds to cover significant portions of the costs of governance. The Nisga'a are not, within the confines of the agreements, permitted to operate without reference to provincial and federal governments; in fact, there are clear requirements to align Nisga'a laws with other laws and regulations and strong accountability provisions. For many years, advocates and critics of Aboriginal self-government described the process as involving the creation of a third order of government. While that description applies in a symbolic sense, Nisga'a self-government means, in the main, that responsibilities typically handled by one of the three standard levels of government in Canada are managed in a delegated and coordinated manner by the First Nation authority.[15]

Champagne-Aishihik First Nation: While the Nisga'a agreement is one of the best-known self-government arrangements, the provisions in the Council for Yukon First Nations umbrella agreement and subsequent individual First Nations accords is equally comprehensive, and a useful illustration of the evolutionary nature of Aboriginal self-government in Canada. The CYFN agreement was signed in 1973; the Champagne-Aishihik First Nation reached a final agreement with the Government of Canada in 1995. Under these accords, self-governing powers are available to the First Nation; once these powers are implemented, the long-standing controls of the *Indian Act* disappear and are replaced by local First Nation governments. Each of the First Nations, including the Champagne-Aishihik and much like the Nisga'a, has the right to make laws to regulate community affairs and to provide services for their members. They also have the right to manage settlement lands, resources, and local commercial and related operations.[16]

The list of administrative responsibilities available for assumption by Champagne-Aishihik First Nation includes the following:

- Management of the affairs of the First Nations;
- Management of the final land claims agreement;
- Provision of education, training, and health care services to citizens;
- Protection and enhancement of Aboriginal languages, cultures, and spiritual beliefs;
- Provision of social services, including welfare, child protection, and adoption;
- Management of personal affairs, such a wills and estates, marriages, and dispute resolution;
- Control and management of land, livestock, resources, harvesting rights, and other uses of settlement lands;
- Regulation of businesses, building permits, transportation, automobile use, zoning, and development processes;
- Sale and use of alcohol and firearms;
- Regulation of public behaviour, including curfews, policing, administration of justice, public health matters, and any threat to public safety and health; and
- Any "matters coming within the good government of Citizens on Settlement Land."

The authority available to the Champagne-Aishihik First Nation is considerable, should the First Nation ever assume all of the powers and responsibilities available to it. What is not clear in the complex language of land claims settlements is perhaps the most important element: the First Nation has a population of less than 1,200 people, in an area covering 41,000 square kilometers. (Prince Edward Island, in contrast, is less than 5,700 square kilometers.) In political terms, however, the Champagne-Aishihik First Nation is a very small political jurisdiction, and the list of potential powers available to the group is, in this context, daunting.

This First Nation has been well-led over the years and has shied away from grandiose or overly fast implementations of self-government. The First Nations 2007 Program and Service Manual outlines a more limited self-governing community than the above list would suggest, and reflects the caution and sense of responsibility in the First Nation.[17] Actual program delivery focuses on social and community services, with a strong emphasis on health, culture, training, and economic development. In the case of Champagne-Aishihik, and indeed many First Nations operating under modern land claims agreements, the accords are a list of what they may do, not what they must do. The First Nation has the authority to pass laws governing its people and lands; the first such laws included the *Income Tax Act*, *Fish and Wildlife Act*, and the *Traditional Pursuits Act*, all passed in 1998 and effective as of the start of the following year.

If the Nisga'a First Nation demonstrates the legal capacity and political ability of a First Nation to assume effective control of wide-ranging administrative powers, the Champagne-Aishihik arrangements illustrate a more normative Canadian approach: a fairly open-ended aspirational agreement, followed by careful and step-wise implementation of actual self-government, focusing on cultural, economic, ecological, and business-related matters. Under this arrangement, self-government is a long-term work in progress, adjusting to the needs and capacities of the First Nation and the unique political circumstances of the province or territory.

Gwich'in and Inuvialuit Self-Government Arrangements: In 2003, the Gwich'in and Inuvialuit of the Northwest Territories reached an historical Agreement-in-Principle (AIP) to work collaboratively on the regional government model for the Beaufort Sea-Mackenzie Delta region. Both groups had been negotiating separate self-government agreements with the federal government and territorial representatives, but decided that the convergence of interests indicated a different approach was required. The agreement represented a significant departure from the standard, single-culture approach to self-government arrangements, in that it drew the Gwich'in and the Inuvialuit into a single governance process. The AIP called for the two cultural groups—whose traditional and contemporary territories overlapped and who had clear needs for collaboration—to negotiate a common agreement with the Government of Canada. Plans called for the creation of new public governments to take over the role of municipal councils and allowed the Gwich'in and Inuvialuit the opportunity to negotiate control and management of the same list of government powers outlined for the Champagne-Aishihik and Nisga'a. The planned Beaufort-

Delta Regional Government would incorporate Gwich'in, Inuvialuit (providing both with assured representation), and non-Aboriginal people, with Aboriginal residents making up three-quarters of the population and thus able to strongly influence, if not dominate, the regional authority. In addition, Gwich'in and Inuvialuit governments would look after group-specific issues and responsibilities.[18]

Negotiations on this promising approach to regional self-government collapsed in 2006, ending the strategy of having a single governance regime manage the broad Beaufort-Delta region.[19] The Gwich'in and Inuvialuit opted for separate negotiations and, eventually, separate agreements, ones sure to be bedeviled by the complex jurisdictional overlaps in the area. While the result was a disappointment, having absorbed a great deal of political energy, time, and resources, both sides agreed that the different priorities and needs of the two groups made a regional government approach unworkable. The Gwich'in-Inuvialuit circumstances illustrate two critical themes in the development of Aboriginal self-government in Canada. First, that experimentation and flexibility remain highly prized and all parties, including federal, provincial/territorial, and Aboriginal governments, are willing to consider a wide variety of models and processes. Second, Aboriginal self-government can be extremely complicated and time-consuming, particularly in areas with overlapping claims and intertwined populations.

Westbank Self-Government: The Westbank First Nation, a financially secure community of slightly more than 600 people in the Okanagan valley of British Columbia, opted for a very different approach to Aboriginal self-government in an agreement they signed in October 2003. The Westbank First Nation had not yet concluded a land claims agreement, meaning that this arrangement was not integrated into a final claims settlement. This meant, in turn, that the self-government accord would not have protection under the *Canadian Charter of Rights and Freedoms*, as did those agreements incorporated within modern treaties. Furthermore, the Westbank community includes a significant number of non-Aboriginal peoples, so the self-government arrangements had to specifically account for their needs and interests.

Under the agreement, the Westbank First Nation would come out from under the *Indian Act* and would take over managerial responsibility for many Indian Affairs and federal government powers and duties. As with the other First Nation agreements, Westbank would have the authority to pass laws in a wide variety of areas relating to land, resources, culture, and community services. Although the self-government agreement focused on the structure and nature of First Nations government, it also included arrangements that allowed non-Westbank member engagement in law-making, albeit only in those areas directly affecting non-members. Because the agreement did not represent a final settlement of land claims, the other characteristics of modern agreements—the end of tax exempt status and the replacement of reserves with settlement lands—did not hold. The agreement was ratified by Westbank members in May 2003, by a vote of 195 to 149. The self-government arrangements came into effect in 2005.[20]

The Westbank agreement continued to broaden the definition of Aboriginal self-government in Canada, for it proceeded in advance of a final agreement and provided for the inclusion of non-member input on selected governance matters. The arrangement attracted considerable opposition from members, other First Nations groups, and the Canadian Taxpayers Federation, with the latter arguing that the arrangements removed the protections of the *Charter of Rights and Freedoms*, continued the process of establishing "third order" governments in Canada and allowed for taxation without representation, specifically relating to non-members living of Westbank land.[21] Westbank, located close to Kelowna and with highly desirable and expensive residential properties, bears little resemblance to the isolated reserve communities that hold much of the country's Aboriginal population. The self-government arrangements, however, demonstrated that accords are possible with First Nations living in close proximity to non-Aboriginal, non-member majorities.[22]

Nunavik Regional Self-Government: The range of options available for Aboriginal communities expanded in the summer of 2007.[23] One of the long-standing criticisms of Aboriginal self-government is that the populations involved would be too small to provide administrative economies of scale. The new government body, membership in which would not be restricted to Aboriginal people, will cover 14 communities in northern Quebec and will, if and when ratified, consist of an elected representative council. The planned regional authority—less than a territory but more than a self-governing community—would not control mineral rights but would stand to benefit economically from resource development in the region. The Regional Government of Nunavik would have key responsibilities for education and health care, two areas of particular concern for the largely Inuit population in the region.[24]

Existing self-government arrangements illustrate the essential characteristics of Aboriginal self-government in Canada:

- Self-government is a process, not a single act;

- Most agreements are aspirational, rather than definitive and mandatory;

- Each region, community, and cultural group has different needs, opportunities, and capacities to address through reforms of governance systems;

- There is a shared and often urgent desire among Aboriginal communities to be free of the control of the Department of Indian Affairs and the *Indian Act*;
- The shape and nature of Aboriginal self-government reflects local circumstances, pressures from non-members, and the imperatives of senior governments;
- Finalizing agreements can be difficult, and controversial and promising developments at the local and regional level have often been reversed when final negotiations or implementation was attempted;
- Governments in Canada have been flexible in drafting and implementing self-government agreements.

Finally, and perhaps most importantly, the standard "third order of government" characterization of Aboriginal self-governing bodies misrepresents the nature of the governance reform established through this process. Self-government agreements take away or delegate the powers of federal, territorial, regional, and municipal authorities in ways that are not properly captured by the concept of a third order of government. Ironically, by assuming responsibilities typically handled by other governments in Canada, self-governing Aboriginal communities inject themselves directly into the governance structures, mandates and ideologies of the Canadian federal system. Rather than representing a stepping away from Canadian political structures, self-government incorporates Aboriginal peoples more fully into the Canadian polity than did the separatist processes of the *Indian Act* and the Department of Indian Affairs. By engaging directly in the standard practices of Canadian governance, self-governing Canadian communities become Canadians with a cultural twist, adapting national, provincial, and regional institutions to the nuances of Aboriginal traditions and values.

Assessing Self-Government

While it is far too early to provide a definitive assessment on the progress of Aboriginal self-government, several important considerations stand out.[24] For one thing, self-government developments have so far attracted little attention from the press and public in Canada. The success of the Eel Ground school system in New Brunswick or the economic development arrangements at Lennox Island, PEI, have created much less of a stir than the water crisis at Kashechewan or the perpetual problems at Davis Inlet. Stories of band governance corruption and mismanagement get many more headlines than major improvements in high school graduation rates, successful local health promotions, or the negotiation of a joint venture agreement with a mining company. Simply, bad news sells better than good, regardless of race. While the progress of self-government has been uneven, it is crucial to remember that this was expected from the outset. It is why self-government was not undertaken as a one-time process, with a single and definitive transfer of responsibilities from the federal and provincial governments to Aboriginal authorities. The re-establishment of Aboriginal self-government is at its very early stages in Canada, with little more than two decades of substantial experience following more than a century and a half of disempowerment and colonial and paternal control.[25] With these understandings and caveats in place, it is nonetheless possible to offer some preliminary assessments of aspects of the Aboriginal self-government enterprise in Canada.[26]

Self-Government as Self-Administration

Critics of Aboriginal self-government, particularly those advocating Aboriginal sovereignty, argue that these arrangements provide for self-administration, not true autonomy. According to this line of argument, the colonial structures remain in place and the policy frameworks do not shift. Instead of having federal civil servants manage local affairs, power shifts to a small group of Aboriginal leaders. They are not given the resources, power and freedom, however, to make real and substantial changes in the management and direction of local government. Put more harshly, self-government in this construction amounts to little more than the downloading of poverty and marginalization to local administrations. This downloading of decisions, furthermore, means that extremely difficult judgments—determining who gets a new home or a post-secondary grant—are placed in the hands of local authorities who find themselves trapped in a complex web of family and community relationships, limited resources, and intense local political pressures.

Self-Government as Community Control

In the early years of Aboriginal self-government, particularly following the signing of the Sechelt Agreement in 1986, commentators claimed that these agreements did not liberate Aboriginal peoples and communities from government intervention. Instead, the complex agreements bound Aboriginal communities financially, constitutionally, and administratively to the Government of Canada, provided only limited, municipal-like powers, and did not recognize Aboriginal cultures. While the First Nations involved rejected the notion that they remained under the influence of Ottawa, the narrow range of powers did not give the local governments much scope for action. Newer accords, which include recognition of culturally based governance structures and provide for a much broader variety of responsibilities, are rarely seen in this light.

Capacity Questions

In the early days of self-government, critics claimed that communities lacked the personnel and local resources necessary to administer their affairs in a competent and systematic fashion. There seemed to be some truth to this claim, particularly when Aboriginal leaders spoke of their intent to secure province-like powers.

Communities and governments recognized that many Aboriginal groups did not have the trained personnel in place ready to assume a full measure of administrative duties. The agreements have all recognized that self-government is a process, not a single event, and that communities need the option of assuming powers only when they deem themselves to be ready. And there are provisions that allow the powers to be shifted back to the federal or territorial governments if circumstances so require. Building capacity for self-government remains a critical element in the development of Aboriginal civic society. The fact that there are some 30,000 Aboriginal people currently in Canadian colleges and universities suggests that capacity-building is proceeding in earnest. Many of these students will, upon graduation, return to their communities or will find work with Aboriginal organizations, providing the trained cadre of managers and professionals that is required for successful administration.

Politics of Smallness

Size matters in political life, and smallness can be a major impediment to successful administration in any culture or political setting. Most Aboriginal communities are small, and most self-governing jurisdictions have relatively few people. In these environments, the politics of smallness can easily take hold—as readily in a Nova Scotian fishing village or Saskatchewan farm town as an Aboriginal settlement. With few members, small political communities suffer from intense attention to political decisions. Avoiding accusations of nepotism and favouritism is virtually impossible. Leaders operate under the glare of community oversight and have great difficulty separating their decisions from personal relationships. Smallness can interfere with effective governance, particularly in democratic settings, and sets conditions that make transparency both essential and a cause for community unrest. Building economies and administrative scale and political distance into self-governing arrangements, as the Nisga'a and Inuit of Northern Quebec have done, will likely prove to be an essential element in long-term self-government structures.

Cultural Elements and Community Engagement

Self-government was intended to reinvigorate the cultural foundations of Aboriginal community life, to reintroduce elders into the decision-making processes and to separate the local governance arrangements from the old colonial, Ottawa-centred systems. Not all communities have opted for such arrangements. Some have adopted elected systems and more standard Canadian democratic arrangements. Many others, however, have opted to reintroduce elements of traditional clan and culturally-centred administrative structures. The use of culturally-based political and decision-making structures has given traditional values and approaches new currency, has helped educate young people in the old ways, and has brought community-based governance back into reality.[27] Not everyone will be pleased with the results—the reliance on clan systems in some self-governing arrangements is not democratic in the usual sense, for example—but the consensus-building approaches that are implicit in Aboriginal decision-making arrangements appear to be serving communities well. If nothing else, these systems broaden local debate and provide for the inclusion of all members in government. In some communities, most notably Six Nations in Ontario, traditional governance and *Indian Act*-type structures (elected chief and councilors) coexist, though not always comfortably.

Relations with Other Levels of Government

While the language of autonomy and separation dominates discussions of Aboriginal self-government, the reality is that collaboration and co-operation with other levels of government is essential to the success of the enterprise. Save for Nunavut, with its entirely Inuit-controlled legislature, and some of the more isolated First Nations communities (like Behchoko in the Northwest Territories), effective and harmonious relations with local, regional, provincial/territorial, and national governments are crucial if self-government is to succeed. Where there have been tensions, for example between the Kamloops First Nation and the city government in the 1980s, progress on economic and community development came to a halt. Where levels of co-operation are high, Kamloops again providing a good example, as do Westbank, the Squamish Nation, Saskatoon, and many northern communities, major changes and advances have been possible. The new Regional Government of Nunavik will have to maintain strong ties with Quebec and Ottawa, and Nunavut's success rests largely on positive relations with the federal government. Self-government is not, therefore, about isolation and separation from the Canadian political system. Instead, the establishment of self-governing Aboriginal communities provides a more equitable distribution of power and allows for Aboriginal collaboration and co-operation with other levels of government. It is important to note that, over time, relations with local and regional governments will ultimately become more crucial to self-governing communities than relations with provincial/territorial and federal governments, as most of the issues of greatest importance to Aboriginal communities are at the local level.

Avoiding Conflict and Scandal

Revelations about political scandals, the mismanagement of funds, or the administrative incompetence of Aboriginal governments are often used as a justification for opposing Aboriginal self-government. Indeed, the presence of systematic scandals and conflict is often used as a rationale for delaying negotiations, with federal and local politicians agreeing that the time is not right to establish self-governing arrangements. If, as critics charge, Aboriginal political organizations are plagued by scandal and corruption, empowering these governments will simply entrench bad governance and political practices. Supporters of self-government will reply that, in the shadow of the Gomery inquiry into political corruption, national and provincial political systems are not without their own significant flaws.[28] They will also point out that most of the revelations about infighting, corruption, and administrative scandal relate to communities that do not yet have self-governing agreements. If there is a pattern worthy of note, it is that there have not been major public scandals relating to the newly empowered self-governing communities. There have been challenges, to be sure, with Nunavut providing the best example of the difficulties inherent in the transition from government control to Aboriginal self-rule. More generally, however, self-governing Aboriginal communities have done a very good job of establishing responsive, accountable, and effective administrations, albeit ones charged with addressing some of the most formidable public government issues in modern Canada.

The Time-Line for Assessing the Impact of Self-Government

The greatest problem with Aboriginal panaceas—the once-and-for-all solutions to the Aboriginal challenges and needs in Canada—is that few people realize how long it takes to set things right. Each of the approaches taken over the past century and a half produced some useful results, along with some problems. For example, the renewed emphasis on community-based education in the 1970s did not bear fruit immediately. But thirty years on, there is abundant evidence that investment in teachers, schools, and locally relevant curricula have produced strongly positive returns. The rapid improvement of high school graduation and post-secondary participation rates in the Canadian North is perhaps the best example of this. Self-government will not solve the problems facing Aboriginal Canadians in five years, ten years, or even two decades. A study on the challenges of Aboriginal self-government completed in 2004 concluded that the system had many problems to overcome, ranging from legitimacy and voices and fairness to the absence of culturally specific governance tools, a limited role for women, the small size of communities, poor accountability systems, and an over-reliance on external funding.[29]

Self-government is not the solution, but it is a major tool that can be used to achieve the ultimate goal of healthy, self-sustaining, and viable Aboriginal communities. There will be bumps along the road and there will be communities that abandon some of their structures and experiments, and some agreements will have to be redefined and renegotiated. But, over time, the authority assigned to Aboriginal communities will build capacity, expertise, and confidence. More importantly, as is already evident in many self-governing communities across the country, the arrangements will build a stronger sense of accountability (for many of the communities are among the most transparent political jurisdictions in Canada), and provide for culturally-appropriate policies and procedures. Self-government has worked to date and it will work even more effectively over time. What the system requires is time to take root, to adapt, and to learn from local successes and challenges.

Conclusion

If any lesson has been learned from the Indian policies of the past century, it is that there are no panaceas or perfect solutions to complex social and cultural problems. Aboriginal Canadians face a vast array of challenges, from language and culture preservation to economic engagement to conquering the social pathology left over from decades of paternal intervention. Deeply imbedded problems and crises will not be overturned in a year or even a decade. The real test of Aboriginal self-government lies in the ability of such initiatives to change the trajectory of Indigenous-newcomer relations. Aboriginal self-government exists. It is no longer an untried concept or a theoretical political option. There are excellent examples where Aboriginal self-government has made a significant and quick impact on communities and residents. There are instances where Aboriginal self-government has failed to flourish, producing dissatisfaction and turmoil in the process. There are First Nations ready to grab the reins of self-government and take wide-ranging control of their community. There are others—and self-awareness on this score is quite strong—that are years away from assuming responsibility for local administration.

Despite the claims of its most ardent supporters, self-government will not solve the many problems facing Aboriginal peoples and communities, either by itself or in short order. The challenges and opportunities are real, but self-government is no more of a panacea than the earlier efforts to address Aboriginal needs and concerns through sweeping federal government programs. It is important to recall, however, than only thirty years ago, provincial governments resisted the very concept of self-government; they are now active participants in shaping the future of Aboriginal administration across Canada. Aboriginal capacity expands yearly. With thousands of Aboriginal students currently in college and university, the ability to attract and retain qualified managers and stewards of Aboriginal governments will continue to improve.

What stands out in the process, moreover, is the realization that Aboriginal self-government is a direction rather than a policy, a goal rather than a specific model or structure. To be successful, self-government arrangements have to reflect, in both timing and formal arrangements, the needs, aspirations, abilities, and cultural roots of specific First Nations. Most importantly, Aboriginal self-government will, in its successes and failures, reflect the actions, priorities, and activities of individual Aboriginal groups. In the final analysis, Aboriginal self-government represents a formidable nail in the coffin of Canadian paternalism and colonialism, transferring authority and resources from the Government of Canada, the provincial, territories, and local governments and thereby empowering Aboriginal peoples and communities across the country.

For the past forty years, Aboriginal activists have focused their energy and attention on convincing other governments to recognize the urgent need for Aboriginal autonomy. Self-government agreements do all of these things, and they turn the political spotlights around. In the coming years, Aboriginal politicians and administrators will turn from government-to-government negotiations and high level constitutional politics to the lower profile work of economic development, educational and health care management, and community-building. If the experience of the past two decades is any guide, the country at large will notice Aboriginal issues less and Aboriginal communities and people will be empowered to address local needs and concerns. While self-government is no panacea, it is a promising and important stage in the revitalization and cultural renaissance of Aboriginal peoples and communities in Canada.

NOTES

1   For a balanced review, see: BC Treaty Commission, *The Self Government Landscape* (Victoria: BC Treaty Commission, n.d.), http://www.bctreaty.net/files/pdf_documents/self_government_landscape.pdf (accessed 15 September 2007).

2   There is a rich and diverse literature on Aboriginal self-government in Canada, including a series of insightful collections produced by Purich Publishing. Many of these are cited by other authors in this book. The references in this essay are designed, in the main, to lead readers to the original documents and agreements behind contemporary self-government arrangements.

3   Dan Russell, *A People's Dream: Aboriginal Self-Government in Canada* (Vancouver: UBC Press, 2000).

4   For a comparative commentary on Indigenous self-government initiatives, David C Hawkes, "Indigenous peoples: self-government and intergovernmental relations," *International Social Science Journal* 53, no. 167 (2001): 153-61.

5   For an overview of the initial efforts to expand Aboriginal self-government, see Royal Commission on Aboriginal Peoples, *Partners in Confederation: Aboriginal Peoples, Self-Government and the Constitution* (Ottawa: Canadian Government Printing, 1993).

6   On the political context for the emergence of Aboriginal self-government, see Alan Cairns, *Citizens Plus: Aboriginal Peoples and the Canadian State* (Vancouver: UBC Press, 2000).

7   This summary is taken from Government of Canada, *Federal Policy Guide, Aboriginal-Self-Government: The Government of Canada's Approach to Implementation of the Inherent Right and the Negotiation of Aboriginal Self-Government,* http://www.ainc-inac.gc.ca/pr/pub/sg/plcy_e.html (accessed 15 September 2007).

8   Charles Marecic, "Nunavut Territory: Aboriginal Governing in the Canadian Regime of Governance," *American Indian Law Review,* vol. 24 (1999-2000): 275-96.

9   Catherine Bell, "Métis Self-Government: The Alberta Settlement Model," in *Aboriginal Self-Government in Canada: Current Trends and Issues* 2nd Ed., ed. John H. Hylton (Saskatoon: Purich Publishing Ltd., 1999), 329.

10 For an early case study of community control of social welfare, in this instance focusing on northern Manitoba, see Sharon Taylor-Henley & Peter Hudson, *Canadian Public Policy/Analyse de Politiques* 18, no. 1 (March 1992): 13-26.

11 The Nisga'a agreement was not implemented without internal debate. For background on a major legal challenge to the accord, see http://www.austlii.edu.au/au/journals/AILR/2001/20.html#Heading (accessed 15 September 2007).

12 For a history of the Nisga'a settlement, see Tom Molloy, *The World is Our Witness: The Historic Journey of the Nisga'a into Canada* (Calgary: Fifth House, 2000); and, D. Raunet, *Without Surrender, Without Consent: A History of the Nishga Land Claims* (Vancouver: Douglas & McIntyre, 1984).

13 For a Nisga'a perspective on Nisga'a Lisims government, see their website at http://www.nisgaalisims.ca/.

14 Carol Etkin, "The Sechelt Indian Band: An Analysis of a New Form of Native Self-Government," *The Canadian Journal of Native Studies* 8, no. 1 (1988): 73-104.

15 The Nisga'a Final Agreement, which includes the self-government provisions, can be found at http://www.ainc-inac.gc.ca/pr/agr/nsga/index_e.html.

16 The *Champagne-Aishihik First Nation Self-Government Agreement* can be found at http://www.eco.gov.yk.ca/landclaims/pdf/casga_e.pdf.

17 *Champagne-Aishihik First Nations, Programs and Services Manual, 2007.* http://www.cafn.ca/pdfs/2007CAFNProgramandServicesManual.pdf

18 The details of the agreement-in-principle can be found at http://www.ainc-inac.gc.ca/nr/prs/j-a2003/2-02285_e.html and at http://nwt-tno.inac-ainc.gc.ca/pdf/pt/pf/PF_BeaufortDelta_e.pdf (accessed 15 September 2007).

19 For a terse announcement of the ending of the combined negotiations, see http://www.daair.gov.nt.ca/what-we-do/InuvialuitSelf-governmentNegotiations.htm. Last accessed 15 September 2007.

20 Details on the ratification process can be found at the Turtle Island website. http://www.turtleisland.org/ discussion/viewtopic.php?p=2865 (accessed 15 September 2007).

21 The opposition of the Canadian Taxpayers Federation is covered in the organization's presentation to the Senate Standing Committee on Aboriginal Rights http://www.taxpayer.com/pdf/Westbank_Selfgovernment_Presentation_(May_4_04).pdf (accessed 15 September 2007).

22 For background on the agreement at Westbank, see http://www.ainc-inac.gc.ca/nr/prs/j-a2004/02472bk_e.html (accessed 15 September 2007).

23 "A Good Headstart for Nunavik," *Nunatsiaq News*, 5 September 2007.

24 For further information on the evolution of the regional Government of Nunavik, including updates on continuing developments, see www.nunavikgovernment.ca.

25 For a very insightful overview of the challenges facing one First Nation planning enhanced governance initiatives, see Stephen Cornell, Cheryl Goodswimmer, and Miriam Jorgensen, "In Pursuit of Capable Governance: A Report of the Lheidkli T'Enneh First Nation," http://www.fngovernance.org/pdf/LTReportFinal.pdf (accessed 15 September 2007).

26 A useful assessment of the challenges of self-government can be found in John Graham and Jake Wilson, "Aboriginal Governance in the Decade Ahead: Toward a New Agenda for Change," unpublished, Institute on Governance, 2004, http://iog.ca/publications/tanaga_framework.pdf (accessed 15 September 2007).

27 The debate about the successes and disappointments of self-government has been going on for some time. See Wayne Warry, *Unfinished Dreams: Community Healing and the Reality of Aboriginal Self-Government* (Toronto: University of Toronto Press, 1998).

28 See, for example, the discussion of the Innu in Adrian Tanner, "The Double Bind of Aboriginal Self-Government," in *Aboriginal Autonomy and Development in Northern Quebec and Labrador*, ed. Colin Scott (Vancouver: UBC Press, 2001).

29 Commission of Inquiry into the Sponsorship Program (Ottawa, 2005), available at http://epe.lac-bac.gc.ca/100/206/301/pco-bcp/commissions/sponsorship-ef/06-02-10/www.gomery.ca/en/phase1 report/default.htm.

30 Graham and Wilson, "Aboriginal Governance in the Decade Ahead."

A CRITICAL ANALYSIS OF THE ROYAL COMMISSION ON ABORIGINAL PEOPLES SELF-GOVERNMENT MODEL

James Frideres, University of Calgary

"Resistance is futile. You will be assimilated!" This warning and belief of the inevitability of a monoculture, held by Canadians for over 500 years, is reminiscent of the Requiremiento of 1513 which was a declaration read in Spanish to Aboriginal people in Latin America to obtain Papal blessing for the massacres that were to follow.[1]

Introduction

Over the past century, assimilation has been the predominant solution to the challenge posed by the existence of Aboriginal peoples as extermination, or blatant exploitation, are acknowledged to be inhumane and inefficient.[2] At the same time, Aboriginal leaders have argued that in order to have the ability to control their own affairs and develop appropriate economic, social, and political institutions, they must have self-government that will lead to self-determination, encompassing such activities such as law, medicine, and spiritual and educational activities.[3] Today, under current conditions, Aboriginal people operate under the guise of the *Indian Act* or some similar provincial jurisdiction which does not allow them to achieve true self-government.

Aboriginal people note that the current form of "Aboriginal government" is one that has been imposed upon them by an external agent. Their resistance to this kind of self-government is based on the fact they understand that this is just one more threat to their independent existence. Aboriginal people have only surrendered their political autonomy under duress. This foreign imposed type of government rejected the Aboriginal family/clan-based community governance that had served them well in the past. Aboriginal culture, with an emphasis on collectivism, egalitarianism, and concern about fairness, has led Aboriginal leaders to argue that the revitalization of prior Aboriginal governance structures, or the creation of culturally relevant forms of governance for First Nations' communities, needs to be established while at the same time linking to the existing Canadian state structure.

Aboriginal leaders have argued over the years that the *Indian Act* created "councils" inappropriate for their communities. Aboriginal people argue that they need to develop some modern versions of their traditional system or to create some innovative forms of representational government.[4] In summary, Aboriginal communities argue for the need to develop a form of Aboriginal self-governance that is built upon Aboriginal customs, traditions, and values but one that is not necessarily limited by tradition. This may mean the re-emergence of a traditional system of "Indigenous ways of knowing and governance."[5] Many Canadians find this perspective unacceptable.[6]

Until the last quarter century, Canadians did not seriously entertain the notion of Aboriginal self-government. In 1983, the Special Committee on Indian Self-Government (the Penner Report) recommended the development of federal legislation to support Aboriginal self-government. Bill C-52 (*An Act Relating to Self-Government for Indian Nations*) was tabled in 1984, but died when Parliament was dissolved the same year. Later, in the mid-1980s, the Federal government, in an attempt to reduce financial liabilities for First Nations people, attempted to implement a "Community-Based Self-Government" policy.[7] There was some initial interest in this new form of self-government, but as the details of how this new policy would be implemented became understood by Aboriginal people, there was a near-unanimous rejection of such a policy. Later, in 1992, the Charlottetown Accord moved forward and would have given constitutional recognition of Aboriginal governments as a "third order." However, this initiative was short lived as the Accord was rejected by Canadians. At each step, when the government pursues Aboriginal self-government action, they do so without a clear understanding of the original features of an Aboriginal community that contribute to its well-being. As a result, serious harm is dealt to each of the communities when it is applied. Moreover, when policies promoting integration are undertaken, their sole aim is to benefit individuals, often at the expense of the community. As such, the federal governments' actions have consistently undermined each community's ability to defend and manage its own resources.[8]

The Royal Commission on Aboriginal Peoples in 1996 presented a formal position paper on the issue of Aboriginal self-government. However, their proposals are at two levels. The macro level of Aboriginal governance focused on how a new structure involving Aboriginal people would integrate into the federal level of government. This presentation focused on how the federal structures and legislation would have to be changed to accommodate Aboriginal governance. The creation of a House of First Peoples (a third house of Parliament), the enactment of a modern Royal Proclamation, and the introduction of several pieces of federal legislation regarding Aboriginal people and the necessity to make Constitutional amendments were all part of the larger scheme.

The second level focused on how local or regional Aboriginal self-governance would be structured. Their proposals for the "mini-level" of government offered an Aboriginal government that would not be a series of mini nation-states but rather a set of governments that would hold distinct jurisdiction within a Canadian framework that involved both the federal and provincial governments. Their position is similar to the argument made in the *Delgamuukw* case where First Nations unequivocally embed their political identity under the sovereignty of the Canadian state. Within each of these distinct jurisdictions, Aboriginal people would have the right to define the form as well as the content of laws and this third order of government would entail the right to develop culturally appropriate political institutions.[9] In the end, Aboriginal people want the Canadian government to recognize the *sui generis* nature of their nationhood while they, at the same time, participate in the legal and political relationships dictated by Western law and politics.[10] Aboriginal people want to achieve self-determination and this will involve full title to their traditional territory as well as political control within it, maintaining a self-sufficient, communal socio-economic system according to their own cultural traditions, and having the appropriate social control mechanisms to deal with issues within the territory as well as issues from outside the territory that may impinge upon them.[11]

In the fall of 2005, the Federal government and the Assembly of First Nations, along with the provinces and territories, agreed to commit to developing increased opportunities for Aboriginal self-government. At the time the Assembly of First Nations noted that this Accord (known as the Kelowna Accord or *Strengthening Relationships and Closing the Gap* produced by the Prime Minister's Office) was the start of Aboriginal control over change ranging from policy to the implementation of programs. This control would allow for culturally appropriate forms of governance across the country and stop the insistence on a "one size fits all" perspective that has been so characteristic of government relations with Aboriginal peoples. Unfortunately, this glimmer of hope was dashed one year later when the Liberal government was defeated and the newly constituted minority Conservative government stated it would not honour or implement the Kelowna Accord.

While Hylton asked the question about the extent and nature of Aboriginal self-government shortly after the Royal Commission completed its final report, the time frame did not allow for a full answer.[12] Now, over a decade later, what can we report on the status of Aboriginal self-government in Canada and the recommendations of the Royal Commission? The answer lies in the historical context of the Royal Commission on Aboriginal Peoples, how it dealt with the issues, the recommendations it made, and the progress it achieved.

The Context

In 1991, the Royal Commission on Aboriginal Peoples received its mandate and it was not until five years later that the final report was made public, although a series of interim reports were published during the life of the Commission. The creation of the Commission reached fruition after several public conflicts involving Aboriginal people took place in the 1980s and early 1990s. The Prime Minister had offered a Royal Commission in 1990 to convince Elijah Harper into a last-minute support of the Meech Lake Accord but then withdrew it when the Manitoban MLA refused to support the federal Meech Lake proposal. The Oka (Kanesatake) issue was fresh in most Canadian minds and other conflicts in Ontario, Labrador, and British Columbia were being reported in the media on a daily basis. Concurrent with these overt events, impacting on the lives of non-Aboriginal Canadians, were media reports about the high rates of poverty, ill health, suicide, and dysfunctional families among Aboriginal people.

The mandate of the Commission, as outlined by Chief Justice Brian Dickson in his report to the government recommending the establishment of same, was broad. The Commission was asked to investigate every aspect of the lives of Aboriginal people in Canada, their history, health, aspirations, and relations with government, land claims, treaties, justice, language and, more generally, their situation in Canada relative to that of non-Aboriginal Canadians. In the end, the Commission held 180 days of public hearings, visited almost one hundred Aboriginal communities, commissioned well over three hundred reports, reviewed innumerable reports already prepared by others, and involved the services of over 1,000 Canadians. With over 3,500 pages and a price tag of $58M it was the most expensive and the most time consuming Royal Commission in the history of Canada.

The Composition and Structure of the Commission

The Commissioners generally were well known to Canadians although some were only known to the Aboriginal, or the non-Aboriginal, community. Moreover, the composition of the Commission followed Canadian tradition of having a "balanced" number from each of the regions of Canada, of each of the sexes, and being Aboriginal and non-Aboriginal. The co-chair, Justice Rene Dussault, was perhaps one of the least well-known commissioners, while the other co-chair, Georges Erasmus, was certainly a household name across Canada at the time in both the Aboriginal and non-Aboriginal community—for different reasons. Allan Blakeney (former premier of Saskatchewan), who left the Commission before it issued its final report, was well known to western Canadians but less likely to be recognized by other Canadians. He resigned because he felt the Commission was spending too much time in hearing grievances and not enough in proposing workable solutions to Aboriginal issues. He was replaced by Peter Meekison, again a westerner, who had been a deputy minister for Alberta. Meekison was a constitutional expert and had been actively involved in developing the amending formula in the *Constitution Act, 1982*, as well as involved in the failed Meech Lake and Charlottetown Accord activities. Paul Chartrand was a Métis and professor of law, well known in the Aboriginal and academic community for his scholarly works in the area of Aboriginal self-government and constitutional analysis. Viola Robinson was a Mi'kmaq, president of the Native Council of Canada (now Congress of Aboriginal Peoples) and would have her law degree three years after the final report. Mary Sillett was the vice president of the Inuit Tapirisat of Canada and long-time community activist. Finally, Bertha Wilson, a familiar name across Canada, had served as the first female Supreme Court judge in Canada.[13]

The first commonality of the group is that many had legal training and focused on the legal aspects of Aboriginal/non-Aboriginal relations—both historically and contemporarily. This particular bias is noted through the 3,500 pages of the Report and the nature of the Report itself. Second, only a few of the Commissioners had any experience with Aboriginal Canada on a day-to-day basis. They had not lived in an Aboriginal community, experienced the realities of life as an Aboriginal, or fully understood the enormity of bridging the two communities. Finally, few of the members of the Commission were linked with the government (provincial or federal), the Aboriginal community, or the private sector.

The Commission created a complex organizational structure to support their efforts, one that involved, in addition to the Commissioners, an office of the executive director, senior advisors, and a number of "departments" such as a secretariat, public participation, policy, administration and finance, communications, and research. In addition, a research advisory committee was created. The research advisory committee members were perhaps the best positioned to ensure that research reports were appropriately carried out but few of these individuals were experts in research and certainly even fewer were experts in "indigenous ways of knowing." As such, research from an Aboriginal perspective was rare. Aboriginal people were likewise scarce on the research and policy section of the Commission. The intervener participation program, administered by David Crombie, yielded over 200 reports. In the end, while there were competent individuals placed on these committees, few of them had the ability to understand and critically evaluate research, understand the criteria required to evaluate the validity and reliability of evidence, or to develop strategies to integrate the hundreds of research reports submitted and the individual testimonials provided to the Commission.

The Proposal

The Commission began its hearing with the belief that they had to accommodate the Aboriginal voice and perspective. To ensure this, they were careful that Aboriginal people had an opportunity to speak to the Commission and to present their research findings, their view of Aboriginal life, and their experiences in Canadian society. In examining the proposal with regard to restructuring the political organization of Canada, it is important to understand the perspectives the authors of the Report brought with them. Four major assumptions held by the Commissioners influenced their recommendations. First of all, the authors insisted that if a renewed relationship between Aboriginal people and the state was to take place, colonialism had to end. Outmoded doctrines (e.g., *terra nullius*), had to be rejected and abandoned in dealing with Aboriginal people in all institutional sectors. Second, the nationhood dimension of Aboriginal social and political organization must be recognized. They believed the relationship between Aboriginal people and the government of Canada still continued to be one of "nation-to-nation" character and this is what differentiated Aboriginal people from other people in Canada. A third element was that Aboriginal nations were historically sovereign, self-governing peoples. As such, Canada would have to incorporate Aboriginal nations that wished to reassume their historical powers. Moreover, this right of self-government was inherent and not something delegated from someone else.

Fourth, non-Aboriginal Canadians had to obtain a better understanding of the place of Aboriginal people in Canadian society. Embedded in this assumption was that the institutional structures of Canada must begin to reflect that understanding. Canadians needed to understand that Aboriginal cultures were sustainable and continue to be regardless of the impact of colonialization. In short, stereotypes and erroneous assumptions held by non-Aboriginal people needed to be dealt with immediately and effectively.

In addition to the above, the Commission's vision of a renewed relationship was premised on the principles of mutual recognition, mutual respect, sharing, and mutual responsibility. They concluded that Aboriginal people were political and cultural groups with values and lifestyles distinct from those of other Canadians. The Commission also noted, at the outset of their Report, that Aboriginal people were legitimate nations. They went on to argue that Aboriginal people's sense of confidence and well-being as individuals remained tied to the strength of their nations, and only with their nations restored could they reach their potential in the 21st century. In this conclusion, they rejected assimilation as a policy in dealing with Aboriginal people.

The Royal Commission on Aboriginal Peoples described three basic models of Aboriginal governance. (See Table 1) They articulated what local/regional Aboriginal self-government would look like, how it would be financed, but not how it would relate to the colonial federal and provincial governments. Later, they identified the specific steps required to restructure the relationship between Aboriginal people and Canada. Embedded in this proposal also were some suggestions as to how the structure of the current Canadian government would need to be reorganized if Aboriginal self-government was to occur.

In developing their proposals for Aboriginal self-government, Aboriginal people have called for a revitalization of traditional values and practices and their reintegration into institutions of government. In short, they feel there is a need to root contemporary governmental initiatives in traditional institutions.[14] They also accept the "rule of law" as a fundamental guiding principle although their concept of law is not equivalent to that held by non-Aboriginal people. Aboriginal people view self-government as having two distinct yet interrelated aspects. The first focuses on authority over traditional territory and its inhabitants, while the second involves control over all other issues that might have an impact on a particular Aboriginal nation.

The Macro Perspective: Aboriginal Nations and Government
The discussion by the Commission on this "macro" level of Aboriginal government focused on what needed to be changed in the existing Canadian political structure and organization as well as what must happen within the Aboriginal nations themselves.

The Commission began by noting that shared sovereignty and Aboriginal government was an idea that Canadians would embrace. Moreover, they took the position that Canadians would accept the idea of having three orders of government—federal, provincial, and Aboriginal—with Aboriginal governments autonomous within their own sphere of jurisdiction and not dependent upon a power delegated from other governments.

To implement the idea of Aboriginal nations and self-governance, the Commission argued that Canada begin with a Royal Proclamation[15] that would embrace sharing and uphold the concept of Aboriginal self-government. Concurrently, the federal government would develop companion legislation that Parliament would accept as part of the new political landscape. Several pieces of legislation were suggested, such as:

- Aboriginal Treaty Implementation Act
- Aboriginal Lands and Treaties Tribunal Act
- Aboriginal Relations Department Act
- An Indian and Inuit Services Department Act
- Aboriginal Parliament Act
- Amend the Canadian Human Rights Act, and
- Aboriginal Nations Recognition and Government Act.[16]

The above would create new laws and institutions to facilitate Aboriginal self-government, committing government to help Aboriginal nations emerge from their present state of fragmentation and marginality, ensure the success of Aboriginal people reclaiming nationhood, create an effective self-government, and allow for new relationships with other political partners in Canada. These companion pieces of legislation also recognized a new role for the federal government in Aboriginal Affairs, including the phasing out of the Department of Indian and Northern Affairs Canada and the creation of a new cabinet position—Minister of Aboriginal Relations. These initiatives would require sustained leadership of the Prime Minister, full commitment of the Cabinet, and support from other agencies of the cabinet (e.g., Privy Council, Prime Minister's Office).

Local/Regional Self-Government
The Commission went on to discuss how local/regional self-government would be structured. An Aboriginal nation (they estimate there will between 60 and 80)

must have a sizeable population, common identity, and constitute a predominant population within a territory. This parallels the federal government's perspective. As such, the Commission disqualified small communities/bands from becoming a nation. Nevertheless, they supported these small communities/bands creating confederacies to increase institutional skill base and/or resources.

The Commission also explicitly noted that self-government was only one path to self-determination. Unfortunately, they did not articulate the other alternatives. While the process of self-government flows from the principles of self-determination, self-government is the ability to assess and satisfy needs without outside influence, permission, or restriction. Moreover, the Commission noted that while many Canadians see "politics" as a separate, distant activity, Aboriginal people have always seen politics as interwoven with other dimensions of their life (e.g., family, the land, spirituality). Aboriginal people have argued that a revitalization of traditional governance, eroded by years of coerced assimilation, needs to take place—government structures grounded in Aboriginal culture and values.

SELECTED DIMENSIONS OF ABORIGINAL SELF-GOVERNMENT

Models	Territory	Citizenship	Jurisdiction	Internal Government Organization
Nation Model	Land and territory based	Dual citizenship (Canada and Aboriginal), each group to determine eligibility	Full core jurisdiction, possibly multi-leveled	Will vary according to the requirements of each Aboriginal nation. Organized centrally or federally confederations
Public Model	Land and territory based Some land to be co-jurisdiction	Non-Aboriginal exclusive Mandatory	Combination of powers necessary to protect Aboriginal rights and culture	Centralized or a federal form
Community-of-Interest Model	Not land based	Voluntary Aboriginal Exclusive	Limited jurisdiction to programs and services relevant to members	One level, sector specific, specific institutions and agencies

Table 1. Royal Commission Models of Aboriginal Government

As noted above, the Commission identified three major models of self-government—public, nation and communal. First Nations tended to prefer nation self-government while Inuit preferred a public form of self-government. Others, such as Métis and non-status Indians, seem to favour a community-of-interest self-government.

The nation self-government model would be appropriate for those Aboriginal nations with exclusive territories and a territorial jurisdiction (e.g., reserves, settlements), and who exhibit a strong sense of shared identity. This self-government form would have exclusive governance on core jurisdictional areas[17] although it would negotiate with other governments on peripheral matters. Moreover, it could incorporate elements of traditional governance, choose a loose federation among regions or communities, or take on a more centralized form of governance. The public self-government model (since undertaken by Nunavut Territory) would exercise jurisdiction over a geographically identified area. All residents within the area would participate equally in the government although non-Aboriginal residents would need to be accommodated. Moreover, the structure and function of the government would be decidedly influenced by Aboriginal culture. For both the nation and public self-government models, there may be different levels of government (e.g., community, regional, territorial). Community-of-interest self-government would be suited for those Aboriginal people who are not land-based or territorial. In general, these would include urban Aboriginals, non-status Indians, and some Métis. This form of self-government could encompass urban reserves, Aboriginal neighbourhood communities, pan-Aboriginal governments, or sector-specific Aboriginal institutions.

For the Commission, to be Aboriginal was to be culturally and politically distinct. Identification with a nation was seen as essential because it is the structures of nationhood that provide the unique cultural elements of identity that make an individual Aboriginal. With this central organizing theme, the Commission detailed how self-government could be brought into existence and sustained for the future.

The Commission recognized that many different self-government models were presented to them. They acknowledged that Aboriginal people were a diverse group and this was reflected in their views of what self-government would look like. (See Table 2)

Nevertheless, the core of their desire for self-government included a greater control over their lives, freedom from external interference, and independence. In short, greater authority over a traditional territory and the people living within, and over external affairs that affected them. Aboriginal people have called for a revitalization of traditional values and practices to root contemporary governmental initiatives in traditional institutions.[18]

The Commission noted that Aboriginal people had two ways to implement their local/regional self-government: to negotiate implementation with the federal government, or to self-initiate. In the end, the suggestion was self-initiation for areas under the core jurisdiction of Aboriginal people, and negotiation with the federal and/or provincial governments for issues considered periphery.

The transition to self-government would require time, funding, and resources. The Commission clearly noted that successful achievement of Aboriginal self-government must have three components: (1) legitimacy (public confidence in and support of the government as well as recognition by other governments); (2)

Models	Land	Citizenship	Jurisdiction	Internal Government Organization
Métis Self-government	Not land based	voluntary	Limited jurisdiction to services relevant to the preservation and promotion of Métis culture	Bureaucratic structure with Métis involvement at all levels
Urban-Satellite	Land within an urban area	mandatory	Urban reservations as identified by the *Indian Act*	Structured by the *Indian Act*
Community	Land based	voluntary	Limited to programs and services relevant to members	Aboriginal involvement at all levels
Single-sector	Not land based	voluntary	Limited to programs and services relevant to members	Aboriginal involvement at all levels

Table 2. Examples of Self-Government Models proposed by Aboriginal Groups[19]

power (the legal capacity to act); and, (3) resources (the physical means of acting). If a land/territorial strategy was undertaken, Aboriginal people would need to increase their land base and become financially self-sufficient. This could be achieved through the settlement of land claims and the incorporation of such additional lands and entitlements through treaties as Canadians found fair. Once that occurred, Aboriginal people would have to introduce a local tax, encourage economic activities in the territory, and so on. The Commission argued that Aboriginal self-government would be a process of rebuilding, obtaining administrative and financial support to facilitate self-sufficiency. Aboriginal communities would engage in consensus-building, initially at an informal level, and later through some formal ratification process. These processes, along with the changing structure of the federal government, would create an effective Aboriginal self-government.

Concerns about the Proposal: A Critical Analysis
Assumptions

The four basic principles (mutual recognition, mutual respect, sharing, and mutual responsibility) the Report is based on are not as prevalent as the Commissioners envisioned. For example, Canadians (and/or their government) are not prepared to recognize Aboriginal people as the original settlers of this land with distinctive rights and responsibilities. The continued push for assimilation is ample evidence that "coexistence" is not a salient value in Canadian society with regard to Aboriginal people. Nor is self-government seen as an inherent right for Aboriginal people, as witness the sustained emphasis on the *Indian Act*. When Canadians hear "Aboriginal self-government," they react with concern. On the other hand, for example, no one is concerned when the province of Alberta makes laws in the field of education and no one else can do any thing about it. Why? There is agreement that the provision of educational services is within provincial jurisdiction and other levels of government cannot amend or reject its decisions. The question is why this could not be the case for First Nations also. These different reactions reflect different values of different populations, i.e., Aboriginal vs. non-Aboriginal.

Aboriginal people have always been cynical about the value of various government committees and commissions. Their reaction to the Royal Commission was no exception though they entered the discussions with a sincere belief that perhaps, this time, things would be different. From an academic point of view, Royal Commissions in Canada are generally a response to growing political pressure on a topic, usually one affecting the social cohesion of society and its effective operation. Indeed, when major political and economic interest groups see increased societal tension negatively influencing operations, pressure is exerted on the government of the day. Others have argued that Royal Commissions are created in lieu of action by disingenuous politicians hoping the pressure on them will be first deflected and then dissipated over the perhaps protracted period such Commissions take to complete their work.[20] For example, within weeks of the release of the report, it was pointed out that the Commission's recommendation about self-government diverted attention from the real issue of Aboriginal government superseding the colonial government of Canada.[21]

As predicted by some, the Commission had no new insights on the nature of the problem. Previous inquiries into Aboriginal issues (as early as the Hawthorn Report in 1966), arrived at the same conclusion and the subsequent action by government has been the same—status quo. For example, in 1991, Prime Minister Brian Mulroney pledged that the government would be able to settle all land claims disputes by the year 2000, through negotiations with provinces and Aboriginals, and through establishing an Aboriginal fast-tracking land claims system. It would not be until the end of 2007 that this new policy would be introduced. Canadians are averse to risk and change is risky for those in power: when your position in society is challenged, there is little incentive to relinquish or share power.[22]

Cairns and Flanagan have been two of the more outspoken critics of the Royal Commission's proposals.[23] They argue that establishing a third order of governance could have negative consequences ranging from creating a politically divisive environment to being institutionally unwieldy and very costly to implement. The Centre for Aboriginal Policy Change argues that Aboriginal government is redundant and any attempts to develop an Aboriginal governance system should be abandoned.[24] The central argument here is that serious mismanagement of current councils is taking place and Aboriginal peoples should be encouraged to assimilate into the mainstream society so that Aboriginal governance structures are not needed. In short, Aboriginal governance structure would be a waste of taxpayer's money since Aboriginal leaders and councils are incompetent and Aboriginal people do not care about good governance because they are "free riders" in a system funded by Canadian taxpayers. Many Canadians, including some of our political leaders, have accepted these arguments and thus were not in support of the Commissions' recommendations.

There also is the argument that Aboriginal self-government as presented by the Royal Commission is just another form of colonialism.[25] Moreover, the enactment of Aboriginal self-government was rejected because not only would the federal government lose financial control but also because little thought had been given as to how a separate administrative system would operate in practice. Clearly, government was unable to transform their own internal mindset of control. Unfortunately, the Royal Commission did not illustrate how the local/regional Aboriginal governments would interface with either the existing, or the suggested amended, federal government. With little direction on how this would take place, people were unwilling to accept the Commission's implicit assurance of, "Trust me, it will work out."

It also has been suggested that Aboriginal governance structures will not protect the rights of individuals, a key component of Western liberalism.[26] Isaac noted that at a philosophical level, people may see self-government as contrary to the liberal concern for individual rights, in short, group rights and individual rights as mutually exclusive.[27] Kymlicka goes on to argue that minority group self-government is a threat to the nation state and will undermine national stability and solidarity.[28] Niezen[29] also points out that Aboriginal claims for self-government do not easily fit into the Western notions of liberalism. For example, the rights of women and individuals who choose to adhere to a Christian religion may be abridged under a traditional Aboriginal governance structure. In these imagined scenarios, Canada could become a series of enclaves of independent nations making a collective Canadian identity impossible. A related concern is that recognition of Aboriginal rights of self-government would lead to multiple "mini-nations" and thus to the development of secessionist states. The creation of the mini-nations would undermine a group's commitment to Canada and jeopardize Canada's future.

As noted earlier, the question as to why the creation of a nation is seen as the only political route capable of developing and preserving Aboriginal culture is not addressed by the Commission. The Commission seems to argue that because Aboriginal nations exist already, and because witnesses told them that "nationhood would create the necessary cohesion for their members," this was the way to go forward. Common identification with a nation was considered the principle bond between Aboriginal people and playing to this perceived strength was better than trying something new. Moreover, since nations need resources to fulfill their cultural mandate, creating nations would be the least costly in terms of time and finances. If the framework of a nation already exists, then there would be no need to develop administrative structures to put some other form of government (administrative structure) in place for Aboriginal people. Moreover, since the federal government already has fiduciary responsibility for Indians, these funds could be directed toward building and maintaining a nation. Finally, the Commission was also cognizant of the fact that the Quebec referendum was taking place (1995) and the idea of having Aboriginal nations was an increasingly important mechanism in containing the secessionist aspirations of Quebec. If Aboriginal people had "nationhood," then Quebec would need to seek permission from Aboriginal people to secede. And, as Flanagan[30] points out, Aboriginal nationalism can disrupt Canadian politics but it cannot threaten the existence of the Canadian state as Quebec secession could. The Commission also felt that if nations have the right to determine (control) the entry and exit of individuals, in both the definitional and physical sense, this would satisfy the concern of Aboriginal communities as to who would decide if an individual was "Aboriginal" and had the right to live in a First Nations community. However, the Commission considered land an essential aspect of self-government (nationhood) and those without land were considered part of the diaspora. Thus, this perspective left some Aboriginal people concerned about the value of self-government as conceptualized by the Commission.

Finally, the breadth of the Commission allowed for their focus to drift and makes it impossible to synthesize and integrate the findings from a disparate set of sources. Moreover, the Commissioners were not trained to critically evaluate evidence presented, integrate findings, and prepare a report that was not only theoretically and philosophically in tune with Canadian values, but also reflected the realities of Aboriginal life in Canada.[31]

Structural Changes

The Commission's report on Aboriginal self-government was based upon the government and courts accepting their interpretation of the *Constitution Act, 1982*. For example, the Commission concluded that section 35 recognized and affirmed the inherent right of self-government as entrenched in the constitution. Furthermore, they concluded that the *Canadian Charter of Rights and Freedoms* applied to Aboriginal nation governments. While the Supreme Court has not addressed these issues, subsequent action by government would require that the Court support such an interpretation. Until then, many leaders argued, it would seem folly to embark upon a "new structure" for Canada and its relationship with Aboriginal people.[32]

The Commission's recommendations would require constitutional and institutional amendments to the structure and functioning of Parliament. For example, the creation of an Aboriginal division within the Senate would require a constitutional amendment. They also proposed a veto be put in place for

Aboriginal peoples on amendments to sections of the constitution that directly affect their rights; that there be constitutional protection for the *Alberta Métis Settlements Act*; and that section 41 of the Constitution be changed so that Aboriginal people have a formal role in the amending procedure. The report also made recommendations with regard to the entrenchment of some measures such as crafting a new Royal Proclamation, establishing an Aboriginal Lands and Treaties Tribunal, promoting equalization of regional disparities and intergovernmental immunity from taxation, and that representatives of Aboriginal peoples be included in all planning and preparations for any future constitutional conferences established by the Government of Canada.[33]

Prior to the Aboriginal Royal Commission, the Royal Commission on Electoral Reform had addressed the question of separate representation of Aboriginal people in the House of Commons.[34] However, they recommended that separate Aboriginal constituencies be established as part of the existing seats allocated to a province and thus no amendment would be necessary. However, the RCAP recommended that Parliament establish an Aboriginal Parliament as the first step toward creating a House of First Peoples or a third house of Parliament.[35] As outlined, it would be:

> ... a body of between 75-100 representatives. Each nation or people would choose representatives, with adjustments made to acknowledge the influence of provincial and territorial boundaries. The primary function of the House of First Peoples would be in relation to federal legislation ... [It would] have the power to veto certain legislation put before it [and passing legislation that impacted upon Aboriginal people would] require a double majority of the House of Commons and the House of First Peoples ... also a role for a third chamber in ratifying constitutional amendments.[36]

A number of options were presented for the selection of Aboriginal representation to the House of First Peoples. The Commission made suggestions as to how the Aboriginal Parliament might be developed and the matters on which it might provide advice to the House and the Senate. In the end, the creation of an Aboriginal Parliament would not be a substitute for self-government but rather an additional institution for enhancing the representation of Aboriginal peoples within Canada. However, establishing separate Aboriginal representation in the House of Commons would require a constitutional amendment. On the other hand, the placement of an Aboriginal member on the Supreme Court would not require any constitutional amendment, although the Commission recommended that such a move receive the support of all Provinces.[37]

The Royal Commission noted that if Aboriginal self-government was to become a reality, substantial changes would need to take place within the current political structure, including a new department, a new minister, and a third level of government. These suggested structural changes were fully understood by the readers of the report and certainly not supported by most Canadians. The Commission also pushed for immediate enactment of a Royal Proclamation and passage of companion legislation. Critics of the proposal argued that this could not happen before the institution of the principled framework was developed. Many non-Aboriginal leaders felt this was an unacceptable strategy and one that could not be supported. Moreover, most political leaders felt that the Royal Commission on Aboriginal Peoples recommendations represented such a major change in the political landscape (and Canadians were giving it so little support), they were not able to endorse the Report's suggestions with regard to structural changes in the political institutions. For example, the social and economic climate of the country had changed from the beginning of the Commission to when the report was released. Polls taken in early 1997 (the closest data we have to the 1996 release of the final Report) show that Canadians were not convinced that Aboriginal people were that disadvantaged, although they were generally in support of Aboriginal self-government. Moreover, the entrenchment and support of the ideology of neo-conservatism that began in the mid 1980s provided a framework for Canadians that focused on blaming the victims. Further, it was clear to the Commission that they could not implement the recommendations in the two- to three-year cycle politicians operate in. A limited political vision of the future prevented the Commission from recommending the enactment of meaningful change: how could a member of parliament possibly take credit or get re-elected on a platform that would take 10 years to conclude? In the end, the Commission's ideas of structural change in Canadian political institutions and their organization fell on barren soil.

There are those who claim that the Commission held out-dated principles such as nationhood being linked to the principle of territoriality. Current transnational perspectives argued that with the global economy and trans-migration in full force, such outdated ideas were no longer applicable.[38] Critics of the Royal Commission also noted that the focus of the Commission was not on the political economy of Canada and how Aboriginal people fit into the structure,[39] rather it was on the legal and historical structure and only somewhat incidentally on Aboriginal marginalization in Canadian society.[40]

The federal government did not wait for the final report and, in 1995, attempted to short circuit what was sure to be a central recommendation of the Royal Commission. The Inherent Rights of Self-Government policy held that the self-government process was dictated by the federal government, a concept solidly rejected by Aboriginal people. At the same time, the government pushed for an aggregated policy of self-government. Aboriginal communities were very clear at the Commission hearings that they wanted local self-government, but, through the strategy of providing large grants to "aggregate" Aboriginal governments, the policy was nominally accepted by many Aboriginal communities/bands and by the year 2000, there were nearly 100 tribal councils in the country. Today, about 80 per cent of bands are affiliated with a tribal council and/or organization. Clearly this strategy has worked.

Self-governing nations around the world make decisions that affect each other. Awareness of this mutual influence has diminished the importance of independence while advancing the notion of interdependence.[41] Aboriginal people are cognizant that asserting their independence (autonomy) at a time when sovereignty in the rest of the world seems to be on the decline, poses a practical and philosophical conundrum. The Royal Commission was aware of the need to strike a balance of Aboriginal autonomy and interdependence and Aboriginal people may need to sacrifice some local autonomy to secure their place in the Canadian federation. But since the Royal Commission did not clearly articulate this balance or how this balance would emerge, Canadians were quick to see this weakness in the recommendations.

Conclusions

The Final Report of the Commission is far-reaching in its vision, complex, and overwhelmingly detailed. Moreover, it presents an "all or nothing" approach to Aboriginal self-government. As discussed above, these facets of the report leave it open to criticism and debate, and leave the issue of Aboriginal self-government unresolved.

To the present day, higher court decisions have treated Aboriginal self-government as though it were any other Aboriginal right and have disregarded its constitutionally protected status. In two major decisions, *Delgamuukw* v. *British Columbia*[42] in 1997, and *R.* v. *Pamajewon*[43] in 1996, the courts have consciously chosen not to rule on the issue of Aboriginal self-government. In *Delgamuukw*, the Supreme Court cited insufficient evidence to make any judicial determination as to the Aboriginal right to self-government. The Supreme Court is well aware of the enormity of a decision (one way or the other) and it is carefully establishing an archive of historical and legal information on the issue before tackling it. Moreover, they see it as a "Pandora's box" that ought not be opened without consideration of the rights within the Canadian legal and political framework.[44] Nevertheless, it should be noted that lower courts have made pronouncements on Aboriginal self-government. In *Campbell et al.* v. *British Columbia* (2000),[45] the presiding judge upheld Aboriginal self-government noting that it was protected by section 35(1) of the *Constitution Act, 1982*. He went on to say that section 91 and 92 of the *Constitution Act, 1867*, were not exclusive and did leave room for the creation of a third order of Aboriginal self-government. However such interpretations are not expected to be upheld in the higher courts.

An empirical and philosophical question arises regarding how Aboriginal traditional governance deals with individual rights: is there something inherently anti-individual-rights within traditional Aboriginal government? Until recently, this question was not considered important. The Commission clearly supported the inherent right of Aboriginal people to engage in self-government, based on section 35(1) of the *Constitution Act, 1982*. They were cognizant that other Aboriginal groups might use additional support (e.g., historical, political), unique to each.[46] However, the Commission went on to argue that while this right is inherent, the constitutional right is exercisable only within the framework of Canada. As such, the Aboriginal right of self-government in Canada involves circumscribed rather than unlimited powers.

To its credit, the Commission noted that assimilating Aboriginal people into the larger Canadian society was not the answer but rather that a strategy of revitalizing Aboriginal economics, political systems, and culture was the correct solution. This position shifted the "cause" of the plight of Aboriginal people away from them and toward the structures and institutions of non-Aboriginal Canada. While activists and academics had pushed this position long before the Commission was created, the publicity and legitimacy of the Commission forced Canadians to rethink their position—a difficult task indeed and one that was not totally successful.

The work of scholars such as Zion, Turner, Tully, and Alfred suggest that Aboriginal people have the potential to transform the political structure of Canada from within, just as other minority groups are attempting to do.[47] They argue that current political structures are adapting to internal forces resulting in alternative and culturally appropriate political institutions. Aboriginal culture has much to offer Canada and the development of alternative political and legal structures can easily be accommodated by mainstream society. What is needed is more support by agencies such as the Royal Commission, the Prime Minister's Office, and Cabinet.

Aboriginal leaders proposing changes to the political structure of Canada are not advocating an independent statehood or secession. The proposed relationship between the federal government and Aboriginal peoples is not the same as ethnonationalism. It is, however, an order of relationship that currently does not exist: as such, there are concerns over the consequences of its establishment. The mechanisms for implementing such a new order already exist, though these interfaces will have to be refined and customized for Aboriginal-federal relations. For example, Aboriginal people negotiate with federal and provincial governments and the private sector over issues of health care, education, and other services. Alternative justice systems already exist. Other linkages between Aboriginal communities and the federal government involving the medical, economic, and education sectors have taken place for many years.

These proposals are not intended to threaten the stability of Canadian society. Nor are they to pave the way for secession.[48] Currently, most Aboriginal people experience a rather "reluctant" Canadian citizenship. The tendered solutions are an attempt to ensure Aboriginal participation in the Canadian social and political structure, making them full citizens of Canada. As the Assembly of First Nations noted, self-government is viewed as part of a new and diverse political order that reflects the changing demography and ethnic composition of Canadian society.[49] Hopefully, this new order will meet the needs and interests of the local and regional Aboriginal communities. In the end, recognition of Aboriginal structures will allow Aboriginals and the mainstream to realize common goals while each supporting their unique cultures. This mutuality and interconnectedness is sufficiently broad to allow for a shared citizenship that both parties fully embrace.

The Commission did not pronounce on future litigation and resolutions, a surprising omission given many of the Commissioners had legal backgrounds. Nor did it address the protection of Aboriginal rights from adverse legislation or judicial decisions. And finally, it does not elaborate upon the extent to which the new Aboriginal governments would be protected.

While the Commissioners certainly knew their Canadian history and law, the report was not accessible to Canadians. For example, the strategy of selling the Report to recoup funds found many people unable/unwilling to obtain a copy at the time. While the dissemination of the Report by CD was innovative, it also meant that if you did not have a computer, access was limited. Finally the sheer size of the report and its division into five volumes reduced its accessibility. And, as time went on, the content of the Report became more distant and irrelevant. For example, a 2004 poll found that Aboriginal self-government was not in the top ten issues of priority for Aboriginal people themselves.[50]

The Commission's concern with ensuring that the history of Aboriginal–non-Aboriginal relations was presented, as well as the massive investigation of the socio-demographic profile of Aboriginal people, was misspent time and money. The Hawthorn Report of 1966 and every annual report from Indian and Northern Affairs Canada for the past three decades have clearly articulated the inequality experienced by Aboriginal people. Academics for the past three decades have documented Aboriginal people's marginalized position in Canadian society and their troubled history with non-Aboriginal people.[51] However, the political agenda of the Commission was more concerned about Aboriginal dependency than self-government. Direct and indirect costs for Aboriginal people, for example, health and social services, had escalated substantially in the previous fifty years and it was clear that something had to be done to bring the costs down.

The Commission would have been better served to concentrate on their over-all conclusion, namely, that the main policy direction, pursued for more than a century and a half by the federal government, was wrong. It might be tempting to suggest that the dismantling of the DIAND regional office in Manitoba and the subsequent transfer of responsibilities to the First Nations of Manitoba is a result of the Commission. However, that agreement occurred before the final report of the Commission and reflects the policy of the government to aggregate Aboriginal communities into tribal councils. Likewise, the *James Bay and Northern Quebec Agreement* and the *Yukon First Nations Self-Government Act* were concluded long before the final report of the Commission. On the other hand, the federal government's transfer of the legislative and administrative jurisdiction for education to the Mi'kmaq was a direct result of the Commissions report.[52]

In the end, the Commissioners wrote a text reminiscent of a legal contract as they followed their legal instincts and training, shaped and wrote their report in the legal tradition.[53] Unfortunately, the report did not reflect the realities of Aboriginal life. From an Aboriginal perspective, life hasn't changed much since the arrival of Europeans. There has been poverty and poor health, and the impact on culture and family has been severe. Nevertheless, they persevered, their ties with their cultural heritage and the unwavering roots of their identity remained in place. The Commissioners came to their community one day, left the next, and there was little communication between the Commission and the public after their departure. Subsequent action on the part of government with regard to Aboriginal self-government has been slow, resistant, and counterproductive.

The Government of Canada is not seriously participating in the development and conduct of the self-government initiative. The pledge to conduct government-to-government relations has failed to lead to serious engagement with Aboriginal communities in pacts that embody the inherent right of self-government. For example, the federal government's *Action Plan* states that "certain provisions in self-government agreements with First Nations, Inuit and Métis and off-reserve people could be constitutionally protected as treaty rights under section 35 of the *Constitution Act, 1982.*"[54] This is a continuance of the Inherent Rights Policy, not an inherent model of Aboriginal self-government. First Nations believe it is their rightful governing role to govern themselves and to hold a recognized position within the realm of the government structure of Canada. Bill C-52 (1984) claimed, among other things, to validate the traditional laws of each nation as long as they didn't conflict with the laws of parliament. Again, this legislation was rejected by Aboriginal people because it did not endorse self-government as an inherent Aboriginal right. The federal government continues to see Aboriginal governance strictly in administrative terms and maintains control over key elements of the political and administrative relationship. There is, for example, an insistence that governance structures embrace Western models and not Indigenous ones, and such restrictions are obstacles to Aboriginal self-government.[55]

Even under conditions of negotiated self-government, accountability for program management rests solely with the federal government, bringing into question the federal commitment to respect the inherent right of Aboriginal self-government. Almost all initiatives and reforms by government to implement inherent self-government have failed.

Neither the Royal Commission nor Indian and Northern Affairs Canada have commented on the examples of Aboriginal self-government tested in the United States.[56] Reinfeld found that the exercise of self-government led to a significant increase in economic productivity of a community and a significant increase in involvement and participation in tribal governance activities.[57] Finally, he found a considerable number of "creative developments" on those reserves as a direct result of the self-government demonstration project.

Was the Commission a waste of time and money? While it has not precipitated a movement toward Aboriginal self-government as Aboriginal people see it, it has played some latent roles. First of all, the process of the Commission involved empowerment that strengthened Aboriginal discourse and facilitated communication among the various Aboriginal communities across Canada. Second, it provided Aboriginal people with a public forum that gave legitimacy to their concerns and their traditional knowledge. Third, it provided a platform that introduced Aboriginal epistemology to Canadians as an alternative to Euro-Canadian thinking. Fourth, the Commission was able to introduce topics such as discrimination, racism, and inequality in such a fashion, (i.e., using a healing metaphor), that it engaged non-Aboriginal people in a dialogue with Aboriginal people on issues that previously had been considered taboo.

In the end, all parties have acknowledged the complexity of the issue. The government has tried to circumvent addressing those complexities by implementing self-government as they define it. They have chosen not to develop a principled framework to discuss the issue and to effectively negotiate and implement the Aboriginal right to self-government. Courts have consciously steered away from making pronouncements on the validity of inherent self-government, waiting until reasoned approaches can be presented. Little action on self-government, as understood by Aboriginal people, has been taken over the past decade. Aboriginal people, in the absence of formal recognition of self-government have gone "underground," giving lip service to the government and the *Indian Act*, but practicing and implementing their own form of self-government. And for the time being, this strategy seems to be working, though, it is clear that in the near future, conflicts will emerge and bring the issue to the forefront once again. However, by that time, many Aboriginal communities will have entrenched their local form of self-government.

NOTES

1   Steve Russell, "The Jurisprudence of Colonialism," in *American Indian Thought*, ed. A. Waters (Maryland: Blackwell publishing, 2004), 217-28.
2   J. Bodley, *Tribal Peoples and Development Issues* (Mountain View: California Mayfield Publishing Company, 1985).
3   Wayne Warry, *Ending Denial* (Peterborough: Broadview Press, 2007).
4   *Ibid.*
5   John Borrows, *Recovering Canada: The Resurgence of Indigenous Law* (Toronto: University of Toronto Press, 2002).
6   Tom Flanagan, "Aboriginal Orthodoxy in Canada," in *Waking Up to Dreamtime: The Illusion of Aboriginal Self-Determination,* ed. G. Johns (Singapore: Media Masters, 2001), 1-19.
7   DIAND (Neilsen Report), *Indian and Native Programs: A Study Team Report to the Task Force on Program Review* (Ottawa: Supply and Service, 1986).
8   Bodley, *Tribal Peoples.*
9   Warry, *Ending Denial.*
10   Dale Turner, "Oral Traditions and the Politics of (Mis)Recognition," in *American Indian Thought,* ed. Anne Waters (Maryland: Blackwell Publishing, 2004), 229-38.
11   Bodley, *Tribal Peoples.*
12   John H. Hylton, ed., *Aboriginal Self-Government in Canada,* 2nd Ed. (Saskatoon: Purich Publishing, 1999).
13   Five years previously, Justice Wilson wrote a unanimous decision for the Supreme Court (*Roberts* v. *Canada,* [1989] 1 S.C.R. 322) holding that the law of Aboriginal title is Federal common law (a body of basic unwritten law that is common to the whole of Canada and extends in principle to all jurisdictions).
14   Royal Commission on Aboriginal Peoples, *Final Report.*

15 The Proclamation would reaffirm Canada's respect for Aboriginal people as nations, acknowledge harmful action by past governments, recognize shared and mutual responsibilities between the federal government and Aboriginal people, affirm that Aboriginal self-government was an inherent right, and acknowledge that justice and fair play are necessary for reconciliation of take place.

16 This *Act* would prescribe Canada's formal recognition to Aboriginal nations.

17 Areas of core jurisdiction consist of issues that are of vital concern to the life and welfare of neighbouring non-Aboriginal communities and are not of federal or provincial interest (e.g. education, language, policing, housing, elections). On the other hand, peripheral areas of jurisdiction are issues that affect the lands, resources, and other interests of neighbouring non-Aboriginal people.

18 Government of Canada, 1996. *Report on the Royal Commission on Aboriginal Peoples,* Ottawa, Canada Communications Group.

19 See K. Krloczi, *The Implications of Self-Government with Respect to Aboriginal Justice Initiatives,* MA thesis, Carleton University, Ottawa, 2004, for more examples and a full explication of each model.

20 Peter Russell, "Indigenous Self-Determination: Is Canada as Good as it Gets?" in *Unfinished Constitutional Business? Rethinking Indigenous Self-Determination,* ed. B. Hocking (Canberra: Aboriginal Studies Press, 2005), 170-89.

21 Kahn-Tineta Horn, "1996 Royal Commission on Aboriginal People Report is a Betrayal and Diversion from the Real Issue of Aboriginal Government Superseding the Colonial Government of Canada," *Canadian Alliance in Solidarity with Native Peoples,* 14 December 1996, www.hartford-hwp.com/archives/44/011.html (accessed 10 September 2007).

22 F. Widdowson, *The Political Economy of Aboriginal Dependency* (Ph.D. Diss., York University, 2006).

23 Alan Cairns, *Citizens Plus: Aboriginal Peoples and the Canadian State* (Vancouver: University of British Columbia Press, 2000); and, Tom Flanagan, *First Nations? Second Thoughts* (Montreal & Kingston: McGill-Queen's University Press, 2000).

24 Tanis Fiss, *Road to Prosperity* (Calgary, Alberta: Centre for Aboriginal Policy Change, 2005).

25 Kiera Ladner & Michael Orsini, "The Persistence of Paradigm Analysis: The First Nation Governance Act as the Continuation of Colonial Policy," in *Canada: The State of Federation 2003: Reconfiguring Aboriginal State Relations,* ed. Michael Murphy (Montreal & Kingston: McGill-Queens University Press, 2003).

26 Will Kymlicka, *Multicultural Citizenship: A Liberal Theory of Minority Rights* (Oxford: Oxford University Press, 1995).

27 Thomas Isaac, "Individual vs. Collective Rights: Aboriginal People and the Significance of *Thomas* v. *Norris,*" *Manitoba Law Journal* 21, no. 3 (1992): 620-43.

28 Kymlicka, *Multicultural Citizenship.*

29 Ronald Niezen, *The Origins of Indigenism, Human Rights and the Politics of Identity* (Berkeley: University of California Press, 2003).

30 Flanagan, *First Nations? Second Thoughts.*

31 J. Bird, L. Land & M. Macadam, eds. *Nation to Nation: Aboriginal Sovereignty and the Future of Canada* (Toronto: Irwin, 2002).

32 The Commission also recommended a Constitutional amendment to protect the *Alberta Métis Settlements Act,* which now has been successfully implemented.

33 A. Doerr, "Building New Orders of Government: The Future of Aboriginal Self-Government," *Canadian Public Administration* 40, no. 2 (1997): 274-89.

34 Canada, *Reforming Electoral Democracy, Royal Commission on Electoral Reform and Party Financing* (Ottawa: Supply and Services, 1991).

35 While this conceptualization is new to Canada, Aboriginal parliaments have been established in northern Europe. The Saami parliaments of Scandinavia have been in operation for a number of years.

36 Royal Commission on Aboriginal Peoples, *Restructuring the Relationship,* Vol. 2 (Ottawa: Canada Communications Group, 1996), Chap. 3, Appendix 3B.

37 Cairns, *Citizens Plus.*

38 R. Todd, "Urban Aboriginal Governance: Developments and Issues," in *Not Strangers in These Parts,* eds. David Newhouse & Evelyn J. Peters (Ottawa: Policy Research Initiative, 2003), 255-66.

39 Widdowson, *Public Economy;* also Curtis Cook & Juan D. Lindau, *Aboriginal Rights and Self-Government* (Montreal & Kingston: McGill Queen's University Press, 2000).

40 Calvin Helin, *Dances with Dependency* (Vancouver: Orca Spirit Publishing, 2007).

41 Robert Mainville, *An Overview of Aboriginal and Treaty Rights and the Compensation for Their Breach* (Saskatoon: Purich Publishing, 2001).

42 [1997] 3 S.C.R. 1010.

43 [1996] 2 S.C.R. 821.

44 M. Lavoie, *The Need for a Principled Framework to Effectively Negotiate and Implement the Aboriginal Right to self-Government in Canada* (LLM. thesis, McGill University, 2003).

45 [2000] 4 C.N.L.R.I.

46 The Commission identified four different sources of Aboriginal right to self-government: (1) the ultimate source is the creator; (2) international law; (3) the colonial powers that recognized them as self-governing nations (e.g. *Royal Proclamation of 1763*); and, (4) *the Canadian Constitution, 1982.*

47 J. Zion, "The 'One Law for All' Myth," in *Justice as Healing: Indigenous Ways,* ed. W. McCaslin (St. Paul: Living Justice Press, 2005); Dale Turner, *This is Not a Peace Pipe* (Toronto: University of Toronto Press, 2006); James Tully, *Strange Multiplicity: Constitutionalism in an Age of Diversity* (Cambridge: Cambridge University Press, 2001); and, Taiaiake Alfred, *Wasáse: Indigenous Pathways of Action and Freedom* (Peterborough: Broadview Press, 2005).

48 Assembly of First Nations, *Our Nations, Our Governments: Choosing Our Own Paths,* Report of the Joint Committee of Chiefs and Advisors on the Recognition and Implementation of First Nation Governments (Ottawa: Queen's Printer, 2005).

49 Assembly of First Nations, *Proposed Framework to Advance the Recognition and Implementation of First Nation Governments,* Special Chiefs Assembly, March 29-31 (Ottawa: Queen's Printer, 2005).

50 Indian and Northern Affairs Canada, *The Landscape of Public Opinion of Aboriginal and Northern Issues* (Ottawa: Public Works and Government Services Canada, 2004).

51 James Frideres & Rene Gadacz, *Aboriginal People in Canada* (Toronto: Pearson, 2005).

52 B. Shepard, "Moving Tenuously Toward Lasting Self-Government for First Nations" (Ph.D. Diss., University of Toronto, 2006); and, R. Shepard & R. Diabo, "A Government-First Nations Dialogue on Accountability: Re-establishing Understanding of the Basics of a Complex Relationship," *Native Studies Review,* 15, no. 2 (2004): 94-104. In 1995, the Program Review for DIAND changed its mandate and made "Indian monies" taxable. It redefined "Indian monies" in such a way that all monies collected, received, or held by the Crown for the use and benefit of Indians could be taxed. Its new mandate also read that "DIANDS core obligations to First Nations are to ensure that basic needs are met," thereby reducing DIAND's obligations.

53 The reader should consult the volume *Aboriginal Self-Government: Legal and Constitutional Issues* (1995) commissioned by the RCAP. The authors, P. Macklem, W. Moss, B. Morse, J. Giokas, D. McMahon, F. Martin, P. Hogg & M.E. Turpel are all prominent scholars in the area of Aboriginal self-government and constitutional experts.

54 DIAND, *Gathering Strength: Canada's Aboriginal Action Plan* (Ottawa: Public Works & Government Services Canada, 1997).

55 DIAND, *Indian and Native Programs.*

56 Stephen Cornell & Joseph Kalt, *Sovereignty and Nation-Building* (Harvard: Kennedy School of Government, 1998).

57 K. Reinfeld, *Draft Study of the Tribal Self-Governance Demonstration Project* (Washington, DC: US Department of the Interior, 1995).

"WE RISE AGAIN:"

Métis Traditional Governance and the Claim to Métis Self-Government

Larry Chartrand, University of Ottawa

My great-great-grandfather, Zacharie Chartrand, lived through the war of 1885 between Canada and the Métis Nation. Zacharie lived in Willowbunch at the time and when he got word of the Canadian police and military attacking up north along the Saskatchewan River valley, he and a few companions packed up for the trip to Batoche to help out their fellow countrymen against the Canadian invaders.

Their travel to Batoche was interrupted shortly after their departure, however, when the local Catholic priest intercepted them. I have been told that the conversation between the Métis compatriots and the priest was heated and bitter, but the result was that the Métis reinforcements from Willowbunch, including my great-great-grandfather, turned back.

We lost the battle at Batoche and I am not sure that the war is yet over between Canada and the Métis Nation. No surrender or peace treaty occurred. The assumption by historians to date has been that the Métis who fought for their Nation and their sovereignty were rebels.[1]

To have hanged Riel for treason on 16 November 1885, was justified only if Canada possessed sovereignty over the territory. I have maintained in earlier writings that the international criteria for territorial acquisition involves both an assertion of sovereignty and effective control over the territory in question.[2] That this was not the case means that Canada killed a prisoner of war, which even at that time (before the Geneva Convention) would most likely have been considered a violation of morality and international law.[3] A just account of the confrontation would show that Canada did not possess adequate governmental control over the territory when the Métis fought the Canadians, and as a result, the Métis were not rebels but the enemy in a war between nations.

Many historians have mistakenly characterized the confrontation as a Métis rebellion on the assumption that Canada had sovereignty over the territory that was the subject of conflict between Canada and the Métis nation.[4] Such statements, imbedded with the baggage of colonial thought, are no longer authoritative. Legal scholars, myself included, who have examined in greater depth the historical application of the legal criteria of territorial acquisition doctrine raise doubts about Canadian sovereignty in the prairies even as late as the 1890s. It is not at all clear who possessed governmental control in the prairie region at the time. At best, the territory was in transition, where small pockets of Canadian control may have existed. Indeed the very fact that the Métis fought and won battles before the final battle of Batoche, and the fact that Cree Chiefs also simultaneously asserted their authority in the area and effectively defied Canadian authority, is powerful evidence of a lack of effective governmental control. Even before the conflicts arose the Métis communities were self-governing and not dependent on Canada's authority as described below.

At the outset, I would like to point out that I do not believe the Métis Nation or communities should be asserting rights within the colonial framework of Canada or using Canada's colonial courts to obtain justice. The right of the Métis nation to exercise self-government, in my opinion, does not flow from any analysis of section 35 of the Constitution, which incidentally requires us to assert a claim to governance in a most undignified manner given the nature of the legal test to be met. It is a test that does not distinguish between an assertion of good governance for the people of the nation to live in harmony with one another and the assertion of an Aboriginal right claim to weave baskets. The fact that both claims must follow the same steps in proving the right in the face of Canadian legislation to the contrary is truly illogical and bewildering. As matters of great importance such as the right to be Métis (guaranteed by exercising the right of self-determination) or to uphold political and governmental authority, one would expect a legal test that is consonant with such fundamental rights. Under current Canadian Aboriginal rights doctrine, both sets of claims are treated equal in their status as Constitutional rights under s. 35.

The right of the Métis to exercise self-government is more appropriately established by international human rights doctrine than by relying on the colonially minded jurisprudence that the courts have adopted in defining s. 35. Within the framework of the Declaration on the Rights of Indigenous Peoples, the right to self-government is given prominence and the respect such an important and fundamental concept deserves. For example, several articles of the Declaration are relevant to the rights of Indigenous peoples to exercise self-government. They are:

ARTICLE 3:

Indigenous peoples have the right to self-determination. By virtue of that right they freely determine their political status and freely pursue their economic, social and cultural development.

ARTICLE 4:

Indigenous peoples, in exercising their right to self-determination, have the right to autonomy or self-government in matters relating to their internal and local affairs, as well as ways and means for financing their autonomous functions.

ARTICLE 26:

1. Indigenous peoples have the right to the lands, territories and resources which they have traditionally owned, occupied or otherwise used or acquired.

2. Indigenous peoples have the right to own, use, develop and control the lands, territories and resources that they possess by reason of traditional ownership or other traditional occupation or use, as well as those which they have otherwise acquired.[5]

There is no comparable level of respect accorded the right to self-government under the doctrine of Aboriginal rights as it is currently defined by Canadian courts in their interpretation of s. 35.

The limitations and reality, however, are that international norms are only as good as the degree to which a state recognizes those norms and abides by them. Canada did not vote in favour of the Declaration when it was presented to the United Nations General Assembly.[6] This disgraceful incident and subsequent actions are indicative of an obstinate Canadian government. One should not hold one's breath waiting for Canada to honour even such minimum human rights standards as contained in the Declaration.

Thus, from a practical perspective, Aboriginal peoples are forced to argue their rights using principles of law that flow from colonial, and I would contend racist, policies. Aboriginal rights doctrine currently does not question the "unilateral assertions of sovereignty" made by the English and Canadian Crowns as a result of the prevailing legal view at the time. Astonishingly, that perspective is still maintained, labelling Aboriginal peoples as not civilized enough to possess a legitimate international personality or to possess a competing sovereignty that would require diplomatic negotiations on the level of state-to-state relations. Canada's adherence to a colonial relationship with Aboriginal peoples violates the contemporary international human rights principle of equality of peoples and is thus an anomaly in international affairs, but one that Canada unconscionably continues to follow. It is inherently discriminatory based on human characteristics (culture, language, skin color, etc.) that are not germane to rational thought.

The adherence to the "doctrine of discovery" as this colonial legal understanding is sometimes called, is precisely why Canadian courts describe the treaties between Indigenous peoples and the Crown as *sui generis* and do not acknowledge them as international treaties. This view of the treaties has been noted and criticized by the United Nations which has studied treaties made by England and Indigenous nations and found that there is no logical basis for making a distinction between these and other international treaties.[7]

Notwithstanding the fundamentally inhumane nature of the doctrine of Aboriginal rights, it is still possible to uphold an Aboriginal right to Métis self-government today by applying the legal tests that inform the doctrine. In other words, the right of Métis communities to make a successful claim to an Aboriginal right to self-government is possible, even within the inequitable and distasteful framework of domestic Canadian Aboriginal rights doctrine.

Métis Rights to Self-Government

I have a right to hunt under the exclusive jurisdiction of the Manitoba Métis Federation (MMF). When I obtain my MMF-issued Métis Harvester's card, I plan on fishing and hunting in Red River territory. In doing so, I will be violating provincial hunting and fishing regulations because I do not plan on obtaining a provincial fishing or hunting license. This is fine because such provincial laws do not apply to me. The rules that apply to me are the rules that the Métis Nation, as represented by the Manitoba Métis Federation, have enacted regarding the management of certain natural resources in the province. Resource management is an evolving function of Métis governance under the MMF. Resource-harvesting rules are currently found in the document entitled "Interim Métis Laws of the Harvest" issued by the MMF after broad community-based consultations.[8]

From time to time—usually during periods of frustration at the lack of progress, either in the legal or political arena, in the movement toward Aboriginal self-government—legal and Aboriginal studies scholars proclaim that we (i.e. Aboriginal peoples) should just do it. In other words, as Aboriginal peoples we should just assert our jurisdiction without obtaining federal or provincial government consent. As a matter of principle, it is a most rewarding experience to see an Aboriginal government just do it as in the case of the Manitoba Métis Federation. Normally, however, Aboriginal governments are fiscally dependent on federal and provincial governments (often due to the historical failure of the Crown to honour its treaty commitments to them) and as a result are financially unable to "just do it." The Manitoba Métis Federation is in a good financial position these days and is able to afford to assert jurisdiction unilaterally; and it is within its right to do so absent provincial government agreement or consent. As a citizen of the MMF, I am very proud of the courage that my Métis government in Manitoba has shown and it stands as a model for other Aboriginal peoples in the ongoing struggle to achieve self-government by just doing it.

However, the Manitoba Métis Federation's independent assertion of autonomy is open to attack by a Canadian government that would have the MMF or its citizens prove their claim under Canadian domestic Aboriginal rights doctrine. Indeed, this attack happens fairly regularly as the MMF has vowed to represent any Métis citizen who is charged by provincial wildlife authorities for hunting while holding a valid MMF hunting permit provided the hunter was following the MMF's resource regulations. There are cases in Manitoba pending where the MMF is supporting hunters charged.[9] The defendants in these cases have no choice other than to raise Constitutional defences under section 35. The number of cases in Manitoba will continue to grow as long as there is no political resolution to the claims of the Métis. In other provinces, various resource-use agreements and policies have been established to allow Métis the right to hunt with agreed-upon restrictions, not unlike those that apply to the First Nations communities in those provinces.

In Manitoba, arguably the birthplace of the Métis nation, the province refuses to act honourably and arrive at a political solution even in the face of their own inquiries that have recommended such action.[10] The province's defiance of Métis' protected constitutional rights to hunt is difficult to comprehend given the clear direction of the Supreme Court of Canada in *Powley*[11] and the provinces of Ontario, Saskatchewan, and (until recently), Alberta's political accords recognizing the Métis citizens of those provinces' freedom to hunt as a manifestation of their Aboriginal status under the Constitution.

Thus, failing a political solution, the only real option in responding to the province's attack is to assert an Aboriginal rights defence under section 35 in the colonizer's courts. Direct defiance is usually not a serious option as such action would likely be too costly in terms of the hunter's life and livelihood as the colonizer maintains overwhelming manpower and firepower.

A right to hunt, relying on *Powley*, could be established and applied to the territory and community in which the Métis hunter belongs.[12] This would not be a difficult challenge to meet as there is considerable evidence to document Métis reliance on hunting, even for commercial purposes, before the advent of effective European control in the territory of the Northwest. However, it is an entirely different matter to assert that the Métis community—in this case, the MMF—has an Aboriginal right to govern its membership in the utilization of certain renewable resources. Courts have been fairly willing to recognize the right to engage in a "practice, custom, or tradition" as this does not, on the surface, threaten the federal or provincial government's regulatory authority; it simply curtails it as applies to the activity in question. On the assertion of a competing right to govern, however, the courts have been at best silent, or at worst ethnocentric, rendering decisions that presume the idea of a competing or overlapping authority in the hands of the Aboriginal group as preposterous.[13]

Asserting Métis Self-Governing Authority

The legal test for establishing an Aboriginal right is for the claimant to assert that his Aboriginal group possesses the right to practice an activity, custom, or tradition that existed prior to effective governmental control in the territory in question and that the practice continues to be of importance to the present day.[14]

The nature of the right being asserted by the MMF, for example, can be characterized as the right to govern and manage certain renewable resource uses by its citizens. The proper characterization of the right is particularly important in the case of asserted governance rights since the Supreme Court of Canada in *Pamajewon*[15] held that it was incapable of assessing self-government claims that were too broadly defined. In *Pamajewon,* the defendants argued that their respective First Nation governments had a broadly defined Aboriginal right to self-government which included the power to regulate gambling in the community. The Court said:

> The appellants [defendant First Nations] themselves would have this Court characterize their claim as to "a broad right to manage the use of their reserve lands". To so characterize the appellants' claim would be to cast the Court's inquiry at a level of excessive generality. Aboriginal rights, including any asserted right to self-government, must be looked at in light of the specific circumstances of each case and, in particular, in light of the specific history and culture of the aboriginal group claiming the right. The factors laid out in *Van der Peet*, and applied, *supra*, allow the Court to consider the appellants' claim at the appropriate level of specificity; the characterization put forward by the appellants would not allow the Court to do so.[16]

However, the MMF has not asserted a broad, all-encompassing right to self-government, but rather a specific and narrowly defined incident of self-government—management of certain renewable resources (primarily wildlife and fish). Arguably, the courts should be able to handle the less conceptually difficult analysis involved in this level of specificity.

In establishing the MMF's claim, it would be beneficial to show that the Métis Nation has traditionally exercised self-government generally and, in particular, the subject-matter area under dispute.

As the Métis Nation grew and developed during the 1800s, so, too, did the institutions that would support it. Elaborate and sophisticated legal and political institutions developed within the Métis communities that comprised the Métis Nation, including the development and organization of community law designed to meet local needs. The governance and legal systems of Métis communities were unique and distinct from both European and First Nations systems, although elements of both can be found in the laws and principles of Métis community government.

Métis communities' governance systems reflected several key values, some of which derive from the very nature of their emergence as a distinct people during the fur-trade era. The fur-trade system contributed to the growth of "freemen" fur-traders on the plains. These freemen married First Nations women, in part, to promote their position within the ranks of the various fur-trade companies and for companionship/partnership in the highly demanding lifestyle of a trader. The children of these unions inherited their father's penchant for freedom, a value that would become a fundamental characteristic of the Métis: Cree kin would often refer to them as *O-tee-paym-soo-wuk,* "their own-boss".[17] Consequently, Métis traditional governance was highly functional with formality of office only arising when necessary in situations where the tools of social order generally associated with smaller and familiar social interactions proved less effective.

Occasions that demanded more formal order took place as communities grew in size and diversity. A notable example of such a process is the community of St. Laurent along the South Saskatchewan River, which included the village of Batoche. Records kept by the local priest, and the careful recording of governance and law-making processes, include the codification of such laws in written form. The growth of this community, particularly after the failure of the Canadian government to implement the treaty of 1870 (with the Métis of Red River) resulted in many migrating to the Saskatchewan country, demanded more formal governance structures, which promoted certainty of expectations. Establishing formal authority structures and enforcement mechanisms facilitated this demand for clear expectations and certainty.

The government processes and much of the substantive content adopted by the St. Laurent community were based on traditions of governance that existed in the Métis community over decades—relied on in past spring seasons when the large-scale bison hunts were organized. The "Rules of the Buffalo Hunt", as they are commonly known, became an institution of the Métis during their bison hunting expeditions. Elements of plains Cree and Ojibway as well as English governance customs were used by the roaming Métis towns of the era.[18]

Cree and Ojibway influence is seen in the structure of the governance of the Métis community expeditions. According to Lawrence Barkwell, the Chief and Council of the plains Ojibway would meet and select one of the hunting party to act as Hunt Chief, whose authority would be paramount throughout the hunt.

> His appointment would last for the duration of that particular hunt. The hunt chief would then select several men to act as police (okitsita). Their duties were to keep order during the march, to watch the enemies and, most importantly, to prevent the younger men from rushing ahead and frightening the herd by firing in advance of the main party and thus spoiling the hunt for the whole band.[19]

The English and Canadian governance influence is evident in the selection processes. All participants gathered to *elect* the leaders who were called captains. The one vote, one person ideal of Western democracy was adopted by the Métis. The captains (often 10) would then name one of their ranks to be the leader of the council (president). Each captain would then appoint 10 soldiers to act as police and enforce the rules of the buffalo hunt and decisions of the council. The council, with the ratification of the Assembly, would then reinstate the rules of the buffalo hunt of previous expeditions, sometimes with minor changes. The Assembly was comprised of all the adult men and women of the community. All decisions had to be ratified and affirmed by the whole of the community before they became official. This adherence to inclusive direct democratic tradition was no doubt the influence of their First Nations kinfolk.[20] It is a tradition of governance that is still highly valued and is reflected in Métis regional and provincial assemblies throughout the homeland today. This democratic requirement is also included in the governing structure adopted by the Métis Settlements of Alberta.[21] For example, Métis Settlement Council bylaw-making decisions are required to be routinely ratified by the community as a whole.

It was the governance traditions of the buffalo hunt that were relied on by Métis communities when they grew and became more permanent as Métis families transitioned from primarily a hunting economy to a farming economy. When these larger, more permanent communities desired a more formal governing authority, they would rely on the tradition of using the Laws of the Buffalo Hunt as the basis for their constitutions.

One of the most well-known examples of this process is, again, the community of St. Laurent. The Community in Assembly would meet once a year (or in special cases other times) to elect their council and ratify all laws and decisions made by the council throughout the year. The first meeting of the Community in Assembly was 10 December 1873, and a constitution was created at that time. Over the years of its existence, laws were enacted that covered a variety of matters from contracts to more elaborate rules for the hunt including rules aimed at conservation, land allocation and use, family matters, and even tax laws.

Early Métis governance traditions were based on egalitarian principles including the recognition that English, French, and First Nations languages were all equally authoritative in official documentation, council meetings, and Community in Assembly. Moreover, all laws and decisions had to be ratified by the entire community and any serious matters needed community approval first. The community practiced a very direct and inclusive form of democracy still valued today as an important tradition of Métis governance.

When the laws were not explicit, the laws of the country (likely Cree or Ojibway) were relied on to fill in the gaps although there is no direct reference to this matter in the literature. Nevertheless, several factors point to the likelihood that this was the case, including references to the commonly relied-on marriage laws of the country. Early in the fur-trade history of the West, the marriage customs of the Cree and Ojibway, for example, were relied on over the distant customs of the English or Europeans. Métis families had close family ties to Ojibway or Cree communities and legal institutions. Moreover, languages of the Cree and Ojibway were understood and considered equally authoritative in the Métis communities. They still are in many Métis communities today (notwithstanding

Canada's insensitive *Official Languages Act* that recognizes only two official languages no doubt based on the endemic myth that there were only two founding nations: the English and the French).

Another factor suggesting that Cree and Ojibway customary law traditions were used in Métis communities to fill in the gaps of Métis specific declarations is that the substantive law, particularly the sanctions employed to ensure enforcement, were based on principles common to Cree and Ojibway societies, although there are also aspects of English or Canadian penal traditions.

In one of the few works documenting Métis traditional governance and laws, Mike Brogden describes Métis traditional justice as follows:

> Its predominant feature was that of mediation, of settling disputes with minimal harm to both parties, rather than of adjudication, of findings of guilt combined with punitive sanctions. Community law was concerned with the restoration of the integrity and harmony of the community, not with the stigmatization of individuals or families through convictions. A central principle was that of restitution. Article XIV, for example, passed on January 27, 1875, [by the St. Laurent Council] provided for the replacement for any horse wounded by another man. Restitution was combined with reparation. Article XIII, passed on the same date, required that where a personal injury was inflicted, the aggrieved party would have the services of the other until the wound was healed.[22]

People familiar with the traditional justice systems of Indigenous peoples in Canada would quickly observe the obvious parallels between these Métis sanctions and Indigenous traditions of resolving disputes that affect their social order.

Métis traditional government was comprised of a unique blending of Indigenous and European (English and French) governance traditions that, despite irreconcilable differences imbedded in the philosophies of each borrowed tradition, worked well and was meaningful to the values and worldview of this self-identifying mixed-blood people. Unfortunately, Canadian imperial aspirations would arise once more in the Northwest. It was not long before the continually evolving and adaptive Métis governance institutions would face a competing authority for governance in the area.

Advancing settlement in the West by Eastern Canadians and immigrants increased the likelihood that Métis community law and governance would conflict with English/Canadian government and law. In fact, the denial of Métis governance began as early as 1875. In the Métis community of St. Laurent, a local Hudson's Bay factor by the name of Lawrence Clarke broke one of the important bison hunting laws. As a result, Gabriel Dumont and others pursued and arrested Clarke. He was fined under Métis community law. However, Clarke complained to the Canadian government via the office of the newly formed

Commissioner of the North West Mounted Police. His letter to the commissioner called for the denial of the legitimacy of Métis law:

> [The Métis] have assumed to themselves the right to make such laws, rules and regulations, for the ... colony and adjoining country of a most tyrannical nature which the minority of settlers are perforce to obey ... This [St. Laurent] court pretends to have the power to enforce the laws on all Indians, settlers and hunters, who frequent the Prairie country in the lower section of the Saskatchewan, and have levied by violence and robbery large sums of money off inoffensive persons who resort to the buffalo country...[23]

Although the Canadian government thought Clarke was somewhat overzealous in his efforts to discredit the Métis, federal officials nonetheless sanctioned Gabriel Dumont by giving him a small fine as a penalty for his actions against Clarke. As Brogden notes:

> Despite the minimal penalty, the result was to undermine the legal process of the Métis community. A North West Mounted Police post was established nearby, symbolizing the extension of the Dominion law and the denigration of communal justice.[24]

Henceforth, the autonomous governance system of the Métis would be viewed as a threat to the Canadian state. The legal system of Canada, as enforced by the better-equipped and more numerous NWMP was to be regarded as the only legitimate government regime in the West. The Métis, however, perceived the NWMP as the coercive arm of a foreign and alien government that had no business interfering with the existing government and processes of their community. It was the Canadian system that was perceived as illegitimate to the Métis. As denial of Métis community government and institutions grew, so, too, did the resistance to that denial. Conflict seemed inevitable. And this conflict between legitimate government institutions was likely a factor that led to the Métis of the Northwest to take up arms when Canada refused to negotiate in peace.

Some might suggest that this history of confrontation supports a view that effective government control under the *Powley* case took place in 1875 when Gabriel Dumont was fined as described above. It does reflect the ability of the Canadian government to effectively assert authority in the area. However, as the events of 1885 show, this authority was tenuous. The determination of a cut-off date (the point in time when the Canadian government established effective government control) is a very important part of establishing Aboriginal rights and cannot be taken lightly.

The international law of prescription offers a principle that we can logically apply here to help assist us in ensuring that we have confidence in the cut-off date being offered. Prescription is one recognized means for a nation to acquire sovereignty and territorial acquisition in circumstances where there already exists a sovereign nation with a government and claimed territory. For the acquisition of territory by prescription to succeed, "[t]here must be, positively, an actual assertion of sovereignty supported by its exercise for a long period, and there must be, negatively, an acquiescence in the claim by the other party."[25]

A qualifying time period may provide the level of assurance that the transition to Canadian government authority was truly effective and enforceable and not merely a temporary intrusion that did not possess the character of permanency to warrant being described as effective government control. Despite the Clarke affair of 1875, the events of 1885 suggest that the Canadian government's control was insufficient to justify confidence in 1875 as being the appropriate cut-off date.

Perhaps a qualifying period of ten to fifteen years later, would be apposite and logical for determining a date at which the Canadian government could be considered possessed of effective government control in the Saskatchewan prairie lands. This would mean that 1895 to 1900 is a reasonable "cut-off date" as required by *Powley* for assessing the Aboriginal rights of the Métis in this area of the country. It is arguable that the date may be sooner in more Eastern and Southern districts and possibly later in more Northern and remote parts of the country, and for some very remote locations, perhaps the cut-off date of effective Canadian government control did not emerge until well into the 20th century. Thus, Métis customs, practices, and traditions, including the tradition of self-government, would need to have been established—as far as the Métis of the Saskatchewan valley is concerned—around 1895-1900. Thus, by the time Canada was able to exert control, a Métis government tradition was in place and while suppressed for many decades afterwards, continued to exist until 1982 when the Constitution was amended to include the protection of Aboriginal and Treaty rights. After 1982, Aboriginal rights cannot be extinguished by the unilateral actions of Canadian governments. It may have been possible for the governments to extinguish the right between 1900 and 1982 by expressly declaring so, but there is no legislation that expressly extinguished the Métis right to self-government during this period. If such Aboriginal rights were not extinguished between 1895/1900 and 1982, then they would be constitutionally protected from government infringement today.

The cut-off date may be earlier in the Red River valley where the question of the MMF's assertion of government over resource use, reflected in the practice of issuing MMF hunting permits to its citizens, is currently at issue. There are additional factors, beyond the scope of this chapter, that would need to be assessed to establish the appropriate cut-off date for the historically rich and diverse area of Red River, but most likely it would be sometime after 1870 when the province of Manitoba was created as a result of the treaty between the Métis and Canada. Regardless, I am positive that a tradition of Métis community governance in the area of hunting and resource use was established well before 1870 as the documentation regarding the "rules of the buffalo hunt" attest.

I promise that I will hunt in Manitoba with a MMF hunting permit and not a provincial one in the future and I will do so without fear of breaking the law of the province since it does not apply to me as a citizen of the Métis Nation manifest in the governance of the Manitoba Métis Federation. This I will do for my child.

NOTES

1   For example see J. R. Miller, *Skyscrapers Hide the Heavens* (Toronto: University of Toronto Press, 1989), 180.
2   See Larry Chartrand, "Métis Aboriginal Title in Canada," in *Advancing Aboriginal Claims,* ed. Kerry Wilkins (Saskatoon: Purich Publishing, 2004), 151.
3   See Daniel Moran, "The Geneva Convention, POWs, and the War on Terrorism," *Strategic Insights* 1, no. 7 (Sept 2002).
4   See in particular, Miller, *Skyscrapers Hide the Heavens.* Miller states that there was "little doubt that Canada was the effective government in the North-West Territories," 180. This statement conjures up a similar statement made by the Supreme Court of Canada in *R. v. Sparrow,* [1990] 1 S.C.R. 1075 at p. 1103, where the Court said that there was "never any doubt that sovereignty and legislative power, and indeed the underlying title, to such lands vested in the Crown." This arrogant colonial view of legal and political national status has been subsequently criticized by legal scholars who have explored the issue of territorial acquisition doctrine under International law and English colonial law more closely. They have found such assertions wanting of fact and legal validity. See, for example, Kent McNeil, "Aboriginal Nations and Quebec's Boundaries: Canada Couldn't Give What It Didn't Have" in *Negotiating with a Sovereign Quebec,* eds. Daniel Drache & Roberto Perin (Toronto: Lorimer & Company, 1992), 107. See also my "Métis Aboriginal Title in Canada," where I extend the arguments established by McNeil to the circumstances of the Northwest.
5   Declaration on the Rights of Indigenous Peoples, United Nations General Assembly, 61st Session (Res/61/295). For a copy of the Resolution and text of the Declaration see http://www.ohchr.org/english/issues/indigenous/declaration.htm (accessed 20 November 2007).
6   The Declaration was adopted on 17 September 2007 by the United Nations General Assembly. The UN Declaration was adopted by a majority of 144 states in favour, 4 votes against (Australia, Canada, New Zealand, and the United States) and 11 abstentions (Azerbaijan, Bangladesh, Bhutan, Burundi, Colombia, Georgia, Kenya, Nigeria, Russian Federation, Samoa, and Ukraine).
7   Special Rappateur, Martinez, Miguel Alfonso, *Study on Treaties, Agreements and Other Constructive Arrangements* (Final Report), (E/CN.4/Sub.2/1999/20; 22 June 1999), www.unhchr.ch/Huridocda/Huridoca.nsf/0/696c51cf6f20b8bc802567c4003793ec?Opendocument.
8   Interim laws found at http://www.mmf.mb.ca/publications/MMF.Harvest.Guide.1.0.pdf.
9   For example, see the Will Goodon case, currently at the Manitoba provincial court level, discussed on the Manitoba Métis Federation website at http://www.mmf.mb.ca.
10 Powley Implementation Committee, Province of Manitoba, *Regarding Métis Harvesting Rights in the Province of Manitoba,* (August 31, 2005). [unpublished]
11 2003 SCC 43.
12 I have addressed the issue of level of community and territorial scope a Métis defendant could assert in the prairies: options range from local Métis community such as Camperville to Métis regional community (such as Zone 4), to Métis provincial community, to Métis nation of the prairies (encompassing all the local, regional and provincial Métis communities). All levels are valid as long as the legal tests are satisfied. My preference is to assert the claim at the nation level.
13 See for example, *R. v. Nikal,* [1996] 3 C.N.L.R. 178 (S.C.C.).
14 *R. v. Van der Peet,* [1996] 4 C.N.L.R. 177 (S.C.C.).
15 *R. v. Pamajewon,* [1996] 4 C.N.L.R. 164 (S.C.C.).
16 *Ibid.,* para. 27.
17 John E. Foster, "The Plains Métis" in *Native Peoples: The Canadian Experience,* eds. R. Bruce Morrison and C. Roderick Wilson (Toronto: Oxford University Press, 2004), 301.
18 I refer to roaming towns as this notion seems appropriate to illustrate the size of some of these expeditions. For example, Barkwell references documentary evidence of Alexander Ross in *Alexander Ross, The Red River Settlement* (Reprint of the 1856 Smith Elder & Co. edition, Edmonton, Hurtig, 248) who reported that the expedition that left Red River in 1840 comprised of some 1,630 people and 1,210 Red River carts along with all the other necessary items needed for a roaming life during the summer on the prairies. Lawrence Barkwell, "Early Law and Social Control Among the Métis" in *The Struggle for Recognition: Canadian Justice and the Métis Nation,* eds. Samuel Corrigan and Lawrence Barkwell (Winnipeg: Manitoba Métis Federation, 1991), 15.
19 Barkwell, 31.

20 George Woodcock, *Gabriel Dumont* (Edmonton: Hurtig Publishers, 1976), 34.

21 See Catherine Bell, *Alberta's Métis Settlements Legislation: An Overview of Ownership and Management of Settlement Lands* (Regina: Canadian Plains Research Center, 1994).

22 Mike Brogden, "The Rise and Fall of the Western Métis in the Criminal Justice Process" in *The Struggle for Recognition: Canadian Justice and the Métis Nation,* eds. Samuel Corrigan and Lawrence Barkwell (Winnipeg: Manitoba Métis Federation, 1991), 45.

23 *Ibid.*, 46. The reference to violence must be seen from the perspective of the writer and is a mischaracterization of the monopoly all governments possess in their police who use violence to enforce the legitimate laws of the state when necessary to do so.

24 *Ibid.*, 47.

25 D. P. O'Connell, *International Law,* Vol. 1 (London: Stevens and Sons, 1965), 488 [emphasis in original omitted].

THE FUTURE OF FISCAL FEDERALISM:

Funding Regimes for Aboriginal Self-Government

Frances Abele, Carleton University
& Michael J. Prince, University of Victoria

I n the pursuit of Aboriginal self-government, fiscal matters and relationships are fundamental. Financing is central to several pressing issues in Canada today: upholding the fiduciary obligation of the Crown to Aboriginal peoples; building economic and social capacity, and rebuilding cultures and languages across many communities; and, negotiating honourable treaties between Canada and Aboriginal peoples to replace colonial attitudes, laws, and structures.

The last forty years have brought major changes to the relationship between Aboriginal peoples in Canada and the various institutions of the Crown. In response to Aboriginal political activism and a long public renegotiation of the balance of political power, the Constitution has been revised, twenty-one modern treaties negotiated, and new public and ethnically exclusive governments created. These changes are reflected also in different standards of accommodation of Aboriginal people and their institutions in Canadian political and economic life. While much remains to be resolved, in jurisprudence and institutional development, there have been significant innovations and improvements.

A massive piece of limiting unfinished business concerns the manner in which the various forms of Aboriginal self-government are financed. As Dene leader and former Northwest Territories premier Stephen Kakfwi observed several years ago:

> Once you have [an idea of the type of political institutions that you need] it also becomes apparent that you don't want to live on a handout and that free housing and free education and free government does not exist any-where in the world. It does not lead to independent, self-reliant individu-als and families and communities. So I mean a government by itself, an agreement (for self-government) by itself doesn't do anything.... Governments need to be financed, they have to be economical and afford-able and they have to be workable. And the people that want to govern themselves have to accept that responsibility.[1]

The need for an independent source of revenue to complete the realization of self-determination is widely recognized. A growing sector of Aboriginal enterprises (held collectively, publicly, and privately), and a network of diverse Aboriginal entrepreneurs and economic policy makers, has emerged. Modern treaty beneficiary organizations manage their members' collectively held capital—funds transferred over (typically) twenty-year periods in substantial amounts in compensation for surrendered lands. Their investments comprise regional transportation or other infrastructure companies, local food production enterprises, real estate development, and a variety of other ventures. The beneficiary organizations manage collectively held capital in trust, and through their investments make an important contribution to regional economies. Many Treaty First Nations operate businesses on and off reserve, through special purpose organizations or development corporations. There is also a growing community of Aboriginal entrepreneurs who operate on and off reserves and traditional territories.[2] In 2001, there were over 27,000 self-employed Aboriginal people in Canada—4.2 per cent of the working-age population, representing an increase of 31 per cent in five years.[3] In addition, the Aboriginal business sector is differentiating. Aboriginal capital corporations provide loans and other assistance, as well as links with mainstream Canadian financial institutions. Over the last twenty years, federal governments have made substantial investments in this sector, usually through "status blind" programs—that is, economic development programs available to Métis, Inuit, and First Nations. In 2005, for example, the federal government reported an investment of approximately $600 million per year in Aboriginal economic development programs delivered through eleven departments and agencies. These programs provide business development assistance, access to capital, infrastructure provision, and skills and technology transfer.[4]

To the extent that Aboriginal businesses generate economic activity on collectively held lands, on reserve, and in Aboriginal communities, they are contributing to the capacity of Aboriginal governments to generate own-source revenues.[5] In addition to relying upon own-source or self-collected revenues, however, virtually all Aboriginal governments in Canada will require transfers from the federal government. In this need they are no different from provincial and municipal governments. Even the richest jurisdictions in the country—the "have" provinces of Alberta, British Columbia and Ontario—receive various transfer payments each year from the federal government. Where Aboriginal governments currently are atypical is in the different rationale that is applied to transfers to them, a circumstance that we believe is unacceptable and counterproductive. There remain important areas of inefficiency and friction, and in many cases the system for transferring funds from the federal to Aboriginal governments is weaker and less effective than the measures that prevail for provinces and municipalities.[6]

In this chapter, we first identify four main pathways to self-determination that are under discussion and under development (to differing degrees) in Canada.[7] Each pathway or model is subject to a different funding regime and even different funding principles. We will describe these funding forms as part of the current overall federal system for intergovernmental fiscal management. We conclude with a discussion of recent trends and their possible implications for the future of fiscal federalism.

Four Models of Self-Government

Understood as pathways to Aboriginal self-determination, each of the four models of self-government comprise a kind of ideal type—an amalgam of ideas about what should be, and about existing and planned practical arrangements.

Features/ Models	Mini- Municipalities	Adapted Federalism	Third Order of Government	Nation to Nation
Notion of sovereignty	Shared between two orders of Canadian government	Shared between two orders of Canadian government	Shared among three orders of government within Canadian federation	Parallel set of two sovereign confederations in a given territory
Origin of law-making powers	Canadian constitution	Canadian constitution	Canadian constitution and some Aboriginal laws and customs	Co-equal sets of Canadian and Aboriginal rules and practices
Basis of Aboriginal- Canada relations	*Constitution Act, 1867 Indian Act, 1876* Other federal laws	*Constitution Act 1867* and *1982* Historic and Modern Treaties *Inherent Rights Policy*	*Constitution Act 1867* and *1982* Historic and Modern Treaties *Inherent Rights Policy*	*Royal Proclamation, 1763* Historic and Modern Treaties *Constitution Act, 1982*
Nature of the relationship	Assimilative neo-colonial	Integrative modified public governments express Aboriginal values and priorities	Integrative Aboriginal governments as semi-sovereign	Coexisting distinct yet co-operative self-governing nations
Source, scope and nature of Aboriginal government powers	Delegated limited bylaws mainly over local concerns	Negotiated mix of jurisdictions and authorities over internal, cultural, and external matters	Negotiated mix of jurisdictions and authorities over internal, cultural, and external matters	Inherent and negotiated comprehensive separate and shared powers
Citizenship status of Aboriginal Peoples	A continued uncertain and tenuous common Canadian citizenship	Canadian citizenship plus rights and obligations under modern treaties	"Citizens plus" possibly a negotiated form of dual citizenship	Distinct citizenship regimes
Concept of Canadian polity and federalism	*BNA Act* federalism centralist if not colonialist relations	Modern federalism asymmetrical	Three-sided federalism administrative/ co-operative relations	Association between two federations: Treaty federalism and *BNA Act* federalism

Figure 1. The four models of Aboriginal self-determination

Each of the four models refers to Aboriginal forms of government upon a defined land base or within a specific territory. They do not describe emergent forms of urban governance. About half of First Nations members and Métis live in small or large Canadian cities, as do a smaller proportion of Inuit. While there has been some discussion of the possible emergence of pan-Aboriginal urban governments, as well as other urban forms, we are not aware of any serious plans to create Aboriginal urban governments, or any models of how these would work.[8] We choose to include self-government for Aboriginal city-dwellers as an aspect of each model. That is, for example, some Aboriginal people who are living in cities are members of groups who have chosen the public government approach to self-government, compatible with our "adapted federalism" model; others are members of First Nations whose treaty places them in a nation-to-nation relationship with the Canadian federation.[9]

The four models range along a continuum, from least independent to most independent, and from most common in practice to existing only in prospect. We describe the models in this order.[10]

The "mini-municipality" model refers to small Aboriginal governments embedded in federalism-as-usual. We use the term "mini" to recognize the generally very small size of the polities who have chosen or continue to accept this model, and the term municipality acknowledges the place of these polities in federalism: they exercise devolved powers from either the federal or provincial orders of government. Examples include the band, or *Indian Act* governments that prevail in most of Canada, and the Métis settlements that exist by virtue of a set of agreements and legislation between Métis in Alberta and that provincial government. The mini-municipality model is certainly the most common, and probably the least popular, form of Aboriginal self-government in existence, and almost everyone sees it as at best a way station or transitional model on the road to something better.

The adapted federalism model entails, as the name implies, a modification to the existing bilateral federation by the addition of a new jurisdiction to accommodate an Aboriginal collectivity. To date, the only existing example is found in Canada's Arctic.[11] In 1999, the former Northwest Territories was divided to create two new territories, Nunavut in the east and a smaller Northwest Territories in the west. This change occurred as a direct consequence of a modern treaty, the *Nunavut Land Claims Agreement* (1993),[12] negotiated between the Inuit of Nunavut and the Government of Canada. Both resulting governments are "public governments;" that is, they are not exclusive to any particular society or ethnic group.[13] In both cases, too, Aboriginal people may rely upon a pronounced demographic advantage and governing traditions that are beginning to make adequate room for Aboriginal aspirations.

The third order of government or trilateral federalism model involves not only the addition of new political entities to the existing federation, but the re-creation of the federation itself. The Canadian federation would become a trilateral federation, with Aboriginal self-governments forming a third order of government alongside the federal and provincial orders. The idea has a long history, going back at least as far as 1983 proposals by the Nishga Tribal Council (as it was then called) and the Assembly of First Nations which were endorsed by a House of Commons special committee.[14] A similar concept was enshrined in the unsuccessful Charlottetown Accord, and in milder form, in the 1995 federal policy statement on the inherent right of self-government.[15] This 1995 policy (and the 1996 final report of the Royal Commission on Aboriginal Peoples) contains an emerging theory of the division of powers and authorities among three orders. The Nisga'a Treaty government was arguably the first working example of trilateral federalism, since joined by the Tlicho and Nunatsiavut governments in Northwest Territories and Labrador respectively.[16]

The nation-to-nation model sees Aboriginal governments as part of a treaty-based alliance between the Aboriginal governments and the Crown in Canada. The treaty relationship is understood to be the governing constitutional relationship, with all else, including the Canadian Constitution, subject to this. Current constitutional provisions recognizing "existing aboriginal and treaty rights" acknowledge the nation-to-nation relationship, but do not create it. Indeed, the provisions on Aboriginal and treaty rights are embedded within the Canadian Constitution, rather than outside and alongside it, which is the vision of the nation-to-nation model as understood here. The nation-to-nation model has its committed advocates, and for some Aboriginal peoples in Canada, it is probably the only acceptable model.[17] At the moment, in Canadian politics and public policy, the nation-to-nation model exists only as a vision of what could be, combined with a particular interpretation of the meaning of the historic and numbered treaties. This is an interpretation shared by some analysts but not embedded in federal policy or arrangements. We explore the potential fiscal aspects of this model, necessarily, in entirely hypothetical fashion.

The Intergovernmental Fiscal Regime

Adopting a broad view of fiscal federalism, grounded in the law, economics, practical politics, and social policy of the country, intergovernmental financial relations include the following elements:[18]

1. The constitutional allocation and division of legislative powers and associated expenditure roles and responsibilities between the levels of government. This division of powers organizes much of Canada's social policy, including the program and service activities of the welfare state and expenditures on education at all levels. Here the federal spending power—constitutionally authorized federal spending in areas of provincial jurisdiction—is also important.

2. The constitutional allocation and division of taxing and borrowing powers, thus specifying the revenue sources available to each order of government.

3. Agreements for the collection and disbursement of revenues, and the coordination and harmonization of income and sales tax systems among governments.

4. The transfer of tax points ("tax room") from the federal government to provincial governments.

5. Equalization payments from the federal government to provincial governments with fiscal capacities determined to be below a national average.

6. Intergovernmental transfer payments from the federal government to provincial and territorial governments. These payments may be conditional specific-purpose grants, semi-conditional general-purpose grants, or unconditional block grants.

7. Federal programs of Canada-wide application that are designed to respond "automatically" to changes in need. The archetypal example of this kind of program is Employment Insurance, a fund created by contributions from employers and workers that is distributed to unemployed workers according to pre-established criteria and on individual application.

8. Executive federalism, the political and administrative structures and processes for consultation, bargaining, planning and, at times, making joint decisions about intergovernmental fiscal arrangements, economic and social policy, and procedural relationships: the "rules of the game."

The principles underlying the federation and the details of its operating principles are often the subject of dispute, but all parties recognize the necessity for a constitutionally determined, orderly sharing of resources and responsibilities among the two orders of government in the federation, and among "have" and "have-not" provinces.[19] Similar principles animate virtually every federation in the world, part of the necessary practical glue that holds them together.

It is perhaps not a large step from these principles to recognize that Aboriginal governments, especially those new governments that are the hope-laden results of long negotiation and earnest development, should logically be included in fiscal federalism. But, just as evidently, changes to the federation's fiscal arrangements to incorporate fully Aboriginal governments of any form will be no simple matter. First, constitutional amendment to include Aboriginal governments in the fiscal federation is unlikely, given the arduous nature of constitutional change and the high political costs of opening such a question particularly in the contentious and vexed area of division of powers. Fortunately, though, some large changes in financing arrangements can happen without constitutional amendment: we have the examples of the Yukon First Nations, Nisga'a, Tlicho, Nunavik, Nunavut, and Nunatsiavut governments, all created pursuant to modern treaties and therefore constitutionally protected—but realized without formal constitutional amendment.[20]

A second complication arises from the complexity and number of mechanisms themselves. Bringing Aboriginal governments into the federal system will require innovations or augmentation to a number of massive financial transfer programs, including but not limited to the complex systems of equalization and transfers in health and social services. In fact, most of the items in the list of eight features of fiscal federalism, above, will have to be adapted. And since Aboriginal governments are all much smaller than any of the other participating governments, special mechanisms for including them will have to be developed.[21]

As we have written elsewhere,[22] including Aboriginal governments of any kind in the policy deliberations and bureaucratic negotiations that fuel federalism immediately raises questions of aggregation and representation. There are many small to extremely tiny Aboriginal governments in Canada; the institutions of federalist interaction could not accommodate their numbers, nor could most of them muster the staff resources to enter the process. Again, political leadership and institutional innovation are required. These difficulties notwithstanding, finding ways to fund Aboriginal self-government through mechanisms that are part of, or very similar to, those of fiscal federalism has a number of advantages, including greater fiscal stability and predictability, and the practical autonomy and planning support that arises from these conditions.

Fortunately, there is substantial experience and experimentation with the negotiation and implementation of financial agreements between federal governments and Aboriginal organizations. Not all of this experience has been positive, as is evident from the law suit launched by Nunavut Tunngavik Incorporated against the federal government for its failure to live up to financial commitments in the Nunavut Agreement, and from research conducted on the implementation of the *Council for Yukon First Nations Agreement*.[23] Unfortunately, implementation of the modern treaties has been assigned to a very small branch of the Department of Indian Affairs and Northern Development which lacks sufficient coordination and evaluation capacity. Nevertheless, experience has accumulated which can be used to inform the development of new mechanisms to transfer funds to modern treaty institutions and to other Aboriginal institutions.[24]

Four Ways to Fund Aboriginal Self-Government?

Peering into Canada's political future, we should anticipate a diverse and fluid set of approaches to financing Aboriginal self-governments, just as there are varied approaches in federal-provincial fiscal relations and in federal-territorial fiscal relations. Each of the four models of self-determination incorporates a distinctive approach to funding. At present, the models also represent varying degrees of realization. There are many existing examples of mini-municipality-style funding, just one of adapted federalism, perhaps four nascent third-order funding regimes, and none that would conform to the regime envisioned under a nation-to-nation approach.

	Mini-Municipalities	Adapted Federalism	Third Order of Government	Nation-to-Nation
Underlying principles	Federal minister remains responsible; capacity development	Adaptation of equalization to small population base; high-cost government	Full extension of executive and fiscal federalism	Fiscal relationship mirrors political one; transfers considered to be "rent" or compensation payments; assumption of significant own-source revenues
Funding mechanism	Devolution of administrative responsibility by way of funding agreements, "contracting out"	Multi-year formula funding agreements	Equalization; automatic inclusion in programs of national application	Multi-year agreements; many shared-cost programs
Degree of autonomy	Low: annual reporting, overall management in federal bureaucracy; control at a distance	Moderate: federal government controls quantum and formula; some negotiation possible	High: Many automatic transfers; full jurisdiction over spending priorities and patterns	Very high: Transfer of funds an entitlement, in perpetuity

Figure 2: Funding regimes for the four models

Figure 2 illustrates the ways in which the four models differ in terms of the funding mechanisms and the degree of autonomy that these provide. At this very high level of abstraction, it is possible to imagine a set of reforms, achieved over time, which would accommodate the full range of institutional situations. It is important to recognize, though, that movement toward the "regularization" of funding regimes for Aboriginal governments will require some changes in prevailing thinking and usual ways of managing change—and most importantly of all, perhaps, a commitment to sustained innovation and program development over many years. In this respect, the incorporation into the federation of Aboriginal governments would follow the pattern of "province building" and federal adjustment that characterized earlier Canadian development. Most provinces took many decades to develop a modern capacity for management and policy development.

Canadian governments and many in the political and bureaucratic elites bring a number of expectations to the reform project. These include, first, an expectation of phased elimination of certain tax relief measures—for example, elimination of personal tax exemptions for First Nations registered members who live on reserve. These tax exemptions originated in the historic treaties; they do not exist for Métis or Inuit, and they have not been incorporated in any of the modern treaties negotiated by First Nations since 1975. Personal tax exemptions will not likely be seen to be compatible with the entry of First Nation governments into the system of fiscal federalism.

A likely second expectation is the gradual expansion of own-source revenues through an active taxing power and revenue collection by Aboriginal governments. Stephen Kakfwi raised this prospect in the interview from which we quoted at the beginning of this chapter, and many Aboriginal and other leaders would support the principle that he is expressing. It is one, of course, that will be much easier for some governments than others. For example, the Government of Nunavut—which we include in our categorization of pathways to self-determination because it is a public government format chosen by an Aboriginal collectivity and protected in a modern treaty—is currently seeking control over Crown lands and natural resources.[25] Eventually this step will provide the territory with substantial own-source revenues. The Nisga'a and Tlicho agreements, among others, similarly provide the signatories with the ability to develop natural resources at their own pace and in their own interests——and they refer to territories that are large enough to provide significant economic opportunities. On the other hand, virtually all First Nations reserves and Métis Settlements are small relative to their populations and compared to other jurisdictions. Absent the rent-taking opportunities that come with substantial and profitable natural resources (such as oil and natural gas), most reserves will struggle to generate sufficient own-source income. First Nation reserves are seeking answers to this problem—essentially one of economic development—in the expansion of their land holdings, including the acquisition of land in cities, and in efforts to develop high-value-added, reserve-based businesses and niche industries.[26]

The connection between economic vitality and self-determination mentioned by Stephen Kakfwi is strong and widely recognized. A quick survey of the Canada-wide experience in this regard yields many interesting examples of the importance of economic enterprise to collective self-determination. For example, the business success of the Inuvialuit of the Northwest Territories, based on investments of the funding received pursuant to their 1984 modern treaty, has sustained their strong presence in the regional economy and in those public institutions that they have identified as important, particularly co-management boards.

Making the Transition: The Route to Reform

Over the last several decades, many activists and observers have held the view that self-determination through revitalized treaties and the negotiation of new political arrangements was the first step toward solving the terrible social problems on many reserves, and improving the generally poor social indicators for Aboriginal people as a whole. To this had been added the conviction, expressed in the Aboriginal Healing Foundation and other measures, that the profound damage inflicted by certain colonial practices had to be repaired before the promise of self-determination—and the means for a healthy life—could be realized. It is also recognized that a third, concomitant measure has to be economic development sufficient to support these other processes of change. This insight is hardly new: it has been expressed by Aboriginal entrepreneurs—in word and deed—for many decades. The contribution of this present chapter, though, is to indicate some of the ways in which economic and political decolonization are joined, and to highlight the importance of attending to the adequate incorporation of Aboriginal governments in the fiscal federation. This is the unfinished business that lies before us.

In this chapter we have noted the need for practice-based research and development into the full range of past and current experience with various funding regimes, and we have stressed that the variety of constitutional arrangements under development suggests that a variety of specific mechanisms must be developed. This work should be undertaken with specific goals firmly in mind. A set of such goals was proposed by the Royal Commission on Aboriginal Peoples. The Commission identified five objectives for financing Aboriginal governments:[27]

- *Self-reliance* by encouraging the development of independent sources of revenue;
- *Equity* in the distribution of resources among and between Aboriginal governments and between Aboriginal and non-Aboriginal people as a whole;
- *Efficiency* in the use of limited resources for service delivery;
- *Accountability* for the use of public funds and for revenue decisions; and
- *Harmonization and co-operation* with adjacent jurisdictions with respect to program and service standards, and tax policies

These principles should underlie the development of a national fiscal framework for Aboriginal governments. The framework should respect the differing choices expressed by Aboriginal collectivities in the forms of self-government that they have chosen, and endeavour to support these by developing enabling mechanisms and practical solutions to long-term problems. Such reform would take all the parties away from the episodic, confrontational, position-protecting, highly guarded style of interaction that characterizes treaty and specific claims negotiations and their implementation to date. Rather, the parties need to move onto the broad plain of Canadian constitutional tradition—pragmatic rather than elegant, incremental rather than "once and for all", and, paradoxically, dedicated to respect for difference in a constitutional setting that provides one law for all.

NOTES

1   Stephen Kakfwi quoted in Lauri Sarkadi, "What Goes Around ... Comes Around," *The Far North Oil and Gas Review* Winter (2000): 25.

2   For an indication of the vitality and breadth of this sector, see http://www.aboriginalcanada.ca.

3   Treasury Board Secretariat 2005. As a proportion of the working-age population, Aboriginal self-employment, at 4.2 per cent, is less than the 7.8 per cent Canadian average for self-employment.

4   See Backgrounder: Federal Aboriginal Economic Development Programs, http://www.pco-bcp.gc.ca (accessed 15 September 2005).

5   Métis and Inuit governments have the power to tax in their territories, as do the Aboriginal parties who have negotiated modern treaties. Since a 1988 amendment to the *Indian Act,* First Nations band governments have

had the power to tax, though the situation remains complicated. See Michael J. Prince & Frances Abele, "Funding an Aboriginal Order of Government in Canada: Recent Developments in Self-Government and Fiscal Relations," in *Canada: The State of the Federation 1999/2000*, ed. Harvey Lazar (Montreal & Kingston: McGill-Queen's University Press, 2000), 337-67. Métis governments in Alberta—the eight Settlement Councils—have authority to impose certain taxes, levies, fees, and charges, with some of these revenues eligible for matching payments from the provincial government. See the *Métis Settlements Act*, RSA, chapter M-14, 2000 and the *Métis Settlements Accord Implementation Act*, RSA, chapter M-15, 2000.

6   For a thorough study of the series of accountability regimes applied to First Nations' financing, see Robert P. Shepherd, "Moving Tenuously Toward Lasting Self-Government: Understanding Differences to Implementing Accountability" (Ph.D. diss., University of Toronto, 2006).

7   We discuss these four pathways in more detail in Frances Abele & Michael J. Prince, "Four Pathways to Aboriginal Self-Government in Canada," *American Review of Canadian Studies* 36, no. 4 (2006): 568-95.

8   The only discussion of possible forms of urban self-government that we are aware of is in the Royal Commission on Aboriginal Peoples, *Final Report*, Vol. 2, part 2, 273-78; and vol. 4, chap 7, 519-613.

9   As the size of urban Aboriginal populations increases, and as successive generations are born into the urban milieu, it is quite possible that a distinct urban Aboriginal identity and sense of political purpose, which is not accommodated within our four models, may indeed emerge. See, for example, Chris Andersen, "Residual Tensions of Empire: Contemporary Métis Communities and the Canadian Judicial Imagination," in *Reconfiguring Aboriginal-State Relations: Canada: The State of the Federation, 2003*, ed. Michael Murphy (Montreal & Kingston: Institute of Intergovernmental Relations, School of Policy Studies, Queen's University, McGill-Queen's University Press, 2005), 295-325.

10   See Figure 1 for more detail.

11   The development of Canada occurred through the addition of territories and provinces to the original four federating colonies of 1867, and of course the formation of the Province of Manitoba in 1871 represents the first direct addition to the federation that came about through the political activism of an Aboriginal group, in this case the Métis.

12   *Agreement between the Inuit of the Nunavut Settlement Area and Her Majesty the Queen in Right of Canada*. (Canada: Indian Affairs and Northern Development, and Tunngavik Federation of Nunavut, 1993), http://www.inac.gc.ca/pr/agr/nunavut/index_e.html (accessed 15 September 2007).

13   For more discussion of Nunavut, see Jens Dahl, Jack Hicks & Peter Jull, *Nunavut: Inuit Regain Control of their Lands and Their Lives* (Copenhagen: International Work Group for Indigenous Affairs, 2000).

14   Canada, *Indian Self-Government in Canada*, Report of the Special Committee. (Ottawa: Queen's Printer, 1983). This study is often called the Penner Report, after the name of the chair, Liberal Member of Parliament, Keith Penner.

15   This policy declares federal recognition of the inherent right to self-government as an existing Aboriginal right, found in section 35 of the *Constitution Act, 1982*, as well as in treaties and in the Crown's fiduciary relationship with treaty First Nations. The jurisdictional scope of the right is spelled out in far more specific detail (and in a more bounded way) than in the 1983 Penner Report, but the 1995 statement does gesture toward what a third order of government would look like. See *The Government of Canada's Approach to Implementation of the Inherent Right and the Negotiation of Aboriginal Self-Government*, (Ottawa: Public Works and Government Services, 1995), http://www.ainc-inac.gc.ca/pr/pub/sg/plcy_e.html.

16   Frances Abele & Michael J. Prince, "Constructing Political Spaces for Aboriginal Communities in Canada," in *Constructing Tomorrow's Federalism: New Routes to Effective Governance*, ed. Ian Peach (Winnipeg: University of Manitoba Press, 2007), 171-200; Michael J. Prince & Frances Abele, "Funding an Aboriginal Order of Government in Canada: Recent Developments in Self-Government and Fiscal Relations," in *Canada: The State of the Federation 1999/2000*, ed. Harvey Lazar (Montreal & Kingston: McGill-Queen's University Press, 2000), 337-67; Frances Abele & Michael J. Prince, "Aboriginal Governance and Canadian Federalism: A To-Do List for Canada," in *New Trends in Canadian Federalism*, 2nd ed., ed. Francois Rocher & Miriam Smith (Peterborough: Broadview Press, 2003), 135-66. The Nunavik Government Agreement is still under negotiation. See Gary Wilson, "The Nunavik Commission and the Path to Self-Government in Arctic Quebec," Presented to the Annual Meeting of the Canadian Political Science Association, 2005. Manuscript available from the author.

17   Gerald Taiaiake Alfred, *Peace, Power, Righteousness: an Indigenous Manifesto* (Toronto: Oxford University Press, 1999); James (Sa'ke'j) Youngblood Henderson, "Empowering Treaty Federalism," *Saskatchewan Law Review* 58, no. 2 (1994): 241-329; James (Sa'ke'j) Henderson, Marjorie Benson, & Isobel M. Findlay, *Aboriginal Tenure in the Constitution of Canada* (Scarborough: Carswell, 2000); and, Patricia Monture-Angus, *Journeying Forward: Dreaming First Nations' Independence* (Halifax: Fernwood, 1999).

18   This discussion of fiscal federalism draws on Michael J. Prince & Frances Abele, "Paying for Self-Determination: Aboriginal Peoples, Self-Government and Fiscal Relations in Canada," in *Reconfiguring Aboriginal-State Relations: Canada: The State of the Federation 2003*, ed. Michael Murphy (Montreal &

Kingston: Institute of Intergovernmental Relations, School of Policy Studies, Queen's University, McGill-Queen's University Press, 2005), 246-53.

19 Our focus here is on federal-provincial fiscal relations; on federal-territorial government fiscal relations, see Frances Abele & Michael J. Prince, "A Little Imagination Required: How Canada Funds Territorial and Northern Aboriginal Governments," in *How Ottawa Spends, 2008-2009,* ed. Allan M. Maslove (Montreal & Kingston: McGill-Queen's University Press, forthcoming 2008).

20 Arguably, though, the gradual alterations to the federation made by the modern treaty and self-government negotiation process are, for Canada, the normal approach to constitutional change: incremental change through negotiated, gradual steps.

21 In a similar spirit and for similar reasons, the formula financing system was developed for territorial governments, where economies of scale, small and dispersed populations, and a harsher climate lead to relatively high-cost governments that could not be adequately funded on the model developed for provinces.

22 Abele & Prince, "Aboriginal Governance and Canadian Federalism: A To-Do List for Canada."

23 Gurston Dacks, "Implementing First Nations Self-Government in Yukon: Lessons for Canada," *Canadian Journal of Political Science* 37, no. 3 (2004).

24 For a comprehensive and very helpful review of successive attempts to reform funding arrangements for First Nations, see Shepherd 2006.

25 Only one of the three territories, Yukon, has anything like province-like control of natural resources, though the Northwest Territories is close.

26 There are hundreds of examples of successful businesses in this category, ranging from a Lake Louise commercial mall development in Alberta to the high-quality maple syrup production and marketing in Kitigan Zibi, Ontario.

27 Royal Commission, *Final Report,* Vol. 2, 280-82; for more discussion of these issues, and the federal government's response, see Abele & Prince, "Four Pathways to Aboriginal Self-Government in Canada," and Prince & Abele, "Funding an Aboriginal Order of Government in Canada: Recent Developments in Self-Government and Fiscal Relations."

Part III:

Trends in the Implementation of Self-Government

COMMUNITY HEALING
AND ABORIGINAL SELF-GOVERNMENT*

Josée Lavoie, University of Northern British Columbia;
John O'Neil, Simon Fraser University;
Jeff Reading, University of Victoria;
Yvon Allard, Consultant

T he concept of Aboriginal self-government has important implications in the field of health, most obviously at the level of community-based health care services, but also in terms of improving the responsiveness of provincial and territorial health care systems and at the federal policy level.[1] At the community level, the emergence of self-governing Aboriginal nations and communities could result in radically different institutional arrangements for the provision of health services. Less obviously, perhaps, self-government is the foundation for social development and is expected to contribute to the healing process currently underway in many Aboriginal communities. At another level, self-government in health matters can also mean Aboriginal communities finding a way to have a voice in provincial and territorial political and health care systems: this option has received considerably less attention. In the health field, therefore, the implementation of self-government has implications for the administration of services, and the general well-being of Aboriginal populations, and for a renegotiation of the political space Aboriginal peoples occupy within the Canadian political landscape. Realizing this objective requires securing increased control over local services, and implementing mechanisms that ensure that Aboriginal peoples have a voice within federal, provincial, and territorial governments. This chapter will examine these expectations in the context of the history of Aboriginal health in Canada.

Health Conditions

H ealth and wellness involves much more than physical health, i.e. the absence of infectious and chronic disease. From an Aboriginal perspective, good health is seen to be a state of balance and harmony involving body, mind, emotions, and spirit. It links each person to family, community, and the earth in a circle of dependence and interdependence, described by some in the language of the Medicine Wheel. Reports continue to show that Aboriginal people bear a disproportionate burden of physical and emotional illness in Canada.[2] Many of the social issues reported as problems by Aboriginal people are closely linked with mental health and social problems, resulting from involuntary rapid cultural change imposed by colonization[3] and multi-generational trauma related to the legacy of oppressive policies and the systematic removal of children to residential schools.[4]

Important variations exist between Aboriginal groups, and from community to community. Despite the recent flurry of activities in creating national health indicators that also capture progress in Aboriginal health,[5] data on the Métis, off-reserve First Nations, and non-status individuals of First Nations ancestry remains sketchy or simply nonexistent. Where available, data on First Nations and Inuit tends to gloss over local and regional differences. Until recently, statistics on Aboriginal health were collected by agencies (governments and universities) external to Aboriginal Nations and interpreted without Aboriginal input.[6] This remains generally the case for the Métis, urban First Nations, and non-status individuals of First Nation ancestry.

The First Nations and Inuit Regional Health Surveys[7] (both the 1999 and 2005 surveys are commonly known as the Regional Health Survey or RHS) have endeavoured to change how health information is produced and interpreted. Both surveys are Aboriginal-led and controlled, and informed by the principles of Ownership, Control, Access and Possession (OCAP).[8] The interpretation of the statistics they produce is entrusted to selected researchers and writers who have expertise in specific health areas and in Indigenous health issues, to ensure that context is understood and reflected in the analysis. The overall survey is informed by a cultural framework that reflects a First Nations understanding of determinants of health.[9] The Aboriginal Peoples Survey (APS) designed by Statistics Canada in partnership with the Congress of Aboriginal Peoples, the Inuit Tapiriit Kanatami, the Métis National Council, the National Association of Friendship Centres, and the Native Women's Association of Canada provides important information on the off-reserve population, albeit with a much more limited level of community engagement in the production of the survey and the interpretation of its results.

The 2005 RHS has shown some progress on indicators of community well-being, including traditional activities, healing, and cultural self-esteem. Overall, nearly 70 percent of First Nations adult and youth respondents stated that they felt in balance physically, emotionally, mentally, and spiritually most or all the time. Despite this, 37.9 percent reported experiences of racism in the past 12 months, and 30.1 percent reported having felt sad, blue, or depressed for two weeks or more in a row. The same study also documented a higher rate of abstinence from alcohol among First Nations (34.4%) than the Canadian population (20.7%). Still, more than double the proportion of First Nations adults reported heavy drinking (16.0%) compared to the Canadian population (6.2%).[10] According to the APS, in 2001, 42.4 percent of non-reserve Aboriginal adults reported excellent or very good health, compared to 61.2 percent for the total Canadian adult population.[11] The APS also documented that 83 percent of parents of Aboriginal children (0 to 5 years of age) living off-reserve rated their child's health as very good or excellent, compared to 90 percent for all Canadians.[12]

The gap in life expectancy that exists between First Nations and non-Aboriginal Canadians is slowly narrowing. In 1996, life expectancy at birth was about five and seven years less for females and males respectively for First Nations living on-reserve, compared to about seven to eight years in 1990.[13] For Inuit, the gap is wider: twelve years for females and eight for males.[14] The available data suggest that the remaining gap in life expectancy can be partly explained by higher rates of infant mortality among registered First Nations peoples living on-reserve (8.0 per 1000) and Inuit (15.0 per 1000), compared to other Canadians.[15]

The rates of injury and accidental death for First Nations on-reserve is four times the rate for all of Canada.[16] According to the 2000/01 and 2003 Canadian Community Health Survey (hereafter CCHS) surveys, about 20 percent of Aboriginal persons aged between 12 and 64 living off-reserve reported having had an injury serious enough to limit their activities in the year prior to the study, compared to 14 percent for other provincial residents.[17] Aboriginal children also have much higher rates of death from injuries than other children in Canada. In 2002-03, 49.5 percent of First Nations youth (aged 12 to 17) reported an injury requiring treatment, compared to 13.6 percent for all of Canada.[18] The rate of death by suicide is 28 per 100,000 for First Nations living on-reserve, compared to 79 per 100,000 for Inuit and 13 per 100,000 for Canada.[19]

Canada's Aboriginal peoples continue to report being at an increased risk of infectious diseases. Table 1 shows the difference in prevalence between groups.

	Aboriginal peoples (non-status)	First Nations on- and off-reserve	Inuit	Métis	Other Canadians
Tuberculosis	21	30	92	5.6	1.3
Chlamydia	n.a.	532 (M) 1366 (F)	1410 (M) 2918 (F)	n.a.	82 (M) 194 (F)

Table 1, Prevalence of Infectious diseases (rate per 100,000/year, 2004 data)[20]

The rate of infection from tuberculosis is much higher among First Nations living on and off-reserve and Inuit than among other Aboriginal groups and non-Aboriginal Canadians. For chlamydia, the rate of infection is seven times that of other Canadians for First Nations, over 15 times that of other Canadians for Inuit. HIV infection and AIDS are of major concern to Aboriginal peoples, especially in northern and remote communities where HIV testing and AIDS treatment is limited or unavailable. The Public Health Agency of Canada reported that as of June 2002, 18,336 cases of AIDS had been reported in Canada, of which 15,713 contained ethnic information. Of these, 459 were reported as Aboriginal persons.[21]

Chronic conditions are sometimes called the diseases of modernization, or western diseases, because they attend the lifestyles typical of western industrial nations: reduced physical exercise; an over-reliance on foods of poor nutritional quality because of limited access to alternatives, especially in northern communities, or economic barriers; high levels of stress; and increased exposure to a wide range of pollutants in the air, water, and food supply. These increase risk, and can be further compounded by an excessive use of caffeine, alcohol, non-traditional use of tobacco, and by recreational drug usage. Cardiovascular disease, cancer, metabolic disorders (particularly diabetes), and respiratory and digestive disorders are significant factors in Aboriginal illness and death. Important differences exist between Aboriginal groups, as shown in Table 2. It appears that the prevalence of chronic diseases is highest among First Nations, with the notable exception of arthritis and rheumatism which is highest among non-status individuals of First Nation ancestry.

	Aboriginal peoples (non-status)	First Nations on- and off-reserve	Inuit	Métis	Other Canadians
Diabetes	9	11(M) 17(F)	2	6	4
Arthritis & rheumatism	26	18(M) 25(F)	9	20	16
Heart problems	7	13(M) 11(F)	5	7	4
High blood pressure	15	22(M) 26(F)	8	13	13

Table 2, Prevalence of chronic conditions (% of the population with the condition)[22]

Diabetes mellitus is a major health and wellness issue among First Nations, Métis and other Aboriginal peoples. The 2005 RHS documented that the number of First Nations living on-reserve with diabetes is rapidly rising, especially among men. The same survey also documented that the age of diagnosis is dropping: 1.5 percent of First Nations youth aged 12 to 19 already have diabetes.[23] Changes in the prevalence of the disease may be at least partially explained by improved screening practices at the community level.[24] Cardiovascular disease and hypertension are also major health problems, with First Nations experiencing, again, the highest prevalence. These health problems also appear to be on the rise.

Aboriginal people suffer more end-stage renal disease (ESRD) than other Canadians. Dyck reports an eight fold increase in the number of dialysis patients between 1980 and 2000. Of 954 Canadian Aboriginal peoples with ESRD studied, 395 (41.3%) had diabetic ESRD.[25]

Both children and adults in the Aboriginal population suffer an increased frequency of acute respiratory infections compared with non-Aboriginal people. Although the reasons why Aboriginal people are at an increased risk of some infectious diseases are unknown, suggested risk factors include poor nutrition related to poverty and access to affordable good quality food, genetic factors, poverty and crowding, and environmental pollutants such as tobacco smoke and wood smoke.[26]

Lung cancer is an emerging health concern among Aboriginal people, due to the non-traditional use of tobacco products. The 2005 RHS indicated that 58.8 percent of respondents smoked either daily or occasionally.[27] The same study documented that 37.8 percent of youth (aged 13 to 17) already smoked on a regular basis. Amongst the 13-year-olds, 9.4 percent of boys and 18.2 percent of girls smoked. The 1999 RHS documented that in 1997, 78 percent of respondents smoked,[28] although, generally, trends in the non-traditional use of tobacco have not been documented. Data for other Aboriginal groups is not available. Still, smoking cessation programs need to be culturally based for use in Aboriginal communities.

The picture of health conditions that emerges indicates that Aboriginal Canadians are increasingly living with chronic conditions requiring access not only to primary but also secondary and tertiary prevention interventions,[29] to ensure that an optimal level of health and autonomy may be maintained in spite of chronic conditions.[30] This is particularly true for First Nations living on-reserve. Yet, secondary and tertiary prevention interventions are lacking on all reserves with the exception of those that are serviced by Nursing Stations (16 per cent of First Nations and Inuit communities' federally funded health services). Beyond access to health care, closing the gap lies in improvements in the fundamental conditions of Aboriginal life including local economies, access to country-grown and other affordable nutritious foods, housing, sanitation systems, community-based healing programs, traditional medicine, and self-determination.[31]

A great deal has changed since the last edition of this book was produced in 1999. National surveys previously produced by governmental departments are now in the hands of First Nations or produced at least in partnership with Aboriginal peoples. The RHS is a first world-wide. It is breaking new ground in the development of variables that reflect an Indigenous worldview, and potentially support a shift in relationship of surveillance.[32] The APS has contributed to improving access to statistics on the off-reserve Aboriginal population. The APS, however, fails to distinguish between Inuit, status Indians living off-reserve, the Métis, and non-status individuals of First Nation ancestry in their reporting. A second important innovation has been the creation of the Institute of Aboriginal Peoples Health (IAPH) in 2000. As one of the thirteen institutes under the umbrella of the Canadian Institutes for Health Research, IAPH is playing a pivotal role in building research capacity among Aboriginal communities, and in the research community, by ensuring that researchers develop meaningful partnerships with

Aboriginal communities throughout the research process.[33] Over time, these innovations will change how research and statistics are generated, interpreted, and used, and lead to the generation of research that not only accurately represents Aboriginal reality, but also offers meaningful solutions.[34]

History of Health Service Development

It is in the creation of the nation of Canada through the *British North America Act, 1867* that the cause can be found for much of the jurisdictional wrangling between federal and provincial governments over who has the responsibility for provision of health care to Aboriginal people today. The BNA *Act* gave legislative authority over Indians and Indian Bands to the federal government. The *Indian Act* of 1876 addressed these federal responsibilities to Indians and forced an arbitrary, but devastating class structure on Aboriginal communities: those who had 'status' and therefore were entitled to special rights and considerations from the new nation of Canada; and those who missed being included in this legal definition, through reasons as diverse as marriage or military enlistment, or in the case of the Métis, for being considered "western enough" to be excluded from the Treaty negotiation process.[35] These Aboriginal peoples became, in essence, a Canadian version of a dispossessed race, or 'non-status'. Any real benefits of "status" are certainly questionable given the *Indian Act*'s prescriptive limitations on permitted activities from birth to burial and the experiences of First Nations in the 130 plus years since the *Act* was passed; the *Act*'s legacy paradoxically remains as a mechanism of both special status and of social control and assimilation.[36] Its assimilation agenda was never in doubt as Canada's first Prime Minister, Sir John A. Macdonald, confirmed in 1887 when he said that civilization's great aim was to assimilate the Indian people in all respects.[37] At the same time, "status" has and continues to confer a measure of visibility and protection to First Nations, unmatched for Métis and non-status individuals of First Nation ancestry.

Prior to the mid-nineteenth century, distinct self-governing Aboriginal societies lived in a harmonious relationship with different ecological regions across the country.[38] Within these environments, Aboriginal societies developed healing systems that emphasized the balanced integration of human beings with the physical, social, and spiritual environment.[39] By living balanced lives according to the principles of their respective traditions, Aboriginal people avoided sickness.[40] In each society, some people had special abilities which made them responsible for assisting individuals and communities to maintain ecological, social, and spiritual balance through ceremonial activity.[41] Additionally, some individuals had specialized knowledge of the medicinal properties of plants and animal parts that they knew to be effective in the cure of common ailments.[42] However, all members of the community shared the responsibility to live balanced lives and all had some knowledge of traditional medicines. Illness was believed to be the result of a failure to respect the basic moral code of the society and in this way, healing systems were also fundamental to the social structure and self-governing systems of each society.[43]

Contact with settlers from Europe undermined this complex system of ecological, social and spiritual balance, and in the process threatened the survival of Aboriginal societies. It is beyond the scope of this chapter to address the phenomenon of social change in depth, except to say that the huge mortality and morbidity from European-introduced infectious diseases, from which Aboriginal people lacked immunity, is often overlooked in historical discussions of Aboriginal contact with Euro-Canadian society.[44] The impact of infectious diseases such as smallpox, influenza, diphtheria, poliomyelitis, and tuberculosis, was not only extremely high mortality (ranging from an average of 40%, to 90% in some parts of Aboriginal North America),[45] but also resulted in major dislocations of individuals and communities, and disruption of traditional social systems. Since most of this mortality would have been among productive adults, and particularly elders, it is indeed an indicator of the strength of Aboriginal traditions that they have endured and flourished.

In response to these changes, First Nations leaders across the prairies sought to negotiate agreements with representatives of the Euro-Canadian state that would ensure the survival of their societies.[46] As compensation for the use of their land and resources, First Nations leaders agreed to relocate their people into villages and reserves if the Crown would guarantee the welfare of future generations.[47] Given the vastly different traditions and languages in which these agreements were negotiated, it is not surprising that Euro-Canadian representatives interpreted their obligation in many different ways.[48]

Of particular relevance is the conflict surrounding the interpretation of federal responsibility for health. The so-called "medicine chest clause" in Treaty No. 6 signed with the Plains Cree in 1876 is the only specific reference to health in any Treaty. This clause charges the federal government with the responsibility to protect First Nations people from pestilence and famine and to provide a "medicine chest" in the house of each Indian agent. The First Nations' perspective on this clause is clearly articulated in the records of Alexander Morris the Treaty Commissioner at the time. Morris writes:

> The Indians were apprehensive of their future. They saw the food supply, the buffalo, passing away, and they were anxious and distressed ... They desired to be fed. Smallpox had destroyed them by hundreds a few years before, and they dreaded pestilence and famine.[49]

Fumoleau as well argues that the Treaty Commissioners negotiating Treaty 8 also promised medicines and medical care, citing a 1919 report by D. McLean, Assistant Deputy and Secretary of Indian Affairs, who wrote that Indians were to be "assured ... that the government would always be ready to avail itself of any opportunity of affording medical service."[50] Fumoleau argues further that the need for a Treaty in the far north was explained by the poor health conditions of the Dene in the region.

A broad approach to treaty interpretation has been supported in the courts. The Supreme Court of Canada has indicated that treaty interpretation should be fair, large, and liberal in favour of the Indians, that the treaty be construed in terms which would be naturally understood by the Indians, that the Crown should avoid sharp dealings, and that interpretations of ambiguous wordings should not prejudice the Indians if another interpretation is possible.[51] Further legislative authority for the federal government's obligation for First Nations health is spelled out in s. 73 of the *Indian Act* where containment of on-reserve epidemics, provision of medical services, compulsory hospitalization for infectious diseases, and provision of sanitary conditions on reserves are described as federal responsibilities.[52]

While First Nations representatives view these provisions as the basis for a full federal obligation for health, the federal government has adopted the position that the provision of medical care is a matter of policy and not of right,[53] basing this position on the 1966 Saskatchewan Court of Appeal decision known as the *Johnston* appeal, which stated that "the [medicine chest] clause itself does not give to the Indians the unrestricted right to the use and benefit of the 'medicine chest' but such rights as are given are subject to the direction of the Indian agent." Therefore, according to this interpretation, it is up to the federal government to determine the legitimacy of Indians' requests for health care and to allocate it free of charge or at a cost.[54] A 1999 ruling on a case brought forth by the Wuskwi Sipihk Cree Nation of Manitoba has however criticised this narrow interpretation, stating instead that "it is clear that the Saskatchewan Court of Appeal took what is now a wrong approach in its literal and restrictive reading of the medicine chest clause in the 1966 decision in *Johnston*. ... In a current context the clause may well require a full range of contemporary medical services."[55] This ruling has yet to influence federal policy initiatives.

Later revisions to the *Indian Act* prohibiting healing ceremonies, such as the sun dance and the potlatch, further extended the colonial society's regulatory control of everyday life in Aboriginal communities, and contributed to the suppression of traditional healing practices.[56] The penultimate act of this assimilation effort was to force Aboriginal children into residential schools where tuberculosis killed 24 percent of all children who attended over a fifteen-year period.[57] In the words of Duncan Campbell Scott, deputy minister for Indian Affairs at the time: "It is quite within the mark to say that fifty percent of the children who passed through these schools did not live to benefit from the education which they had received therein."[58] Of those who survived, harsh discipline and incidents of sexual and physical abuse coerced children away from their language and tradition, and inflicted psychological scars that continue to this day.[59]

Resistance to these destructive forces was for the most part underground. The most visible symbol of opposition, the 1885 Métis resistance in Manitoba and Saskatchewan was crushed through armed force.[60] Imprisonment, fines, and relocation were used in other regions of the country to enforce assimilationist policies.[61] Otherwise, the "welfare" of Aboriginal societies was systematically neglected.[62] Famines and tuberculosis virtually decimated Aboriginal communities, unaided except for relocation of survivors to state institutions. Housing provided was of the poorest quality, and health care and education were left to the Churches, which used these institutions as opportunities for Christianization.[63]

After decades of ignoring the health of First Nations people, in the 1930s the Canadian state began to develop a system of primary care clinics, a public health program, and regional hospitals. Initiated primarily in response to the threat that epidemics of tuberculosis posed to the external society, this system adopted an authoritarian approach that contributed to further undermine community cohesion and self-reliance.[64] In practice, this meant people had little choice but to be relocated to medical facilities away from their communities for treatment, and accept public health campaigns which were often insensitive to local social and cultural systems,[65] and, in the worst case, unwillingly accept medical procedures like sterilization.[66] Until quite recently, virtually all providers of services were non-Aboriginal and behaved according to Euro-Canadian cultural standards with little interest in or understanding of Aboriginal cultural practices and values. Encounters were often clouded by suspicion, misunderstanding, resentment, and indeed racism.[67] Further, health care providers generally assumed that Aboriginal medicine was non-existent. Traditional healing was characterized as superstition or witchcraft, when Western medical practitioners were aware of it at all, and most believed that such beliefs were destined to disappear.

It was not until the 1960s that Canada's disinterest in fulfilling its obligation to Aboriginal societies was met with systematic resistance. Aboriginal organizations formed to represent the interests of their people in the courts and legislatures of Canada.[68] Ironically, Aboriginal political development was kindled in part as a critical response to the federal White Paper policy proposal of 1969, which recommended the dismantlement of the *Indian Act,* considered by many people as colonial and genocidal but nonetheless protective in its provisions of federal responsibility. Fundamental to these initiatives were Aboriginal interpretation of treaties, the assertion of Aboriginal identity and rights by people otherwise excluded from treaties, the establishment of Aboriginal claim to traditional territories, and the right to self-government.[69] These initiatives further insisted that the institutions which structure the relationship between Aboriginal communities and Canadian society (i.e. schools, legal and social services, and medical care) be recast to ensure that Aboriginal cultural principles including community autonomy were entrenched.[70]

Self-Government and Colonial (Western) Medicine

The first nation-wide initiative to exercise influence over colonial medicine occurred in 1978, when the federal government attempted to reduce the provision of uninsured services (i.e. services such as drugs and eyeglasses that are not provided to all Canadians through the medicare system) to First Nations. This action provoked a forceful reaction from Indian organizations such as the National Indian Brotherhood (now known as the Assembly of First Nations) who argued that Treaty rights were being abrogated.[71]

Following the 1979 national election, the newly elected Progressive Conservative government led by Prime Minister Joe Clark tabled the first Indian Health Policy, nominally intended to restore Indian health through community development, a reaffirmation of the traditional relationship of Indian peoples to the federal government, and by strengthening the relationships within the Canadian health care system (including provincial and privately delivered medical services). This document has been further interpreted as providing a stimulus for both the recognition of important traditional medicines and greater First Nations and Inuit control over the delivery of services. Also in 1979, the *Report of the Advisory Commission on Indian and Inuit Health Consultation*, authored by Justice Thomas Berger, provided the first systematic inquiry into Aboriginal dissatisfaction with the health care system. Berger recommended that Inuit and Indian health be addressed separately, given the vastly different traditions and problems faced by each group. He further recommended that consultation funding be provided to a National Commission Inquiry on Indian Health, a subcommittee of the National Indian Brotherhood, to develop a National Indian Health Council that would ultimately be responsible for assisting First Nations communities to develop locally controlled health care systems. While influential, this recommendation was largely ignored. Inuit health service development would occur largely in the context of land claims and ongoing political development, particularly the proposal for a distinct Inuit Territory (Nunavut) and the Inuvialuit land settlement in the Northwest Territories.[72] Further, these developments continued to exclude the Métis and non-status individuals of First Nation ancestry.

Prior to these national initiatives, the *James Bay and Northern Quebec Agreement* was signed by representatives of the James Bay Cree, the Inuit of Nunavik, and the federal and Quebec governments, creating the first Cree and Inuit Boards of Health and Social Services in Canada.[73] While debate continues concerning this agreement's applicability as a self-determination model, significant changes to health and social services have resulted.[74] In Puvirnituk, for example, the Inuit-controlled hospital board has established an indigenous midwifery program in which Inuit midwives provide a full range of care.[75] Puvirnituk also provides a model for Aboriginal people in other jurisdictions who regard the expropriation of childbirth from their communities as a significant threat to community development.[76]

One of the first federal health programs to be devolved to the administrative authority of First Nations and Inuit communities was the National Native Alcohol and Drug Abuse Program (NNADAP), established in 1975. This program is responsible for the creation of hundreds of community-based alcohol prevention and treatment projects across the country. Since the early eighties, this program has contributed to the emergence of some of the most significant healing initiatives in the country including the Four Worlds Development Project, the Nechi Institute, and the Alkali Lake prohibition strategy. Early experience with the program suggests that despite the remarkable efforts and success of First Nations and Inuit organizations involved in community mental health and alcohol treatment, frustration occurred over the program's responsiveness to community needs.[77] A more recent evaluation concludes however, that the majority of people feel that NNADAP services do meet community needs.[78] This review also concludes that NNADAP workers require broader infrastructural support such as training, and recognition by management and external agencies, in order to remain effective. This can be at least partially attributed to funding. The program is funded for service delivery during regular office hours (9 to 5, Monday to Friday), and at pay scales that are too low to attract qualified individuals.[79]

Likewise, Community Health Representatives (CHRs) were included as essential components of the community-based health care system. These roles were devolved early to community control. The role of the CHR has changed over time, historically at the whims of the Nurses-in-Charge who defined the extent of the CHR's involvement in health care delivery based on their own comfort level,[80] and, more recently, as a result of scope of practice legislation constraining the role of nurses and by extension, that of the CHR.

In 1981, the federal government initiated the Community Health Demonstration Program (CHDP) in an attempt to assess the costs, timing, and implications of future transfers of control.[81] The program, although portrayed as an exercise in self-determination, was roundly criticized because it was implemented without prior Aboriginal consultation and because the connotations of "demonstration" implied the unlikelihood of long-term transfer. The program funded a mere 31 projects, only seven of which directly addressed the transfer of community health services. One project—the Sandy Bay reserve in western Manitoba—was given a critical evaluation.[82] The reviewers argued that local control was lacking in the CHDP due to an unavailability of global budgeting combined with a withholding of training resources. This ultimately prevented the establishment of a community-based health development plan.

Since the 1990s, the majority of community-based health development in First Nations and Inuit communities south of the 60th parallel has occurred under the auspices of the Health Transfer Policy (HTP) of 1989, which evolved out of the CHDP. The policy is administered by the First Nations and Inuit Health Branch of Health Canada (formerly the Medical Services Branch, hereafter FNIHB). The policy has three stated objectives:

- To enable Indian Bands to design health programs, establish services, and allocate funds according to community health priorities;
- To strengthen and enhance the accountability of Indian Bands to Band members; and,

- To ensure public health and safety is maintained through adherence to mandatory programs.[83]

This policy enables communities to assess their health needs and develop appropriate and responsive community health plans and programs. Allocated funding was largely based on historical expenditures, with some provisions made for administration. Culhane Speck argued that transfer initiatives might be driven by federal efforts to off-load programs and contain costs rather than an interest in responding to local needs.[84] These concerns have since been reflected in various assessments and evaluations.[85] Nevertheless, First Nations and Inuit groups have sought to take advantage of the opportunities afforded by this policy: as of June 2007, a total of 158 Transfer Agreements, representing 279 First Nations and Inuit Communities (or 46 per cent of eligible communities) have been signed.[86] In 1994, FNIHB introduced an alternative integrated agreement, allowing smaller communities to assume a measure of control over local health services, without shouldering the concomitant level of responsibility. As of 2007, 169 communities (33 per cent) have elected to follow this path.[87] It is clear that the policy has at least partially contributed to meeting First Nations and Inuit expectations.

A program evaluation conducted in 2005, concluded that the HTP had met its stated objectives and that mechanisms should be continually made available to First Nations and Inuit communities/organizations to: (1) support the flexible development and delivery of community-based services; and, (2) promote local governance in health policy, programs, and priority-setting.[88] The evaluation nevertheless highlighted serious shortcomings while offering a number of correctives. A major area of concern is related to inequities exist in the way First Nations and Inuit communities are funded: this prompted three recommendations. First, establish a process to develop funding formulae that reflect needs, recognise the unique conditions existing in each community, reflect the cost of service provision, and are mindful of sustainability. Second, all funding agreements should include a built-in, automatic, yearly index reflecting the cost of living and price and volume increases. Finally, take into account the specific needs of small and isolated communities in the formulae-based funding mechanism. The evaluation highlighted an inequitable reporting burden for First Nations and Inuit communities. In 2003-04, First Nations in British Columbia alone submitted an estimated 5,815 reports to fulfil their FNIHB accountability requirements. The report recommended that reporting requirements be streamlined by altering the monitoring agreement clauses and how activities and indicators that cannot be aggregated be reported in to a cost-effective reporting framework that reflects the performance of on-reserve services as well as the accessibility of all services.

In terms of programs, the evaluation recommended that FNIHB support First Nations and Inuit in taking the lead in developing strategic linkages with federal and provincial public health authorities to address First Nations and Inuit public health needs. It also recommended that investments be made in holistic mental health and wellness as a core component of Health Transfer to reflect a broader and more current understanding of the consequences of multi-generational trauma.

The evaluation report was accepted by FNIHB in September 2005. The report led to a submission to the Treasury Board Secretariat in March 2006, for the renewal of program authorities. Plans for the implementation of a new and more flexible framework, building on the strengths of transfer, and addressing some of the shortcomings highlighted in the evaluation, have been under discussion.[89] At the time of writing, this is still in the planning stage.

Other examples of Aboriginal control over health services have emerged, both at the local and regional levels. The Kateri Memorial Hospital Centre (KMHC) was established in 1955 when a local Mohawk elder secured funding from the Mohawk Council of Kahnawake and the Quebec government to continue local hospital operations. Through over 50 years of tumultuous relations with federal, provincial, and university (McGill) agencies, KMHC provides curative and preventative services to Aboriginal residents of the Kahnawake reserve and nearby Montreal.[90]

Urban Aboriginal Health Centres (UAHCs) have emerged since the 1980s to serve the specific needs of the Aboriginal urban population. Anishnaawbe Health Toronto (AHT) was funded in 1988 by the provincial government as a multi-service, urban community health centre, grounded in the principles of the medicine wheel, and mandated to provide services to the off-reserve, non-status, and Métis Aboriginal population of Toronto.[91] The Vancouver Native Health Society was established in 1992 with funding from the provincial government, to reach out to the estimated 20,000 Aboriginal people living in Vancouver Downtown Eastside, one of Canada's poorest neighbourhoods.[92] The Aboriginal Health and Wellness Centre was established by the Aboriginal community in Winnipeg in 1988 with a similar mandate.

The Alberta Indian Health Commission (AIHCC), established in 1981 to promote provincial First Nations health concerns was recognized, together with the Blood Tribe Board of Health as a First Nations health authority at the 1989 Health Transfer Forum. In addition to consultation and liaison with various Aboriginal and provincial organizations, the AIHCC also provides urban community health representatives in Edmonton and Calgary.[93] The Labrador Inuit Health Commission (LIHC) was created in 1979, in response to the specific exclusionary policies of the International Grenfell Association which failed to recognize Aboriginal rights. The Labrador Inuit Association refused to witness the signing of the 1986 *Canada-Newfoundland Native Peoples of Labrador Health Agreement* and established the LIHC instead, concentrating on CHR-delivered health education and promotion.[94] The Commission is currently in the process of negotiating a self-government agreement that will include health services until now delivered by the Government of Newfoundland & Labrador.

Response to pressure from Inuit Tapirisat of Canada in the early 1980s led to the devolution of health services to the Northwest Territories. By 1988, transfer of authority for health to the territorial government and regional health boards was complete. Evaluations of this process have been largely critical. O'Neil has argued that little real empowerment of regional health boards occurred, initially resulting in increasing tension and alienation between Yellowknife and the regional Inuit,[95] exacerbated by the reluctance of former government administrators to assist in a meaningful transfer of power. Inuit have been concerned that control over health services be embedded in the context of self-government, and particularly the creation of Nunavut, strategies resisted by the territorial bureaucracy reluctant to facilitate this process. Nevertheless, devolution paved the way to the establishment of the Nunavut Department of Health and Social Services in the new territory.

Recently, three reports of national significance offer avenues to expand opportunities for Aboriginal peoples' participation in national and provincial policy and planning processes. In October 2002, the Standing Senate Committee on Social Affairs, Science and Technology tabled *The Health of Canadians—The Federal Role* (the Kirby Report). The report focused its recommendations on improving the performance of the health care sector through investments in infrastructure. While the report acknowledged that Aboriginal peoples are underrepresented in, and underserved by, the health-care sector, specific recommendations focused on strategies for increasing the supply of Aboriginal health care professionals.[96] This report was followed that November by the report of the *Royal Commission on the Future of Health in Canada* (also known as the Romanow Report). In particular, Chapter 10 was dedicated to Aboriginal health issues and echoed the Royal Commission on Aboriginal Peoples findings that systemic barriers continue to undermine Aboriginal peoples' ability to fully benefit from the Canadian health care systems. In an effort to mitigate conflicting constitutional assumptions, fragmented services and inadequate access, and different cultural and political influences, the Romanow Report recommended pooling current funding for Aboriginal health services provided by all levels of government into consolidated budgets in each province and territory to integrate Aboriginal health care services, improve access, and provide adequate, stable, and predictable funding. This funding should be used to fund new Aboriginal Health Partnerships that would be responsible for developing policies, providing services, and improving the health of Aboriginal peoples. Finally, in 2003 the report of the *National Advisory Committee on SARS and Public Health* (the Naylor Report) was released.[97] The issue of Aboriginal health was literally side-stepped except for this brief mention:

A continuing challenge in mounting appropriate responses is a recurring tension between the right and aspirations of Aboriginal peoples to greater self-determination within the Canadian federation, and the uncertain effectiveness and efficiency of reinforcing the existent pattern of separate health systems for First Nations and Inuit communities.[98]

Additional reports have at times served as catalysts for a number of important health developments, including:

- The Manitoba Intergovernmental Committee on First Nations Health (ICFNH) was set up in 2001 with representatives from the Assembly of Manitoba Chiefs (AMC), Manitoba Health (MH), the First Nations and Inuit Health Branch of Health Canada Manitoba region (FNIHB), Indians and Northern Affairs Canada (INAC), the Department of Aboriginal and Northern Affairs (ANA), and the Department of Family Services and Housing (FSH): the Public Health Agency of Canada (PHAC) is a recent addition. The Committee's mandate is to resolve jurisdictional issues and promote joint policy development.[99] This has resulted in the creation of a cross-jurisdictional primary health care policy framework,[100] and a number of research projects prioritized by the Committee, including First Nations health care financing and documenting jurisdictional gaps.

- A special meeting of First Ministers and Aboriginal leaders held September 2004, resulted in a commitment to design an action plan to improve access to health services for all Aboriginal peoples. What followed was 18 months of discussions and consultation by Aboriginal groups to design a blueprint for improving First Nations, Inuit, and Métis health. The blueprints were tabled and debated at a meeting of the First Ministers in November 2005, in Kelowna. The result was the Kelowna Accord, a $5.1 billion, long-term plan. The Accord and associated financial commitment was short lived, ending with a shift of government at the federal level.[101]

- In November of 2005, the Province of British Columbia, the First Nations Leadership Council, and the Government of Canada signed the landmark Transformative Change Accord.[102] The Accord has three ambitious objectives: (1) to close gaps in the areas of education, health, housing, and economic opportunities over the next 10 years; (2) to reconcile Aboriginal rights and title with those of the Crown; and, (3) to establish a new relationship based on mutual respect and recognition. To close the gap in health, the Accord proposes to prioritize investments in mental health and youth suicide prevention programs, chronic disease prevention, pilot projects integrating acute care and community health services for First Nations, the training of First Nations health care professionals, and telehealth. The Accord also commits to improving cross-jurisdictional coordination through Health Partners Groups, and to improve Aboriginal participation in planning and decision-making. Planning is progressing, in spite of the federal government's decision not to follow through with the Kelowna Accord.

- The Assembly of First Nations published its report, *First Nations Public Health: a framework for improving the health of our people and our communities*, in November 2006.[103] This document was structured to help guide governmental efforts to improve the performance of the public health sector in meeting First Nations' needs. The report offers additional steps to remodel what its authors perceived to be inadequacies in both the Kirby and Romanow documents.

Different opportunities have emerged to provide Aboriginal peoples some measure of control over health services. This has had a profound impact on how services and programs are planned. Aboriginal capacity in health care planning and delivery has grown tremendously. Still, with the exception of UAHCs where they exist, most opportunities have by-passed the Métis and non-status individuals of First Nations ancestry. Emerging in the last decade have been increased opportunities for First Nations, Inuit, and Métis to engage at the provincial and national levels in policy and planning processes. Tripartite opportunities, however, depend on the goodwill of the provinces. Opportunities vary from province to province, and are vulnerable to political shifts.

Aboriginal and Treaty Rights

An official recognition of existing Aboriginal and treaty rights is included in section 35 of the *Constitution Act, 1982*. The constitution defines Aboriginal peoples to include the Indian, Inuit and Métis peoples of Canada. However, the definition of what Aboriginal rights entails in the Constitution has never been resolved, as the constitutionally mandated conferences on this issue during the 1980s resulted in a stalemate. The courts have provided the mechanism for determination of specific Aboriginal rights; however, the Aboriginal right to health care has never been acknowledged by the courts or the federal government. A fiduciary obligation for the provision of health and health-related services to First Nations and Inuit was recognized by the federal Minister of Health in a 1997 meeting with the Assembly of First Nations.[104] Métis health was not explored.

The concept of a federal fiduciary obligation to Aboriginal peoples has its roots in the first agreements, which were negotiated by Aboriginal people with representatives of the British Crown. A fiduciary relationship is defined as "an expression ... which exists whenever one man trusts and relies on another. It exists where there is a special confidence reposed in one - who in equity and good conscience is bound to act in good faith and with due regard to interests on one reposing the confidence."[105] Fiduciary obligation may encompass a wide scope of issues including self-government, Aboriginal title, compensation for breach of faith, duty to consult, and the principle of partnership.[106] For historical reasons, Métis affairs have generally been considered a provincial jurisdiction, or outside the realm of the fiduciary duty. This did not stop the First Ministers Meeting in Kelowna in 2005, or then-Prime Minister Paul Martin, from making an unprecedented announcement recognizing the federal government's primary fiduciary responsibility for the Métis Nation.[107] It remains unclear whether and how the Conservative government of Stephen Harper will uphold this commitment.

Despite the assurance by the federal government that it recognizes a fiduciary responsibility to the provision of health services to First Nations and Inuit, an area of contention is whether or not that role becomes diminished as First Nations and Inuit assume more responsibility for providing health services. The courts have provided some direction in this issue, ruling that a fiduciary responsibility cannot be overridden based on other priorities or considerations[108] and that government actions cannot be unreasonable or create undue hardship for First Nations and Inuit people. In contrast to the undefined area of Aboriginal rights to health care, an historical record exists to prove treaty entitlements, although again the extent of this entitlement has never been judicially determined. At issue is the broadness of the treaty terminology "pestilence" and "medical care" in a contemporary context. There is no dispute that a promise to provide relief for pestilence was made in certain treaties, and history has recorded Crown Treaty Negotiator Lieutenant-Governor Alexander Morris as promising the Cree that it was the Queen's way to provide relief in the case of national famine and medical care in the case of national pestilence. Furthermore, Governor Morris assured the Cree that writing appropriate provisions in the treaty would not affect these policies.[109] Modern courts have upheld the validity of oral records. In particular, the Supreme Court has put forward a broad, common-sense approach in defining a treaty to include "agreements in which the word of the whiteman is given and by which the latter makes certain of the Indians' cooperation."[110]

In an attempt to rectify the situation, the Liberal Party of Canada made a commitment in 1993 to "seek the advice of treaty First Nations on how to achieve a mutually acceptable process to interpret the Treaties in contemporary terms giving full recognition to their spirit or intent."[111] Unfortunately, to date the provincial and federal crowns and Aboriginal people have petitioned the courts for relief of the majority of confrontational issues, and these cases demonstrate that there is a clear disconnect between jurisprudence and policy. In the complex area of Aboriginal and treaty rights, some First Nations are unwilling to proceed with transfer, or self-government, agreements as they fear it will jeopardize their treaty rights. The federal government has not allayed this concern, as it in the past has stated that it regards a transfer of responsibility between the federal government and a First Nation to trigger a corresponding reduction in any fiduciary responsibility of the federal government.[112]

Self-Government and Traditional Medicine

Canada is one of the few countries in the world where medical pluralism is not taken for granted. The medical profession in Canada has assumed greater control over healing activities than anywhere else in either the industrialized or developing world. Perhaps the best example of this is the situation of midwifery which has been defined as a medical act in Canada, but is a separate, legal, and widely used professional service in most of the rest of the world including the United States, Europe, and Australia. In other countries, healing systems such as homeopathy, chiropractic medicine, acupuncture, and naturopathy are also well established, regulated by professional organizations, and in some instances, state supported through health insurance, for example, in Britain. Ayurvedic and Chinese medicine are examples of ancient and widely utilized healing systems for much of the world's population (in India and China respectively). While it is beyond the scope of this chapter to address the social history of Aboriginal medicine in Canada, traditional medicine has been, and continues to be, misunderstood and underestimated by mainstream health care providers. Indeed, for a period of time, one might describe the interaction as systematically condescending and discriminatory toward the traditional Aboriginal healing methods.

Traditional Aboriginal medicine in Canada should be understood, historically at least, as a diverse and heterogeneous phenomenon, albeit with some consistent principles and values such as the importance of spiritual well-being and balance in everyday life. Considerable variation exists from the medicine societies of the Kwakwaka'wakw and Anishina'beg to the family-based *angatquq* of the Inuit. Additionally, within each society, other healers such as midwives and herbalists were recognized. In those Aboriginal societies where traditional healing was organized into a more institutional framework, resistance to the destructive forces described above was possible; in situations where healers functioned independently, such as among the Inuit, resistance was weaker.

The purpose of this brief review is to underscore the historical basis for contemporary differences in Aboriginal response to the renewal of traditional medicine. The resurgence of ceremonial activity for healing purposes has made a profound change in the lives of many Aboriginal people and now constitutes a widely utilized alternative to Western medicine in many communities, particularly in Western Canada. Moreover, Western health care providers are proving increasingly interested and open to its potential, as evidenced by the increasing demand on traditional healers to introduce and orient health care workers to the concepts of traditional Aboriginal medicine.[113]

It would be a mistake however, to characterize all Aboriginal communities and individuals as participants in traditional medicine. Many communities and individuals have adopted Christianity to provide a spiritual basis for well-being and remain sceptical of "Indian or traditional medicine." Many communities and individuals regard Christian spirituality as a legitimate and important component of their culture and look to these values as a basis for community healing. Even then, traditional medicine and Christianity at times coexists in the same communities, families and individuals.

Traditional medicine must also be understood in more holistic terms than Western medicine.[114] Attempts to compare the two systems from a Western institutional perspective fail to grasp the pervasive way in which Aboriginal medicine is constituted as foundational to cultural practices, independent of the state-imposed regulatory structures of contemporary Aboriginal life. Aboriginal medicine works largely because participants accept the authority of medicine people to effect changes in their everyday lives. This authority derives from an altogether different source than the authority delegated from the Canadian state. Aboriginal medicine, in this sense, is a way of life, complete with guidelines for behaviour, systems of authority, and in some instances, punitive mechanisms.[115] As such, it should also be considered in the context of self-government. It is not a system that can be simply regulated by community, band, or tribal governments in the same way governments can control institutions of colonial medicine. It is more likely that various levels of Aboriginal government will be regulated by the authority structure of traditional medicine.

An example of the potential role for traditional medicine in community health programs in the context of self-government can be found in the experience of the Peguis First Nation in Manitoba.[116] During the 1980s, increasing numbers of band members approached health centre staff (previously transferred to band control) for assistance in accessing traditional healers. In 1985, citing FNIHB's mission statement as defined in the 1979 Indian Health Policy, health centre staff were able to facilitate referral to traditional healers by negotiating the provision of travel costs as part of uninsured service benefits from FNIHB. Demand for these services has grown to the point where a traditional healer now travels to Peguis at least once every three months to hold "clinics" at the Matootoo Lake traditional healing centre. This healing centre was established by Mide Megwun Bird, who is one of seven traditional Chiefs appointed by the female elders of the Three Fires (Midewiwin) Society. These clinics usually see an average of thirty to forty clients. Between July 1991 and March 1993, the health centre reported 325 client referrals for traditional healing: these numbers did not include people who approached the healers directly. The success of the traditional clinic has raised questions about limitations in FNIHB support, referral systems with hospitals, and regulatory systems to ensure quality of care. For Peguis people involved, raising the awareness of Western health professionals and maintaining internal control over regulating the practice are essential for future development.

In 1998 the federal government created the Aboriginal Healing Foundation (AHF). It has an eleven-year mandate to allocate $350 million toward addressing the legacy of physical and sexual abuse of Aboriginal students in residential schools. A central part of its mandate is to fund healing services, provided through healing centres and community activities that may utilize traditional or Western approaches to treatment. All funded projects must involve a holistic approach, encompassing the four domains of the Medicine Wheel. The program themes which guide the Foundation's funding activities are: community-based healing and healing centres; restoring balance in the community through early detection and prevention of abuse; developing and enhancing Aboriginal capacities to provide healing activities; and disclosures of abuse through a historical record. Traditional healers will be self-regulating in this system, through a central advisory council that will ensure the credibility of healers operating as a result of funds from the Foundation.[117] As of April 2007, the AHF has funded 1,345 separate projects, mostly in the areas of mental health and healing, thereby filling a service gap that has been repeatedly documented.[118] It remains unclear as to how the mental health and healing needs of communities will be served once the mandate of the AHF ends in March 2009. A recent report raised this issue, stating that should these services not be replaced at the community level, provincial mental health services could see a rise in demand for their services,[119] raising concerns over continuity, responsiveness, and appropriateness.

Contemporary Issues in Self-Government and Health

The *British North America* (*BNA*) *Act*'s stipulation of the federal responsibility for Indians has already been described. In addition, section 92 provided for provincial roles and responsibilities in establishing and delivering health services. Perhaps unwittingly, this laid the groundwork for the federal and provincial governments to disclaim responsibility for health services provided to Aboriginal people. The provinces interpret the *BNA Act* as a clear statement that the federal government should bear the burden of financing the delivery of First Nations and Inuit community-based health services (and indeed in some cases, even off-reserve health programs), outside of those prescribed in the *Canada Health Act*, namely, accessible hospital and physician services to all Canadians. Although Aboriginal people are included in the financing formula to provinces and territories (through the Canada Health and Social Transfer), reimbursement strategies have been engineered with the federal government, who has contracted university medical faculties to provide services to those communities which are too isolated to access hospitals and physician offices in towns and cities.

The jurisdictional disputes between federal and provincial governments concerning the provision of health and social services to Aboriginal people have served to diminish the effectiveness of the Canadian health system in addressing health concerns of this population. A number of key issues have emerged to illustrate this point. First, until 1999, the *Indian Act* allowed First Nations to restrict voting rights to those First Nations members living on reserve only. A 1999 Supreme Court decision, *Corbiere v. Canada,* however ruled that section 77 of the *Indian Act* violated the Canadian Charter of Rights.[120] First Nations now find themselves politically and legally obligated to First Nations members living off-reserve, while at the same time receiving virtually no funding to provide services to them.

Second, individuals of First Nation ancestry not eligible for registration under the *Indian Act* are generally called non-status or non-registered Indians. For these individuals, funding for health and social programs does not come from the federal government. They are instead understood to fall under provincial jurisdiction, and as such have the same rights of access to programs and services such as health care, income assistance, and education as any other Canadian resident of their province or territory. In theory, the jurisdictional carving is neat. In practice however, Bill C-31 is expected to result in increasing numbers of individuals of First Nation ancestry not eligible for registration.[121] Those who may be born on-reserve, and share the culture, language, practices, and needs of their cultural peers and a parent, may be denied access to the same culturally appropriate services, including the right to live on-reserve, as a result of a bureaucratic provision. The bureaucratic construct of "Indian" is a poor proxy for cultural affiliation. Further, population projections show that Bill C-31 will result in a rapid increase in the number of non-registered individuals living on-reserve,[122] who will require access to primary health care. Current policies suggest these individuals should seek care outside the reserve and in provincial facilities. While seemingly reasonable, this is not without challenges as a result of poverty, lack of access to public or private means of transportation, geography, and winter weather conditions. In reality, most First Nations communities who now manage their on-reserve health services, find themselves morally obligated to serve all residents living on-reserve, partially because many of the non-status residents are the dependent children of community members who themselves have status. A recent study completed by Lavoie & Forget[123] estimates that, by 2029, Bill C-31 may cause Manitoba First Nations Health Organizations to face an additional $23M (2004 constant dollars) in the costs of providing health care without a corresponding increase in funding, thereby further stretching already limited resources.[124]

Third, the federal role for health services extends to public health and nursing services in most First Nations and Inuit communities: in remote communities, treatment is provided by nurses with an expanded scope of practice. The Non-Insured Health Benefit (NIHB) program provides some federal benefits whether resident on- or off-reserve. The NIHB program is a payer of last resort for health services (meaning those services not provided by provincial resources or paid by third-party insurers), and an eligible list of benefits is determined through medical or dental necessity. Even with this program, many areas of First Nations and Inuit needs have slipped between federal and provincial jurisdictions, including home care and mental health services. New areas are emerging following FNIHB's delisting of medication from the formulary.[125] The federal government's view of what constitutes a 'health service' is narrowly defined to include primary prevention services. This has created further fragmentation in the provision of health services and presents a barrier to an integrated holistic approach to health.

Fourth, as one of the most vulnerable groups in the Canadian population, residents of Aboriginal communities are particularly sensitive to downsizing and other cost-cutting measures in provincial health systems. Escalating health costs in the 1980s collided with constantly declining federal transfer payments, and a dramatic overhaul of provincial health systems. The regionalization model now in place in most provinces has pushed health program development and resource allocation decisions down to the level of regional health boards and/or community councils. This has added a third level of government making decisions on health services which impact Aboriginal people. This closer-to-home approach has created an opportunity for Aboriginal communities, both rural and urban, to liaise with one board to ensure that changes to health services are developed taking their needs into account. The effectiveness of this communication varies from region to region, depending on the proximity of the Aboriginal community to the major service centre in the region, the receptivity of the regional health board to deal with Aboriginal concerns, and, in the case of First Nations, their preference to deal only with the federal government. Regional health boards, for their part, sometimes exclude First Nations communities from consultations, because they are seen as a federal responsibility and therefore present no obligation for the board to seek input. Still, a phenomenon is emerging. As transferred communities and regional health authorities meet for joint planning, jurisdictional issues of joint interest are identified.[126] In these processes, regional health authorities may find themselves caught between their obligation to follow directions from the provincial government, and their interest in increasing their responsiveness to communities. In joint planning sessions, politicized issues are being taken on by the First Nations leadership, on behalf of all communities. In effect, First Nations and Inuit communities are emerging as the only voice in the Canadian health care system that is independent from provincial governments and their centralized planning processes.

Fifth, downsizing and restructuring of health services to a population which relies on services from different jurisdictions creates scenarios of cost shifting.[127] In the early 1990s, Indian and Northern Affairs Canada's unilateral decision to no longer cover NIHB for First Nations living off-reserve on social assistance forced the provinces and FNIHB to pick up these expenses. In the late 1990s, it was the unilateral shift to home care by the provinces that forced FNIHB to create the First Nations and Inuit Home and Community Care program. Delays in response by either level of government have at times resulted in gaps in services. As the federal program is capped, the end result may be that certain First Nations and Inuit health needs will not be met by either provincial or federal governments for extended periods of time. Provincial health care (PHC) initiatives, such as delisting of previously insured services, early discharge from hospital and increased need for home care, user fees for prescriptions, as well as delisting of "federal clients," has placed greater demands on the federal NIHB Program and on-reserve services which are also operating in a capped-budget envelope. Provincial reforms are redirecting institutional care resources to community-based care. Although the provinces do not dispute their responsibilities for hospital care to First Nations and Inuit, the refocusing to community-delivered care moves these resources to an area considered the mandate of the federal government. Thus it is difficult, if not impossible for First Nations and Inuit communities to benefit from increased provincial resources for home care or outreach mental health programs. Meanwhile, FNIHB has imposed caps on funding to transferred communities. This has resulted in an impoverishment trend, whereby transferred communities have access to fewer and fewer resources on a per capita basis to provide for a growing population with increasingly higher needs for community-based interventions resulting from complex morbidities.[128] Evidence showing a disproportionate utilization of secondary and tertiary care services for ambulatory-care-sensitive conditions[129] suggests barriers to accessing PHC services.[130] Moreover, a 2002 study by Martens et al. found the number of Aboriginal amputations resulting from diabetes complications was 16 times higher than that of other Manitobans. This suggests that adequate local access to primary health care is indeed compromised.

And finally, jurisdictional issues also impact Métis and non-status individuals of First Nation ancestry living off-reserve, as the provinces largely disclaim responsibility for these groups, again citing federal jurisdiction in non-*Canada Health Act* matters. FNIHB, in delivering the mandate of federal legislation, is not responsible for Métis and non-status individuals of First Nation ancestry, whether or not they reside in Métis communities or in rural or urban settings. The parliamentary standing committee that undertook a study of the health of Aboriginal peoples has documented jurisdictional issues resulting in health service gaps for urban non-status and Métis people (Standing Committee on Health, 1995). Some examples include:

- Native Council of Nova Scotia: off-reserve people are 'pitted in a jurisdictional void';

- Métis Nation of Alberta: Métis people are often excluded from new provincial health services as these governments do not want to acknowledge a fiduciary responsibility to Métis peoples as one of the Aboriginal peoples;

- National Association of Friendship Centres: one of the biggest problems facing urban Aboriginal peoples is the jurisdictional issue among federal, provincial, territorial, and municipal governments, and the general government designation of "who's Indian, who's not Indian, who's Métis, who's status, or who's Inuit;"

- Vancouver Native Health Society: in reference to the downtown east side of Vancouver, a community which is the poorest in Canada and which has the largest population of Aboriginal people in western Canada, "the downtown east side certainly has all the markings one might expect to find on any typical reserve in Canada" including poverty, unemployment, and poor health. People in this community cannot access federal funds directly, and when approaching the provincial government, they "wind up getting all of the crumbs after the administration from the provincial bureaucracies ... and all of the other distributions take place;"

- Manitoba Métis Federation: Métis and Indians are treated differently even if they live in neighbouring communities. The federal government health facilities and services are on First Nations reserves, and the federal government pays medical transportation costs of First Nations to urban hospitals and specialists. Nearby Métis people may access the on-reserve facilities, but not any of the transportation resources.[131]

The list of factors which are barriers to an effective, sustained First Nations, Inuit, Métis and other Aboriginal health strategy include:

1. The Canadian health system's emphasis on curative services and the poor health of Aboriginal people means that limited health resources go to treatment which leaves few resources for developing innovative approaches to preventing the cause of poor health. As described above, First Nations and Labrador Inuit communities have the option of assuming the administrative responsibility for health services through Health Transfer. However, the immediate demands of service provision in a financial system that does not allow program enrichment has meant that those communities that signed an agreement early in the 1990s have grown progressively poorer as population growths and costs soar, while resources remain the same. Both inequalities in per capita funding and an impoverishment trend have been documented in the recent National Evaluation.[132]

2. The health system's emphasis on the physical and mental domains to the exclusion of spiritual and cultural components of well-being, and the lack of culturally based health programming, does not provide the holistic approach which Aboriginal people have clearly stated is crucial to improving community and individual well-being.

3. Lack of integration of social and health services at federal and provincial levels means that there is no single, concerted approach to improve health through addressing the determinants of health, such as economic development, employment, housing, and education. Communities are left to negotiate through contradicting processes and priorities, with little leverage. Nowhere is this more apparent than in First Nations emergency planning discussions.

4. The erosion of the traditional role of women through the imposition of western models of governance, such as elected band councils, which have replaced the traditional hereditary system, is contrary to the proven role of women in Indigenous cultures as focal points sustaining health of a community.[133]

5. The legacy of the enforced dependency on the Canadian government, or in the case of urban Aboriginal and Métis, the neglect by the Canadian government, has meant communities have relied on provincial government-directed approaches to health services and have yet to be afforded the opportunity to develop integrated, effective Aboriginal health strategies.

Some provincial governments are now rethinking their roles in the provision of service in First Nations and Inuit communities, and services aimed at meeting the specific needs of Aboriginal peoples. For example, the Ontario Aboriginal Health Policy was adopted in 1994, resulting in the inclusion of Community Wellness Workers in the provincial health care system, the funding of ten Aboriginal Health Access Centres in urban environments as well as eight healing lodges and treatment centres.[134] Provincial governments in Manitoba, Saskatchewan, and Alberta have established Aboriginal health policy units within their provincial health departments to promote dialogue and coordinated planning. The *Future of Health Care in Canada*[135] and the SARS crisis[136] both highlighted serious gaps in services, especially in the area of public health. Intergovernmental processes bringing together First Nations leadership and federal and provincial government departments have emerged in both Manitoba and British Columbia to promote joint planning to address jurisdictional issues and gaps in services.[137]

Recently, the federal government has started to provide some resources for targeted programming to all Aboriginal groups, including the Métis and non-status. The approach has, however, been pan-Aboriginal, and criticized by the Métis National Council, the Assembly of First Nations, and the Inuit Tapiriit Kanatami.

Aboriginal people believe that true community healing and well-being can only be found through the path of self-government and self-determination that gives them full control over services provided to their communities, not merely the administration of separate federal efforts through a patchwork of programs. The federal government has recently affirmed a major recommendation of the Royal Commission on Aboriginal Peoples when it recognized the inherent right to self-government for Aboriginal people as an existing Aboriginal right within section 35 of the *Constitution Act, 1982*.[138] Self-government negotiations are taking many forms in Canada. Although most Canadians might equate self-government with high profile agreements such as the Nisga'a Treaty in British Columbia or the creation of the new territorial government of Nunavut in April 1999, much more modest initiatives are being negotiated at both an organizational and a community level. For example, Métis and off-reserve Aboriginal negotiation processes are being designed which include for discussion, self-government institutions, devolution of programs and services, and public government. The federal government has also indicated a commitment to work with First Nations who have existing treaties to achieve self-government in the context of this treaty relationship. What this means, however, in terms of health care, falls dramatically short of aspirations, as self-government agreements continue to include the funding of the same programs provided by FNIHB, which are funded at historical expenditure levels, fail to resolve issues related to jurisdiction, and do not reflect needs.

Conclusion

The preceding section described the connection between self-government and control over health services. However, health services alone do not determine the health of a community. Indeed, current evidence suggests that health is determined more by broad social factors than it is by health services.[139]

This final section will consider the relationship of self-government to health status from a population health perspective. Poverty has been known to be an important determinant of health for the last fifty years.[140] Mortality is significantly affected by social class.[141] Likewise, longevity can be linked to adequacy of income.[142] Aboriginal people suffer a high degree of unemployment, a high dependency on social assistance, and a low income relative to other Canadians: they live in poverty.[143] As noted, they also suffer disproportionate mortality rates. Insofar that self-government will improve the economic status of Aboriginal people it is reasonable to expect that health status will improve, likely from at least two sources. First, self-government is linked to land claims, the satisfactory negotiation of which will provide resources, in cash or land, to Aboriginal people. Second, self-government will create jobs or displacement in favour of Aboriginal people, and will provide wage employment for an expanded proportion of the population.

The real improvements in health, as reflected by self-government may stem from improvements in self-esteem and empowerment.[144] In 1986, the Honourable Jake Epp released a document entitled *A Framework for Health Promotion*.[145] Within it he cited the challenges of reducing inequities, increasing prevention, and enhancing coping by self-help, mutual care, and healthy environments. Strengthening community participation is a cornerstone of this framework. Grounding self-government in the traditional social values of Aboriginal medicine teachings further facilitates political, cultural, and health development. Self-government and its impact on health can well be seen within a health promotion context. Improvements in health can be expected from the act of empowerment that self-government will provide. This empowerment will foster the re-establishment of traditional health networks. It will likely change the policy-setting agenda for health that has to date been set externally. The likely rebalancing of the system in favour of Aboriginal values will improve the self-esteem of those working within it, and of those whom it serves.

The change in policy direction could well have an impact on health. If crowding can be reduced, and water and sewage systems improved, there will be coincident decrease in the incidence of infectious diseases. If employment, self-esteem, and personal empowerment are inherently improved, there will be a diminished number of the injuries, suicides, and homicides that plague communities today.

Finally, with the control implicit in self-government, Aboriginal people will assume roles now filled by non-Aboriginal people. The positive impact of this role modelling on young Aboriginal people will provide direction that will diminish alcohol, drug dependency, and violence within that cohort. Self-government, then, should be an enormous step in breaking the cycle of poverty, disadvantage, and hopelessness. As such, it will significantly alter the web of causation now defining the extensive burden of illness of Aboriginal people. These gains may be secured through self-government, if self-government agreements respect and reflect the needs, interests, and aspiration of Aboriginal peoples. On this last matter, doubts remain. While considerable progress can be seen for First Nations and Inuit, the Métis and non-status individuals of First Nations ancestry, however, have so far remained largely invisible and side-stepped by these developments.

NOTES

---

*   This chapter is a revised and updated version of John O'Neil, Laurel Lemchuk-Favel, Yvon Allard, and Brian Postl, "Community Healing and Aboriginal Self-Government," in *Aboriginal Self-Government in Canada: Current Trends and Issues*, 2nd Ed., ed., John H. Hylton, (Saskatoon: Purich Publishing, 1999). We extend our thanks to the authors of that chapter.

1   "Aboriginal people" is an umbrella term encompassing First Nations, Inuit and Métis, and is entrenched in the Constitution as amended in 1982. The term however glosses over cultural, legislative, and administrative complexities. "First Nations" is the preferred self-referent used by the Indigenous peoples of Canada historically known as "Indians." This collective term veils a multiplicity of nations, including Nisga'a, Cree, Ojibway, Salish, Mohawk, Mi'kmaq, and Innu, to name a few. In administrative terms, there are currently 627 First Nations recognised by the federal government (Indian and Northern Affairs Canada, 2002). These are political and administrative organizations that emerged to satisfy the requirements of the *Indian Act*. They may or may not be members of one of the 76 regional Tribal Councils. These numbers do not represent the whole of Indigenous organizations, nor the number of Indigenous cultures: Inuit and Métis are excluded.

   Inuit is also a collective self-referent that refers to the Arctic people historically known as Eskimos. Inuit themselves recognise local groups with different names (Pallurmiut, Inuvialuit, etc.) reflecting the complexity of Arctic history and a subtlety in cultural differences glossed over by outsiders. Finally, Métis refers to the descendants of French or Scottish traders and Cree or Ojibway women who settled on the Red River area, north of what is now Winnipeg, Manitoba, developing their own blended culture and their own language, Metchif. After Confederation, the Métis were not entitled to sign treaties. Like non-status Indians, themselves descendents of status Indians and non-Aboriginals, Métis do not benefit from the special provisions made by the federal government for a number of programs, including community-based health services.

   For the purpose of this chapter, the term Aboriginal will be used only when statements apply to First Nations living on and off-reserve, Inuit, Métis and non-status individuals of First Nation ancestry, inclusive. In other cases, individual self-referents will be used. The term Indian will only be used when quoting historical documents, or when speaking of the *Indian Act*'s legal term "Indians" which defines access to certain federal programs and benefits.

   We have coined the expression "non-status individuals of First Nation ancestry" to refer to individuals who lost their Indian status as a result of provisions embedded in the *Indian Act*, and who find themselves in jurisdictional limbo. This is a growing yet largely invisible group in Canada, facing specific challenges (Clatworthy & Four Directions Project Consultants, 2001; Clatworthy, 2003). The term indigenous will also be used when speaking of a collective experience that crosses national boundaries.

2   Naomi Adelson, "The Embodiment of Inequity." *Canadian Journal of Public Health* 96 (2005): S45-S61; Canadian Institute of Health Information, *Improving the Health of Canadians* (Ottawa: Canadian Institute of Health Information, 2004); First Nations Regional Health Survey National Committee, *First Nations Regional Longitudinal Health Survey (RHS) 2002/03 Results for Adults, Youths and Children Living in First Nations Communities* (Ottawa: First Nations and Inuit Regional Health Survey National Committee, 2005); First Nations and Inuit Regional Health Survey National Steering Committee, *First Nations and Inuit Regional Health Survey* (Ottawa: Health Canada and the Assembly of First Nations, 1999); Health Canada, *Healthy Canadians: A Federal Report on Comparable Health Indicators 2002* (Ottawa: Health Canada, 2002); Health Canada (FNIHB), *A Statistical Profile on the Health of First Nations in Canada* (Ottawa: Health Canada (FNIHB), 2003); and, Health Council of Canada, *The Health Status of Canada's First Nations, Métis and Inuit Peoples* (Ottawa: Health Council of Canada, 2005).

3   Judith Bartlett, "Involuntary Cultural Change, Stress Phenomenon and Aboriginal Health Status," *Canadian Journal of Public Health-Revue Canadienne de Sante Publique* 94(3) (2003): 165-6.

4   Linda Archibald, "Promising Healing Practices in Aboriginal Communities" in *Final Report of the Aboriginal Healing Foundation,* vol III (Ottawa: Aboriginal Healing Foundation, 2006).

5   Canadian Institute for Health Information, *Pan-Canadian Primary Health Care Indicators: Pan-Canadian Primary Health Care Indicator Development Project* (Ottawa: Canadian Institute for Health Information, 2006).

6   John O'Neil, Jeff Reading & Audrey Leader, "Changing the Relations of Surveillance: the Development of a Discourse of Resistance in Aboriginal Epidemiology," *Human Organization* 57 (1998): 230-7.

7   First Nations Regional Health Survey National Committee, *First Nations Regional Longitudinal Health Survey (RHS) 2002/03 Results for Adults, Youths and Children Living in First Nations Communities* (Ottawa: First Nations and Inuit Regional Health Survey National Committee, 2005) [2005 RHS].

8   Brian Schnarch, "Ownership, Control, Access, and Possession (OCAP) or Self-determination Applied to Research: a critical analysis of contemporary First Nations research and some options for First Nations communities," *Journal of Aboriginal Health* 1 (2004): 80-95.

9   First Nations Regional Health Survey National Committee, *First Nations Regional Longitudinal Health Survey.*

10   *Ibid.*

11   Michael Tjepkema, "The Health of the Off-Reserve Aboriginal Population," Supplement to *Health Reports,* Statistics Canada 13 (2002), 1-17.

12   Martin Turcotte & John Zhao, "Well-being of Off-Reserve Aboriginal Children," *Canadian Social Trends* 75, (2004): 22-7.

13   Royal Commission on Aboriginal Peoples, *Gathering Strength,* Vol. 3 (Ottawa: Royal Commission on Aboriginal Peoples, 1996).

14   Canadian Institute of Health Information, *Improving the Health of Canadians* (Ottawa: Canadian Institute of Health Information, 2004).

15   *Ibid.*

16   *Ibid.*

17   Michael Tjepkema, "Non-fatal Injuries among Aboriginal Canadians," *Health Reports* 16 (2005): 9-22.

18   First Nations Regional Health Survey National Committee, *First Nations Regional Longitudinal Health Survey (RHS) 2002/03 Results for Adults, Youths and Children Living in First Nations Communities.*

19   Canadian Institute of Health Information, *Improving the Health of Canadians.*

20   *Ibid.*

21   Public Health Agency of Canada, *HIV/AIDS Among Aboriginal Persons in Canada: A Continuing Concern* (Rep. No. April 2003) (Ottawa: Public Health Agency of Canada, 2003).

22   Canadian Institute for Health Information, *Improving the Health of Canadians.*

23   First Nations Regional Health Survey National Committee, *First Nations Regional Longitudinal Health Survey.*

24   Josée Lavoie, John O'Neil, Lora Sanderson, Brenda Elias, Javier Mignone, Judith Bartlett et al., *The National Evaluation of the Health Transfer Policy, Final Report* (Winnipeg: Manitoba First Nations Centre for Aboriginal Health Research, 2005).

25   *Ibid.*

26   David Young, Grant Ingram & Lisa Swartz, *Cry of the Eagle: Encounters with a Cree Healer* (Toronto: University of Toronto Press, 1989).

27   First Nations Regional Health Survey National Committee, *First Nations Regional Longitudinal Health Survey.*

28   First Nations on Reserve and Inuit Adults, and Reading, The Tobacco Report (Ottawa: First Nations and Inuit Regional Health Survey, 1999)

29   Primary prevention activities refer to early interventions designed to prevent the onset of chronic conditions. Secondary prevention activities focus on assisting in the management of chronic illness to avoid or delay the development of complications. Tertiary prevention activities are designed to assist in the management of complications once they manifest themselves, to ensure that optimal autonomy is retained.

30   Josée Lavoie, "The Transformative Change Accord, a Step in the Right Direction? Sure, Any Others?" in Prince George: Unpublished conference presentation, Northern Aboriginal Health Research Gathering, March 2007.

31   Michael Chandler, & Chris Lalonde, "Cultural Continuity as a Hedge Against Suicide in Canada's First Nations," *Transcultural Psychiatry* 35 (1998): 191-219.

32   O'Neil, Reading & Leader, 230-37.

33   Jeff Reading, "The Canadian Institutes of Health Research, Institute of Aboriginal People's Health: a global model and national network for Aboriginal health research excellence," *Can.J.Public Health* 94 (2003): 185-9.

34   *Ibid.*

35   Jacqueline Peterson & Jennifer Brown, *The New Peoples: Being and Becoming Métis in North America* (Winnipeg: University of Manitoba Press, 1985).

36   Canada, *Indian Self-government in Canada: Report of the Special Committee on Indian Self-government,* House of Commons, (Ottawa: Supply and Services Canada, 1983).

37 Augie Fleras & Jean Elliot, *The 'Nations Within': Aboriginal-State Relations in Canada, the United States, and New Zealand* (Toronto: Oxford University Press, 1992).

38 Jane Buikstra & Della Cook, "Paleopathology: an American Account," *Annual Review of Anthropology* 9 (1980): 433.

39 Dara Culhane Speck, *An Error in Judgment: The Politics of Medical Care in an Indian/White Community* (Vancouver: Talonbooks, 1987); Mark St. Pierre & Tilda Long Soldier, *Walking in the Sacred Manner: Healers, Dreamers, and Pipe Carriers – Medicine Women in the Plains Indians* (New York: Simon & Schuster, 1995); James Waldram, Ann Herring & T. Kue Young, *Aboriginal Health in Canada: Historical, Cultural and Epidemiological Perspectives*, 2nd ed. (Toronto: University of Toronto Press, 2006); and Cynthia Wesley-Esquimaux and Magdalena Smolewski, *Historic Trauma and Aboriginal Healing* (Ottawa: Aboriginal Healing Foundation, 2004).

40 Irving Hallowell, *Contributions to Anthropology: Selected Papers of A. Irving Hallowell* (Chicago: University of Chicago Press, 1976); and Linda Garro, "Resort to Traditional Healers in a Manitoba Ojibwa Community," *Arctic Medical Research* 47 (1988): 317-20.

41 Walter James Hoffman, *The Midewiwin or 'Grand Medicine Society' of the Ojibwa*. Seventh Annual Report of the Bureau of Ethnology to the Secretary of the Smithsonian, 1885-86 (Washington: US Government Printing Office, 1981); Wolgang Jilek & N. Todd, "Witchdoctors Succeed where Doctors Fail: Psychotherapy among Coast Salish Indians," *Canadian Psychiatric Association Journal* 19 (1974): 351-5; and Christopher Vecsey, *Traditional Ojibwa Religion and its Historical Changes* (Philadelphia: American Philosophical Society, 1983).

42 Young, Ingram & Swartz, *Cry of the Eagle*.

43 Joseph Jorgensen, *The Sun Dance Religion: Power for the Powerless* (Chicago: University of Chicago Press, 1972).

44 Russell Thornton, *American Indian Holocaust and Survival: a Population History since 1492* (Norman: University of Oklahoma Press, 1987).

45 Wesley-Esquimaux & Smolewski, *Historic Trauma*.

46 Harold Cardinal, *The Unjust Society: the Tragedy of Canada's Indians* (Edmonton: Hurtig Publishers, 1969).

47 Roger Gibbons & J. Rick Ponting, "Historical Overview and Background," in *Arduous Journey: Canadian Indians and Decolonization*, ed. J.R. Ponting (Toronto: McLelland and Stewart, 1986), 18-57.

48 George F. Stanley, "As Long as the Sun Shines and the River Flows: An Historical Comment," in *As Long as the Sun Shines and the River Flows: A Reader in Canadian Native Studies*, eds. A.L.Getty & A. Lussier (Vancouver: University of British Columbia Press, 1983).

49 Alexander Morris, *The Treaties of Canada with the Indians of Manitoba and the North-West Territories including the negotiations on which they were based*, 1991 ed. (Toronto: Belfords, Clarke & Co., 1880), 177.

50 René Fumoleau, *As Long as This Land Shall Last* (Toronto: McClelland and Stewart Ltd; 1973), 113.

51 *The Queen* v. *Sparrow* [1990] 1 S.C.R. 1075; *R*. v. *Nowegijick* [1983] 1 S.C.R. 29.

52 *Claxton* v. *Saanichton Marina Ltd*. [1989] 3 C.N.L.R. 46.

53 Yvonne Boyer, "The International Right to Health for Indigenous Peoples in Canada," Discussion Paper Series on Aboriginal Health, Legal Issues: No. 3 (Ottawa: National Aboriginal Health Organization, Native Law Centre, University of Saskatchewan, 2004).

54 *The Queen* v. *Johnston* [1966] 56 D.L.R. (2d) 749.

55 *Wuskwi Sipihk Cree Nation* v. *Canada* [1999] 164 F.T.R. 276, cited in *Danika Littlechild, The Treaty Right to Health*. Aboriginal Health and Remote Access Forum, presentation (Calgary, AB: February 22, 2007).

56 E. Brian Titley, *A Narrow Vision* (Toronto: University of Toronto Press, 1989).

57 P.H. Bryce, *The Story of a National Crime: An Appeal for Justice to the Indians of Canada* (Ottawa: James Hope and Sons, 1922).

58 Cited in J.R. Miller, *Skyscrapers Hide The Heavens: A History of Indian-White Relations* (Toronto: University of Toronto Press, 1989), 125.

59 Wesley-Esquimaux & Smolewski, *Historic Trauma*.

60 Mike Brogden, "The Rise and Fall of the Western Métis in the Criminal Justice Process," in *The Struggle for Recognition: Canadian Justice and the Métis Nation*, eds. Samuel W. Corrigan & Lawrence J. Barkwell (Winnipeg: Manitoba Métis Federation, 1991), 39-68.

61 Titley, *A Narrow Vision*.

62 George Graham-Cummings, "Health of the Original Canadians, 1867-1967," *Medical Services Journal* (1967): 115-66; Walter Vanast, "Hastening the Day of Extinction: Canada, Quebec, and the Medical Care of Ungava's Inuit, 1867-1967," *Etudes/Inuit/Studies* 15 (1991a): 55-84; and Bryce, The Story of a National Crime.

63 Mary Ellen Kelm, *Colonizing Bodies: Aboriginal Health and Healing in British Columbia, 1900-50* (Vancouver: UBC Press, 1998).

64 Corinne Hodgson, "The Social and Political Implications of Tuberculosis Among Native Canadians," *Canadian Review of Sociology and Anthropology* 19 (1982): 502-12; Robin McGrath, "Inuit Write About Illness: Standing on Thin Ice," *Arctic Medical Research* 50 (1991): 30-6; and Walter Vanast, "The Death of Jennie

Kanajuq: Tuberculosis, Religious Competition and Cultural Conflict in Coppermine, 1929-31," *Etudes/Inuit/Studies* 15 (1991): 75-104.

65 Sally Weaver, "Smallpox and Chickenpox: an Iroquoian Community's Reaction to Crisis, 1901-1902," *Ethnohistory* 18 (1971): 361-78.

66 John O'Neil & Patricia Kaufert, "Irniktakpunga!: Sex Determination and the Inuit Struggle for Birthing Rights in Northern Canada," in *Conceiving the New World Order: Global and Local Intersections in the Politics of Reproduction,* ed. F. Ginsberg & R. Rapp (Los Angeles: University of California Press, 1997).

67 Dara Culhane Speck, *An Error in Judgment;* Patricia Kaufert & John O'Neil, "Biomedical rituals and informed consent: Native Canadians and the negotiation of clinical trust," in *Social Science Perspectives on Medical Ethics,* ed. G.Weisz (Dordrecht: Kluwer Academic Publishers, 1989), 41-63.; Kelm, *Colonizing Bodies,* and her "Wilp Wa'ums: Colonial Encounter, Decolonization and Medical Care Among the Nisga'a," *Social Science & Medicine* 59 (2004): 335-49; Lavoie, "Shared concepts and conflicting meanings: public health politics in Nunavik health care" (MA Thesis, McGill University, 1993); O'Neil, "Health Care in the Central Canadian Arctic: Continuities" and "Change Health and Canadian Society: Sociological Perspectives," in *Health and Canadian Society: Sociological Perspective,* eds. David Coburn, Carl D'Arcy, George Murray Torrance (Toronto: Fitzhenry and Whiteside, 1981); and O'Neil, "The Cultural and Political Context of Patient Dissatisfaction in Cross-cultural Clinical Encounters: a Canadian Inuit Study," *Medical Anthropology Quarterly,* 3, (1989): 325-43.

68 J. Rick Ponting & Roger Gibbons, *Out of Irrelevance: A Sociopolitical Introduction to Indian Affairs in Canada* (Toronto: Butterworths, 1980).

69 Leroy Little Bear, Menno Boldt, & J. Anthony Long, *Pathways to Self-Determination: Canadian Indians and the Canadian State* (Toronto: University of Toronto Press, 1989).

70 Frank Cassidy & Robert Bish, *Indian Government: Its Meaning in Practice* (Lanztville, BC: Oolican Books, 1989); and David C. Hawkes, *Aboriginal People and Government Responsibility: Exploring Federal and Provincial Roles* (Ottawa: Carleton University Press, 1991).

71 Auditor General of Canada, *Department of National Health and Welfare* (Auditor General of Canada: Ottawa, 1982).

72 Thomas Berger, *Report of the Advisory Commission on Indian and Inuit Health Consultation* (Ottawa: National Health and Welfare, 1980).

73 Evelyn J. Peters, "Federal and provincial responsibilities for the Cree, Nascapi and Inuit under the *James Bay and Northern Quebec,* and the *Northeastern Quebec Agreements,*" in *Aboriginal Peoples and Government Responsibility: Exploring Federal and Provincial Roles,* ed. David C. Hawkes (Ottawa: Carleton University Press, 1989), 173-242.

74 Richard Salisbury, *A Homeland for the Cree: Regional Development in James Bay 1971-1981* (Montreal: McGill-Queen's University Press, 1986); and Josée Lavoie, "The Decolonization of the Self and the Recolonization of Knowledge: The Politics of Nunavik Health Care," in *Aboriginal Autonomy and Development in Northern Quebec and Labrador,* ed. Colin Scott (Vancouver: UBC Press, 2001).

75 Jennifer Stonier, "The Innuulitsivik Maternity," in *Childbirth in the Canadian North: Epidemiological, Clinical and Cultural Perspectives,* eds. John D. O'Neil & Patricia Gilbert (Winnipeg: Northern Health Research Unit, 1990), 61-74.

76 O'Neil & Kaufert, *Irniktakpunga.*

77 Four Worlds Development Project, "Survival Secrets of NNADAP Workers," *Four Worlds Exchange* 2 (1990): 24-39.

78 Richard Jock, John Paul, & Virginia Toulouse, *National Native Alcohol and Drug Abuse Program General Review* (Ottawa: Final Report Submitted to the NNADAP Review Steering Committee, 1998).

79 Lavoie, et al. *Health Transfer Policy, Final Report.*

80 Lavoie, *Shared concepts: Nunavik health care.*

81 Monique Bégin, "Discussion paper: Transfer of Health Services to Indian Communities" (Ottawa: National Health and Welfare, 1981).

82 Linda Garro, Joanne Roulette, & Robert Whitmore, "Community Control of Health Care Delivery: The Sandy Bay Experience," *Canadian Journal of Public Health* 77 (1986): 281-84.

83 National Health and Welfare & Treasury Board of Canada, "Memorandum of Understanding between the Minister of National Health and Welfare and the Treasury Board concerning the Transfer of Health Services to Indian Control" (Ottawa: 1989).

84 Dara Culhane Speck, "The Indian Health Transfer Policy: a step in the right direction, or revenge of the hidden agenda?," *Native Studies Review* (1989) 5(1): 187-213.

85 See Assembly of First Nations, *Assembly of First Nations comments on M.S.B. response to the Recommendations made at the AFN National Indian Health Transfer Conference in November of 1987;* and its *Special Report: The National Indian Health Transfer Conference* (Ottawa: Assembly of First Nations, 1988); R. Browning & A. van de Sande, "Long Term Evaluation of the Health Transfer Initiative: Major Findings," *Native Social Work*

Journal 2 (1999): 153-62; Institute for Human Resource Development, *Long term evaluation of the Health Transfer Initiative* (1995); A. Gibbons, *Short-term evaluation of Indian Health Transfer* (Victoria, BC: Adrian Gibbons and Associates, 1992).

86 Health Canada FNIHB, *Transfer status as of March 2007.* (Ottawa, Health Canada, First Nations and Inuit Health Branch, 2007).

87 *Ibid.*

88 Lavoie et al., *Health Transfer Policy, Final Report.*

89 Health Canada (FNIHB), "Health Contribution Funding Framework - Moving Forward" (powerpoint presentation) (Ottawa: Health Canada (FNIHB), 2005).

90 Ann Macaulay, "The History of a Successful Community-oriented Health Service in Kahnawake, Quebec," *Canadian Family Physician* 34 (1988): 2167-9; Louis Montour & Ann Macaulay, "Diabetes Mellitus and Atherosclerosis: Returning research results to the Mohawk community," *Canadian Medical Association Journal* 139 (1988): 201-2.

91 V. Johnston, "Health: Yesteryear and Today," in *Multiculturalism and Health Care: Realities and Needs,* ed. R. Masi (Toronto, Ontario: Canadian Council on Multicultural Health, 1990); and C.P. Shah, "A National Overview of the Health of Native Peoples Living in Canadian Cities," in *Inner City Health—The Needs of Urban Natives: Proceedings,* ed. Y. Yacoub (Edmonton: University of Alberta, 1988).

92 Cecilia Benoit, Dena Carroll & Munaza Chaudhry, "In Search of a Healing Place: Aboriginal Women in Vancouver's Downtown Eastside," *Social Science & Medicine* 56 (2003): 821-33.

93 R.N. Nuttall, "The development of Indian health boards in Alberta," *Canadian Journal of Public Health,* 73(1982): 300-03.

94 I. Allen "Community health representatives working in Labrador Inuit communities," in *Circumpolar Health 90,* ed. Brian Postl, et al. (Winnipeg, University of Manitoba Press, 1990).

95 John O'Neil, "The Impact of Devolution on Health Services in the Baffin Region, NWT: a case study," in *Devolution and Constitutional Development in the Canadian North,* ed. Gurston Dacks (Ottawa: Carleton University Press, 1990).

96 Michael Kirby, *The Health of Canadians: The Federal Role* (Ottawa: The Standing Senate Committee on Social Affairs, Science and Technology, 2002).

97 National Advisory Committee on SARS and Public Health, *Learning from SARS - Renewal of Public Health in Canada, A report of the National Advisory Committee on SARS and Public Health* (Ottawa: Health Canada, 2003).

98 *Ibid.*, 79.

99 Assembly of Manitoba Chiefs, *The Intergovernmental Committee on First Nations Health* (Winnipeg: Assembly of Manitoba Chiefs, 2006).

100 The Intergovernmental Committee on First Nation Health (ICFNH), "Intergovernmental Primary Health Care Policy Framework on First Nation Health Care," Draft #1, version 2 (Winnipeg, 2006).

101 CBC News, *"In-Depth: Aboriginal Canadians, Undoing the Kelowna Agreement,"* (Ottawa, Nov 21st, 2006, accessed November 23rd, 2007), http://www.cbc.ca/news/background/aboriginals/undoing-kelowna.html

102 British Columbia Assembly of First Nations, First Nations Summit, Union of British Columbia Indian Chiefs & Government of British Columbia, *The Transformative Change Accord: First Nations Health Plan, Supporting the health and wellness of First Nations in British Columbia* (Vancouver: Government of British Columbia, 2005).

103 Assembly of First Nations, *First Nations Public Health: A Framework for Improving the Health of Our People and Our Communities* (Ottawa: Assembly of First Nations, 2006).

104 Assembly of First Nations, *Meeting the Health Needs: First Nations in Crisis* (Ottawa: Assembly of First Nations, 1998)

105 Brian Garner, *Black's Law Dictionary,* 4th ed. (St. Paul, Minn.: West Publishing Co, 1968)

106 D. Pharand, "Annex II. Canada's Fiduciary Obligation under General Principles of Law Recognized in National Legal Systems," in *Canada's Fiduciary Obligation to Aboriginal Peoples in the Context of Accession to Sovereignty by Quebec,* ed. Royal Commission of Aboriginal Peoples (Ottawa: Minister of Supply and Services Canada, 1995).

107 Métis Nation of Alberta (2005). "First Ministers Meeting 2005, Historical turning point for the Métis Nation," Métis Nation of Alberta http://www.albertametis.com/firstministers.aspx.

108 *Kruger* v. *the Queen* [1985] 17 D.L.R. (4th) 591.

109 George Brown and Ron Maguire, *Indian Treaties in Historical Perspective.* (Ottawa: Department of Indian Affairs and Northern Development; 1979).

110 *R.* v. *Sioui* [1990] 1 S.C.R. 1025.

111 Liberal Party of Canada, *Creating Opportunity: The Liberal Plan for Canada* (Ottawa: Liberal Party of Canada, 1993).

112 Jerome Berthelette, Medical Services Branch. Letter to Gina Whiteduck, First Nations Health Commission,

dated June 12, 1995. This was also cited in the original *Transfer Handbook* (Health and Welfare Canada (MSB), 1991). This has since been deleted.

113 For example, in June 1993, the Manitoba Medical Association, together with Brokenhead First Nation organized a Workshop on Traditional medicine which drew over 120 participants, 45 of whom were physicians.

114 Young, Ingram, & Swartz, *Cry of the Eagle.*

115 Claude Denis, *We Are Not You: First Nations and Canadian Modernity* (Peterborough: Broadview Press, 1997); Chief Thomas Fiddler & James Stevens, *Killing the Shamen* (Moonbeam ON: Penumbra Press, 1986).

116 B. Cohen, *Health Services Development in an Aboriginal Community: The Case of Peguis First Nation* (Peguis First Nation: Peguis First Nation, 1993).

117 Aboriginal Healing Foundation, *Annual Report 2005, Aboriginal Healing Foundation* (Ottawa: Aboriginal Healing Foundation, 2006).

118 John Elias & J. Greyeyes, "Report on an Environmental Scan of Mental Health Services in First Nations Communities in Canada for the Assembly of First Nations," 60. (Prince Albert, 1999); and Javier Mignone, John O'Neil, & Clarke Wilkie, *Mental Health Services Review, First Nations and Inuit Health Branch, Manitoba Region* (Winnipeg: University of Manitoba, 2003).

119 Josée Lavoie & Evelyn Forget, "A Financial Analysis of the Current and Prospective Health Care Expenditures for First Nations in Manitoba" (Manitoba: Centre for Aboriginal Health Research, 2006).

120 *Corbiere* v. *Canada* (Minister of Indian and Northern Affairs) [1999] 2 S.C.R. 203.

121 Stewart Clatworthy, "Impacts of the 1985 Amendments to the *Indian Act* on First Nations Populations" Clatworthy & Four Directions Project Consultants, First Nations Membership and Registered Indian Status (Winnipeg: Assembly of Manitoba Chiefs, 2001); and Stewart Clatworthy & Four Directions Project Consultants, *Membership and Indian Registration: Population Impacts of Bill C-31 on First Nations in Northern Manitoba* (draft) (Winnipeg: Assembly of Manitoba Chiefs, 2005).

122 Clatworthy, *First Nations Membership and Registered Indian Status.*

123 Lavoie & Forget, *A Financial Analysis.*

124 The recent British Columbia Supreme Court challenge to section 6 of the Indian Act (*McIvor et al.* v. *The Registrar, Indian and Northern Affairs Canada* [2007] BCSC 26) could potentially change registration rules. At the time of writing, the impact of this court case on the *Indian Act*, policy, and practices remains undefined.

125 Lavoie & Forget, *A Financial Analysis.*

126 Lavoie, *A Cross-jurisdictional Decision-making Process for Northern Saskatchewan, volume I: Findings, Analysis and Recommendations: Final Report* (Winnipeg: Manitoba First Nations Centre for Aboriginal Health Research, 2006).

127 Lavoie & Forget, *A Financial Analysis.*

128 Lavoie, Forget, & O'Neil, "Why Equity in Financing First Nations On-Reserve Health Services Matters: Findings from the 2005 National Evaluation of the Health Transfer Policy," *Healthcare Policy,* 2 (2007): 79-98.

129 Ambulatory Care Sensitive Conditions (ACSC) are conditions for which hospitalization is very sensitive to the provision of PHC, such as hospitalization for complications related to Type 2 Diabetes Mellitus.

130 Patricia Martens, R. Bond, Laurel Jebamani, et al., *The Health and Health Care Use of Registered First Nations People Living in Manitoba: a Population-based Study* (Winnipeg: Manitoba Centre for Health Policy, Department of Community Health Sciences, Faculty of Medicine, University of Manitoba, 2002); Patricia Martens, D. Sanderson, & Laurel Jebamani, "Health Services Use of Manitoba First Nations People: is it related to underlying need?" *Can.J.Public Health,* 96 Suppl 1, (2005): S39-S44; Baiju R. Shah, Nadia Gunraj, & Janet E. Hux, "Markers of Access to and Quality of Primary Care for Aboriginal People in Ontario, Canada," *American Journal of Public Health,* 93, (2003): 798-802.

131 Standing Committee on Health, *Toward Holistic Wellness: the Aboriginal Peoples* (Ottawa: Public Works and Government Services Canada, 1995).

132 Lavoie et al. *The Health Transfer Policy, Final Report.*

133 Mona Etienne & Eleanor Leacock, *Women and Colonization, Anthropological Perspectives* (New York: Praeger, 1980); Laura Klein & Lillian Ackerman, *Women and Power in Native North America* (Norman: University of Oklahoma Press, 1995).

134 Government of Ontario, "New directions: Aboriginal health policy for Ontario," Executive Summary (Toronto: Government of Ontario, 1994).

135 Roy Romanow, "Building on Values, the Future of Health Care in Canada," Final Report, (Ottawa. 2002).

136 National Advisory Committee on SARS and Public Health. *Learning from SARS - Renewal of Public Health in Canada, A report of the National Advisory Committee on SARS and Public Health* (Ottawa, Health Canada, 2003).

137 Assembly of Manitoba Chiefs, *The Intergovernmental Committee on First Nations Health* (Winnipeg: Assembly of Manitoba Chiefs, 2006); and, British Columbia Assembly of First Nations, First Nations Summit, Union of British Columbia Indian Chiefs, & Government of British Columbia, *The Transformative Change Accord: First Nations Health Plan, Supporting the Health and Wellness of First Nations in British Columbia* (Vancouver: Government of British Columbia, 2005).

138 Government of Canada, *Gathering Strength: Canada's Aboriginal Action Plan* (Ottawa: Minister of Public Works and Government Services Canada: Ottawa, 1997).

139 Robert Evans, Morris Barer, & Theodor Marmor, *Why are Some People Healthy and Others Not? The Determinants of Health of Populations* (New York: A. de Gruyter, 1994); and Michael Marmot & Richard Wilkinson, *Social Determinants of Health* (Oxford: Oxford University Press, 2006).

140 Margaret Whitehead, Peter Townsend, & Nick Davidsen, *Inequalities in Health: The Black Report* (Middlesex: Penguin, 1982).

141 Margaret Whitehead, "The concepts and principles of equity and health," *International Journal of Health Services* 22 (1992): 429-45.

142 Lisa Berkman & Lester Breslow, *Health and Ways of Living: the Alameda County Study* (New York: Oxford University Press, 1983).

143 J. Hagey, G. Larocque, G. & C. McBride, *Highlights of Aboriginal Conditions 1981-1989.* Parts I, II, and III, Quantitative Analysis & Socio-Demographic Research Working Paper Series 89-1, 89-2, and 89-3 (Ottawa: Finance and Professional Services, Indian and Northern Affairs Canada, 1989).

144 Michael Chandler & Chris Lalonde, "Cultural continuity as a hedge against suicide in Canada's First Nations," *Transcultural Psychiatry* 35, (1998): 191-219; and, Ilona Kickbusch, "Health Promotion: A World Health Organization Discussion Document on the Concept and Principles," *Canadian Public Health Association Health Digest* 8 (1984): 101-2.

145 Jake Epp, *Achieving Health for All: A Framework for Health Promotion* (Ottawa: Health & Welfare Canada, 1986).

UNFINISHED BUSINESS:

Self-government and the James Bay Northern Quebec Agreement Thirty Years Later [1]

Gabrielle A. Slowey, York University

As early as the 1950s, the Quebec government considered exploiting the energy potential flowing into James Bay. However, lack of political will compounded by the remoteness of the resource and the high costs of extraction undermined any interest in development. All that changed in 1971, when the provincial government, under the leadership of the newly elected premier, Robert Bourassa, unveiled plans to develop hydroelectric power by constructing dams in the watershed of eastern James Bay.[2] While the Quebec government believed development would proceed quickly given the "sparse population" of the territory, it was soon confronted with outrage and protest by the almost eleven thousand Aboriginal peoples living in the region: 6,500 Cree (or "Eeyouch," who call their land Eeyou Istchee) and 4,200 Inuit (who call their land Nunavik), who felt that the government's actions violated their Aboriginal rights.[3]

For the provincial government, the James Bay project promised prosperity, with cheap power attracting new industry and creating jobs. For the Cree, it threatened their traditional way of life. Battle lines were drawn until a legal challenge, the *James Bay Development Corporation* v. *Kanatewat*[4] pushed the province to negotiate with the Indigenous inhabitants of northern Quebec.[5] On 11 November 1975, the Cree and Inuit of Northern Quebec, through the *James Bay Northern Quebec Agreement* (JBNQA) surrendered their claim to land and withdrew their opposition to development in return for $225 million dollars, unrestricted hunting rights to 170,000 square kilometres of land and, for the first time in Canada's modern treaty period, the opportunity for self-government.[6]

The JBNQA is the longest-standing example of a comprehensive treaty negotiated with people not previously covered by historic or existing treaty.[7] The agreement includes provisions concerning but not limited to lands, resource and environmental management, self-government, financial compensation, economic development, education, health and social services. More specifically, through self-government, the JBNQA promised the Cree powers to protect their traditional way of life and the opportunity to participate in development occurring within their territory. In the thirty years since the agreement was signed, transformative and dramatic social, economic, and governance changes have taken place. Many of these have been positive changes for the lives of Cree people. But has the promise of self-government been fulfilled? That is, do the Cree enjoy self-government or does it continue to exist only in theory? A review of Cree self-government over the last 30 years indicates that although the JBNQA set the stage for self-government, Cree governance has only begun to grow since the signing of the *Cree-Naskapi (of Quebec) Act* in 1984 (CNQA) and the Paix des Braves in 2002. In fact, it was only very recently, in July 2007, that the federal government finally announced a deal with the Cree of northern Quebec that sets the stage for the realization of regional self-government. Together, these more recently negotiated agreements provide the organization and resources required to realize the promise of self-government made initially, thirty years ago, under the JBNQA.

This chapter begins by considering ways in which the promises of self-government contained in the JBNQA have yet to be fulfilled. It contemplates ways in which self-government of the Cree has been challenged by the agenda of the state and the consequences for its own political and economic development. It connects both an internal (Cree) and external (government) appetite for self-government to globalization, the development of resources and neo-liberal ideology. It concludes that increased intergovernmental co-operation is necessary to fulfill the promise of Cree self-government and suggests that many of the struggles currently confronting the Cree, from implementing self-governance to delivering programs to managing economic development, are not unique, but are in fact experiences common among other treaty First Nations in Canada.

The Promise of the JBNQA

Although the Cree possess an inherent and permanent right to govern their own territory, they have been denied that right since Ottawa assumed control over the governance and administration of all Indian bands in Canada in 1867. Under Ottawa's strict scrutiny, the scope of Cree governance was limited by government policy which held there were no Aboriginal rights. Instead, Aboriginal governments were constrained by and supervised under the terms of the *Indian Act* (1876). Because the *Indian Act* was an impediment for the proper exercise of local autonomy and local government, it became a focus for change in Cree-Canada relations. The Cree recognized that progress in self-government could not be made within the context of the *Indian Act*. Hence, the Cree seized the opportunity to advance beyond a relationship legislated unilaterally by Canada, and sought recognition and autonomy of the Cree as a people and a nation, through a negotiated relationship. In particular, the Cree wanted to redefine their relationship with the Governments of Canada and Quebec and seize control over local decision-making by negotiating the JBNQA. For its part, the federal government wished to extinguish Aboriginal title to the land while the province was also keen to off-load responsibilities for the provision of services to regional and community authorities. Regardless, the JBNQA offered the Cree the opportunity to reclaim control and achieve a vision of governance premised on political control over land, resources, and development and dedicated to the enhancement and advancement of their people.

The JBNQA covers a large amount of territory, spanning over 1.07 million square kilometers, initially encapsulating eight (now nine) permanent communities on the James Bay coast and in the Eeyou Istchee interior.[8] This includes the communities of Whapmagoostui, Chisasibi, Wemindji, Eastmain, Waskaganish, Nemaska, Waswanipi, Mistassini, and Oujé-Bougoumou.[9] Moreover, it is an extremely complex legal document, a complexity exemplified by provisions describing the three categories of land applied throughout Eeyou Istchee. Category 1 lands are those lands allocated for the exclusive use of the Cree and Inuit in and around their communities. Of a total 14,000 square kilometres of Category 1 lands, almost 5,600 belong to the Cree and form the land base upon which their governance is situated. Within the category, there are two further subcategories: Category 1A lands (3,300 square kilometres) which are subject to federal jurisdiction and Category 1B lands (2,300 square kilometres) which are under provincial jurisdiction.[10] Category II lands are those lands over which the Cree and Inuit have exclusive hunting, fishing, and trapping rights but no special right of occupancy. Of almost 155,000 square kilometres set aside as Category II lands, 68,790 square kilometres are allocated to the Cree. Finally, Category III lands make up the remainder of the territory covered under the agreement (910,711 square kilometres). Within the Category III area, the Cree and Inuit possess traditional harvesting rights, the right to participate in environmental protection and wildlife management regimes, the right to participate in the economic development of the area and also participation in a regional governance structure—such as it was in 1975. The general public is allowed access and use of the lands as they also have the character of provincial crown lands. So, even though the land regime was viewed by the signatories to the agreement as providing enough land to protect the traditional economy and culture of the Cree, lands assigned under Category 1 were ultimately "of minimal importance in relation to the total economy of Quebec."[11] That is, the lands set aside for the Cree, while of significant importance and value to the traditional practices and governance of the Cree did not jeopardize the development of Quebec's resources or hinder its economic development plan.[12] Moreover, throughout Eeyou Istchee the province retained surface and subsurface rights to all Cree territory.

Treaties, as instruments defining relationships between First Nations, Canada, and the provinces, must possess significant flexibility to accommodate evolving relationships. While the JBNQA is an excellent example of what co-operation between government and First Nations can achieve, it also demonstrates how treaties can be "iconic documents with no real significance for the people living under them."[13] This has been evident in the post-JBNQA era where the Cree have continued to fight for its implementation. Whether it was the failure to build remote roads (despite consultation with the Cree in the mid-1980s to build roads in the north, the roads were eventually built, not in James Bay, but on the north shore) or the failure to initiate an environmental protection regime which would involve Cree in decisions about development occurring in their region (supplanted instead in the 1990s by the *Canadian Environmental Assessment Act*), the fact is that the governments of Canada and Quebec failed to implement the JBNQA even though any building or development on any part of their territory is considered by the Cree to fall under the purview of their self-government.[14] Instead of working with the Cree on a government-to-government basis, the state relegated Cree involvement (i.e. in environmental assessment and co-management) to consultation and participation without decision-making power.[15] Without implementation of the 1975 treaty, therefore, the promises of the JBNQA are hollow and empty; just fancy words written on pieces of paper.

Cree co-operation in the 1970s soon turned to frustration in the 1980s as Canada abandoned its responsibilities. As former Grand Chief Ted Moses writes, "I want to be very clear about this. The federal government signed the *James Bay and Northern Quebec Agreement* and walked away."[16] In the 1980s the Cree successfully mounted opposition to the province's proposed Great Whale hydro project. However, Cree opposition to development occurring in the region further stymied their relationship with the government which refused to discuss implementation of the agreement. During this tumultuous time the Cree felt they missed out on important opportunities to participate in the development occurring around them. Based on this reality, the Cree chose to return to the negotiating table in an ongoing effort to have the potential of the JBNQA realized.

The Politics of Implementing Self-Government
The Cree-Naskapi (of Quebec) Act, 1984

Under the terms of the JBNQA, the federal government was obligated to negotiate special federal legislation with the Cree which would extend the powers of the band councils as new community governments and replace the provisions of the existing *Indian Act*.[17] However, it was not until 1984, almost ten years later, that the *Cree-Naskapi Act* (CNQA) was tabled to Parliament as the first example of Indian self-government legislation of Canada liberating the Cree from the confines of the *Indian Act*.[18] The development of the CNQA followed immediately upon the recommendations produced by the Penner Report (formally known as the Special Committee of Parliament on Indian Self-Government) in 1983 which strongly recommended that Aboriginal self-government be regarded as an Aboriginal right and entrenched in the Constitution. It was in the context of this new era, in which the government promoted a new bilateral and co-operative approach to making Aboriginal policy, that the Cree nation was involved in formulating its self-government framework.[19]

The CNQA represents an important step toward the realization of self-government. However, according to John Ciaccia, former member of the National Assembly for Mount-Royal, the JBNQA provided only for the Cree communities to be governed by local administrations equal to the other local communities and municipalities throughout Quebec.[20] It was, in the province's view, an agreement for a self-administration style of self-government. Yet this critique ignores the importance of authority and direct control returned from the Department of Indian Affairs to the Cree. As pointed out by the Waskaganish Band in its initial presentation to the Cree-Naskapi commission, "The elected band council became the head of a legal entity rather than performing a purely administrative function for the Department of Indian and Northern Affairs (INAC) as the case was under the *Indian Act*."[21] Furthermore, in a ruling handed down by Justice Ouellete of the Quebec Provincial Court, it was determined that the band council, operating under the CNQA, constituted an "autonomous level of government" responsible to its own members for its administration and the exercise of its powers and not to Parliament.[22] The removal of INAC control from the daily governance of First Nations thus signified an important departure from previous practices and contradicted the province's view at the time that Cree self-government was mere self-administration. It was not yet, however, officially self-government.

Between 1975 and 1984, Cree leaders like Billy Diamond and Ted Moses were entrenched in a fight for implementation of the JBNQA. With the finalization of the CNQA, however, these leaders returned home to begin the long and arduous process of building communities and constructing governments. In the post-CNQA era, the scope of self-governance enjoyed by the Cree grew to include real participation in the management of hunting, fishing, and trapping rights and social and environmental protection, Cree-controlled health and education authorities, the enactment of measures relating to policing and justice, and the establishment of local self-government. The CNQA also provided that bands be incorporated to allow them to function as legal entities with the rights, powers, and privileges of a natural person. This means the band governments can enter into contracts, own property, and take legal action. In short, the CNQA established a new legal regime that gave rise to a new political reality.[23] It provided for Cree governance on Cree land, promoting Cree traditional ways of life and practices and simultaneously incorporating new elements into Cree governance and institutions. That Cree government is now responsible and accountable to community members rather than INAC is a significant step toward self-government. Greater control over internal affairs and the management of Category IA lands enabled by the passage of the CNQA provided for conditions within which Cree self-government could finally begin to take shape. Consequently, it was not until the post-CNQA era that the governance of the Cree was noticeably transformed.

Like the JBNQA, however, implementation of the CNQA has been a challenge for the Cree because "when the parties left the negotiation table they went away without a framework for the orderly implementation of the CNQA and the harmonious evolution of their new relationship."[24] To elaborate, under the terms of the CNQA, the Cree-Naskapi commission is required to report on the status of the implementation of the CNQA every two years. However, the first commissioners were not appointed until February 1986, and since that time, the Commission has submitted ten biennial reports to the Minister of Indian Affairs on the status of implementation, reporting both on matters within the *Act* and within its enveloping legal framework of the *James Bay and Northern Quebec Agreement*, though the JBNQA framework itself remained an unaddressed issue. Moreover, while Canada and Quebec had initially believed that the costs of implementation of that agreement were low, it was soon apparent that this would not be the case. As far as the federal government was concerned, implementation of the CNQA rested with the Cree governments and their members, while the Cree felt it imperative that the government set aside the necessary resources in regard to the *Act*, and also that the *James Bay and Northern Quebec Agreement* required implementing self-government.[25] This discord concerning financial responsibility dominated the post-CNQA era as Cree compensation dollars and federal financial transfers proved an insufficient base upon which to support regional social orders and economies.[26]

The Paix des Braves, 2002

A significant flaw of the JBNQA is that it has been treated by governments as a static document lacking the flexibility that was earlier noted as an essential element for effective implementation. This, of course, contrasts with Hydro-Québec's approach and the Cree approach, which have been to seek amendments needed to accomplish their mutually agreed-to goals in respect to proposed new developments. With regard to governments however, as former Grand Chief Moses remarked, the JBNQA remains "a rigid, inflexible and unchanging instrument as it fails to evolve with the changing realities and dynamics of Eeyou local government."[27] For instance, in 1975, there were less than 7,000 Cree. Today that number has more than doubled and there are over 16,000 Cree living in the area.[28] While the JBNQA was supposed to provide the basis for a new relationship to grow, the denial of treaty promises and lack of good faith on the part of Canada and Quebec stunted any progress toward building a new partnership. This was a highly problematic position on the part of governments, because Cree communities are not stagnant or trapped in time. They have rapidly changing demographics and live in dynamic social, political, cultural, and natural environments. Communities constantly change and grow; adapting to changing conditions has been the key to Cree survival. Cree society has changed more rapidly in the past thirty years then most have in the past one hundred. In contrast, the JBNQA's main failure has been its entrenching Cree-Canada/Quebec relations in a specific time and place without anticipating the changes and future needs of either party. Furthermore, funding formulas negotiated in 1984 for program and service delivery do not take into account the costs of technological advances or changing needs of a rapidly growing population. And a major obstacle to the successful implementation of the JBNQA and CNQA has been insufficient financing.[29]

So it was with great fanfare on 7 February 2002 that a deal with the Quebec government was signed that allowed for continued hydro development in northern Quebec in exchange for $3.5 billion over 50 years, more control over their communities and economies, and the promise of more Hydro-Québec jobs.[30] The *Agreement Concerning a New Relationship between the Government of Quebec and the Crees of Quebec*, also referred to as 'the Paix des Braves' (PDB), received a vote of almost 70 per cent in favour of the deal. Viewed as a flexible agreement which will allow problems to be worked out through ongoing interaction, the ways in which it exceeds the JBNQA are significant. First, it provides the Cree with an annual payment of $70 million over the 50 year term of the Agreement, indexed to the value of the output of the hydroelectric, mining and forestry industries in the territory. Second, it provides Quebec with permission to further develop La Grande Complexe (Eastmain 1 and Eastmain 1A) but requires further social and environmental impact review including consultation before being licensed to be built.[31] Finally, it enables the Cree to assume, for 50 years, the implementation of many of the obligations assigned to Quebec under the JBNQA. This is critical as it increases the scope and authority of the Cree.

Although the Paix des Braves has been likened to an Impact Benefit Agreement, this comparison is false since the money for the Cree provided in the Paix des Braves is not tied to a specific development project but instead comes from the province. Monies provided reflect the total economic value of industry activity occurring in Eeyou Istchee, hence, the Paix des Braves is a type of revenue-sharing agreement that ensures the Cree finally benefit from development.

Agreement Concerning a New Relationship
between the Government of Canada and the Cree of Eeyou Istchee, 2007
On 16 July 2007, five years after the Cree signed an historic deal with the Government of Quebec, the federal government and the Grand Council of the Crees formally announced that a new deal had been reached which would put an end to years of controversy concerning the outstanding obligations of Canada to the Cree under the terms of the JBNQA.[32] In what was deemed an "historic step in federal-native relations," the federal government reached a $1.4 billion dollar settlement with the Cree of Quebec, "ending three decades of complaints that the federal government hadn't lived up to its treaty obligations."[33] The new deal, which sets the stage for the creation of a Cree constitution and provides for future talks on regional self-government, sets up a "nation-to-nation relationship" according to the current Grand Chief of the Grand Council of the Crees, Matthew Mukash.[34] To elaborate, in addition to settling grievances arising from the failure to implement the original agreement, the new agreement aims to set up new governance arrangements for the next twenty years (a period beginning when the new deal comes into effect). In response, the Cree have agreed to with-

draw lawsuits launched against the Government of Canada that accuse Ottawa of failing to deliver all the benefits promised under the JBNQA. In essence, the new agreement sets up a process for the establishment of a Cree Nation Government which will assume the responsibilities of the Canadian government concerning certain provisions promised under the JBNQA, responsibilities that include the administration of justice and social and economic development along with the federal share of capital costs, operations, and maintenance. Indeed, the new deal will finance infrastructures such as community centres, administrative buildings, and courthouses. The monies will also be used to compensate the Cree for village development for which they paid but which fell under the responsibility of the Government of Canada under the terms of the JBNQA. The deal, however, is not yet a *fait accompli* and represents only the first phase in an effort to modernize the Cree governance regime. In fact, both the Government of Canada and the Cree population have to ratify the deal (a Cree referendum is scheduled for October, 2007) although it is anticipated that the deal will pass easily among the Cree as it does not concern new hydro developments as was the case in the Paix des Braves. While the new deal does not erase the pain and suffering endured over the past thirty years, the Cree can now look forward to new housing and medical benefits initially promised over thirty years ago. "It feels great to have this," said Chief Billy Katapatuk.[35]

Governing in a Neo-liberal Era

Like other governments across Canada, the Cree already struggle to govern in a neo-liberal era, the primary characteristics of which include trying to address the needs of a burgeoning population with dwindling financial resources available in an environment dominated by government cutbacks, downsizing, and the devolution of more and more power to the regional, provincial, and municipal/local level. Some bands, like the Whapmagoostui First Nation (formerly known as the Great Whale River Band), and more recently the Cree Nation of Mistissini, have reduced some services and deferred development plans due to lack of capital and trained personnel.[36] The result is more pressure on communities to better manage their funding so they can provide high levels of service.

Cree community governments continue to suffer the effects of federal government cuts and costs-reducing measures. Grand Chief Matthew Mukash recently lamented the loss of a substantial program to train and employ Cree workers that was cancelled by Indian and Northern Affairs Canada (INAC). He pointed out that the Cree Human Resources Territorial (CHRT) program was funded under INAC's treaty obligations but the Ministry unilaterally decided to cut the program. He concludes that "this decision by Ottawa has had a significant impact on the ability of Cree youth and workers to obtain training and certification in trades to work on new projects in the area."[37] This poses a significant challenge for the Cree who wish to make it possible for the youth to remain in the communities while also striving to take advantage of opportunities promised by local industry.

Cutting programs like the CHRT undermines the ability of the Cree to improve their economic situation and sabotages their self-governance.

To elaborate, in 2000 the rate of unemployment in the Cree communities hovered around 40 per cent with almost 400 young Cree entering the workforce annually.[18] The unemployment rate and lack of opportunities has been exacerbated by the lack of resources available for economic development and the failure of the Canada and Quebec governments to fulfill section 28 (Economic and Social Development) of the JBNQA. With Cree governments already constrained by a lack of capital necessary to provide services to members, there is little left over to fund much-needed economic development, further aggravating the situation respecting employment and economic development. In addition, the development of local resources has not resulted in increased employment for local Cree. While the building of the Eastmain hydroelectric project promises to generate over 2,000 jobs for Cree members, the lack of qualified workers means that Cree labour will continue to be used to build roads and clear land, in work camp cafeterias, and housekeeping services as opposed to serving in managerial or administrative positions.

What is of note, therefore, is that in the ten years following the signing of the JBNQA, the Cree fought for implementation of the agreement. The first step toward that goal was the signing of the CNQA. With an agreement finalized, Cree leaders were free to return to their communities and begin organizing their government. Although funding for band governments increased under the CNQA, the Cree would fight almost twenty years more, until the Paix des Braves in 2002, to secure a new resource-sharing arrangement that provided the much-needed funds necessary to begin to fulfill promises made under the JBNQA.[39] However, while a newly negotiated relationship with the province promises change, only time will tell if federal government promises of funding will prove adequate to support the successful implementation of self-government.

The Economics of Implementing Self-Government

Although the Cree were brought into the market economy through the fur trade, by the 1970s it was apparent that the Cree could no longer make a living off the land. Profitability in the fur trade declined as costs required to go out on the land and procure the furs drained already limited finances.[40] So, with the development of a hydroelectric complex, the Cree were given an opportunity to once again become actors in the global marketplace. As part of their vision for a healthier community, the JBNQA promised that the Cree could maintain a traditional way of life while also benefiting from the economic development that was occurring around them. In addition to being a self-governing people, the JBNQA intended for the Cree to become self-sufficient, strengthening their economy by playing an important role in the development and administration of lands and resources. The Cree have long maintained that they are not against development. They simply want a voice in how it proceeds and to share in any potential benefits. As Brian Craik of the Grand Council of the Cree puts it:

With globalization, independence, political, cultural or in economic terms, is won or maintained not by striving for isolation but by becoming inter-dependent with the world at large. The value of the resources that a community or nation makes available to the global economy allows them some ability to define their place in the larger polity and economy.[41]

The Cree believe that resources should be considered in the broadest possible terms, to not only include forests, minerals, and labour but also pristine land-scapes, fresh air, and even the existence of an isolated people pursuing a tradition-al way of life.[42] However, as the trade of resources is increasingly interdependent, the Cree recognize that they can no longer live in isolation or exclusively as a traditional people.

The Cree live in an interconnected and globalized world and their economic development is increasingly predicated on their ability to participate effectively in the global market economy. To do this, they have to be able to exercise their economic power as stakeholders in the development of resources lying within their traditional territory. Unfortunately, at the same time that customary practices like hunting and trapping were recognized and protected under the treaty, Cree title to land was extinguished. That is, while the Cree succeeded in securing greater control over their own governance, they lost significant control over the resources and development occurring on their lands.

Given their focus on economic development, it is not surprising that the Cree no longer view resource development as anathema to their cultural survival. The change in perspective correlates to a change in objectives and opportunities. Achieving political independence and economic self-sufficiency are critical goals of self-government. Although the desire to end dependency and poverty and achieve a better quality of life or self-determination is a primary factor driving Cree development, they appear (like many other First Nations governments) increasingly convinced that outstanding social, political, and economic issues are best resolved through direct access to the free market as opposed to state interven-tionism.[43] In short, promises of choice and employment are attractive and so shar-ing the rhetoric of neo-liberalism represents a pragmatic and strategic approach by the Cree who recognize the value of being involved in globalization processes rather than being victims of it. Hence, groups like the James Bay Cree appear now to be embracing neo-liberal globalization as a building block to more equitable power-sharing, or, at the very least, as a way to ensure they exert some degree of influence in the development process while also ensuring the fiscal autonomy and security of their governments.

In addition to much-needed government-funded training programs, the 2000 Report of the Cree-Naskapi Commission concludes that "measures are needed to assist the private sector of the economy and increase its importance in the local economy."[44] And the Cree agree. They too believe that to achieve economic devel-opment in the region requires increased private sector activity. As Brian Craik puts it, "Who is best at doing economic development? The private sector is."[45] The Cree argue, however, that there is an important role for government to play; that is, to provide conditions conducive to economic development, including establishing infrastructure and roads to ensure regional economic development occurs. Even if government does not directly train Cree workers, it should at a minimum create an economic environment conducive to investment which can benefit Cree members either directly, through employment or tax revenue, or indirectly, through economic spinoffs. While the Cree have been promised millions of dollars in contracts from new development projects, they struggle to develop the capacity to meet the demands of their new clients.

Expanded and sustained economic development is an integral part of self-government and, where the JBNQA failed, it is believed the Paix des Braves can succeed as it takes a concerted approach to economic development occurring in the James Bay region. With its provisions covering financial assistance, job creation, economic development, and the awarding of contracts to the Cree it is designed to make certain that the Cree share in the resources and spinoffs accompanying development occurring on their lands. More specifically, Hydro-Québec has promised to employ 150 Cree by the year 2017. Under the terms of the *Boumhounan Agreement* and other similar agreements (e.g. *Apatawissiwin Agreement*) signed at the same time as the Paix des Braves in 2002, Hydro-Québec commits to supporting Cree in obtaining the technical skills needed to work in hydro management as well as to providing contracts to the Cree which could lead to long-term job creation.[46]

Furthermore, under the terms of the Paix des Braves, the Cree assume the obligations of Quebec concerning economic and community development previously assigned to them under the JBNQA. To assist, the Quebec government has agreed to pay the Cree an annual amount that will be indexed in accordance with the valuation of hydroelectric production, mining exploitation, and forest harvesting in the region. According to Moses, "The assumption of these obligations by Eeyou for Cree community and economic development with annual payments from Quebec will definitely advance Eeyou governance."[47] In other words, the Paix des Braves moves Cree self-government forward by implementing important economic development provisions of the JBNQA which had not been addressed previously.

Until the mid-1990s most Cree employment was primarily located in Cree institutions. These included the school board, the health board, and community governments. It is only since 2002 that the Cree have been able to introduce the type of development plan required to implement the JBNQA. For instance, they have begun to increase their employment in the forestry sector with the opening of forestry companies like Eenatuk in Mistissini, Geeweytin Inc. in Oujé-Bougoumou, and Nibagatuk Sawmill in Waswanipi.[48] Although these companies have only enjoyed intermittent success they remain open and provide seasonal as well as some full time employment.

In the 1990s, mining development began to occur in the area and the Cree opened development companies in an effort to be involved. The workforce at the Troilus mine for instance, operating near Oujé-Bougoumou, was approximately one-third Cree, with the company employing 130 Cree at its peak production and almost 100 Cree throughout its 10 year-operation. The Government of Canada has also worked to enhance Cree entrepreneurship and employment in the area by encouraging employers to hire Cree people and train them though programs like the Aboriginal Business Canada program and through the Aboriginal Human Resources Development Strategy (AHRDS). Other regional companies, like Air Creebec and the Cree Construction and Development Corporation, however, have proven to be much more successful at expanding Cree economic development and employment opportunities and Cree employment, Air Creebec being 100% Cree owned. All in all, since the signing of the Paix des Braves, the employment of the Cree can be roughly divided into three categories: one third work in Cree institutions; one third work in part-time employment and receive income security for trapping (as set out in the JBNQA); and one third work in the private sector or are unemployed, which represents a significant step forward.[49] And, like many other First Nations across Canada, the Cree are linking with the corporate sector to provide jobs and employment opportunities.

Protecting traditional lifestyle pursuits while at the same time seeking out new opportunities to participate in the market economy and secure benefits from the development occurring on their lands is a dilemma that confronts many First Nations in Canada. For the Cree, the key to achieving their vision of self-government lies in their self-governance as they make important development decisions in an effort to enjoy both. Self-government provides mechanisms to allow all parties to work together in regard to the development of mining, forestry, and hydroelectric resources in the region while also providing the Cree with a voice in environmental protection and sustainable development. Across the Canadian north, however, there is growing discussion concerning royalty-sharing agreements. Currently, royalties on resource development are paid into provincial coffers. However, the Cree believe that these windfalls should be reinvested in those areas from which they emerge. To elaborate, Craik argues that "right across Canada in the north you have a lack of capital and the only places that have capital are the ones that are tied right near an oil well or oil sands or sitting on top of some kind of mineral deposit."[50] Hence, these communities suffer when resource exploitation is complete. Instead, royalties collected need be reinvested in the local economy to buffer them from the boom and bust cycle associated with non-renewable resource development.

Conclusion

In sum, it is impossible to separate Cree self-government from the development of one of the world's largest hydroelectric complexes. Cree opposition initiated the process leading to Canada's first modern-day treaty. The JBNQA thus forms the cornerstone of Cree-Crown relations in Eeyou Istchee, their newly acquired rights constitutionally entrenched and beyond the unilateral reach of other governments. It is the "charter of Eeyou Treaty rights," including the right to self-government.[51] What this chapter has proven, however, is that the completion of a land claim or a treaty like the JBNQA does not represent the end of negotiations; in fact it is just the opposite. For the Cree, the treaty was only the beginning as they embarked on a new era of conflict and confrontation in an effort to settle the "unfinished business" of the JBNQA.

It is in the context of increasing global demand for power and energy that the Cree continue to negotiate the terms and scope of their governance and work toward fulfilling the promises of the JBNQA. This is also the case for many other First Nations who are engaged in self-government negotiations, or have negotiated claims and are working to achieve implementation. As the push for development of resources across the north expands, so too does the opportunity for self-government. Whether it is the Cree of Northern Alberta and the development of oil sands or the Dene of the Northwest Territories and the Mackenzie Valley Pipeline, it is of constant concern that the future for self-government is intimately tied to global market demands for resources that are predicated upon less government intervention. Instead of seeing neo-liberal globalization as a force of domination and disempowerment, however, these First Nations see only the potential for liberation and empowerment. And why not? Neo-liberal globalization promises that societies around the world will be taken in new, interwoven, and positive directions. It promises that government (federal and provincial) will no longer act as an impediment to development but instead will stand in support, devolving many of the responsibilities for program design and delivery, which is the underlying aim of self-government.

In the end, the JBNQA was not just an agreement dealing with Cree governance, land, and territorial issues. It was not just an agreement between two orders of government. It was a license to develop the James Bay region. As Grand Chief Matthew Mukash put it, "Governments only understood our treaty as providing them the right to develop, while ignoring the obligations they had undertaken in favour of the Cree Nation."[52] This is why Cree self-government remains unrealized. For the Cree, the land, water, and associated economic, social, and cultural activities remain at the heart of their vision for self-governance.[53] Fortunately, the potential for self-government first articulated under the JBNQA has begun to be fulfilled, and this is in large part due to the CNQA, the Paix des Braves, and the new *Agreement Concerning a New Relationship between the Government of Canada and the Cree of Eeyou Istchee* which fill important gaps, providing government organization, authority, and financing. To achieve the full vision of the Eeyouch, however, requires the concerted support, co-operation, and coordination of other orders of government in Canada. This is where the challenge for the future continues to be for all parties involved as agreements like the Paix des Braves and the *Agreement Concerning a New Relationship between the Government of Canada and the Cree of Eeyou Istchee* are set to expire in fifty years (2052) and twenty years (approximately 2027) respectively. The aim for the future must be for more resource-sharing and governing agreements that are continued in perpetuity, thereby assuring the continued security and governance of the James Bay Cree within Eeyou Istchee.

NOTES

1   The author gratefully acknowledges the information and insight provided by Brian Craik of the Grand Council of the Cree (GCC) as well as comments on earlier drafts provided by Stephanie Irlbacher-Fox and Ailsa Henderson. She also acknowledges the research assistance provided by Emily Rozitis and Altaf Kassam.

2   Responsibility for the project would be overseen by the Société d'énergie de la Baie-James, a newly created mixed corporation (public/private) controlled by Hydro-Québec.

3   In the interest of space, this chapter focuses on the experiences of the Cree and does not, unfortunately, attend to the concerns and experiences of the Inuit.

4   [1975] Que. C.A. 166.

5   Hans M. Carlson, "A Watershed of Words: Litigating and Negotiating Nature in Eastern James Bay, 1971-75," *The Canadian Historical Review* 85, no. 1 (2004): 64; and, Paul Rynard, "Welcome In, But Check Your Rights at the Door: The James Bay and Nisga'a Agreements in Canada," *The Canadian Journal of Political Science* 33, no. 2 (2002): 216. In 1972, lawyers for the Indians of Quebec Association (IQA) initiated court action to obtain an injunction against hydro development that would further damage Cree lands. Development of the James Bay project proceeded while the matter was before the courts. On 15 November 1973, Justice Malouf of the Superior Court of Quebec granted the injunction which was then overturned, one week later, in the Court of Appeal on the basis that the balance of interest lay in favour of completing the project as it would benefit all Quebeckers. However, as Rynard writes, in light of *Calder* and Cree claims, the government could no longer deny the existence of Aboriginal rights (216).

6   The JBNQA was actually signed by the Grand Council of the Cree (GCC) on behalf of eight Cree communities because it is the political body that represents the Cree people in all matters affecting Cree status, lands, rights, and society. While heterogeneity exists amongst Cree people and Cree communities, this paper refers to the "Cree" as one homogenous group given their confluence under the GCC and the JBNQA.

7   Colin Scott, *Aboriginal Autonomy and Development in Northern Quebec and Labrador* (Vancouver: UBC Press, 2001), 6.

8   Rynard, "Welcome In," 222.

9   The Oujé-Bougoumou Eenouch, as a distinct First Nation, are not party to the JBNQA because, at the time of negotiations, they were registered as members of the Mistassini Band by the federal Department of Indian and Northern Affairs for administrative purposes (making them beneficiaries under, but not signatories to, the agreement). At the time of negotiation, however, the Cree and governmental parties acknowledged the unique situation of the Cree of Oujé-Bougoumou, who numbered about 200 in 1974, and promised it would be addressed after the JBNQA came into force. Finally, the Oujé-Bougoumou Cree signed an agreement with the province on 6 September 1989, and the federal government on 22 December 1990, providing them with recognition and a land base. See: Cree-Naskapi Commission, "Report of the Cree-Naskapi Commission 2000," (Ottawa, ON) 40-41.

10 Department of Indian Affairs and Northern Development, *Principal Provisions of the JBNQA and NEQA*, http://www.ainc-inac.gc.ca/pr/agr/que/cin005_e.pdf (accessed 22 May 2007).

11 *James Bay and Northern Quebec Agreement*, 1975, 5. In part, the Cree did not want to be placed on reserves but wanted to retain the right to hunt, trap, and fish over the entire area of Eeyou Istchee.

12 In the years just prior to the JBNQA, in those cases where Cree interests challenged the development of resources, be it forestry or mining or hydro development, they were displaced. Examples of communities include Chisasibi, Nemaska, and Waswanipi, which were displaced and/or relocated for administrative or development purposes. See the "Report of the Cree-Naskapi Commission 2000," 58; and Scott, *Aboriginal Autonomy Quebec*, 17.

13 Brian Craik, personal communications, 14 November 2003.

14 For more on the environmental dimension, see Evelyn J. Peters, "Native People and the Environmental Regime in the James Bay and Northern Quebec Agreement," *Arctic* 52, no. 4 (1999): 385-410.

15 Scott 2001, *Aboriginal Autonomy Quebec*, 13.

16 Ted Moses, "Eeyou Governance Beyond the Indian Act and the James Bay and Northern Quebec Agreement," 2, http://www.gcc.ca/archive/article.php?id=1 (accessed 15 September 2002).

17 Moses, "Eeyou Governance," 4. Specifically, section 9 of the JBNQA established a government obligation to recommend "special legislation" relating to local government on the lands held by Canada for the use of the Cree and Naskapi bands.

18 The CNQA supersedes the *Indian Act* which remains in place for federal purposes of status.

19 Although an outgrowth of the JBNQA, the CNQA is not separate from it. As Moses writes, the JBNQA and the CNQA "are inseparable and must be considered as a whole to capture the intent and spirit of the exercise and practice of Eeyou self-government."

20 John Ciaccia, "Philosophy of the Agreement," in *The James Bay and Northern Quebec Agreement,* http://www.gcc.ca/.

21 "1986 Report of the Cree-Naskapi Commission" (Ottawa: 1986), 6.

22 *Ibid.,* 11.

23 For more specific details on the provisions of the Act that set out the roles and responsibilities of the Cree band governments, refer to the "1986 Report of the Cree-Naskapi Commission," 7 10.

24 *Ibid.,* 29.

25 The Cree now form part of the Land Claims Agreement Coalition (LCAC) which is a forum designed to bring together comprehensive claims groups to press common implementation issues.

26 Scott, *Aboriginal Autonomy Quebec,* 14.

27 However, it is important to distinguish that the JBNQA did not "freeze" Cree/Aboriginal rights in time.

28 "2000 Report of the Cree-Naskapi Commission" (Ottawa: 2000), 20.

29 Lack of financial capital along with capacity and qualified or trained personnel represents another important obstacle to implementation. This can be said of the JBNQA prior to the Paix des Braves and is still true for Canada and the JBNQA.

30 The Paix des Braves was also accompanied by an agreement on health services, an agreement on a Cree regional police force—a first for Canada—and a commitment to buy some Cree wind power.

31 While the Cree enjoy a high level of social cohesion, since thirty per cent of the Cree did not endorse the Paix des Braves it is important to acknowledge that dissent does exist. More notable, however, is that dissent typically emerges in the face of pending development projects. See, for instance, Steve Bonspiel, "Cree Reject Rupert River Diversion Project: 3 Communities Vote Leaders Propose using Wind Power Iinstead," *Montreal Gazette* (2 December 2006): A-9. See also Susanne Hilton, Stephane Sirois, & Patricia Desgagne, *Opinion Leaders Perception Study of the Nine Cree Communities of Eeyou Istchee,* prepared for the Eastmain-1-A Rupert Diversion Project (Hydro-Québec), 2005.

32 Grand Council of the Crees 2007, "Canada's New Government and the Grand Council of the Crees Reach Agreements on Renewed Relationship," http://www.gcc.ca/newsarticle.php?id=107 (accessed 11 September 2007).

33 Tu Thanh Ha, "Ottawa, Cree Reach 'Historic' $1.4 billion Accord: Deal Paves Way for Quebec Bands to Govern Themselves," *Globe and Mail* (17 July 2007): A-1, A-6.

34 *Ibid.,* A-1.

35 *Ibid.,* A-6.

36 "1986 Report of the Cree-Naskapi Commission," 18-19; "Report of the Cree-Naskapi Commission 2004" (Ottawa: 2004), 50.

37 Matthew Mukash, "Grand Chief Matthew Mukash's Remarks at Premier's Event at Hydro-Québec, Montreal," http://www.gcc.ca/newsarticle.php?id=98 (accessed 15 September 2007).

38 "2000 Report of the Cree-Naskapi Commission," 57.

39 An example includes housing. Current federal funding is insufficient in that it assumes low population growth. Under the JBNQA this was a significant issue as almost 90 per cent of Cree remain in Cree communities. This number far exceeds the federal standards. Thus, under the *Paix des Braves* the Cree could begin to address this housing deficiency and build more houses. It is interesting to note, however, that there is also an increase in privately built housing in the communities as employed members are now able to build their own houses.

40 For instance, costs associated with travelling by air to the remote hunting and trapping territories became prohibitive.

41 Brian Craik, "Aboriginal Peoples and Hydro-Power in the Quest for a Meaningful Place in a Global Economy." *Presentation at Large Dams: Who Wins? Who Loses? Hydro-power, the Environment and Indigenous Peoples.* Montreal: McGill University (19 April 2007), 2.

42 *Ibid.*

43 Brian Craik, "Crees," email to author, (9 May 2007), Toronto, ON.

44 "2000 Report of the Cree-Naskapi Commission," 57.

45 Craik, personal communication, 2003.

46 Hydro-Québec, *Eastmain-1-A Powerhouse and Rupert Diversion. Supplement to the Environmental Impact Statement.* Vol. 4 (2005): iv, 85-88.

47 Moses, "Eeyou Governance," 8.
48 Craik, "Aboriginal Peoples and Hydro-Power," 1.
49 *Ibid.*
50 Craik, Personal communication, 14 November 2003.
51 Moses "Eeyou Governance," 6.
52 Mukash, "Grand Chief Matthew Mukash's Remarks," 1.
53 Scott, *Aboriginal Autonomy Quebec,* 5.

SELF-GOVERNMENT IN NUNAVUT[1]

Ailsa Henderson, University of Toronto

I n 1993, representatives of the Canadian government, NWT, and Nunavut Tunngavik signed a land claim agreement that created Nunavut, the third Canadian territory. The product of twenty years of negotiations between Inuit and government officials, the *Nunavut Land Claims Agreement* (NLCA) recognized Inuit title to land in the eastern Arctic and established co-management boards so Inuit had a say in the development of their land. The NLCA also contained provisions for a political accord, which established a new territory, to begin in 1999, with a new territorial legislature and bureaucracy. Nunavut covers one fifth of the Canadian land mass, two thirds of its coast line and contains approximately 30,000 residents.

It has become de rigueur to note that Inuit represent 85 per cent of the Nunavut population and therefore that the claim provides de facto Aboriginal self-government in the eastern Arctic.[2] The de facto element—the distinction between ethnic self-government and self-government through public government—is assumed to be unimportant, given the extent of Inuit control over the levels of a public government. In other words, because Inuit outnumber non-Inuit in the territory, and because Inuit members have so obviously outnumbered non-Inuit members in the legislature and in the cabinet, it is considered that public government (government by and for all within the territory) can provide an avenue for Inuit self-government (government by and for Inuit).

And yet we know that public expectations of the claim have not been met. Optimism in 1999 has led to concern about public funding and falling perceptions that the claim is having an impact. Social indicators suggest levels of poor health, poverty, and social dislocation are either unchanged or have worsened since 1999. Beyond mere discontent, critiques of the current situation articulated within the legislature and the bureaucracy suggest that Nunavut is failing to meet expectations in very specific ways. The following chapter explores the nature of the Nunavut settlement, public expectations, evaluations, and critiques and argues that key to understanding perceptions of Nunavut is the 'de facto' nature of the settlement.

How do we distinguish between self-government and de facto self-government?

Within the Canadian literature it is typical to distinguish among models of self-government by exploring the level of autonomy exercised by the polity. Models compare self-government to municipalities, provinces, or sovereign states. We can distinguish, for example, between weak models of self-government, where group members have control over a limited number of areas, and strong models of self-government, where group members have control over a considerable degree of authority. Self-government for one group might include, for example, all the powers cities typically exercise, such as bylaws, property taxes, sewage and water, or zoning regulations. Self-government for another group, however, might include full fiscal autonomy, the right to engage in foreign affairs, or possession of a separate international personality. The authority to determine group membership— to identify who has access to rights—is, of course, an important element of self-government. From this perspective, self-government can be seen as a continuum along which groups may be located.

There are other ways to distinguish self-government. The Nunavut settlement is unique because it pursues simultaneously two separate models of self-government: one the ethnic model typically pursued in bids for Aboriginal self-government, the other modelled on public government or what in Nunavut is referred to as 'de facto' self-government. According to the land-claims model, territory is relevant because land claims seek legal recognition of title to land; any land covered under the claim thus becomes the property of a particular group. For the public government model, land is important because it identifies a territory over which a particular government exercises authority. This distinction—land as property versus land as territory—is an important one, because it highlights the separate bases for authority. In the public government model, the boundaries of government authority are the physical borders of the territory. For the land-claims model, land as property has a weaker relationship to authority. The boundaries of land claim authority are the social boundaries of a group, whether concentrated geographically or dispersed, rather than the physical boundaries of a territory.

Who is in the group?

Any measure of self-government relies on an identification of 'self', the group that is going to govern itself. In nation-states, citizenship becomes the determinant of group membership, so that individuals who are citizens can participate fully in the decisions of the polity. There are, of course, variations on this definition. Individuals who are not citizens but reside within the geographic boundaries can be included. Substate units such as provinces don't have the authority to patrol the boundaries of citizenship. For this reason, residency in the province can also be an indicator of group membership. If self-government is pursued by a group that exists within or across existing political jurisdictions, then some additional mechanism for determining group membership is required. For Aboriginal peoples, membership has often been identified either by blood ties or by residency in a community. The identification of a group—who belongs and who doesn't, what binds the group—is an essential component of self-government.

It is important to note that self-government need not be defined ethnically. A people living in proximity can decide that their membership in a territorially-based political community forms the basis for self-government. Nationalist movements in Catalonia and Scotland include within the nations members who are resident within the territorial boundaries of the polity, regardless of their ethnicity, race, or religion. Debates about whether Quebec is an inclusive nation or not typically focus on whether the goals for self-determination include only a subset of the population or include all within the borders of the province.

Land claim self-government stands, in some respects, in conflict with the notion of public government. If public government seeks to provide policies for all within the boundaries of a territory, regardless of whether they belong to a particular social group, self-government is concerned predominantly with group members. This division is easier to understand if public government is offered at the level of a province or a state and self-government is offered to members within a small area, such as a band or reserve. The division is less clear, however, when the territorial boundary for self-government is large enough that it includes non-members.

If we are to analyse the *Nunavut Land Claims Agreement*, three things are worth noting. First, beneficiaries of the NLCA must be registered with the Nunavut Tunngavik Incorporated (NTI) by a particular Nunavut community. In some cases this is the community in which an individual is currently resident, in other cases this is the community of birth or family origin. Second, the claim allows for certain elements of self-government, for it provides financial compensation to Inuit. These funds, managed by NTI, are used to create programs targeted at beneficiaries of the claim. Third, the new territorial legislature, by comparison, exercises far greater jurisdiction, legislating on education, health, community government, transportation, language, and justice. Created by the political accord, the legislature, its government, and administration, are modelled on public government rather than self-government. The legislature is elected by all adults within the territory, and passes legislation and administers programs and services aimed at the entire population of Nunavut. It would have been possible—unlikely, but possible—for non-Inuit candidates in the 1999 election to have won in each of the 19 constituencies, and for the Nunavut electorate to have a legislature composed entirely of non-Inuit.

While the dominance of Inuit within the population makes it more likely that Inuit will be represented in the legislature and will form the government, and makes it more likely that Inuit preferences will be implemented as territorial policy, there is nothing automatic about this situation. Indeed nationalism in Quebec in the 1960s and 1970s drew on this specific point. The demographic weight of francophone Quebecers within the province did not guarantee that language policy fostered self-government for a francophone majority. The 1977 *Charter of the French Language* is, therefore, a useful example of how a group can use public government to further self-government, just as it is an example of the fact that public government does not always guarantee self-government for the majority group within a territory.

To understand why the Nunavut settlement contains elements of both Aboriginal self-government and de facto self-government through public government, and to understand the current critiques of the devolution settlement, we must explore three things. First, we must look at how Inuit were integrated into the Canadian political system; second, we must look at the arguments made by Inuit claims negotiators; and third, we must examine the expectations Inuit had of the land claim and territory.

Public government and political integration

Inuit negotiators pursued two models of self-government: a land claim, which offered a model of ethnic self-government, and territorial division, which offered de facto self-government through public government. This dual pursuit is understandable when we examine how Inuit were integrated simultaneously into ethnic and public institutions in the 1950s and 1960s. The Supreme Court declared Inuit to be a federal responsibility in 1939[3] and the 1951 revision of the *Indian Act* explicitly referred to Inuit for the first time, a change that coincided with an increase in federal efforts to administer social policy to its eastern Arctic population. Education, health care—if at a distance—housing, and social benefits were all extended, serving both to disrupt and to empower the local population. If federal approaches to Aboriginal peoples in Canada have employed the twin threats of assimilation and paternalism then federal approaches to Inuit as objects of social policy were fairly typical: a solid education would serve as a tool of emancipation, enabling Inuit to integrate into a wage economy whether in northern or southern Canada; sickness and starvation as documented by federal workers were perceived to justify government intervention.[4] First ignored by the federal government Inuit were then treated as objects of policy rather than as political citizens. And yet, unlike other Aboriginal groups, Inuit were not excluded from political participation by policies that juxtaposed Aboriginal identity and citizenship.

Exclusion from political participation was justified on practical rather than ethnic grounds. All residents of the eastern Arctic were excluded from electoral participation in the north. In 1962, the federal government created an electoral constituency of the entire Northwest Territories, and although elections to the territorial council began in 1951, it was another fifteen years before eastern Arctic residents were afforded an opportunity to cast a ballot. As the bulk of the eastern Arctic population was Inuit this provided a de facto bar to Inuit participation in political life;[5] the population was perceived to be too small, and the logistics of organizing a campaign and vote too complicated, to justify their inclusion before special by-elections in 1966. Even then, the failure to translate election materials and the refusal to translate more than the maiden speech in the council served to exclude those unable or unwilling to read and speak English. Other barriers would have differentially affected Inuit, including the hefty deposit required for candidature.[6] If the *Indian Act* presented systemic barriers to participation for some Aboriginal peoples, in the eastern Arctic political and logistic barriers tended to inhibit Inuit involvement in the formal political process.

The slow pace at which electoral constituencies were created in the north, and the haphazard way in which Inuit participation in elections was courted, would suggest that the government was indifferent to the particularities of life in the eastern Arctic. This is not the case. Although electoral democracy arrived slowly and imperfectly, this was but one of several strategies aimed at understanding the policy preferences of Inuit and encouraging their political participation. First, the Territorial Council pursued a policy of bringing politics to the people by holding territorial council meetings in their midst. Second, the federal government took the lead in inviting 'appropriate' Inuit, in small numbers, to sit on the various non-elected governmental bodies that sought to administer policy in their name. Third, a desire to encourage a democratic spirit among Inuit prompted the use of Northern Service Officers (NSOs) charged with generating local councils where residents could voice their concerns about local issues. These last two strategies had an obvious impact on Inuit as membership on committees became an important gateway to greater participation, with early participants later sitting on the electoral council or occupying leadership positions within community councils or Inuit organizations. There was, however, a mismatch in the expectations of committee members on the one hand, and territorial council members or officials on the other. This is most evident when we look at the activities of the various community councils created by the NSOs.

The community councils could run either in a public-government or a self-government model. In some communities, where the Inuit population dwarfed the non-Inuit population, the community councils were effectively Inuit councils. In other communities, where the non-Inuit population was larger, NSOs could at their discretion create separate Eskimo Community Councils, as occurred in Baker Lake, Cape Dorset, Cambridge Bay, and Frobisher Bay. These separate Eskimo councils later met on a regional basis. In 1966, the Keewatin regional Eskimo council met with delegates from Rankin Inlet, Baker Lake, Coral Harbour, Whale Cove, Arviat, and Churchill and was followed two years later by the Baffin regional Eskimo council. These regional councils, in which Inuit could speak freely in Inuktitut, provided the best opportunity to discuss common issues raised by their cultural, economic, and political 'integration'. Upon return to their communities, delegates began campaigns of correspondence with community councils and the territorial council to communicate the conclusions of their discussions. As the territorial council viewed the community councils as the only official channel of communication these requests largely fell on deaf ears. As one official noted, "the government cannot operate by petition, particularly if our policy on placing increased responsibility in the hand of local governing bodies is to be successful. We must listen to the people as they speak through their own chosen representatives."[7] The Eskimo councils, both local and regional, were seen to be ancillary bodies, clearly separate from public government, useful as a means of gauging Inuit public opinion but not perceived as agents of Inuit self-government. They were seen differently by their members, however, who viewed them as political organisations in which Inuit could voice their goals for development in the north. Certainly they were not seen as an expression of existing self-government, for much of the discussion focused on how northerners could adapt to the reality of Canadian and territorial governance of the north. If not engines of Inuit autonomy, they were certainly perceived as vehicles for Inuit political expression.

The political system into which Inuit were integrated in the 1960s and 1970s therefore offered a spectrum of political opportunities. At times, government officials appeared geographically remote and ambivalent, while at others Inuit participation was courted, providing a venue for political expression. The spectrum did not run from public government to self-government. Although the local and regional bodies allowed Inuit to discuss political affairs, there was no assumption that their requests or criticisms would prompt action from the territorial council or federal government. Instead, they provided the opportunity of participation with no prospect of self-determination.

Self-Government and Self-Determination

Formed in 1971, the Inuit Tapirisat of Canada (ITC) advanced a land claim in 1972—before the Supreme Court *Calder* decision, before the distinction between specific and comprehensive claims, and before the *James Bay Northern Quebec Agreement*.[8] At this time, ITC called together experts to determine the type of documentation that would be necessary to pursue the claim. The project later became known as the Inuit Land Use and Occupancy Research Project and sought to document Inuit traditional use of the land in the eastern Arctic. The claim was linked, certainly in the minds of Inuit if not the federal government, to self-determination:

> The Inuit and Dene, through their Brotherhoods, have made the claim that they have a right to a homeland of their own in which they are free to develop the political institutions which will ensure their cultural survival...We want to hear the Minister of Indian and Northern Affairs, and Northern residents like the Territorial Councillors for Yellowknife and Hay River say categorically: "We hold it as a matter of principle that the Inuit and Dene people of the Northwest Territories have the right, within Canada's constitution, to political self-determination within their homelands."[9]

In three documents published from 1976 to 1979, the ITC outlined its vision of the social, economic, and political future for Inuit in Canada. The three documents vary in the degree to which they emphasize self-government and they ground their authority in different methods. Throughout, documents portray a land claim and self-government as two sides of the same coin, together offering the level of economic and political autonomy necessary to secure cultural and political self-determination.

Completed in 1976, *Nunavut: a proposal for the settlement of Inuit Lands in the Northwest Territories*, was grounded heavily in research that eventually appeared in a three-volume document highlighting the extent of Inuit land use in the Arctic.[10] This focus on occupancy was tied to the requirements of a 1973 federal Comprehensive Land Claims Policy, namely that the group had occupied the land to the exclusion of other groups, and employed the land and its resources for traditional uses. The 1976 document carefully locates the legitimacy of any land claim in longstanding Inuit occupation of the eastern Arctic. It also advocates equal participation of Inuit, security of Inuit identity and traditional way of life, sound environmental stewardship of the land, and just compensation. With respect to self-government, the document calls for a new territory "where Inuit, by their number and right to vote, will have control of their future": "En soi, ce territoire et ses institutions refléteront mieux les valeurs et les vues des Inuit que les Territorires du Nord-Ouest actuels."[11] The territory was not expected to confer additional rights to Inuit but the document called for 10-year residency before gaining the right to vote (Article 404), three official languages (Article 405), and a territorial police force (Article 406). Article 410 calls for a representative public service and can be seen as a precursor to Article 23 in the *Nunavut Land Claims Agreement*, which calls for increases in Inuit employment within the federal and territorial civil service in Nunavut to a "representative" level. Interpreted in the south as a radical call for change, the 1976 document was perceived in the north as reflecting the southern legal hands that held the pen and was later withdrawn by ITC in favour of one following extensive public consultations with Inuit throughout the eastern Arctic.[12]

The 1977, *Speaking for the First Citizens of the Canadian Arctic* sets out more clearly the call for self-government, linking it with property rights and locating its authority in public consultation rather than academic research. The document criticises the lack of consultation with Inuit about their own future and land. Both this and the 1976 document deliberately couple economic self-determination made possible by the property rights afforded by a land claim and political self-determination through self-government: "...We want the opportunity to run our own affairs."[13] The document also notes, however,

This in no way implies that Inuit are thinking in terms of a separate sovereign nation. We want to co-operate with the rest of Canada as partners in Confederation. We are not opposed to development. We are realistic enough to know that some development is inevitable. But we want to run our own affairs, and we seek guarantees that our land will not be destroyed.[14]

Beyond the document, clarifications provided by ITC staff and Inuit politicians underlined the importance of self-government: "We've mostly talked about political self-determination. Political self-determination means taking over our own government."[15] *Nunatsiaq News*, the weekly Iqaluit-based paper, noted that this "new government would include 'the type of changes necessary to ensure that our culture and language survive'."[16] In media interviews, land claims director John Amagoalik reiterated the possibilities of language legislation, significant education reform, and five-to-ten-year residency requirements for non-Inuit to acquire full political rights in Nunavut. The political structures themselves warranted renovation to a style more in keeping with grassroots community-level decision-making rather than a trustee model of political representation.[17] The 1977 document not only perceived the territory as the political corollary to the claim, but also called for differentiated citizenship rights within the territorial population. The third document, *Political Development in Nunavut* continues with this theme and calls on Ottawa to negotiate self-government for Inuit. The proposal identifies a territory not as an end in itself but as a path to acquiring provincial status.

There are, of course, different sources of opinion concerning self-government and public government. Certainly the ITC documents calling for a land claim and separate territory in the eastern Arctic help us to understand the ideal structures identified by the Inuit organizations. Equally relevant are responses to other attempted political reforms in the 1970s and 1980s. Territorial and federal reactions to Inuit calls for self-determination through self-government display considerable unease at the coupling of land claims and self-determination. A 1977 territorial executive statement on northern political development expressed concern over the creation of an ethnically-defined polity. Federal reaction took the form of a Special Representative, Bud Drury, to identify an appropriate path to political development. The Office of the Special Representative (OSR) was charged with wading into the issue of territorial division, the transfer of control over resources, the possibility of provincial status for a united or divided territory, and the matter of local or regional development. Bound up in all of these issues were two separate debates about political development in the north. First, whether the chief avenue would be public or ethnic institutions, and, second, whether constitutional or local issues would take priority.

During its investigation of different political structures for the north the staff of the OSR began pushing a model of development that would decentralize and devolve territorial decision-making to the regional level, providing greater autonomy to regions and in so doing provide the same measure of de facto self-government offered to Inuit in the NLCA but on a regional rather than a territorial scale. Inuit opposition targeted both the substance of the plan and the process by which potentially significant political developments were being identified. At a time when ITC was busy negotiating a claim it seemed absurd to them that rival political developments should be promoted by a non-Inuit public body:

It annoys us that we were not consulted as to how an inquiry should be set up and what its terms of reference should be...This compromises the negotiation process and attempts to lower the status of the [Inuit Land Claims] Commission to that of a Rotary club...change your terms of reference to integrate your work into the framework of negotiations.[18]

At issue was not just that non-Inuit were seeking to determine how Inuit might 'develop' politically, but the very separation of political development from the land claim itself. The considerable hostility with which such a plan was met also emphasizes that de facto self-government through public government was not seen as an ideal by those campaigning for the land claim.

[Y]ou don't know how the Inuit live, you have never lived as an Inuk and you've never been born here. We will not give you recommendations to change the government because we have our own people doing this for us.[19]

The campaign for a land claim demonstrates that Inuit perceived self-government to be an integral part of their economic and political self-determination, a view not shared by territorial and federal officials who advocated greater autonomy for regions within the NWT. The resulting land claims agreement adopts neither view, facilitating public government on a scale opposed by the territorial commissioner, but lacking elements of self-determination advocated by ITC.

Self-Government and the Nunavut Land Claim

The extent to which the land claim deviates from what ITC had called for during the 1970s is best seen in the language used within the claim. Self-determination and self-government are not mentioned, let alone more overtly political terms such as "emancipation" or "colonial rule." The preamble to the claim identifies as one objective "to encourage self-reliance and the cultural and social well-being of Inuit," self-reliance being quite distinct from self-determination. Of course, the claim itself does not set out the grounds for division. These are contained within the Nunavut Political Accord. Federal opposition to including provisions for territorial division within a land claim were eventually resolving by separating these two issues in the legislation. As a result, the *Nunavut Land Claims Agreement* (NLCA) outlines the requirements of the claim, while the separate Political Accord outlines the basis for territorial division. The Accord indicates that the powers of the new territory will be consistent with the former Northwest Territories and the cited areas of jurisdiction are consistent with those enjoyed by the NWT. One might argue that the Accord locates public territorial government so wholly within an existing system that any efforts to provide a radical departure from existing political institutions would seem unlikely to succeed.

Neither the claim nor the Accord has any vestiges of the 'ethnic' approach to political development so feared by territorial administrators. References to the 'public' good—to public government, public land, and public purpose—are frequent. The well-known Article 23 mandates proportional hiring for Inuit in the territorial bureaucracy (and Nunavut-based federal bureaucracy) across all levels of employment, something that is designed to prevent an Inuit clerical ghetto. The same article mentions cross-cultural training for staff bureaucracy, suggesting training would be directed toward both Inuit and non-Inuit staff. In terms of self-determination, the clearest language surfaces in Article 32, which outlines the role of the Nunavut Social Development Council:

> 32.1.1 Without limiting any rights of Inuit or any obligations of Government, outside of the Agreement, Inuit have the right as set out in this Article to participate in the development of social and cultural policies, and in the design of social and cultural programs and services, including their method of delivery, within the Nunavut Settlement Area.

Later in the same Article government obligations are identified as:

> (a) providing Inuit with an opportunity to participate in the development of social and cultural policies, and in the design of social and cultural programs and services, including their method of delivery, in the Nunavut Settlement Area; and
> (b) endeavouring to reflect Inuit goals and objectives where it puts in place such social and cultural policies, programs and services in the Nunavut Settlement Area.

The Article doesn't refer to self-government or self-determination but to the specific cultural traits of a particular group and that programs and services should reflect this difference. That Inuit influence is linked specifically to cultural policies rather than self-determination suggests that the NLCA has more in common with multiculturalism policy than the accommodation of desires for self-government.

The Political Accord provides us with the clearest view of how remote the idea of self-government had become. In its reference to the Accord the claim notes explicitly that it will set out the structure of public government and that the Accord is not intended as a claim agreement or treaty right. That the Political Accord is a separate document suggests victory for those seeking to treat economic/cultural and political self-determination as distinct. Its opening section, where it draws an explicit comparison to the political structure of the Northwest Territories, and later sections highlighting that territorial powers "shall be generally consistent with those in the present Northwest Territories," are also telling. The sole reference to residency (7.3) identifies the aim for employment of local residents. The capacity for innovation exists: the legislation calls for electoral districts and no fewer than ten legislative members but does not specify an electoral system; it outlines capacity to establish "such schools as [ratepayers] think fit", suggesting a capacity for innovation within the education system. It explicitly mentions the "preservation, use and promotion of the Inuktitut language" but adds "to the extent that the laws do not diminish the legal status of, or any rights in respect of, the English and French languages." Since the 1950s, territorial and federal officials have advocated local and regional public government rather than ethnic self-government as a means of integrating Inuit within the Canadian political system, and we can certainly see their stamp on the *Nunavut Land Claims Agreement*.

The Political Accord noted that the specific design of the territorial institutions, including a timetable for assuming power, the structure of the bureaucracy, the location of the capital, the process for the first election, and the creation of electoral districts, as well as other issues such as the division of assets and liabilities, would be the responsibility of a Nunavut Implementation Commission. The nine-member NIC held public consultations throughout the territory and issued a first full report in 1995, a follow-up in 1996, and several topic-specific reports. The recommendations outlined possibilities for a decentralized civil service, proposed an innovative electoral system modelled on gender parity that ultimately failed at the hands of a public referendum, and offered three options for the location of a capital, which was later decided in another public referendum.

The first elections for the Nunavut legislature were held in February 1999, and the territory opened its doors on 1 April 1999. Many of the institutional features are familiar to observers of NWT politics. The nineteen-member legislature is structured along the lines of consensus politics, so candidates run as independents and then elect from amongst themselves a speaker, premier, and members of the cabinet. The absence of political parties as the basis of territorial political organization—described as consensus politics—is one of the most distinct features of political life in Nunavut. The civil service is decentralized throughout the territory, with Iqaluit housing a plurality of positions and the ten largest other communities receiving a share of Government of Nunavut employees.

Evaluations of De Facto Self-Government

If the claim provided de facto self-government, it is worth noting that expectations for the new territory emphasised cultural self-determination for Inuit. Asked, in 1999, to identify the expected consequences of the new territory, Nunavut residents displayed high hopes that the situation would be 'much better or somewhat better' for Inuit values and languages and more than half expected positive consequences for all policy areas save the teaching of English and French. If we compare the reactions of Inuit and non-Inuit, we see significant differences in all but one area, the incorporation of Inuit values, where both groups agreed that values would be better represented. In most cases Inuit held more positive views than non-Inuit.

Area of improvement	Nunavut	Inuit	Non-Inuit
Respect for Inuit values	**81.2**	80.2	85.2
Teaching of Inuktitut and Inuinnaqtun	**76.5**	77.1	74.1
Inuktitut and Inuinnaqtun	**70.8**	71.1	69.4
Education programs	**63.8**	68.9	44.1
Economic development	**63.7**	62.9	66.2
Environment	**63.3**	65.4	55.6
Community government	**61.5**	62.8	56.4
Justice system	**54.9**	58.4	42.3
Community health	**53.3**	56.8	40.3
Health services	**51.5**	55.0	38.6
Teaching of English and French	**37.5**	43.0	17.6

Table 1: Expectations of Nunavut % indicating positive impact

Source: 1999 NWT Labour Force Survey (number (n)=814)

The results suggest a considerable level of optimism about the capacity of the claim to deliver change both with respect to Inuit values and languages but also that it would affect the economic and social future of the territory. If we turn to evaluations of the claim after 1999, however, we can distinguish evaluations of the claim itself from evaluations of de facto self-government. Here we see optimism for self-government has declined since 1999, though the decline has not been drastic.

	1999	2001	2004	Change
Implementation of NLCA positive impact on me	51.4	56.7	57.6	+6.2
Inuit	57.2	60.6	61.9	+4.7
Non-Inuit	31.0	36.2	39.4	+8.4
Nunavut positive impact for me personally	62.9	67.2	65.0	+2.1
Inuit	68.2	68.3	63.4	-4.8
Non-Inuit	42.8	61.3	72.0	+29.2
Nunavut opportunity for all to govern lives better	85.9	79.3	76.5	-9.4
Inuit	86.5	78.8	74.0	-12.5
Non-Inuit	83.8	81.5	86.9	+3.1
Nunavut positive impact on my community	80.5	74.4	73.3	-7.2
Inuit	79.6	73.0	69.7	-9.9
Non-Inuit	84.0	82.1	89.0	+5.0

Table 2: Support for the Nunavut land claim and new territory
% indicating positive impact or agree with statement

Sources: 1999 NWT Labour Force Survey (n=814), 2001 Nunavut Housing Survey (NuHS) (n=5816), 2004 NuHS (n=900). Results are for unweighted responses. Results in 1999 are for over-18 population.

Belief that the land claim has had a positive effect has increased since 1999, despite the drop in support in 2001. When asked about their views of the territory, however, we see stable or falling proportions of happy respondents. Most telling is the decline in the proportion that believes the territory provides an opportunity for better governance. Evaluations of the land claim itself, therefore, remain positive but there has been a 7-point drop in the proportion that believes the territory is good for the community and almost a 10-point drop in perceptions of governance. We should, of course, put this into context. If sitting governments were able to receive supportive evaluations from three quarters of survey respondents they would be very happy indeed. Absolute levels of support for the territory, according to these measures, remain high. If we want to understand why individuals might be disappointed, however, we must explore the differing responses of Inuit and non-Inuit.

There are meaningful differences between Inuit and non-Inuit in terms of support for the public territory. We might have expected gaps in support among Inuit and non-Inuit for the land claim itself, since only Inuit can be beneficiaries of the claim (notwithstanding the possible benefits to communities as a whole as a result of the claim). When evaluating Nunavut as a new territory, non-Inuit were initially more pessimistic than Inuit but the gap has grown so that there are now significant differences between the two groups. For each question probing evaluations of the territory, the proportion of Inuit that believes the territory has had a positive impact has dropped, while the proportion of non-Inuit that believes the same has increased. So evident an ethnic divide in evaluations of the territory suggests that the territory is letting down Inuit more than non-Inuit.

Respondents expected the territory to have a positive impact on the integration of Inuit values, and the territory, rather than the claim, has had the greater drop in support, so it is not surprising that critiques focus on how the territory is integrating Inuit values into its ethos. This is best seen in criticisms that the government has done an insufficient job integrating Inuit Qaujimajatuqangit.

Inuit Qaujimajatuqangit: the Gap Between Public and Self-Government

Critiques of the Nunavut land claim are not difficult to find. In southern Canada, criticism surfaces from those who believe the Nunavut government is an expensive, ill-advised experiment, a model that artificially props up a way of life that is untenable in a modern world.[20] Within Nunavut, the critique is different, attacking not the extravagance or false ambition of the claim, but the extent to which it is underperforming, leaving the hopes and wishes of Inuit beneficiaries unrealised. The most cogent critique calls for greater attention to Inuit Qaujimajatuqangit (IQ), or "that which Inuit have long known". IQ proponents not only discuss elements of traditional knowledge relevant to contemporary existence but articulate also a vision of the future that is closest to calls for self-government in the 1970s. In this context, the problem in Nunavut is not the way that public government delivers services relevant to the social and economic well-being of Inuit, but the extent to which it deviates from self-government.

Before division, departments of the NWT government attempted to cope with the considerable diversity that existed within the territory in various ways, decentralizing local decision-making through the creation of regional health boards and educational authorities, and, within its central bureaucracy, organizing traditional-knowledge working groups. Attention to IQ did not start with the creation of Nunavut, although in the years between the signing of the claim and the first elections nascent departments devoted increased attention to Inuit traditional knowledge. The Nunavut Social Development Council, whose mandate is described in Article 32 of the claim, played a key role, and its 1998 Igloolik meeting provided the first explicit mention of Inuit Qaujimajatuqangit. Although seemingly rooted in the past, the term has since expanded to include: "The Inuit way of doing things: the past, present and future knowledge, experience and values of Inuit society"[21] and has become a handy catch-all for "Inuit values."

In a political system without a formal opposition, or a coherent partisan plank from which to subject the government to scrutiny, IQ has become an obvious topic for critics of government ministers, policy, and devolution itself. This is not to say that it is the only criticism possible, but it has been the best and most consistently articulated, and as such has become the chief form by which criticisms are expressed: the government of Nunavut insufficiently incorporates IQ in its daily decision-making process, in its policy output, and in its structures, and as a result is failing Inuit in Nunavut. Understanding IQ helps us to understand why de facto self-government is falling short of expectations.

Current critiques of the Nunavut political settlement argue there has been insufficient attention to Inuit Qaujimajatuqangit. The Nunavut Implementation Commission focused far less on the integration of Inuit values than on other topics. In its discussion paper on the design of the government, the commission made four points on how to address "the distinctiveness of Nunavut." While the first argued that Inuktitut should be the working language of the bureaucracy, the other three were less inventive, arguing for the standardization of oral and written Inuktitut and better communications networks. Its solution for how the government could be "sympathetic to the cultural identity and history of Nunavut" was to set aside a budget to purchase and display Nunavut art in government buildings.[22] Since 1999, government departments have attempted to provide flexible working hours or days on the land but such activities appear as piecemeal and token efforts to make the culture of public government more reflective of Inuit.

Admittedly, the diverse definitions of IQ have provided difficulties. As one newspaper editorial noted, "in two short years it's degenerated into, well, whatever anyone wants it to mean."[23] That the lead department (Culture[s], Languages, Elders and Youth) is the smallest department might also account for the pace of change. Two things are apparent. First, frustration over a lack of IQ is frustration over the inability of a public government to accommodate the values of the population it is designed to serve. As Arnakak notes, IQ concerns "the right to exercise and institute the values and principles of conduct of [Nunavut's] citizenry into its constitution,"[24] and the failure to implement IQ is a failure to put Inuit at the centre of the political settlement. Second, I would argue this frustration is precisely targeted at the gap between de facto and real self-government.

Calls for greater attention to IQ focus both on the substantive aspects of policy—that there should be more Inuktitut education, greater relevance of the educational curriculum to northern lives, a justice system that takes advantage of traditional approaches to dispute resolution—and the interaction of individuals as they reach decisions. It is not just about Inuit content to legislation, something we might equate to Canadian content legislation for broadcasting. Is it also about the values of collective decision-making and as such butts up against very rigid bureaucratic values about the importance of hierarchy and credentialism.[25] As the government IQ Task Force noted, it has been very difficult to shift the entrenched values of public government and to incorporate within them Inuit approaches. This prompted the task force to call for a land-bridge between government services and the "primary relationship needs" in Inuit culture: relationships to the land, family, spirit, and organizations.[26] In this, calls for the integration of IQ are as much about difference as they are about symbolic power and self-determination:[27] "confirming the value of Inuit Qaujimajatuqangit will restore Inuit pride and increase individual self-esteem."[28] If, as has been suggested, IQ is itself a means of resistance,[29] it is a form of resistance within public government. While government departments seek to meet demand for the substantive elements of IQ, public demand for this symbolic role have increased.

We know that claims negotiators in the 1970s sought a settlement where property rights and political self-government would guarantee self-determination. We know that division of the territory was perceived to be an essential step in the integration of Inuit values in the governance of the eastern Arctic. We know that survey respondents in the 1990s believed the new territory would be better for the integration of Inuit values. It is not surprising to see, then, that the extent to which the territory has integrated Inuit values is the main benchmark by which the success of de facto self-government in Nunavut is measured.

And yet how can we be certain that the problem is de facto self-government? In part this stems from existing models of self-government. Proposals for Aboriginal self-government in Canada are assumed to follow three possible models—municipal, provincial, and sovereign—escalating by geographic size and autonomy. Self-government as offered to bands and proposed in the 2002 *First Nations Governance Act*, for example, is based on a municipal model. In trying to distinguish between self-government and public government, the existing literature suggests that self-government is really just government for Aboriginal peoples modelled on one of the three existing orders of public government in Canada. This suggests that it is unremarkable in its institutional structure, decision-making process, or leadership selection; that majority or plurality voting will determine decisions; and that the chief innovation will be the substance of policy, offering greater Aboriginal content for education, language rights, or community-based justice. Deviations are thus expected to be policy-based, rather than structural or procedural. This, really, is self-government through institutions of public government. Throughout the 1970s, however, ITC possessed a vision more radical than that described above, more ambitious than the carbon copy territorial administration in the eastern Arctic. Territorial and federal leaders who feared the existence of an ethnic state in the eastern Arctic advocated political development for the north as a way to divert attention away from self-government. The failure of Inuit to attain their vision in the *Nunavut Land Claims Agreement* can account for contemporary critiques of political developments in Nunavut.

This should not lead us to conclude that there is little prospect for meaningful change. Part of the unrealised vision in Nunavut lies not in what is prevented by the claim, but how the various provisions of the claim and the accord have been under-utilized, with unequal attention paid to the various articles. There is far greater attention to, for example, Article 23 and the proportion of Inuit in the civil service than Article 32, outlining the role of the Nunavut Social Development Council and the role of Inuit in determining their own social and cultural programs and services. The NSDC played an important role in the years between the signing of the accord and the first territorial executive, but, since 1999, has assumed a less public role, something that is likely to the detriment of the settlement as a whole. Greater attention to the territory rather than the claim has undermined the extent to which it can be perceived as a meaningful step toward self-determination.

Within the structures of the territory there are obvious changes that would bring the current settlement closer to the model espoused by land claims advocates. Although extended residency requirements for voting rights would not likely survive a *Charter* challenge, language legislation expanding the scope of Inuktitut education in the public school system and the provision of Inuktitut second-language training for all Inuit and non-Inuit GN staff could provide a fundamental shift. In March 2007, the executive introduced languages legislation akin to the *Charter of the French Language* introduced in Quebec thirty years earlier. The legislation is designed to elevate the status of Inuktitut in public spaces, schools, and work. It is unlikely that the Government of Nunavut will truly be seen as an agent of self-determination if the public service continues to operate in English. Hiring policies based on practical experience and a flatter organizational structure would make the bureaucracy appear less rooted in a Westminster government model. Last, very little attention has been paid to the relationship between local communities as the site of democratic discussion and decision-making. There is clear demand for political participation, as seen in healthy rates of turnout and the number of candidates for elected positions, and this should be seen as an untapped resources. The early models raised by ITC suggested a more dynamic role for local communities would be more in keeping with a polity operating according to self-government rather than public government. A bottom-up rather than top-down approach to the relationship might provide the sort of cultural shift necessary to effect meaningful change. If de facto self-government has failed to reflect the values of its electorate there is every reason to believe that this can be a temporary rather than permanent state of affairs.

NOTES

1   The author would like to thank Gabrielle Slowey, Annis May Timpson, and Graham White for their helpful comments and suggestions.
2   Gurston Dacks, "Nunavut: Aboriginal Self-Determination through Public Government," in *Report for the Royal Commission on Aboriginal Peoples* (Ottawa: Canada Communications Group, 1993); Mark Dickerson, *Whose North?: Political Change, Political Development, and Self-Government in the Northwest Territories* (Vancouver: UBC Press, 1992); Ailsa Henderson, "Northern Jurisdiction: Government Structures in Nunavut," *Hemisphere* 9, no. 3 (2001): 31-34; Jack Hicks & Graham White, "Nunavut: Inuit Self-Determination Through a Land Claim and Public Government?" in *Inuit Regain Control of Their Lands and Their Lives,* eds. Jens Dahl, Jack Hicks and Peter Jull (Copenhagen: IWGIA, 2000); André Légaré, "Le gouvernement du Territoire du Nunavut: Une analyse prospective," *Études/Inuit/Studies* 20, no. 1 (1996): 7-43, and his "The Process Leading to a Land Claims Agreement and its Implementation: The Case of the Nunavut Land Claims Settlement," *Canadian Journal of Native Studies* 16, no. 1 (1996): 139-63; John Merritt et al., *Nunavut: Political Choices and Manifest Destiny* (Ottawa: Canadian Arctic Resources Committee, 1989); John Merritt, "Nunavut: Canada Turns a New Page in the Arctic," *Canadian Parliamentary Review* Summer (1993): 2-6, and his "Nunavut: Preparing for Self-Government," *Northern Perspectives* 21, no. 1 (1993): 3-6.
3   *Re Eskimos* [1939] S.C.R. 104.
4   "Human Problems in the Canadian Arctic," *Department of Northern Affairs and National Resources 1958-1959 Annual Report* (Ottawa, 1959).
5   Inuit living in the western Arctic were provided with the right to vote earlier and indeed one of the first elected members was Inuk politician Abe Okpik.
6   Ailsa Henderson, Nunavut: *Rethinking Political Culture* (Vancouver: UBC Press, 2007).
7   E.R. Horton, *State in Connection with Frobisher Bay Visit* (1968), 1 [NWT Archives].
8   For a review of the claims process see Kirk Cameron & Graham White, *Northern Governments in Transition: Political and Constitutional Development in the Yukon, Nunavut and the Western Northwest Territories* (Montréal: Institute for Research on Public Policy, 1995); Gurston Dacks, *Nunavut: Aboriginal Self-Determination;* Dahl, Hicks & Jull 2000, *Inuit Regain Control;* Dickerson, *Whose North?* ; and Légaré, "The Process Leading to a Land Claims Agreement."
9   Ludy Pudluk et al., "Political Development in the North," *Nunatsiaq News* 22 October 1975.
10 Milton Freeman, *Inuit Land Use an Occupancy Project* (Ottawa, Department of Supply and Services, 1976).
11 *Speaking for the First Citizens of the Canadian Arctic* (Ottawa, Inuit Tapirisat of Canada, 1977), 15.
12 Légaré, "The Process Leading to a Land Claims Agreement."
13 *Speaking for the First Citizens of the Canadian Arctic,* 4.
14 *Ibid.,* 7.
15 John Amagoalik, "Letter to Warren Allmand," 9 June 1977.
16 Gilda Meckler, "Amagoalik Responds to Territorial Council's Attack on Nunavut," *Nunatsiaq News* 29 June 1977.
17 *Ibid.*
18 Amagoalik, "Letter to Warren Allmand."
19 Peter Kattu, "Letter to OSR Commissioner E.H. Drury," 29 January 1977.
20 Albert Howard & Frances Widdowson, "The Disaster of Nunavut," *Policy Options* July/August (1999): 58-61; also, Frances Widdowson & Albert Howard, "Corruption North of 60," *Policy Options* January/February (1999): 37-40, and their "Duplicity in the North: A Reply to Graham White," *Policy Options* September (1999): 66-68, and "The Aboriginal Industry's New Clothes," *Policy Options* March (2002): 30-34.
21 Nunavut IQ Task Force, *The First Annual Report of the Inuit Qaujimajatuqangit Task Force* (Iqaluit: CLEY 2002), 4.
22 *Discussion Paper Concerning the Development of Principles to Govern the Design and Operation of the Nunavut Government* (Iqaluit, Nunavut Implementation Commission, 1994).
23 "Defining Inuit Qaujimajatuqangit," *Nunatsiaq News* 30 November 2001.
24 Jaypeetee Arnakak, "Northern IQ," Management 12, no. 1 (2001): 17.
25 Graham White, "Traditional Aboriginal Values in a Westminster Parliament: The Legislative Assembly of Nunavut," *Journal of Legislative Studies* 12, no. 1 (2006): 8-31.

26 Nunavut IQ Task Force. *The First Annual Report*, 2.

27 Henderson, *Nunavut: Rethinking Political Culture.*

28 Government of Nunavut, *The Bathurst Mandate. Pinasuaqtavut: That Which We've Set Out to Do* (Iqaluit: Government of Nunavut, 1999).

29 Nunavut IQ Task Force, *The First Annual Report*, 2.

COWESSESS FIRST NATION:

Self-Government, Nation-Building, and Treaty Land Entitlement

Robert Alexander Innes, University of Saskatchewan
& Terrence Ross Pelletier, University of Saskatchewan

On 25 April 1995, Cowessess First Nation reached a tentative agreement with Canada and the Saskatchewan government for its Treaty Land Entitlement (TLE) settlement subsequently ratified by the band membership on 7 December 1995. At a public ceremony held at Cowessess First Nation, Minister of Indian Affairs Ronald Irwin, Saskatchewan Minister of Indian and Métis Affairs Joanne Crofford, and Cowessess Chief Lionel Sparvier signed the agreement, 14 March 1996. Calling for the federal and provincial governments to pay Cowessess more than $46.6 million, the deal was, at the time, the second largest TLE settlement in the province and the largest in southern Saskatchewan. Of the twelve installments, the first, $12.8 million, was deposited into the Cowessess' trust accounts in April 1996 with the final TLE payment of $1.1 million to be paid in 2008. The TLE negotiation and ratification process was different for Cowessess than it was the other TLE First Nations, circumstances that were partially due to its advantageous bargaining position as well as the urban/reserve composition of the band. Furthermore, while the TLE settlement has offered Cowessess new economic development opportunities, the combined TLE negotiation process and implementation demonstrate Cowessess First Nation's assertion of self-government, a position that corresponds with the nation-building model established by the Native Nations Institute and the Harvard Project on Indian Economic Development.

TLE, while making reparations for policy inadequacies and in certain cases for the outright disregard of First Nations interests, provides a much-needed infusion of cash necessary to facilitate self-government. Hence, the importance placed by Saskatchewan First Nations, in particular, on negotiating an equitable TLE with federal and provincial officials. With these ideas in mind, this chapter examines the evolution, negotiations, and implementation of the Cowessess TLE using the Harvard Project's nation-building criteria as the analytical framework, specifically the five principles for successful economic development. What is apparent is that economic development is not an economic concern outright but rather is considered imperative to developing effective governing institutions. Interestingly, Cowessess separately negotiated their TLE, which had not been validated by the federal government in time to participate in the historical processes that led to the negotiation and ratification of the 1992 *Treaty Land Entitlement Framework Agreement* (TLEFA) signed between the federal government and 25 Saskatchewan First Nations. Utilizing the nation-building principles enables a critical examination of how First Nations self-governing standards can in fact guide tri-partite negotiations processes, suggesting that to negotiate is not to acquiesce to government demands or pressure. In this case, Cowessess negotiators following through on community stipulations proceeded to exercise agency resulting in a negotiated agreement reflecting their constituent's desires.

Principles of Nation-Building

Beginning in the early 1990s, the Harvard Project on Indian Economic Development and the Native Nations Institute for Leadership, Management, and Policy at the University of Arizona have studied patterns of economic development on American Indian reservations, and, more recently, in a handful of Canadian First Nations.[1] It was discovered that indicators such as high education levels, access to natural resources, and proximity to large markets did not necessarily translate into localized economic success. Furthermore, examples persisted of isolated albeit economically successful communities demonstrating comparatively low education attainment levels with limited to no access to natural resources. The question of why some communities were economically successful and others were not drove further research.

Over time, the Harvard Project on Indian Economic Development and the Native Nations Institute have put forth five characteristics to explain why some economies struggled, with an additional five characteristics developed to clarify why other economies were so successful. Unsuccessful economies, it was argued, are characterized by short-term planning that lacks a strategic orientation; decision-making authority that rests with outside interests, usually the federal government; economic development is seen as strictly an economic concern; Native culture is perceived to be an obstacle to development; and, the role of the leadership seem primarily as distributor of resources.[2] Conversely, successful economies are characterized by groups asserting practical sovereignty; demonstrating effective governing institutions; matching these institutions with the contemporary political culture of the community; implementing strategic long-term planning; and, transforming the concern of the leadership from distributing resources to implementing "institutional and strategic foundations for sustained development and enhance[d] community welfare."[3] As Cornell and Kalt indicated, "the 'nation-building' approach, thanks to its dual focus—conscious or unconscious—on asserting tribal sovereignty and building the foundational, institutional capacity to exercise sovereignty effectively, thereby provid[es] a positive environment for sustained economic development."[4]

They went on to further describe two crucial aspects for groups who assert practical sovereignty. First, Aboriginal people need to assume control of the decision-making process. This usually means that economically successful communities were guided by leaders who, with input from local populations, set agendas reflecting their interests and concerns rather than those of outsiders. Assuming control of the decision-making process results in leaders who are solely responsible for their decisions. Therefore, in the opinion of Cornell and Kalt, Aboriginal people benefited directly from good decisions while suffering the consequences of bad decisions: "Once decisions move into Indians hands, then the decision-maker's themselves have to face the consequences of their decisions." This, the authors argue, over time, provides a learning curve resulting in "the quality of their decisions" improving.[5] Additional research demonstrated that sustained reservation economic development was directly related to Aboriginal people as primary decision-makers. Practical sovereignty, they concluded, "appears to be a *necessary* (but not sufficient) condition for reservation economic development."[6] (Emphasis in original.)

This practical sovereignty, or effective governing institutions, facilitates a group's ability to assert their sovereign powers thereby implementing laws, policies, and rules of conduct that are not apt to be easily or frequently changed. The resulting stability enables the governing institutions to make tough decisions without worrying about immediate consequences. Such stability is also predicated upon separation of politics and the day-to-day operations, which enables politicians to concentrate their efforts on policy design and implementation rather than micromanaging band programs. Finally, stable institutions nurture competent and reliable bureaucrats with job security who are generally more effective, which in turn reduces staff turnover while maintaining corporate memory. Nation-building also requires operational governing institutions that reflect the local political culture, responding to local needs and political desires to gain legitimacy and the confidence of the community. To be a cultural match, governing institutions have to be culturally appropriate and be effective, although in this instance culture does not necessarily mean traditional culture. Rather, the evolutionary quality of culture means that governing institutions should reflect contemporary beliefs and norms of the community as opposed to being guided by a romantic historic notion of how things should be.

The other necessary element of nation-building is leadership with a demonstrated willingness to develop and implement effective governing institutions. Many tribal community leaders are more concerned with maintaining their own power than promoting an effective governance structure, according to Cornell and Kalt:

> ... members of tribal council get to make the decisions, hand out the goodies, and reward supporters, but the nation as a whole suffers as *its* power— its capacity to achieve its goals—is crippled by an environment that serves

the individual interests of office-holders but not the interests of the community as a whole. Equally crippling is a community attitude ... that sees government not as a mechanism for rebuilding the future but simply as a set of resources that one faction or another can control.[7] (Emphasis in original.)

According to the nation-building approach, leadership willing to promote community rather than individual interests by relinquishing some power facilitates community well-being by creating effective political institutions. Accordingly, institutions that discourage self-serving leadership "will encourage forms of leadership that better serve the nation."[8] Cowessess leadership responded to the political environment (local, provincial, and federal) that eventually led to their signing a TLE package.

Context of Treaty Land Entitlement

Following the signing of the Numbered Treaties in the 1870s, surveying for reserves was to follow a formula allocating 640 acres to each family of five, or an average of 128 acres per person. Determining the amount of land to survey for a band was problematic, however, as band membership wildly fluctuated in the 1880s. This led to errors in many a band's census.[9] Some First Nations people did not immediately want to settle on a reserve, preferring instead to follow the last of the buffalo, while still others moved back and forth between bands in an effort to meet their social and economic needs. Not all was the fault of itinerant populations; in some cases, surveyors simply did not provide enough land. As Peggy Martin-McGuire has observed, even though each reserve's history is unique, once "bands and individuals completed migrating, relocating, and settling, most reserves fell short of the required size."[10]

Saskatchewan entered Confederation in 1905, resulting in certain obligations, including providing provincial lands to augment existing reserves. In most cases, the province failed to follow through, though some attempts were made. Prior to 1930, for example, the Department of Indian Affairs attempted to fulfill TLE in Manitoba, Saskatchewan, and Alberta, but as time passed the process became more complicated.[11] In 1930 the Natural Resources Transfer Agreement (NRTA) was passed, which transferred jurisdiction for control over resources on Crown land from the federal government to the prairie provinces. Section 10 of the agreement, in particular, recognized that the federal government had yet to fully meet its TLE requirements, and took steps to ensure that: (1) the provinces would have a role in TLE; and, (2) provincial Crown land would be needed to fulfill First Nations TLE. The provinces fully acknowledged TLE obligations in the northern provincial regions, but officials were not overly concerned with expediting the process in regions of limited settlement. In the case of the southern regions, officials of each province worked from the assumption that the TLE obligations had been met.[12] In cases where additional lands were added, a new land survey was needed. First Nations argued that their initial population estimates were too low, necessitating additional lands and another survey. Despite all of this work, in most cases, a shortfall remained.

Required nonetheless to provide the lands, provincial authorities had to decide whether to use the population of the band at the date of the first survey (DOFS) or the population at the most recent survey. The first formula multiplied the population at DOFS by 128 (the number of acres allowed by treaty for each member), and then subtracted the amount of land originally allocated, to best determine the amount still owed the First Nation. For example, if the population of a band at DOFS was 100, and they originally received 9,800 acres, then the formula would be:

100 * 128 = 12,800 acres the First Nation should have received.
12,800 − 9,800 = 3,000 acres owed the First Nation.

The second formula meant multiplying the most recent official population by 128, and then subtracting that total from the amount of land originally received to arrive at the amount still owed the First Nation. For example, if the current population was 300 band members, the formula would be:

300 * 128 = 38,400 acres
38,400 − 9,800 = 28,600 acres owed the First Nation.

The Department used the latter population formula from the late 1800s until the 1960s, when the provinces began to lobby for its elimination.[13]

In the early 1960s, the TLE process came under fire. Manitoba, and later Alberta and Saskatchewan, all objected to the second population formula, instead arguing for the use of the DOFS formula. The federal government proposed a compromise formula that would still use the existing population as its base, but in this version, the acres already received would be used to derive the percentage of land still owed. The First Nation cited above, for example, received 77 per cent of the land they were deemed "entitled" to (9,800 ÷ 12,800 = 76.5%), or a shortfall of 23 per cent. To make up the shortfall, the First Nation would receive 23 per cent of 38,400 amounting to 8,832 acres.[14] Federation of Saskatchewan Indians (FSI) research in the early 1970s showed that there were five bands in northern Saskatchewan and ten in southern Saskatchewan owed upwards of one million TLE acres in total.[15] Using the compromise formula, between 1968 and 1973, the Province of Saskatchewan set aside nearly 185,000 acres in northern Saskatchewan for TLE claims.[16]

Progress on TLE in southern Saskatchewan stalled after the election of the Trudeau government in 1968. The *Calder* decision would soon reanimate grassroots support for TLE resolution ultimately resulting in changes to the federal government's Indian policy. Shortly after the *Calder* decision was handed down, the federal government issued a *Statement on Claims of Indian and Inuit People*, which contained a description of two kinds of land claims. Comprehensive claims were claims where Aboriginal people had never extinguished their Aboriginal title through treaty; and specific claims were those based on non-fulfillment of a treaty, a breach of an *Indian Act* or other statutory responsibility, the breach of an obligation arising out of government administration of First Nation funds or other assets; or an illegal sale or other disposition of First Nation land by government. Treaty Land Entitlements in this case fell under the specific claims category. Anticipating an influx of claims under the new policy process, that year the government established the Indian Claims Commission which in and of itself spurred tremendous activity on the TLE front in Saskatchewan.

Over the next fourteen years, TLE negotiations were nevertheless stymied by federal/provincial acrimony. Still, Saskatchewan's First Nations were determined to push the governments to work toward a settlement. In 1973, the federal government responded by informing the province of the need to resolve TLE for five First Nations in the south. In 1975, the FSI identified another 25 First Nations with outstanding TLE claims, with the federal government recognizing 15 of those as valid. These numbers came as a surprise to a provincial government expecting a dramatically lower figure.[17] This motivated the FSI to request the federal and provincial governments to enter into discussions to resolve the claims.[18] In August of that year, Minister of Indian Affairs Judd Buchanan wrote to all the provincial premiers seeking their support in resolving TLE.[19] A year later, the Saskatchewan government responded, proposing a new formula for settlement of the claims. Under the proposed Saskatchewan Formula, the entitlement would be based on band population as of 31 December 1976.[20] Additionally, it was recommended that federal funds be used for the purchase of private land to fulfill outstanding TLE requirements.[21] The Saskatchewan Formula was praised by the FSI, which was not surprising given how it favoured the TLE nations.[22] The federal government took its time in responding, however, and initially provided only conditional support. Although publicly supportive of the measure, the main stumbling block was the use of federal funds to purchase private lands. The Saskatchewan Formula ultimately fell into limbo, and for the next three years only six bands resolved their TLE.[23]

At the time of the Progressive Conservative defeat of the New Democratic Party government in the May 1982 provincial election, only 90,000 acres, amounting to less than 10 per cent of the potential TLE lands, had been transferred to provincial First Nations. In this period, the number of claims the federal government recognized as valid increased from 15 to 21.[24] The change in provincial government, unfortunately, further delayed TLE settlement. The Progressive Conservative government quickly suspended all TLE negotiations, claiming it wanted to initiate a review period and study the issue.[25] In June 1984, following two years of review, a new provincial TLE policy was announced which contained four main points:

1. Negotiations would be carried out on a band-by-band basis, resulting in different settlement packages for different bands;

2. The 1976 population base would be used as a guide for quantifying band entitlement (whether in land or land and add-on elements);

3. Financial compensation for third-party interests would be made by the federal government;

4. Tax exemptions, mineral rights, resource revenue sharing, and cash settlement were considered legitimate substitutes for land.[26]

Of course, the new policy was based on the assumption that the Saskatchewan Formula was legally binding and that the province could lose a court challenge should they deviate from its prescribed criteria.

Both the provincial and federal governments were pleased with the new TLE policy, even if the recently renamed Federation of Saskatchewan Indian Nations (FSIN) had serious misgivings. Criticism was in this case directed at both levels of government with the FSIN steadfast in its claims that individual band settlements should not take place, bands should receive all the lands to which they were entitled, and that bands should be granted the authority to choose the lands to meet finalized TLE provisions. The FSIN believed that the new policy undermined the previously acceptable Saskatchewan Formula while openly stating that the province was "seriously jeopardizing the federal government legal and trust obligations under the Constitution and the Treaties."[27] In response, Indian Affairs sought out legal advice that November, at which time it was informed that the federal government was legally obliged only for the shortfall acreage based on the population at the date of the first survey.[28] As a result, one year later the federal government publicly withdrew its support of the Saskatchewan Formula.[29] Some TLE claims were nevertheless still processed, the most notable being the Muskeg Lake First Nation claim that led to the creation of an urban reserve in the city of Saskatoon.[30] For all intents and purposes, however, the TLE process in Saskatchewan had ground to a halt.

Saskatchewan's TLE First Nations were not pleased with the latest developments. The chiefs of Muskowekwan, Ochapowace, Piapot, and Star Blanket First Nations (referred to as the MOPS bands) even threatened to initiate a court action if the federal government did not reinstate the Saskatchewan Formula. In an effort to placate the chiefs and avoid being dragged into court, Indian Affairs agreed to appoint an independent third party to mediate a settlement process.[31] However, delays in this appointment led the FSIN in conjunction with Star Blanket and Canoe Lake First Nations to file a statement of claim against the federal government in 1989.[32] In response to the statement of claim, that April and May the federal government reached a quick agreement with the FSIN which resulted in the creation of the Office of the Treaty Commissioner (OTC) followed by the appointment of former Saskatoon mayor, Clifford Wright, to the position of treaty commissioner.[33] Heralded for his role in the creation of the Muskeg Lake urban reserve in that city, Wright was charged with establishing a model to settle the outstanding TLE claims.

Wright proposed a new model—a proportion of a band's current population based on a percentage of individuals or families for which no land was surveyed, what he called the equity formula.[34] While the equity formula adhered to the government's treaty obligations, it was also consistent with the recent legal interpretation of the treaties in addition to adhering to the principles of treaty interpretation. Wright provided an example of how the equity formula should work:

Band A had a reserve surveyed for it in 1890. The survey allotted 10,000 acres. However, the population of the Band at the time was 100; therefore, the treaty land entitlement should have been 12,000 acres (100 * 128 acres). The per capita reserve allotment was therefore only 100 acres (10,000 divided by 100 people) instead of the 128 acres per capita as required by the provisions of Treaty. The percentage of per capita shortfall was thus 22 per cent. This percentage of shortfall in relation to the total amount land received by Band A would likewise be approximately 22 per cent.

The population in Band A in 1990 is 500. To calculate the treaty land entitlement due now, the following formula would apply:

500 people * 128 acres = 64,000 acres * 22 per cent (percentage of shortfall expressed on either an individual or Band basis) = 14,800 acres.
The quantum of entitlement would therefore be 14,800 acres in 1990.[35]

In other words, the band's shortfall acres would be 2,000 and its equity acres would be 4,800. In order to resolve land entitlement, the treaty commissioner proposed a willing buyer/willing seller system of acquiring land. This resulted from the fears expressed by rural municipalities anxious that they in fact could lose a portion of their tax base (due to private rural lands converting to tax-free reserve status). The commissioner argued his formula could alleviate any such situation through a one-time payment to municipalities large enough to generate the interest that would be needed to cover lost tax revenue.[36] The OTC further argued that both levels of government should enter into a cost-sharing agreement to finance the purchase of land while urging swift settlement of TLE not only as a means of honouring the spirit and intent of the treaties, but also to curtail spiraling settlement costs.

After the release of the treaty commissioner's recommendations, officials from both the federal government and entitled First Nations met to strategize.[37] Although neither legally binding nor comprehensive in scope, the OTC's recommendations provided "the equity formula, the purchase policy and the creation of a mutually acceptable political climate" which formed a foundation for discussions on a framework agreement.[38] A protocol agreement was signed in January 1991, setting out the TLE process guidelines. That September the federal and provincial governments agreed to the cost-sharing terms, which were amended several times before becoming entrenched in the *Treaty Land Entitlement Framework Agreement* (TLEFA).[39] On 22 September 1992, officials representing 26 First Nations and the federal and provincial governments signed the TLEFA.[40] Following its signing, each First Nation was responsible for negotiating its own Band Specific and Band Trust Agreements with the federal government. The TLEFA stipulated that each First Nation had until 22 September 1995 to ratify their agreements with a community referendum as required or the settlement would be withdrawn. On 31 August 1995, Keeseekoose First Nation became the last of the First Nations to ratify their agreement and only Joseph Bighead First Nation failed to ratify its agreement, choosing instead to opt out of the process.[41]

Management of TLE funds was strictly regulated. Each First Nation established a TLE trust into which the funds were to be deposited over a 12-year period and trustees were charged with fund administration. Funding awards were based on equity acres (the equity acres are greater than the actual shortfall acres). Funds deposited were only to be used to purchase the equivalent in shortfall acres, though a small amount could be used for special projects, such as elders' payment or for paying the TLE related expenses for the First Nation council and TLE trustees. Interest from the TLE funds, however, could be used at the First Nation's discretion, as could revenue generated from TLE lands. Once the shortfall acres had been purchased, First Nations could either purchase more lands, up to the total equity acres, if they chose or divert the funds into any other project.[42]

The TLEFA was hailed as a positive step forward for First Nations and the province. At the news conference announcing the TLEFA, Dan Bellegarde, FSIN's first vice-chief, noted (later confirmed by the OTC) that the First Nations land base could double as a result of TLE.[43] The OTC later noted that reserve land comprised about one percent of the provincial land base, a number that would double as a result of the TLEFA. The FSIN's chief negotiator and former University of Regina president, Lloyd Barber, pointed out that First Nations would not be restricted to acquiring Crown land; they could buy land from anyone willing to sell. OTC executive director Toby Stewart stated that TLE "will certainly be a shot in the arm for everyone involved with the land purchases; the ripple effect will be felt in many sectors of our economy."[44] Certainly, the provincial economic development spinoffs made TLE more palatable for those either indifferent or directly opposed to the process. This can be seen in the Association of Saskatchewan Taxpayers (AST) endorsement of the process. Responding to the TLEFA, AST president Kevin Avram concluded that from a moral and economic perspective, using tax dollars to settle TLE was ultimately in the taxpayers' best interests: "Native people can't build a sound economic future on government handouts. They must be allowed to control some of the economic levers to make them more independent and self-sufficient."[45]

The new TLE process was not immune to criticism, however. As early as 1995, TLE First Nations experienced problems converting their land selections to reserve status. This was an important issue due in part to the unique status reserve land is afforded by the *Indian Act*, and the impact of that on economic development and like projects. According to the FSIN newspaper, the *Saskatchewan Indian*, the FSIN and TLE First Nations initially worked with federal and provincial representatives to streamline reserve creation, a slow process resulting in many First Nations waiting years for their selected lands to be converted to reserves.[46] In her thesis examining the Witchekan Lake First Nation's TLE, Brenda McLeod was critical of the TLEFA negotiations, arguing that there was a problem when it came time to providing accurate documentation for the treaty population. McLeod argued that there was a problem in properly providing accurate documentation for the historical population, which was the basis for shortfall acreage, thereby limiting a more beneficial entitlement claim. She also suggested that First Nations' oral history was not given enough credibility in comparison to written documents utilized by federal and provincial officials to substantiate (or deny) First Nations claims.[47] The issue of using annuity pay lists to document nineteenth century First Nations populations is frequently criticized. As Kenneth Tyler stated, "These pay sheets were not designed to keep track of the number of Indians. They were designed to keep track of the amount of money the Agent had doled out."[48] Annuity pay lists recorded the names of individuals who received their five-dollar annuity in any given year. If a person did not receive their payment, the annuity would be paid in arrears the next time that person appeared to receive his or her money. McLeod suggested that researchers may have limited their efforts to the annuity pay list because they were "the most convenient and easily accessible" documents.[49] McLeod was however referring specifically to Witchekan Lake First Nation, a band that adhered to Treaty 6 in 1950. McLeod argued that available census records were not used to crosscheck the data in the annuity pay lists. Also, the TLE distilled cultural differences between First Nations into a homogenous group of Native bands. This approach, according to McLeod and notwithstanding the fact that the FSIN and entitlement chiefs were in favour of it, ignored socio-economic and cultural distinctiveness and therefore reduced bands' potential benefits. McLeod argued further that lack of research during the TLE process came from the "motivation to settle TLE lay in potential election pressures that each side could exert. Given the many years this outstanding debt remained unresolved, its settlement would be somewhat of a political coup for those seeking re-election."[50]

A few First Nations have experienced problems with the management of TLE funds. In spite of strict guidelines designed to prevent administrative mismanagement, regulatory loopholes have nevertheless resulted in misspending, albeit justified by how those particular First Nations interpreted regulatory framework. The few legitimate ways for First Nations to access TLE funds not used to purchase shortfall acres is paying the TLE-related expenses of council members and TLE trustees. Some trustees recorded unreasonable expenses, in certain cases completely draining TLE funds. These First Nations not only lost out on purchasing their shortfall acres, but once discovered, they become responsible for repaying that money to the federal government. These cases have received significant media attention even if they do not represent the norm.

Criticisms notwithstanding, the overall TLE impact has been positive for First Nations and the province. Much of the TLE-purchased land in southern Saskatchewan has been agricultural land which the First Nations have subsequently leased to Aboriginal and non-Aboriginal farmers, generating significant revenues. A number of First Nations have used their TLE money to purchase lands in urban areas. On these urban reserves, First Nations have bought or built office and/or retail buildings, sites that have been leased primarily to First Nations businesses and government agencies often employing thousands of people, many of whom happen to be First Nations. Urban First Nations have benefited not only from available urban employment, but also from *Indian Act* exemptions available to status Indians working on-reserve.

There are also a number of First Nations, including Cowessess, who are still receiving their TLE installments. These First Nations were not a part of the TLEFA because their claims had not been validated by the federal government at the time of its signing in 1992. As a self-governing entity, Cowessess officials chose to pursue a separate strategy that, to outside interests, may have appeared foolhardy. These actions will be evaluated in the following section.

Negotiating the TLE: Cowessess First Nation Asserts Self-Government

For Cowessess First Nation, obtaining INAC validation of their TLE claim was a long and drawn-out process. Cowessess leaders had long believed that they had a TLE claim but could not produce substantiating evidence. In the early 1970s, an Indian Affairs official, Lou Lockhart, completed a review of Cowessess 1880s annuities pay lists, and, based on his assessment, concluded that the community had sufficient numbers to qualify for TLE. Others at Indian Affairs believed that Cowessess would never qualify for a claim and therefore rejected Lockhart's assessment. According to former Cowessess TLE coordinator and former chief, Terence Pelletier, "It is important to remember, that when those other INAC people said that, it made Lou Lockhart more determined to research and prove Cowessess' claim. He eventually did. So he is kind of like the Luke Skywalker of Cowessess."

A number of long-term band councillors followed up the Cowessess' TLE claim, even though Cowessess chiefs seldom participated for extended periods. The chiefs, however, worked toward settling the TLE claim. Chiefs for Cowessess, unlike the councillors, are seldom re-elected to second or third terms in office, making it difficult to commit for extended periods while at the same time permitting the councilors to maintain their focus. Councillors who worked on the claim in the 1970s and 1980s, include Edwin Pelletier, Harold Lerat, Henry Delorme, and Howard Young. In the 1980s and early 1990s, Councillor Hubert Gunn, in particular, pursued the TLE claim, participating in the actual negotiations and initial ratification process. Unfortunately, Gunn died in 1996; he was unable to benefit from the land claim he spent so many years lobbying for.

Even with all the work devoted to the claim, the Indian Affairs validation process moved slowly. By the late 1980s, Indian Affairs acknowledged that Cowessess had a land shortfall, but before accepting a TLE claim the band would have to meet some specific criteria. In other words, the band had to demonstrate that the band population used to survey the reserve was significantly short of the actual band population. Annuities pay lists were the only means available to government to keep track of reserve populations to substantiate the TLE claims, and Indian Affairs officials accepted these data due to their detailed information. For instance, the pay lists contained information such as the individual's name, year of payment, location of payment, and to which band the individual belonged. Yet in the Cowessess TLE claim, a problem arose concerning which years were to be used to substantiate populations. From Indian Affairs' perspective Cowessess' TLE claim was questionable as the date of the first survey (DOFS) was the year the pay lists were counted against the acres surveyed. The problem was that multiple surveys for the reserve existed. The first survey was completed in 1878, when Louis O'Soup led a splinter group to Crooked Lake. A second survey was conducted in 1881 after Chief Cowessess brought the remainder of his band from Cypress Hills to join O'Soup's group. This issue presented a major stumbling block that prevented Cowessess from gaining validation in 1992.

The October 1993 validation of Cowessess' claim did likewise not translate into a quick TLE agreement. Yes, the federal government agreed that Cowessess had a significant shortfall, and, yes, the evidence pointing out that the reserve survey of 1881 showed 480 people when the Cowessess band membership was actually 680 was provocative. According to the equity formula, Cowessess was entitled to receive $27 million from the federal government to settle their outstanding claim. Cowessess leaders rejected this offer, arguing that, in fact, there were considerably more original members than the 680 claimed by the federal government. Again, Indian Affairs officials disagreed and recommended that Cowessess substantiate their claim with the pay lists. Interestingly enough, and contrary to the argument made by McLeod and Tyler against pay lists as a reliable source of documentary evidence, for Cowessess researchers the use of the pay lists proved to be beneficial.

Cowessess negotiators came across files that indicated there were many people who accepted annuities one year and failed to ever again appear on the pay lists. One of the stipulations of the TLE claim was that an individual had to appear on a band's annuity pay lists for two consecutive years in order to be counted as part of the claim. Cowessess argued that these people did not appear the second time because they had died. Indian Affairs responded that those people might have gone to other bands, taken scrip, or even left Canada to join relatives on American reservations in Montana or North Dakota. Cowessess researchers determined that the people in question in fact did not appear on any other Canada or US band lists, nor did they show up in the scrip records or in the records of the Hudson's

Bay Company. Cowessess argued for including those people in their claim by linking their 'disappearance' from the historical records to Edgar Dewdney's 1880s starvation policy.

Briefly, in 1881, Indian Commissioner Edgar Dewdney decided to close the agency farms and relocate farm instructors, while refusing to survey the Cypress Hills reserves that had been promised to various bands.[51] Even more significantly, Dewdney decided to close Fort Walsh, which had acted as the distribution centre for rations for the thousands of Aboriginal people living in the region. He, in effect, implemented a policy of starvation aimed at subjugating the chiefs.[52] Dewdney's starvation policy had a devastating effect on the First Nations population. Chief Big Bear, the last chief to sign treaty, was forced to move his band to the Battleford region to establish his reserve. His band's 21-day journey was arduous, as a majority of the 550 people had to walk. Big Bear's granddaughter described the journey:

> The trek to our former home was a hard one to live through because of the lack of food and the scarcity of game. We travelled forever northwards and ran into severe storm. Deaths were numerous. We stopped only briefly to bury our dead; amongst the victims were my mother and sister.[53]

Cowessess argued that their people were also greatly affected by the starvation policies. Cowessess linked the pay lists to Dewdney's policies. Cowessess claimed that these persons died on the prairies during the year between treaty payments. As the federal government policy at the time was to withhold food or rations from certain First Nations people, many First Nations people starved on the plains. Many Cowessess members were unable to show up for the pay list counts because they were among those who died. So Cowessess argued that the federal government should not now benefit from this policy that lead to many deaths. The federal government has never acknowledged the starvation policy or its devastating effects on Saskatchewan's First Nations people, perhaps reluctant to debate publicly such a disgraceful episode of Canadian history.

In any case, Indian Affairs agreed to include those people whose deaths Cowessess attributed to the federal government's starvation policy with Indian Affairs checking each name to determine if it merited inclusion to Cowessess numbers. Reviewing close to three hundred additional names from the original band list was a time-consuming process, and the government's chief negotiator decided to strike a deal with Cowessess in hopes of reaching a quicker settlement, suggesting that the government would accept half of the remaining names on Cowessess' list without a review process. Such an arrangement benefited Cowessess by fast-tracking the agreement while also guaranteeing the community a large settlement. Cowessess agreed, which meant that Cowesses, unlike other First Nations, reached a negotiated figure for the claim. Cowessess' TLE settlement, then, was based on a negotiated band population of 804, even though band officials estimated that the population could be as high as 1,000. Arguably, other First Nations may have limited their claims by using the pay lists, as McLeod and Taylor asserted; in this case, the pay list combined with acknowledgment of the impact of the federal starvation policy was a crucial aspect of the Cowessess' settlement. It is not certain, however, whether other First Nations' could have negotiated better settlements if they had employed the starvation policy argument.

According to the equity formula, the band's present population figure was as important as the historical population. First Nations children are not automatically given Indian status at birth; their parents have to fill out a form and register them through Indian Affairs. It was common for parents not to register their children because status Indians benefits could still be accessed until the child reached eighteen years of age. However, for the purpose of the TLE, only those registered, including children, would count toward the claim. During the period of negotiations, then, Cowessess sent out numerous letters to band members to remind them to register their children for Indian status. In addition, band leadership told its members to encourage any relatives to apply whom they believed were eligible for Indian status through Bill C-31. The band offered assistance to help in the application process.

Implementing Cowessess TLE

In total, the TLE entitled Cowessess to a minimum of 53,312 acres (actual shortfall acres) and to purchase up to 189,367 acres (their equity acres). The Cowessess TLE agreement adhered to the same principles found in the original TLEFA, but since Cowessess was not a part of that agreement, it was able to negotiate additional terms. Chief Lionel Sparvier outlined these concessions in a letter addressed to his band members:

1. The ability to withdraw from the Trust funds an amount not exceeding $1,147,000, of which $800,000 may be utilized for Band development purposes, and $347,000 for the providing of one time lump sum payment to elders of the Band over the age of 65. The $800,000 could be used for any project deemed suitable to the First Nation without being subject to the constraints of the TLE agreement. Money was set aside for elders because it was believed that they would have the least to gain from the long-term benefits derived from TLE.

2. The ability to establish Trusts in the areas of Band development, education, culture and recreation for the use of all band members living on and off the reserve. The funds for these projects could come from one of two sources. The first was from interest generated from income in trust property, but it would need prior approval from TLE trustees. The second source was from the actual principal of the TLE fund. The use of this source could

be problematic as it could lead to a draining of the TLE accounts. It would, therefore, need approval of the band membership through a band-wide ratification vote.

3. The inclusion of an amendment clause that allows the Band Council and its Trustees to address any future changes in the tax system that may put in jeopardy the taxability of income generated from the Trust property. Other First Nations are required to conduct a ratification vote to amend their trust agreement, but Cowessess was able to negotiate a more time-effective measure. As Chief Sparvier noted to his membership, this was "a substantial concession, and one which will allow the Band and Trustees the ability to react quickly to any changes in the current tax system."

4. The inclusion of a floating upper limit on the purchase price of land, and the ability to purchase lands, prior to acquisition of the shortfall acres, without the purchase of underlying mines and minerals up to maximum of $4,000.

The upper limit, which varies community to community, is the maximum amount of money that a band can spend to purchase a piece of property. The floating upper limit takes into consideration the amount of money that Cowessess has already received and the amount that it has spent to purchase land throughout the land acquisition process; as a result, the upper limit will change as purchases are made. As Chief Sparvier noted, these new clauses were important because, they "will allow the Band greater flexibility in the structuring of land acquisition arrangements, particularly as they relate to the acquisition of urban land."[54]

After Cowessess and Indian Affairs reached an agreement on the TLE settlement, First Nation leaders had to ratify it by holding a band-wide referendum. Like the other TLE First Nations, Cowessess had to obtain a simple majority of band members to authorize the agreement, but Cowessess distribution, combined with Indian Affairs ratification regulations, made this process very arduous. Each First Nation was required to have 80 per cent of the eligible voters' addresses on file. At the time of the agreement, Cowessess' population exceeded 2,500, which would have meant a database of close to 1,400 names. Eighty per cent of Cowessess lived off-reserve, and band officials only had addresses for approximately 300 people. Because every non-vote was counted as a "no" vote to the TLE agreement, ratifying the deal required that Cowessess officials locate as many members as possible. The band embarked on an exhaustive campaign to ascertain membership whereabouts, finding sizeable numbers in several communities in the province. Large populations were located in Regina and a lesser number in Saskatoon. Significant numbers were also found in Vancouver, Calgary, Edmonton, and Winnipeg. Finally, many community members lived throughout Canada and in foreign countries such as Australia, Russia, and the United States. One was serving in the military as a sailor on undisclosed duty aboard a Canadian warship, necessitating forwarding of his ballot by the military to make the final count.

In addition to compiling its membership's addresses, Cowessess had to tackle the time-consuming and costly process of explaining the TLE agreement to those interested parties. Copies of the agreement were mailed to band members along with a summary prepared by the band's lawyers. Two documents comprised the final agreement: (1) *Cowessess Treaty Land Entitlement Agreement*; and, (2) *Cowessess Treaty Land Entitlement Trust Agreement*. Two hundred pages of densely legalistic and intimidating language led Cowessess leadership to schedule reserve and off-reserve informational meetings to help explain the documents. At first, the off-reserve meetings were only scheduled for major western cities but later meetings were added, in cities in Ontario, for instance, to not only allow First Nations TLE officials to better explain the agreement, but also as a venue to connect with the urban membership, many of whom had never lived at Cowessess. At these meetings, TLE officials Terrence Pelletier and Hubert Gunn encouraged urban members to visit and reconnect with their relatives and homeland. Indian Affairs covered the costs for the meetings while also agreeing to fund the ratification process. A sliding-scale formula partially reimbursed Cowessess for each member who lived in Saskatchewan with more allocated for those who lived outside the province and those living abroad. The band, however, was unable to arrange for meetings outside the country.

It took nearly three years from the time of the TLE settlement to the ratification vote, the latter of which provided a number of options. People could vote on the reserve or in a number of urban voting stations located throughout western Canada. Those members not living near these stations could vote by mail. Cowessess TLE officials spent significant time, energy, and resources—in all, over $300,000—but their efforts were rewarded: on 7 December 1995, the membership voted overwhelming in favour of the agreement.

The time and resources spent travelling to the various urban centres and meeting urban members was crucial to the final vote, the significance of which was recently witnessed in the 2001 failed ratification of the *Cowessess First Nation Lands Management Act*. In 1996, Cowessess First Nations became one of 14 First Nations nationwide who signed the *Framework Agreement on First Nations Land Management*, which was later passed by Parliament as the *First Nations Land Management Act*. The framework agreement provided these First Nations with "the option to manage their reserve lands outside the *Indian Act*."[55] Each First Nation had to develop its own land management act and pass a simple majority ratification vote. However, the Cowessess' lands management act ratification vote did not pass. Even though a majority of those who did vote supported the new act, non-votes—primarily representative of the urban membership—outnumbered the yes vote. Cowessess is currently attempting to hold another ratification vote on its land management act and will no doubt be seeking higher urban participation rates. The implementation and management of their TLE is the responsibility of the TLE trustees.

Principles of Nation-Building and Cowessess First Nation

The first experience Cowessess had with practical sovereignty was with the implementation of the 1996 TLE agreement. Cowessess also had the unique experience of observing the first group of TLE bands who settled earlier with the 1992 TLE agreements. Public controversies within these bands highlighted issues of good governance at a time when Cowessess was delivering public information sessions to their members. As a direct result, suspicions of Cowessess elected leadership led to initiatives that lent credibility and legitimacy to Cowessess land claim funds management. An initial weakness identified in the 1992 agreement was that the annual financial reporting system bypassed the band membership and simply required submitting a cursory audit to INAC. Cowessess instituted an amendment requiring the TLE trustees to report to the membership in person by 30 March each year. It was surmised (correctly) that making the trustees directly accountable to the membership would have a positive effect on their management practices.

Another weakness identified was the authorized expenses rules. The 1992 agreement authorized lands acquisition expenses to be withdrawn from the main capital trust. No limits were in place for expenditures nor did it describe what constituted authorized lands acquisition activities or specify by whom such activities could be undertaken. As a result, it was later verified, there was misuse of this rule. Chief Sparvier stated to the senior TLE management that he witnessed misuse on a large scale occurring on a certain reserve and stated emphatically that this would not happen on Cowessess. He wanted basic financial procedures and policies in place to address this major concern.

First, the Cowessess trust agreement set a limit on funds from the capital monies for initial start up costs of the TLE office. Thereafter, a lands management policy would be implemented to ensure that all purchased lands were available for immediate cash lease, and that subsequent operational expenses, including lands acquisition costs, were taken from this pool of funds. Second, since, along with trustees, chiefs and councils were involved in major spending activities, the Cowessess trust implemented a policy stating that the chief and council would not be authorized to receive funds from TLE. Furthermore, a related policy statement disqualified band programs from being funded from TLE funds. This prevented under-funded or poorly managed band programs from utilizing membership TLE funds to offset deficits. As well, a general principle stated that TLE would not fund areas designated as treaty rights such as education and health. However, one of the first major authorized expenditures was for a computer classroom for the reserve school; an education item not funded by INAC until about 2003.

Effective governing institutions facilitated the growth of the TLE funds and property creating wealth in land and capital for the band.[56] A decision was made to provide workshops on trust law to potential trustees among the band membership. A professor specializing in trust law from the College of Law, University of Saskatchewan, offered this workshop. It made everyone aware of the many trustee obligations contained in the TLE agreement and in Canadian law. A second important step was to require the trustees to operate as a board of directors; that is, adopt board governance style for conduct. Learning from guidelines for a provincial board ensured reasonable reimbursement rates for trustees were followed, working chair was adopted, no band-level administrators were allowed to sit as trustees, and senior trust management was competent and reliable; all of this contributed to precedents providing long-term stability.

In terms of a cultural match, there have been numerous examples of poor administration among other bands styled on models of self-serving bureaucracy. For Cowesscss, the cultural match followed that proposed by public meetings prior to the trust being voted on by everyone. Membership concerns were implemented in the laws, policies, and rules of conduct that were consistently followed over time.

These practical policies, combined with good leadership, promoted the public goals and purpose of the trust. By protecting the interests of the trust property from the beginning, Cowessess now has enough capital and wealth to initiate any capital project involving land either in an urban or rural setting. After 11 years, the trust has $26 million in trust money and 74,000 acres of land leased out, valued at $18 million. These monies and land leases produce about $1.5 million in gross revenue. The influence of Cowessess economically and socially will be magnified over time in the southern Saskatchewan region.

Conclusion

The TLE signing ceremony was held before a capacity crowd at Cowessess First Nation community hall representing both reserve and off-reserve community members, and officials from the FSIN and the provincial and federal governments. Gifts were given and appreciation expressed to the TLE committee and the volunteers who worked at the various voting stations. Minister Irwin took the time to inform the gathering:

> This agreement confirms my government's commitment to resolving Aboriginal land claims and fulfills its treaty obligation to the people of Cowessess First Nations. ... With the purchase of new land, the Cowessess First Nation will forge a link with the past and create an opportunity for the future. This settlement will provide an economic base which will benefit current community members as well as future generations.[57]

Minister Crofford noted that "[the] agreement fulfills provincial obligations and provides Cowessess First Nations with the resources necessary for future economic development that will benefit all of Saskatchewan."[58] And Chief Lionel Sparvier stated, "Treaty 4 contained an obligation to provide land to our people. ... This agreement settles our people's right to receive land as a reserve. It is my hope that the resources acquired by the settlement of this outstanding promise will promote the well-being of our people."[59] At the end of the signing ceremony, Cowessess officially became a TLE First Nation.

Cowessess' TLE process is noteworthy for a number of reasons. First, the negotiations demonstrated Cowessess' perseverance in obtaining the best possible deal for all its band members. Seeking to extract as much money from the federal and provincial governments as possible, and, clearly, the use of the starvation policy argument achieved that goal, community leaders were also intent on compelling federal recognition of Canada's treaty responsibilities to those people who had died, if not, at the very least, acknowledgement of the government's complicity in their deaths. As a result of this recognition, the ancestors leave a tangible legacy to the present-day Cowessess band members. The efforts to count as many people as possible as contemporary band members have also enabled Cowessess to not only obtain more money; it has maximized the number of descendants of the original Cowessess band benefiting from the treaty. Another important aspect of the TLE process was that Cowessess has strengthened its financial and social capabilities. Financially, the band has been and will continue to be able to create and partner economic development ventures that benefit both reserve and urban First Nations members. Socially, because the First Nation had to make contact with long lost members, either indirectly through the many mail-outs or directly through informational meetings, Cowessess has (re)ignited its social relations with off-reserve members. Fundamentally, the TLE process has provided Cowessess the opportunity to increase its nation-building capacity.

NOTES

1   Stephen Cornell & Joseph P. Kalt, *Two Approaches to Economic Development on American Indian Reservations: One Works, the Other Doesn't* (Massachusetts: Harvard Project on American Indian Economic Development and the Native Nations Institute for Leadership, Management, and Policy on behalf of the Arizona Board of Regents, 2006); Stephen Cornell, Miriam Jorgensen, Joseh P. Kalt & Katherine A. Spilde, *Seizing the Future: Why Some Native Nations Do and Other Don't* (Massachusetts: Harvard Project of American Indian Economic Development, 2005).

2   Cornell and Kalt, *Two Approaches.*

3   *Ibid.,* 17.

4   *Ibid.,* 11.

5   *Ibid.,* 14.

6   *Ibid.*

7   *Ibid.,* 17.

8   *Ibid.,* 18.

9   Brenda McLeod, "Treaty Land Entitlement in Saskatchewan: Conflicts in Land Use and Occupancy in the Witchekan Lake Area" (M.A. thesis, University of Saskatchewan, 2001).

10   Peggy Martin-McGuire, "The Importance of the Land: Treaty Land Entitlement and Self-Government in Saskatchewan," in *Aboriginal Self-Government in Canada: Current Trends and Issues,* 2nd Edition, ed. John H. Hylton (Saskatoon: Purich Publishing, 1999).

11   James Pitsula, "The Blakeney Government and the Settlement of Treaty Indian Land Entitlements in Saskatchewan, 1975-1982," in *Historical Papers: A Selection of the Paper Presented at the Annual Meeting held at Quebec,* 1989 (Ottawa: Canadian Historical Association, 1989), 191-192.

12   *Ibid.,* 192.

13   *Ibid.,* 193.

14   *Ibid.*

15   Noel Dyck, "The Negotiation of Indian Treaties and Land Rights in Saskatchewan," in *Aborigine Land and Land Rights,* eds. Nicolas Peterson and Marcia Langton (Canberra: Australian Institute of Aboriginal Studies, 1983).

16   Richard Bartlett, "Native Land Claims: Outstanding Treaty Land Entitlements in Saskatchewan, 1982-89," in *Devine Rule in Saskatchewan: A Decade of Hope and Hardship,* eds. Leslie Biggs and Mark Stobbe (Saskatoon: Fifth House, 1990), 138

17   *Ibid.*
18   Peggy Martin-McGuire, "Treaty Land Entitlement in Saskatchewan: A Context for the Creation of Urban Reserves," in *Urban Indian Reserves: Forging New Relationships in Saskatchewan,* eds. F. Laurie Barron and Joseph Garcea (Saskatoon: Purich Publishing, 1999).
19   David C. Knoll, *Unfinished Business: Treaty Land Entitlement and Surrender Claims in Saskatchewan* (Saskatoon: Native Law Centre, 1987).
20   Clifford Wright, Report and recommendations on treaty land entitlement, presented to Roland Crowe, Treaty Indian Nations of Saskatchewan and the Honourable Tom Sidden, Minister of Indian Affairs by Treaty Commissioner Cliff Wright (Saskatoon: Office of the Treaty Commissioner, 1990), 5.
21   Bartlett, "Native Land Claims," 7.
22   Pitsula, "The Blakeney Government."
23   Martin-McGuire, "Treaty Land Entitlement," 63.
24   *Ibid,*; Bartlett, "Native Land Claims," 140.
25   Bartlett, "Native Land Claims," 142; Martin-McGuire, "Treaty Land Entitlement," 66.
26   As summarized by Bartlett, "Native Land Claims," 143.
27   *Ibid.*, 144.
28   *Ibid.*, 145.
29   Martin-McGuire, "Treaty Land Entitlement," 69.
30   Lester Lafond, "Creation, Governance and Management of the McKnight Commercial Centre in Saskatoon," in *Urban Indian Reserves: Forging New Relationships in Saskatchewan,* eds. F. Laurie Barron & Joseph Garcea (Saskatoon: Purich Publishing, 1999.)
31   Bartlett, 146.
32   *Ibid.*; Wright, Report and recommendations, 17.
33   Bartlett, "Native Land Claims," 146; Martin-McGuire, "The Importance of the Land," 276.
34   Wright, Report and recommendations.
35   *Ibid.*, 39.
36   *Ibid.*, 57.
37   Martin-McGuire, "Treaty Land Entitlement," 71.
38   *Ibid.*
39   *Ibid.*
40   "Treaty Land Entitlement Ratifications Now Complete," *Saskatchewan Indian* Fall (1995): 22.
41   *Ibid.*
42   Martin-McGuire, "Treaty Land Entitlement."
43   Trevor Sutter, "Land Entitlements: Legal Wording and Few Hurdles Stand in Way," *Regina Leader Post* 2 May 1992, A-3.
44   *Ibid.*
45   *Ibid.*
46   *Saskatchewan Indian,* 22.
47   McLeod, "Treaty Land Entitlement," 209.
48   Kenneth Tyler cited in McLeod, "Treaty Land Entitlement," 210.
49   *Ibid.*, 201.
50   *Ibid.*, 225.
51   Michel Hogue, "Disputing the Medicine Line: The Plains Cree and the Canadian-American Border, 1876-1885," *Montana: The Magazine of Western History* 52 (2002): 2-17.
52   John Tobias, "Canada's Subjugation of the Plains Cree, 1879-1885," in *Out of The Background: Readings on Canadian Native History,* eds. Robin Fisher and Kenneth Coates (Toronto: Copp Clark Pitman Ltd., 1988).
53   Hugh Dempsey, *Big Bear: The End of Freedom* (Lincoln: University of Nebraska Press; Vancouver: Douglas & McIntyre, 1984), 114.
54   Chief Lionel Sparvier, "Cowessess First Nations - Treaty Land Entitlement," (Cowessess Indian Reserve, Office of the Chief, October 10, 1995), 3.
55   *First Nations Land Management Agreement* http://www.tleoffice.com/home/ (accessed 15 September 2006).
56   See Cowessess Treaty Land Entitlement Office, "Trust Financial Report." Audit prepared by Meyers, Norris and Penny LLP, 2006. Cowessess Treaty Land Entitlement Office provides access to all financial reports through its website, http://www.tleoffice.com/home/.
57   Government of Canada, "Cowessess First Nations Signs Treaty Land Entitlement Agreement" News Release (1996), 1.
58   *Ibid.*
59   *Ibid.*

GOVERNMENT ON
THE MÉTIS SETTLEMENTS:

*Foundations and Future Directions**

Catherine Bell, University of Alberta
& Harold Robinson, Métis Settlements Appeal Tribunal

Introduction

The Métis Settlements of Alberta are Canada's only legislated, land-based Métis government. Approximately seven thousand Métis live on eight Métis settlements in central and northern Alberta. Together, settlement lands total approximately 1.25 million acres. Understanding the unique landholding and governance structure on the settlements requires consideration of the historical, legal, and political context for negotiation; settlement government and justice objectives; and the ultimate goal of creating a practical, flexible, and functional regime in which governmental institutions respond to the experiences and needs of a particular people. Similarly, the strengths and weaknesses of this system of government are best measured by the extent to which institutions and policies of Métis settlement government promote the well-being of the settlements affected.[1] However, the Métis settlement scheme and history of its development also offer some interesting lessons for others engaged in self-government negotiation and implementation.

The foundational principles and framework for transfer and allocation of Métis settlement lands and resources; protection of settlement lands; and executive, legislative, and judicial branches of government are found in the 1989 *Métis Settlements Accord* (hereafter the Accord)—a bilateral agreement between the government of Alberta and the then Federation of Métis Settlements. Legislation was subsequently enacted in 1990 to implement negotiated agreements in these areas and, as acknowledged in amendments to the original legislation, "for the purpose of enabling the Métis to attain self-governance under the laws of Alberta."[2] Although settlement leaders advocated recognition of Métis Aboriginal rights to land and government at constitutional conferences and dealings with the province, this rights-based strategy was eventually set aside to avoid provincial negotiations being mired in the complex legal issues that resulted in the failure to reach a national agreement on the existence and scope of Métis constitutional rights. Negotiating a unique, results-oriented, "made in Alberta" approach to self-government was seen as the most practical means to achieve concrete results for settlement members at the time.

At the core of the settlement model is an understanding that what is important is not that "ideal institutions are created" but that there is a commitment on the part of Métis Settlement Government and the Government of Alberta "to the ideal of continued co-operation in adapting institutions to meet new challenges."[3] Unlike rights-based agreements, certainty and extinguishment of Aboriginal constitutional rights is not central to the agreement reached. Indeed, it is only with the 2004 amendments that the goal of self-governance is clearly articulated. Concerned about issues of jurisdiction and potential impact on Aboriginal rights, a paragraph was included in the *Constitution of Alberta Amendment Act, 1990* to clarify that the Métis settlements legislation is not to be construed so as to abrogate or derogate from Aboriginal rights.[4] Despite this intent, the legislation raises complicated constitutional questions. Further, although certain provincial mechanisms are adopted to protect the settlement land base and ensure the continued existence and make up of the Métis Settlements General Council (MSGC), the binding effect of these mechanisms on future governments is debatable. Thus, the success of this system is largely dependent on its flexibility and co-operation and good will between the parties affected.

Paradoxically, one of the key ingredients for the success of this model—its ability to adapt to experience, change, and the needs of the settlements—is also a fundamental weakness. As provincial statutory entities with delegated authorities, the institutions of Métis government are vulnerable to unilateral change. However, settlement members have adopted a pragmatic response to this vulnerability by achieving what is possible within a delegated framework and looking to new opportunities for increased protection and control. As with any relationship, the partnership between MSGC and Alberta has had its ups and downs, but generally, intergovernmental relations to date have been positive and respectful of Métis political autonomy in negotiated fields of jurisdiction.

Over the past fifteen years, regional and local Métis settlement government institutions have assumed jurisdiction in a wide range of areas and significant progress has been made on the ground in the areas of community, and social and economic development. Jurisdictions of the MSGC have been expanded and the office of the Métis Settlements Ombudsman (MSO) has been established. Some proposals to expand Métis Settlement Appeal Tribunal (MSAT) jurisdiction and the creation of the MSO resulted from a joint initiative to review MSAT's mandate (MSAT Task Force). Other changes are in response to the continuing demand for good government by settlement members and the natural evolution of new structures and approaches that ultimately improve local and central governance functions and thereby enhance local autonomy. However, some changes are under negotiation. Others, such as the unilateral increase of regulatory powers of the minister, requirements for General Council Policies on such matters as its personnel manual and rules for meeting (Robert's Rules), creation of an executive committee for MSAT, and changes to the role of the MSAT Chair seem inconsistent with the trend to greater autonomy set out in the Accord.

Essential to the functioning of any government is adequate financing and strong economic development. Métis settlement government is currently financed in a number of ways including: a financial commitment of $310 million allocated over a period of 17 years commencing 1 July 1990; revenues from surface and sub-surface development of settlement land; the ability to charge fees, dues, and levies on settlement and non-settlement members for services provided, permits, licenses, and other authorizations; and the ability to access federal and provincial grants available to other Aboriginal and municipal governments. Taxation powers over interests in settlement lands also exist.

In 2007, unconditional funding provided as part of original Accord package will no longer be available. In anticipation of this event, the Transition Assessment and Planning (TAP) Project was initiated by the MSGC and Alberta in 2004. Together, the partners have taken stock of the progress made over the first 15 years of the Accord. The TAP Project has entered into the planning and development phase and work is now being done to identify new approaches to promote continued progress toward the Accord goals of improved land security, self-governance, and economic self-sufficiency.

Today, we are in a new era in which Métis constitutional rights are being addressed in legal and political fora and federal jurisdiction over Métis is again being given serious consideration. The recent *Powley* decision recognizing the existence of Métis Aboriginal rights and the creation of the Office of the Federal Interlocutor for Métis and Non-Status Indians have opened new avenues of negotiation that were not available when the original Accord was negotiated in the late 1980s.[5] In response, the MSGC has negotiated a new provincial harvesting agreement for hunting, trapping, and fishing outside of settlement lands (which is similar to an agreement negotiated by the Métis Nation of Alberta Association). The MSGC is also creating a database of traditional land use activities and ancestral connections to historical Métis communities through a grant provided by the Federal Interlocutor's Office. In order to improve the federal government's awareness of the settlements, the MSGC opened up an outreach office in Ottawa in 2005.

The purpose of this chapter is to outline the basic structure and operations of Métis settlement government and changes that have occurred, or are proposed, to the initial settlement scheme, financing, and operations of government over the last fifteen years. We conclude with reflections on practical issues in the exercise of government functions and complicated questions that arise as we enter a new era of Métis Aboriginal rights. What we present is not the end of a history of negotiations, but part of an ongoing journey toward new partnerships between the Métis settlements, and federal and provincial governments.

Historical and Political Context

Pursuant to federal policy, in the late 1800s Métis people in Manitoba, and later Saskatchewan and Alberta, were offered treaty if they lived among and were accepted by First Nations or scrip (a certificate redeemable by individual Métis for land or money).[6] Métis who were not eligible for treaty were offered scrip only. These processes failed to protect the collective existence of Métis in communities and to provide them with sufficient lands and resources to sustain themselves. In Manitoba, this resulted in some Métis migrating west to join other Métis communities in central and northern Saskatchewan and Alberta. In northern Alberta Métis communities of Ojibwa, Cree, and Chipweyan descent also emerged near, or within the present geographical boundaries of, some contemporary Métis settlement communities. Concerned about some of the more destitute Métis populations in Alberta and following the Northwest Métis Resistance of 1885, Father Lacombe approached the federal government to set up a farming colony in northern Alberta for the benefit of the Métis. *St. Paul de Métis* was established in 1895, but ten years later declared a failure and opened up for settlement. Only a small number of Métis claims in the area were recognized.[7]

Métis from the colony joined others throughout the province struggling to survive.[8] Although some were successful establishing farms in southern Alberta, those who remained in central Alberta lived in tents along road allowances and tried to make a living as farm hands. In addition to suffering from poverty and homelessness, many Métis were without schooling, housing, medical services, and social relief. Malnutrition became an issue for those in the north as wildlife resources were depleted or disrupted by settlement. Non-status Indians of mixed blood suffering from a similar fate were, for the purposes of federal and provincial policy, referred to as "half-breeds"—a term used interchangeably at the time with "Métis." This was the situation when the Natural Resources Transfer Agreements (NRTA) were being negotiated. Although a provision in these agreements was included to protect the "Indian" lifestyle of hunting, fishing, and trapping, its application to any or all Métis has been a matter of political debate with Métis peoples arguing for inclusion. Settlement Métis also take the position that the Crown's duty to address scrip claims was a trust encumbering federal lands and Alberta acquired land under the NRTA subject to this trust. Although still a contentious issue, the relevant provision in the Manitoba NRTA, identical to Alberta's NRTA, has been interpreted by the Supreme Court of Canada to exclude the Métis.[9]

During this time many Métis also moved to the Fishing Lake area to join a number of families who had settled on forest reserve land.[10] Perccived threats to the continued existence of this settlement arising from the NRTA resulted in the creation of the first Métis regional political organization in Alberta (later to become known as the Métis Association of Alberta or MAA). Following a 1931 meeting of two hundred Métis representing six communities, Jim Brady, Malcolm Norris, and Joseph Dion (an enfranchised Indian) submitted a petition with over

500 names to the Alberta government on behalf of the Métis seeking assistance in obtaining land, education, medical care, and free hunting and fishing permits. The government responded with a questionnaire completed by over 1000 Métis and non-status "half-breeds" addressing issues such as failure to receive scrip and homestead lands, ownership of livestock, and attitudes toward farming. Shortly thereafter the MAA was formed. The primary goals of the organization, approved by 32 councillors representing as many communities, were to see that adequate provision was made for "homeless and destitute families," including education and medical services.[11] These issues "were contained, depended upon, and were expressed in one clear and unmistakable demand: the demand for land."[12]

As the federal government asserted "half-breeds" were a provincial responsibility, Métis leadership focused on pressing the provincial government into action.[13] The province appointed the Ewing Commission to look into the "problems of health, education, and general welfare of the Half-breed population of the province."[14] Although all Métis executive members emphasized social welfare needs in their submissions, Brady and Norris also argued Métis had rights to land arising from the failure of the scrip system, and an independent economic base for Métis self-determination. However, the latter position was viewed by the Commission as a "leftist" radical opinion and the Chair refused to hear rights-based arguments.

The Commission operated on the assumption that if Métis had rights to land by virtue of Aboriginal ancestry, such rights were extinguished by the scrip system. The Commission recommended: allotment of Crown land for the creation of farm colonies to be free from intrusion by white settlers, a paternalistic system of local governance consisting of elected advisory boards and provincially appointed settlement supervisors; and that Métis be given preferential rights in harvesting fish, game, and furs. The Commission also recommended that girls be educated in homemaking skills, boys in agriculture and for both, writing, and arithmetic.

Following these recommendations the province enacted the *Métis Population Betterment Act,* later known as the *Métis Betterment Act.* Although similar to federal Indian legislation in many respects, it differed in others. The *Métis Betterment Act* preamble recognized that it was in the public interest that the ways and means of giving effect to the Ewing Commission recommendations should be arrived at by "means of conferences and negotiations." Somewhat disillusioned by the Commission recommendations, Brady pulled back from political life which resulted in Norris also not taking part in the negotiations. Tomkins and Dion worked with the province and, despite the emphasis on agriculture, selected lands for the colonies (later to be known as the settlements) in areas where Métis had traditionally sustained themselves. Their belief in the goodwill of the government, a leadership vacuum in the MAA, the emergence of a new organization which challenged the creation of the colonies in favour of individual titles, and the priority of securing a land base were likely some of the reasons Tomkins and Dion did not place as much emphasis on administration and governance of the colonies as Brady and Norris.[15]

Several events occurred in the administration of the legislation that resulted in a call for new arrangements. The original vision was for co-operative settlement management, but by the 1950s the system became very top-down with supervisors appointed without consultation and accountable only to the Minister of Welfare. By the 1960s, more administrative power was delegated to the settlements and unworkable sections of the *Métis Betterment Act* were ignored. However, increased administrative power also resulted in uncertainty about the extent of settlement powers, their status to enter into binding legal relationships, and the continual need to involve the Métis Development Branch in contractual and other arrangements. Of particular significance was the disestablishment of four colonies without consultation or consent (Touchwood, Marlboro, Cold Lake, and Wolf Lake). At the time only one was occupied by Métis, but the unilateral action of the province generated concerns about security of the Métis land base. Further, Métis believed the province was more concerned with developing oil and gas under settlement lands than acting for the "betterment" of the Métis.

In 1972, a Task Force was established in response to these concerns. It recommended that the settlements move toward a form of local self-government and that land be set aside perpetually for their benefit. In 1977, the Federation of Métis Settlements (the Federation), a representative body of the remaining eight settlements, was also formed and commenced litigation on behalf of settlement members accusing the province of misappropriating resource revenues that, pursuant to Orders-in-Council under the *Métis Betterment Act,* were allegedly to be placed in trust for the benefit of the Métis.[16] Following the Task Force report the Métis Development Branch adopted a policy to devolve more responsibility to settlements, which by then had assumed administrative powers for delivery of local housing, education, and economic and cultural programs. Two years later an investigation into seizure of settlement files in the course of the natural resource litigation resulted in the provincial ombudsman recommending that a new joint Métis-provincial commission be formed to review the administration of the *Métis Betterment Act.*

After consultations with settlement members, the MacEwan Committee made many recommendations designed to enhance Métis control, protect Métis culture, provide adequate financial resources to build viable communities, and protect the survival of Métis culture. Unanimous recommendations included securing a permanent land base, increased local government over settlement lands, clarification of legal status, and greater control by settlement members over social and economic development. The Federation included Aboriginal rights to land and government in their submissions and subsequent negotiations with the province.[17] The Committee proposed that new legislation recognize Métis Aboriginal ancestry and their distinct role in the history and culture of Alberta, but matters of Aboriginal rights were considered to be outside the Committee's provincial mandate.[18]

At this time, the Federation was also involved in national conferences held to clarify Aboriginal rights recognized and affirmed in section 35 of the Canadian

Constitution. During these conferences identification and membership became contentious issues that were never resolved and both federal and provincial governments denied jurisdiction over Métis peoples. At the root of provincial concerns was the potential impact of Métis claims on provincial lands, revenues, and resources. Further, to the extent that Métis Aboriginal rights were acknowledged, governments asserted they had been extinguished through scrip distribution. Although Federation representatives appreciated that other Métis people had little success in negotiating with provincial governments, it was in a unique position to develop a relationship with the Government of Alberta. Alberta had responded positively to the MacEwan Committee recommendations and was prepared to negotiate pursuant to its jurisdiction over property, municipal governance, and civil rights.[19] Also, even if the federal government had jurisdiction, there was no guarantee it would be exercised. Concerns about federal reluctance to exercise jurisdiction proved true in subsequent negotiations. A similar position for recognition of joint jurisdiction was maintained by settlement leaders and the government of Alberta during the negotiation of the failed Charlottetown Accord.[20]

The MacEwan Report, released in 1984, gave rise to a fresh set of negotiations and eventually a resolution by the Lougheed government to protect settlement land through an amendment to the *Alberta Act.*[21] However, this critical resolution was conditional upon settlements developing fair and democratic procedures for membership and land allocation.[22] Resolution 18 also called for transfer of *fee simple* title to Métis government, delegated self-government jurisdictions exercised by institutions proposed by the Métis, and introduction of new legislation to replace the old regime. Ensuing negotiations were conducted without prejudice to Aboriginal and treaty rights and resulted in the signing of the Métis Accord. Hundreds of community and Métis government meetings were held throughout the Accord process. In the end, 77 per cent of those who voted supported the Accord. The greatest opposition came from members of Paddle Prairie who were concerned about implications of the Accord on their Aboriginal rights and felt that all title and jurisdiction to enact laws affecting settlements should rest at the settlement level.[23]

Contemporary governance goals flowing from this history are land security, local autonomy, and self-sufficiency. The Accord was implemented in 1990 with the enactment of four pieces of legislation: The *Métis Settlements Act* (MSA), *Constitution of Alberta Amendment Act* (CAA), *Métis Settlements Land Protection Act* (MSLPA), and *Métis Settlements Accord Implementation Act* (MSAIA).[24] Eight settlement councils, and one central authority, the MSGC, have the powers of a natural person in law and enjoy delegated authority to pass policies and bylaws in relation to land, membership, governance, and matters related thereto. Another key feature was the creation of MSAT.

The leadership agenda in the early 1930s, through to the Alberta-Métis Settlements Accord, and today continues to focus on results without prejudicing potential legal rights. What follows is a discussion of some of the main features of the original land and governance system followed by changes brought about through, and proposed by, the 2004 *Métis Settlements Amendment Act.*

Government and Membership

There are four key features of settlement government: settlement councils, the MSGC, the minister responsible for administering the Act, and MSAT. Settlement councils are comprised of five elected members from the settlement and exercise bylaw powers similar to a municipality.[25] Settlement councils can also enact bylaws relating to membership and land allocation, as well as other jurisdictions given to them under MSGC policies (e.g. surface access, allocation of settlement share of subsurface royalties). bylaws must comply with MSGC policy and be given three separate readings by a settlement council, presented at a public meeting, and approved by the majority of settlement members in attendance. These governments also run local programs and services such as water systems, garbage pick-up, housing, and local economic development. Matters such as election procedures, resignations, disqualifications, delegation of authority, and conflicts of interest are modeled on provincial municipal law.[26]

The MSGC is the central government composed of members from each settlement council and a four-person executive elected by the 40 settlement councillors for a total of forty-four members.[27] It has delegated jurisdiction in specified areas to enact policies binding on settlement councils in specified areas of collective interest formerly within the jurisdiction of the province, manages collective settlement funds, and holds *fee simple* title to the settlement land base under letters patent.

Within General Council there are also several committees established to carry out the responsibilities of the MSGC. The Strategic Training Initiative (STI) is primarily concerned with delivering training programs to settlement residents under the federal Aboriginal Human Resources Development Agreement. The tripartite unit was established to negotiate agreements with Canada and Alberta. Various standing advisory committees (SACs), including the Land and Resources SAC, Finance SAC, Governance SAC, and the MSGC Board, enable the MSGC to attend to its executive functions as holder of letters patent, partner in co-management processes, and manager of the Future Fund, which currently sits at $100 million.

The MSA only provides a framework for settlement government and jurisdiction. Many of the settlement laws are found in MSGC policies, ministerial regulations, settlement bylaws, and decisions of MSAT. General Council has jurisdiction to enact, amend, or repeal policies and model bylaws after consultation with the minister in a range of areas including membership and residency; finance; land and resource development and allocation; creation, transfer, and devolution of interests in settlement lands; administration of estates; and taxation, levies, and fines.[28] Policies inconsistent with provincial laws, subject to a few exceptions noted in the MSA, are of no effect to the extent of being inconsistent with provincial law. This has resulted in numerous consequential amendments to legislation to enable its application to the interests created under the MSA, such as dower and family relief legislation. Policies are published in the *Alberta Gazette* and have the force of law within the settlements after 90 days from the date of submission to the minister, provided that the minister does not veto the policy, or a portion of it. Although unpopular with settlement government, the veto power has yet to be exercised. Particularly important in negotiations was preservation of traditional lifestyles and the ability to enact policies relating to hunting, fishing, trapping, and gathering in the settlement area. As these are given priority over other provincial laws, they are developed with the minister and approved by the Lieutenant Governor in Council.[29]

The desire to protect Métis values also resulted in community consultation and consensus requirements being incorporated into bylaw-making powers of settlement councils, the composition of the MSGC as an "all council," and the original process for enacting General Council policies.[30] The practice of MSGC is to develop policies through committees and institutions of the MSGC and to circulate them to affected third parties and settlements after first reading. Polices are posted in settlement council offices following the second reading.[31] The MSA also requires that most policies have unanimous support by MSGC members before being adopted and implemented. At the time, this provision was central to the decision of Paddle Prairie to support the Accord.

General Council also works together with several central governance institutions and corporations. These include the Settlement Investment Corporation (SIC), Settlement Sooniyaw Corporation (SSC), Land and Membership Registry, and Region 10 Child and Family Authority (CFA). The SIC is a $4-million company that provides settlement members with small business loans. The SSC was established to promote economic development through business incubation and promotion of joint ventures and new partnerships, but has been largely silent during the first 15 years of the Accord. This will change as the settlements are now poised to move from investing in critical infrastructure and housing to investing in people and business. The Métis Settlements Ombudsman (MSO), and new authorities anticipated in the TAP proposals are discussed later in this chapter.

Before leaving structures of government, mention should be made of the Transition Authority (comprised of the Minister of Intergovernmental Affairs and the President of the MSGC) and Transition Commission created to assist in the transition from government administration through the Métis Settlements Branch to self-government. The Transition Commission was also responsible for certain aspects of training, financial management, and maintaining the Métis Settlements Land and Membership Registry. Intended to expire after seven years, the commission was extended for four years by agreement of the MSGC and the minister. With the exception of the Land Registry, MSGC has assumed many of the former powers of the Transition Commission. The Land Registry is currently being administered by the Province. Under the TAP Project, however, the MSGC's and Alberta's relationship to all Métis institutions is being reviewed and some may be brought under the MSGC umbrella, while others will remain at arm's length.

Four significant changes to this system are brought about by the 2004 amendments. Under the original system, settlement councillors were elected annually for staggered terms of three years with at least one new councillor appointed each year. The original rationale for this system was to ease the settlements into the role of government and to ensure consistency of experienced and new councillors. However, it proved unworkable in the actual operations of government because local decision-makers were always in election mode. Consequently, elections were changed to every three years commencing October 2004 and all councillors are now appointed for a term of three years. Terms of office that expired before this date were extended and those that expired after were deemed to end with the election.[32] New election provisions were to be reviewed jointly or independently no later than December 31, 2005. At the time of writing the review was underway.

A second change is the mechanism by which the MSGC enacts policy. The requirement of unanimity proved problematic in practice because it gave every settlement a de facto veto over critical policy development, without providing an effective dispute-resolution mechanism to deal with the inevitable disagreements. The MSA was amended by Alberta so that all policies and amendments could be passed by special resolution (six of eight settlements). A further amendment enabled the MSGC to develop a new review policy that enables settlement Councils that oppose a policy to apply to the MSAT on the grounds that a newly passed policy unfairly discriminates against their members.[33]

Further, under the original MSA the minister exercised regulatory power to clarify application of the *Act*,[34] but only at the request of General Council. The minister may now make regulations of his/her own motion in areas of MSGC policy jurisdiction. However, such regulations expire on the earliest of: the coming into force of MSGC policy, two years, or the day on which they are repealed.[35] Although well-intentioned, this power has the potential to significantly undermine the autonomy of the MSGC by having the minister set priorities for policy development. Hopefully, this provision, too, will only operate as a safety net and, like the minister's veto power, not be exercised. In keeping with the spirit of flexibility and commitment to co-operation, this change and others in the *Act* are subject to review, both through the TAP Project and through the *Act* itself. The MSGC may make proposals to change the Act or regulations that are "directed to the creation of a more effective and culturally appropriate structure for self-governance" and set out "workable alternatives" to existing structures and institutions.[36]

Finally, under the MSA, a Métis person is defined as "a person of aboriginal ancestry who identifies with Métis history and culture."[37] Applications to settlement council must be accompanied by proof of Métis identity, which could include affidavits of two Métis recognized as Elders. Applications could not be approved if an applicant was a registered Indian or Inuk unless he or she was removed from the registry or was registered under the age of 18, lived on the settlements, had one or both parents as members of the settlement, and a bylaw was passed approving membership. With the 1985 amendments to the *Indian Act* (Bill

C-31), some settlement and non-settlement Métis regained Indian status sometimes without knowledge of the effects this could have on their existing and potential membership in the settlements or their inability to remove themselves from the Indian register once status was granted.[38] This issue was dealt with in part by a Transitional Membership Regulation requiring each settlement council and the minister to provide the Transition Commissioner with a list of existing members as of November 1990. Members on both lists were affirmed as members and those deemed of uncertain status could apply to MSAT to confirm or deny membership based on whether the applicant was treated as a member under previous legislation and fairness dictated that membership be maintained.[39] MSAT can also hear appeals from membership denials, several of which have involved consideration of Bill C-31 status. On some settlements, this issue has also been litigated and continues to result in the denial of membership, residence, and other services.

In addition to the above processes, the MSGC can now enact its own policies and criteria to determine whether an Indian or Inuk can become a settlement member. MSGC did not seek this jurisdiction, has not enacted a policy on this issue, and is reluctant to do so given the divided and strongly held opinions of different settlement councils. However, through workshops and its traditional-use studies, the MSGC is examining the underlying principle of what it means to be a member of the Métis settlements. Rather than focusing on the legalistic definitions contained in federal statutes, which inevitably create division, the MSGC is focusing on the elements that unite community members, such as common cultural practices, language, and the settlements' own unique history and development.

Land Rights and the Land Registry

Fundamental components of the Accord are greater control over settlement lands and the creation of a secure land base for the Métis. This is accomplished through transfer of title, two protective legislative enactments, jurisdictions delegated to MSAT and MSGC, and the co-management agreement for mineral rights appended to the MSA. *Fee simple* title is held by the MSGC by way of letters patent (including beds and shores, road allowances, and highways but excluding water, mines, and minerals). *The Métis Settlements Land Protection Act* (MSLPA) confirms the terms of the letters patent, restricts rights of expropriation to interests less than *fee simple* and includes mechanisms to resolve disputes, prevents the giving of *fee simple* as security for a debt (other interests are addressed in the Land Policy), and requires consent of both the affected settlement and MSGC for entry to settlement land to exercise subsurface rights. It also prohibits alienation of a *fee simple* interest without the consent of the Crown, MSGC, and the majority of members of the affected settlement, and majority of all settlement members is necessary before any of this land can be sold to non-settlement members.

The *Constitution of Alberta Amendment Act* (CAA) also provides some security by preventing changes in the MSLPA, alteration or revocation of MSGC ownership under the letters patent, and dissolution or changes to the composition of the

MSGC without the agreement of the MSGC. However, the ability of one provincial government to bind another on matters relating to enactment, repeal, and amendment is a matter of debate. Although contemporary academic opinion suggests a distinction must be drawn between binding the substance of, and procedures for, enacting legislation and that the later is acceptable, this is not clear in law.[40] Because federal involvement would make it more difficult for the province to amend or repeal its constitution, and provincial constitutions are instruments which form part of the Canadian constitution, the MSGC and Alberta sought greater protection through federal involvement in the amending process. To date, the Federal government has denied this request on the opinion that it is a wholly provincial matter covered by s. 45 of the Canadian Constitution, which allows provinces to enact laws to change provincial constitutions.

MSGC policy provides for a unique system of landholding on the settlements and acquisition of leasehold and lesser interests by non-settlement residents.[41] Métis title to settlement land is held by settlement councils unless Métis title to a specific parcel is registered in the name of a settlement member in the Métis Land Registry. Métis title gives the holder exclusive rights to use, occupy, improve, and grant lesser interests to settlement and non-settlement members in accordance with MSGC policy and settlement bylaws, and transfer *inter vivos* or on death to other members of the settlement. It is acquired through conversion under the Land Interest Conversion Regulation, inheritance, or application to the settlement council. Provisional Métis title provides exclusive use and occupation for five years with the ability to renew for another five. The Land Policy anticipates members with converted equivalent interests or subsequently acquired provisional Métis title will make improvements the settlement council deems necessary to acquire Métis title. Métis title is limited to 175 acres; however, settlement council can grant allotments of up to 167 additional acres necessary for farming, ranching, or business purposes. The nature of an allotment is similar to leasehold under common law.

Métis settlement lands do not form part of the provincial land titles system but are administered through a unique registry created to enable registration of collective and individual interests, lesser interests of non-settlement members, and estate instructions. Like other registry systems it is intended to provide proof of entitlement and public notice of interests in settlement land, facilitate efficient disposition, indicate priorities of interest holders, and provide compensation for loss arising through errors or unauthorized registrations. Unlike the federal Indian registry system, the Métis land registry system closely resembles provincial land titles systems and has generally not hindered commercial development through lack of clarity or priority of interests. As a joint initiative of the MSGC and the province, it was intended to promote Métis control through the appointment of a registrar and local staff to monitor and record the transfer of interests. As discussed earlier, at the time of writing, the function of the registrar has been temporarily assumed by the Department of Aboriginal and Northern Affairs

(Alberta). However, settlement members continue to have an active role monitoring the creation of new interests and preparing documents for registration.

A fundamental component of the landholding system is control by Métis government over renewable surface resource development and increased participation by the Métis settlements over subsurface development. Significant oil and gas deposits and surface resources (including timber, peat, gravel, and marl) are found under and on settlement lands. Settlement council has the sole authority and responsibility for managing the non-renewable surface resources of the settlement area.[42] However, the management of these resources must benefit the community and minimize damage to wildlife resources and the environment. Should a dispute arise as to whether the surface resources are being properly managed, an adversely affected party (including the MSGC) can ask MSAT to review a settlement council's decision.

Schedule 3 to the *Métis Settlements Act* provides for the co-management of subsurface resources under settlement land. The Co-management Agreement enables the MSGC to propose terms and conditions on public offerings of resources under settlement lands. These terms and conditions have now become standard, and amongst other terms concerning matters such as environmental protection, cultural impact, and employment, also require successful bidders to offer participation rights of up to 25 per cent to General Council and the affected settlement and to commit to negotiating overriding royalties (which range from 3 to 10 per cent). While the participation right and overriding royalties were managed for a period of time by an oil and gas company incorporated by the MSGC called RESCO, these rights are now directly managed by the MSGC in concert with affected settlement councils. As set out in the MSGC Oil and Gas Resource Sharing Policy,[43] the MSGC and affected settlement split the overriding royalty down the middle (12.5/12.5 per cent) and the MSGC receives the first 3 per cent of any negotiated overriding royalty.

Dispute Resolution

One way to improve justice for Aboriginal peoples is to minimize incompatibilities by making the system more sensitive to particular cultural traditions, laws, and justice objectives. This means increasing Aboriginal input, representation, laws, traditions, and values in dispute resolution while correspondingly reducing complexity, formality, and rigidity of process. Tribunals can lend themselves to these objectives because they are created to adjudicate issues requiring expert knowledge and to implement policy goals. MSAT expertise includes knowledge in Accord negotiations and intent of the legislation, the landholding and registry system, membership matters, community practice and custom, and land and resource development. Tribunals can also be given broad discretion and remedial powers to help implement the self-government and justice goals of the legislation that creates them. For example MSAT can provide for any means of alternative dispute resolution it considers appropriate and has a wide range of remedial power including "any remedy, that in all circumstances, fairness requires."[44] With greater emphasis being placed more recently on alternative processes, approximately two thirds of appeals brought before the Tribunal since 2005 have been resolved in this manner without a hearing and imposition of an MSAT order.

Specific justice goals of settlement members arising from the administration of former Métis legislation are inextricably linked to self-government goals and include "providing an internal check on the exercise of government power; resolving disputes that arise in the interpretation of Métis legislation and settlement laws; and providing fair, impartial, and accessible justice to settlement members."[45] If necessary, by leave of the Court of Queen's Bench, its decisions may be enforced as a judgment of that court. A tribunal can also take on extra-judicial functions that assist in the resolution of disputes such as investigation, research, and educational functions. This may make it more desirable than a court. All of these functions are performed by MSAT and its staff, an important consideration given the differing levels of resources, education, comfort, and familiarity of legal process by disputants. Finally, tribunals also have procedural flexibility that enables them to create procedures more grounded in and responsive to the culture of a specific community and to utilize alternative processes that share common ideologies with indigenous systems.

MSAT has extensive jurisdiction over settlement land, membership, and surface rights (formerly exercised by the Alberta Surface Rights Board). Unlike other tribunals, it also has jurisdiction arising from written consent of parties to a dispute and its jurisdiction is dynamic, increasing through delegations under new policies and bylaws. Through its surface access jurisdiction, MSGC policy, bylaws, and the co-management and other mineral agreements, MSAT jurisdiction extends to non-settlement members, mainly but not exclusively oil and gas companies. Like a court, MSAT has the ability to interpret and enforce legislation.[46] It has also contributed to the development of a unique contemporary Métis common law. Although it is not bound by previous decisions, where possible the decisions fuse together legislation, common laws, custom, and community practice and offer some predictability for resolution of disputes. MSAT also has unique features not commonly shared with other tribunals including: ADR jurisdiction; the ability to hold hearings on settlement lands; joint review processes and accountability to two governments; and input of affected constituencies into its design and operation.

Creating a tribunal was viewed as a practical response to self-government aspirations as it was not possible to engage the federal government in the creation of a settlement court or to achieve agreement on inherent jurisdiction. Because the federal government was not prepared to negotiate and under s. 96 of the *Constitution Act, 1867* they have jurisdiction to appoint judges to superior courts, the only option available was creation of a quasi-judicial tribunal with delegated jurisdictions in areas of provincial responsibility. The challenge was to invest MSAT with sufficient powers so it could act like a Métis court and at the same time include enough safeguards so that it could survive a section 96 challenge.

Safeguards include minimizing but retaining supervisory powers of the superior court, inclusion of extra-judicial functions such as research and investigation capabilities, and inclusion of judicial functions and remedial powers which can be defended as necessarily incidental to a novel social policy goal.[47]

Like lower courts, the decisions of MSAT are subject to appeal on questions of jurisdiction and law to the Alberta Court of Appeal and challenges can be made to its jurisdiction before or during a hearing. As of December 2005, 167 orders had been issued and only eight had been appealed (one withdrawn) and only one has been challenged on jurisdiction. Subject to one exception, the experience of MSAT has been judicial deference to its decisions and understanding of the broader political purpose it serves. For example, in the *Chalifoux* case, Madame Justice Picard upheld a verbal agreement for transfer of an interest in settlement land and acknowledged that "the policy and intent of the legislation is to put power in the hands of Métis people to deal with lands disputes within the framework of the Act."[48] Similarly, in *Paramount,* a case concerning a challenge by an oil and gas company to Métis jurisdiction, Justice Wilkins notes that the province developed a "unique legislative regime which is intended to assist the Métis people in achieving self-sufficiency and local autonomy" and later in the decision "to enable the Métis people to govern their own relationships in matters concerning their lands."[49]

The current structure of MSAT consists of a chairman appointed by the minister from a list provided by MSGC, three members appointed by MSGC, and three appointed by the minister. Important for support of oil and gas companies was the creation of the Existing Leases Land Access Panel (ELLAP) consisting of a chair appointed by agreement of MSGC and the minister, two members appointed by MSGC (usually two of the three already appointed), one by the Ministry of Energy, and one by Industry Associations. This panel only deals with access matters arising under leases in existence before 1 November 1991, and has authority to issue right of entry orders and issue compensation orders. The Land Access Panel (LAP), consisting of at least three members appointed by the chair with agreement of MSGC and the minister, exercises jurisdictions formerly exercised by the surface rights board in relation to all other surface and subsurface development. Other panels of MSAT include: the land panel, the majority of whom must be Tribunal members appointed by MSGC, with jurisdiction to hear all other matters relating to settlement land; and the membership panel, the majority of whom must be MSAT members appointed by the minister.

It is beyond the scope of this chapter to review all of the changes that have occurred in the evolution of this system. However two important events are worthy of note: (1) the MSAT Task Force (equal representation from the settlements and government); and, (2) amendments proposed in 2004. The Task Force held public meetings on each settlement, and heard representations from experts who had worked on projects involving MSAT and representatives of the oil and gas industry. Concerns raised included: difficulties caused by unanimity provisions of the MSA; limited jurisdiction over civil matters; MSAT jurisdiction over settlement council decisions and MSGC policy; lack of jurisdiction over election issues and removal of councillors from office; MSAT's inability to provide support in criminal cases (for example, justice committees); politicization of the appointment process and the need for more settlement representation; the need for settlement council approval before members can agree to MSAT jurisdiction; misconduct by elected councillors; timeliness of MSAT's decisions and its consequential ability to deal with expanded jurisdiction; and use of legal counsel. The oil and gas industry supported MSAT's role but called for "a clearer statement of the purpose of MSAT", consolidation of LAP and ELLAP, more detail in MSAT decisions, and the right to appeal compensation awards, public availability of MSAT decisions, and "fair and impartial membership."[50]

The Task Force made several important recommendations relating to MSAT adopted in amending legislation yet to be proclaimed. A new s. 187.1 proposed MSAT exercise its powers "with a view to preserving and enhancing Métis culture and identity and furthering the attainment of self-governance by Métis settlements under the laws of Alberta." MSAT jurisdiction would be extended to include: validity of elections; and the right to hold office (formerly exercised by the Court of Queen's Bench) and to review MSGC policy regarding assessment and taxation of interests in settlement land on request. Acting on a report from the ombudsman or minister and after a hearing, MSAT would also have jurisdiction to dismiss a settlement council, councillors, employees, and officials, or direct specific actions to be taken. LAP and ELLAP have not been consolidated, likely in the interest of maintaining a majority of settlement members, but their jurisdiction to terminate right of entry orders has been clarified. MSAT could also bring its own application to the Court of Queen's Bench for an opinion on a question of law or jurisdiction and can act jointly with another board, commission, or other body if considered expedient or in the public interest. The Task Force did not recommend extending jurisdiction in other areas but called for these matters to be considered in implementing recommendations from the provincial justice summit and subsequent reviews of MSAT. Their recommendations that MSAT determine if settlement council approval is necessary for exercising consensual jurisdiction over members, and that MSAT be designated a friend of the court to assist in issues relating to the settlements, were not adopted.

The 2004 amendments also propose changes to the composition of MSAT and the process for appointing chairs, vice chairs, and members.[51] Membership includes three full time members and eight part time members from each settlement, persons appointed by the minister, and a newly created Selection and Review Committee composed of the chair and vice-chairs. Of the three full time members, one is appointed as MSAT's chair by the minister on recommendation of the Selection and Review Committee and the other two, appointed by MSGC and the minister, are vice-chairs. Appointments would be made in accordance with criteria, if any, established by MSGC policy. The chair and vice-chairs also form an

Executive Committee, which may make rules concerning procedure for conducting MSAT business and administrative matters relating to its quasi-judicial functions, processes for hearings and appeals, and ethical conduct. Many of these functions, although not specified in the MSA, were formerly exercised by the chair. Amendments would also clarify that alternative dispute resolution processes apply to jurisdictions acquired under policies and bylaws and can be made mandatory by the Executive Committee.

The Task Force also called for an independent conduct advisor office to address complaints against settlement councillors as this was not considered compatible with MSAT's primarily judicial role. In response to this recommendation, the minister is given additional regulatory power to establish the office of the Métis Settlement Ombudsman (MSO). Amendments also address confidentiality and immunity from personal liability. Pursuant to this power an ombudsman office was created and is accountable to the Minister of Aboriginal and Northern Affairs (Alberta). The 2005/2006 Annual Report indicates that, from the creation of the MSO in September 2003, a total of 1033 complaints and requests for information were received. Of the 354 complaints received in 2005/2006 the largest number related to housing, employment, professional conduct, and nepotism. Of the 293 complaints relating to administrative fairness and conflict of interest, 197 were not in the form of formal complaints or supported with sufficient evidence to investigate, 18 were withdrawn, 64 were resolved informally, 11 resulted in referrals or facilitated resolution, and only 2 went to mediation or arbitration. Not all complaints were legitimate while others revealed a range of concerns including mismanagement of funds, administrative unfairness in provision of services, unfair hiring practices, and the need for forensic audits on some settlements. [52] The existence of these types of problems are common to all governments and even more understandable in this context given the size of the settlement populations, given the constant turn-over in settlement government; education levels in regard to governance rules, operation, administration and other matters; and the need for resources for capacity-building. Over time and with the new changes to election procedures it is hoped that the number of complaints will decrease.

Financing Métis Government

The preamble of the Métis Settlements Accord aims for the settlements "to achieve ... economic self sufficiency." How to do that is a key question being explored in the TAP Project. Below are the key findings from the Stage I TAP Report concerning the settlements' socio-economic situation.

The settlements and their members face a number of challenges, including workplace discrimination, politics mixed with commercial transactions, land that cannot be used as collateral, services and infrastructure that are expensive to set up and maintain, and limited linkages to today's technology. With limited economic activity on the settlements most members work off-settlement. The result-

- Settlement Councils provide many more services than a regular municipal government, including membership, land allocations, housing, education, oil and gas operations, investment decisions, business development and management, and participation in General Council meetings.

- Over the first 15 years of the Accord, the emphasis has been on infrastructure and housing, not economic development per se.

- Settlement members now have a higher level of education and employment than they did before the Accord. However, members still trail Albertans in terms of education, engagement in the workforce, and individual and household income.

- It is difficult to get a conventional loan to start a business on the settlements. It is also difficult to find qualified people to manage and work in a settlement business. Lack of marketing and coordination services also hampers business development on the settlements.

- With some work, institutions such as the Settlement Sooniyaw Corporation (SSC) and Settlement Investment Corporation (SIC) could provide the expertise and (non-political) framework needed for an economic diversification effort.

- Working with regional partners will help the economic growth efforts by tapping into existing pools of expertise, business networks, capital, and increasing marketing power.

Findings - Stage 1 TAP Report (May 11, 2005)

ing Labour Outflow Model may work for individuals, but communities suffer because members and revenues are absent. Some people are making more money, but it doesn't translate into the local council having money, unless they introduce ways to translate individual income to local government revenue.

As identified through the TAP Project, a possible starting point for appropriate development is the Community Development Model, which invites community members to explore the traditions and practices that positively set settlement communities apart from surrounding municipalities. It draws attention to communal resources like ecological attractions, recreation facilities, and cultural events. The Community Development Model builds on western and traditional capacities—ranging from improved education and business supports to reclaimed language and cultural practices—that are essential to building successful Métis communities. With these cultural benchmarks in place, the foundation is set for the next stage of community development. The Corporate Development Model sees community members translating the mix of western and traditional capacities into new business partnerships and new companies. The development envisioned by the Corporate Development Model anticipates support through business incubation, entrepreneurship training, loan guarantees, and direct financial, logistical, and marketing assistance for new or growing businesses. The goal is to graduate successful, financially sound firms that can compete in the regional economy. While successful application of the Corporate Development Model would represent a significant step forward, it is not the final step. Ultimately, the goal is to facilitate participation in the global economy (where the real money is).

The TAP findings and the models for economic development provide three lessons: (1) economic development takes time and you have to ensure that what you do in the short term works toward a longer-term vision; (2) economic development takes place in an increasingly global environment and will require that businesses are run like businesses, not as by-products of local government; and, (3) economic development is not the same as building fiscal capacity to run local government because much economic development is done by private individuals and companies.

As evidenced by the Stage 1 TAP findings, in which settlement councils are all things to all people, the proposed models for community and economic development present a serious challenge to the settlements' legislated governance structure. In particular, they call for a shift in the pervasive culture of reliance through which members have come to depend on a small group of individuals to deliver not only core services such as water and road services, but to also deliver training grants, jobs, and social housing allocations.

New Directions

Looking forward necessitates first looking back at the 1989 Alberta-Métis Settlements Accord. This critical document committed Alberta and the MSGC to the shared goals of settling the oil and gas lawsuit, securing settlement lands, establishing self-governance, and achieving economic self-reliance. In the MSGC's opinion, the last three goals of land security, increased autonomy, and economic sustainability are not end points, but starting points in a continuing partnership. In 2004, the TAP was established by the MSGC and Government of Alberta to determine how far the settlements have advanced toward the Accord goals and to jointly develop new action plans and agreements wherever the goals remained unmet.

The Stage 1 Tap Report, released May 2005, found that tremendous progress was made (especially with respect to new housing, roads, gas and water services) over the past 15 years but more needs to be done to achieve Accord goals. Of particular importance is the finding that continued progress will not be possible unless changes are made that enable increases in local employment, revenues, and business and cultural opportunities. Stage 2 of the TAP Project is intended to identify the changes and new partnerships needed to make sure the settlements continue to move forward. The chairs from each settlement were invited to work on the Stage 2 planning process and to form a new group called the Accord Review and Renewal Council (ARRC). Together, settlement leaders are working hard to develop new and improved ways for the settlements and Alberta to meet the Accord goals of security, autonomy, and prosperity. However, rather than taking a top-down approach, ARRC is committed to talking with settlement members about the developmental models currently under consideration: community meetings were underway at the time of writing to get member feedback on new models for housing, economic development, governance, and the delivery and payment systems for core services.

From the community meetings held so far, many members are concerned that the final payment under the Accord will spell the end of the settlements. While it is true that the last payment under the *Accord Implementation Act* was scheduled for 1 April 2006 (which covered the 2006/07 fiscal year), this did not spell the end of the settlements. Further, the land protection framework and governance powers, including the MSGC's statutory authority to make budgets, pass laws, and negotiate participation interests in oil and gas activities, for example, stayed in place. However, like municipal governments and districts, securing ongoing funding through provincial municipal grant and other provincial and federal support in designated program areas remains crucial to self-governance and the economic viability of the settlements.

The MSGC is trying to avoid a rights-based approach to this issue and is working with the Government of Alberta to develop appropriate plans for community viability and prosperity. To this end, the MSGC signed a *Goals and Guidelines Agreement* with then-minister Pearl Calahasen to work together on future planning. To further solidify the Government of Alberta's commitment to the planning process, the MSGC also secured the Premier's commitment through an *Affirmation Agreement* on 1 November 2005.[53]

Though the settlements' main partnership rests with the Government of Alberta, the MSGC has also made concerted efforts to enhance and expand its relationship with the federal government. With its tripartite office entering its tenth year of operations, the MSGC has accessed over $5 million in federal grants and has accessed over $2 million in new grant money this past year alone. The MSGC's new satellite office in Ottawa is intended to increase awareness of the settlements among federal politicians and officials and to monitor key activities and trends within the federal government.

Critical Reflections, Emerging Issues, and Conclusions

The structure and operation of Métis settlement government has generated many challenges and raised broader legal questions in need of further exploration. Practical problems include: issues of generating prosperity when the usual prerequisites to growth, such as education, business acumen, and access to capital are in short supply; and the ever-present challenge of ensuring effective and accountable government in small remote communities that are often dominated by extended families. Another practical challenge is finding the appropriate method and forum to ensure maximum community participation in decision-making. Although printed information is circulated to members, MSAT has visited communities to educate them about its functions; hearings are public and held in communities; and law-making processes include community participation. Ironically, some communities are meeting less frequently than in the past. Although committed to traditional values of community participation and consensus, the development and ensuring enactment of MSGC policies has been slow, difficult, and labour-intensive, sometimes bringing progress to a standstill. As Ken

Noskey, former president of the MSGC, acknowledged, "there are circumstances in which consensus need not mean unanimity" and where there is division of opinion "all communities, no matter how highly they value consensus, require some mechanism whereby division of opinion will not make decision-making come to a halt."[54]

Other cultural institutions, such as reliance on elder opinion, have also been affected. For example, the original vision for dispute resolution was for each settlement to have an elder advisory and appeal committee. However, it soon became apparent this was unworkable given the extension of MSAT jurisdiction beyond local matters, the need for specialized knowledge in addition to the cultural expertise of elders, and the fact some members had lost touch with the role of elders in dispute resolution. In the end, elder expertise was incorporated into membership provisions of the MSA and potential participation in dispute resolution processes through appointments to MSAT by MSGC. Despite the potential avenues for participation, the failure to include specific institutions of Métis Eldership in the legislation may have indirectly contributed to decline of their traditional dispute resolution roles. In recognition of this, MSGC has hosted a series of Elders conferences, some settlements have created advisory committees, and MSAT has developed a mediation model which incorporates participation by elders if desired by settlement members.

There are, of course, many objections that can be raised against relying on tribunals as a means to achieve Aboriginal justice objectives. Tribunal decisions are subject to review by non-Indigenous courts, governed in the main by non-Indigenous laws, and only give effect to Indigenous laws when non-Indigenous governments determine such laws should be considered. The hierarchy of decision-making, the dominant role of non-Indigenous law and normative values, and the ability of non-Indigenous governments to alter jurisdiction and processes runs contrary to goals of those who seek a separate justice system and their own system of checks and balances to constrain potential bias and abuse of authority. However the reality of the federal and political environment in which the settlements operate does not support separate justice, nor was this considered in Accord negotiations as necessary to make justice more accountable to settlement members.[55]

Recognition of Métis Aboriginal rights to hunt and the broader implications of *Powley* raise issues about the eligibility of settlement members to exercise Aboriginal constitutional rights, rights to commercial hunting and sustenance hunting outside of settlement lands, reconciliation of mutual interests and legal rights, and legal characterization of the Accord, to name a few. In *Powley*, the Supreme Court of Canada recognized a Métis Aboriginal right to hunt for food and articulated a process for proving Métis Aboriginal rights to hunt, fish, and trap for sustenance in a specified geographical area.[56] The decision also stands for the broader proposition that Métis rights (asserted independent of claims to title) are sourced in particular practices, customs, and traditions integral to a distinctive Métis community and its relationship to the land at the date of effective European control over a particular Métis community and area. Therefore, *Powley* also provides a general framework to prove rights, other than title, claimed in a specified geographical area inhabited by a contemporary community asserting a historical, practice-based right. As Arthur Pape, co-counsel for the Powleys, stated after the victory: "The court has now made it possible for ... interests in land, in resources, in self-governance to in fact be enjoyed and operate for the benefit of the Métis people, as the Constitution has extended similar kinds of protections to First Nations and Inuit."[57]

A challenge in identifying the historical foundation of Métis rights, and contemporary communities entitled to exercise those rights, is the impact of social, political, and economic forces on the formation and sustainability of Métis identity and communities. The Court acknowledges this in the flexibility it applies to community identification and issues of continuity.[58] However, it also sets out certain criteria for Métis identity for the purpose of exercising s.35 harvesting rights and calls for membership requirements in contemporary Métis political organizations to "become more standardized so that legitimate rights-holders can be identified."[59] In practical terms, this may mean identifying those members who meet the judicial definition of a Métis person given in *Powley*; conducting land use and other studies to establish reasonable continuity of activities and connection of existing members to a historic Métis community in a given geographical area at the date effective European control; historical research to periods that may qualify as the date of effective European control; and consideration of whether members who cannot trace ancestry to a particular historic Métis community can be considered to have sufficient ancestral connection by "birth, adoption, or other means."[60]

The criteria given in *Powley* raise some interesting, but not insurmountable, challenges for the Métis settlements. For example, the definition of a Métis under the *Métis Settlements Act* is "a person of aboriginal ancestry who identifies with Métis history and culture" and membership criteria are broad enough to include some who are of Aboriginal ancestry, but are not necessarily descendants of a distinctive historic Métis community.[61] Secondary literature on the settlements and research conducted pre-*Powley* in the settlements suggests that many members are descendants of distinctive Métis communities and for whom the scrip distribution system failed. Those who are not, identify as Métis and at some point acquired status and became accepted as part of the Métis settlement community through application of legislation or a history of family connections dating to the original purpose and creation of the first colonies. Pragmatic, personal, and economic consequences arise in attempting to distinguish among members for existing governmental relations, consultation mechanisms, reconciliation of statutory and constitutional rights, and life within the settlement communities. It is difficult to conceive of disentitling settlement members from exercising rights enjoyed by other settlement members when they identified as Métis prior to Métis rights recognition in the Constitution, are legally recognized as such by statute, and are accepted by a contemporary Métis community with a clearly defined territory and identifiable representative government. It may well be that this type of situation is what the Supreme Court had in mind when it suggests that "an individual's self-identification need not be static or monolithic" as long as it is not "recent in order to benefit from s. 35" and proof of ancestral connection can be proved by "other means." Indeed equitable and legal arguments can be developed to support this conclusion.[62]

Another complication may arise in identifying the relevant geographic land base. Some settlement lands set aside in 1938 (after the date a court would likely consider to be the assertion of effective control) were selected on the basis that Métis communities were established in those areas, but other factors came into play including availability of fish and suitability of land for agricultural purposes. Thus, traditional territories over which hunting, fishing, trapping, and other practices were exercised may not always coincide with, and may extend beyond, settlement areas. Indeed, given the migratory nature of the Métis, these areas may overlap with other contemporary Métis or other Aboriginal communities that trace land use and ancestry to the geographic area in question. Failure to establish exclusivity does not vitiate a First Nation or Inuit claim to harvesting rights in a given area and should not for the Métis. This challenge requires more consideration of references in *Powley* to rights being located in a community's traditional hunting grounds. As Jean Tiellet explains, "In *Powley*, it was not necessary for the court to determine whether the Métis community at Sault Ste Marie formed part of a larger Métis people that extended over a wider area such as the Great Lakes because the Powley/LaSage family had always lived in the environs of Sault Ste Marie and because Steve Powley shot his moose within minutes of Sault Ste Marie."[63] Also of interest is *Laviolette*, in which the Provincial Court of Saskatchewan identified the relevant geographic area to identify community and relevant lands as all of Northwest Saskatchewan, rather than just fixed settlements with significant Métis populations, based largely in part on Dr. Frank Tough's evidence that Métis in the area had a regional consciousness based on trade and family connections and were highly mobile.[64]

Although Alberta has entered into an Interim Métis Harvesting Agreement (IMHA) with the MSGC for members to hunt, fish, and trap for sustenance on unoccupied Crown lands in Alberta, this and an IMHA entered into with the Métis Nation of Alberta are being re-examined in light of significant opposition by non-Métis interest groups. Given the membership criteria and history of these Métis organizations, as a practical matter, these agreements assume that the vast majority of members in these organizations meet the *Powley* criteria for Métis identity and do not require that each Métis person who is a member of the MNA or Métis settlements prove identification for the purpose of exercising rights under the agreement. Like the lower courts in *Powley* (upheld by the Supreme Court) and *Laviolette*, the agreement takes into account the historical migratory lifestyle and regional consciousness of the Métis in defining areas where harvesting rights can be exercised. However, despite these influences, the IMHAs acknowledge in their preamble that there is "uncertainty in the law relating to Métis Harvesting in Alberta" and provide in paragraph 4 that they do not "affect, abrogate, or derogate from, or recognize or affirm any constitutional or Aboriginal rights of the Métis Settlement General Council or its members." The recent Alberta Provincial Court decision in the *R. v. Kelley*[65] case, now on appeal, suggests that the IMHAs may grant more rights than recognized under s. 35 (1) of the *Constitution Act, 1982*[66] and therefore are contrary to equality provisions found both in s. 15 of the *Charter* and the *Alberta Bill of Rights*.[67] Although this ruling can be challenged on many grounds, it underscores numerous issues that need to be explored in their application to the settlements, including the importance of clarifying the concept of community and territory applicable to the exercise of Métis rights in Alberta. Given the diversity of case law on this issue, this may not be resolved until these issues are again before the Supreme Court.

Another issue that arises from *Kelley* is the ability of a province to enter into agreements or terminate or limit the exercise of Métis Aboriginal rights by other means. The IMHAs specifically indicate they are not concerned with this, but could they be if the parties wished this to be the case? The question is complicated because it is not clear who has jurisdiction over Métis Aboriginal rights and indeed, the recent decision of the Supreme Court in *Blais* may have significant ramifications for the ability of a province to terminate Aboriginal harvesting rights through regulation.[68] The complications of jurisdiction are discussed in detail elsewhere by the author and in this volume. They are raised here simply to demonstrate another area the settlements must explore in developing new paths for negotiation. Further, a finding that Métis are solely within federal jurisdiction has ramifications for assessing the constitutional validity of provincial legislation that singles out Métis.

Experiences responding to the 2004 amendments and some provisions in those amendments, although well-meaning and perhaps necessary, raise issues of meaningful participation and negotiation and could have significant implications for Métis autonomy. Even if settlement autonomy remains intact, concern about long-term sustainability of the settlements has arisen as questions about the enforceability of government obligations under the Alberta-Métis Settlements Accord in the post-2007 era begin to be tested. Add to this the outstanding need for constitutional amendment to permanently protect the Métis land base, and one begins to understand the mounting pressures on the MSGC.

However, to understand the MSGC, one must also consider that whatever the legal or political milieu, the great constant of settlement leadership and settlement members has been their unwavering practicality and pragmatism. While this does not exclude pursuing a rights-based agenda (which is sometimes the most practical approach to addressing critical issues), it does mean that the settlements will first look to conferences and negotiations to develop lasting solutions to the challenges of the day.

*   Used with the permission of Irwin Law Inc. A version of this chapter appears in *Rights, Identity, Jurisdiction and Governance: Current Issues in Métis-Government Relations,* eds. Melanie Mallet and Frederica Wilson (Irwin Law Inc. forthcoming 2008).

1   The approach advocated is similar to the "well-being" approach applied to an early analysis of settlement legislation by Tom Pocklington in which he also discusses the impact of the model on other citizens of the province. In his work he considers not only issues of political autonomy but also specific areas of well-being such as political health, administrative skills, and self-esteem. See, for example, Tom C. Pocklington, T*he Government and Politics of the Alberta Métis Settlements* (Regina: Canadian Plains Research Centre, 1991). See also Catherine E. Bell, "Métis Self-Government: The Alberta Settlement Model," in *Aboriginal Self-Government in Canada,* 2nd Ed., ed. John. H. Hylton, (Saskatoon: Purich Publishing, 1999), 330. For more detailed discussion of matters raised in this chapter including Métis settlement government, land rights and administration, historical and political context, self-government justice objectives, the Métis Settlements Appeal Tribunal, and decisions, see Catherine E. Bell, *Alberta's Métis Settlement Legislation: An Overview of Ownership and Management of Settlement Lands* (Regina: Canadian Plains Research Centre, 1994); and Catherine E. Bell and the Métis Settlements Appeal Tribunal, *Contemporary Métis Justice: The Settlement Way,* (Saskatoon: Native Law Centre, 1999).

2   *Métis Settlements Amendment Act,* S.A. 2004, c.25, s. 41 (Assented to May 11, 2004 with sections applying to MSAT awaiting proclamation. These are sections 3(b) and (d), 10-18, 24-27, and 43.)

3   Alberta, Task Force To Review the Mandate of the Métis Settlements Appeal Tribunal, *Métis Settlements Appeal Tribunal Mandate Review Task Force Report* (Co-chairs: Denis Ducharme, MLA and Fred V. Martin, LL.B.)1.

4   R.S.A. 2000, C. 24.

5   *R. v. Powley,* [2003] 2 S.C.R. 207.

6   The issue of entitlement to land as a result of problems arising in the scrip distribution system is the subject of ongoing litigation in Alberta, Saskatchewan, and Manitoba. There are many academic commentaries on the scrip distribution system. See, for example, Paul Chartrand, *Manitoba's Métis Settlement Scheme of 1870* (Saskatoon: Native Law Centre, 1991); Thomas Flanagan, *Métis Lands in Manitoba* (Calgary: University of Calgary Press, 1991), 35-55; Joe Sawchuk, Patricia Sawchuk, and Theresa Ferguson, *Métis Land Rights in Alberta: A Political History* (Edmonton: Métis Association of Alberta, 1981); Douglas Sanders, "Métis Rights in the Prairie Provinces and the Northwest Territories: A Legal Interpretation," in *The Forgotten People: Métis and Non-Status Indian Land Claim,* ed. Harry Daniels (Ottawa: Native Council of Canada, 1979), 5; Douglas Sprague, "Government Lawlessness in the Administration of Manitoba Land Claims, 1870-1887" (1980) 10(4) Man. L.J. 416; and Douglas Sprague, *Canada and the Métis, 1869-1885* (Waterloo: Wilfred Laurier Press, 1988).

7   For more extensive discussion of the circumstances leading to the creation of St. Paul de Métis, see Joe Sawchuck et al., *ibid.* at 172-8; and George Stanley, "Alberta's Half-Breed Reserve St. Paul de Métis 1896 -1909" in *The Other Natives: The Métis,* vol. 2, eds. A. S. Lussier and D.B. Sealey, (Winnipeg: Métis Federation Press and Editions Bois-Brules, 1978), 105-7; Bell, *Contemporary Métis Justice, supra* note 1 at 1-14.

8   The following discussion of the history leading to the Ewing Commission and the Commission hearings and outcomes draws on the following sources: Commission, A. Gaz. 1934, 941 in Native Affairs Secretariat, *Alberta's Métis Settlements: A Compendium of Background Documents* (Edmonton: Policy and Planning Division, n.d.) [Ewing Commission]; Murray Dobbin, *The One-and-a-half Men: The Story of Jim Brady and Malcolm Norris* (Vancouver: New Star Books, 1981; second publication Regina: Gabriel Dumont Institute, 1987), 88-106; and Joe Sawchuk, *The Dynamic of Native Politics: The Alberta Experience* (Saskatoon: Purich Publishing, 1998), 53-5; and including testimonials from settlement members see Bell, *Contemporary Métis Justice, supra* note 1 at 7-14; and Pocklington, *supra* note 1 at 12-21.

9   *R. v. Blais,* [2003] 2 S.C.R. 207. Prior to this decision, case law in Alberta supported the inclusion of some Métis who "live an Indian way of life" (sustenance hunting, fishing, gathering). See *R. v. Ferguson,* [1993] 2 C.N.L.R. 148 at para. 19 (Prov. Ct.). For a more in-depth treatment of this issue and arguments against Blais see Frank Tough, "The Natural Resources Transfer Agreements and Indian Livelihood Rights, ca. 1925-1933" (2004) 41 Alta. L. Rev. 999 at 1000-1; Frank Tough, "Introduction to Documents: Indian Hunting Rights, Natural Resources Transfer Agreements and Legal Opinions from the Department of Justice," (1995) 10 Native St. Rev. 121; and Catherine Bell and Clayton Leonard, "A New Era in Métis Constitutional Rights: The Importance of Powley and Blais" (2004) 41 Alta L. Rev. 1049 at 1063-1067.

10   Dobbin, *supra* note 8 at 56.

11   *Ibid.,* at 63.

12   *Ibid.*

13   Tom Pocklington, *supra* note 1 at 11-12; Sawchuk et. al., *Métis Land Rights in Alberta, supra* note 6 at 188-90; and Fred Martin, "Federal and Provincial Responsibility in the Métis Settlements of Alberta" in *Aboriginal*

Peoples and Government Responsibility: Exploring Federal and Provincial Roles, ed. David Hawkes, (Ottawa: Carleton University Press, 1989) 255.

14   Ewing Commission, *supra* note 8, Tab 2.
15   Ewing Commission, *supra* note 8 at 104-9 and Catherine Bell, *Contemporary Métis Justice, supra* note 1 at 14.
16   *The Métis Settlements Population Betterment Act* is cited as *The Métis Betterment Act*, S.A. 1938, c.6. As am. S.A. 1940, c.6, in s. 8(j) it provided that the minister could make regulations which have for their purpose "the advancement and betterment of any Settlement Association, or any members thereof, or the administration of the affairs of any Settlement Association...." Pursuant to this section, Order-in-Council 1785/43 was promulgated providing for the creation of a Métis Population Betterment Trust Account funded by natural resource revenues accrued from settlement lands. Litigation over whether the wording of the relevant section, and subsequent related regulations, included subsurface resources provided significant impetus for negotiation on the part of Alberta during a time when other provinces denied jurisdiction and refused to negotiate with the Métis. See Catherine Bell, *Alberta's Métis Settlement Legislation, supra* note 1 at 9-10.
17   See e.g. *Metissm: A Canadian Identity* (Edmonton: Federation of Métis Settlements, 1982).
18   *Foundations For the Future of Alberta's Métis Settlements: Report of the MacEwan Joint Committee on the Métis Betterment Act and Regulations* (Chair: Dr. G. MacEwan)(Edmonton, 1984), 11, 59. For a general discussion see Tom Pocklington, *supra* note 1 at 141; and Catherine Bell, *Alberta's Métis Settlement Legislation, supra* note 1 at 11-14.
19   *Constitution Act, 1867*. (U.K.). 30 and 31 Vict., c.3, ss. 92(13) and (18).
20   For more detailed discussion of these issues see Catherine Bell, "Self-Government," *supra* note 1 at 331-3.
21   Originally the *Alberta Act*, 1905, 4-5 Edw. VII, c.3 now identified as part of the Constitution of Canada by s. 52(2)(b) of the *Constitution Act, 1982*, being Schedule B to the *Canada Act, 1982* (U.K.), 1982, c.11.
22   Alberta Legislative Assembly, *A Resolution Concerning an Amendment to the Alberta Act*, No. 18 (3 June 1985).
23   Tom Pocklington, *supra* note 1 at 151-2.
24   *Métis Settlements Act*, R.S. A. 2000. C. M-14 as am. S.A. 1998 c. M - 14.3 and by the *Métis Settlements Amendment Act*, S.A. 2004, c. 25 [MSA]; *Constitution of Alberta Amendment Act 1990*, RSA. 2000 c. 24 [CAA]; *Métis Settlements Land Protection Act*, R.S.A. 2000 c.M-16 [MSLPA]; and the *Métis Settlements Accord Implementation Act*, R.S.A.2000 c. M-15 [MSAIA].
25   Bylaw powers cover a range of areas including matters of internal management, health, safety, welfare, public order, fire protection, nuisance, pests, animals, airports, advertising, refuse disposal, parks, recreation, control of businesses, water, sewage, development levies, and land use planning. See Schedule One to the MSA, *ibid*.
26   Structure, function, and jurisdiction of settlement councils are elaborated in MSA, *ibid*. ss. 8-71 and bylaw powers are elaborated in schedule one.
27   Structure, function, and jurisdiction of MSGC are elaborated in MSA, *ibid*., ss. 214-232.
28   Several policies have been enacted by the MSGC concerning business activities, assessments and levies, financial allocation, public utilities, and business property contributions. Important ones relating to lands and resources include the Non-Renewable Surface Resources Policy (G.C.P. 9807), A. Gaz 1999. I. 266; Timber Policy and Model Timber Bylaw (No. 9806), Alta. Gaz. 1999. I. 243; Mineral Projects Policy and Model Bylaw (No. 9603), Alta. Gaz. 1992. I. 919; Land Policy (No. 90003), Alta. Gaz. 1992. I. 2592; and Hunting, Fishing, Trapping and Gathering Bylaw (No. 90001) O.C. 642/90, Alta. Gaz. 1991. I.1719 [HFTG]. The mineral projects policy is currently being revised and new hunting agreements are being negotiated in light of *Powley*.
29   Under the HFTG policy, hunting and fishing for food during any season and trapping are limited to licensed settlement members. Pursuant to settlement bylaws, special permits can also be issued to families of members and non-members. Members can also gather wild plants within the settlement area during any season. Licenses and permits are issued by settlement councils.
30   For a discussion of traditional and contemporary community values and the challenge of incorporating traditional values into the settlement scheme see Bell, *Contemporary Métis Justice, supra* note 1 at 43-52.
31   Ken Noskey, President, MSGC, presentation to the Royal Commission on Aboriginal Peoples at Elizabeth Métis Settlement (16 June 1993) at 68, available on CD-ROM: *For Seven Generations: An Information Legacy of the Royal Commission on Aboriginal Peoples* (Ottawa: Libraxus Inc., 1977).
32   *Métis Settlements Amendment Act, supra* note 2, ss. 3-14 and 42.
33   Métis Settlements General Council Review Policy (GCP 0408), Alta. Gaz. 2005, 316.
34   Examples include, among others, the Land Interest Conversion Regulation, Alta. Reg. 362/91; Métis Settlements Land Registry Regulation, Alta. Reg. 361/91; and Transitional Membership Regulation, Alta. Reg. 337/90.
35   *Métis Settlements Amendment Act, supra* note 2, s. 40.
36   *Ibid.*, s. 41.
37   MSA, *supra* note 24, s. 1(j) and regarding applications, proof of membership, registered Indians and Inuit, ss. 74-84.
38   *An Act to Amend the Indian Act*, S.C. 1985, c. 27 and see Catherine Bell, *Contemporary Métis Justice, supra* note 1 at 21-2, 67-71.

39 For elaboration, see Catherine Bell, *Alberta's Métis Settlement Legislation, supra* note 1 and *Contemporary Métis Justice, supra* note 1 at 25 and 66-71, respectively, citing sample MSAT decisions.

40 For elaboration see Catherine Bell, *Alberta's Métis Settlements Legislation, supra* note 1 at 81-2. See also R. Elliott, "Rethinking Manner and Form: From Parliamentary Sovereignty to Constitutional Values," (1991) 21 Osgoode Hall L.J. 215.

41 The source for this discussion is the Métis Settlements General Council Land Policy, *supra* note 32.

42 Métis Settlements Non-Renewable Surface Resource Policy (No. 9807), Alta. Gaz. 1999, I. 266, s.2.2.

43 Métis Settlements General Council Oil and Gas Sharing Policy (GCP 0502), Alta Gaz. 2005, 2180.

44 MSA, s.190(1)(o). The structure, jurisdiction and operations of MSAT are elaborated in MSA, ss. 180-232.

45 Catherine Bell, *Contemporary Métis Justice, supra* note 1 at 7.

46 Some of this analysis draws on arguments that MSAT is more analogous to a Métis court developed by Fred Martin, lead negotiator for the Federation, "Self-Government and the Métis Settlements" (paper presented at the Faculty of Law, 20/20 Celebration, 18 September 1992) at 8 [unpublished].

47 This and other criteria set out in *Reference re An Act to Amend Chapter 401 of the Revised Statutes, 1989, the Residential Tenancies Act,* S.N.S. 1992, c. 31, [1996] 1 S.C.R. 186 at para 74 and *Re Residential Tenancies Act of Ontario,* [1981] 1 S.C.R. 714, 41-4; and elaborated in Catherine Bell, *Contemporary Métis Justice, supra* note 1 at 52-3.

48 *Paddle Prairie* v. *Arthur Challifoux, Bernice Risdale and MSAT,* [1998] 1 C.N.L.R. 134 (Alta. C.A.) at para. 16. The exception is a decision of Madame Justice Trussler concerning the status of the settlement member to challenge a subdivision appeal in which MSAT held settlements are held for the benefit of all settlement members, all settlement members are directly affected by subdivision applications, and therefore have status to challenge them. Madame Trussler held this was too wide a definition of "directly affected" and that MSAT must look at each case to determine if an individual is directly affected. See *Anderson* v. *MSAT,* [1994] 2 C.N.L.R. 15 (Alta. C.A.).

49 *Paramount Resources Ltd.* v. *Métis Settlements Appeal Tribunal,* [1999] 3 C.N.L.R. 199 (Alta. Q.B.) 203 at 211.

50 Task Force Report, *supra* note 3 at 4.

51 MSAA, *supra* note 2, s. 23 regarding the ombudsman, and with respect to MSAT ss. 7, 16-19, 22, 24-35, 43-46.

52 Métis Settlements Ombudsman, Annual Report (1 April 2005 - 31 March 2006) at 13 and 16, www.metisombudsman.ab.ca.

53 Both documents can be found on the MSGC's website, Métis Settlements General Council www.msgc.ca.

54 Ken Noskey, *supra* note 31 at 72-3.

55 For further discussion, see Catherine Bell and David Kahane, eds. *Intercultural Dispute Resolution in Aboriginal Contexts* (Vancouver: U.B.C. Press, 2004).

56 For elaboration of these arguments, see Catherine Bell, "Toward an Understanding of Métis Aboriginal Rights: Reflections on the Reasoning in *R.* v. *Powley,*" in *Aboriginal Rights Litigation,* eds. Joe Magnet and Dwight Dorey, (Markham: LexisNexis Butterworths, 2003) 387; and Catherine Bell, "A New Era," *supra* note 9.

57 Quoted in Cristin Schmitz, "Historic SCC ruling affirms aboriginal rights of Métis," (2003) 23(21) *The Lawyers Weekly* 1 at 24.

58 Individuals must self-identify as Métis and have an ancestral connection to an historic Métis community by "birth, adoption or other means." *Powley, supra* note 5 at para. 32. However, in assessing the historical foundations of a right, focus should be on continuity of the practice grounding the right not continuity of community.

59 *Powley, supra* note 5 at para 29.

60 *Supra* note 58.

61 MSA, *supra* note 24 s. 1(j) and see ss. 74 and 75.

62 *Powley, supra* note 5 at paras. 31 and 32.

63 Jean Tiellet, *Métis Law Summary 2006* online:, Pape Slater Tiellet www.pstlaw.ca at 16.

64 *R.* v. *Laviolette* (2005) SKPC 70 (Can LII).

65 *R.* v. *Kelley* [2006] 3 C.N.L.R. 324 (Alta. Prov. Ct.).

66 Being schedule B to the *Canada Act 1982* (U.K.), 1982. c.11.

67 R.S.A. 2000 c. A-14.

68 *R.* v. *Blais,* [2003] S.C.R. 236. See also, Bell, "A New Era," *supra* note 9.

FIRST NATIONS SATELLITE RESERVES:

Capacity Building and Self-Government in Saskatchewan

Joseph Garcea,[1] University of Saskatchewan

Introduction

Two major goals of First Nations governments and communities are to foster capacity building within both the governmental and societal spheres and to enhance self-governance. Among the various strategies and means recently used in pursuit of those goals is maximizing the utility of available resources. To that end, First Nations in several provinces have been investing resources to the creation and development to what have been dubbed 'satellite reserves' both in urban and non-urban areas.[2] This has been particularly evident in the province of Saskatchewan, where the past quarter century has seen more than thirty satellite reserves created in urban areas and hundreds created in non-urban agricultural areas.[3] Moreover, additional ones are in progress of being created and still others are being contemplated by First Nations both in Saskatchewan and in other provinces.[4]

The creation of such reserves has been strongly supported by First Nations leaders. Unlike the reserves of earlier times, which were created largely at the behest of federal government officials to segregate, isolate, marginalize, and subordinate Aboriginal communities and to circumscribe the land holdings and mobility of their members, the new satellite reserves are being created at the request of First Nations leaders who see them as a means to advance their economic, social, cultural, and political development objectives. Such leaders are intent on adapting what, for the most part, has been a negative and counterproductive legacy in order to create a positive and productive one.

The purpose of this chapter is to provide an overview of the following aspects of satellite reserves in Saskatchewan: their key characteristics; their location, types and number; the factors contributing to their creation; the politics surrounding their creation; the policies and processes for their creation; a brief assessment of their value; and some suggestions for further research.

Key Characteristics of Satellite Reserves

Satellite reserves are parcels of land with reserve status that are either contiguous to or completely separated from the original First Nations reserves.[5] Such reserves are established by the acquisition of Crown lands or privately owned lands, either individually or jointly by First Nations. As is the case with the original reserves, under the *Indian Act* these satellite reserves are communally owned lands that belong to an entire band rather than to any particular member or members. They are subjected to the same regulations regarding, among other things, land ownership, land use, and financial management as the original reserves. Some satellite reserves, particularly those established either in urban areas or in rural areas in close proximity to an urban area, may be subject to special regulatory provisions related to land use and development which may not apply to either the original reserves or new satellite reserves established in rural remote areas relatively far from any urban area. Reserve land has a different legal status than land held by First Nations which has not been conferred reserve status. This status has important implications for the policies related to matters such as taxation and disposition of such land and any buildings on it. In provinces such as British Columbia, these lands are exempt from municipal taxation, but grants or service fees are normally forwarded to the municipality in lieu of taxes. However, in Saskatchewan and Manitoba, legislation upholding this exemption was repealed. Consequently, in these two provinces all lands not conferred reserve status are taxable by the municipality[6] but reserves continue to be exempt from municipal taxation.

The conversion of land acquired by First Nations to reserve status is not automatic. To achieve a conversion a formal decision-making process must be followed that starts with an application by the First Nation and concludes with an order-in-council. For their part First Nations make strategic decisions regarding if and when they want land converted to reserve status. The conversion process entails costs and benefits that First Nations councils must assess before deciding whether to proceed. In some cases, the financial and political resources needed, as well as the resulting encumbrances on the use and disposal of reserve lands, have led First Nations to decide not to proceed with conversion. Land not converted to reserves is technically referred to as "land held in trust for a band of Indians."

The Location, Number, and Types of Satellite Reserves

In Saskatchewan, satellite reserves have been created in the southern and the northern part of the province, in both urban areas (urban reserves) and rural areas (rural reserves). What follows provides a brief overview of each of these two major types of satellite reserves based on information compiled by the federal government's Department of Indian and Northern Affairs.[7] Between 1981 and 2006 thirty-two urban satellite reserves were created on land located within the corporate boundaries of existing urban communities in Saskatchewan. Whereas only seven were created during the first fifteen years, twenty-five were created during the decade from 1996-2006 (see Table 1). Of the thirty-two urban reserves created since 1981, twenty-four have been created in southern Saskatchewan and eight in the Northern Administration District (NAD). Of those in the NAD six are what are known as community transfers consisting of various types of properties and two are commercial properties.

Urban Reserve Creation by 5 Year Period	
1981-1986	3
1986-1991	1
1991-1996	3
1996-2001	12
2001-2006	13

Table 1

Four major categories of urban satellite reserves have been created—commercial, institutional, agricultural, and northern community transfer (i.e., transfer of all or part of a northern community). Of these twenty-one are commercial reserves, four are institutional reserves, six are northern community transfer reserves which serve a combination of purposes (i.e. residential, institutional, and commercial), and one is an agricultural reserve. The agricultural reserve exists within the boundaries of the City of North Battleford.

Urban Reserves By Category			
Commercial	Agricultural	Institutional	Northern Community Transfer
21	1	4	6

Table 2

To date, urban satellite reserves have not been created for residential purposes, although bands have consistently insisted on their right to build accommodations. In 1996, the Muskeg Lake Cree Nation, for example, tried to purchase and convert city-owned land to reserve status in Prince Albert for residential purposes, but those efforts were blocked by protests by city residents living in what would have been the neighbouring subdivision.[8] Other plans for establishing residential urban reserves by the Peter Ballantyne Band on a tract of land adjacent to its Opewakoscikan Reserve in Prince Albert and another on 320 acres just 6.5 kilometers from Saskatoon have not materialized.[9] The interest in the creation of residential reserves is based on the dual consideration of generating revenue by renting properties to their own members as well as other Aboriginal and non-Aboriginal persons, meeting some of the housing needs of their members, and expanding reserve-based membership because off-reserve band members are not counted in the federal assessments of reserve population that are used to determine funding allocations.[10]

Reserves have been created in various types of municipalities (i.e. cities, towns, villages, resort villages, etc.) with populations ranging from approximately 200,000 to less than 100. To date, only one has been established in a municipality with a population of approximately 200,000, ten have been established in municipalities with populations ranging from approximately 5,000 to 50,000, and the remaining twenty-one have been established in relatively small municipalities with populations ranging from approximately 100 to 5,000. Most of those have been established in municipalities with populations less than 50,000 whereas the majority of them have been established in municipalities with populations less than 5,000.

Urban Reserves By Community		
Community	Population	Reserves
Cochin	208	1
Denare Beach	785	1
Deschambault Lake	700	1
Duck Lake	610	2
Fort Qu'Appelle	1,919	4
Kinoosao	80	1
Kylemore	960	1
Lebret	203	1
Leoville	341	2
Meadow Lake	4,471	1
North Battleford	13,190	2
Pelican Narrows	599	1
Prince Albert	34,138	4
Sandy Bay	1,175	1
Saskatoon	202,340	2
South End	35	1
Spiritwood	911	1
Sturgeon Landing	139	2
Yorkton	15,038	3

Table 3

Forty-five different First Nations have been involved in the creation of the existing urban satellite reserves. Thirty of those are members of the Treaty 4 First Nations which jointly created two reserves in the Fort Qu'Appelle area. The only other urban reserve that has been created jointly by First Nations (i.e. Beardy's & Okemasis and One Arrow) is located in Duck Lake. Whereas some First Nations have established only one satellite reserve, others have established two or more (see Table 4). The Peter Ballantyne Cree Nation established twelve, either in the Prince Albert region or in several communities within the Northern Administration District; the Pelican Lake First Nation established three in communities located between Prince Albert and Meadow Lake; Starblanket established two in Fort Qu'Appelle and Lebret; Sakimay established two in Yorkton; the thirty Treaty 4 First Nations established

Urban Reserves By Band	
Beardy's & Okemasis	1
Joint Holding Beardy's & Okemasis with One Arrow	1
One Arrow	1
Kahkewistahaw	1
Little Black Bear	1
Mosquito, GBH, Lean Man	1
Flying Dust	1
Fishing Lake	1
Muskeg Lake	1
Red Pheasant	1
Saulteaux	1
Sakimay	2
Star Blanket	2
Treaty 4 (30 Sask. Bands – Joint Holding)	2
Pelican Lake	3
Peter Ballantyne	12

Table 4

two in Fort Qu'appelle; and Beardy's & Okemasis established two in Duck Lake (one on its own and one jointly with the One Arrow First Nation).

The first few urban satellite reserves were created on Crown lands that First Nations acquired as part of their land claims negotiations with the federal government. Furthermore, they were created using lands and buildings that the federal government had used earlier as residential schools. This was the case, for example, both in the city of Prince Albert and in the village of Lebret. Others were created on federal Crown lands that were either used, or to be used, for a variety of federal institutions, such as post offices, Royal Canadian Mounted Police detachment offices, or prisons. Ironically, some of these had been institutions that the state and its agents had used either to indoctrinate or to control First Nations members. More recently, reserves in urban areas are also being created on lands acquired by First Nations from private interests.

The thirty-two urban reserves comprise a total of approximately 1,300 acres and roughly half this land is located in three communities in northern Saskatchewan, two of which were so-called northern community transfers (Deschambault Lake 249.42 acres, and Pelican Narrows 163.17 acres) and one of which was commercial land (Sandy Bay, 148.07 acres). Approximately one quarter of this land is the agricultural urban reserve in North Battleford (347.14). The remaining land (393.10 acres) is located in twenty-eight urban reserves, of which five range in size from 30 to 85 acres, five from 10 to 30 acres, eight from 1 to 30 acres, and ten are less than one acre. Those smaller than one acre are residential and commercial lots.

The 1,300 acres of land that have been transferred to reserve status in urban areas constitute a very small fraction of the approximately 711, 984 acres that have been set aside in urban and rural areas through the *Treaty Land Entitlement Framework Agreement* (TLEFA) and does not even include lands in rural areas set aside under the dozens of Specific Claims processes.[11] Of these, approximately 70 have been concluded, 41 are under initial review, 14 are under review by the Department of Indian Affairs, and 14 are under review by the Indian Specific Claims Commission.[12] Roughly 1,400 parcels of land have been set aside to date under the two processes. Approximately 50 per cent (345,176 acres) of the total acres converted to reserve pursuant to the TLEFA were located in the North West District of the province along the Saskatchewan-Alberta border; approximately 30 per cent (229,792 acres) were located in the South District; and approximately 20 per cent (115,476 acres) in the North Central District. Most, though by no means all, of these conversions produced satellite reserves; the rest did not because they were physically attached to the original reserves. Most of the satellite reserves in rural areas are standard-sized farms ranging from one 160 to 640 acres. However, there are several which consist of 1,000 to 15,000 acres, and one created in 2003 for the Onion Lake First Nation is 87,126 acres of largely forest land that previously had been held by Mistik Forestry to produce lumber and lumber products.[13] Although most of these lands have been purchased primarily for their agricultural or forestry industry potential, some have been acquired for future residential or commercial purposes.

Factors Contributing to the Creation of Satellite Reserves

Five major interrelated factors contributed to the creation of so many new satellite reserves during the past quarter century.[14]

Land Claims Factor
The primary factor that has contributed to the creation of satellite reserves has been the decisions of First Nations leaders to pursue the resolution of outstanding land claims, and the decisions of the federal and provincial governments to honour those claims. It is doubtful that any new reserves would have been created in Saskatchewan without this opportunity to acquire the necessary lands and financial resources. Land claims processes also provided essential co-operation and support from Canadian governments. Equally important, they provided First Nations leaders with an opportunity to consider how additional land holdings in various parts of the province could be used to pursue their development objectives.

Demographic Factor
The second major factor that has contributed to the creation of satellite reserves in urban areas has been the demographic trends among Aboriginals. One study projects that between 1995 and 2045, the Aboriginal population will increase from 13 per cent to 32 per cent of the province's total population.[15] At least 48 per cent of Indians in Saskatchewan live off-reserve.[16] This is the result of the continuing migration of First Nation members to urban areas and the relatively high birth rate among them. These demographic trends contributed to bands creating resi-

dential subdivisions and schools on some satellite reserves. Currently, however, in the southern part of the province, the creation of residential subdivisions and Indian-controlled schools on reserves remains a lower priority than commercial and industrial developments.

First Nations Autonomy Factor

The third major factor that has contributed to the creation of satellite reserves has been the decision by the federal government to devolve more decision-making authority and autonomy to band councils. Since the late 1980s, and especially since the failure of the Meech Lake and Charlottetown Accords, the federal government has accelerated the devolution of authority for program decisions to First Nations particularly through various co-management agreements and self-governance agreements in various policy sectors, as well as the enactment of the *First Nations Land Management Act* in 1999. Although the federal government has been resistant to the notion of sovereignty, it has been responsive to calls for some increased autonomy for Aboriginal governments.

Development Objectives Factor

The fourth major factor has been the economic, social, cultural, and political development objectives of the First Nations leadership.[17] Those objectives have emanated from the Aboriginal self-governance and self-sufficiency paradigm, within the context of which leaders view satellite reserves as a means for providing communities with greater and more diversified economic activity and increased financial resources.[18] Reserves can generate lease and taxation revenues. Agricultural, commercial, and institutional properties provide Indian bands and their members with several financial benefits. One is the tax immunity enjoyed by band councils and by First Nations members who work or operate businesses on reserves. This minimizes tax loads and, theoretically at least, maximizes income. Tax immunity optimizes returns on investment through rental income and provides First Nations with leverage in negotiating partnerships with commercial entities both in and outside the Aboriginal sector. These factors have resulted in such reserves being referred to as "economic development centres" both in the TLEFA and other documents of the early 1990s.[19]

Satellite reserves are seen as instruments that contribute to meeting the social service needs of band members living in towns and cities. Some are logical places for First Nation band councils, regional tribal councils, and provincial umbrella organizations to locate social and educational services. Similarly, creation of these reserves makes it possible for First Nations to, among other things, obtain and preserve culturally important lands and to establish educational and cultural centres devoted to the preservation and development of First Nations cultures.

First Nation leaders have also seen satellite reserves as important for achieving significant political development objectives. Those used for institutional and commercial purposes, in particular, are seen as places where band councils, regional tribal councils, and provincial First Nations organizations can establish offices and conduct their political and governance activities. This can provide opportunities to develop political management skills which are as important as commercial and institutional management skills for First Nations to achieve their other development goals.

Self-Government Factor
The fifth major factor has been the belief by First Nation leaders that new satellite reserves are important instruments for advancing their self-government goals.[20] This includes both the more limited form of self-government under the *Indian Act*, and the broader form of self-government embodied in the notion of the inherent right of self-government for Aboriginal peoples. The *Indian Act* embodies a system of self-government, though by no means a highly autonomous one, which is inextricably tied to the reserve land base. Under the *Indian Act*, First Nations governments exist primarily to govern reserves and band members who have strong links to reserves. Within this framework, therefore, the creation of new reserves is an important means of expanding the land base and the number of people, organizations, and enterprises that will be subject to First Nations governing regimes. Additionally, new satellite reserves are seen by First Nations leaders as a way to advance the inherent right of self-government for Aboriginal people. The initial concept of an inherent right of self-government embodied the notion of a nation living on a defined land base and exercising extensive internal autonomy, even sovereignty, derived from some supra-authority, often described as the Creator. In the past, however, land base was conceptualized as existing Indian reserves located primarily in the remote, rural areas of Canada. During and since the various rounds of negotiations on constitutional reform, arguments have been advanced that the inherent right should be viewed as portable, applicable to newly acquired Indian lands, and even to Aboriginal people with no defined land base.[21] Even in these formulations, a more limited version of self-government (that is to say, self-administration and qualified Aboriginal rights) is often envisioned,[22] making the creation of satellite reserves an important vehicle for extending the reach of the inherent right beyond the traditional limited reserve land base.

The Politics of Creating Satellite Reserves
Satellite reserve creation initiatives have generated some interesting political dynamics. Rarely, if ever, has there been unanimous support for or opposition to the creation of a satellite reserve. This is true even among members of First Nations involved in the creation of the reserves. Support or opposition tends to depend on an array of factors, most notably the perceptions stakeholders and residents of the effect the reserve would have on their pecuniary personal interests and their broader community interests.

The Proponents of Satellite Reserves

Invariably, the strongest proponents of new reserves are the leaders and members of the First Nations who want to see them created for all the reasons noted above. Typically, the leaders promote the benefits because they want their members as well as members of the general public and governmental and non-governmental stakeholders to understand the contributions that a new reserve could make to the development of local and provincial economies and communities. Successive federal and provincial governments over the past two decades have also been quite supportive both because reserve creation has helped in the resolution of some outstanding land claims and because they believed, or at least hoped, that new reserves would contribute to economic and social development in First Nations communities. Proponents have also included elected and appointed municipal officials who have generally seen the potential benefits for their economies and communities.[23] These officials have had a major effect both on the dynamics of reserve creation and on how quickly the processes have proceeded. In some instances, the proponents of new reserves have also included entrepreneurs and residents of the communities in which the reserves are being created. Although all of these are supporters, it should not be assumed that they had no concerns regarding either the proposed creation of such reserves or their intended uses.

The Opponents of Satellite Reserves

Opposition to the creation of satellite reserves has emanated from non-Aboriginal people as well as Aboriginal people both in southern and northern communities. In southern communities it has emanated primarily from non-Aboriginal elected and appointed municipal officials as well as members of the general public. Their opposition is generally based on concerns regarding negative effects that a proposed satellite reserve might have on a range of things including the following:

1. the land use complexion and future development of a particular subdivision, since municipal planning and development bylaws do not automatically apply to reserves;

2. the tax base of the municipality if a First Nation refuses to pay municipal taxes or service fees that normally accrue to non-reserve land;

3. the commercial interests of some local entrepreneurs on the uneven playing field created by the tax exemptions commercial activities on reserves enjoy;

4. the real-estate value of existing neighbouring properties; and

5. the quality of life of people living on neighbouring properties.

The first two concerns have been articulated primarily by elected and appointed municipal and school board officials, the third by business owners, and the last two by residents both within and somewhat beyond the geographic area in which the proposed reserve would be created.

One of the interesting aspects of opposition to the creation of satellite reserves in northern Saskatchewan is that a substantial proportion of it was expressed by Aboriginal members of the proposed communities where the majority of the population was and continues to be of First Nations ancestry. Opposition came from First Nations and Métis residents alike. In some cases it even came from members of the First Nation establishing the satellite reserve. In the so-called 'northern community transfers,' whereby either part or all of a community would be converted from municipal to reserve status,[24] opposition was based on concerns about one or more of the following:

1. ability of residents to retain freehold titles to residential or commercial properties;

2. even after compensation for the transfer of lots to reserve status, such lots would have to be leased back from the First Nation if the current owners wanted to stay there; and,

3. creation of the reserve could lead either to the municipality reverting to a lower classification and thus a loss of governance autonomy and capacity, or to the complete loss of municipal status.

Such concerns were very evident, albeit to a varying extent, in all six of the northern community transfers, but arguably most pronounced in the conversion of the entire community of Deschambault Lake from municipal to reserve status. This serves as a reminder that it cannot be assumed that a high proportion of First Nations members in a community precludes concerns, controversy, and conflict over the creation of satellite reserves.

The opposition to the creation of satellite reserves has abated considerably, but not entirely, in recent years for several interrelated reasons. One is that the negative scenarios painted by vocal critics did not materialize anywhere. A second is that the Muskeg Lake Cree Nation urban reserve in Saskatoon served as a positive model of best practices that have been emulated extensively in the creation and operation of other such reserves. Third, the policies and processes regarding the creation of reserves have generally provided all stakeholders with the necessary degree of clarity, certainty, and protections. And fourth, officials of the Saskatchewan Association of Rural Municipalities (SARM) and officials of individual rural municipalities eventually received a tax-loss compensation formula that they found more acceptable than what initially had been proposed by the federal government. SARM rejected the initial proposal and in 1997 it launched a lawsuit against the federal government in an effort to resolve the issue. Eventually they agreed to a formula of 22.5 times the annual taxation levied for the municipal portion of the property taxes levied the previous year.

This did not include the compensation for the education portion of the property tax that would be paid through a separate fund (i.e., the School Division Tax Loss Compensation Fund).

Despite the relatively positive experience with the creation of satellite reserves to date, opposition to new proposals has not disappeared. The most recent example of this was the controversy surrounding the creation of a 347-acre satellite reserve by the Red Pheasant First Nation for agricultural purposes adjacent to North Battleford. The opposition was spearheaded by political, administrative, and commercial leaders in that community ostensibly over concerns that the site had extensive potential for real estate development and commercial use by the First Nation that would adversely affect existing real estate and commercial holdings in the city. The negotiations between City and First Nation representatives for the purpose of producing agreements were very acrimonious and eventually came to a standstill. Section 9.01 of the TLEFA states that if no agreement is signed within five months, where the Band is willing to negotiate in good faith but the municipality is not, the case can be brought to arbitration. In 2001, the case was referred to an arbitrator who ruled that the City of North Battleford did not act in good faith in its negotiations with Red Pheasant First Nation. In January 2003, the land was officially designated reserve land, despite the City's concerns, and currently there is no municipal services agreement in place and the land is still only used for agriculture. Lack of a municipal services agreement means the city receives no tax-loss compensation for the land, and there are no bylaw-compatibility or dispute-resolution mechanisms for the city and the reserve. This stands in contrast to the creation of the satellite reserve for the Indian-run casino in that city. In that case, the First Nation and the City negotiated and signed the requisite agreements related to service provision and payments as well as bylaw compatibility without much debate or acrimony. The main reason for this is that the City knew and supported the current use of the property because it benefited the economy, and it was unlikely that the use would be altered in the near or more distant future.

Policies and Processes for Creating Satellite Reserves

Two major sets of policies and processes impinge on the creation of satellite reserves, one of which has been promulgated by the federal government and the other by the provincial government. Before providing a brief overview of those policies, an important caveat is in order. The precise process for the creation of such reserves is contingent on, among other things, whether the land is in an urban or rural area and whether the land that is being converted is held by the Crown or private individuals.

National Policies

The policies and processes for creating satellite reserves are outlined in two documents: the *Treaty Land Entitlement Framework Agreement* (TLEFA) and the federal *Additions to Reserves Policy* (ARP). The former is a province-wide land claims agreement signed in 1992 by the federal government, the province of Saskatchewan, and twenty-six entitlement bands in the province.[25] The latter is the national policy of the federal government that applies to lands acquired by bands (whether through land claims agreements or any other means) and earmarked for conversion to reserve status.[26] In the TLEFA, the reserve creation policy is articulated in Article 9 for urban reserves and Article 11 for rural reserves. The ARP has been articulated in Chapter 9 of Indian and Northern Affairs (INAC)'s 1991 Land Management Manual and Chapter 10 of the 2001 *Land Management Manual.*[27] The major difference between Chapter 9 and Chapter 10 in terms of ARP is not in the nature of the key provisions, but in the degree of clarity related to some key provisions.

The general reserve creation process for satellite reserves in rural areas outlined in Article 11 of the TLEFA and the ARP consists of six major stages. The first stage is for the First Nation's council to ratify and submit a Band Council Resolution (BCR) to Indian and Northern Affairs Canada (INAC). The second stage is for INAC and that First Nation to discuss all requirements to move the proposal forward, and determine their respective roles and responsibilities for carrying out the following steps: communication and consultation with local communities and municipal governments; and environmental audits and surveys. The third stage is for the regional Additions to Reserve (ATR) committee to analyze the proposal to ensure requirements of the ATR policy have been met. The fourth stage is for the ATR committee to forward its report to the Regional Director General (RDG) either recommending that the proposal for approval in principle (AIP) be approved or rejected. The fifth stage is for the RDG or DM to either grant or refuse the AIP to recommend a proposal to the Minister for consideration of reserve status through the Governor in Council. An AIP can be granted with or without conditions. If conditions are attached they must be dealt with fully before the AIP is referred to the Privy Council Office to be approved by Governor in Council by means of an Order in Council (OIC). The sixth stage is either approval or rejection of the AIP by the Governor in Council.

The policies and processes for the creation of urban satellite reserves differ from those for creating them in rural areas in at least one very important respect. In both TFLEA and ARP policy, after the First Nation has acquired a parcel of land and has indicated its intention to have it transformed into an urban reserve, it is required to undertake negotiations for an agreement with the neighbouring municipality on a number of key issues. These include: (1) whether compensation will be paid for the loss of municipal and school taxes once the land is placed beyond those taxation domains; (2) the type and financing of municipal services to be delivered to the new reserve; (3) bylaw compatibility between the municipality and the reserve, particularly where reserve development has the potential to affect neighbouring municipal lands and residents; and, (4) a joint consultative process, especially a dispute-resolution mechanism, for addressing matters of mutual concern.

By contrast, the policy for the creation of rural reserves requires no comparable negotiations with the rural municipality in which the lands are located. Indeed, the only provision in the TLEFA regarding any such negotiations involving land in rural municipalities only applies to land that is adjacent to an urban or northern municipality. Even in that case, however, that provision is quite permissive regarding such negotiations. Article 11.10 of the TLEFA contains a very flexible post-reserve creation undertaking that reads as follows: "In the event Entitlement Land is set apart as Entitlement Reserve adjacent to an Urban Municipality or Northern Municipality, the Entitlement Band agrees to give favourable consideration to establishing compatible zoning bylaws consistent with those in place, from time to time, in any adjoining portion of the Urban Municipality or Northern Municipality."[28] The provision only applies when a reserve adjoins an urban or northern municipality, and even in that case it only requires First Nations to give favourable consideration to negotiations, but there is no requirement for them to undertake such negotiations. The interesting and important aspect of this provision is that it neither compels nor encourages First Nations to undertake any consultations with rural municipalities regarding zoning or anything else either prior to or after the establishment of the reserve. The major reason for this is that zoning in rural areas, where most lands are used strictly for agricultural purposes, is not as a significant as it is in urban areas. However, that is not true in all cases. A few rural municipalities that border on urban municipalities, especially those that border on the cities of Saskatoon, Regina, and Prince Albert, have some sizeable residential subdivisions within their own boundaries that could benefit from negotiated bylaw compatibility agreement if a reserve were established adjacent to them.

Finally, it is important to note that First Nations lands in urban areas that are not designated to be converted to reserves require no negotiation of the types of agreements noted in the policy. Nevertheless, there are some instances in which First Nations and municipalities have signed services agreements and bylaw-compatibility agreements in anticipation of the creation of an urban reserve, though no such reserve has yet been created. This is the case with two office towers in Saskatoon owned by the Battlefords Tribal Council and the Yellow Quill First Nation where agreements have been signed but the First Nations have either chosen not to apply for or have not been granted reserve status. It is also the case with an 80-acre parcel of land acquired by the Red Pheasant First Nation in the planning district which is jointly managed by the City of Saskatoon and the RM of Corman Park. This particular land acquisition resulted in the signing of a unique tripartite agreement in November 1999, between the Red Pheasant First Nation, the RM of Corman Park, and the City of Saskatoon that dealt with the provision and payment of services and compatible land-use bylaws.[29] Similarly, the City of Regina and two First Nations have signed comparable, albeit bilateral, agreements for each property in anticipation that reserves would be created within the city boundaries, though to date they have not. The agreements between the

City of Regina and the Nekaneet First Nation were signed in 2002, and those between the City of Regina and the Piapot First Nation were signed in January 2007. In all of the aforementioned cases First Nations and municipal councils have agreed to comply with the provisions of those agreements because they deem them to be mutually beneficial, even though technically they are not required to do so until the land is converted to reserve.

Both the TLEFA and the ARP stipulate that such agreements must be negotiated in good faith and that where a municipality fails to do so in response to the reasonable proposals of a band the federal government may proceed to create the reserve in question, notwithstanding the objections of the municipality. This is precisely what happened in at least two cases. In 1982 the first urban reserve was proposed in Prince Albert, and the city simply refused to negotiate with the First Nation and tried to mount a national municipal campaign within the municipal sector against the creation of that reserve.[30] The second case occurred in the first quinquennium of the new century when a proposal emerged for creating a reserve in North Battleford. This case was dealt with pursuant to section 9.01 of the TLEFA whereby the First Nation approaches municipal council to negotiate service provision and payment agreements as well as bylaw compatibility agreements and if an agreement is not signed within five months the matter may be subjected to arbitration. This was the case in North Battleford in the year 2000, when Red Pheasant First Nation purchased 347 acres of agricultural land. Although the First Nation had no plans to develop the agricultural land for residential, commercial, or institutional purposes, there was community concern that the land would be developed in a way that would adversely affect the development plans of the city and its commercial sector. In 2001, the case was taken to arbitration, and the arbitrator ruled that the City of North Battleford had not acted in good faith in its negotiations with the Red Pheasant First Nation. Despite the city council's concerns and objections, the federal government designated the land as a reserve in January of 2003. Consequently the city and the reserve operate adjacent to each other in the absence of any agreements and any coordinative or dispute-resolution mechanisms.

Provincial Policies

The TLEFA necessitated the enactment of some provincial legislation related to the creation of reserves—the *Treaty Land Entitlement Implementation Act*.[31] The *Treaty Land Entitlement Implementation Act* contains a number of amendments of consequence to the province's municipal acts, the *Education Act*, the *Crown Minerals Act*, and the *Water Corporation Act*.

The amendments to the municipal acts are largely designed to empower municipalities to enter into agreements with Indian bands on four key matters: (1) tax-loss compensation or grants in lieu of taxes for Indian reserve lands; (2) the application, enforcement, and compatibility of the bylaws of the municipality and the Indian band; (3) the provision of municipal services to an Indian band or persons on a reserve; and, (4) the mechanisms for resolving disputes that may arise between the municipality and the Indian band on any matter. The amendments to the statute which applies to rural municipalities contain additional provisions. These require every municipality that receives (or is entitled to receive) tax-loss compensation from the rural municipal tax-loss compensation fund established under the TLEFA to maintain roads adjacent to Indian reserves for which tax-loss compensation has been paid. These provisions were included in part as a reminder to municipalities that tax-loss compensation was being paid for the continuance of at least certain basic road services to the lands converted to reserves.

The provincial government also promulgated three primary amendments to the *Education Act*. The first authorizes school divisions to enter into agreements with First Nations regarding loss of revenue resulting from lands within the division being converted to reserve status. The second authorizes the provincial minister of education to establish a trust fund (i.e. the School Division Tax Loss Compensation Fund) for the purpose of collecting payments from Canada for tax-loss compensation and to distribute payments to school divisions that lose tax revenues as a result of lands being converted to reserves pursuant to the TLEFA. The third permits a board of education to enter into agreements with another board of education, the council of a municipality, a First Nation band, and either the provincial or federal government, to sell, transfer, or exchange property without having to request public tenders or arrange for a public auction, provided this action is taken to facilitate community or school planning, or to achieve another educational or public purpose. Another important policy provision related to education in the *Treaty Land Entitlement Implementation Act* states that when a board of education has agreed to sell a school in the NAD to an entitlement band, and the parties cannot agree on a purchase price, either party can submit the matter to an arbitration board established pursuant to provisions in the TLEFA.

The amendments to the *Crown Minerals Act* authorize the minister to enter into agreements with Indian bands or the federal government regarding the transfer of the administration and control of Crown lands and minerals. Similarly, the *Water Corporation Act* authorizes the minister to conclude agreements with the Canadian government or Indian bands relating to the management, administration, development, conservation, protection, and control of any water and related land resources in Saskatchewan. Moreover, it authorizes the minister to conclude agreements for the creation of co-management boards and provides for the delegation of any of the related powers of the corporation to these boards. Another major amendment authorizes the provincial Crown to transfer the water or the use of water situated within an Indian reserve to the federal Crown. A further amendment gives Indian bands the following rights in relation to any reserve lands set aside for them under the TLEFA: the right to place a dock, wharf, or pier on the land forming the bed or shore of any surface water that is adjacent to any such reserve lands; and water rights with respect to the use and occupation of any land that is adjacent to any surface water.

The initiative by the provincial government to enhance this statutory framework is beneficial and laudable, though to date it has still not developed a policy or procedures manual. Such a manual has been produced by the Manitoba government to assist municipal governments and band councils in creating development and services agreements.[32] Equally important, a detailed policies and procedures manual on the general process and negotiations related to the creation of reserves is still needed.

Conclusion

The objective in this concluding section is to provide some observations regarding the prospects for additional satellite reserves in the near and distant future, the prospects for residential developments on reserves, the value of current satellite reserves in advancing the objectives for which they have been established, and areas for further research.

Prospects for Additional Reserves

The prospects for additional satellite reserves in the near future are quite good, and for several reasons. First, TLEFA First Nations have not completed their acquisition of lands. Second, some First Nations have outstanding Specific Claims that they have not completed processing, or outstanding claims they have not yet initiated. Third, a number of other urban reserves are either in the process of being created or are planned. Fourth, several First Nations have properties in urban and rural areas which may be converted to reserves in the near future. In Saskatoon, for example, this includes two office towers (i.e. Canterbury Towers, Avord Towers), and in Regina it includes land zoned for commercial use.[33] Fifth, some are likely to be created as a result of First Nations amassing capital through their land holdings, commercial activities, and investments. The greater the amount of financial resources that they have at their disposal after meeting the needs of their communities and members, the greater the likelihood that they will have resources to create additional satellite reserves. The number of reserves that will be created is contingent on a range of factors, especially the following two: (a) how well the existing ones perform in terms of the benefits that they generate for First Nations, their members, and the broader community; and, (b) the degree to which First Nations are able to operate such reserves in a way that they foster benefits and minimize problems for neighbouring municipal governments and their communities. Such matters will likely weigh heavily in the decisions that the federal government will make in approving the creation of such reserves in the future.

Prospects for Residential Reserves

The prospects for residential developments on satellite reserves in or very near to urban areas are quite good. Various First Nations have explored such options in the recent past, they continue to do so today, and they are likely to continue to do so in the near and distant future. The major question is whether such developments would be exclusively for their members, exclusively for non-members, or some combination of the two, comparable to those in other parts of Canada.[34] The precise configuration of such residential developments could range from apartment buildings, conventional residential subdivisions, or special subdivisions such as those integrated with golf-courses, depending on the principal goals of the First Nation involved.

Value of Satellite Reserves

A detailed quantitative analysis of the value of satellite reserves is difficult and somewhat beyond the scope of this chapter. Nevertheless, it is possible to make some observations regarding their value not only in advancing the economic, social, cultural, and political development objectives pursued by the First Nations leaders, but also in making positive contributions to neighbouring municipalities. The prevailing view, particularly among governmental stakeholders, is that there is positive value both for First Nations and their neighbouring municipal communities.[35] To date, there has not been any substantial or sustained assertion of demonstrable negative effects. Indeed, some reserves have been so successful that they have become models for other communities, such as Winnipeg, where the creation of comparable reserves has been considered.[36]

Although some satellite reserves have been more successful than others in advancing economic objectives, the consensus is that on the whole they have generated revenues both for First Nations and for individual members of First Nations. First Nations have acquired revenue streams largely through commercial and institutional property rentals in urban areas, and the revenues generated through farming on agricultural lands in the rural areas and to a lesser extent the sale of timber from forest lands. Such benefits in urban areas are particularly good for reserves with housing, commercial, and institutional operations. The most profitable in this respect are those that have businesses, banks, head offices for First Nations organizations, offices for educational and social service organizations, and casinos. For some First Nations members the satellite reserves have provided opportunities to establish businesses or work for business and organizations located on them. All of the aforementioned economic benefits will differ from case to case depending on the First Nation and the individual members involved. In this respect it is important to note that only a few of the 32 urban reserves are used for commercial purposes that provide either First Nations or individual First Nations members with substantial direct financial benefits. The same is undoubtedly true of rural reserves, at least on aggregate, because some First Nations have many more acres than others, even if the financial returns per acre are comparable.

The extent to which the satellite reserves have advanced social, cultural, and political development objectives is much more difficult to assess because they are somewhat less tangible and less visible than economic benefits, however, general consensus is positive. The handful of satellite reserves that have been used for various types of institutional purposes (i.e., governance, education, and community service provision) in places such as Prince Albert, Saskatoon, Yorkton, and Lebret certainly contribute directly to such objectives. Moreover, these, along with all the other satellite reserves, have contributed to the political development objectives of First Nations in at least two ways: (1) they have provided more land over which to exercise governance jurisdiction; and, (2) they have provided leaders and members with more opportunities to engage in and observe a wider range of governance and political management activities—including intergovernmental relations—related to the establishment and operations of such reserves.

Another prevailing view is that satellite reserves have had a positive effect on the neighbouring municipal communities and non-First Nation members of those communities.[37] This is particularly true in the handful of urban areas where the satellite reserves have included relatively large commercial and institutional developments (i.e. Prince Albert, Saskatoon, Yorkton, and North Battleford). For such communities, spinoffs from the economic returns on commercial operations, and the payrolls of commercial and institutional entities, are quite important for the local economies. In rural areas it has provided many retiring farmers with opportunities to sell their land. Moreover, by extension, the local and provincial economies benefited if either those who sold farmland, or at least the money they acquired from such sales, remained in Saskatchewan.

In summary, the prevailing view is that satellite reserves have been beneficial both for First Nation and municipal communities.[38] There is a widespread recognition, however, that the extent to which such benefits continue is highly contingent on the extent to which First Nation and municipal governments are able to coordinate their respective planning, development, land use, and service-provision initiatives in ways that are consonant, constructive, and mutually beneficial.[39] For this purpose, more protocols such as those signed by the City of Regina and the Nekaneet First Nation may be beneficial.[40]

Further Research

Further research regarding satellite reserves is warranted in at least two major areas. One area is the geographic distribution of rural satellite reserves, reserve lands attached to original reserves, and new reserves. Such research should be conducted by geographers and planners who deal with geographic location issues. Another area for further research is the economic impact of all satellite reserves. Impact analyses should examine the following: the real estate value of the satellite reserve land base over time; the financial returns of that land base given the various types of activities on it over time; the distribution of the monetary and non-monetary benefits of satellite reserves among governments and members of First Nations communities; and the economic benefits of satellite reserves to the economies of adjoining non-reserve communities. These are but a few of the interesting and important areas for further research on what, to date, has been an interesting and important phenomenon and one that is likely to continue to be so in the future.[41]

1   This is a substantially revised and updated version of the following article: F. Laurie Barron & Joseph Garcea, "Aboriginal Self-Government and the Creation of New Indian Reserves: A Saskatchewan Case Study," in *Aboriginal Self-Government in Canada: Current Issues and Trends,* 2nd ed., ed. John H. Hylton (Saskatoon: Purich Publishing, 1999), 289-309. The author would like to express his appreciation to Devin O'Neal for his valuable research assistance for this chapter.

2   F. Laurie Barron & Joe Garcea, "Reflections on Urban Satellite Reserves in Saskatchewan," in *Expressions on Canadian Native Studies,* eds. Ron F. Laliberte, Priscilla Settee, James B. Waldram, Rob Innes, Brenda Macdougall, Lesley McBain & F. Laurie Barron (Saskatoon: University of Saskatchewan Extension Press, 2000), 400-28.

3   Theresa Dust, *The Impact of Aboriginal Land Claims and Self-government on Canadian Municipalities: The Local Government Perspective* (Toronto: Intergovernmental Committee on Urban and Regional Research, 1995); Donovan Young, "Some Approaches to Urban Aboriginal Governance," in *Self-government for Aboriginal People in Urban Areas,* ed. Evelyn J. Peters (Kingston: Institute of Intergovernmental Relations, Queen's University, 1995); F. Laurie Barron & Joe Garcea, eds., *Urban Indian Reserves: Forging New Relations in Saskatchewan* (Saskatoon: Purich Publishing, 1999).

4   Union of BC Municipalities, *Local Government and Aboriginal Treaty Negotiations: Defining the Municipal Interest* (Vancouver: Union of BC Municipalities, 1994); and, Lillian Thomas, *Report on Implementing Treaty Land Entitlements and Toward the Establishment of "Urban Aboriginal Reserves" in Winnipeg* (Winnipeg: 2005).

5   Barron and Garcea, "Reflections on Urban Satellite Reserves."

6   Dust, *The Impact of Aboriginal Land Claims.*

7   Canada, *Saskatchewan Urban Reserves (as of July 2007)* (Ottawa: Indian and Northern Affairs Canada, 2007); and, Canada, *Treaty Land Entitlement Reserve Creation Report* (Ottawa: Indian and Northern Affairs Canada, 2007).

8   Barron & Garcea, eds., *Urban Indian Reserves.*

9   Darren Bernhardt, "Saskatoon land becoming hot item for Indian bands," *Saskatoon Star Phoenix,* 6 January 1999.

10 Leslie Perreaux, "Natives file lawsuit against tax collection," *Saskatoon Star Phoenix,* 4 February 1999.

11 Canada, Saskatchewan Treaty Land Entitlement Framework Agreement, 1992.

12 Canada, *Treaty Land Entitlement Reserve Creation Report.*

13 *Ibid.*

14 Canada, *Facts on File: First Nations in Saskatchewan: Urban Reserves* (Ottawa: Indian and Northern Affairs, n/d).

15 Kelly Lindsay, Marv Painter, & Eric Howe, "Impact of the changing Aboriginal population on the Saskatchewan economy, 1995-2045," in *Saskatchewan and Aboriginal peoples in the 21st century: Social, Economic and Political Changes and Challenges* (Regina: Federation of Saskatchewan Indian Nations, 1997), 37-144.

16 Canada, Lands and Trust Services, *Urban Reserves: Presentation to Senior Policy Committee* (Ottawa: Indian and Northern Affairs, 1998).

17 Barron & Garcea, "Aboriginal Self-Government," 289-309; see also their *Urban Indian Reserves* and "Reflections on Urban Satellite Reserves."

18 Royal Commission on Aboriginal Peoples (RCAP), *Final Report of the Royal Commission on Aboriginal Peoples* (Ottawa: Queen's Printer, 1996).

19 See Federation of Saskatchewan Indian Nations, *Options for Creating First Nations Urban Development Centres* (Saskatoon: Federation of Saskatchewan Indian Nations, 1993); Federation of Saskatchewan Indians and Saskatchewan Urban Municipalities Association, *Establishing Urban Development Centres* (Saskatoon: Federation of Saskatchewan Indian Nations, 1994).

20 Evelyn J. Peters, ed., *Self-government for Aboriginal People.*

21 See for example the Royal Commission on Aboriginal Peoples.

22 John Weinstein, *Aboriginal Self-Determination Off a Land Base* (Kingston: Institute of Intergovernmental Relations, Queen's University, 1986).

23 Marty Irwin, "A City's Experience with Urban Aboriginal Issues," in *Continuing Poundmaker and Riel's Quest,* eds. Richard Gosse, James Youngblood Henderson & Roger Carter (Saskatoon: Purich Publishing, 1994), 397-402; Terry Mountjoy, "Municipal Government Perspectives on Aboriginal Self-Government," in *Aboriginal Self-Government in Canada: Current Issues and Trends,* 2nd Ed., ed. John H. Hylton (Saskatoon: Purich Publishing, 1999), 310-28; and, Perreaux, "Natives file lawsuit."

24 Ron Merasty, "Indian Reserve Status Granted in Sandy Bay, Deschambault Lake," *Cree Nation News,* 10 July 1996.

25 Canada, *Amended Cost-Sharing Agreement between Canada and Saskatchewan signed as part of the Treaty Land Entitlement Framework Agreement* (Ottawa: Indian and Northern Affairs Canada, 1992).

26 Canada, "Additions to Reserves/New Reserves," Chapter 9 in *Land Management and Procedures Manual* (Ottawa: Indian and Northern Affairs Canada, 1991); and, Canada, *Lands and Trust Services* (August 24, 1998): *Urban Reserves: Presentation to Senior Policy Committee.*

27 Canada, "Additions to Reserves/New Reserves," Chapter 10 in *Land Management and Procedures Manual* (Ottawa: Indian and Northern Affairs Canada, 2003).

28 Canada, *Amended Cost-Sharing Agreement between Canada and Saskatchewan signed as part of the Treaty Land Entitlement Framework Agreement,* 95-96.

29 Red Pheasant First Nation, Rural Municipality of Corman Park (City of Saskatoon, 1999), *Compatible Land Use Agreement* [Mimeographed].

30 Barron & Garcea, "Urban Indian Reserves."

31 *Treaty Land Entitlement Implementation Act,* S.S. 1993, c. T-20.1.

32 Manitoba, *Guide for Municipal-First Nation Development and Services Agreements* (Winnipeg: Department of Rural Development, 1998).

33 Neil Scott, "Urban Reserve ok'd," *Regina Leader-Post,* 1 June 1999.

34 Joe Garcea, *Residential Urban Reserves: Issues and Options for Providing Adequate and Affordable Housing.* Prepared for the Bridges and Foundations Project on Urban Aboriginal Housing in Saskatoon: A Community University Research Alliance Project (CURA), 2004.

35 Canada, "Urban Reserves in Saskatchewan" (Western Economic Diversification Canada, 2006), http://www.wd.gc.ca/rprts/research/urban_reserves/1a_e.asp (accessed 10 September 2007); and, Canada, "Have Urban Reserves Made a Difference?" (Western Economic Diversification Canada, 2006), http://www.wd.gc.ca/rprts/research/urban_reserves/1a_e.asp (accessed 10 September 2007).

36 Thomas, *Report on Implementing Treaty Land Entitlements.*

37 See Irwin, "A City's Experience;" Mountjoy, "Municipal Government Perspectives;" and, Lorne A. Sully & Mark D. Emmons, *Urban Reserves: The City of Saskatoon's Partnership with First Nations.* Presentation to Conference hosted by Pacific Business & Law Institute in Calgary Alberta, 22 April, 2004.

38 Canada, "Urban Reserves in Saskatchewan;" and, Canada, "Have Urban Reserves Made a Difference?"

39 Theresa Dust, *Economic Development on Aboriginal Lands and Land Use Compatibility* (International Municipal Lawyers Association, 2005), http://www.tdust.com/res/econ_dev.pdf (accessed 10 September 2007).

40 City of Regina, *Protocol Declaration of Understanding between the City of Regina and File Hills Qu'Appelle Tribal Council* (2007)[Mimeographed]; and, City of Regina, *Protocol Declaration of Understanding between the City of Regina and File Hills Qu'Appelle Tribal Council* (1998) [Mimeographed].

41 Canada, "Have Urban Reserves Made a Difference?"

Part IV:

Issues and Debates

CONSTITUTIONALIZING THE SPACE TO BE ABORIGINAL WOMEN:

The Indian Act *and the Struggle for First Nations Citizenship*

Jo-Anne Fiske, Ph.D., Dean, School of Graduate Studies
and Professor of Women's Studies and Anthropology, University of Lethbridge

Introduction

In their quest for self-governance, First Nations have faced and continue to face numerous struggles internally and externally. Shaped by complex, and some would argue contradictory, implications of the Canadian Constitution, these struggles take place within a national sociopolitical terrain that on the one hand upholds the ideology of democracy and on the other constrains democratic practices. These struggles take on particular meaning for women as they seek to balance themselves within polarizing views of national and state citizenships that are ambiguously marked by shifting notions of rights and traditions. Acknowledging colonial history and contemporary politics, my focus is twofold: to offer a chronology of the impact of the *Indian Act* on First Nations women and to decode the discursive practices that shape perceptions of Aboriginal[1] women, citizenship, and nationhood. The chapter unfolds as follows: it begins with a history of the sexist implications of the *Indian Act*. It then addresses contemporary provisions of the *Act* and their implications for women's citizenship within evolving measures to advance the quest for self-governance. The chapter then turns to understanding the discursive context that constructs Aboriginal women's perceptions of citizenship, womanhood, and nationhood. By discursive context I mean the socially produced meanings that are embedded within public conversations. The manner in which concepts are framed and deployed have simultaneous political, social, and cultural connotations. Discourse analysis extends our understanding beyond language to embrace the underlying meaning and power affected by social and textual contexts. I conclude with a discussion of emerging notions of citizenship and nationhood that are women-centred and stand in distinction from traditional concepts of citizenship arising from private property and fraternal associations grounded in individual rights.

Impact of the *Indian Act* on First Nation's Women

By upholding implicit and explicit assumptions of fraternal nationhood and patriarchal privilege, legislation that defines 'Indians' and exercises control over them and their lands has had pernicious consequences for generations of women. From the pre-confederation colonial world through to today, women and men are granted different protections and privileges with respect to their rights. Since 1850, "Indian" has been legally defined by a series of colonial and federal acts that provide legislation governing Aboriginal peoples recognized in law as Indians. In early legislation, the term embraced any person of Indian "birth or blood," and anyone alleged to belong to a specific group of Indians including persons married to Indians or adopted into Indian families.[2] From 1857 onward, the concept of "Indianness" and entitlement to registration (that is, to hold Indian status) has been specifically gendered. Colonial governments, guided by patriarchal and racist assumptions, placed family authority in the role of a father/husband whose wife was constituted as his dependant. In consequence, the definition of Indian became narrower and, over time, came to privilege descent through the male line and to privilege men with full citizenship within their First Nation while denying women the same rights to participate in community governance and to enjoy both land and economic benefits.

Social evolutionary premises constructed "progress" as the movement of Aboriginal men toward "civilization" through mimicking masculine attributes of the colonizing society. Government authorities and Christian missionaries marked individual men as "civilized" when they acquired private property, formal schooling, military service, or employment away from their home communities. Always desiring the assimilation of Indian peoples into the Canadian polity, Canada introduced enfranchisement practices for revoking Indian status that were meant to encourage men to embrace Canadian identity and values. Prior to 1960, when all First Nations people registered under the *Indian Act* finally received the right to vote in federal elections, enfranchisement denoted a policy that granted individuals (and in rare cases entire First Nations) Canadian citizenship through voluntarily relinquishing Indian status. Enfranchisement granted individuals property rights and, in post-confederation years, the federal vote. Initially (1857) only men were able to voluntarily enfranchise: in 1918 unmarried women and widows could do so. Enfranchisement was not always voluntary. Canada imposed it upon individuals whose education and employment history qualified them whether they desired it or not.

In 1857, the colonial government stripped status from women married to status Indians, and the children of these marriages, when the husband/father's status was voluntarily or involuntarily revoked. Thus through enfranchisement of their husbands, women were denied any autonomous identity; they were classified automatically as non-status Indians—often without their knowledge—when the men were enfranchised. The *British North America Act* of 1867, now known as the *Constitution Act, 1867,* gave the federal government authority over

Indians and their lands and Canada used this authority to deny legal Indian status to women who married men not holding legal status and to the children of those marriages.

In 1876, Canada consolidated colonial acts into the *Indian Act*. From 1876 to 1985, the *Indian Act* continued to discriminate against women by denying them their rights to Indian status by virtue of marriage to a non-Indian. Under section 12(1)(b), marriage to a status man of another band forced a woman to leave her natal community and to have her membership transferred to her husband's band. Policies regarding voluntary and involuntary enfranchisement of men continued to affect women; at various times they were initiated to rescind the status of men in exchange for voting rights and property ownership. Status was involuntarily revoked when an Indian earned a university degree, practised medicine or law, or entered the Christian clergy.[3] Women who lost status through marriage could only regain status through a successive marriage to a status man. Their daughters might also gain status through marriage to a status man. Under these provisions their sons, of course, could never be registered since men could not gain status through marriage.

The sexual discrimination women endured afflicted them and their children in a number of ways. Women stripped of their status could never return to reside in their home community, share in collective property of their bands, nor even hold the right to burial on reserve lands. Whether widowed or divorced, they remained non-status. Once designated non-status, women no longer enjoyed rights to resources as protected by the *Indian Act*, for example, fishing and hunting rights. Nor did they have access to the education and health benefits provided to status Indians.[4]

Under the *Indian Act*, Canada granted limited governing authority. In a gesture to democratic principles, Indian bands were to be governed by an elected council holding minor capacities to form and enforce civil bylaws and manage access to property. Until 1951, women also suffered further disadvantages under the *Act* with respect to participation in community governance; they could neither vote for the elected chief and council nor hold elected office. In 1956, women gained a degree of privacy insofar as amendments to the *Act* permitted children born out of wedlock to be registered provided they faced no protest. A woman and her out-of-wedlock children were jeopardized if she married a non-Indian. Marriage conferred "legitimacy" on children born prior to the marriage and with it came involuntary loss of status in accordance with the husband/father's standing. This practice remained until challenged in the courts in 1982.[5]

In the 1970s, two cases protesting section 12(1)(b) advanced to the Supreme Court of Canada where they were heard together.[6] In its 1973 decision, the Supreme Court of Canada upheld the sovereign power of Parliament to rule who is/is not Indian, and thereby brought to an end Indian women's access to legal redress in Canada. The offending sections of the *Indian Act* remained and women found themselves in conflict with the major, male-dominated Aboriginal organizations and the leadership of their communities.[7] In consequence, women of Tobique, a Maliseet First Nation of New Brunswick, turned to international law.[8] Sandra Lovelace appealed to the International Human Rights Committee on the grounds that the *Indian Act* violated the International Covenant on Civil and Political Rights. On 30 July 1981, Canada, which had signed the covenant in 1976, was found to breach Indian women's rights "to enjoy their own culture ... religion [and] language."[9] The decision embarrassed Canada and the government moved toward redressing the offending sections of the *Indian Act* while it confronted the growing demand for self-governance and First Nations sovereignty. In 1981, Canada issued a proclamation that foreshadowed legislative reforms that would come four years later. The Governor General's proclamation permitted Indian bands to remove themselves from 12(1)(b). Because each First Nation could decide this issue, Indian women did not have universal access to this provision. Only 19 per cent of Indian bands chose to protect women's interests by suspending 12(1)(b).[10]

The 1985 amendments to the *Act* are commonly known as Bill C-31. The amendments were brought into force to redress the *Act*'s sexist regulations and to bring the *Act* in line with the equality provisions of the *Constitution Act, 1982,* which took effect in 1985. Bill C-31 is a complex piece of legislation that is now perceived as creating a conflict between individual rights and the collective rights of the bands to maintain social, cultural, linguistic, and customary legal practices. The Bill safeguarded the status of all who were registered prior to 1985. As a consequence of C-31, status can no longer be removed or gained upon marriage. Voluntary and involuntary enfranchisement came to an end. However, women who acquired status by marriage prior to 1985 retain it and their rights to band membership. Women of the 19 bands who suspended the application of 12(1)(b) remained registered under 6(1)(a), that is without any change in their original status.

Under section 6(1)(c), women who had lost status when they married out are now entitled to reinstatement of their status and are automatically restored as members of their natal band. Their children, having only one registered parent, gained the right to be placed on the Indian Register under section 6(2). Adult children with 6(2) status are not automatically registered in their mother's band. Their membership depends on the membership rules applying to that band. If the band membership is regulated by Indian and Northern Affairs Canada (INAC), their membership is assured. However, under section 10 of the *Indian Act* if the band regulates its own membership it will regulate the inclusion of individuals registered under 6(2).[11] C-31 has not eliminated sexual inequality between girls and boys born to unmarried Indian men and non-Indian women between September 4, 1951 and April 17, 1985. Girls born in these circumstances are now entitled to be registered, but only under section 6(2). Sons born out of marriage to status fathers fare differently. In 1983, in *Martin* v. *Chapman,* the Supreme Court ruled that "illegitimate" sons could not be treated differently than sons born in wedlock to status fathers. With this ruling, sons born to this combination of parents were entitled to be registered prior to 1985, and thus are now eligible to be registered as 6(1).[12]

Discrimination with respect to entitlements that come with registration through the *Indian Act* remains a barrier to women's equality within First Nations communities. After two successive generations of intermarriage between status and non-status persons, as defined by section 6(2) of the current *Indian Act,* results in the termination of Indian status. Descendants of out-marrying women do not have the same access to status as the descendants of men who married non-Indians. Women who have been reinstated are registered under section 6(1)(c) of the *Act*. Because their non-Indian male spouses have never acquired status, their children are registered as 6(2) and are prohibited from transferring status to the third generation unless they partner with someone who is also registered.

In a further move to control First Nations through regulating Indian status, the federal government introduced the policy requiring mothers to disclose the names of their children's fathers. Documented proof of the father's status is required to determine an infant's registration; if no proof that the father has status is provided, the infant is registered under 6(2) if the mother is 6(1). Of course if the mother is categorized as 6(2), she is unable to register her children unless the listed father is also registered. If the father is not named, the children of a 6(2) mother are not registered. If the parents are both 6(2), the child is registered 6(1), which provides greater possibility of transferring status down the generations.

The consequences of section 6 are complex, and read in light of section 10, which provides for First Nations to write their own membership codes, are seen by some to violate First Nations rights. The complexity of C-31 can be best viewed in light of the court case indexed as *Sawridge Band* v. *Canada (T.D.)*. This case originated in 1986 and remains unresolved. Three Alberta First Nations, Sawridge, Tsuu T'ina, and Ermineskin, challenged Canada's right to determine membership as being in violation of section 35 of the Constitution. The plaintiffs argued that sections 6 to 14.3, both inclusive, of the *Indian Act,* as amended by section 4 of an *Act to Amend the Indian Act,* s.c. 1985, c.27, are inconsistent with the provisions of section 35 of the *Constitution Act, 1982* to the extent that they infringe or deny the right of Indian bands to determine their own membership and therefore to that extent are of no force or effect. The court in turn asserted that there are no existing Aboriginal or treaty rights that provided Indian bands with the power to control membership. Furthermore, had there been such a right, it would have been extinguished by section 35(4), which provides for equality between women and men. The plaintiffs' claim was dismissed. This delighted women whose rights to reinstated membership in the three nations had been disputed. They experienced their exclusion as discrimination based on gender and birth. However, the First Nations' leaders argued that this was not the case; rather their exclusion was grounded in cultural traditions that determined community boundaries. The leaders also argued that the issue at stake was one of self-governance, as discussed further below.

In a press release a few days after the judge gave his decision, the late Chief Walter Twinn of Sawridge denounced the decision as "the most anti-Indian pronouncement of recent judicial history."[13] The plaintiffs' actions, Twinn argued, were neither discriminatory against the women the three First Nations refused to recognize nor against their mixed racial children. Rather, the legal challenge against the *Act* and the *Charter* constituted a defense of the inherent and constitutional rights of First Nations to determine citizenship and to uphold customary practices of membership and identity. The plaintiffs also expressed fear that off-reserve and newly reinstated members could form a voting bloc against long term residents that would shift the economic interests of the status quo.[14] The plaintiffs filed an appeal on 29 September 1995.

The plaintiffs' appeal resulted in a ruling that the trial judge's conduct constituted a reasonable apprehension of bias and a new trial was ordered.[15] In March 2003, the federal court issued a mandatory order to restore band membership to the excluded women. "The plaintiff and the persons on whose behalf she sues, being all the members of the Sawridge Band, are hereby ordered, pending a final resolution of the plaintiff's action, to enter or register on the Sawridge Band List the names of the individuals who acquired the right to be members of the Sawridge Band before it took control of its Band List, with the full rights and privileges enjoyed by all Band members."[16] Canada argued this was necessary to meet the needs of the now elderly women.

Currently, a number of issues respecting evidence are before the courts that will require resolution before the second trial can be heard. The Native Council of Canada, Native Council of Canada (Alberta), Non-Status Indian Association of Alberta, and Native Women's Association of Canada (NWAC) are now interveners in the *Sawridge* case. While NWAC shares concern that First Nations, not the federal government, should exercise authority over membership, it does not accept assertions that the *Sawridge* case is free of gender discrimination. NWAC has long held the view that the equality rights of women and their children must be protected before greater powers pass from Canada to First Nations.[17] At present, the Sawridge First Nation is asking that limits be placed on the interveners in this case.

Sawridge established the social and legal context in which women reinstated under C-31 and their descendants contest limitations on their access to band membership and to Indian status. These conditions are particularly troublesome for women whose children and grandchildren are not registered due to the second generation cut-off and who are affected by the policies regulating disclosure of paternity. As Joyce Green has pointed out in her study of C-31 and the *Sawridge* case, women do not share common views on questions of identity and membership. Nor, she argues, will granting First Nations true control over citizenship protect women's equality any more than federal legislation has done.[18]

The issues taken up by Sawridge First Nation were, in part, addressed recently by the British Columbia Supreme Court. As of 15 June 2007, all of the provisions that treat women and men born before 1985 differently were revoked when Sharon McIvor, a noted Aboriginal lawyer and activist, succeeded in the B.C. Supreme Court in her application to have matrilineal descent recognized as a legitimate claim to Indian status. The court rejected part of the existing legal definition on the grounds that it discriminates against Canadians who trace their Aboriginal roots through their female relatives rather than through their father or grandfather. Madam Justice Ross concluded "that s. 6 of the *1985 Act* violates s. 15(1) of the *Charter* in that it discriminates between matrilineal and patrilineal descendants born prior to April 17, 1985, in the conferring of Indian status, and discriminates between descendants born prior to April 17, 1985, of Indian women who married non-Indian men, and the descendants of Indian men who married non-Indian women." She concluded "that these provisions are not saved by s. 1" and declared "that s. 6 of the *1985 Act* is of no force and effect insofar, and only insofar, as it authorizes the differential treatment of Indian men and Indian women born prior to April 17, 1985, and matrilineal and patrilineal descendants born prior to April 17, 1985, in the conferring of Indian status."[19] Canada has appealed the decision. It is unclear how the legal complexities will be resolved. The future is uncertain and the strategies espoused by women remain varied: for some women, the answer appears to lie in seeking fuller protection from domestic and international human rights laws. For others, the answer is sought through a delicate balancing of traditional laws, sovereignty, and human rights protection.[20]

The *Indian Act* and Self-Government

The move toward greater degrees of self-governance followed the 1985 amendments. Of particular significance for women was the passing of the amendments altering property rights on reserve. In 1999, 14 First Nations signed on to the *First Nations Land Management Act* (FNLMA).[21] The FNLMA, which "provides the term 'first nation' [as meaning] an *Indian Act* band named in a schedule," was signed "in order to improve their capacities and opportunities for economic development." INAC described the legislation as "a government to government agreement within the framework of the constitution of Canada;" it is not a treaty within the meaning of s. 35 of the *Constitution Act, 1982*.[22] Limited protections are provided in general terms for sexual equality with respect to matrimonial property on the breakdown of marriage but not to other property rights. However, as INAC reports, there exist no unequivocal means by which an individual can enforce the mandatory requirements.

The requirement for non-discrimination on the basis of sex refers only to the rules and procedures—not to the law that is ultimately enacted. Furthermore, it is not clear if marriage includes customary and common law relationships. The signatory First Nations are empowered to adopt land codes "pursuant to the custom of the first nation," and effectively withdraw their lands from the *Indian Act*'s management provisions, but it is unclear how conflicts between customs and the matrimonial land provisions might be reconciled.[23] In 1995, Canada adopted the Aboriginal self-government policy that includes law-making authority over marriage and property rights on reserve.[24] Reference to land codes grounded in custom has particular significance for First Nations women who seek *Charter* protection of their rights. The FNLMA is grounded in Canada's self-government policy. Insertion of the term 'first nation' in the legislation is more than symbolic. It is a clear statement of Canada's commitment to a new understanding of government relations and anticipates future devolution of power to First Nations government and increasing autonomy from the *Indian Act*.

The BC Native Women's Association challenged the *Act* in federal court. They argued that the FNMLA violated Canada's fiduciary obligations to Indians which must apply equally to women and men. The issues were whether the Crown owes a fiduciary duty to the plaintiffs, and whether such a fiduciary duty may be delegated. The women lost their case on the grounds that they failed to prove a "recognizable threat" as opposed to a hypothetical or speculative threat.[25] In consequence, many would argue, property rights remain contentious as the federal government now seeks reconciliation between protecting women's matrimonial property rights on terms equitable to provincial law while not undermining First Nations authority as the move toward devolution of federal powers to local governance continues. The AFN in partnership with NWAC began a country-wide consultation process to find remedies to matrimonial property issues. They were directed by INAC to consider legislative solutions if consensus was not reached; however, the AFN "calls for the development of options to recognize and implement First Nations jurisdiction over matrimonial real property on reserve lands."[26]

The social and political tensions that shape emerging forms of self-government are not confined to specific issues of sexist discrimination but embrace additional questions of the entitlements and obligations of all off-reserve First Nations people. Prior to 1999, section 77(1) of the *Indian Act* limited voting rights to band members "ordinarily resident on the reserve." Non-residents protested being denied the right to vote in First Nation council elections on the grounds that this exclusion violated section 15 of the *Charter*. Their protest was upheld when on 20 May 1999, the Supreme Court of Canada (SCC) found section 77(1) of the *Indian Act* to be inconsistent with the section 15 equality provisions of the *Charter*.[27] The decision was rendered in specific reference to "Indian Act band council election." Whether this decision would prevail if new legislation recognized greater powers under self-government is not known, and this ambiguity contributes to arguments that First Nations governments be subject to the *Charter* and potentially the standards of international human rights.

Human rights provisions have failed Aboriginal women in the past. In what was to be a temporary measure, in the 1970s, the *Indian Act* was exempted from the *Canadian Human Rights Act* (CHRA) under section 67 in order for Canada to comply with its commitment not to amend the *Indian Act* before consultations with the National Indian Brotherhood (now AFN) and other Aboriginal organizations were concluded. This shielded both First Nations and Canada from any complaint that arose from discrimination in the *Indian Act*. With the passage of C-31, women with reacquired status have brought complaints of discrimination against First Nations governance that have been dismissed due to this shield. In consequence, it is widely perceived that women more often than men are affected by the absence of human rights protection.[28] Despite several attempts to amend the CHRA, section 67 still stands, with the most recent effort to remedy the situation being made in spring 2007.

As they had done in other circumstances, NWAC took the position that women's rights must be safeguarded and that this is consistent with protections provided by the *Charter*. In their brief to the Human Rights Review Panel, NWAC called for a provision similar to s. 25 of the *Charter*[29] but reminded the panel that

> it should be recognized that some of Canada's most prominent foes of the rights of Aboriginal women have argued that the right to discriminate against and exclude women is part of the traditional heritage of Aboriginal peoples ... any provision drafted pursuant to recommendation 2 should include a safeguard to the same effect as subsection 35(4) of the *Constitution Act, 1982*, that aboriginal and treaty rights are extended equally to men and women. ...[30]

Once again, while all Aboriginal women's groups consulted by the Canadian Human Rights Review Panel (CHRRP) strongly endorsed repeal of section 67, the positions of First Nations governments and the AFN are mixed.[31] The AFN has responded to the current remedy, Bill C-44, with caution. While declaring commitment to human rights and equality, as evidenced in the accord AFN and Canada signed in 2005,[32] AFN challenges Canada to bring forth amendments that balance collective and individual rights, to protect treaty and charter rights, and to provide infrastructure necessary for First Nations to address complaints within the principles of customary laws and social and cultural traditions.[33] The National Aboriginal Section of the Canadian Bar Association worries that bringing First Nations governments under the CHRA will divert scrutiny away from Canada's fiduciary duties, place First Nations under unfair surveillance, render customary law and traditions vulnerable, and undermine protections of the *Indian Act* by opening it up to amendments without due consultation with First Nations—the express concerns raised 30 years ago that originally led to exemption of the *Indian Act* from the CHRA.[34]

The current contestation over the CHRA exemplifies the complex, emotional, gendered legal struggles embodied in reform of the *Indian Act*. Moreover, the political arena is further complicated. First Nations women's battle to achieve full citizenship takes place within legal struggles and sociopolitical arenas marked by a series of discursive maneuvers that frame their claims to citizenship in dichotomous terms. Over the past four decades, women, in particular urban women with restored status, have been construed variously as a threat to and a burden on First Nations communities. The discursive construction of women shapes emerging notions of nationhood and citizenship.

The Discursive Context

First Nations women have been constituted as a threat to self-government on three grounds: imperiling collective rights, undermining cultural differences, and unraveling the special status protected by the *Indian* Act. During the 1970s, women who contested section 12(1)(b) of the *Indian Act* were portrayed as a threat and viewed as traitors. Leading lawyers and political leaders argued women's claim to equality created a tension between individual and collective rights. In 1975, Doug Sanders, a noted legal scholar, attempted to delineate gendered relations in Aboriginal communities through marking clear boundaries around women's rights and roles. Implicitly, he marked Indianness as a male identity and prerogative. In 1984, he carried this position further when he posed the question, "Indian Status: A women's issue or an Indian issue?" and the hostile stage was set. Legal and political discourses thence became embedded in dichotomous gendered thinking that never questioned the nature of men's rights within the collective but implicitly and explicitly assumed masculine collectivity.[35] A fierce legal debate followed that on the one hand acknowledged the provisions in section 12(1)(b) were based on sexual discrimination and on the other argued the need to create limited membership qualifications in order to protect cultural and political boundaries. Sanders, as the legal scholar Whyte had earlier, accepted the premises of patriarchy and male dominance as the normative social order. As early as 1974, Whyte argued that 12(1)(b) "ensured the maintenance of Indian culture and political values," and within the "normal" process of male domination, the section was necessary to protect a "vulnerable enclave." He concluded that sexual equality could be the "instrument of cultural genocide" and did not contest male Indian representation of the women activists' agenda as "sinister."[36]

While this argument was most marked in the resistance of male leadership to women's equality rights, it was not restricted to it, leading to divisions within and between Indian Bands that revealed distinct differences between women who had and those that had not married out. Lines were drawn between status and non-status women on the same grounds as those between married-out women and men: women's identity, citizenship, and rights were seen as acquired through men and marriage out signaled a willingness to leave one's community and identity for another.[37] Some women in reserve communities resisted descriptions of male leadership as biased while others condemned women for speaking out on their own terms.[38]

The dominating legal debate, from the 1970s to the 1990s, positioned collective rights in competition with individual rights. Following the divisive campaign that led up to C-31, the Treaty 8 Group complained that women with restored rights, who could potentially return to reserve communities, would

> ... have little, if any, appreciation of the concept of collective rights. These rights are the pillar of the way of Life of Indian band communities. Crowding reserves with persons who are unfamiliar with or not committed to collective rights will undoubtedly have a deleterious effect upon, if not destroy, our communal lifestyle. WE FEEL THREATENED [emphasis in original].[39]

For the past two decades, politicians and social critics have persisted in the position espoused by the Treaty 8 Group and other First Nations. Reinforcing the notion that reinstatement has occurred on false premises, Karamitsos and Smith declared that C-31 has "blossomed into an all-encompassing call to anyone and everyone with even the slightest native ancestry to reclaim their 'heritage'!"[40] In defense of the Sawridge First Nation's opposition to reinstatement by Canada, they declaim that the effects of reinstatement on "smaller, close-knit bands will be culturally destructive, since the infusion of any new members can radically affect the decision-making process at the council level" and fear the "new members ... will be unable or unwilling to bond with the communal entity of the band" while the smallest of First Nations "will be too small to assimilate them."[41]

Treating women with reacquired rights as 'new' members has also been advocated by Macklem. He represents reinstated women as not sharing the interests of "indigenous difference" with members of their natal community. He presumes that women who have married and moved into another cultural milieu either have lost contact with or never known the culture of their natal communities. He positions them as 'others' by labelling them as "newcomers" or "new members" who by virtue of their numbers "dramatically threaten interests associated with indigenous difference."[42] He advocates against Bill C-31 on the grounds that constitutional protection of cultural difference must take priority over *Charter* guarantees of equality and individualism. Thus he argues "the *Charter* should be interpreted in a manner that respects the constitutional significance of Indigenous difference."[43]

Entwined within arguments regarding cultural difference and collective rights are allegations that activist women, in particular, urban women, have internalized values of white liberal feminism,[44] an argument Isaac and Maloughney cogently summarize as presenting women's rights as a "conflict between imposed 'white' norms and the well-being of all Aboriginal people."[45] Even women whose rights have not been disrupted by loss of their Indian status suffer from the prevailing view that their claims for equity and justice threaten the collective and self-government. Property rights on reserve remain contested; Canada's determination to alter existing practices respecting home ownership, possession of reserve lands, and property rights after marital breakdown have been, and continue to be, viewed by some as merely another of the state's justifications for intruding into First Nations affairs and diminishing the scope and powers of self-governance. In 1986, when writing about the court decisions that provincial matrimonial property laws are not applicable to First Nations reserves, Bartlett captured the very issues that persist today.

> From one perspective the cases, *Derrickson v. Derrickson* and *Paul v. Paul*, did involve a contest between the rights of men and women to share in family property. But at another level the cases involved the question of the right and jurisdiction of the larger society to impose its rules and values upon Indian society. A grant of jurisdiction to the larger society enables and assumes the assimilation of the Indian people and the denial of Indian self-government.[46]

Women's challenges for legal protection within First Nations governance, Bartlett argues, contradict the intent of C-31, for any recognition of women's rights would explicitly be grounded in values of the dominant society and not in First Nations values. By accepting the notion that any claim by First Nations women for equality is foreign to First Nations, he is able to conclude "the restoration of Indian status [will] have meant nothing" should governments external to First Nations erode the potential of self-government in favour of equality of the sexes.[47]

Arguments that women with reacquired status are, or will become, an economic and social burden on their home community underlie perceptions of reinstated women as a threat to collective well-being. These arguments are grounded in the fact that First Nations communities are under-resourced and any additional residents will create untold economic stresses. Women are construed as being "thrust" upon their communities where they "undermine and fracture these communities even further."[48] Political leaders, pressed to provide adequate social and economic resources to their communities, also present the on-reserve housing shortage as just cause to deter reinstated women from residing on reserves.[49] Reinstated women desiring to do so are constructed as a burden on their natal community.[50] Individual communities and national leaders protest that Canada has consistently failed to provide sufficient financial resources, in particular for housing, to accommodate reinstated women and their children who wish to move to the reserve communities.[51]

Despite the AFN's 1984 claim that discrimination against women was imposed upon First Nations and " 'equality' does already exist with the traditional 'citizenship code' of all First Nations people,"[52] gender divisions continue to run deep within struggles for First Nations self-government. In 2001, Rebecca Atkinson described the conflict over self-governance and equality as "a 30-year gender war that has pitted the political aspirations of aboriginal leaders against the rights and needs of female band members."[53]

Gender divisions have, as Borrows illustrates, resulted in a prolonged "dialectical interaction between traditional practices and modern precepts."[54] Within this discursive context, wherein women struggle not only against the colonial legacy of sexism and patriarchy but also against political and scholarly discourses that deny their authentic identity and cultural affiliation, oppositional discourses have surfaced that locate women at the centre of society and advocate a new understanding of citizenship and First Nationhood. The discourses simultaneously contest allegations of cultural outsiders insensitive to collective well-being and the allegations of assimilation into dominant feminism. Nurture and kinship are primary organizing concepts around which they theorize citizenship and nationhood within a women-centered presentation of tradition.

Citizenship and Nationhood

Aboriginal women give primacy to principles of care and responsibility in their construction of gendered traditions and social cohesion. These assertions are found across the political spectrum, from the anti-feminist position of Monture-Angus[55] to the pro-feminist activism of the Native Women's Association of Canada.[56] Through the deployment of kinship, Aboriginal women locate themselves at the centre of Aboriginal community and survival. Aboriginal women criticized as being individualistic for their activism imagine motherhood beyond narrow patriarchal definitions. Mothering, they argue, is not a practice restricted to nuclear family obligations or even to extended kinship relations. Rather, mothering stands as the social praxis that offers care for all community members from infants to elders. Care-giving relations arise from kin relations and extend beyond to intergenerational transfer of traditional knowledge and spirituality, which are the foundations of identity. Lavell-Harvard and Corbiere Lavell, for example, explicitly politicize reproductive labour as they claim Aboriginal mothering is essential to Aboriginal survival. Writing of the "commonality of difference" Aboriginal mothers share, they assert "... Aboriginal mothers specifically, are distinguished from other Canadians by particular legal statuses and historical, social, and cultural experiences."[57]

NWAC advances a similar position. In the 1980s, to counter the divisive stance adopted by Native Indian Brotherhood (later the Assembly of First Nations) and to make their position more palatable to male leaders who opposed women's return to their communities, the Native Women's Association Canada adopted an ideology of traditional motherhood.[58] Arguing that mothering extends from care of infants to wider community responsibilities, women of the Native Women's Association positioned themselves as acting within the traditional responsibilities of mothers, grandmothers, aunties, and sisters, a stance reinforced in recent position papers.[59] NWAC proclaims its obligations to Aboriginal nationhood as caregivers and leaders and represent their association as

> a 'Grandmother's lodge'. In this Grandmother's Lodge we as Aunties, Mothers, Sisters, Brothers, and Relations collectively recognize, respect, promote, defend, and enhance our Native ancestral laws, spiritual beliefs, language, and traditions given to us by the Creator.[60]

Insofar as the extended family is vital to individual well-being so is the nation. Without the sacrifice of nurturing relations, Aboriginal peoples cannot survive as distinct peoples united by collective values and reciprocal relations of obligations between women and men. The Ontario Native Women's Association expressed this cogently in their study of violence against women: "The extended family is vital to our Nations; it is the premise of our community-life. The welfare of any one of our members of our communities is important to everyone."[61]

Bysiewicz and Van de Mark also view the responsibility to nurture not only as the pivotal action upon which community revolved in the past, but also as the essential relationship that has allowed Aboriginal societies to survive the physical, mental, social/cultural, and spiritual violence of colonialism and neocolonialism.[62] This theme is repeated by McGadney-Douglass, Apt, and Douglass. Indigenous caregiving, they claim, is found globally as an expression of a social order grounded in the people's relationships to the creator, Mother Earth, and to one another. Relationships are envisioned within a spiritual frame that epitomizes the holistic world view espoused by Aboriginal peoples.[63] For self-governments to be Aboriginal they must be structured in the interests of women and men and take into account traditions women espouse as well as those advanced by men. Contrary to the criticisms brought against them, women espouse a classical discourse of nationhood: a unity founded in common history, shared culture and language, descent, and place of origin.

Napoleon moves the discussion of citizenship and nationhood beyond metaphors of kinship and caregiving as she embraces the concept of relational autonomy. First proposed by feminist theorist, Jennifer Nedelsky,[64] relational autonomy envisions "an understanding of autonomy that recognizes the inherently social nature of human beings."[65] By recognizing the complexity of social relations, Aboriginal people can "develop and sustain the capacity to find their own internal law, and ... figure out what social relationships and personal practices foster this capability."[66] Within this paradigm, Aboriginal women's struggle for emancipation from colonialism through participatory citizenship grounded in tradition is not only feasible, it is a constitutional right. As Greschner asserts, constitutional rights "are a promise of constitutional space for aboriginal peoples to be aboriginal."[67] To women, this means a space for Aboriginal citizenship and nationhood that draws from traditional principles that respect and honour women and men and value equally gender-distinct contributions to society.

Constitutional space to be Aboriginal as defined by feminine principles of care and equality dissolves the allegations that protection of human rights is contrary to protection of collective well-being and Aboriginal cultural difference. This is particularly true of Bill C-31 and the return of women and their families to their natal communities. Protection of human rights is not in conflict with traditions women espouse. Napoleon contends that, "pre-contact aboriginal societies practiced forms of nationhood that were deliberately inclusive in order to build strong nations with extensive international ties."[68] She argues that the exclusive practices of the current and past *Indian Act* regimes could not have had traditional precedents; without intermarriage between pre-contact societies survival would have been impossible. Although the restoration of Indian status can be construed as an example of individualism and 'white' or liberal values, it can also be understood as bringing families together and thus as consistent with traditional actions that strengthen Aboriginal caring practices. Growth in populations that followed from restoration of status is as much a continuity of Aboriginal practice as an intrusion of external values. Ladner makes this case in reference to Blackfoot women and nationalism, and argues that there is considerable evidence to suggest that, traditionally, Aboriginal societies not only embraced democracy and respect for individual freedoms but that these values "wielded an enormous influence over Eurocentric traditions."[69]

From the perspective of Ladner and Napoleon, Aboriginal women's human rights are inseparable from their rights and responsibilities as Aboriginal women. Their citizenship within First Nations merges with the broader context of Aboriginal identity: it is the sum of their identities that defines their citizenship. Within the frame of caregiving and women's responsibilities and leadership citizenship is reconceived. Citizenship takes on new meanings in shifting neocolonial relations and imagined postcolonial futures as Aboriginal women struggle to (re)gain central roles in self-governing nations. Writing of the Blackfoot, Ladner asserts a holistic view of nationality and citizenship that embraces this view.

> According to the Elders, it is a world where women were members of society, where all people (human beings and non-human beings) regardless of gender were respected and honoured for the gifts they were given by the Creator and for the roles they played within the circle of life. It was a world where women existed at the centre of society—economically, spiritually, politically, and culturally. It was a society in which women could choose their own path in life, as wives, mothers, spiritual leaders, as owners of property, even as warriors and chiefs.... Moreover, Siiksikaawa nationalism did not emerge in a manner that excluded women or relegated them to a subordinate position as mere producers of nationalists.[70]

Napoleon reminds us that Aboriginal constructs of citizenship differ dramatically from western precepts grounded in liberal democracy, which structure society and political regimes in hierarchical relationships. Divergent cosmologies account for fundamental differences. "For instance, many aboriginal nations make no fundamental distinction between the history of humans and the history of the world, and they fuse human power with the power of the land."[71] Recognition of commonalities in cosmology, however, must not ignore cultural and legal distinctions between Aboriginal peoples. As First Nations articulate new formations of citizenship and nationhood, they must imagine themselves beyond discourses of tradition and competing rights to take up new concepts of law and social relations. Power within communities and between communities must be reconfigured to address the barriers to women's participation in Aboriginal societies' core institutions.

Green's analysis of citizenship and rights addresses the complexity of women's struggles within the frame of on-going discrimination within the hierarchal powers of the state. She addresses the constraints women face as they struggle to reconceptualize their identity and First Nations citizenship. To exclude women from the process by which First Nations "*will* their existence and determine [their] collective forms," denies them the defining feature of citizenship and the fundamental right citizenship is meant to protect: the right "*to be.*"[72] Thus, she argues, Canada's obligation is to protect Aboriginal women's rights in their specificity: as Aboriginal women located in particular communities asserting their identity and benefiting from specified treaty and Aboriginal rights. Her argument recognizes the centrality of Aboriginal identity for women and the centrality of women to Aboriginal citizenship and nationhood. This raises two questions: How should women's citizenship be conceptualized? Will women-centred Aboriginal citizenship fundamentally alter Aboriginal women's location within state relations of power?

Women-centred visions of the past and future have been conceptualized under a number of terms: gynocentric, matriarchal, matri-centred, gender egalitarian, for example. Each of these terms can be opposed to male-centred views that seek to represent patriarchy as a 'natural' bias that protects Aboriginal cultures from dissolution through assimilation and to arguments that pre-contact societies were marked by male privilege and domination.[73] However, these fail to offer a theoretical basis for developing models of citizenship and nationhood, as both Green and Napoleon have demonstrated.[74] Citizenship most frequently connotes assigned membership in a nation state either through birth (*jus soli*) or ethnicity (*jus sanguinis*) or an acquired membership through processes of naturalization, whereby a person acquires a different citizenship than the one assigned at birth. In democratic countries, citizenship grants rights to political participation through holding the vote in national and subnational polities and through citizen consultation in legislative and policy reform. Green also worries that reconceptualizing citizenship may not provide a viable solution. Citizenship, she asseverates, is "an elastic term that is being stretched past recognition."[75] Application of the term has moved beyond defining membership in a state and the rights and duties that arise from it to

> include relationships within the state between communities, and the state's obligation to pursue for its citizens and communities the ideals articulated in international law to which Canada is signatory, as well as the rights and freedoms contained in the Canadian Charter of Rights and Freedoms.[76]

In this context, Aboriginal women are challenged to conceptualize citizenship in terms that can confront antagonistic discourses of Aboriginal male leadership and discriminatory practices of the state.

Earlier I argued that the premises of nationhood postulated by NWAC among others could be conceptualized as a 'feminine nationhood'. I argued that nationhood grounded in western democracy historically has referred implicitly to a fraternity, as for example in the French traditions.[77] Fraternity connotes a male-centred nation where collective and individual rights merge (often unconsciously) in the conflation of a male national identity and state defined rights, privileges, and obligations. Aboriginal women contest these premises and practices as they argue for an Aboriginal nationhood and citizenship grounded in traditional premises that honour women and place women's reproductive roles at the centre of society.[78] Because women's location within the nation cannot be taken for granted, "women's virtues have to be enunciated and defended. For it is on this very basis they are denied full humanity; they are alienated from nationhood by their sexuality and reproductive capacity."[79] I now suggest that emerging notions of relational citizenship in conjunction with politicization of women's reproductive labour within state-wide and global leadership might be more aptly captured by the concepts 'caring citizenship' and 'sororeal nationhood,'[80] which refer to a consciousness of identity and membership grounded in relationships of mutual respect and responsibility and constituted through women united by sisterhood whether through kinship or social ties.

As Tronto has argued, expanding notions of citizenship grapple with values of inclusion based on rights and obligations that address notions of identity, the common good and social participation.[81] The concept of caring citizenship builds on the latter principles and in particular addresses these from a woman-centred perspective. While this is foreign to western democratic praxis, Aboriginal women view their reproductive and voluntary work within a frame of communal relations and cultural continuity carried out within traditional values. Thus caring citizenship is grounded in metaphors of essential womanhood and kinship but extends beyond relations in Aboriginal nations to address values and virtues of civic leadership devoted to cultural and social survival within the state and the neo-colonial relations that form the global economy. Citizenship takes on new meanings in shifting neocolonial relations and imagined postcolonial futures as

Aboriginal women struggle to (re)gain central roles in self-governing nations. Aboriginal citizenship is envisioned in terms that resonate with egalitarian, complementary relations of precolonial life. It has come to mean membership in a community with balanced sites of power, where authenticating discourses that construct nationhood and define national culture are defined from women's perspectives in harmony with male views. As early as 1988, NWAC opposed Canada's control over First Nations citizenship and composed model citizenship codes based on traditional practices that sought gender balance and complementarily.[82] In keeping with this vision, women's claims for equality within Aboriginal nations are grounded in collective social responsibilities including a responsibility to be leaders along side men.[83]

I coined the term 'feminine nationhood' to embrace the discourse that Aboriginal women had advanced. On the one hand they spoke in opposition to what they saw as male privilege within the nation state, First Nations, and their quasi-political male dominated association the Assembly of First Nations. On the other they distinguished themselves from prevailing ideologies of mothering and womanhood in the dominant society. I now move beyond my earlier understanding to propose 'sororeal nationhood' to capture emerging articulations of women's reproductive and altruistic practices as the core relationship upon which communities are founded, survive, and interrelate across state boundaries. Just as notions of fraternal citizenship signify national ties grounded in human rights and democratic participation, sororeal nationhood draws on sisterhood expressed through global Indigenous commonalities. By reconceptualizing citizenship and nationhood, Aboriginal women are moved to argue for new forms of civic relations that would embrace harmonious ways of thought, living, and being. They emphasize partnerships and participatory politics and remind us that patriarchal models of family and nationhood are not inevitable.

Emerging concepts of citizenship and nationhood grounded in Indigenous women's specificity are commensurate with international law. Just as Greschner asserts that Canadian constitutional rights promise the constitutional space for Aboriginal peoples to be Aboriginal, on a global scale international law offers the same promise. Consistent with these concepts of citizenship and nationhood is the duty of states to protect women and children from violations of their rights as members of Indigenous nations existing within the state. Understanding women in relation to multiple kinship roles and their care-giving obligations places them fully within the collective as protected by international covenants on Aboriginal rights and as realized through human rights protection.

While the significance of developing new discourses of citizenship and nationhood should not be discounted, the context in which they emerge must not be overlooked.[84] Aboriginal women's citizenship within First Nations communities and the challenges of self-governance cannot be isolated from their position within the nation state. Currently, the barriers First Nations women confront are exacerbated by recent actions of the state that constrain democratic measures. Two notably affect women: the stance adopted by Status of Women Canada with respect to political advocacy, and the withdrawal of the Court Challenges Program. In the past, First Nations women turned to the policy research branch of Status of Women Canada. This research program established an Aboriginal women's advisory group to address critical and urgent policy issues, including self-government, health, *Indian Act* reform, and a range of other topics. The mandate of the research branch included disseminating research results to key policy offices throughout the federal government, having copies of work posted on their website and providing free copies to women's organizations, educational institutions, and public libraries. Equally problematic for First Nations women, Status of Women Canada has removed from its mandate equality issues and support for social advocacy.

The same women were further disempowered when the government withdrew funding formerly available under the Charter Challenges program. The Court Challenges Program has been an important source of funding for individuals and equality-seeking organizations to ensure that the rights of marginalized and vulnerable groups are protected under the *Charter of Rights and Freedoms*. Without this important source of support, the capacity of First Nations women to advance their Aboriginal and equality rights have been greatly undermined. Recourse to international law is available only when appeals to domestic law have been exhausted. Aspirations for participatory democracy are hindered; when access to legal redress is denied, women's lives within their community are sorely diminished. Denial of the protections of international law, as Sandra Lovelace has demonstrated, restricts women's social and political participation in their First Nations communities. Discontinuance of the Court Challenges Program brings into question Canada's recognition of First Nations as "peoples" and their right to self-determination insofar as it denies avenues of redress for First Nations women struggling for citizenship within their communities. Denial of protections also reminds us that the impact of women-centred citizenship within First Nations will not by itself address their disadvantaged location within the relations of power of the Canadian state.

Conclusion

Aboriginal women's struggles for full citizenship within First Nations and the nation state have been stymied by the underlying assumptions of a fraternal nationhood and its constraints on caring citizenship. Strategies denying women full rights are ostensibly grounded in past Eurocentric, patriarchal practices that subordinated women to the rule of father and husband. However, the colonial legacy runs deeper within both nation state and First Nations politics. As Canada moves, however awkwardly, toward affirming self-governance for First Nations communities as constituted through the *Indian Act*, it continues to fail Aboriginal women. Their location as minorities within minorities is not addressed.

Hierarchies of domination persist that compel them to simultaneously address social dislocation within their nations of origin and within the state. Protection under human rights legislation remains limited and ambiguous, confounded by a lack of clarity of the meaning and scope of self-governance. This position renders First Nations women vulnerable to attacks that their claims for women-centred citizenship lack Aboriginal authenticity even as they are seen to be calling for a privileged location within the state contrary to principles of democratic equality. Expanded forms of relational citizenship, which I have conceptualized as sororeal, through appealing to global commonalities in Indigenous women's historic experience as defined within Indigenous cosmologies offer the hope of resolution of the doubly disadvantaged position from which Aboriginal women in Canada assert their Aboriginal and human rights to be Aboriginal.

Notes

1   The terms Aboriginal and First Nations are used interchangeably except where specific use of First Nation is found in legislation and policy or in reference to specific First Nations. Indian is used only where it follows from use in law and past policies. Indigenous is employed to reference international meanings such as are found in nongovernmental organizations and international law.

2   Megan Furi & Jill Wherret, *Indian Status and Band Membership Rules* (Ottawa: Parliamentary Research Branch, Library of Parliament, 2003), 2.

3   *Ibid.*

4   Kathleen Jamieson, *Indian Women and the Law: Citizens Minus* (Ottawa: Minister of Supply and Services, 1978).

5   Larry Gilbert, *Entitlement to Indian Status and Membership Codes in Canada* (Scarborough: Carswell, 1996), 57.

6   *Attorney General of Canada* v. *Lavell; Isaac* v. *Bédard*, [1973], 38 D.L.R. (3d) 481 (also reported: 23 C.R.N.S. 197, 11 R.F.L. 333, [1974] S.C.R. 1349).

7   Jamieson, *Indian Women and the Law.*

8   Janet Silman, *Enough is Enough: Aboriginal Women Speak Out* (Toronto: Women's Press, 1987).

9   *Lovelace* v. *Canada* [1981] 36 U.N. GAOR Sup. No. 40 annex XVIII at 166, R.D. Doc. A/36/.4/.0. Sandra Lovelace Nichols was appointed to the Canadian Senate by then-Prime Minister Paul Martin in 2005. She earned this honour in recognition of her achievements as "a driving force in securing rights for Aboriginal women in Canada, and is also a wonderful example of the impact one woman can have when she sets out to correct an injustice."

10   Bonita Lawrence, *"Real" Indians and Others: Mixed-Blood Urban Native Peoples and Indigenous Nationhood* (Lincoln NE: University of Nebraska Press, 2004), 61.

11   Furi & Wherret, *Indian Status and Band Membership Rules,* 5.

12   *Ibid.*, 6; and Gilbert, *Entitlement to Indian Status,* 53.

13   Native Council of Canada, Comment. "Classroom edition: Topic Bill C-31," *Windspeaker,* 1995.

14   *Ibid.*

15   *Sawridge Band* v. *Canada* [1997] 3.F.C 583 (C.A.).

16   *Sawridge Band* v. *Canada* [2003] 4 F.C. 748.

17   Sharon McIvor, "Aboriginal Women Unmasked: Using Equality Legislation to Advance Women's Rights," *Canadian Journal of Women and the Law,* 16 (2004): 113.

18   Joyce Green, "Exploring Identity and Citizenship: Aboriginal Women, Bill C-31 and the Sawridge Case" (Ph.D. diss., University of Alberta, 1997); and her "Constitutionalizing the Patriarchy: Aboriginal Women and Aboriginal Government," in *Expressions in Canadian Native Studies,* eds. Ron F. Laliberte et al (Saskatoon: University of Saskatoon Extension Press, 2004), 328-54.

19   *McIvor* v. *The Registrar, Indian and Northern Affairs Canada,* (2007) B.C.S.C. 827.

20   McIvor, "Aboriginal Women Unmasked"; Green, "Exploring Identity and Citizenship"; Jo-Anne Fiske & Evelyn George, *Seeking Alternatives to Bill C-31: From Cultural Trauma to Cultural Revitalization through Customary Law* (Ottawa: Status of Women Canada, 2006).

21   S.C. 1999, c.24.

22   Indian and Northern Affairs Canada, Discussion Paper: "Matrimonial Real Property on Reserves",

http://www.ainc-inac.gc.ca/pr/pub/matr/fnl_e.html (accessed 19 June 2007).

23 *Ibid.*

24 Jill Wherret, *Aboriginal Self-Government* (Ottawa: Parliamentary Research Branch, Library of Parliament, Ottawa, 1996).

25 *B.C. Native Women's Society v. Canada* [2000] 1 F.C. 304 (T.D.).

26 Assembly of First Nations, *Matrimonial Real Property: Our Lands, Our Families Our Solutions,* http://www.afn.ca/article.asp?id=3069 (accessed 19 October 2007).

27 *Corbiere v. Canada* [1999] 2 S.C.R. 203.

28 Wendy Cornet, "First Nations Governance, the Indian Act and Women's Equality Rights," in *First Nations Women, Governance and the Indian Act: A Collection of Policy Research Reports* (Ottawa: Status of Women Canada, 2001), 117-66.

29 Section 25 reads "The guarantee in this Charter of certain rights and freedoms shall not be construed so as to abrogate or derogate from any aboriginal, treaty or other rights or freedoms that pertain to the aboriginal peoples of Canada including (a) any rights or freedoms that have been recognized by the Royal Proclamation of October 7, 1763; and, (b) any rights or freedoms that now exist by way of land claims agreements or may be so acquired."

30 Mary Eberts, *Aboriginal Women's Rights are Human Rights* (Ottawa: NWAC, 2005).

31 Canadian Human Rights Review Panel, *Promoting Equality: A New Vision* (Ottawa: Department of Justice, 2000), 129.

32 On 31 May 2005, the Government of Canada and the Assembly of First Nations signed a Political Accord. The Accord is based on 11 principles "that are to be read together and are mutually supportive." These principles include: upholding the honour of the crown; constitutionalism and the rule of law; and recognition of the inherent right of self-government and Aboriginal title. The eighth principle, "Human Rights," states: First Nations and Canada are committed to respecting human rights and applicable international human rights instruments. It is important that all First Nations citizens be engaged in the implementation of their First Nation government, and that First Nation governments respect the inherent dignity of all their people, whether elders, women, youth or people living on or away from reserves.

33 Assembly of First Nations, *First Nations Perspectives on Bill C-44 (Repeal of Section 67 of the Standing Committee on Aboriginal Affairs and Northern Development)*, www.afn.ca/misc/C-44.pdf (accessed 19 October 2007).

34 Canadian Bar Association, National Aboriginal Section, Submission on Bill C-44 *Canadian Human Rights Act* Amendments (application to the Indian Act), http://64.233.167.104/search?q=cache:Ao-74Z-XB0UJ:www.cba.org/CBA/submissions/pdf/07-23-eng.pdf+AfN+c-44&hl=en&ct=clnk&cd=9&gl=ca (accessed 19 October 2007).

35 Douglas Sanders, "Indian Women: A Brief History of their Roles and Rights," *McGill Law Journal* 21 (1975): 656-672; and, "Indian Status: An Indian Issue or a Women's Issue?" *Canadian Native Law Reporter* 3 (1984): 30-39.

36 John Whyte, "The Lavell Case and Equality in Canada," *Queens Quarterly* 81 (1974): 33.

37 Judith Sayers & Kelly MacDonald, "A Strong and Meaningful Role for First Nations Women in Governance," in *First Nations Women, Governance and the Indian Act: A Collection of Policy Research Reports* (Ottawa: Status of Women Canada, 2001), 16; and Dan Russell, *A People's Dream: Aboriginal Self-government in Canada* (Vancouver: UBC Press, 2000), 132.

38 Margaret Jackson, "Aboriginal Women and Self-government," in *Aboriginal Self-government in Canada: Current Trends and Issues,* ed. John. H. Hylton (Saskatoon: Purich Publishing, 1994), 188.

39 Quoted by Michael McDonald, "Indian Status: Colonialism or Sexism?" *Canadian Community Law Journal* 9 (1986): 25-6; original in *Globe and Mail*, 2 April 1985.

40 Keith Karamitsos & Melvin H. Smith, "Opening the Floodgates: Bill C-31 and Native Membership," *Options Politiques* (December 1997): 40.

41 *Ibid.*, 42.

42 Patrick Macklem, *Indigenous Difference and the Constitution of Canada* (Toronto: University of Toronto Press, 2001), 130.

43 *Ibid.*, 227.

44 Katherine Beatty Chiste, "Aboriginal Women and Self-government: Challenging Leviathan," *American Indian Culture and Research Journal* 18, no. 3 (1984): 19-43.

45 Thomas Isaac & Mary Sue Maloughney, "Dually Disadvantaged and Historically Forgotten?: Aboriginal Women and the Inherent Right of Aboriginal Self-government," *Manitoba Law Journal* 21 (1992): 461; see also John Borrows, "Contemporary Traditional Equality: The Effect of the *Charter* on First Nations Politics," *University of New Brunswick Law Journal* 43 (1994): 31.

46 Richard H. Bartlett, "Indian Self-government, the Equality of the Sexes, and Application of Provincial Matrimonial Property Laws," *Canadian Journal of Family Law* 5, (1986): 188.

47 *Ibid.*, 195.

48 Glen S. Coulthard, "Culture, Consent, and the State in the Struggles of Indigenous Peoples for Recognitions and Self-Determination: Social Constructivism and the Politics of Critique," 11, http://www.law.uvic.ca/demcon/papers/Essentialism.doc (accessed 19 October 2007).

49 Chiste, "Aboriginal women and self-government," 39.

50 Borrows, "Contemporary traditional equality," 36-7.

51 Jamieson, *Indian Women and the Law,* 132; Russell, *A People's Dream,* 132; Macklem, *Indigenous Difference and the Constitution,* 229.

52 Borrows, "Contemporary Traditional Equality" 31.

53 Jim West, *Aboriginal Women at the Crossroads,* First Nation Drum [2002], http://www.firstnationsdrum.com/Fall2002/PolWomen.htm.

54 Borrows "Contemporary Traditional Equality," 31.

55 Patricia Monture-Angus, *Thunder in my Soul: A Mohawk Woman Speaks* (Halifax: Fernwood Publishing, 1995); and *Journeying Forward: Dreaming First Nations' Independence* (Halifax: Fernwood Publishing, 1999).

56 Native Women's Association of Canada, *Violence against Aboriginal Women and Girls: An Issue Paper,* http://www.nwac-hq.org/en/documents/nwac-vaac.pdf (accessed 19 October 2007).

57 D. Memee Lavell-Harvard & Jeannette Corbiere Lavell, eds. *Until our Hearts are on the Ground: Aboriginal Mothering, Oppression, Resistance and Rebirth* (Toronto: Demeter Press, 2006).

58 Jo-Anne Fiske, "The Womb is to the Nation as the Heart is to the Body: Ethnopolitical Discourses of the Canadian Indigenous Women's Movement," in *Feminism, Political Economy and the State: Contested Terrain,* eds. Pat Armstrong & M. Patricia Connelly (Toronto: Canadian Scholars' Press, 1999), 293-325; Lilianne Krosenbrink-Gellissen, *Sexual Equality as an Aboriginal Right: The Native Women's Association of Canada and the Constitutional Process on Aboriginal Matters, 1982-1987* (Saarbrucken: Verlag Breithenbach, 1991).

59 Native Women's Association of Canada, *Violence Against Aboriginal Women and Girls,* 3, 12.

60 Native Women's Association of Canada, *Voice of Aboriginal Women: Aboriginal Women Speak out about Violence* (Ottawa: Canadian Council on Social Development and Native Women's Association Canada, 1991), 22.

61 Ontario Native Women's Association, *Breaking Free: A Proposal for Change to Aboriginal Family Violence* (Thunder Bay, ON: Author, 1989), 45.

62 S. Bysiewicz & R. Van de Mark, "The legal status of the Dakota Indian woman," *American Indian Law Review* 3 (1977): 262.

63 Brenda F. McGadney-Douglass, Nana Araba Apt, & Richard L. Douglass, "Back to the Basics: Mothering and Grandmothering in the Context of Urban Ghana," in *Until our Hearts are on the Ground: Aboriginal Mothering, Oppression, Resistance and Rebirth,* eds. D. Memee Lavell-Harvard and Jeannette Corbiere Lavell (Toronto: Demeter Press, 2006), 105.

64 Jennifer Nedelsky, "Reconceiving Autonomy: Sources, Thoughts and Possibilities," *Yale Journal of Law and Feminism* 1, no. 1 (1989): 1.

65 Val Napoleon, "Aboriginal self-determination: Individual selves and collective selves," *Atlantis* 29, no. (2005): 5.

66 *Ibid.*

67 Donna Greschner, "Aboriginal Women, the Constitution and Criminal Justice," *University of B.C. Law Review,* Special Edition on Aboriginal Justice (1992): 342.

68 Napoleon, "Aboriginal self-determination," 10.

69 Kiera Ladner, "Women and Blackfoot nationalism," *Journal of Canadian Studies* 35, no. 2 (2000): 37.

70 Ladner 2000, 36.

71 Napoleon, "Aboriginal self-determination," 17.

72 Green, "Constitutionalizing the Patriarchy," 716.

73 Paula Gunn Allen, *The Sacred Hoop: Recovering the Feminine in Native American Traditions* (Boston: Beacon Press, 1986); and, Monture-Angus, *Thunder in my Soul: A Mohawk Woman Speaks* and *Journeying Forward: Dreaming First Nations' Independence.*

74 Green, "Constitutionalizing the Patriarchy"; and, Napoleon, "Aboriginal self-determination."

75 Green, "Constitutionalizing the Patriarchy," 736.

76 *Ibid.*, 721-22.

77 Fiske, "The Womb is to the Nation as the Heart is to the Body."

78 See for example Leanne Simpson, "Birthing an Indigenous Resurgence: Decolonizing our pregnancy and birthing ceremonies," in *Until our Hearts are on the Ground: Aboriginal Mothering, Oppression, Resistance and Rebirth,* eds. D. Memee Lavell-Harvard & Jeannette Corbiere Lavell (Toronto: Demeter Press, 2006), pp. 25-33.

79 Fiske, "The Womb is to the Nation as the Heart is to the Body," 304.

80 The terms fraternal and sororeal are drawn from the Latin for brother and sister respectively. Fraternal notions of citizenship and nationhood have a long history in European nation-states. The battle cry of the French revolution, "liberté, égalité, fraternité," is perhaps the best known example of explicit association of male kinship with democratic citizenship. Associated with the French Revolution in 1789, it remained a primary slogan of subsequent struggles for freedom in France during the 19th century. Fraternity is used in metaphorical terms

and has not been explicated with respect to citizenship in First Nations, although as I have demonstrated elsewhere it is an underlying if unspoken assumption guiding visions of a future third order of government (Fiske 1999); see also Dana D. Nelson, *National Manhood: Capitalist Citizenry and the Imagined Fraternity of Whitemen* (Durham, NC: Duke University Press, 1998). Sororeal, on the other hand, does not emerge in discussion of citizenship and has no precedent in European political philosophy or application to the constitution of the citizenry of any nation-state with European roots. As will be elaborated below, I apply it here in contradistinction to implicit notions of fraternity and as a way of capturing Aboriginal women's explicit referencing of kinship ties as the source of nationhood. Fraternity is defined in the Oxford English Dictionary as "brotherliness" and "set of men of the same class"; notably sororeal is not listed.

81 Joan Tronto, "Care as the Work of Citizens: A Modest Proposal," in *Women and Citizenship*, ed. Marilyn Friedman (New York: Oxford University Press, 2005): 130-48.

82 Mary Ellen Turpel, "Aboriginal Peoples and the Canadian Charter of Rights and Freedoms: Contradictions and Challenges," *Canadian Woman Studies* 10, nos. 2&3 (1989), 154-5.

83 Krosenbrink-Gellissen, *Sexual Equality as an Aboriginal Right*, 93; Fiske, 1999.

84 Mary Ellen Turpel, "Patriarchy and paternalism: the legacy of the Canadian state for First Nations women," *Canadian Journal of Women and the Law* 6, no. 1 (1993): 174-92.

THE SIGNIFICANCE OF BUILDING LEADERSHIP AND COMMUNITY CAPACITY TO IMPLEMENT SELF-GOVERNMENT

Brian Calliou, Banff Centre,
Aboriginal Leadership and Management Program

Aboriginal self-government is a major issue for Aboriginal peoples, and is also a major policy issue for the Canadian state. However, much of the literature on Aboriginal self-government addresses either the legal or political context. There has been far less focus on how to effectively implement self-government.[1] This article is an attempt to explore some of the issues that must be addressed to actually implement self-government in an effective and efficient matter, that is, to actually do the stuff of self-government.

The global certainly affects the local. In the current highly technological and competitive global economy, there is a growing need for Aboriginal communities to build the capacity to deal effectively in the world system. Aboriginal leaders must also build their own leadership capacity to communicate with multiple levels of governments, industry, and a global economic market. Capacity-building would see Aboriginal leaders develop leadership competencies, in particular, the knowledge, skills, attitudes, beliefs, and values that help communities meet the current challenges of contemporary life. In developing these competencies, Aboriginal leaders need not discard their traditional principles. Rather, they could reconcile the modern tools with their cultural needs.[2] In this way, leaders have the knowledge and skills to successfully lead their communities and organizations into the modern, global environment while achieving and maintaining their own vision of self-government.

Self-Government

The literature regarding Aboriginal self-government is growing rapidly,[3] reflecting a variety of approaches. The federal government negotiates self-government agreements according to a particular policy approach and framework that results in a restricted delegation of federal powers, akin to a municipal style of government.[4] On the other hand, Aboriginal communities generally begin from the perspective that such policies and frameworks are too restrictive and instead argue that they have an inherent right to self-government based on their original sovereignty or rights as peoples.[5] Although Aboriginal leaders generally say that it is too restrictive, some legal commentators are exploring a more effective use of the *Indian Act*.[6] Yet another approach is to negotiate self-government as part of a modern land claim agreement or treaty[7]; or to see healing and health as a prerequisite for the success of self-government and economic development.[8] Similarly, there are arguments that self-government starts with strong individuals, who take responsibility for their families and communities, and require overcoming the negative effects of oppression by the state.[9] Yet another approach sees institutions such as private property as the key to self-government.[10] Finally, self-government can be discussed as political pluralism where Aboriginal peoples seek equality as governments, more power in their relations with other governments, and the respect to construct their own identity.[11] All these approaches examine various aspects of Aboriginal self-government that need to be considered and explored. Meanwhile, Aboriginal community leaders struggle to implement their version of the inherent right to self-government and negotiate self-government agreements.

The federal government's approach has led to a number of self-government agreements but the negotiation process is time consuming, especially since Aboriginal leaders enter negotiations from the rights-based approach. Issues of extinguishment of existing rights, jurisdictional space, and resource control, all slow the process down because of the significant legal consequences.

Many Aboriginal community leaders are frustrated with this slow negotiation process and are instead taking a pragmatic, or business, approach to self-government and are achieving economic success as a result, generating wealth to create own source revenue.[12] The leaders who take this business approach set out a vision to be self-governing and not dependent upon outside agencies for money. They set out to build the institutions, systems, structures, processes, controls, measurement mechanisms, and human resources they need to run a stable government, and establish community-owned businesses, often through economic development corporations, that operate independent of political interference.[13] They use modern business management tools. These leaders see successful business and economic development as a key to true self-determination and freedom from dependence upon government transfer payments.[14]

Aboriginal communities that set up structures and processes for good governance build stability so that collective enterprises can flourish to provide jobs and wealth. Self-generated revenue is reinvested back into the community for social programs, infrastructure, as well as culture and language revitalization. Partnerships with other industries or businesses are only likely to occur if an Aboriginal community illustrates that it governs well and is stable. Indeed, the Membertou First Nation in Nova Scotia recognized this and worked to obtain ISO certification, an international standard of management. Successful Aboriginal communities place great emphasis and effort on building capacity of their general membership, leadership, and administrative departments. They see capacity-building and organizational development as key elements.[15] Community leaders and some commentators feel that by achieving economic success, they are achieving a truer form of self-government because they are not as dependent on government transfer payments as they once were.

When Europeans began to settle in what they called the new world, they found autonomous Aboriginal communities that were self-governing nations with their own laws, traditions, and defined territories.[16] When Canada formed, its federal structure gave jurisdiction over "Indians and lands reserved for Indians" to the national government, rather than to the provinces, under section 91(24) of the *Constitution Act, 1867*. The federal government exercised its jurisdiction by passing the *Indian Act*, which defined who was an "Indian" and imposed a municipal form of leadership and governance with limited powers upon First Nations. The federal government only formally recognized the imposed elected chief and council system as legitimate. This resulted in the traditional forms of leadership and governance being driven underground. Since the first *Indian Act*, Aboriginal peoples have always resisted this imposition and have struggled for self-government.[17]

Aboriginal peoples also adapted to the imposed economic system.[18] However, by being dispossessed of their traditional lands, marginalized from the local economy, and controlled by the Department of Indian Affairs (est. 1880), First Nations came to depend upon government to set their policy direction and for transfer payments. This political economic context reflects the relationship between Aboriginal peoples and the settler state that led to the expropriation of Aboriginal lands, and the oppression of Aboriginal peoples—all in the service of capitalist interests. The result of this internal colonialism sees the political and economic elite making legal and policy decisions in the metropolitan core that affect the hinterlands and periphery.[19]

Although the federal government moved away from their policy of overt assimilation after WWII, their 1969 White Paper nevertheless proposed the elimination of any special status or recognition of Aboriginal rights.[20] In response, Aboriginal peoples rallied and began the new Indian rights movement. When the constitution of Canada was being repatriated from England, Aboriginal peoples lobbied strongly for protection of their rights, and achieved success with s. 35(1) *Constitution Act, 1982*.[21] Although First Ministers' meetings with the Aboriginal organization leaders failed to reach any agreement on defining self-government, Aboriginal leaders increasingly expressed their inherent right to self-government.[22]

Many contemporary Aboriginal community leaders publicly state they have an inherent right to self-government or argue that Aboriginal peoples should just assert their jurisdiction over their local affairs. Others have negotiated self-government agreements. However, even having self-government and full jurisdiction over local matters does not ensure success unless a number of elements are also in place.

Research on Aboriginal economic development has found that it is closely tied to successful self-government, that is, in order to be economically successful, a community needs to govern successfully and build a stable environment and culture of growth.[23] In the Canadian context, one scholar found that communities that had few or no external influences imposing planning and administrative control were able to be more autonomous and coherent in their own planning for economic change.[24]

The Harvard Project began in the mid-1980s by examining why some US tribes were economically successful even when they had less land and fewer natural resources available than other tribes. The Project initially looked at local economies comparing number of jobs and businesses. What they found was broader than just economic—it was social, holistic. Economic development had to be part of community development and self-determination: a well-governed and stable community with a vision to grow businesses. Their research found that successful tribal economic and business development required four key elements: local autonomy; effective institutions; strategic direction; and strong leadership.[25] Firstly, successful tribes exercised *de facto* sovereignty. They did not follow the policy directions of funders or Indian Affairs; rather, they assumed local autonomy and set their own direction and made their own decisions. In other words, they took ownership and control over local decision-making and actually practiced self-government, taking responsibility for their decisions while learning from their mistakes leading to constant improvement. Secondly, successful tribes needed to establish effective institutions, setting up rules and mechanisms on how to relate in a community committed to business growth. Thus, there were rules and regulations that treated businesses and enterprises fairly; a dispute resolution mechanism; separate spheres of politics and business; and a competent bureaucracy with clear, transparent policies for the local government. In this way, good governance and a stable environment meant local members and outside investors felt comfortable risking their investment in that tribal community. Thirdly, successful tribes set a strategic direction for the tribe. The leaders set a vision and a mission for the community along with plans for the long term. Strategic plans assisted the community leaders in making decisions, and assisted in focusing their limited resources on achieving their collective goals. Fourthly, the Harvard Project found that successful tribes had strong, action-oriented leaders with the education, knowledge, and skills to carry out their roles and responsibilities for implementation of the strategic plan and for monitoring and evaluating performance and results. Strong leaders set out strategic action items with timelines attached and with someone accountable to ensure they were being acted upon. These strong leaders were proactive rather than reactive and they made things happen.

The Harvard Project's nation-building model is a useful holistic framework for community economic development. If Aboriginal communities, through strong leadership, set their own long-term strategic direction and establish institutions of good governance, and make well-informed decisions, they too can achieve success in their self-government and their economic development. However, in order to effectively implement self-government, Aboriginal leaders need to build the necessary capacity. The remainder of this article will concentrate on capacity-building, first at the community level through the establishment of effective institutions for good governance, and second, at the individual leader level.

Building Capacity

Capacity-building is important if Aboriginal communities are to become capable of taking advantage of economic opportunities. Because of the new regulatory environment, modern claims settlements, and recent court cases on the duty to consult, any industrial development on traditional Aboriginal territories must provide economic benefits to the effected Aboriginal communities, something not all Aboriginal communities are capable of taking advantage of. Furthermore, since Aboriginal communities are demanding increased powers and jurisdiction, there is a real need for capacity-building to take on more self-government duties. Capacity development can be viewed from two perspectives: (1) building the capacity of the community; and, (2) building the capacity of the leadership.

Building Community Capacity

Building community capacity has been recognized as an important factor to successful community economic development.[26] A community needs to have the collective capacity to capitalize on opportunities, deal with threats, and solve shared problems. Robert Chaskin and others have come up with a community capacity-building model.[27] Each community, through its individuals, organizations, and networks, can carry out essential functions such as: governing, planning and decision-making; producing goods and services; sharing of information; as well as organizing and advocating. Chaskin and his collaborators found that each community has specific conditions that influence everything within such as: stability; safety; density; opportunity structure; migration patterns; class and power distribution. These contextual factors are influential and may either promote or constrain community capacity.

The core of the community capacity-building model focuses on strategies such as leadership, organizational development, organizing for action, and organizational collaboration. These categories are somewhat similar to the Harvard Project's conclusions on key elements, namely: the need to build capacity in the areas of strong leadership; organizational development through the establishment of institutions and processes for good governance; and organizing and doing what is necessary to put the plans into action. The Chaskin model of community capacity-building also refers to organizational collaboration, an area that Aboriginal communities must also focus on, especially within their governments and bureaucracies where various departments or agencies too often work in isolation, form silos, and, on occasion, have conflicting agendas. Aboriginal communities must build the capacity to align such diverse departments and agencies so that they work collaboratively to achieve the collective vision. Aboriginal communities and their organizations also need to collaborate with external partners that they can leverage their scarce resources with. They must continue to build these external relationships as they become more self-governing. Self-government is not about isolation—rather it is about interdependence.

Collective capacity-building prepares the entire community to take advantage of opportunities and to face any threats or problems they encounter. It is imperative that Aboriginal communities build stable governing systems in order to effectively carry out their inherent right to self-government. Part of building community capacity for Aboriginal peoples is to establish good governance institutions.

Establishing Institutions of Good Governance

The Royal Commission on Aboriginal Peoples' (RCAP) final report set out a definition of governance identifying three fundamental attributes: power, legitimacy, and resources. Power refers to the political and legal capacity to act as a government. Aboriginal peoples exercise their power to govern through self-government agreements, existing statutory models such as the *Indian Act*, or attempts to implement the inherent right to self-government on their own. Legitimacy refers to the support and public confidence of a government. The Harvard Project states that there needs to be a cultural match for the institutions, structures, and leadership of governments. Essentially, community members need to feel the government, its structure, processes, and leadership are theirs, and culturally relevant as well as fair and effective. Resources refer to all tangible and intangible things required to run a government and includes land and natural resources, as well as human, economic, information, and technological resources.

The concept of governance can be defined as "the art of steering societies and organizations." Governance, in essence, is about how strategic policy direction is set, how decisions are made, and how stakeholders are engaged. Governance occurs "through interactions among structures, processes and traditions" and is fundamentally about "power, relationships and accountability."[28] With the appointment or election of a leader to govern over a community or organization comes a level of authority and the power to set direction and control assets and resources. With this power comes a tremendous level of responsibility—to act with integrity in the best interests of the collective and to be accountable to the various stakeholders who have a relationship to the governed entity.

Setting up good-governance institutions is an essential element for successful self-government and community economic development.[29] Institutions mean rules and ways of relating. Economist Douglas North has written on how certain institutions helped democratic societies achieve economic success.[30] For capitalist countries, this includes laws supporting contracts, private ownership of property, and the rule of law. Aboriginal communities need to consider establishing a constitution, a legal land system, a conflict resolution system, and a system for zoning lands and licensing businesses.[31]

Aboriginal communities need to build community capacity. They need to establish institutions of good governance such as structures, systems, processes, and controls, along with a vision and strategic direction to give meaning and hope to the effort being made. In order to carry out the functions of good governance and successful economic development, an Aboriginal community needs to build the capacity of another of the key elements to success—leadership.

Building Leadership Capacity

The second aspect of building capacity relates to development of individual leaders who often require a specific knowledge-based skills set. Government and industry hire personnel and leaders with high levels of post-secondary education. Government and industry also invest substantial resources in leadership development. Aboriginal communities are often at a disadvantage because the levels of post-secondary education are much lower than the national average. Furthermore, there is not enough emphasis on leadership development. Too often, Aboriginal leaders rely on outside expertise in their senior management roles or as advisors. Leadership development is a form of building personal capacity, and if Aboriginal leaders placed greater emphasis on their own leadership development, they would lead their communities, their organizations, and their businesses more effectively and efficiently with the knowledge, skills, and tools to help them deal with government and business elite.

The root of leadership, "lead", has been defined as "to guide on a way ... to direct the operations, activity, or performance of ... to tend toward a definite result."[32] Some argue that leadership is more an art than a science and that it is difficult to teach.[33] Much early thought considered strong leadership to mean "command and control," a view that grew out of strategic and military approaches, the hero approach to leaders, and the "scientific management" studies of Frederick Taylor and Henri Fayol.[34]

In the literature on leadership and management, the old command and control method has been replaced with the "stewardship" and "servant leadership" approach, which sees the leader set the strategic direction, empower others, and share leadership by allowing others to lead their own ideas to achieve results.[35] These servant leaders determine how to help their workers achieve their respective goals and find ways and resources to assist them. Servant leaders build learning cultures and help their workers be all they can be. Success is measured, not by how well the leader is doing, but by how well the workers are doing in their role and in their personal growth. This new perspective includes "transformational leadership" where the leader makes meaning for the group by creating an inspirational vision and strategic direction, and mobilizing energy in carrying out the goals, in contrast to the old "transactional leadership" where the leader cajoled, controlled, and threatened employees to perform.[36] This new leadership sees leaders as stewards of the assets and resources of the community or organization.[37]

Many studies regarding Aboriginal community economic development have shown the importance of capacity development, especially of training for leadership and management roles.[38] In the mid-1980s, Menno Boldt and Anthony Long argued that there was a new university-educated group emerging among Aboriginal peoples and optimistically stated "the emerging educated elite has the expertise to establish and staff the political and administrative infrastructures needed for Aboriginal self-government" and continued that "one of the most urgent needs confronting Aboriginal peoples today is for personnel trained to facilitate economic and social development within their communities."[39] Yet in 2005, John Borrows and Sarah Morales, referring to the RCAP Report, state that "Recent trends imply major shortages of Aboriginal people educated in fields such as economics, community planning and development, business management, forestry, biology, resource conservation, wildlife management, geology and agriculture."[40] Aboriginal leaders are either elected or appointed to their leadership roles often without formal management or business training, a lack that leaves them under-qualified to carry out their roles, or relying on outside experts to either advise them or run their top managerial roles.

Contemporary Aboriginal leaders continue to struggle with the effects of colonialism at both the community and the personal level.[41] Furthermore, the Office of the Auditor General of Canada in one of its reports noted, "the need for more effective capacity development of First Nations" and mentioned that those without adequate competencies to manage effectively, occasionally experienced third-party management.[42] Thus, strong leadership is an important ingredient for successful economic development and good governance: both the Harvard Project and the Chaskin model for community-capacity building found strong leadership a key strategy.

Human-capital theory assists us in understanding that investing in education and training shows a good return, providing individuals with knowledge and skills to do more complex work and thereby increasing chances for a better paying job with more responsibility.[43] This investment in human capital benefits both the individual leader and the collective, and generates more networks and interdependence in the community thereby increasing the social capital.[44] As one commentator on adult education states, "The contribution of education and training to overall economic development and growth, as well as to an individual's economic future, has been recognized for some time."[45] It is crucial for Aboriginal leaders to obtain the training they need in order to lead and manage effectively and efficiently.

What then are the competencies that Aboriginal leaders need to lead in this new global economy? Besides being familiar with the nation-building model mentioned earlier, Aboriginal leaders also need to learn the modern management principles and competencies. Peter Scholtes argues that the new leadership competencies include: the ability to engage in systems thinking and knowing how to lead systems; the ability to understand the variability of work in planning and problem solving; understanding how we learn, develop, and improve; leading true learning and improvement; understanding people and why they behave as they do; understanding the interdependence and interaction between systems, variation, learning, and human behaviour and knowing how each effects the others; and giving vision, meaning, direction, and focus to the organization.[46]

Some research has gone into what types of competencies Aboriginal leaders feel they need to carry out their roles and responsibilities effectively. For example, Brian Calliou and Robert Breaker conducted competency map research for the Aboriginal Leadership and Management program area at The Banff Centre by holding a series of focus groups with Canadian and American Aboriginal leaders, managers, and directors of boards to assist in designing their own competency map to use in their programs.[47] Competencies that Aboriginal leaders consistently identified as necessary were the following: knowledge of community identity, culture, and history; spiritual harmony and a balanced life; a holistic and global world view; strategic thinking and long term planning skills; responsibility and accountability; team-building skills; vision; risk-taking ability; an action orientation and plan implementation skills; strong integrity; a willingness to delegate authority and share power; an ability to resolve disputes; strong communication skills; business management skills; open-mindedness and objectivity; and problem-solving and decision-making skills.

To learn these modern organizational design and management skills and knowledge, Aboriginal leaders do not have to forego their own cultural and traditional ways of being, knowing, and doing. Rather, they can reconcile these modern competencies, and any modern systems such as capitalism, with their traditional principles to meet their collective needs.[48]

How should Aboriginal leaders learn these competencies? Formal credentials can be obtained through most colleges and universities via business and management programs or Native Studies. Other institutions also provide this type of professional development, for example: The Banff Centre, Aboriginal Leadership and Management; the National Centre for First Nations Governance; the Aboriginal Leadership Institute; Institute on Governance; Aboriginal Financial Officers Association; Council for the Advancement of Native Development Officers; and in the US, the Native Nations Institute. These institutions use adult education principles such as the experiential learning approach and engaging the students rather than the university lecture method.[49] Continuing education conferences and seminars, or even reading books, also help in this regard.

Capacity-building for leaders and managers in Aboriginal communities is crucial to successful community economic development and for good governance of the local government, its organizations and its business enterprises. The following two best-practice case studies illustrate the business approach to community economic development and self-government and the significance of capacity-building of leadership and the community.

Best Practice Case Study Examples

There are examples of successful Aboriginal leadership. In the US, one amazing story is the Mississippi Choctaw. Chief Phillip Martin took the Mississippi Choctaw from an impoverished tribal community to one of the state's leading economic engines.[50] One commentator called the story "nothing less than an economic miracle" and that "the key, essential factor was the leadership provided by one Choctaw in particular: Chief Phillip Martin."[51]

Chief Martin used the business approach to self-government and economic success for his community. He left the poverty of his reservation to attend and graduate from a boarding school before joining the air force and achieving the rank of sergeant. When he returned from service he could not find employment on the reservation so he worked as a clerk at an air naval station and took night classes at a local college graduating with an associate of arts degree.

Phillip Martin returned to the reservation and in 1959 became elected leader of an impoverished community with high unemployment, many social problems, and virtually no hope for tribal members. His vision was to take his community out of dependency and see it self-governing and self-sufficient. He used federal government grants to leverage other grants which enabled him to hire accountants, bookkeepers, personnel managers and planners. In order to attract private investment, Chief Martin "understood that corporations wanted cheap labor, low taxes, and an honest, consistent, and stable government policy."[52] He and his council worked to put in place good governance processes. Then they set up a tribal company, Chahta Enterprises, and built an industrial park. Martin's persistence eventually attracted Packard Electric to enter an agreement to train Choctaws to assemble wiring harnesses for General Motors automobiles. That commitment allowed the tribe to obtain government grants and loan guarantees to build an assembly plant. The Choctaw had their challenges and at one point Chahta Enterprises was deep in debt and near bankruptcy. Chief Martin decided to hire a professional manager who worked at General Motors to manage Chahta Enterprises allowing that individual to operate the enterprise without input/interference from Martin and the tribal council. This resulted in a professionally run business, and profits. The Choctaw also diversified into many areas such as a plastic injection molding plant, a greeting card plant, a car speaker plant, a construction company, a shopping center, and eventually a resort hotel and casino, with an 18-hole golf course. The Choctaw are now an economic driver for the entire region, employing not only their own but thousands of people from the surrounding communities. The Choctaw have almost full employment for their members and only 2.7 per cent are on social assistance.[53] Economic success has allowed the Choctaw to reinvest in their culture and language. Over 90 per cent of their members speak their language, they have revitalized a traditional Choctaw stick game, and they hold regular traditional dances and ceremonial events.

In the Canadian context, there are some shining examples as well. Chief Terrance Paul and the Membertou First Nation in Nova Scotia are an example of the business approach to self-government and have been very successful in economic development and business partnerships.[54] Referring to the decisions by the Membertou First Nation to assert its local sovereignty in its direction and decision-making and the resulting economic progress, one commentator stated, "Significant changes in the way it managed those resources and made decisions was needed, changes that required strong leadership and a pool of managerial and technical skills." She continues: "Significant institutional changes were made to alter the structure and processes of band governance so that band leadership could make and implement economically sound decisions."[55]

As recently as 1995, about 85 per cent of Membertou adults were on some form of social assistance. The band was running a deficit budget and some attempts at economic ventures had failed because of their lack of both managerial and community capacity. Taking responsibility for the accumulated debt, failed economic ventures, and the possibility of third-party management, Membertou Council led by Chief Terrance Paul decided it was time for change. Chief Paul knew that answers had to come from within the community if they were going to break the "dependence psychology" of reliance on federal and provincial governments. In the mid-1990s, the leaders decided to build a team to lead the change toward economic independence and began by recruiting a community member, Bernd Christmas, who had left the reserve and was a Toronto Bay Street lawyer. Christmas was hired as the CEO and General Council for the band. Chief Paul and his new CEO worked on bringing home other community members who had gained success in the outside world including a financial officer. The new band organization, modeled as a corporate structure, was to be run as a business, treating members as shareholders and reinvesting profits into community-building projects. With their previous record of business failures, poor financial position, and no successes to springboard from, the leadership team decided to obtain ISO certification, an international standard for management and internal governance. They began the ISO certification process in 2000, following a two-year program that enabled their organizations and bureaucracies to control their operations effectively and efficiently. This certification sent a strong message to the international corporate world that Membertou First Nation was serious about economic partnerships and had the capacity to deliver their end of the bargain.

To connect with the business community, Membertou opened an office in downtown Halifax, the political and commercial capital of Nova Scotia. Membertou used the procurement strategy for Aboriginal business as a tool to obtain contracts with major corporations. Callaghan and Christmas indicated that while it was "difficult to know what exactly motivates partnerships," a combination of ISO certification, new leadership processes and innovative business strategies "seemed to open the door to many new opportunities."[56] Membertou's partnerships include: Lockheed Martin, where Membertou assists with the maritime helicopter project bid; SNC-Lavalin, where Membertou provides engineering services and environmental technologies; Sodex'ho Canada, where Membertou offers onshore and offshore catering; and Fujitsu Consulting, where Membertou assists in health records management for military personnel. Membertou also developed other revenue-generating sources such as: Membertou Trade and Commerce Centre and Business Park; Membertou Fisheries; Mi'kmaq Gas Bar and Convenience; and gaming operations on the reserve. Band revenues have grown substantially as a result and now are well over $40 million annually. Furthermore, unemployment has been reduced significantly, education levels are rising, and the Mi'kmaq language is being successfully reintroduced. As Scott concludes, "Membertou is undeniably a great success story today, and one that resulted from good long-term planning and skill" and that it was a result of "strong patient leadership, human capital development, and governance changes."[57]

Other well-known examples of Aboriginal leaders in Canada who have set up successful businesses and economic development are: Chief Jim Boucher of Fort McKay First Nation in north eastern Alberta; Chief Darcy Bear of Whitecap Dakota First Nation in central Saskatchewan; Chief Clarence Louie of Osoyoos First Nation in southern interior of British Columbia; and Chief Victor Buffalo of Samson Cree Nation in central Alberta. These Aboriginal leaders all took the business approach to community economic development and their version of self-government. They built capacity in their community in order to have the capability to build economic success.

Conclusion

There are many approaches to self-government in Canada. Some Aboriginal leaders are fed up with the slow process of litigating and negotiating and have instead taken a pragmatic approach that has produced some successful examples and can be characterized as the business approach to self-government.

Having self-government and asserting jurisdiction is not enough, however. Aboriginal communities need the capacity to implement self-government. Indeed, if Aboriginal leaders take on self-government but do not have the capacity to deliver it well, then they are only letting their own people down. There needs to be capacity-building for both the individual leaders as well as their communities. Leadership education and training must be undertaken in order for Aboriginal leaders to carry out their roles and responsibilities effectively. There also needs to be capacity development for the community: building institutions and systems of good governance in order to establish a stable local environment. The stability created can lead to investment and thereby create a sustainable economy. The nation-building model is a useful holistic framework for community economic development and self-government. It provides key elements that need to be developed to achieve successful community economic development. Like the Chaskin model of community capacity-building, the nation-building model emphasizes the importance of continuing education and capacity-building for leadership and community. This capacity-building for leaders is no different than the life-long learning our Elders tell us we need with respect to our traditional knowledge.

1   See for example the collection of articles in Michael Murphy, ed., *Canada: The State of the Federation* 2003 -
     Reconfiguring Aboriginal-State Relations (Montreal & Kingston: Institute of Intergovernmental Relations,
     Queen's University & McGill-Queen's Press, 2005). Even some writers who look at implementation focus on
     legal and political issues, for example Peter Hogg & Mary Ellen Turpel, "Implementing Aboriginal Self-
     Government: Constitutional and Jurisdictional Issues," *Canadian Bar Review* 74, no. 2 (1995).

2   An excellent example of how the leadership strategies employed by traditional Chief Sitting Bull could teach and
     influence the modern business manager is Emmett C.Murphy with Michael Snell, *The Genius of Sitting Bull: 13
     Heroic Strategies for Today's Business Leaders* (Englewood Cliffs: Prentice Hall, 1993). Brian Calliou sets out a few
     traditional leadership characteristics and discusses modern competencies in, "The Culture of Leadership: North
     American Indigenous Leadership in a Changing Economy" in *Indigenous Peoples and the Modern State,* eds.
     Duane Champagne, Karen Jo Torjesen & Susan Steiner (Walnut Creek: AltaMira Press, 2005), 47-68.

3   For example, see Yale Belanger & David Newhouse, "Aboriginal Self-Government in Canada: A Review of
     Literature Since 1960," *Canadian Journal of Native Studies* 24, no. 1 (2004): 129-222; and Albert Peeling & Val
     Napolean, "Aboriginal Governance: An Annotated Bibliography." Prepared for the National Centre for First
     Nations Governance, www.fngovernance.org (accessed 15 September 2007).

4   Canada, *The Government of Canada's Approach to Implementation of the Inherent Right and the Negotiation of
     Aboriginal Self-Government* (Ottawa: Minister on Indian and Northern Development, 1995).

5   See for example Ed Allen, "Our Treaty, Our Inherent Right to Self-Government: An Overview of the Nisga'a
     Final Agreement," *International Journal of Minority and Group Rights* 11 (2004), 233; John Borrows, "A
     Geneology of Law: Inherent Sovereignty and First Nations Self-Government," *Osgoode Hall Law Journal* 30
     (1992): 291; and, Mary Ellen Turpel, "Indigenous People's Rights of Political Participation and Self-
     Determination: Recent International Legal Developments and the Continuing Struggle for Recognition"
     Cornell International Law Journal 25 (1992): 579.

6   For reviews of the self-governance powers in the *Indian Act,* see Shin Imai, *Aboriginal Law Handbook,* 2nd ed.
     (Toronto: Carswell Thomson Professional Publishing, 1999); and Brian A. Crane, Robert Mainville & Martin
     W. Mason, *First Nations Governance Law* (Markham: LexisNexis Canada, 2006).

7   For a brief overview, see Chapter 4 entitled "Self-Government Agreements" in Crane, Mainville, & Mason,
     First Nations Governance Law, 69; and Jack Hicks & Graham White, "Nunavut: Inuit Self-Determination
     Through a Land Claim and Public Government?" in *Nunavut: Inuit Regain Control of Their Lands and Their
     Lives,* eds. Jens Dahl, Jack Hicks & Peter Jull (Denmark: International Work Group for Indigenous Affairs,
     2000), 30.

8   See for example the chapter entitled "Health and Healing" in Royal Commission on Aboriginal Peoples, *Final
     Report* (Ottawa: Minister of Supply and Services, Canada, 1996), 316; Wayne Warry, *Unfinished Dreams:
     Community Healing and the Reality of Self-Government* (Toronto: University of Toronto, 1998).

9   Patricia Montour-Angus, *Journeying Forward: Dreaming First Nations' Independence* (Halifax: Fernwood
     Publishers, 1999).

10   Terry L. Anderson, Bruce L. Benson & Thomas E. Flanagan, eds., *Self-Determination: The Other Path for
     Native Americans* (Stanford: Stanford University Press, 2006).

11   Tim Schouls, *Shifting Boundaries: Aboriginal Identity, Pluralist Theory, and the Politics of Self-Government*
     (Vancouver: University of British Columbia Press, 2003).

12   The business approach can also be termed the corporate model. See for example, Edith G.J. Callaghan and
     Bernd Christmas, "Building a Native Community by Drawing on a Corporate Model" in *Legal Aspects of
     Aboriginal Business Development,* eds. Dwight Dorey and Joseph Magnet (Markham: LexisNexis Butterworths,
     2005).

13   See for example, Michael Cameron, "A Prototypical Economical Development Corporation for Native American
     Tribes" in *What Can Tribes Do? Strategies and Institutions in American Indian Economic Development,* eds. Stephen
     Cornell & Joseph P. Kalt (Los Angeles: American Indian Studies Center, UCLA, 1992), 61; Daria Caliguire &
     Kenneth Grant, *A Foundation for Economic Development for the Hualapai Nation: Building an Enterprise Board*
     (Cambridge: Harvard Project on American Indian Economic Development, John F. Kennedy School of
     Government, 1993). See also, Government of Canada, *Comprehensive Community Planning: Experiences in First
     Nations, Inuit and Northern Communities* (Ottawa: Indian Affairs and Northern Development, 2004); see also
     Dean Howard Smith, "Managing Tribal Assets: Developing Long-Term Strategic Plans," in *Modern Tribal
     Development: Paths to Self-Sufficiency and Cultural Integrity in Indian Country,* ed. Dean Howard Smith (Walnut
     Creek: AltaMira Press, 2000), 93; Theodore S. Jojola, "Indigenous Planning and Resource Management" in
     Trusteeship in Change: Toward Tribal Autonomy in Resource Management, eds. Richard L. Clow & Imre Sutton
     (Boulder: University of Colorado Press, 2001), 303.

14   For example, Calvin Helin, *Dances With Dependency: Indigenous Success Through Self-Reliance* (Vancouver:
     Orca Spirit Publishing, 2006).

15 See Edith G.J. Callaghan & Bernd Christmas, "Building a Native Community by Drawing on a Corporate Model," 42-43. Robert Anderson also describes the importance of capacity-building through education and training for the success of the Meadow Lake Tribal Council in Robert Brent Anderson, *Economic Development Among the Aboriginal Peoples in Canada: The Hope for the Future* (North York: Captus Press, 1999), 203-206.

16 Brian Slattery, "The Hidden Constitution: Aboriginal Rights in Canada" in *The Quest for Justice: Aboriginal Peoples and Aboriginal Rights,* eds. Menno Boldt & J. Anthony Long (Toronto: University of Toronto Press, 1985), 114-138.

17 For an historical overview of the development of the *Indian Act,* see John L. Leslie, "The *Indian Act*: An Historical Perspective" *Canadian Parliamentary Review* (Summer 2002): 23. John S. Milloy, "The Early Indian Acts: Development Strategy and Constitutional Change" in *As Long as the Sun Shines and Water Flows,* eds. Ian Getty & Antoine Lussier (Vancouver: University of British Columbia Press, 1983), 59, stated that "Immediately upon publication of the [Indian] act, tribal councils recognized its intent and rejected it."

18 See the description of how Aboriginal peoples adapted, played a role in, and contributed to the new economy in Cora Voyageur & Brian Calliou, "Aboriginal Economic Development and the Struggle for Self-Government" in *Power and Resistance: Critical Thinking About Canadian Social Issues,* 4th ed., eds. Wayne Antony and Les Samuelson (Halifax: Fernwood Publishing, 2007), 135.

19 James Frideres, "The Political Economy of Natives in Canada" in *Native Peoples in Canada: Contemporary Conflicts,* 3rd ed., ed. James Frideres (Scarborough: Prentice-Hall, 1988), 366. See also Frances Abel, "Understanding What Happened Here: The Political Economy of Indigenous Peoples" in *Understanding Canada: Building on the New Canadian Political Economy,* ed. Wallace Clement (Montreal: McGill-Queen's University Press, 1997), 129.

20 See for example Roger Gibbins & J. Rick Ponting, "Historical Overview and Background" in *Arduous Journey: Canadian Indians and Decolonization,* ed. J. Rick Ponting (Toronto: McClelland and Stewart, 1986), 18.

21 Douglas Sanders, "The Indian Lobby" in *And No One Cheered: Federalism, Democracy and the Constitution Act,* eds. Keith Banting and Richard Simeon (Toronto: Methuen Publications, 1983), 301.

22 See for example the Aboriginal voices such as Chief Gordon Peters in Frank Cassidy, ed., *Aboriginal Self-Determination: Proceedings of a Conference Held September 30-October 3, 1990* (Lantzville: Institute for Research on Public Policy and Oolichan Books, 1991), 33, who states "There is only one source of authority that we have, and that is the Creator."

23 Stephen Cornell & Joseph P. Kalt, "Pathways From Poverty: Economic Development and Institution-Building on American Indian Reservations," *American Indian Culture and Research Journal* 14 (1990): 89; Stephen Cornell & Joseph P. Kalt, "Reloading the Dice: Improving the Chances for Economic Development on American Indian Reservations" in Cornell & Kalt, *What Can Tribes Do?*; and, Joseph P. Kalt, "Sovereignty and Economic Development on American Indian Reservations: Lessons from the United States" in Royal Commission on Aboriginal Peoples, *Sharing the Harvest: The Road to Self-Reliance - Report of the National Round Table on Aboriginal Economic Development and Resources* (Ottawa: Minister of Supply and Services and Canada Communications Group, 1993), 35; Miriam Jorgensen, ed., *Rebuilding Native Nations: Strategies for Governance and Development* (Tucson: University of Arizona Press, 2007).

24 Edward J. Hedican, "Governmental Indian Policy, Administration, and Economic Planning in the Eastern Subarctic," *Culture* 25 (1982).

25 See summary in Brian Calliou, "Final Activity Report: A Forum to Explore Best Practices, Policy and Tools to Build Capacity in Aboriginal Business and Economic Development" available online at www.banffcentre.ca/departments/leadership/aboriginal/pdfAwP1%20Final.pdf or in Brian Calliou, "The Culture of Leadership".

26 For a sampling, see Hubert Campfens, ed., *Community Economic Development Around the World: Practice, Theory, Research, Training* (Toronto: University of Toronto Press, 1997); Freeman H. Compton, "Community Development Theory and Practice" in *Citizen Participation: Canada,* ed. James A. Draper (Toronto: New Press, 1971); and, William E. Rees, "Stable Community Development in the North: Properties and Requirements, An Econo-Ecological Approach" in *Northern Communities: The Prospects for Empowerment,* eds. Gurston Dacks & Kenneth Coates (Edmonton: Boreal Institute for Northern Studies, University of Alberta, 1988), 59. See also, Rolf Gerritsen, Jack Crosby & Christine Fletcher, *Revisiting the Old in Revitalizing the New: Capacity Building in Western Australia's Aboriginal Communities: A Discussion With Case Studies - Final Report* (Casuarina: North Australia Research Unit, The Australian National University, 2000); Lewis Williams, "Culture and Community Development: Toward New Conceptualizations and Practice," *Community Development Journal* 39, no. 4 (2004): 345; B.J. Reed & D. Paulson, "Small Towns Lack the Capacity for Successful Development Efforts," *Rural Development Perspectives* 6 (1990): 26; M. McGuire, R. Rubin, R. Agranoff & C. Richards, "Building Development Capacity in Nonmetropolitan Communities," *Public Administration Review* 54, no. 5 (1994): 426. For a critical view of capacity-building see Lynne Phillips & Suzan Ilcan, "Capacity-Building: The Neoliberal Governance of Development," *Canadian Journal of Development Studies* 25, no. 6 (2004): 393.

27 Robert J. Chaskin, Prudence Brown, Sudhir Venkatesh, & Avis Vidal, *Building Community Capacity* (New York: Aldine De Gruyter, 2001).

28 Institute on Governance, "Understanding Governance in Strong Aboriginal Communities - Phase One: Principles and Best Practices From the Literature," www.iog.ca/view_publication_section.asp?area=1#pub_5 (accessed 15 September 2007).

29 Stephen Cornell & Joseph P. Kalt, "Where's the Glue? Institutional Bases of American Indian Economic Development," *Journal of Socio-Economics* 29 (2000): 443; Stephen Cornell & Marta Cecilia Gil-Swedberg, "Sociohistorical Factors in Institutional Efficacy: Economic Development in Three American Indian Cases," *Economic Development and Cultural Change* 43 (1995): 239. See also the Canadian example, J. Rick Ponting, "Institution-Building in an Indian Community: A Case Study of Kahnawake (Caughnawaga)" in *Arduous Journey,* 151.

30 Douglas North, *Institutions, Institutional Change and Economic Performance* (Cambridge: Cambridge University Press, 1990); Douglas C. North, "Institutions, Transaction Costs, and Economic Growth" *Economic Inquiry* (July 1988): 419.

31 See for example, Paul Nissenbaum & Paul Shadle, "Building a System for Land Use Planning: A Case Study for the Puyallup Tribe" in *What Can Tribes Do?*, 133; Stacy Paul Healy, "Constructing a Legal Land System That Supports Economic Development for the Métis in Alberta," *Journal of Aboriginal Economic Development* 2, no. 1 (2001): 61; Andrea Skari, "The Tribal Judiciary: A Primer for Policy Development" in *What Can Tribes Do?*, 91. See the *First Nations Gazette,* published by the Native Law Centre, University of Saskatchewan, which publishes examples of First Nations zoning, business licensing, and taxation laws and includes which First Nations in Canada have such laws.

32 *The Merriam Webster Dictionary* (Springfield: Merriam Webster Inc., 1997), 423.

33 Max DePree, *Leadership is an Art* (New York: Dell Publishers, 1989); Calliou, "The Culture of Leadership."

34 See Frederick W. Taylor, *Principles of Scientific Management* (New York: Harper & Row, 1911); Henri Fayol, *General and Industrial Management* (New York: Pitman, 1949); and, see generally U.K. scholar Keith Grint, *The Arts of Leadership* (Oxford: Oxford University Press, 2000).

35 DePree, *Leadership is an Art,* discusses this very well. See also D. Coyhis, "Servant Leadership: The Elders Have Said Leadership is About Service: They Say We Are Really Here to Serve the People," *Winds of Change* 1-3 (1993): 23; R.K. Greenleaf, *Servant Leadership* (New York: Paulist Press, 1977).

36 For a sampling see B.M. Bass, "From Transactional to Transformational Leadership: Learning to Share the Vision," *Organizational Dynamics* 18, no. 3 (1990): 19; A.E. Rafferty & M.A. Griffin, "Dimensions of Transformational Leadership: Conceptual and Empirical Extensions," *Leadership Quarterly* 15 (2004): 329.

37 Peter Block, *Stewardship: Choosing Service Over Self-Interest* (San Francisco: Berrett-Koehler, 1992).

38 See for example, Anderson, *Economic Development Among the Aboriginal Peoples in Canada,* 184-187 and 203-206; Calliou, *Final Activity Report,* 16-19, 34; Callaghan & Christmas, "Building a Native Community by Drawing on a Corporate Model," 41-45.

39 Menno Boldt & J. Anthony Long, eds., *The Quest for Justice: Aboriginal Peoples and Aboriginal Rights* (Toronto: University of Toronto Press, 1985), 9.

40 John Borrows & Sarah Morales, "Challenge, Change and Development in Aboriginal Economies," in *Legal Aspects of Aboriginal Business Development,* eds. Dwight Dorey and Joseph Magnet (Markham: LexisNexis Butterworths, 2005), 147.

41 See for example, Taiaiake Alfred, *Peace, Power and Righteousness: An Indigenous Manifesto* (Toronto: Oxford University Press, 1999); and, Menno Boldt, *Surviving as Indians: The Challenge of Self-Government* (Toronto: University of Toronto Press, 1993).

42 Office of the Auditor General of Canada, "Chapter 5: Management of Programs for First Nations" in Office of the Auditor General of Canada, *Report of the Auditor General of Canada - May 2006* (Ottawa: Office of the Auditor General of Canada, 2006), 68, www.oag-bvg.gc.ca (accessed 15 September 2007).

43 Gary S. Becker, *Human Capital: A Theoretical and Empirical Analysis With Special Reference to Education* (New York: Columbia University Press, 1975).

44 J. White & Paul Maxim, "Social Capital, Social Cohesion, and Population Outcomes in Canada's First Nations Communities" in *Aboriginal Conditions: Research as a Foundation for Public Policy,* eds. J. White, P. Maxim & Dan Beavon (Vancouver: University of British Columbia Press, 2003), 8.

45 Bruce Spencer, *The Purposes of Adult Education* (Toronto: Thompson Educational Publishing, 2006), 30-32.

46 Peter R. Scholtes, *The Leader's Handbook: Making Things Happen, Getting Things Done* (New York: McGraw-Hill, 1998), 21.

47 Calliou, "The Culture of Leadership"; Manley Begay Jr., "Leading by Choice, Not Chance: Leadership Education for Native Chief Executives of American Indian Nations" (Ed.D. diss., Harvard University, 1997); Manley Begay Jr., *Designing Native American Management and Leadership Training: Past Efforts, Present Endeavors, and Future Options,* Harvard Project Report Series No. 91-3 (Cambridge: John F. Kennedy School of Government, Harvard University, 1991); Jacqueline Ottmann, "First Nations Leadership Development

Within a Saskatchewan Context" (Ph.D. diss., University of Saskatchewan, 2005); Sixdion Inc., "Skills Acquisition for Devolution" [unpublished research report for the Department of Indian and Northern Development, Government of Canada, 1998].

48 Wanda Wuttunee, *Living Rhythms: Lessons in Aboriginal Economic Resilience and Vision* (Montreal & Kingston: McGill-Queen's University Press, 2004); Dean Howard Smith, *Modern Tribal Development: Paths to Self-sufficiency and Cultural Integrity in Indian Country* (Walnut Creek: AltaMira Press, 2000); Colleen O'Neill, "Rethinking Modernity and the Discourse of Development in American Indian History: An Introduction" in *Native Pathways: American Indian Culture and Economic Development in the Twentieth Century,* eds. Brian Hosmer and Colleen O'Neill (Boulder: University Press of Colorado, 2004).

49 For comment see D.A. Kolb, *Experiential Learning: Experience as the Source of Learning and Development* (Englewood Cliffs: Prentice Hall, 1984).

50 For published accounts see Benton R. White & Christine Schultz White, "Phillip Martin: Mississippi Choctaw" in *The New Warriors: Native American Leaders Since 1900,* ed. R. David Edmunds (Lincoln: University of Nebraska Press, 2001); Peter J. Ferrara, *The Choctaw Revolution: Lessons for Federal Indian Policy* (Washington, D.C.: Americans for Tax Reform Foundation, 1998); and Robert H. White, "The Mississippi Band of Choctaw Indians" in *Tribal Assets: The Rebirth of Native America,* ed. Robert H. White (New York: Henry Holt & Company, 1990).

51 Ferrara, *The Choctaw Revolution,* 14.

52 White & Schultz White, "Phillip Martin: Mississippi Choctaw," 198.

53 *Ibid.,* 203.

54 For published accounts see Callaghan & Christmas, "Building a Native Community by Drawing on a Corporate Model;" Jacquelyn Thayer Scott, "'Doing Business With the Devil': Land, Sovereignty, and Corporate Partnerships in Membertou, Inc." in *Self-Determination: The Other Path for Native Americans,* eds. Terry L. Anderson, Bruce L. Benson & Thomas E. Flanagan (Stanford: Stanford University Press, 2006).

55 Thayer Scott, "'Doing Business With the Devil'," 245.

56 Callaghan & Christmas, "Building a Native Community by Drawing on a Corporate Model," 45.

57 Thayer Scott, "'Doing Business With the Devil'," 267-268.

WHERE IS THE LAW
IN RESTORATIVE JUSTICE?

Val Napoleon, University of Alberta;
Angela Cameron, University of Victoria;
Colette Arcand, University of Alberta;
& Dahti Scott, University of Alberta

Ways of Thinking about Law

Restorative justice is seen by some as an important tool in moving toward, and sustaining, Aboriginal self-government.[1] The main purpose of this chapter is to explore whether restorative justice can be usefully considered an expression and form of practice of local law, with a view to its implications for Aboriginal self-government. Specifically, the chapter explores how analysis changes with a shift from understanding restorative justice as a "program" to considering it an expression of local law, and therefore a critical aspect of on-the-ground self-government. The chapter addresses experiences and trends in the implementation of local law by examining the work of the Alexis First Nation Justice Committee (the Committee)[2] in the Nakota community of Alexis First Nation, just outside Edmonton, Alberta.[3]

Considering the work of the Committee as being founded on local and/or Nakota law[4] could enable Alexis First Nation community members to (1) find other expressions of local and Nakota law at work in the community, (2) extrapolate how the legal obligations, legal norms, and legal principles of local and Nakota law might be applied elsewhere, perhaps to local governing institutions, and (3) critically examine how legal norms, obligations, and principles might be applied to other issues or conflicts. These are self-governing acts and are part of what self-government should encompass. The chapter will first develop a legal framework within which to discuss the concepts of local law and, to a lesser extent, restorative justice. This framework will then be applied as a lens to discern and describe the parameters and functions of local law that derive from the work of the Committee.

Legal Framework
A legal framework can be understood as a way of talking about, thinking about,

and working with laws and legal orders—in this case, Indigenous laws and legal orders. Such a conceptual framework is formed, in part, by asking critical and unsentimental questions about the sources[5] and functions of law, the legitimacy and authority of law, the ways in which laws change, and the internal power imbalances and oppression within legal orders.[6] This legal framework advances an understanding of law as whole and separate from the dominant understanding of formal, centralized law created and perpetuated by the common and civil law in Canada. It asks how Indigenous laws and legal orders relate to these dominant understandings of law.[7] When applied to Nakota law, this legal framework helps us to better understand local manifestations of Nakota law in Alexis, identify and deal with internal contradictions and conflict, and develop non-colonial relationships between Aboriginal peoples and Canada.

The process of carving out an understanding of local law is in itself an exercise in self-determination. We are encouraging Aboriginal people and groups to create the political space in which they can consider such critical questions as: What are we beyond our resistance to colonialism? What do we want our contemporary legal institutions and laws to look like? and, How do we develop the political space that is necessary for the exercise of intellectual capacity to articulate, interpret, and apply Indigenous laws to contemporary issues?[8] At the end of the day, Indigenous societies (like every healthy society) must have the political space in which to consider and manage their own laws and legal orders. It follows, similarly, that Indigenous legal orders and law are fundamentally about citizenry—and therefore part of the collective social capital.[9]

Restorative Justice

In Canada, the term "restorative justice" is applied to a wide variety of theories and practices ranging from justice committees to victim-offender mediation.[10] It is a term commonly used by Canadian federal and provincial governments and courts to describe criminal justice programs for Aboriginal people in conflict with the law.[11] There are a large number of restorative justice programs across Canada with varying degrees of control and participation by Aboriginal people. The Alexis First Nation Justice Committee is one such program.

Understanding the link between restorative justice and Aboriginal self-government is confusing for several reasons. First, most restorative justice programs in Canada are not run autonomously by an Aboriginal group. While federal and provincial governments may grant certain levels of autonomy to Aboriginal groups deploying a restorative justice program, such as the Committee, the reality is that any potential for self-governance is often curtailed by extensive government reporting requirements, lack of resources, and indirect control (e.g., qualification criteria, evaluation standards, etc.).[12] Second, most government-sanctioned restorative justice programs, even those that deal exclusively with non-Aboriginal clients, acknowledge or claim roots in pan-Aboriginal[13] concepts of justice or law.[14] Meanwhile, they are often completely unrelated to the laws and legal orders of the local Indigenous peoples where they are applied. Finally, while Aboriginal and restorative justice initiatives are obviously considered to be about justice, they generally say nothing about Indigenous legal orders and law. Usually the only references to law are statements that are diametrically opposed to the Western criminal justice system. This binary approach is founded on the erroneous assumption that there is only one type of law—that of centralized states with formally enacted systems of law.[15] Thus, a false dichotomy between restorative justice and the Western criminal law is created, which unfortunately constrains other creative possibilities for Indigenous peoples.

This chapter argues that despite the ways in which restorative justice programs may be administered as ambiguous tools of self-governance, Indigenous laws and legal orders may still form the foundation for these programs. In other words, Indigenous laws and legal orders may continue to function and flourish just beneath the visible surface of the justice programs at an implicit and informal level. The Committee is recognized by the Alberta government as a restorative justice program closely linked to the criminal justice system and operating within limited parameters. However, in talking to the people who work within the Alexis program, it is evident to us that the successes of the program are at least in part due to the Nakota legal order and laws[16] which are alive and persist within this primarily Nakota community.

The label "restorative justice" does not reduce crime, or heal offenders and victims. The rhetoric or descriptions in government working papers and evaluations, or the *Criminal Code*,[17] do not make changes in Aboriginal communities.[18] In fact, the rhetoric of restorative justice usually obscures forms of local law. We understand government-mandated restorative justice as a political, economic, legal, and institutional scaffold that both supports and, at times, distorts local law within Western law and politics. While the tenets and rhetoric of restorative justice may sometimes overlap, or enhance, the ways in which local laws are functioning, we argue that local laws themselves are more interesting and promising in terms of strengthening self-governance.

Local Law
As the authors of this chapter, we come from a variety of cultures and legal traditions. Three of us are Aboriginal, but none of us are Nakota, nor do we live in the Alexis community. This has been both a great source of insight and a challenge.[19] In this project of trying to understand forms and functions of law across cultures (i.e., Western, Cree, Dunnezah, Dene, and Nakota), we must begin by recognizing our own cultural blinders and accepting that these may impair our efforts, no matter how well intentioned our desire to understand.[20]

The Committee is constituted by an agreement with the Province of Alberta to provide services and support to persons in Alexis who are charged with criminal offences.[21] The work that the Committee does is, in its relation to Canadian law, created and bounded by this agreement. However, we argue that much of the work that is being done by the Committee is better viewed within a different framework—that of local law.

Alexis local law is historically rooted in but no longer identical to Nakota law. Nakota law is part of a complete Nakota legal order[22] that historically extended more broadly (geographically and normatively) across the larger Nakota society and its territory. As with all law, Nakota law is not static, but is constantly changing. Local law consists of the ways that Nakota law is presently understood, interpreted, and practiced in the specific geographic community of Alexis. In other words, the settlement of Alexis in its present geographic location has caused Nakota law to localize into the single community of Alexis First Nation. This situation is further complicated because, with ongoing intermarriage with other Aboriginal and non-Aboriginal peoples, Alexis is no longer completely Nakota.[23] Today, Alexis is geographically separated from other Nakota groups and surrounded by Cree communities in historic Cree territory.[24] The ways that Nakota law is understood and used in social interactions is influenced by historic and contemporary realities that are unique to Alexis.

Local law locates law in the on-the-ground, day-to-day self-governance performed (in this case) by Aboriginal people according to Aboriginal laws and legal orders. Local law operates simultaneously with State law, but is usually either invisible or only visible in the form of traditions, customs, or practices.[25] A local-law framework turns the focus away from what is happening in relation to the provincial and federal governments, and instead examines Aboriginal laws and legal orders, and the ways they function as institutions in and of themselves. In this chapter we examine the work of the Committee, and ask ourselves whether what they are doing on a day-to-day basis can be understood as an expression and form of practice of local law deriving from Nakota law.

Frequently within Western (State) law, Aboriginal laws and legal orders are reduced to essentialized and simplistic rules or practices such as prayer or smudging.[26] We want to examine what gives those practices meaning and what the information is that underlies the traditions.[27] We might ask, for example, "Why is that smudge conducted at this particular time?" Our focus is not on the rules themselves, but on the intellectual and reasoning processes that are necessary for the collaborative practices of law, management of conflict, and governance generally.[28]

Our view is that underlying the practices or "rules" are a set of philosophical and legal norms that are constantly accessed and interpreted. We want to look closely at processes such as legal reasoning, deliberation, and interpretation of laws, rather than at the bare rules or practices alone.[29] It is difficult to see these intellectual processes, or at least more difficult than to see State-law legal reasoning, as local law does not have a separate dedicated institution (such as a law school) to explain and teach it. The law instead derives from and rests within the everyday social interactions, practices, traditions, lives, place names, and kinship relations of Indigenous groups.[30]

In every legal culture, including Aboriginal laws and legal orders, the ways that we understand and fulfill these norms are constantly contested and debated. Law lives in each new context. In fact, one of the most important things to understand about law is how it changes in our own and in other cultures.[31] It has to change in order to fulfill an effective governance function—it must be appropriate to new contexts and circumstances or it will lose its legitimacy. This contestation of legal norms occurs as societies themselves change and face new challenges or new ways of being together as people.[32] In part, local law functions as a dispute-management system when these norms are contested. It is local law that provides the mechanisms that ensure such ongoing contestation happens within boundaries generally accepted by that culture. Moving from focus on the practice itself to the philosophical basis of the practice allows us to see more clearly the norms that are at work, the ways that those norms are contested, and the dispute management mechanisms, or local laws, that mediate this contestation.

Contrary to prevailing stereotypes, Indigenous laws and legal orders are not static or frozen in historical rituals or practices. Understanding and using local law is not about trying to go back in time, but about drawing on strengths and principles of the past to deal with modern problems and situations.[33] We think that the Committee does this in several important ways, and we discuss examples of their application of local law below. We also find places where local law could be used to address modern problems and situations, but where it seems not to have been applied—in particular in assisting the victims of domestic violence in that community.

Alexis First Nation

The specificities of Alexis local law lie in part in the history of this group of people. We include some of this history here for two reasons related to self-governance. First, stereotypes about Aboriginal peoples abound, including the notion that Aboriginal "traditions" exist only in the frozen past. Discussing the complexities of Aboriginal history provides a more flexible, nuanced understanding of where local laws come from, how laws may have changed, and how they may continue to change. Second, as with all peoples, the history of Aboriginal groups shapes the conflicts, laws, and understandings they hold today. This history needs to be acknowledged and understood to provide context for further positive social change.

The Alexis Nakota Sioux Nation is situated on the north shore of Lac Ste Anne, approximately 72 kilometres west of Edmonton, Alberta. By adhesion, Alexis is a Treaty 6 signatory and is situated in an area that is traditional Cree territory. The history and circumstances of how this band of Nakota Sioux came to be formally established in its present location provides some context to their cultural uniqueness and the development of local law. The Nakota Sioux settlement in Cree territory was made possible by the operation of Nakota Sioux and Cree international laws and protocols.

It is difficult to piece together the history of the Alexis Nakota Sioux prior to the signing of the adhesion to Treaty 6. The archival records contain conflicting accounts of the migration of the Sioux in Canada. According to the Alexis Nakota History and Culture Program, "the Alexis Nakota Sioux Nation is the most northern member of the Siouan language family. Although closely related to their Cree neighbours through intermarriage and centuries of neighbourly interaction, Alexis maintained its cultural uniqueness as a Nakota Nation."[34]

What we can gather of the history of Alexis begins in the East with a group of Sioux who had alliances and intermarriage ties with the Saulteaux (Chippewa-Ojibwa)[35] and the Cree.[36] Alexis members contend that their ancestors were Nakota who broke away from the other divisions of the Sioux and migrated westward to Alberta during the fur trade. The two main points of variation are geographical origins and international alliances. Alexis First Nation's assertion that they originated in the East, near the Mississippi, is supported by Peter Grant.[37] However both Paul Carlson[38] and Helen Buckley[39] contend that the geographical origins of the current northwest Nakota are in the Great Plains and then the forests of Minnesota. According to Alexis First Nation, they were members of the Sioux nation and had alliances with the Cree and Saulteaux. According to Peter Grant, however, the Sioux were historically at odds with the Saulteaux.[40] And according to Carlson, the northern Nakota became the enemies of the Sioux, from whom they originally separated in the Great Plains.[41] According to all accounts, however, the Nakota Sioux had allied relations with the Cree, a pattern of international conduct that continues today in Alexis. Nevertheless, the present location of the Alexis First Nation is the result of a complex and turbulent history that spans hundreds of years and thousands of miles. Despite often harsh historical experiences, the Nakota have maintained a political and cultural identity, and a strong sense of collectivity. This is the historic backdrop to the present-day community of Alexis First Nation.

Alexis First Nation Justice Committee

Colette Arcand, Angela Cameron, and Val Napoleon met several times with members of the Committee in January 2007. The discussions were open-ended, with a series of questions intended to prompt conversation. We asked about the members' roles and responsibilities, relationships and kinship system, conflicts and community issues, and historic connections with other peoples and communities. Our goal was to encourage critical discussions about how the Committee members understood their legal obligations according to local and/or Nakota law. We also asked about contradictions in local and/or Nakota law, and whether the members saw the Alexis Court Project as a way to fulfill their legal obligations according to local and/or Nakota law.

By and large, the Committee members found it very difficult to respond to or engage with the questions. Two reasons for this discomfort were identified. First, the Committee members are used to discussing their work as a restorative justice program—not as law. This is the usual basis for their relations with government and the judiciary, as well as program evaluators, other Aboriginal groups, and outside researchers. Second, the term "law" became a major stumbling block because they associate it with their work with the *Criminal Code* and the courts. Given this experience, it was very difficult for the Committee members to imagine law in terms of being local and/or Nakota. This is discussed further in the next section.

Under the Court Services Division of Alberta Justice and Attorney General, Alexis First Nation has had provincial court sitting in the community for many years. Referred to as the Alexis Provincial Court, the Alexis program is described on the Alberta government website as follows:

A unique First Nations Court and Restorative Justice Initiative has been developed at the Alexis First Nation where Provincial Court Judges and Stony Plain Crown prosecutors share information about the criminal justice system and court procedures with the Alexis Justice Committee, Elders, and other community members. In turn, judges and prosecutors have the opportunity to build relationships with the Aboriginal community and learn about its culture, traditions, and social resources. This relationship-building and sharing of knowledge supports a community-based approach to justice that promotes respect for the law and safe communities.

The court, working with the community and justice stakeholders, has incorporated court-ordered supervision of offenders, interim reviews, and accountability to the community into the Alexis Restorative Justice process. The justice committee acts as a sentencing resource that augments pre-disposition or pre-sentence reports by identifying cultural and social resources available at the Reserve. The justice committee also assists the probation officer in monitoring the probation of some offenders, and in providing the court with community reviews of the probationer's compliance. These interim reviews are an important and unique component of the Alexis Restorative Justice process.[42]

Under the Alberta Solicitor General and Public Security, Alexis First Nation has a formally established Youth Justice Committee, a Community Tripartite Agreement under the First Nation Policing and Law Enforcement Initiatives, an Aboriginal Crime Prevention Program, and a Community Supervision Program for Aboriginal Offenders.[43] According to the online description, this latter program emphasizes the "culture and traditions of local Aboriginal communities." Supervision is provided to "Aboriginal persons with probation, temporary absence, pre-trial or fine option status."[44]

In 2003, a government-funded evaluation of the Committee concluded that the restorative justice program had been successful on a number of fronts during its ten-year existence. In particular, the evaluation notes that "the offenders find the structure of the sentences ... and the ongoing support from the Justice Committee and Probation Officer to be critical in changing their behaviour and lifestyles. The recognition by the Justice Personnel of the underlying causes of their lifestyle and the upfront willingness to assist the offenders to reintegrate into the community are keys to success."[45]

Local Law in Alexis—Experiences and Issues
It Is Hard to Talk about Law

Indigenous law flows from sources that lie outside of the common law and civil law traditions. As described in 1973 in the *Calder* case by the Supreme Court of Canada, such a unique source resides in the fact that "when the settlers came, the Indians were there, organized in societies and occupying the land as their forefathers had done for centuries." These laws have no need for dependence "on treaty, executive order or legislative enactment." They are "pre-existing" and have their own logic, as the Court said, "indigenous to their culture [though] capable of articulation under the common law."[46]

The purpose for our meeting with the Committee was to engage in a discussion about how the Committee members understand their work in the community and whether this understanding reflects their local and/or Nakota laws. Local law in this context is the way community members manage themselves as a group over time. Historically, Nakota society's governance was without a hierarchical or centralized authority. In keeping with the theory of law that recognizes law as deriving from social interaction rather than solely from centralized formal state processes,[47] local law is about how people make decisions and conduct themselves in a social context. Local law may be described as "a language of interaction" that is necessary for people's social behaviour to be meaningful and predictable over time. It is this language of interaction that makes possible social settings where people's behaviours generally fall within expected or known patterns.

This is a more complex and subtle way to think about local and/or Nakota law because, since much of this law is implicit or beneath the surface of our consciousness, it usually remains invisible. It becomes that which we do not know that we know. However, Indigenous societies also made implicit law explicit, complete with collective processes for deliberation, reasoning, interpretation, and application. We know that these processes have been damaged and undermined by recent history. Consequently, most Indigenous peoples, including Alexis, have difficulty discussing Indigenous law and legal orders in any critical, rigorous, and practical way.

Our starting premise is that local law and Nakota law in Alexis (and the equivalent in other communities) can be drawn out by examining the activities and experiences of the Committee members. In this way, legal norms and legal obligations can be discerned in people's behaviours over time—that "network of tacit understandings and unwritten conventions rooted in the soil of social interaction."[48] According to Gerald Postema, "We cannot fully understand law, we cannot appreciate its dynamic character, the role it plays in human affairs, or the kind of public good it offers, if we fail to attend to this implicit dimension of law."[49] Postema contends that implicit rules do not arise from conception, but from conduct:

> Although implicit rules arise from the conduct of determinate agents, typically they have no precise date of birth and no determinate authors. They presuppose no relations of authority and subordination; thus, their practical force depends neither on authority nor on enactment, but on the fact that they find "direct expression in the conduct of people toward one another."[50]

So, while the Committee members were unable to explicitly discuss local and/or Nakota law, it is arguable that their examples demonstrated a fulfillment of legal obligations and are a form of local and/or Nakota law at work. The committee members' language conveys the implicit nature of this particular discourse: "That's how things are," they say, and, "It's natural." In this way, what people know is "how things are," and natural, and invisible. Some members described their local and Nakota laws as a way of life, again exemplifying a more internal perspective and a more holistic way of understanding.

For the most part, the Committee members discussed their work within the boundaries of a justice program intended to deal with people charged with criminal offences. This is congruent with their mandate as a formalized, community-based Aboriginal justice initiative under the Criminal Justice Division of Alberta Justice and Attorney General. As previously outlined, the community is actively involved in various Aboriginal justice initiatives in many areas, and from the Committee's perspective, it makes good sense that the Committee discuss their work within these terms of reference.

As the discussion began about local and Nakota law being applied in the Committee's work, we observed that the Committee members were uncomfortable with the language of "law" and were having difficulty in articulating their own laws. We did introduce our questions by explaining that in our theoretical framework, law is not just rules, it is how law is practiced and how it is thought about. Further, we hoped that by looking at the interactive process of the Committee, we could learn how people figure out how to interpret and apply the rules, and how to act on the rules generally. The authors listened to the Committee members as they discussed why they care about the work they do.

John Borrows provides some useful examples from Anishinabek law that are helpful to our consideration of local or Nakota laws at work in Alexis. Borrows explains that Anishinabek legal traditions use precedential, standard-setting criteria to guide and judge action. He finds that the trickster Nanabush is a useful intellectual instrument for teaching law: "Nanabush turned to what was there, what was familiar, what was nearby, and he was able to take those things that were familiar and nearby and transform them—transform them in such a way that he got people involved with what was going on in the community."[51]

The Committee incorporates sacred ceremonies when the members work with offenders. It may also arrange to have clients work closely with Elders in the community as part of their community supervision. One example provided by Committee members was how a thirty-day continuous fire was employed to inspire the youth in the community and promote spirituality. One Committee member explained that the Committee "takes what works and uses it." These are examples of what Borrows describes as expressions of normative values being reflected in day-to-day affairs. Borrows writes, "The professionalization of the decision-making through lawyers takes law out of the hands of people.... Why should you need to hire somebody at $100 an hour when through kin, through story, through ceremony, through speaking with elders, you can deal with challenges on other bases?"[52]

These are the sort of processes used by Alexis to deal with circumstances that are presented to them by the actions of their community members. Alexis is drawing on principles of legal obligation to one another in order to confront problems. There are similarities between the work of Alexis and how Borrows discusses Anishinabek law and interactions: "Go with our friends; form a council; be unanimous; and act in such a way that you take responsibility for the decision you make."[53] The Committee has decided that is what they will do. They meet with clients, discuss the circumstances, make recommendations to the court, and are involved with follow-up with clients via interim reviews to the courts. Borrows explains:

> You study indigenous words and you get a world view focused on relationships people should have with one another in terms of their obligations and responsibilities. This is the case with environmental law; there are things that people are trying in the criminal justice context. In fact, as Morris Rosenberg mentioned, the idea of sentencing circles has some of its roots in indigenous legal traditions, in gathering together and trying to come to a resolution in that format.[54]

In Alexis, the Committee reconciled an internal community conflict in the early 1990s that resulted in the ongoing acceptance of diverse spiritual practices. One Committee member described this as a heated political issue that affected the Committee's work. Another Committee member described how they decided to work through this issue because they needed to co-operate to help the people. The members discussed how they worked this out themselves without the provincial judge who usually participates in the Committee meetings. They described how they came to consensus about prayer, higher powers, and the acceptability of different means and practices as an individual's personal choice. Now, spirituality among

Alexis community members is generally some form of Christianity, or Nakota traditional spirituality, or a blend of the two. This acceptance of spiritual diversity by the Committee is an example of successful ongoing conflict management.

Spirituality is supported because the members believe it is more important to nurture spirituality than to worry about how an individual practices it. Today, for example, all members support the idea that programs like Alcoholics Anonymous are just as effective as a traditional sweat ceremony. No one method is better than the other, just different—the method does not matter so much as ending up with sober people. From the Committee members' discussion about this experience, it becomes apparent that they were involved in an active and deliberative process to find solutions to their conflicts. The experiences of the Committee are similar to how Postema describes interactive processes involving informal and implicit law:

> Because parties engaged in interaction frequently face new situations and new practical problems, they must adjust, reinterpret, or even replace existing rules. These revising activities are possible only because the parties develop shared abilities to negotiate the network of expectations and together to arrive at new, relatively stable understandings. Participating in such practices we learn how to anticipate the solutions our counterparts will hit upon as they attempt to anticipate our decisions and actions. Interpretation and extension or contraction of existing rules in such a practice, then, is itself an essentially interactive process.[55]

If we follow Postema's and Fuller's line of argument, the importance and effect of the presence of implicit law in modern legal systems becomes even more substantial and critical to thinking about self-government for Alexis. According to Postema, Fuller's claim is that "dependence on implicit interactive practice is a common feature of modern law, but also that law is not possible without it, that it is essential to our idea of legal order."[56] According to Fuller's congruence thesis, "a substantial degree of congruence between enacted laws and background informal social practices and conventions governing horizontal relations among citizens is necessary for the existence of law."[57] In Alexis, the Committee's social interactions are congruent with the understood rules or social norms in the community. In other words, the explicit work of the Committee is founded inextricably on the implicit and informal law that derives from Nakota law. Again, turning to Fuller (in Postema's words), "Legal norms and authoritative directives can guide self-directed social interaction only if they are broadly congruent with the practices and patterns of interaction extant in the society generally."[58] Alexis legal norms are not just "understanding the meaning of the words in which [they are] formulated, but understanding the institutions, practices, and attitudes of the community to which [they are] addressed."[59] In other words, legal norms make sense as "practical guides for self-directing agents ... only when they are set in a context of concrete practices, attitudes, and forms of social interaction."[60]

There are times and circumstances when a projected norm does not make sense. For example, statements about "respect" were made during the meeting with the Committee. One member talked about respect for other people's ways, and another talked about treating offenders with respect. Members also talked about the importance of not judging clients, not kicking someone who is down, and giving all people a second chance. These comments are important. However, when respect is articulated in an abstract form, problems can be created because of the difficulty in understanding the contextual and relational subtleties of "respect." Julie Cruikshank provides an example in her discussion about her work in the Yukon, in which one speaker of a panel addressed the audience at an environmental conference:

A second speaker adopted a different strategy, one that works effectively in many meetings. He spoke of the concept of respect—respectful behaviour toward other human beings and between humans and non-humans. Accustomed to using this language to speak to large audiences, he may have seemed to some to over generalize by using such phrases as "we always respected our elders" and "we always respected our women." When an audience member requested a clearer definition of the term "respect," this panellist responded, again conventionally, that it is impossible to translate some concepts from Indigenous languages to English. The previous panellist, trying to formulate a more optimistic response, proposed that while "respect" is indeed an English word used only recently, it might be thought of as referring to attention to subtlety, especially in the relationships among humans, and between humans and other living things.[61]

Cruikshank's point is that in attempting to reach broad audiences "who come with universalistic expectations and expect to understand what they hear, familiar strategies are inevitably the most effective in the short term, but they too have costs."[62] The cost Cruikshank is referring to occurs when the abstract formulation becomes an obstacle to making the practical sense of the norm known. She writes: "The inescapable lesson seems to be that removing oral tradition from a context where it has self-evident power and performing it in a context where it is opened to evaluation by the state poses enormous problems for understanding its historical value."[63]

At Alexis, one Committee member explained that people used to tell stories that contained laws, but these did not work out when interpreted in English. She talked about the old teachings that were based on having to answer for one's actions in the spirit world after death. Another example is about the purpose and meaning of the smudge at the beginning of a meeting. The Committee members explained that the smudge and prayer at the beginning of a meeting are important to settle the room, settle peoples' minds, and humble the participants (i.e., where are we in the universe?). Before a court hearing, the smudge settles the room, humbles the young people, and helps to deter aggressive behaviour by reminding them of their relationship to the Elders in the room. Postema apprehends this process: "Law has a social depth which we must recognize if we are to understand adequately the nature and modes of functioning of these salient surface phenomena. By its very nature, law is deeply implicated in the practices and conventions of the communities it governs."[64]

Borrows argues that there is a crisis in the rule of law in Aboriginal communities—not because Aboriginal peoples do not have the rule of law, but because the legitimacy of the rule of law in Aboriginal communities has been undermined.[65] For Alexis, this is not the only difficulty. It is also difficult to describe how local or Nakota law works because these institutions and constructs have been displaced, damaged, and arguably distorted by Western law (more on this later). However, what remains in Alexis (and in other similarly situated Aboriginal communities) is the underlying implicit and informal law.

Another difficulty that became apparent in Alexis is that it is difficult even to find a useful language with which to create constructive (i.e., non-colonial) intellectual bridges between Nakota law and Western law. Also, it is difficult to discuss either local or Nakota law solely on the basis of what was shared during the meeting with the Committee. Local law and Nakota law are deeply embedded in the practices and day-to-day interactions in the community. Without participating first-hand in the Committee's activities over time, and without further information from the Committee, it can only be argued that there is evidence of local and Nakota law at work in this community—but dialogue is elusive.

Kinship

Local law functions as a conflict-management tool during the contestation of social norms. In Alexis, it derives in part from and rests within the kinship system. At the same time, kinship units have been flexible, allowing this form of local law to act as a primary form of conflict management.

Nakota society is organized along kinship lines with extended family groupings that are fluid, enabling people to operate and move within the larger group according to matrilineal, patrilineal, or bilateral lines of descent. These kinship relationships in part provide members with their identities while determining their rights and obligations to one another. Historically, this social organization determined the distribution of goods; regulated the utilization of resources; provided domestic, political, and spiritual leadership; and established standards of behaviour and punishments for deviation.[66] In describing the Dakota Sioux, Ella Cara Deloria wrote, "The ultimate aim of Dakota life, stripped of accessories, is quite simple: One must obey kinship rules; one must be a good relative. ... Without that aim and the constant struggle to attain it, the people would no longer be Dakotas in truth. They would no longer even be human."[67]

Kinship and responsibility

It was clear that most Committee members viewed the work they did as more than just working within the Alexis restorative justice program. This was evidenced in part by the ways in which members carried their "Committee" work with them outside of the time and space allotted to restorative justice work. For instance, several Committee members noted that they get visits at home from young clients in crisis seeking guidance. There was a clear sense among the members that the work within the Alexis restorative justice program was primarily the work they were already required to perform as a good relative. This was closely tied to local legal understandings of responsibility for young people within that kinship system, extending well beyond the nuclear family.

For instance, one female participant notes that she cares about the Committee's work in part because she is the second oldest girl in her family. She had the responsibility to look after her younger siblings and the younger children in her extended family, and as an adult she still has that kind of responsibility. Another female member, with eleven children and thirty-four grandchildren, joined the Committee in part because her children are all grown up, leaving her time and energy to fill a (grandparent) role for other young people in Alexis. She notes that this is the work she does because "that is what parents and grandparents did."

Committee members actively teach kinship principles to young people who participate in the Alexis restorative justice program. One male member, for example, talked about kinship language and the names used to address particular family members such as nephew, cousin, brother, and little brother. He noted how young people do not use the names from the language, and that the Committee members advise clients that they are going to have to learn because they are going to have to teach their own kids. A female member echoed that laws were oral, passed on in the conduct of individuals in their relationships with their families and communities.

Gender roles, parenting, and grandparenting

Several Committee members referred to the existence of gender roles within Nakota law. One female member talked about how the male offenders do their individual work with male elders and female offenders with female elders to provide a setting for learning gender roles and proper protocols. Nakota kinship laws established gendered norms within families and the larger community, allocating responsibilities and duties to one another, as well as the division of work.[68] For instance, one female member noted that older sisters were seen as second mothers, and brothers as second fathers. Verbal greetings by these names locate each person in the kinship network.[69] Each role and relationship carries legal obligations, including setting out who will be responsible for the welfare of children in case of future harms to the parents.

In Alexis, a number of circumstances have challenged these norms. For example, the demands of contemporary living have disrupted the practice of dividing work and responsibility along gendered lines. Rather than accepting this practice as a static "rule," Alexis local law has maintained and fulfilled the philosophical basis of the practice (teaching children how to be a good relative) while allowing for gendered norms to be contested. Importantly, the underlying philosophy of being a good relative has remained intact and guided the changes to the practice itself. This ensures that Alexis children who lack a relation of a particular gender have others in the community fulfilling that role. The social circumstances that supported the gendered division of responsibility have changed, and therefore so have the practices and norms.

Contemporary pressures on gender roles reflect a number of social changes. Also, there is a dearth of adults of both gender who understand and follow Nakota laws about kinship responsibility generally. Alexis local law has intervened to allow gendered norms to be fulfilled within that challenging contemporary context. In several cases, this has meant that committee members of one gender will perform the kinship work of the opposite gender in order to ensure that children in Alexis are learning Nakota kinship principles. In addition, paid work generally has provided opportunities for several Committee members of both genders to teach Nakota kinship principles and responsibilities to Alexis children. The responsibilities of kinship extend beyond the particular young people who come before them in committee.

For instance, some female Committee members choose to work outside the home, sharing their role as Nakota woman/mother with other roles as a paid worker. One female Committee member spoke about preparing the smudge before court, which she described as a man's job. One female member said that being a school-bus driver and raising her own children fulfills her role as a Nakota woman, and is her contribution to Alexis. Another female member says that she has had to play a grandfather role in her paid work because some of the youth don't have a grandfather who can do this. She notes that this "isn't her role" and reiterates that she is in fact a "younger sister." Another female member talked about how she plays the role of grandfather to her grandson, whose father is deceased, and emphasized the need for these roles.

Reciprocation, respect, and role modeling
Throughout the roundtable discussion, several other principles of Alexis local law emerged. These were discussed either in terms of reasons for joining and staying with the Committee, or as tools used to teach and guide young people who came before the Committee.

There was a sense among some members of the importance of reciprocity, or giving back. One male member was helped by the Committee and then joined as a member afterwards. One woman stated she got involved as a way to give back because they had accepted her when she married a community member. Another woman said that work on the Committee is her way of giving back to the community in general.

Over the course of the roundtable, the word "respect" was used frequently to characterize good relations within families and within the Alexis community.

Elders were seen as an important source of knowledge for how to conduct yourself with respect. A female member said, "There are three Ls in 'Indian country'—Look, Listen, Learn—and try to be as good as the practicing Elders." There was an acknowledgement that Elders are important, and several members expressed fears about losing their Elders as they pass on. One female member stated that the Elders are an important part of the Committee. Another female member said that the Elders maintain the history and remember the changes. This was echoed by another woman who said that the Elders watch who makes changes and breaks unhealthy patterns.

Finally several Committee members understood their work on the Committee to include being a role model. The elder male Committee members in particular discussed their commitment in terms of acting in ways to model the behaviour of a good relative. One male Committee member talked about how he felt that was important, otherwise who would listen to him? Two male Committee members talked about how they did not want their grandchildren to perceive them as alcoholics, but instead as models of how to remain sober. One elder female noted that having used alcohol herself, and knowing how to overcome it, gives her knowledge to share with younger people on how to get clean.

Two younger members—a man and a woman—also talked about being good role models and teachers to their own children and to other children in Alexis. They said that they in turn look to Elders as role models and as sources of knowledge. According to one man, being a good role model also goes beyond yourself, as you are representing your family.

Gender

A recent evaluation of the restorative justice program in Alexis,[70] discussions with justice officials, and our roundtable discussion with Committee members revealed a lack of adequate resources available for the victims of crime. The evaluation reported that most of the program's strength lies in treating offenders, and that dealing with victims is a serious challenge.[71] For example, the report notes that "some victims find it difficult to provide statements and evidence in front of their own community" and "some victims are fearful of providing statements since the offender's family might be in court."[72] The evaluation also highlights how the Alexis restorative justice model is not including victims in the process to the extent that it could, and that the Committee and the criminal justice service providers recognize this gap and are attempting to acquire funds to start a victim services unit on the reserve.[73] The evaluation goes on to recommend that victim services be developed to enhance the Alexis restorative justice model.

In a recent conversation with an Alexis community member who does paid work with the Committee, the problem of victim services was raised and recognized. Scarcities of financial and human resources were identified as key factors contributing to this problem. Although Committee members have received government training on how to deal with offenders, they currently do not have government training to address the needs of victims. In the past, the Committee tried to establish a subcommittee to work with victims. Unfortunately, it proved to be beyond the capacity of the Committee, and resulted in an unmanageable workload for the Committee members. The Committee member also mentioned that the Committee has tried to recruit other agencies to help them improve the situation for victims, but the substantial commitment required between agencies to allow for such an alliance with the Alexis program has not yet been realized. This means that victims have limited options when seeking local resources. The nearest victim services facility is located in Mayerthorpe, which is approximately a forty-five minute drive west of Alexis.

It also became clear to us that very many of the generic "victims of crime" referred to in the evaluation and by the Committee are women who have been assaulted by their intimate partners.[74] In our opinion, this represents a piece of the larger pattern of violence against women, which cuts across cultures in Canada and which warrants particular attention and analysis. Violence against women is a gendered crime, regardless of the community where the crimes occur, and helps to perpetuate and entrench the legal, social, economic, and cultural subordination of women. Framing the issue within Aboriginal self-government does not erase the need to address these issues in a gendered way. Issues that have been marginalized and ghettoized as "Aboriginal women's issues" need to be contextualized within the larger Aboriginal political frame, and Aboriginal political issues, including self-government, require a gendered and feminist analysis.[75]

The efficacy and safety of restorative justice in cases of intimate violence[76] has been explored from various positions,[77] with particular attention to the survivors[78] of intimate violence. In this chapter, however, we are interested in the ways that local law has (not) dealt with women survivors of intimate violence. We argue that, to an important extent, the funding and parameters of the restorative justice project have also set boundaries around the functioning of local laws and legal orders in relation to these issues. The availability of financial and human resources earmarked for offenders, albeit limited, has steered the Committee toward local legal work that supports offenders. We argue also that Alexis local law itself has the potential to assist women survivors in similar ways.

All law, including local law in Alexis, changes over time. In order to maintain its legitimacy as a governance function, local law provides parameters within which norms can change and adapt to contemporary social issues. We discussed above how Nakota norms of gendered kinship roles have adapted to contemporary challenges. In the context of intimate violence, Alexis local law has the potential to adapt in similar, helpful ways to cope with this contemporary social issue outside the parameters of the restorative justice project. This must be done, in part, through legal reasoning—by applying Alexis local law to this issue in ways that are intellectually rigorous, critical, flexible, and inclusive of women. Committee members have already done this to some extent with offenders.

Solving contemporary social problems will likely require Alexis local law to continue to recognize and adapt resources from non-Nakota sources. For instance, in treating/healing offenders, many committee members referred to the extensive and successful use of Alcoholics Anonymous. Survivors of intimate abuse also require such services, including specialized victim service providers with training in the gendered dynamics of intimate abuse, and resources such as individual counselling.[79]

There remains, however, the important issue of resources. In helping offenders, Committee members give above and beyond the paid parameters of their work. They speak of this extra work in terms of a local legal kinship obligation. The restorative justice program, however, also plays a role. It acts as a scaffold for the local law at work in Alexis and simultaneously provides limited financial and human resources which the committee stretches into use in their kinship work. The Committee, and the paid staff who support them, are already stretching these resources to an incredible extent and using them to do far more local legal work than the restorative justice program demands of them. These resources, however, are simply insufficient to meet the needs of survivors as well. We argue that, given some restorative justice resources specifically earmarked for survivors, Committee members would and could stretch them beyond their programmatic capacity, and use them to augment local legal work. With these resources, in conjunction with the conscious, critical application of Alexis local law to the circumstances of women survivors, the Committee has the potential to fill a legitimate local governance role in relation to crimes of intimate violence.

Norms versus Values

All legal orders, of whatever kind, have to have mechanisms for fashioning these collective positions out of the welter of disagreement. This does not undermine the key insights of the theorists of social law, but it does warn us against the tendency to treat the social law as natural, as emerging harmoniously from practice. Instead, it insists on the existence of contestation and dissent and focuses attention on the means by which contestation is settled. ... Indeed, the very essence of law—and of normative orders generally—involves the fashioning of an emphatically social outcome in the face of disagreement.[80]

This section considers the implications of focusing on values, rather than on norms, within the restorative justice field. It then asks, what difference would a focus on norms make, if any? The primary concern here is whether the focus on values might represent a failure to recognize agency in the interpretation of values. There are some similarities as well as wide variations between the identified values listed in the following discussion, but they are all described as basic beliefs underlying the practice of restorative justice, including many discussions, conferences, and government and community programs. And yet this critical, predominantly values-based approach remains unquestioned.[81]

Within the vast literature on restorative justice, much is written about the importance and centrality of values. For example, in a recent book on peacemaking circles, the "circle values" are listed as forgiveness, love, respect, honesty, humility, sharing, courage, inclusivity, empathy, and trust.[82] The authors argue that each individual must strive to "shift to living more mindfully aligned with our values" and "learn how to act in more value-consistent ways."[83] The peacemaking circles are spaces where, among other things, one can learn to act in harmony with one's values.[84]

Barb Toews works inside penitentiaries. From her perspective, restorative justice is grounded in four core values that affirm and build strong webs of relationships: respect, care, trust, and humility.[85] According to Toews, acting on these values in restorative justice practice requires recognizing other needs and behaviours such as accountability, healing, responsibility, restoration, honesty, dependability, and confidentiality.[86] From a national Canadian perspective, the former Law Commission of Canada identified restorative justice values as: participation, respect for participants, community empowerment, commitment to agreed outcomes, and flexibility and responsiveness of process and outcomes.[87] From an international perspective, Daniel Van Ness draws a distinction between normative values and operational values.[88] The list of normative values includes active responsibility, peaceful social life, respect, and solidarity. The operational values are directed to the parties affected by the offence and include amends for the harm, assistance to become contributing citizens, collaboration to develop solutions, empowerment, encounter, inclusion, moral education, protection, and resolution.[89]

The Alexis evaluation report refers to incorporating cultural and spiritual values into sentencing and to restoring moral values to the community.[90] During the discussions in Alexis, Committee members referred more generally to traditional, cultural, and moral values. From the perspective of the Committee members, the term "value" seems to express deeply held beliefs about their work, culture, community—basically, that which is good and to be aspired to as people, sometimes including that which is held sacred.

It is not our intent to question the deeply held beliefs of the Alexis people or anyone else. Rather, because our interest is law, we are concerned with the questions of individual and collective agency. People can only interpret values according to their experiences and circumstances, and within their cultural horizons. In the restorative justice discourse, these propounded values are assumed to be absolutely universal, leaving no place to consider how people are interpreting them. Nor is there any place to consider whether people disagree with the values or how they weight them when values conflict (e.g., family versus work). Also, within the prevailing restorative justice discourse, it would be exceedingly difficult for anyone to actually disagree or acknowledge contradictory values. Interpretation of values matters because this determines what our expectations are insofar as ultimate success or failure of our experience with restorative justice. Specifically, failing to recognize interpretive differences can lead to conflict about whether particular restorative justice requirements have been fulfilled.[91]

Why, then, does agency matter to law? If we understand that there are different forms of law beyond centralized, formal State law, then we can imagine decentralized and collaborative law that is more reflective of decentralized, non-state Indigenous societies. And if we understand law as an intellectual process that subsumes rules and practices by including legal reasoning and interpretation, then we need to recognize individual and collective agency as integral to a thinking citizenry.

From this perspective, it makes more sense to consider norms, in this case legal norms that carry an obligation. Legal norms are a part of what makes law. And, all norms are constantly contested and change over time. The health of a legal order is determined by whether it can withstand the ongoing contestation and whether the citizens recognize the legal order as legitimate. According to Jeremy Webber, all law, including non-State as well as State law, is inherently non-consensual:[92]

> The socially-grounded law is portrayed as a unified and harmonious body of norms, highly adapted to a particular social milieu and exempt from disagreement and contention. It is not so much that disagreement is denied but that it has no point of entry into the theory. The law is given directly by social interaction, not by processes of human debate and decision-making.[93]

When we shift our analysis from restorative justice to considering local law, we create the necessary space in which to think critically about agency and norm contestation as integral to law. Such a shift enables people to deliberately take into account the importance of citizenry, intellectual capacity, and conflict management. In other words, such an approach encourages communities to build their social capital in the form of local law.

To conclude, in order to remain alive and therefore legitimate, Indigenous legal orders and law must be able withstand internal challenges and change. It is this ongoing challenge to norms that keeps a culture alive and vital—and ensures continued relevance for younger people. Otherwise, Indigenous law will fail to be useful in today's world, and there will be no point in teaching or practicing it. All that will be left will be cultural remnants.

Conclusion: Local Law and Self-Government

Fundamentally, law is about governing ourselves—managing ourselves in large groups and determining how we relate to other people from other large groups. It is the thesis of this chapter that we might learn about local or Indigenous law by changing how we look at contemporary community practices such as the Alexis Court Justice Project. To take this argument one step further, recognizing the contemporary manifestations of local law creates opportunities to support and strengthen it—as opposed to inadvertently continuing to obscure it in the language of programs.

There is a troubling general perception that there is a broad dichotomy between the level of sophistication of Aboriginal societies and the Canadian state. On one side is an assumption that the Canadian state possesses complete systems of governance, law, economics, and social structures. On the other is the assumption that, although Aboriginal peoples possess values, practices, and various notions of culture, they lack complete systems of governance or law or anything else, except perhaps spirituality. This supposed asymmetrical relationship is founded on a usually unstated,[94] but very real, assumption of various cultural deficits on the part of Aboriginal peoples. In the case of "Aboriginal justice," for instance, Aboriginal values and practices have usually been "extracted" from Aboriginal culture and added to the *Criminal Code*. Removing these from the complete systems that give them meaning is a distortion and should be recognized as such.

So what might a symmetrical relationship look like? Such a relationship would be founded on an understanding that Aboriginal peoples have complete systems of governance and law (albeit damaged by recent history), and that practices and norms have to be appreciated from within that which gives them meaning. So rather than imagining Canadian criminal law relating to Aboriginal values and practices, there would be some effort to take a pluralist approach, relating Canadian criminal law to how Aboriginal peoples dealt with harms and offences in their entirety. This is not about trying to go back in time, but about starting the conversation between Aboriginal people and the state at a different place rather than from an assumed cultural deficit.[95]

For Alexis First Nation, perhaps considering the work of the Alexis Justice Committee as being founded on local and Nakota laws could provide community members with an opportunity to rigorously and critically examine them. Then they would be in a position to consider how their own laws might relate to those of Canada and Alberta on a corresponding basis. In other words, perhaps this is a way that the internal conversations among Aboriginal citizens will change the nature of the external relationships between Aboriginal peoples and Canada.[96] This work of deliberating on local and Nakota law does not require the sanction of the state until Alexis (or other Aboriginal community) decides to formalize these aspects of their relationship with the state.

A related, ongoing issue before Alexis and other small Aboriginal communities is that of scale. For the most part, these questions about self-government require Aboriginal peoples to look beyond band structures in order to consider scale—the concepts of the public good and personal interests,[97] accountability, and the full extent of the relationships and responsibilities within the society. The reserve boundaries created by the *Indian Act*, which divided and grouped Indigenous peoples into bands, cut across Indigenous legal orders. This division of Indigenous peoples and lands has undermined the management of our legal orders and has undermined the application of Indigenous laws. At the band level, the larger legal order becomes unworkable, and some co-operative arrangements must be established to enable bands to draw upon broader-based relationships at a national level to more effectively implement their laws. For Alexis, this might involve international alliances with the Cree.[98]

NOTES

1   For instance, see generally, Wanda D. McCaslin, ed., *Justice as Healing: Indigenous Ways* (St. Paul, MN: Living Justice, 2005); P.A. Monture-Okanee & M.E. Turpel, "Aboriginal Peoples and Canadian Criminal Law: Rethinking Justice," *U.B.C. Law Review* 26 (1992): 248; and, A.C. Hamilton, *A Feather Not a Gavel: Working Toward Aboriginal Justice* (Winnipeg: Great Plains, 2001). Others are more cautious about the role of restorative justice as it is currently practiced in the self-government project. See for example, Jonathan Rudin, "Aboriginal Justice and Restorative Justice," in *New Directions in Restorative Justice: Issues, Practice and Evaluations,* eds. Elizabeth Elliott & Robert M. Gordon (Portland: Willan, 2005), 89-114; and, Larissa Behrendt, "Lessons from the Mediation Obsession: Ensuring that Sentencing 'Alternatives' Focus on Indigenous Self-Determination," in *Restorative Justice and Family Violence,* eds. Heather Strang & John Braithwaite (Cambridge: Cambridge University Press, 2002), 178-90.

2   The authors are grateful to Sandra Potts and the other members of the Alexis First Nation Justice Committee who so generously shared their experience, knowledge, and laughter with us.

3   Alexis First Nation is an Indian Band pursuant to the *Indian Act,* R.S.C. 1985, c. I-5. In deference to their preference for the spelling "Nakota", as in "Alexis Nakota Sioux Nation" (see http://www.alexisnakotasioux.com), we have retained that spelling here, as opposed to "Nakoda," which is used elsewhere in Canada.

4   The distinction between "local law" and "Nakota law" is examined below in the section "Local Law."

5   This is an important question for Indigenous peoples who had decentralized forms of governance.

6   See generally, Christoph Eberhard, "Toward an Intercultural Legal Theory: The Dialogical Challenge," *Social and Legal Studies* 10, no. 2 (2001): 171-201.

7   See generally, Law Commission of Canada, *Indigenous Legal Traditions in Canada* by John Borrows (Ottawa: Law Commission of Canada, 2005).

8   Boaventura de Sousa Santos views the naming of non-officially recognized law as emancipatory in an even broader sense. According to de Sousa Santos, by naming Indigenous laws and legal orders, we add to the global "ecology of knowledges," disrupting binary or "abyssal" categories fostered by modern, liberal Western thought that supports and sustains socio-political inequality. De Sousa Santos points to "other" forms of knowledge—such as Indigenous laws and legal orders—as key to challenging universality because they provide positions from which to see real alternatives to capitalism and other forms of dominant neo-liberalism. See Boaventura de Sousa Santos, "Beyond Abyssal Thinking: From Global Lines to Ecologies of Knowledges" (paper, Demcon Conference, University of Victoria, December 1, 2006), 19.

9   Javier Mignone describes social capital in the context of northern Manitoba First Nations as the extent to which resources are socially invested: a culture of trust, norms of reciprocity, and collective action are present; participation is facilitated; and inclusive, flexible, and diverse networks are in place. See Canadian Institute for Health Information, "Measuring Social Capital: A Guide for First Nations Communities" by Javier Mignone (Ottawa: Canadian Institute for Health Information, 2003), University of Manitoba, http://www.umanitoba.ca/faculties/human_ecology/family/Staff/pdf_files/Measuring%20social%20capital%20A%20guide%20for%20FN%20Communities-1.pdf (accessed 21 May 2007).

10 Susan Sharpe, "How Large Should the Restorative Justice 'Tent' Be?" in *Critical Issues in Restorative Justice,* eds. Howard Zehr & Barb Toews (New York: Criminal Justice, 2004), 17.

11 For example, see *House of Commons Debates,* vol. IV (1st Sess., 35th Parl.), 5873 (Minister of Justice Allan Rock); *R. v. Gladue,* [1999] 1 S.C.R. 688, para. 21; *R. v. Wells,* [2000] 1 S.C.R. 207, para. 27.

12 One notable exception was the Hollow Water Healing Circle Process, which functioned with minimal oversight from outside of the Aboriginal group that it served (Native Counselling Services of Alberta). See, Solicitor General Canada and Aboriginal Healing Foundation, *A Cost-Benefit Analysis of Hollow Water's Community Holistic Circle Healing Process* by Joe Couture and others (Ottawa: Solicitor General, 2001), http://www.sgc.gc.ca (accessed April 2007).

13 This is also the case with "cultural" programs in penitentiaries. For an excellent example, see Joane Martel and Renée Brassard, "Painting the Prison 'Red': Constructing and Experiencing Aboriginal Identities in Prison," *Br. Journal of Social Work.* (October 31, 2006), http://bjsw.oxfordjournals.org.login.ezproxy.library.ualberta.ca (accessed 22 May 2007).

14 Rudin, "Aboriginal Justice and Restorative Justice," *supra* note 1.

15 Warwick Tie, *Legal Pluralism: Toward a Multicultural Conception of Law* (Aldershot, UK: Dartmouth, 1999), 248.

16 This includes any local version of the Nakota legal order and laws. See the section " Local Law" below.

17 *Criminal Code.* R.S., 1985, c. C-46.

18 "Aboriginal communities" here refers broadly to settled geographic communities and cultural groupings of Métis, First Nations, and Inuit peoples. With further thought and research, this local law approach might be helpfully applied to the more diffuse and "intercultural" urban Aboriginal communities.

19 However, Colette Arcand worked with the Alexis Justice Project for some years, and is closely connected to some community members. While this work of cross-cultural understanding is difficult, it is crucial to socio-political change. According to Boaventura de Sousa Santos, this difficult work requires "a theory or procedure of translation, capable of creating mutual intelligibility among possible and available experiences." See his "A Critique of Lazy Reason: Against the Waste of Experience" (University of Victoria, December 1st, 2006), 4.

20 See generally, "On the Limits of 'Grand Theory' in Comparative Law," *Washington Law Review* 61 (1986): 945-56.

21 Barbara Allen & BIM Larsson and Associates, *Alexis Restorative Justice Model: An Evaluation* (Edmonton: Alberta Justice, 2003), 3.

22 Indigenous legal orders are characterized by law that is embedded in the social, political, economic, and spiritual aspects of each person's everyday life, rather than in a separate institution with legal experts who are wholly responsible for law. See Harold J. Berman, *Law and Revolution* (Cambridge: Harvard University Press, 1983), 49-50.

23 However, international relations, trade, and intermarriage have always been a part of Aboriginal societies.

24 There are four Nakota communities in Alberta. See below for a more detailed history of the Alexis First Nation.

25 Gerald Postema, "Implicit Law," *Law and Philosophy* 13, no. 3 (August, 1994): 361.

26 For a discussion on the dangers of essentializing the law in legal pluralism, see Brian Z. Tamanaha, "A Non-Essentialist Version of Legal Pluralism," *Journal of Law and Society* 27, no. 2 (2000): 296-321.

27 H. Patrick Glenn, *Legal Traditions of the World, Sustainable Diversity in Law,* 2nd ed. (Oxford: Oxford University Press, 2004), 13-14ff. Glenn argues that tradition is not merely rote or a practice, but rather should be perceived as information. That is, tradition is composed of information and there are important questions about the nature of the information that constitutes the tradition. As such, tradition is constitutive of identity and society.

28 For a broader discussion of Indigenous legal traditions as tools of governance, see John Borrows, "Indigenous Legal Traditions" (on file with author, University of Victoria); and Law Commission of Canada, *Justice Within: Indigenous Legal Traditions* by John Borrows (Ottawa: Law Commission of Canada, 2007).

29 Gerald J. Postema, "Classical Common Law Jurisprudence (Part II)," *Oxford University Commonwealth Law Journal* 3, no. 1 (2003): 1, 3-10. According to Postema, there are six distinctive features of legal reasoning in the common law:
    (i) It focuses on problem solving.
    (ii) There is deliberate regard for the larger public good beyond individual interests.
    (iii) It requires skilled and knowledgeable adjudicators or mediators.
    (iv) It cannot be turned into technical formulas to be followed by rote without thought.
    (v) There is a deliberate and planned reasoning process.
    (vi) The legal reasoning and decisions are considered common or shared among the collective.

30 See for instance, "The Habitat of Dogrib Traditional Territory: Place Names as Indicators of Bio-Geographical Knowledge," *West Kitikmeot Slave Study,* http://www.wkss.nt.ca/HTML/08_ProjectsReports/08_habitat/08_habDogribTT.htm (accessed April, 2007). Also see Glenn, *Legal Traditions,* n. 27. Glenn argues that tradition and the human behaviour surrounding it ought to be considered a source of information: "The necessity of massaging the information of tradition thus extends through the entire range of attitudes toward it. It occurs amongst the most faithful of adherents to it, as they seek to perpetuate it; it occurs amongst the most vigorous of opponents to it, as they seek to overcome it; and it occurs between both groups. In the theoretical discussion of tradition, this emerges in the conclusion that tradition never reaches definitive form, but rather, in the present, a series of interactive statements of information."

31 See Katharine T. Bartlett, "Tradition, Change, and the Idea of Progress in Feminist Legal Thought," *Wisconsin Law Review,* (1995): 303-43.

32 See generally, Roderick Alexander Macdonald, *Lessons of Everyday Law* (Montreal: McGill-Queen's University Press, 2002).

33 Bartlett, "Tradition," 331 (see n. 31).

34 "Alexis Nakota History and Culture Program," 1, Alexis Nakota Sioux Nation, http://www.alexisNakotasioux.com/default.aspx?ID=0-6 (accessed 24 Nov. 2007).

35 "Saulteaux" is the common spelling in Canada. Members of the Saulteau First Nation living at Moberly Lake, BC omit the final x. Historian Peter Grant uses the spelling "Salteau."

36 Alexis Nakota Sioux Nation, *Escabi (Alexis Stoney)* by Fedirchuk McCullough & Associates, (Cultural Properties Study-Cheviot Mine Project, January 1996), 29, 31.

37 Peter Grant was a fur trader who commented on the division of the Sioux from the perspective of circa 1804 in his chapter, "The Salteau Indians about 1804," in *Les Bourgeois de la Compagnie du Nord-Ouest,* ed. L.R. Masson (New York: Antiquarian Press, 1890). See *Escabi,* 30 for excerpts.

38 Paul H. Carlson, *The Plains Indians* (College Station: Texas A & M University Press, 1998), 2.

39 Helen Buckley, *From Wooden Ploughs to Welfare: Why Indian Policy Failed in the Prairie Provinces* (Montreal: McGill-Queen's University Press, 1992), 28.

40 *Escabi,* 30; Peter Grant, "Salteau Indians," 346-47.

41 Carlson, *Plains Indians,* 34. According to Carlson, "Dakotas (as they called themselves), or Sioux, ...formed part of the larger Oceti Sakowin, or the Seven Council Fires, a group of distinct peoples who under pressure from the Ojibwas in the 1600s separated into three broad divisions. The eastern or Santee division, living on the prairies and woodlands of Minnesota, included four groups: the Mdewakantonwan, Wachpekute, Wachpetonwan, and Sisitonwan (Sisseton). The middle division included two groups, the Yankton and Yanktonai, who lived on the prairies and plains stretching west to the Missouri (and who are sometimes called Nakota). The western division included only the nomadic Lakotas (Tetons), but representing about half the Oceti Sakowin population, it was the largest, with some of its subgroups (Oglalas and Brules) having populations larger than most of the other council-fire peoples."

42 Solicitor General and Public Security, "Aboriginal Justice Programs and Initiatives Summary 2003," 2-3, Alberta Solicitor General and Public Security, http://www.solgen.gov.ab.ca/publications/default.aspx?id=2678 (accessed 24 Nov. 2007).

43 *Ibid.,* 7, 8, 9, 10.

44 *Ibid.,* 7.

45 Allen & Larsson, *Alexis Evaluation,* viii.

46 John Borrows, "Creating an Indigenous Legal Community," *McGill Law Journal* 50, no. 1 (2005): 160.

47 Lon L. Fuller, "Human Interaction and the Law," *Am. Journal of Jurisprudence* 14 (1969): 2. Since many Indigenous peoples were decentralized, but nonetheless had legal orders and law, Fuller's theory of law being generated by social interaction over time is very useful.

48 Postema, "Implicit Law," 361.

49 *Ibid.*

50 *Ibid.,* 363.

51 Borrows, "Indigenous Legal Community," 166-68.

52 *Ibid.,* 177.

53 *Ibid.,* 171.

54 *Ibid.,* 176.

55 Postema, "Implicit Law," 365.

56 *Ibid.,* 367. This is because centralized systems of law can only operate if there are decentralized, interactive customary laws around them. Central systems of law require peoples' co-operation in order to function. If people do not co-operate with and uphold central systems of law, they fail. See Fuller, "Human Interaction," 23.

57 *Ibid.,* Postema, 368.

58 *Ibid.,* 373-74.

59 *Ibid.,* 375.

60 *Ibid.,* 375-76.

61 Julie Cruikshank, *The Social Life of Stories: Narrative and Knowledge in the Yukon Territory* (Vancouver: UBC Press, 1998), 66-67.

62 *Ibid.,* 68.

63 *Ibid.,* 64.

64 Postema, "Implicit Law," 377.

65 Borrows, "Indigenous Legal Community," 168.

66 Rose Stremlau, "'To Domesticate and Civilize Wild Indians': Allotment and the Campaign to Reform Indian Families, 1875-1887," *Journal of Family History* 30 (July 2005): 266.

67 Ella Cara Deloria, *Waterlily* (Lincoln: University of Nebraska Press, 1988), x, quoted in Stremlau, *ibid.,* 266.

68 *Ibid.,* Stremlau, 266. Also see Val Napoleon, "Raven's Garden: A Discussion about Aboriginal Sexual Orientation and Transgender Issues," *Canadian Journal of Law and Society* 17 (2002): 149-71, for commentary on other Aboriginal legal orders where gender norms also proved flexible.

69 Daniel Jutras asserts that law manifests itself in small but important ways, such as greetings, in everyday life: "Brief encounters are evidence of the existence of true legal systems on a very small scale: micro-normative systems display characteristics that are fundamental to any form of legal ordering." See "The Legal Dimensions of Everyday Life," *Canadian Journal of Law and Society* 16 (2001): 46.

70 Allen & Larsson, *Alexis Evaluation.*

71 *Ibid.,* 26.

72 *Ibid.,* xii.

73 *Ibid.,* 26.

74 Statistics were not available. However one justice employee noted in conversation that almost all of the files have a domestic violence component.

75 Val Napoleon, "Indigenous Discourse: Gender, Identity, and Community" in *Indigenous Peoples and the Law: Comparative and Critical Perspectives,* eds. Kent McNeil and Benjamin J. Richardson (N.p.: Osgoode-Hart, forthcoming in 2008).

76   In this chapter, we use the term "intimate violence" to denote physical, sexual, emotional, financial, psychological, or spiritual abuse by adult males of adult female partners in intimate relationships. We follow Anne McGillivray & Brenda Comasky, Canadian feminist legal scholars, in using this term in lieu of wife battering, battered woman syndrome, wife abuse, spousal assault, family violence, domestic abuse, domestic assault, and domestic violence. Intimate violence is used instead because it speaks to the close, personal relationship between abuser and survivor and the "deep trust presumed to exist among family members, between intimate partners." Anne McGillivray & Brenda Comasky, *Black Eyes All of the Time: Intimate Violence, Aboriginal Women, and the Justice System* (Toronto: University of Toronto Press, 1999), xiv.

77   See for example, Angela Cameron, "Sentencing Circles and Intimate Violence: A Canadian Feminist Perspective," *Canadian Journal of Women and the Law* 18 (2006): 1019-52; Barbara Hudson, "Restorative Justice: The Challenge of Sexual and Racial Violence," *Journal of Law and Society* 25, no. 22 (1998): 237-56; and, Joan Pennell & Gale Burford, "Feminist Praxis: Making Family Group Conferencing Work," in *Restorative Justice and Family Violence,* eds. Heather Strang & John Braithwaite (Cambridge: Cambridge University Press, 2002), 108-27.

78   We choose to use the word "survivor" rather than "victim." "Victim" erases the complex ways that women resist, recuperate from, return to, and eliminate violence from their own lives. "Survivor" more easily captures the emotional, financial, political, employment, and parenting strategies that women who live with violence deploy from day to day. It is partly in supporting and augmenting these strategies of agency, survival, and resistance that the solutions to intimate violence lay.

79   See generally, Joanne C. Minaker, "Evaluating Criminal Justice Responses to Intimate Abuse through the Lens of Women's Needs," *Canadian Journal of Women and the Law* 13 (2001): 74-106.

80   Jeremy Webber, "Naturalism and Agency in the Living Law," 2 (working paper, on file with author, University of Victoria, 2007).

81   For a very interesting critique of how harmony is used to stifle internal conflict and challenges to the status quo, see Laura Nader, *Harmony Ideology: Justice and Control in a Zapotec Mountain Village* (Stanford: Stanford University Press, 1990).

82   Kay Pranis, Barry Stuart & Mark Wedge, *Peacemaking Circles* (St. Paul, MN: Living Justice, 2003), 47. Other publications focus on restorative justice principles. See for example, Howard Zehr, *Changing Lenses,* 3rd ed. (Scottsdale, PA.; Herald, 2005); and, Howard Zehr, *The Little Book of Restorative Justice* (Intercourse, PA.: Good Books, 2002). Zehr is often described as the grandfather of restorative justice.

83   *Ibid.*, Pranis, et al., 46.

84   *Ibid.*, 47.

85   Barb Toews, *The Little Book of Restorative Justice for People in Prison: Rebuilding the Web of Relationships* (Intercourse, PA: Good Books, 2006), 23.

86   *Ibid.*

87   Law Commission of Canada, *Transforming Relationships Through Participatory Justice* (Ottawa: Minister of Public Works and Government Services, 2003), xvi. The Commission also provides a list of "consensus-based justice values" at xviii. The Law Commission of Canada closed its offices in 2007 after the federal government terminated funding.

88   Daniel Van Ness, "An Overview of Restorative Justice Around the World" (paper, Eleventh United Nations Congress on Crime Prevention and Criminal Justice, Bangkok, April 22, 2005), International Centre for Criminal Law Reform, www.icclr.law.ubc.ca/Publications/Reports, 5 (accessed 23 May, 2007).

89   *Ibid.*

90   Allen & Larsson, *Alexis Evaluation,* xi, 18 (see n. 21).

91   Jennifer Haslett, Restorative Opportunities Program (Alberta), Correctional Services of Canada, in discussion with Val Napoleon, 17 March 2007. Jennifer has worked extensively with victims and offenders in restorative justice processes since 1996.

92   Webber, "Naturalism," 2 (see n. 80).

93   *Ibid.*, 1.

94   But see the work of academics like Thomas Flanagan and others who advance racist notions of a single evolution of civilizations. See for example, Thomas Flanagan, *First Nations? Second Thoughts* (Montreal: McGill-Queen's University Press, 2000).

95   For a very interesting argument for political pluralism, see Tim Schouls, *Shifting Boundaries: Aboriginal Identity, Pluralist Theory, and the Politics of Self-Government* (Vancouver: UBC Press, 2003).

96   For an excellent discussion about legal pluralism, see Jeremy Webber, "Legal Pluralism and Human Agency," *Osgoode Hall Law Journal* 44, no. 1 (2006): 167-98.

97   John Ralston Saul argues that some distance creates a level of personal disinterest that is necessary in order for people to effectively maintain and protect the larger public good. See, *The Unconscious Civilization* (Concord, ON: Anansi, 1995), 167.

98   Alexis already has various working arrangements with other communities.

ABORIGINAL EDUCATION AND SELF-GOVERNMENT:

Assessing Success and Identifying the Challenges to Restoring Aboriginal Jurisdiction for Education

Jean-Paul Restoule, Ontario Institute for Studies in Education (OISE)

Aboriginal education and self-government are inextricably linked, and if Aboriginal people are to survive as members of distinct nations, education respecting Aboriginal cultures, languages, and spiritual traditions is a necessity. To protect these areas, Aboriginal peoples in Canada have to date utilized a variety of strategies to compel federal recognition of the inherent right to control Aboriginal education. Ranging from treaty negotiations to public government models, as well as self-government agreements devoted exclusively to defining educational jurisdiction, Aboriginal efforts to establish control over education have taken many forms resulting in the creation of many unique and innovative models. An exploration of the latter is the concern of this chapter: I will survey these models focusing on explicating the challenges to the restoration of areas of control. The National Indian Brotherhood (NIB) policy document *Indian Control of Indian Education*, released in 1972, provides the starting point for the overall discussion. Specifically, how have demands for greater local control of schooling been met by First Nations governments and Canada since this landmark call to action?

Aboriginal education is at a crossroads. At once a colonial endeavour and increasingly informed by traditional Aboriginal education models, in the face of federal and provincial resistance to augmented First Nations control, the 1972 NIB pronouncement is understandable. But what was the NIB striving for when it demanded 'Indian Control of Indian Education'? What does this represent? Long a critic of federal offloading of responsibility for Native education, Dianne Longboat, a respected Mohawk educator, traditional teacher, and healer, has identified five core areas that, once recognized and assigned to First Nations jurisdiction, would result in true Indian control of Indian education:

1. Administrative
2. Political
3. Financial
4. Personnel
5. Curriculum

Longboat's framework is informative and will guide the interpretation of First Nations attempts to regain control over jurisdiction for education.

We will see that, in some instances, First Nations are taking control over more than administration. In some cases, even where they have recognition of their right over the control of curriculum and certification, they may choose to defer to the provincial standards. In other cases, these standards are not freely chosen by Aboriginal governments but rather imposed. I argue that this issue of choice is tied to the long-standing disagreement of the source of the right to control education. When First Nations talk control over education, the assumption is that it is an inherent Aboriginal right. When they enter into treaties, they are exercising the inherent right that provides the basis for sovereignty and the right to enter into treaty talks in the first place. Canada prefers to use treaties as a form of special contract, ultimately resulting in the devolution to specific communities various aspects of Aboriginal education delivery while demonstrating reluctance to recognize inherent rights in law. The notion of inherent right informs the various attempts examined in this chapter to circumvent federal and provincial control of Aboriginal education. That is this chapter's starting point.

Treaty Rights and Inherent Rights

Aboriginal peoples consider the right to an education an inherent Aboriginal right protected by s. 35 of Canada's *Constitution*. Canada has nevertheless been slow to recognize this right in practice. Formal acknowledgement notwithstanding, many First Nations may exercise this right by putting into practice customary law or passing their own laws over education. Even so, the lack of resources and funding are difficult operational barriers to overcome following a unilateral assertion of jurisdiction. While it is the most direct way of assuming control, it may not be the most successful approach due to its confrontational scope. Engaging in treaty discussions has proven more successful in enabling First Nations to assume control over education. Already in place, the treaties offer First Nations and Canadian officials' common ground from which they can negotiate a new treaty interpretation germane to improving First Nations jurisdiction over education. Negotiating new treaties or amending the context of existing treaties requires the agreement of both treaty parties, and the final product needs to be something both sides can live with. In Saskatchewan and Alberta, for instance, progress has been made toward implementing control over education based on the spirit and intent of the numbered treaties, which included provisions respecting education.

In 1996, for example, the Federation of Saskatchewan Indian Nations (FSIN) asserted First Nations jurisdiction over education based on historic treaty implementation of the 1870s. By 2000, a tripartite framework agreement had been formally negotiated and was signed initiating further negotiations on new governance and fiscal arrangements. Education and family services were given priority and an education working group was established. Among the objectives of the Saskatchewan First Nations with treaties are to:

- establish institutions for early childhood education, kindergarten, elementary, secondary, and post-secondary education;

- secure First Nations' jurisdiction in the area of education that is personal and territorial in nature;

- attain a First Nations' legislative framework that would govern education and that would be subject to ratification by Treaty First Nations; and,

- have educational institutions organized under the laws of First Nations.[1]

Additionally, "First Nations' jurisdiction in education in urban areas can be achieved through First Nation controlled institutions such as FNUC [First Nations University of Canada] and SIIT [Saskatchewan Indian Institute of Technologies] at the post-secondary level; and through First Nations controlled and shared institutions at the primary and secondary levels. The institutions would not be restricted to Treaty First Nations and attendance would be a matter of individual choice." Finally, "the scope of jurisdictional discussions shall include: standards, curriculum, accreditations, special education, administration, languages, cultures, tuition agreements, educational level equivalencies, teaching methodologies, or pedagogies, teacher certification, evaluation of First Nation education systems, and complimentary health, social and cultural services which support educational developments."[2] Ultimately, the provincial treaty First Nations will exercise the level of jurisdiction currently held by the Province of Saskatchewan pursuant to s. 92 of the *Constitution Act, 1867* and treaty First Nations' jurisdiction over education will be constitutionally protected.

Other initiatives include establishing a provincial language immersion program from early childhood to Grade 12, taking into consideration the different language needs of the various cultural groups. In consultation with existing or planned regional education authorities, the merits of establishing a provincial Aboriginal education board and system are also being considered. First Nations believe also in the treaty right to post-secondary education, technical trades, occupational skills training, language, and culture—an interpretation most governments do not share. First Nations in Saskatchewan anticipate researching and challenging for the legal recognition of post-secondary education as a treaty right within the meaning of Treaty 6. In concert with this initiative, a database will also be created to facilitate research, cataloguing statistics, in essence providing evidentiary support needed to pursue this action. Establishing constitutional protection of this interpretation, Saskatchewan Treaty nations could potentially obtain jurisdiction over education.

In 2005, six Saskatchewan First Nations agreed to move forward with the First Nations education council. The Northwest Nations Education Council will establish an education authority complete with board of directors, professional public services, and financial accountability framework. The council, made up of representatives from the participating First Nations, "will work with local school committees to design and implement programs for the new education system. It will focus on improving student performance by strengthening the effectiveness of classroom instruction; improving cultural programs in order to strengthen the identities of First Nations people; and developing programs that more actively involve families and community members."[3] The council is moving forward under existing arrangements suggesting further that First Nations are not bound by lengthy treaty talks to begin implementing programmatic enhancements aimed at greater parental and community involvement.

On the Alberta side of Treaty 6, the Confederacy of Treaty 6 First Nations also identified the need to acknowledge the treaty right to education while establishing appropriate legislation and funding arrangements that support authentic and full First Nations jurisdiction over education.[4] Treaty 6 educators consider jurisdiction over education an inherent right that affirms the First Nations right to create, manage, and evaluate educational systems that honour the languages, cultures, and traditions of their communities.[5] Arguably, colonialism is a significant impediment to obtaining jurisdiction over education, a process that is embedded within the larger and continuing struggle for self-determination.[6] Levels of financing provided by Canada, for example, are constantly being disputed. Critics argue that First Nations asserting sovereignty and inherent rights ought then to be funding their own initiatives without Canadian government support. Perhaps, but often overlooked is the fact that the treaties with Canada promised schools and schoolmasters. In this case, First Nations may not be receiving fair compensation in the form of adequate education for the lands and resources obtained *vis-a-vis* treaties that continue to fuel Canada's economic growth.

In Treaty 7 territory, located in southern Alberta, extensive grassroots consultation about education raised several issues of local concern. Despite a handful of language immersion programs, the leaders of many communities spoke of the need for greater cultural immersion.[7] Proposing that securing appropriate cultural immersion would be best accomplished through First Nations jurisdiction over education, and that the need to preserve languages was receiving some attention in the public schools, it was clear that other needs were not being addressed. In one instance, it was identified that Kainai children needed to learn clan songs and that "It is easier for First Nations controlled schools to base their actions on appropriate cultural protocol."[8] This focus on cultural immersion often means that First Nations controlled schools can accommodate flexible attendance schedules that permit participation in seasonal cultural ceremonies. The First Nations also have greater control over tuition agreements, teacher contracts, and the integration of services to support students and their families. These involve, for instance, providing social workers in the schools, developing educational initiatives on Fetal Alcohol Spectrum Disorder, and making tutors available. In the area of post-secondary education, the Treaty 7 nations have developed a First Nations Accreditation Board and two post-secondary education institutions: Blue Quills First Nations College and Red Crow Community College. However, funding gaps were identified as troublesome with one report highlighting inadequate funding in several areas of education, including special education, post-secondary education, and transportation for off-reserve members and parents.[9] Even with jurisdiction clarified and restored, the report's authors argued that stable funding be in place prior to First Nations realizing control. Based on Longboat's 5 principles, it appears that they are further ahead than many First Nations in several relevant areas of control. However, limited financial arrangements with INAC combined with its insistence that First Nations educators offer Alberta curriculum have restricted what Treaty 7 First Nations can do even with their recognized control over education.

In northern Alberta, the Chiefs of Treaty 8 First Nations have secured a formal mandate to proceed with developing an education system. They have also established a representative Education Commission, which is linked to the Treaty 8 bilateral process as a practical measure. The Treaty 8 Education Commission has assumed management of the following targeted programs: Youth Employment Strategy, Teacher Recruitment and Retention, and the Parental and Community Engagement Strategy. In addition to completing practical tasks such as developing a Grade 1 social studies unit and its companion Teacher Guide, the Treaty 8 Education Commission has established a working relationship with Alberta Ministry of Education while providing their member nations a forum that enables information sharing and discussions about education issues that invariably make it back to the desks of provincial and federal departments.[10] The education provisions in particular reflect the elders' understandings of treaty principles:

> By virtue of First Nation Language and Culture Protection (Way of Life) the traditional process of lifelong learning was not to be disturbed with respect to First Nation governance and programming of the education/learning processes dedicated to First Nations peoples. ... It was understood that as a result of Treaty and increased migration of "newcomers" into the Treaty 8 territory there would be impacts upon the First Nations and their peoples that would require relevant assistance for well-being, coexistence and parity. ... Where the governance and programming of lifelong learning exceeds that which would [be] beyond a comparable level to the Crown's subjects/citizens the responsibility would be the First Nations from their access to livelihood resources.[11]

Once again, briefly utilizing Longboat's criteria, there is some control gained over personnel issues but curriculum standards remain in the hands of Alberta. These initiatives could likely have been entered into regardless of treaty but the constitutional protection provided by treaty right ensures First Nations control is the highest law of Canada.

Modern Day Treaty Model

Modern treaties arising from comprehensive land claims agreements often contain explicit provisions assigning First Nations jurisdiction over education while clearly articulating education as a treaty right. The federal government has been reluctant to call this right inherent. Nevertheless, s. 35 protection applies to these agreements at First Nations' insistence. The *Sechelt Self-Government Agreement*, passed in 1986, is an early example of this process. With their law-making powers clearly outlined in the Agreement, the Sechelt maintain control over education for band members living on Sechelt lands. In the Northwest, the Dehcho Dene First Nations, working from the assumption that their rights are inherent, initiated negotiations among their member communities and with local communities seeking augmented control over education. Without contacting federal or territorial representatives, they held talks with participating Dene communities and local communities at the municipal level and were guided by Dene Tha ideas concerning education. In a draft AIP signed with federal and territorial representatives, the Dehcho regional government obtained exclusive jurisdiction over the following relevant areas: language; culture and arts; training; education, including post-secondary; regional education services, including capital planning; distance education; and specialized education. The agreement provides that annual block funding for education, as required by treaties 8 and 11, will be disbursed by the Dehcho government. Reflecting on Longboat's standards, several areas of control over education would be restored, but the dependence on annual block funding could result in similar disputes and gaps that were identified by Treaty 7 Nations. Although previous examples suggest that the Dehcho may be unable to achieve some education goals, it as yet remains to be seen.

Other AIPs such as those signed in the Yukon demonstrate that certification and curriculum standards remain the purview of the territorial government. In their Self-Government Agreement-in-Principle the Gwich'in and Inuvialuit retain some jurisdiction over education. Similarly, the Sahtu Dene and Métis SGA allows settlement corporations to engage in education activities although the AIP sets out restrictions in areas of curriculum framework, and educator and caregiver certification for Early Childhood Education and K-12, while restricting the ability of the community to set standards for Grade 12 graduation and equivalency examinations. The territorial government retains control over these areas according to the AIP, a prevalent theme for those negotiating modern treaties and Self-Government Agreements (SGAs).

Take for example the Nisga'a Final Agreement and the Tlicho First Nation's Land Claims and sga. The Tlicho First Nation has specific powers to enact laws in relation to education in their communities and on their lands. This includes law-making abilities as they relate to teaching the language, history, and culture of Tlicho First Nation. They may also enact laws in relation to pre-school and early childhood development programs. However, restrictions are placed on the Tlicho First Nation's ability to establish a community-based teacher certification process and law-making concerning post-secondary education. The Final Agreement's limitations suggest that the equivalency requirements expected of students attending schools under Tlicho authority will need to adhere in part to territorial curriculum and examination guidelines and frameworks. Besides language teachers, the Tlicho will not have power to enact certification standards.

Similarly the Nisga'a Treaty identified the Nisga'a ability to enact laws in Nisga'a Lands with respect to pre-school to Grade 12. These laws must ensure that standards in the areas of curriculum, examination, and teacher certification are comparable to British Columbia's. These standards may already be what the Nisga'a would choose to aspire to and it may be pragmatic to adhere to them. However, mandating their comparability is not the restoration of Aboriginal control over education. The Nisga'a Lisims Government may make laws in respect of post-secondary education on Nisga'a Lands, including establishing institutions that grant degrees, diplomas and certificates, and determining the curriculum for these institutions. The Nisga'a Treaty also contains provisions for, and coordination of, all adult education programs in Nisga'a Lands. But the Nisga'a must ensure the standards for the institution's accountability structures, admissions, instructor qualifications, curriculum standards, and degree, diploma and certificate requirements are all comparable to the provincial standards for post-secondary education. The language of "transfer without penalty" carries with it a paternalistic assumption that the students from an Aboriginal system will inevitably underachieve in a provincial school absent mandated standards. At the present writing, the Nisga'a have chosen not to establish their own education authority on their lands although they have the power to do so. They instead control bc School District 92, established under provincial law.

The Nisga'a School District recalls the situation in Northern Quebec. Often referred to as the first modern day treaty, the *James Bay and Northern Quebec Agreement* (jbnqa) was signed in 1975. The agreement established Cree and Inuit school boards, which remain under provincial jurisdiction. The boards are similar to other Quebec school boards but are distinct in that they have a special mandate and powers negotiated in the Agreement ensuring cultural relevance in education programs from elementary to secondary and adult education. The Cree school board has operated well since early on. Reflecting on the agreement 10 years later, Billy Diamond, then Chair of the Cree School Board, said:

Indian control of Indian education is not an easy thing to bring about, even when you have signed an agreement which is designed to facilitate the process. Our fights with Canada and the province continue, but we feel we have gained their respect because of our ability to properly operate our board. We are convinced that, in the end, Cree education will be provided to all of our people in the manner that we proposed in the agreement.[12]

In Nunavik, the area of the JBNQA largely populated by Inuit, the Kativik School Board has been in operation since 1978.

The Kativik School Board is governed by a Quebec provincial law entitled "The Education Act for Cree, Inuit and Naskapi Native Persons". It has the exclusive jurisdiction in Nunavik to provide pre-school, elementary, secondary and adult education, and the responsibility to develop programs and teaching materials in Inuktitut, English and French; train Inuit teachers to meet provincial standards; and encourage, arrange and supervise post-secondary education.[13]

Kativik School Board programs must meet the objectives prescribed by the Quebec Ministry of Education. However, the content and language levels have been adapted for Inuit second language learners—the language of instruction from Kindergarten to Grade 2 is Inuktitut. Parents of Grade 3 children are then given the choice of placing their children in English or French immersion. The Inuit culture and language continue to be taught throughout primary and secondary school. As well, the Kativik School Board has begun to actively pursue a policy of balanced bilingualism emphasizing Inuktitut. Kativik-run schools offer culture classes and excursion classes on the land to learn survival skills. They also maintain a Teacher Training Program to provide Inuit teachers with the skills to become certified according to provincial standards. The Kativik's mandate reads: "To develop a curriculum that embraces Inuit traditions, culture and language, and prepares students for active participation in the modern world."[14] In finding this balance, some First Nations are content to leave curriculum and certification to the province. I argue that the choice to leave these matters with the province should be up to the Aboriginal people.

Public Government Models

These aforementioned school boards, specifically those arising out of the JBNQA, are protected by s. 35 of the *Constitution Act, 1982*. It must be noted that the treaty and comprehensive claims processes are but two of the avenues available to Aboriginal people seeking greater control of education. In instances where Aboriginal people constitute the majority population, the opportunity exists to operate education activities through existing public education models. For the Métis in Alberta, there are school districts whose boundaries ensure they are the majority population. The province in turn maintains jurisdiction even if the demographically superior Métis maintain "local" control. The province makes decisions on curriculum, certification, and other standards. The Métis have a voice insofar as they are part of the local school districts even if full control or jurisdiction remains elusive. In the Northwest Territories, a public government model contained within the Dehcho draft agreement results in Dehcho control over education (the rules governing elections ensure Dene control). The agreement will permit all regional residents in the area for five years or more to vote and run as candidates in elections, although 50 per cent of the seats are reserved for Dene as is the main leadership position.[15] With law-making powers extending to education, this means Dene control of education through what is essentially a public government model.

In New Brunswick, provincial policy consultation is enabled through the First Nations Education Initiative Committee, and is aimed at incremental improvements to the status quo. Supported by the federal and provincial governments, the New Brunswick Education Initiative represents an alliance of 14 provincial First Nations who have joined together to address issues such as tuition agreements, access to special education services, and the relationships between First Nations and the New Brunswick Department of Education and local school districts. Focusing their attention on helping Aboriginal students, the goal is to secure funding for initiatives such as cultural resource centres, computer labs, Aboriginal language teachers, First Nations history teachers, Aboriginal education coordinators, teachers' assistants, and intervention workers for at-risk Aboriginal students.[16] Such improvements to the public system are encouraging as this is where the vast majority of Aboriginal students receive their formal education, and thus would not benefit from greater control over education exercised exclusively on reserves.

British Columbia has also demonstrated some willingness to incorporate Aboriginal perspectives and initiatives into the public education system. In Qualicum district, for example, an Elder-In-Residence program provides an elder with the Qualicum First Nation to "spend one day a week at schools demonstrating traditional cultural activities and teaching life lessons, such as the importance of respect. The elder also acts as a leader for Aboriginal students and staff in the district."[17] Similar programs exist in Burnaby district and Haida Gwaii-Queen Charlotte. According to a recent BC press release, "The BC government has signed Aboriginal enhancement agreements that integrate First Nations culture[s] in public schools in 22 districts and aims to complete agreements in all 60 districts."[18] Some public funds are also allocated to language and culture programs, Aboriginal student support service programs, and other local education programs.

Developments such as those in New Brunswick and British Columbia are a welcome change from what I would portray as the completely assimilative assumptions that historically buttressed efforts to integrate Aboriginal students into provincial schools. While the amount of control exercised is limited, it is a presence that has potential to offer public perceptions of Aboriginal life and aspirations. The positive support of Indigenous self-esteem and identity could have an impact on graduation rates. Both efforts potentially enhance self-government efforts and capacity by ensuring there is an Indigenous human resource base as well as the public will to see it enacted. However, it continues to be an additive approach where culture is simply added on to the base curriculum. When the culture is added it can also be taken away; unless it forms the core of school activities and expectations this is only treating the symptoms that lead students to become disengaged. When the provincial standards are placed in the context of the learning of Indigenous cultural knowledge, interesting things can happen.

A couple of inspiring examples from Manitoba demonstrating what is possible even while under provincial jurisdiction exist in Niji Mahkwa and Children of the Earth schools in Winnipeg. Children of the Earth is a secondary school that delivers "the Manitoba curriculum plus plus plus."[19] The pluses include Ojibway and Cree language skills and exposing students to traditional knowledge through participating in sweat lodges, the Sundance, and shaking tent and pipe ceremonies. Even though this is an additive approach, it does go quite far indeed. Located on the same campus is elementary school Niji Mahkwa. Their vision statement is painted on the wall and reads: "Niji Mahkwa School and community upholds the belief that all children have an inherent right to the highest quality, holistic education. Integration of traditional, cultural teachings in a supportive learning environment will provide students with the strength to meet the challenges of life." Niji Mahkwa has integrated provincial requirements into a cultural approach, or, as Principal Myra Laramee has stated, "We don't integrate Aboriginal perspectives in the curriculum. We integrate learning outcomes into our way of living."[20] For example, during a field trip to pick sage, the Niji Mahkwa students also learn science, social studies, ancestral medicine, and the Cree and Ojibway vocabulary for plants. In each lesson, the school strives to support academics, culture, technology, and linguistic ability. This is an exciting approach that promotes culture first while still respecting provincial curriculum requirements that can be found and built around the cultural activities. In this way it goes much further than merely to add culture to the curriculum.

In Nunavut, the Inuit form the majority population, which greatly influences the territorial government, meaning that the Inuit exercise by default Aboriginal control of Aboriginal education. This ability to enact laws respecting education is articulated in the *Nunavut Act*. This authority however is shared with all residents of Nunavut, Inuit and non-Native. Since Nunavut's earliest days as a territory, there have been attempts to pass a *Nunavut Education Act*. The initial effort was introduced to the legislative assembly in 2002 and withdrawn a year later. Working from this draft and further bottom-up consultation with communities, attempts to bring the act back started in 2005-06. Nunavut has struggled to make its own education law and policy, and some critics suggest literally no difference exists between the *Nunavut Education Act* and the NWT education laws and policies.[21] Since Nunavut's creation, more Inuit culture is incorporated into classrooms and high school graduation rates have risen, in some cases reaching 30 per cent.[22] Programs promoting elders in the classroom are common when it comes to teaching history and culture. Training programs for nurses and teachers were also introduced, as were programs to increase Inuit participation in the fields of law enforcement and justice.[23]

Nunavut is composed of District Education Authorities (DEAs). Each DEA is responsible for the appointment, discipline, and termination of school principals; hiring of teachers; control of school budget for recurring expenses; school operations; scheduling; reporting to the community; and the development and implementation of student discipline policies. DEAs are composed of elected officials representing parents and are considered to be democratic institutions controlling education at the local level. Recent initiatives include a Nunavut Adult Learning Strategy, and aggressive recruitment of Inuktitut-speaking teachers. Preparations are also being made to ready the population to participate in mining, fishing, tourism, and construction industries. All the same, priority was placed on enhancing Inuit languages as "living, working languages of choice in all spheres of life in Nunavut."[24] Three models were adopted by the territory, and communities were encouraged to adopt that most appropriate to their needs. The first model promotes early immersion in regions where language fluency has eroded. The second model, Qulliq, is aimed at communities with strong Inuktitut first-language skills and use where students will learn reading and writing in Inuktitut followed by the introduction of English as a second language. Inuktitut is the primary medium of instruction through to Grade 12 with English used in some other courses. The third model, a dual language model, is proposed for communities who can organize programs to ensure students receive instruction in core courses in their first language, while learning a second language and receiving non-core courses taught in either language.

Nunavut continues to use curricula inherited from the Northwest Territories and the Western Northern Canadian Protocol for grades K-9. For Grades 10-12, Nunavut continues to rely on Alberta curriculum; however, "There is no coordinated K-12 curriculum that combines Inuit and Qallunaat perspectives with the supporting teaching materials and student-learning resources required to ensure instruction in classrooms meets bicultural expectations."[25] Nunavut recognizes that developing curriculum and resources to properly reflect two cultures and three languages is a complex and time-consuming endeavour. Currently, few teaching and learning resources exist for teachers' use that reflect Inuit culture, history, and perspectives. Canada has committed itself through the Inuit Relations Secretariat to "enter into discussions with Inuit Tapiriit Kanatami and other relevant Inuit education organizations, about identifying measures and initiatives to improve the Inuit education system and articulate some outcomes and suggestions for concrete actions."[26]

Outside Nunavut, Aboriginal people do not have the population numbers needed to "run" things. In the early 1990s, the Assembly of First Nations (AFN) proposed a *First Nations Education Act* recognizing First Nations jurisdiction over education nation-wide. Such an approach could vary from being open to implementation at the local level (simply providing the local First Nations with enabling powers) to being highly centralized, prescriptive, and detailed. Although it was not introduced as a bill by the federal government, the idea still has its supporters.[27] The consolidated school boards would provide supervision, develop curriculum, and ensure quality education for reserve schools with the raised academic expectations such a board could have. The boards would be under the control of First Nations and would have the sole purpose of education for the children. Mendelson[28] advocates for regional control over the form the board takes as each region's First Nations would have particular needs and situations to consider.

Specific Education Agreements

Little progress has been made toward a national legislation on Aboriginal or First Nations education and trends suggest that First Nations and Aboriginal communities prefer to work on their own agreements on a nation-to-nation basis with provincial or territorial participation. In many cases, this form of control over schools and programs is delegated to specially created and legally recognized education authorities established by First Nations. Perhaps the best known and closely scrutinized is the Mi'kmaw Kina'matnewey operating under the *Mi'kmaq Education Act* in Nova Scotia.

In 1998, the *Mi'kmaq Education Act*[29] was passed by the federal and Nova Scotia governments activating a 1997 agreement between Canada and nine of the thirteen Nova Scotia Mi'kmaq communities. The new act released the communities from the education sections of the *Indian Act* and set out the nature and scope of jurisdiction transferred for elementary and secondary education and support for post-secondary education. The Mi'kmaq have a specific mandate: "The long-term goal, which all parties recognize, is the full recognition of the inherent right to self-government through a treaty. Until that has been done it is agreed that the best approach is to have Mi'kmaq jurisdiction in education recognized by Federal Government legislation."[30] Renewed in 2005 with a tenth Mi'kmaq community (Bear Island) participating, the *Mi'kmaq Education Act* sets out the powers and responsibilities of the education authority (Mi'kmaw Kina'matnewey), that is peopled by the community chiefs. With federal funding in place, the communities must meet provincial curriculum standards. The communities also have the power to pass education laws that reflect their language and culture. The act also provides for power over administration and financing including support for post-secondary education for community members wherever they may reside. Mi'kmaw Kina'matnewey also manages the Nova Scotia Mi'kmaw Language Centre of Excellence, which provides curriculum and services to all 13 Mi'kmaw communities.[31]

The Mi'kmaw control resources earmarked for facilities, teachers, instructional materials, and technologies for grades K-12, several of the areas that Longboat had mentioned. The communities have developed Mi'kmaq-specific curricula particularly in language development and for teaching history while also focusing efforts on teacher training and preparing for self-governance. INAC has reported that the agreement has led to increases in high school graduation rates, although the increase measured reflected the period 1991 to 2001.[32] INAC also trumpets the stable enrollment of students in band-operated schools. In the eight years since the first Mi'kmaw Kina'matnewey agreement, four new secondary schools were established in four communities.[33] The immersion programs have been hailed a success: "After four years, students in the immersion programs are now fluent speakers who can hold conversations in Mi'kmaq with elders in their community—like their grandparents."[34] Thirty-eight Mi'kmaq teachers received training at St. Francis Xavier University.[35] The Mi'kmaw Kina'matnewey claim that their programs are inadequately funded. For example, in one year MK had 130 students attending post-secondary institutions but only received funding for 80 from INAC.[36]

Many First Nations are watching the Mi'kmaw Kina'matnewey. The protection of language and the persistence of students are encouraging but the funding challenges must give pause to many First Nations. INAC clearly views the *Mi'kmaq Education Act* and the recent *First Nations Jurisdiction Over Education in British Columbia Act*[37] as models for future education self-government arrangements in other provinces.

> On July 5th, 2006, INAC signed a Tripartite Agreement on Education Jurisdiction with Xweme'lch'stn Estimxwawtxw School Squamish Nation Community, which clears the way for First Nations in British Columbia to assume control over education. This agreement now in place in British Columbia and the Mi'kmaq Education Authority in Nova Scotia can serve as models for other provinces.[38]

As noted, the federal government passed enabling legislation (*First Nations Jurisdiction Over Education in British Columbia Act*, hereafter *First Nations Education Act)* in 2006 providing legal authority to the Agreement on Education Jurisdiction. The agreement restores jurisdiction over education to First Nations chiefs and council. Community Education Authorities (CEA) can be established in First Nations to govern one or multiple schools, or in some cases, one school from multiple communities. The CEAs will be composed of varying numbers of representatives who may be appointed, elected, or otherwise chosen, who have authority over several key policies respecting language of instruction, school calendar, program and standards of education, arrangements and agreements with external agencies for education delivery, and other services, such as health and social services. The CEAs will be regulated by the First Nations Education Authority, who will primarily operate as a resource to BC First Nations who wish to take control of their education processes. Any First Nation in BC seeking to assume jurisdiction need only pass a Band Council Resolution (BCR). The sections of the *Indian Act* respecting education will cease to apply, specifically sections 114-122. INAC nevertheless has a fiduciary obligation to provide resources for education and communities will continue to be accountable to the department for information on finances and results.

One of the interesting aspects of the *First Nations Education Act* is the notion of reciprocal tuition. Under the agreement, the province will pay First Nations schools' tuition for students attending who do not ordinarily reside on reserve, whereas prior to the agreement First Nations schools did not receive tuition for those students. First Nations schools will also be able to grant their own graduation certificate as well as apply to grant the BC high school certificate. In each of these cases, the school must be a member of the First Nations Education Authority (FNEA). The First Nations schools participating will have to meet the standards of a certification system established by First Nations schools. The FNEA is a regulatory body supporting the First Nations participating in jurisdiction over education. It will have the power to certify teachers and schools and establish curriculum standards, its power delegated from the First Nations that agree to participate: each participating First Nation will have seats on the FNEA, thus determining the standards.

Participating communities will have to develop capacity to sign on and ratify the agreement before implementing jurisdiction over education. Each community determines its own readiness although recommendations have been made for self-assessment with benchmarks such as whether or not the school has gone through an assessment process and if the Board has some governance capacity. Some First Nations have this capacity in place and could sign on within three years. Currently, the agreement applies only to K-12 education. However, it was agreed that this was phase one and that subsequent phases will address early childhood development and education, and post-secondary education and training. According to Longboat's criteria, many areas will be controlled by the local First Nations. However, federal funding could result in disputes similar to those experienced in the Mi'kmaq example. There is also the need to offer education that will permit students to "transfer without penalty" into the provincial system, again presenting a paternalistic tone and subtly but nonetheless reinforcing the offending sections of the *Indian Act* they worked so hard to escape.

In Ontario, the Union of Ontario Indians (UOI) is currently seeking ratification for a similar draft final agreement, implementation of which is expected to begin in 2008. The draft final agreement with the province and Canada will allow participating First Nations to acquire control over elementary and secondary schooling on reserves and funding for post-secondary education and adult education for members irrespective of residency. The 42 Anishinaabe First Nations participating in the UOI represent one-third of the province's registered Indian population, and by the end of 2006, 27 had passed band council resolutions supporting the Agreement-In-Principle. The UOI is engaging in two concurrent self-government negotiations processes, one solely about education and the other focused on self-government. The Kinomaadswin Education Body (KEB) will oversee Anishinaabek education once the agreement is in place and implemented. The KEB acts as a centralized authority overseeing seven Regional Education Councils within the Anishinaabek Nation (the UOI membership). It will not have any law-making powers unless the participating First Nations delegate such power. Each of the seven regions is composed of several First Nations all of whom are encouraged to establish a Local Education Authority to which the *Indian Act*'s education sections will not apply. The participating First Nations will be able to develop Anishinaabe language, spirituality, and culture in the education system and mention has been made of negotiating with the province for the creation of an Anishinaabek post-secondary education institute.

First Nations throughout Ontario are negotiating agreements and hoping for a more favourable outcome than that of the United Anishinaabeg Council's. Their much touted "first self-government agreement to be negotiated outside of a land claim or treaty process" fell apart following community rejection in 2005.[39] The Nishnawbe-Aski Nation, representing 49 communities in northwestern Ontario, is at the agreement-in-principle stage with the federal government. In the Treaty 3 area, 26 First Nation communities in northwest Ontario and two in eastern Manitoba are at the framework agreement stage while continuing to consult with the communities on governance generally. On 12 November 2002, chiefs from eight Fort Frances area First Nations signed a framework agreement.

In Treaty 3 territory, ten bands in the Rainy Lake Tribal Area formed their own Education Authority in 1985, "because of the desire to maintain traditional cultural and linguistic values and to improve economic status, social status and community interactions. Education was seen as a driving force in the quest for political self-determination. Each of the ten bands appointed one member to a Board of Directors, which functions with the leadership of the Executive Director."[40] The focus of Seven Generations Education Institute is adult education, specifically skills training and assisting adult learners returning to their education. The ability of Seven Generations to set their own agendas and partnerships with powers similar to the Nova Scotia authority suggests that First Nations do not necessarily have to enter into negotiations for restoration of jurisdiction over education. They already have the power to set up their own education authorities. It leads one to question why self-government agreements are necessary to pursue local control of education.

Balancing localization and centralization

One of the criticisms leveled at supporters of local control is that it is unworkable at worst and impractical at best for most First Nations, in particular for remote and small communities. In the absence of centralized bodies devising curriculum units and providing the necessary resources for all members, local communities have the potential to become bogged down in work and expenses as they attempt to cultivate their own resources. McCue advocates for a centralized body developing the goals, philosophies, and visions of Aboriginal education more generally while permitting local communities the control over whom they hire and how to direct finances.[41] Accreditation, curriculum achievements, and other standards are likely to be set by provinces and territories, or at least to be developed by First Nations in conformity with the province or territory's guidelines for seamless integration. The centralized body makes sense as it would benefit from economies of scale and would allow for expertise to be applied more evenly. That is, rather than have each community develop curriculum and materials, in some cases with little or no experience in the area, the task would be undertaken by a committee that has greater expertise and be distributed to all the First Nations. Those with the skills would be able to make effective contributions that have the greatest possible impact. It also provides a clear point of contact for the collection and storage of exemplary curriculum or teaching resources.

Sharing resources among and between different Aboriginal schools is one of many suggestions.[42] There could be some good reasons to seek a national body developing or setting curriculum for Aboriginal schools. Another option is to develop a hybrid whereby the body represents an Aboriginal cultural group throughout the territories where the communities are located. That is, instead of each community developing curriculum, there would be an Anishinaabe education body for all the Anishinaabe communities, a Mi'kmaq body for all the Mi'kmaq communities, a Haudenosaunee body for the Haudenosaunee communities, and so on.

One region where there is more centralization is Manitoba. In 1990, the Assembly of Manitoba Chiefs (AMC) and Canada signed an Education Framework Agreement setting out an agenda for increasing control and jurisdiction over First Nations education. A Manitoba First Nations Education Resource Centre was established in late 2004 to provide education specialist service delivery to First Nation schools.[43] The provincial curriculum has Aboriginal content and the province has an Aboriginal Education Directorate that has as its mandate to support the success of Aboriginal students in all areas of education and training. Focused primarily on increasing retention and access to the system through to post-secondary options, recruiting Aboriginal teachers and developing Aboriginal policy with Aboriginal education councils are also significant objectives. The directorate has also supported original language curriculum development.

What governance structures are needed for successful schools?

The Society for the Advancement of Excellence in Education (SAEE) undertook 10 case studies examining schools considered successful at "producing tangible progress for Aboriginal students." Governance structures differed with three schools under the authority of school districts, one under the Yukon Department of Education, and the remaining six band operated. The common success factors were:

- Strong leadership and governance structures
- High expectations
- Focus on academic achievement and long-term success
- Secure and welcoming climate for children and families
- Respect for Aboriginal culture and traditions
- Quality of staff development and a wide range of programs and supports for learning.

The major issues identified in the report included:

- Overlapping jurisdictions
- Uneven resource allocation
- Literacy
- Hiring and retaining qualified and experienced staff
- Transition from elementary to secondary school
- Lack of a national policy to evaluate Aboriginal education.[44]

Indian Act revisions were recommended, as was the establishment of a national centre for Aboriginal language and culture. Additional recommendations included offering access to secondary education in home communities, stressing Aboriginal issues in teacher education programs, placing pre-schools under jurisdiction of education, and establishing better measuring, tracking, and reporting measures for evaluating the progress of students.

Three years later, 13 more schools fitting that same description of "success" were studied. Fulford, author of the second study, wrote:

> In the previous volume of *Sharing Our Success,* Bell noted that "the fully independent band-operated model provides Aboriginal communities with the greatest control of their educational systems." He noted that band-operated schools are better able to integrate the delivery of education from Pre-K to post-secondary into an overall community plan, citing Peguis School as an example. Se't A'newey, Kitigan Zibi, Eskasoni, the two Waskaganish schools and the three schools in Akwesasne support this assertion in the present study. On the other hand, Nuiyak School has aggressively linked all levels of learning and community development, yet is administered through the Nunavut Department of Education. Both Nuiyak and Chief Jimmy Bruneau are notable for their strong connection to local capacity building and the degree of autonomy from their respective territorial governments in matters pertaining to education delivery.

In Fulford's study, only two of the schools did not have elected boards and nine of the 13 participating schools had advisory parent councils or DEAS. "The degree of community involvement in schools varied considerably, with the greatest 'buy in' generally achieved in community schools and those with active parent involvement."[45]

It is interesting to note that in both SAEE studies, "governance and leadership" was the success factor identified most often by researchers. However, the forms of governance for the schools, all of which are considered successes, varied from band-run to provincial to hybrid versions of the two. "Associated factors include visionary and exceptional leadership, innovative management models, strong local governance, forging community and research partnerships, challenging the status quo, long-term planning, mentorship and capacity-building."[46] Myra Laramee, when asked about the success of students attending Niji Mahkwa, was adamant about the very basic foundation of effective schooling: the parents and the community.[47] Commenting on how *Indian Control of Indian Education* has been interpreted, Verna Kirkness, one of its architects, reminded Native educators that "the greatest challenge is to be radical, to ask the right questions within the community, to ask the families what they want for their children. Only then will we be practicing what we set out to do in 1972, which was to have the parents set the agenda for education in our communities."[48]

The more things change the more they stay the same. Local control and parental responsibility, the pillars of the NIB's *Indian Control of Indian Education*, remain the critical components to Aboriginal student success. There are a number of models that exist with a range of degrees of Aboriginal control and jurisdiction over varying elements of education and it will be up to the local communities to decide which of these forms is the most appropriate to adopt and that best reflects the needs of its members. What is possible in Aboriginal education is largely a matter of vision and creativity.

NOTES

1   Federation of Saskatchewan Indian Nations, "Treaty Right to Education: A Presentation Report from the Federation of Saskatchewan Indian Nations Education and Training Secretariat," http://www.fsin.com/educationandtraining/downloads/Treaty%20Context%20for%20Education.pdf (accessed 12 May 2007).
2   *Ibid.*
3   James Parker, *Agreement Lays Foundation for Education Council for Battlefords-Area First Nations* (Indian and Northern Affairs Canada, Ottawa: 2005), http://www.ainc-inac.gc.ca/nr/prs/m-a2005/2-02696_e.html (accessed 12 May 2007).
4   Confederacy of Treaty 6 First Nations, "Images of Persistence: Reclaiming Educational Jurisdiction in Treaty 6 Territory," in Nancy Morgan, *If not now, then when? First Nations Jurisdiction over Education: A Literature Review* (Ottawa: A Report to the Minister's National Working Group on First Nations Education, 2002).
5   *Ibid.*, 5.
6   Morgan, *If Not Now, Then When?*
7   Treaty 7 First Nations Education Systems, *Shared Voices and Visions: Treaty 7 First Nations Dialogue on Education* (Alberta: 2000), http://www.education.gov.ab.ca/nativeed/nativepolicy/Treaty7.pdf (accessed 12 May 2007).
8   *Ibid.*
9   *Ibid.*

10   Indian and Northern Affairs Canada, *Indian and Northern Affairs Canada, Canadian Polar Commission, and Indian Specific Claims Commission 2004-2005 Departmental Performance Report* (Treasury Board Secretariat, 2005), http://www.tbs-sct.gc.ca/rma/dpr1/04-05/INAC-AINC/INAC-AINCd45_e.pdf (accessed 11 May 2007).

11   Treaty 8 First Nations of Alberta, *Treaty Exploration Discussion Paper on Treaty Principles* (Alberta, 2006), http://www.treaty8.ca/page.aspx?ID=4-5 (accessed 11 May 2007).

12   Billy Diamond, "The Cree Experience," in *Indian Education in Canada,* eds. Yvonne M. Hebert, Don N. McCaskill, & Jean Barman (Vancouver: UBC Press, 1987).

13   Kativik School Board, www.kativik.qc.ca (accessed 12 May 2007).

14   Brian Callaghan, "Inuit Education in Nouveau Québec 1912 - 1991," (M.A. thesis, McGill University, 1992).

15   *General Agreement in Principle between Dehcho First Nations, Government of Canada and the Government of the Northwest Territories, March 5, 2007,* http://www.dehchofirstnations.com/documents/negotiations/07_03_05_general_agreement_in_principle.pdf (accessed 12 May 2007).

16   Indian and Northern Affairs Canada, *New Brunswick Education Initiative Receives Funding,* http://www.ainc-inac.gc.ca/nr/prs/m-a2005/2-02658_e.html BG (accessed 12 May 2007).

17   Bob Kennedy, *Bringing Elders into Classrooms to Support Aboriginal Students and Encourage Them to Do Better in School,* http://www.turtleisland.org/discussion/viewtopic.php?p=6569#6569 (accessed 20 May 2007).

18   *Ibid.*

19   Diane Poulin, *Children of the Earth Fosters Belonging, Respect* (Manitoba Teachers Society, n.d.), http://www.mbteach.org/Aboriginal%20educ/aborchildrenofearth.htm (accessed 12 May 2007).

20   Diane Poulin, *Niji Mahkwa School: Integrating Learning into Culture* (Manitoba Teachers Society, n.d.); [http://www.mbteach.org/aboriginal%20educ/aborniji.htm (accessed 12 May 2007).

21   See ongoing commentary in *Nunatsiaq News,* for example.

22   Nunavut Department of Education, "Bilingual Education Strategy for Nunavut 2004-2008," ed. Nunavut Dept. of Education (2004).

23   Ann Meekitjuk Hanson, *Commissioner's Address Opening of the Third Session of the Second Legislative Assembly of Nunavut; Nov. 15, 2005,* http://www.commissioner.gov.nu.ca/english/commissioner/speaches/ commissioner_address.html (accessed 12 May 2007).

24   Hanson, *Commissioner's Address.*

25   Nunavut Department of Education, "Bilingual Education Strategy," 5.

26   Indian and Northern Affairs Canada, *Policy Directions in Aboriginal Education South of 60° for the First Ministers' Meeting* (Ottawa: 2005).

27   Michael Mendelson, "Improving Primary and Secondary Education on Reserves in Canada," in *Caledon Commentary* (Ottawa: Caledon Institute of Social Policy, 2006).

28   *Ibid.*

29   S.C. 1998, c. 24; S.N.S. 1998, c. 17.

30   Mi'kmaw Kinamatnewey, http://www.kinu.ns.ca (accessed 12 May 2007).

31   Jennifer McCarthy, *Mi'kmaw Kinamatnewey: A Case Study in Aggregation* (Institute On Governance, 2001) 2, http://www.iog.ca/publications/MKCaseStudy.pdf (accessed 12 May 2007).

32   Indian and Northern Affairs Canada, *Renewed Agreement Benefits Mi'kmaq Students* [News release 2-02620], http://www.ainc-inac.gc.ca/nr/prs/j-a2005/2-02620_e.html (accessed 12 May 2007).

33   Indian and Northern Affairs Canada, *Renewed Agreement Benefits Mi'kmaq Students.*

34   Indian and Northern Affairs Canada, *Backgrounder* (May 9, 2005), http://www.ainc-inac.gc.ca/nr/prs/j-a2005/02620bk_e.html (accessed 12 May 2007).

35   Indian and Northern Affairs Canada, *Renewed Agreement Benefits Mi'kmaq Students.*

36   McCarthy, *Mi'kmaw Kinamatnewey.*

37   S.C. 2006, c.10.

38   Indian and Northern Affairs Canada, "2005-2006 Departmental Performance Report," in *Canadian Polar Commission, and Indian Specific Claims Commission,* ed. Indian and Northern Affairs Canada (Canada: Treasury Board Secretariat, 2006).

39   Morgan, *If Not Now, Then When?* 49.

40   Seven Generations, *Mission Statement / Who We Are,* http://www.7generations.org/About%20Us/aboutUs.html (accessed 12 May 2007).

41   Harvey McCue, *The Establishment of Centralized Governments for First Nations and for the Primacy of Local Community Governments in First Nations Affairs,* http://www.turtleisland.org/discussion/viewtopic.php?p=4631 (accessed 12 May 2007).

42   Verna Kirkness, "Our Peoples' Education: Cut the Shackles; Cut the Crap; Cut the Mustard," *Canadian Journal of Native Education* 22, no. 1 (1998): 10-15.

43   The Manitoba First Nations Education Resource Centre (n.d.), http://www.mfnerc.org/pages.php?page_id=mission (accessed 12 May 2007).

44   David Bell, *Sharing Our Success: Ten Case Studies in Aboriginal Schooling* (Kelowna: Society for Advancement of Excellence in Education, 2004).

45   George Taylor Fulford, *Sharing Our Success: More Case Studies in Aboriginal Schooling,* SAEE Research Series; 2 (Kelowna: Society for the Advancement of Excellence in Education, 2007), 300.

46   *Ibid.,* 323.

47   Poulin, *Niji Mahkwa School.*

48   Kirkness, "Our Peoples' Education."

Part V:

Future Prospects

FUTURE PROSPECTS FOR ABORIGINAL SELF-GOVERNMENT IN CANADA

Yale D. Belanger, University of Lethbridge

Following publication of the Parliamentary Task Force on Indian Self-Government final report in 1983, Roger Gibbins and J. Rick Ponting responded that, prior to endorsing the Committee's myriad suggestions, "close attention be paid to the linkages that might be established or retained between Indians and the existing Canadian governments." They added prophetically, "Without such linkages, the Penner recommendations could widen rather than bridge the tragic gulf that now exists between Indian First Nations and the broader Canadian community."[1] A quarter century after the Aboriginal self-government ideal came to prominence nationally, it is imperative to reflect back on the evolution of a concept and its impact on Aboriginal people in Canada. This volume confirms that the proposed linkages identified in the Penner Report such as the formal constitutional entrenchment of Aboriginal self-government, the appropriate enabling legislation to recognize those governments, or creating defined realms of authority for education, child welfare, heath care, membership, social and cultural development, land and resource use, for example, have yet to fully materialize. At the same time, it has also made clear that self-government continues its evolution—the result of effective grassroots organization and dedication to belief in self-government.

The fact that the linkages lack definition—a challenging obstacle to developing effective self-government—can be distilled to two points. From an Aboriginal perspective, the linkages have been in place for centuries in the form of official political and treaty relationships that both implicitly and explicitly recognize Aboriginal people and their communities as self-governing nations. Hence, the goal should be reanimating these relationships. On the other hand, the Canadian belief in self-government as an inherent right is found, in substance, in the federal transfer of financial responsibility for programs to Aboriginal governments—this occurs once community-based political values and ideologies have been sufficiently altered to conform to the municipal models long advocated by federal officials. The resulting tensions, many of which are identified in this book, require further investigation and remedial action if the Aboriginal self-government ideal is to become mutually acceptable as opposed to a model negotiated in adversarial fora.

Despite these concerns, several unique and innovative Aboriginal self-government models have emerged as Aboriginal leaders adjust their political strategies to better reflect their constituents' socio-economic needs and desires. Federal officials have responded cautiously to First Nations demands for representative self-governing models intended to expand self-government from a delegated right to an inherent form of governance within Canadian Confederation based on the accepted sovereignty of First Nations and the attendant responsibility for governing oneself, though there has been some progress on this front as well.

Reflecting on 'A New Era'

In 1994, John Hylton suggested that Canada was on the precipice of a new era. Writing while the Royal Commission on Aboriginal Peoples (RCAP) was in the midst of its research mandate, a period in which the idea of Aboriginal self-government was gaining political currency, Hylton predicted that "a new era in Canada's relations with the Aboriginal Peoples, based in self-government, may be on the horizon."[2] In the 1999, he identified six features characteristic of this new era, ideas he claimed would

"fuel the momentum to implement more self-governing programs and institutions in the future. Specifically, the following may be noted:

- Aboriginal people in Canada are increasingly engaged in the practice of self-government. Furthermore, a number of Aboriginal nations have already negotiated far-reaching self-government agreements. Significant progress can be noted, even in the five years since the first edition of this book was published.

- In terms of support for self-government, there has been an expression of considerable political will on the part of Canadian governments. Although this has not always translated into the type of concrete action that Aboriginal people want and deserve, nonetheless this support contributes to a positive outlook for the future.

- Despite delays and uncertainty, the current federal government appears more ready than previous administrations to enter into new arrangements with Aboriginal people.

- The final report of the Royal Commission on Aboriginal Peoples (RCAP), as well as a number of important interim reports, have served to focus public and political attention on the need for a fundamental restructuring of relations.

- Public opinion appears at least cautiously supportive of a "new deal" for Canada's Aboriginal peoples.

- Finally, self-governing arrangements with Aboriginal people are consistent with the broader values and practices that governments are adopting to respond to a wide range of social and economic challenges facing the country.[3]

In the years between the two editions of *Aboriginal Self-Government in Canada*, self-government evolved from a concept with limited operating models to draw from for guidance to eight self-government agreements becoming operational between 1995 and 1999. The next nine years proved equally productive with an additional seven final agreements activated as self-government continued its evolution.

But has this evolution been for the better? Has our understanding of self-government improved? Are Canadians accepting of self-government? What impact do the differing Aboriginal and Canadian conceptions of self-government have on its development? And, is the emergent self-government ideal flexible enough to embrace multiple agendas while still contributing positively to both Aboriginal community development and Canadian Confederation? The last nine years have witnessed significant social, political, and economic transformations nationally making it incumbent upon us to reflect on those changes and their potential impact on the continued evolution of Aboriginal self-government.

Self-Government: A Reality in Canada

First Nations leaders in Canada would argue that self-government is not a new concept but rather one preceding the arrival of newcomers to North America, inherent, and based upon local sovereignty, resulting, therefore, in a right to govern local affairs. When we use the term Aboriginal self-government we are speaking about a contemporary concept borne of Canadian Confederation perhaps more accurately described as modern-day Aboriginal self-government in the same way that we differentiate historic and modern-day treaties. The modern-day form of Aboriginal self-government was realized first with the *Cree Naskapi Act* of 1984, and more formally in the *Sechelt Act* of 1986, both of which were followed by two decades of negotiations between various First Nations and the federal officials.

Each province and territory now boasts various self-governing regimes, and, as indicated by Morse in this volume, there are currently 72 national self-government negotiating tables in place representing 445 Aboriginal communities (this total includes 427 First Nations, 18 Inuit communities, and some Métis locals). Several agreements-in-principle are also in process. Clearly self-government in Canada is here to stay. But one must stop and consider how we arrive at self-government considering that it is approached from two distinct poles. Promoting mutual coexistence *sans* interference from outside parties, political or otherwise, Aboriginal leaders seek local government operations that reflect community needs whereas Canada sets the stage for how self-government negotiations will transpire while promoting First Nations municipalize to better fit within the overall self-government matrix.

Arguably, this is not as troubling as our collective inability to create an ideology to guide all parties seeking self-government. This is a tricky proposition that would require each party to concede a level of political influence. With controlling interest of the self-government agenda, Canadian officials are unwilling to capitulate to Aboriginal demands; Aboriginal leaders, on the other hand, are loath to yield whatever limited powers they may bring to the negotiations. But despite what could be considered a contentious environment, as this volume confirms significant progress has been made and Aboriginal people are steadily taking a lead role in self-government's design and implementation, leading to their participation in Canadian politics at various levels. And with 14 finalized self-government agreements, 16 agreements-in-principle awaiting ratification, and numerous federal, provincial, and community-based programs that are components of larger self-government aspirations, Hylton was accurate when he suggested that self-government "finds many different expressions in Canada."[4]

It is important to note that the effect is cumulative—as self-government capacity expands, innovative governing models materialize. Provincial, territorial, treaty, and independently negotiated models have demonstrated their staying power as have the "just do it" models employed by communities such as Kahnawake in Quebec. This diversity of models attests to the willingness and ability of Aboriginal leaders to consider alternative governing processes when pursuing self-government. This often entails Aboriginal communities and non-governmental organizations such as tribal councils adopting responsibility for programming through federally sanctioned negotiations that cover every conceivable area of government and community service, including but not limited to: justice services, education, community infrastructure, housing, health care and social services, sport and recreation, economic development, employment, as well as many other realms.

The recent proliferation of negotiations also suggests that self-government is gaining in popularity, and that, once at the negotiating table, all interested parties work together developing democratic institutions and interactive jurisdictional agreements at the national, provincial, and municipal levels. This may indeed be true, but, as Coates and Morrison point out in this volume, neither Aboriginal nor Canadian leaders consider self-government a perfect solution to complex social and cultural problems confronting their respective communities. Many Aboriginal leaders, like many Canadian officials, pursue self-government negotiations cautiously, while still others avoid pursuing the self-government ideal, ever aware of the impact of past federal assimilation policies and the inadequacies of historic and modern treaty negotiations.

A variety of issues continue to wreak havoc on the existing system, in terms of how we both conceptualise and negotiate self-government, and many argue for a complete procedural overhaul. The lack of a clear self-government policy at the federal and provincial levels and continued reliance on existing policy and funding environments to define the basis of self-government relationships encapsulated in final agreements is problematic. What is more, existing models are not inclusive, and rely upon constitutional definitions that often leave the Métis and urban Aboriginal populations beyond the scope of current self-government negotiations. The complexity and evolutionary aspect of Aboriginal self-government suggests that more issues will arise as negotiations move forward, but the evolutionary aspect will also permit correctives to be developed.

Political Will: The Conservative Agenda

The shift from a Liberal to a Conservative government in 2006, and Prime Minister Stephen Harper's demonstrated indifference toward Indian affairs, caused concern among Aboriginal leaders for the condition of the Aboriginal-Canada relationship. This apprehension became amplified as Harper unhurriedly made public his Government's agenda concerning Aboriginal people, reaching a fever pitch following his withdrawal of the $5.1-billion Kelowna Accord proposed by the previous Liberal administration. This was indeed a bold move, for the Kelowna Accord tabled by Prime Minister Paul Martin was supported by First Ministers and Aboriginal leaders alike, all of whom envisioned utilizing the five-year accord to improve education, housing, economic development, health, and water services. Specifically, the plan included:

- $1.8 billion for education to create school systems, train more Aboriginal teachers, and identify children with special needs;
- $1.6 billion for housing, including $400 million to address the need for clean water in many remote communities;
- $1.3 billion for health services; and,
- $200 million for economic development.[5]

Martin's minority government collapsed 72 hours after the Accord's conclusion.

Indian Affairs Minister Jim Prentice (Calgary Centre North) played a leading role early on, openly promoting the need for improved band council accountability while funnelling cash into various infrastructure projects designed to enhance the water quality on many reserves. Moreover, Prentice appeared open to consultation and optimistic concerning Aboriginal issues, and he soon became popular with Aboriginal leaders nationally. Despite Prentice's efforts, however, the Conservative government's failure to disclose its Indian affairs agenda was disquieting, leading to a brief albeit politically destabilizing fifteen-month period that inevitably precluded many political organizations from developing strategies to bolster Aboriginal participation in the federal policy process. The federal budget announcement of 19 March 2007, which resulted in $70 million allocated for Aboriginal training, justice, and a commercial fisheries program, and $300 million to develop a program of private home ownership on reserves, was a harbinger of things to come.

Assembly of First Nations (AFN) Grand Chief Phil Fontaine reacted publicly, proclaiming support of the budget was tantamount to supporting an apathetic government that demonstrated minimal concern for Aboriginal issues which was akin to outright rejection of First Nations and their concerns.[6] He added, "They will judge this lack of courage to act, to do the right thing and to truly honour Canadian values of justice, fairness, and compassion."[7] Fontaine was frustrated by what he described as the federal government's recognized lack of accomplishments related to Aboriginal issues, and he called for national day of action (June 29) that potentially involved interfering with road, rail, and port service across the country.[8]

In response to both Fontaine and Assembly of Manitoba Chiefs (AMC) Grand Chief Ron Evans' corresponding threats to obstruct development projects, Prentice published an open letter in the *Winnipeg Free Press* March 29 indicating that he was willing to sanction any participating First Nations and Aboriginal organizations, thereby threatening the financial viability of Aboriginal political organizations deemed objectionable to Conservative policies. Specifically, in reference to the AMC's anticipated use of a portion of its $50.8-million in federal funding for protest activities, Prentice stated that he was "prepared to order forensic audits of every organization that participates in blockades and civil disobedience to ensure that monies intended for children were not used to plan these activities."[9] Notably, this episode represented the AFN and INAC's first public dispute since the election of the Conservatives to power, an event most observers anticipated well in advance of the mid-2007 budget announcement. These three recent episodes, however, offer particular insight into the Conservative Party's policy orientation extending beyond land claims to self-government:

- it appears that its proposed private property program is structured to eliminate existing reserves;

- related to point one, the Conservatives have once again breathed life into the age-old strategy of promoting Aboriginal assimilation into the Canadian cultural aesthetic; and,

- former Minister of Indian Affairs Jim Prentice's threats to initiate forensic audits represented an obvious effort on his part to restrict the actions of and free speech exercised by Aboriginal political organizations, which in turn could potentially handicap their ability to act as the official voice of national Aboriginal concerns related to Indian policy creation and implementation.

The Aboriginal day of action came and went without incident, although First Nations-Canada relations remain strained. In September 2007, Canada refused to sign the United Nations Declaration on the Rights of Indigenous Peoples along with Australia, New Zealand, and the United States. Despite its non-binding nature, the Declaration took two decades to negotiate and represented an impressive vote of confidence for Aboriginal peoples in Canada. Prentice's successor, Chuck Strahl (Chilliwack-Fraser Canyon), cited inconsistencies between the Declaration and the Canadian Constitution, the *Charter of Rights and Freedoms*, various Parliamentary acts, and existing treaties. Further undermining the spirit of self-government Strahl also rejected the sections compelling the Canadian government to consult with First Nations leaders about the potential impact of proposed legislation upon Aboriginal people, adding, "We'd have to consult with 650 First Nations to do that. I mean, it's simply not doable."[10]

These episodes suggest that some of the political will crucial to self-government's continued progress may have evaporated with the Liberal's demise replaced by a Conservative government with demonstrably little interest in escalating the dialogue while continuing to promote settling land claims negotiations, reaching three agreements in BC alone in 2006. Yet Harper personally endorsed the *Westbank First Nation Self-Government Act*, described at the time as the model for future deals with First Nations, an incident that threatened both caucus support and party stability. Specifically, those opposed to Harper's plan were upset that non-native residents and business owners would be afforded no voting rights and that local government abuse of Aboriginal citizens could potentially be shielded from a Charter challenge by leaders claiming their actions to be an aspect of the Aboriginal right to govern.[11] Finally, additional funding was directed at improving reserve infrastructure, specifically water treatment facilities in various Aboriginal communities nationally. Coates and Poelzer offer four explanations suggesting why the Conservatives have been able to resolve land claims, which they argue could likely lead to movement on self-government agreements:

1) Aboriginal settlements are good for business: unsettled land claims create significant encumbrances on economic development.
2) Conservatives have historically viewed Canada as a community of communities: The accommodation of Aboriginal communities is not the ideological stretch for Tory conservatism that it has been historically for Liberals.
3) Conservatives value local and regional community, and decentralized power: Self-government and land-claims settlements are consistent with decentralization and the empowerment of local communities.
4) Conservatives have historically valued tradition and the collective wisdom passed down.[12]

With these ideas in mind, political will may still exist as regards Aboriginal self-government even if the spectre of mistrust continues to guide Aboriginal leaders in their dealings with Conservative officials.

The Royal Commission on Aboriginal Peoples

The Royal Commission on Aboriginal Peoples (RCAP) was established in 1991 during a period when the push for self-government appeared stalled. The Royal Commission's research mandate was wide-ranging and probed every aspect of Aboriginal life, exploring relations between Aboriginal peoples and the Canadian state, and making recommendations about how to improve conditions confronting Aboriginal people. Costing more than $60 million, the RCAP's final report was five-volumes consisting of 3,536 pages. In total "the Commission met 100 times, had 178 days of hearings, recorded 76,000 pages of transcripts, generated 356 research studies, published four special reports, and two commentaries on self-government."[13]

Importantly, the report concluded that the Aboriginal right to self-govern was recognized in both international and domestic law, and that Canada should adopt the principles of mutual recognition, mutual respect, sharing, and mutual responsibility to help define "a process that can provide the solutions to many of the difficulties afflicting relations among Aboriginal and non-Aboriginal people."[14] In sum, the Royal Commission envisaged a renewed Canadian partnership where people would "acknowledge and relate to one another as equals, coexisting side by side and governing themselves according to their own laws and institutions."[15]

Despite its promise, the RCAP faded quickly from sight. There is little question that it significantly influenced the federal government's 1995 Inherent Rights Policy, but the bulk of its recommendations have yet to be implemented. Ten years after its release, the Assembly of First Nations (AFN) released *Royal Commission on Aboriginal People at 10 Years: A Report Card* summarizing Canada's response to the Commission's major recommendations. Of the 66 key recommendations contained in the report's four volumes, only 29 were assigned passing grades, and most of those were marginal at that. The overall RCAP experience was given a failing grade. "[T]he reality for First Nations communities today is *ongoing poverty*, and an increasing gap in living conditions with other Canadians, which were reported during the RCAP hearings. Any major improvements in individual communities or regions have been led *by* those communities *for* those communities."[16] Since the Royal Commission tabled its final report, Canada provided no "sustained investment in meeting the basic needs of First Nations communities, or in addressing key determinants of health/well-being."[17]

To be fair, the final RCAP report was commissioned by the Progressive Conservatives and tabled during the Liberal regime; however, the ideas in the report were aimed at renewed commitment to rebuilding the First Nations-Canada relationship and were not specific to any one party. And the limited critical reviews reflecting on the process, the recommendations, and inaction on the part of Canada in response to RCAP since its release and its subsequent fading from our collective memory is disappointing. Many of the recommendations would have accomplished what existing self-government policy and agreements are unable to: reconciling the Aboriginal-Canada relationship by promoting English, French, and

First Nations as partners in confederation. Arguably, prior to reconciliation and partnership becoming central aspects of modern-day self-government, the process will remain inherently adversarial and contentious, and apt to fail.

Public Opinion

Public opinion influences federal and provincial politicians, and at various times in recent history Aboriginal leaders have garnered the sympathy required to compel the government to respond. Most noticeable was Mulroney establishing the RCAP in 1991 following the Oka crisis while a study the same year indicated that, despite a general misunderstanding about what self-government represented, most Canadians opposed it.[18] Moreover, the reasons were fuelled by concerns related to how self-government's implementation might negatively affect the economic security of non-Native citizens.[19] It was evident that self-government was not fully understood by the public and therefore not supportable. Yet a subsequent survey following the Charlottetown Accord's demise in 1992 indicated that 60 per cent of all Canadians supported the proposed constitutional changes related to Aboriginal issues. Half of those questioned were also in favour of the government giving high priority to Aboriginal self-government.[20]

The level of public support for Aboriginal self-government was estimated to be between 65 and 85 per cent in the mid-1990s.[21] And by 1998, Canadians believed that Aboriginal self-government should be a government priority despite a lack of consensus concerning how self-government powers were to be defined and implemented.[22] Perhaps most disturbing, in this instance, was the fact that Canadians did not distinguish between self-government and cultural adaptation, leading the study's authors to conclude that self-government may be publicly understood as a means of further assimilating Indians.[23] By 2000, public opinion had once again shifted with an Angus Reid poll submitted to Indian and Northern Affairs Canada (INAC) indicating the following Canadian attitudes about Aboriginal self-government:

- Twenty-five per cent of those surveyed in the poll believed Aboriginal peoples have a historic right to self-government;

- Thirty-four per cent felt the government should set up a framework for Aboriginal self-government, while 40 per cent indicated that Aboriginal people had no more right to self-government than other ethnic groups in Canada;

- On the issue of land claims, 16 per cent said they feel native people have "no claim to any more land in Canada" while the same percentage felt land claims are "legitimate and should be fully compensated in land, money or both."[24]

This low level of support is troublesome, especially in light of the fact that at the time of the survey Canada had finalized several self-government agreements and was involved at several other tables. Arguably, the issues had to do with both the lack of information made public about self-government and the inability of politicians to assist the public to decipher self-government's complexities. Self-government was consistently presented as a nebulous yet all-inclusive concept that failed to respect the cultural complexity of individual communities, hence difficult for those not immersed in the ongoing dialogue to comprehend.[25] The lack of information disseminated in sound bytes and short media overviews continues to be insufficient to provide the required context to fully comprehend or appreciate self-government's legal and social complexity and its importance to Canadian confederation. Enhancing the public's understanding would, as several studies suggested in the early 1990s, likely result in superior support for self-government.[26]

A political catch-22 has arisen as the increasing complexity of Aboriginal self-government and the variety of models currently being utilized means that politicians and Aboriginal leaders must be necessarily ambiguous when trying to illustrate what Aboriginal self-government is and what it embodies. This represents yet another obstacle to overcome.

Further complicating the public's understanding of Aboriginal issues could be the mixed signals it received from provincial politicians during the British Columbia referendum in 2002. Even with the federal government's demonstrated support for self-government negotiations and resolution of land claims, a referendum challenged the legitimacy of ongoing treaty negotiations when Liberal Gordon Campbell disputed the *Nisga'a Treaty*'s validity on the grounds that the constitutional right to Aboriginal self-government did not exist. The courts quickly struck down this argument even if Campbell's comments stirred controversy.

This provincial initiative made national headlines, and many Aboriginal leaders publicly condemned what they depicted as the referendum's racist scope. Others equated Campbell's attitudes as characteristic of all Canadians' beliefs about Aboriginal people and self-government. Inflaming the situation further was BC Attorney General Geoff Plant's comments suggesting that the referendum provided ordinary British Columbians a say in the treaty process. This in effect signalled to provincial citizens and national media consumers that self-government was a potentially threatening process that could be curbed only through extreme measures such as referenda and plebiscites. Those responsible for drafting the questionnaire crafted a document of questions structured to elicit a yes response to all queries, leading veteran pollster Angus Reid to describe the referendum as "one of the most amateurish, one-sided attempts to gauge the public will that I have seen in my professional career."[27] Furthermore, many of the issues dealt with on the ballot were beyond provincial jurisdiction, meaning that the referendum was a waste of time and $9 million. The plebiscite nevertheless demonstrated overwhelming support for the BC government, with an estimated 80 per cent voting "Yes" to all eight proposed principles.

Clearly public support for self-government vacillates. Some recent opinion polls indicate that 80 per cent of Canadians believe treaties signed by the Canadian government and First Nations should be honoured because they are binding agreements, up from 75 per cent in a 2006 survey, and 55 per cent recommend honouring the treaties even if they hinder or prevent economic development within the local communities they affect. Even though treaties are generally seen to be documents signed by political opponents engaging in political diplomacy, the fact that they were negotiated by the leaders of political communities is accepted by and large. Does the support for maintaining the treaties suggest that there is also public support for self-government? That is difficult to determine, but self-government support will continue to decline until more detailed information begins to appear in public media and as soon as events similar to the BC referendum cease to materialize.

Barriers to Change

Future prospects for Aboriginal self-government are at best unknown due to a range of variables. Many of the issues are time tested, and Hylton identified several that continue to stand in the way of rapid and even continued progress.[28] These obstacles, discussed below, have yet to be fully addressed, something that needs to take place if the momentum generated during the last two decades is to be maintained.

Constitutional Renewal

Many of Canada's leading constitutional scholars contend that the right of self-government exercised by Aboriginal people and formally acknowledged by the Crown in the *Royal Proclamation of 1763* has never been relinquished.[29] James [Sákéj] Youngblood Henderson, for example, argues in this volume that treaties with the British Crown represent colonial acknowledgement of the inherent sovereignty of the tribes, their system of law and rights, and their right to choose their destiny, relationships, and way of life.[30] Brian Slattery highlights the consequences associated with these viewpoints: "when Section 35 of the *Constitution Act, 1982,* took effect, the right of self-government was still extant and featured among the 'existing aboriginal and treaty rights' recognized in the section."[31]

Despite such pronouncements and the fact that contemporary Aboriginal leaders continue to advocate for the Constitutional entrenchment of the inherent right to self-government, the Canadian government has to date given no indication that Constitutional renewal is on its radar, instead promoting treaty negotiations as a means of establishing relationships with Aboriginal leaders. Implicit with treaty negotiations is the formalization of political relationships that encourage the recognition of cultural values, customary practices, and fundamental political traditions. As well, they are also considered formal agreements between two (or more) sovereign nations negotiated by appointed emissaries and ratified by each signatory's government.[32] The nation-to-nation aspect inherent in treaty negotiations resonates with Aboriginal leaders who subscribe to the RCAP's characterization of the Aboriginal-Canada relationship as one of equals "coexisting side by side and governing themselves according to their own laws and institutions."[33] Similar to the modern-day self-government negotiations process, the modern treaty process is also imperfect. The Métis and other groups lacking a demarcated land base are excluded from treaty talks. It is also an incredibly slow process. For example, the six-stage treaty process in BC has, since its inception in 1992, produced one ratified agreement and one initialled final agreement.

The policy approach to self-government has also come under scrutiny, specifically the government's Inherent Rights Policy (IRP). Announced in 1995, the IRP recognized the right to self-government as an existing right within section 35 of the *Constitution Act, 1982,* in matters "internal to their communities, integral to their unique cultures, identities, traditions, languages and institutions and with respect to their special relationship to their land and their resources."

Both the federal government and First Nations have since taken the position that the inherent right to self-government is an existing Aboriginal right constitutionally recognized and protected within s. 35(1). However, federal officials contend that the rights must first be conferred upon a band prior to their being recognized from a legal standpoint.

The sense of urgency attached to expanding the inherent right to self-government has not abated, especially in light of ongoing negotiations that configure self-government agreements based on federal policy demanding a First Nation surrender all Aboriginal rights and adopt a municipal-style model of governance. Many Aboriginal leaders consider this to be a modern policy of assimilation, if you will.[34] Furthermore, it is awkward to negotiate for a right that may or may not legally exist. Lacking a formal definition requires federal officials to ask First Nations to take an incredible leap of faith, especially when one stops to consider that the Supreme Court of Canada has adopted a wait-and-see approach regarding the evolution and meaning of the inherent right to self-government.

Federal officials still take the lead when developing Aboriginal policies and legislation. The *First Nations Governance Act* (FNGA), first proposed in 2001, is a case in point. In addition to pronounced AFN opposition, BC's Interior Alliance spokesperson Chief Arthur Manuel described the proposal as a "gross violation of Indigenous peoples' inherent right to self-determination" and said it would accelerate the extinguishment of Aboriginal title and rights. Seeking to establish leadership selection codes, modern standards for financial and operational accountability *vis-à-vis* the bands' ability to establish financial management codes, the ability to tailor their governing structures to suit their needs, the legal capacity of bands, the scope of their law-making powers, and improved capacity to enforce band laws, notably absent from the proposed legislation was any clarification concerning the issue of status and band membership, First Nations women's concerns relating to land, the delivery of programs and services, or a broad review of the *Indian Act.* Importantly, the FNGA defined self-government as a legislative by-product as opposed to being tied to the land base or as an inherent right. These proposed changes to the *Indian Act* were withdrawn in 2003 but not soon forgotten.

Community Development

Existing policy approaches to helping improve local Aboriginal development continue to be guided by *Indian Act* criteria which insist upon government overview of all initiatives and Aboriginal compliance to related federal and provincial legislation and policy guidelines. As other non-Native communities in Canada struggle with similar development issues, they are provided the chance to develop innovative solutions to unique problems, an option Aboriginal communities currently lack. As an example, economic development was identified in the 1980s as a necessary step in the move toward self-government. Prime Minister Pierre Elliot Trudeau responded with the Native Economic Development Program in October 1983. Employing a strategy of creating a pool of capital owned, controlled, and managed by Aboriginal peoples, the resultant loan and trust companies, development corporations, and venture capital operations were ineffectual. Over the years various similar strategies have been employed in an effort to generate what has come to be a limited level of success.

Building on this theme, the Royal Commission described an urgent need to support self-government and community-based initiatives to rebuild First Nations economies. It also warned that "self-government without a significant economic base would be an exercise in illusion and futility." Drastic measures were needed "to rebuild Aboriginal economies ... severely disrupted over time, marginalized, and largely stripped of their land and natural resource base." The Commission also warned, "under current conditions and approaches to economic development, we could see little prospect for a better future" while further cautioning that establishing "a more self-reliant economic base for Aboriginal communities and nations will require significant, even radical departures from business as usual."[35] The prevalent theme to emerge was that Aboriginal leaders and the Canadian officials shared a historic relationship that necessitated the two sides working with one another for the mutual benefit of all Canadians.

From an Aboriginal perspective, fostering economic self-sufficiency is paramount to community well-being and is considered a means of stimulating and maintaining localized economic development thereby leading to economic and political independence. Despite the Royal Commission's dire pronouncements, the federal government has yet to shift its focus from an *Indian Act*-guided approach to economic development to fostering proven community development principles. Barriers to economic development also include inadequate education, limited access to capital, and fruitless government coordination, capacity-development issues self-government should be combating. The Harvard Project on American Indian Economic Development has connected sustained development to the recognition of effective exercise of tribal sovereignty, as discussed by Calliou in this volume.

The importance of economic development to the structure and operations of self-government cannot be ignored. Not only is an independently generated source of funding required to promote Aboriginal self-government, but officials in Ottawa will only acknowledge self-government after a band has met the criteria necessary to a stable reserve economy. Specifically, the Inherent Rights Policy of 1995 clearly states:

> All participants in self-government negotiations must recognize that self-government arrangements will have to be affordable and consistent with the overall social and economic policies and priorities of governments, while at the same time taking into account the specific needs of Aboriginal peoples. In this regard, the fiscal and budgetary capacity of the federal, provincial, territorial and Aboriginal governments or institutions will be a primary determinant of the financing of self-government.

Federal politicians justify this stance arguing that reserve-based economic ventures have rarely succeeded, and in many ways continue to play an insignificant role related to securing personal incomes and generating general band revenue.

The Need for Healing

Community development is more than promoting economic development, however. Synonymous with this concept is the need to heal Aboriginal communities, physically and emotionally. There has been a consistent desire to create healthy and stable governments that in turn could take a lead role in fostering community well-being and in building healthy relationships with the world around the community, an idea consistent with indigenous political philosophies reflecting the nature of the desired political relationships, the need to renew and formalize these relationships, and the need for appropriate governing structures. An interim Royal Commission report summarized the feelings expressed by Aboriginal leaders nationally: "Health is the core of the well-being that must lie at the centre of each healthy person and the vitality that must animate healthy communities and cultures. Where there is good health in this sense, it reverberates through every strand of life."[36]

The nature of healing and well-being is hotly contested by Aboriginal leaders in Canada. Many argue that prior to engaging in self-government healing must first occur. Others contend that resources must be produced and then channelled into appropriate healing strategies. Despite the merits of either conviction, the reality is that most Aboriginal communities remain isolated from functioning economies and are forced to contend with myriad social issues *sans* funding and other required resources. Artificial welfare economies are still the main economic drivers in many Aboriginal communities nationally, meaning that there exists limited economic capacity to become self-governing. Dollars often leave as quickly as they enter Aboriginal communities, resulting in minimal currency circulation further depressing local Aboriginal economies. For example, it is estimated that the Blood Reserve (pop. 10,000) in southern Alberta leaks upwards of $100 million annually into the Lethbridge economy, whereas in 1992 it was estimated that the Blood and Peigan Reserves combined spent $30 million in the city.[37]

At times, it also appears that little in the way of public sympathy exists which, as described above, is needed to provoke political response. Take the recent writings of *National Post* columnist Jonathan Kay, when he concluded that "Each year the federal government spends over $8-billion on reserve-resident natives, or $80,000 per reserve-resident household (a statistic I never get tired of quoting, because it puts to rest the idea that natives are somehow being nickel-and-dimed under the current system)."[38] Although his commentary was knowledgeably countered one week later by McMaster University instructor Hayden King,[39] such tried and true attitudes influence political will while also portraying Aboriginal people as irreparably damaged, hence unable to manage their own affairs. Also fostering change are changing demographics. For example, recent statistics demonstrate that close to 80 per cent of Aboriginal people live off-reserve. Since only those Aboriginal people working and living on-reserve are exempt from paying personal taxes, this suggests that the vast majority of Aboriginal people nationally contribute significantly to Canada's tax base. Although no data exists to date, the costs of INAC's operations are likely funded by these tax dollars, and if there remain additional monies they are channelled into funding non-Native programming. This tax base alone, if properly managed, could fuel self-government for decades to come.

It is generally accepted however that prior to improving local health, meaningful self-government is not possible. With this in mind, statistics gleaned from the AFN report card are telling:

- One in four First Nations children live in poverty, compared to 1 in 6 Canadian children. They have double the rates of disability, and over one third of their homes are overcrowded.

- Year-end 2003 data from DIAND indicated that 9,031 First Nations children on reserve were receiving child welfare assistance representing a 70 per cent increase from 1995.

- A recent report has found that 0.67 per cent of non-Aboriginal children were in child welfare care as of May 2005 compared to 10.23 per cent of status Indian children.

- One in three First Nations people consider their main drinking water unsafe to drink, and 12% of First Nations communities have to boil their drinking water.

- Six percent (over 5,000 homes) are without sewage services, and 4 per cent lack either hot water, cold water, or flushing toilets.

- First Nations communities rank 76th out of 174 nations when using the United Nations Development Index 2001. This is compared to Canadian communities who rank 8th.

- First Nations are more likely to require health services than Canadians: for example, diabetes is at least three times the national average, and tuberculosis is eight to ten times more prevalent among First Nations.

* Life expectancy for First Nations men is 7.4 years less, and 5.2 years less for First Nations women, compared to Canadian men and women respectively.[40]

But, as Lavoie *et al* discuss in this volume, Aboriginal health is increasingly compromised by provincial and federal governments' refusal to accept responsibility for health care. Such inter-jurisdictional disputes leave many people waiting for health services, a conflict that will become more prominent as urban Aboriginal populations continue to grow. Often lost in the mix are those First Nations and Aboriginal communities managing their own health facilities—as reserve and rural Aboriginal populations grow so does the need to expand health services. In most cases, there is a moral imperative to care for community members notwithstanding status, which in turn compromises community well-being due to a lack of financial resources.

Self-Government: Still Many Meanings

First Nations are clearly taking action to determine what is needed prior to developing forms of self-government, which can be defined generally as the need to promote the recognition of community-based rights and jurisdiction while fostering the economic development needed to drive local political and economic initiatives.[41] At the same time, the ongoing debate as to what self-government truly represents and how this will affect both Aboriginal people and the national political environment continues to impede negotiations and the realization of self-governance at the community level. Dating back to the 1960s and the Hawthorn Report's recommendations aimed at paving the way for improved social and political control on reserves, and the controlled and precise response to the White Paper proposal aimed at emphasizing the historic and as-yet-extinguished right to self-govern, the two definite approaches to the self-government debate discussed above are difficult to overcome.

Aboriginal leaders have adapted whereas Canadian officials tend to be inflexible in their attitudes about and approach to negotiating self-government, and this is arguably the foremost impediment to realizing successful self-government: positioning Aboriginal people as legislative artifact and/or multi-cultural minority within a system purporting the existence of two founding nations. There are currently more than 600 First Nations communities featuring distinctive cultures, traditions, and languages. Each community has different needs, different wants, different capacities, and different priorities. Self-government in this environment becomes simply another policy initiative the evolution of which is guided almost exclusively by Ottawa's politicians. And even though Aboriginal voices continue to be heard in this debate and influence federal officials, at the end of the day, Aboriginal self-government remains an idea nestled with the political elite in the nation's capital and transformed only once negotiations with a First Nation begin.

The federal approach described above masks the multitude of ways of envisioning Aboriginal self-government. The Royal Commission described the variations this way:

> Self Government means different things to different Aboriginal groups. For some, it may mean reviving traditional governmental structures or adapting them for modem purposes. For others, if may mean creating entirely new structures or participating more actively in new or existing institutions of public Government at the federal, provincial, regional or territorial levels. For certain groups, it may involve developing structures of public Governments that would include all the residents of a particular region or territory. For still other groups, it may mean greater control over the provision of governmental services such as education and health care. In discussing the implementation of self-Government, it is important to remember that there is more than one way for Aboriginal peoples to achieve the goal of greater autonomy and control over their lives. No single pattern or model can be adequate given the great variety of aspirations and circumstances among Aboriginal peoples.[42]

Hylton saw that "a singular approach to self-government involving the all-too-familiar, centrally defined, top-down techniques of government institutions will not be very effective. A more flexible, community-oriented, bottom-up approach will be required."[43] This latter approach resonates with the original principles outlined in 1983's Parliamentary Task Force on Indian Self-Government report wherein Ontario Member of Parliament (MP) Keith Penner urged federal officials to forge a new relationship with Aboriginal people across Canada. Unfortunately, the four constitutionally-mandated First Minister Conferences (1983-1987) and the subsequent two decades spent trying to shoehorn Aboriginal conceptions of self-government into existing federal, provincial, and municipal templates have undermined, rather than reinforced, this early work. Again, such attitudes require changing prior to self-government advancing ideologically and therefore on the ground.

Final Thoughts: A Framework for the Future

In recent years various federal programs have been established to accommodate Aboriginal circumstances and national aspirations while self-government negotiations continue and land claims are slowly resolved. The contextual nature of Aboriginal self-government, necessitating site-specific programming, continues to be characterized largely by discrete, isolated experiments and pilot projects instead of institutions of perceived legitimacy and permanence. As a result, many important initiatives or contributions are overlooked or undervalued, which is problematic in three ways: (1) these programs are vulnerable to funding cuts resulting from shifting government priorities; (2) the innovative nature of these programs is often obscured from individuals who could potentially benefit from new and unique frameworks in their pursuit of self-government; and, (3) the existing ad hoc approach distorts reporting and accountability relationships, forcing Aboriginal groups to devote significant amounts of time maintaining accountability to funding agencies as opposed to focusing their energies on community betterment.

Current funding mechanisms are inadequate to promote program stability, leaving Aboriginal agencies unable to establish the proper infrastructure and administrative procedures needed to offer a full range of services, and often operating within a policy or legislative vacuum, at the periphery of mainstream programs. This results in barriers to self-governing success. For instance, the nature of service operations and its function and placement must be defined when developing a new program or extending an existing program into a new community. Further questions concerning program mandates and outcomes must also be adequately addressed prior to implementation, a time-consuming process tapping available resources that could better be channelled into combating issues negatively influencing Aboriginal people nationally.

Aboriginal programs and institutions cannot continue to be seen as add-ons to the mainstream service-delivery system. But unlike mainstream programs, Aboriginal programming operates in an ad hoc fashion without an appropriate legislative base; clearly defined mandates; appropriate funding; and clear policies and standards that typify government services and guide interface with mainstream systems. Limited progress has been made in recent years, as devolution of social services to various bands and tribal councils has positioned Aboriginal people to guide service delivery. The Métis and the urban Aboriginal populations once again bear the brunt of a poorly crafted policy environment that fails to meet these peoples' needs.

Several innovative solutions have been developed in an attempt to indigenize federal Indian programs while ensuring the participation, albeit limited, of the Aboriginal community. A number of these initiatives include:

- Adopting affirmative action or employment-equity hiring practises.

- Establishing specialized Aboriginal units, staffed by Aboriginal employees, within larger non-Aboriginal programs and agencies.

- Promoting greater awareness among non-Native staff of Aboriginal people through cultural sensitivity and awareness programs.

- Allowing Aboriginal input into decision-making in non-Aboriginal programs. Elders, for example, may be consulted about the sentencing of offenders, band councils may be asked about the apprehension of a child, or a committee may be established to provide community input into the work of a non-Aboriginal agency.

- Introducing traditional Aboriginal practices into non-Aboriginal programs. Correctional institutions, for example, sometimes permit sweat lodges, sweetgrass ceremonies, and the attendance of elders and spiritual leaders.

In many cases, these initiatives have had a positive influence. Unfortunately, they reflect the ad hoc approach characteristic of the federal government's approach to engaging Aboriginal people and their concerns. As Hylton concluded in 1999, words that continue to resonate today, "The task of establishing funding, policy, and legislative frameworks or the operation of Aboriginal programs and agencies will require a substantial commitment of time and resources. The task cannot be completed by governments alone. It will require a co-operative effort that involves Aboriginal agencies, Aboriginal governments, and Canadian governments."[44] To date, Aboriginal leaders and agencies have demonstrated an interest in creating this interactive environment: perhaps it is time for the federal government to respond in kind.

Notes

1   Paul Tennant, Sally Weaver, Roger Gibbins & J. Rick Ponting, "The Report of the House of Commons Special Committee on Indian Self-Government: Three Comments," *Canadian Public Policy* 10, no. 2 (June 1984): 211-24.
2   John H. Hylton, *Aboriginal Self-Government in Canada: Current Trends and Issues* (Saskatoon: Purich Publishing, 1994), 15.
3   John H. Hylton, *Aboriginal Self-Government in Canada: Current Trends and Issues,* 2nd ed. (Saskatoon: Purich Publishing, 1999), 432-3.
4   Hylton (1999), 433.
5   See Lisa L. Patterson, *Aboriginal Roundtable to Kelowna Accord: Aboriginal Policy Negotiations, 2004-2005* (Ottawa: Political & Social Affairs Division, 2006).
6   "Tory Budget may Provoke Blockades, Chiefs Warn," *St John's Telegram* (21 March 2007), A-9.
7   Phil Fontaine, "Budget a Blow to First Nations' Hopes: First Nations Rejected by Budget 2007," *Toronto Star* (22 March 2007), 21.
8   Paul Barnsley, "Native Leaders Ask: Where's our Canada?" *Windspeaker* (April 2007), 8.
9   Jim Prentice, "Budget Generous to Aboriginals, Minister Says," *Winnipeg Free Press* (29 March 2007), A-12.
10 "Canada Votes Against UN Aboriginal Declaration," CTV News (13 September 2007), http://www.ctv.ca/servlet/ArticleNews/story/CTVNews/20070913/aboriginal_rights_070913/20070913?hub=TopStories (accessed 19 November 2007).
11 Peter O'Neil, "Conservative Caucus Split Over Native Self-government Bill," *The Ottawa Citizen* (22 April 2004), A-4; see also "Fatally Pragmatic: Opposition's Support of Race-based Government Abandons Principle," *Calgary Herald* (26 April 2004), A-10.
12 Ken Coates & Greg Poelzer, "A Friend to First Nations," *National Post* (16 January 2007), A-15.
13 Quoted in Alan C. Cairns, *Citizens Plus: Aboriginal Peoples and the Canadian State* (Vancouver: UBC Press. 2000), 116.
14 The Royal Commission on Aboriginal Peoples, *For Seven Generations: An Information Legacy of the Royal Commission on Aboriginal Peoples,* vol. 1 (Ottawa: Queen's Printer, 1996), 677-8.
15 *Ibid.,* 678.
16 Assembly of First Nations, *Royal Commission on Aboriginal People at 10 Years: A Report Card* (Ottawa: Assembly of First Nations, 2006), 2.
17 *Ibid.*
18 Marlene Wells & J.W. Berry, "Attitudes Toward Aboriginal Self-Government: The Influences of Knowledge, and Cultural and Economic Security," *The Canadian Journal of Native Studies* 12, no. 1 (1992), 76.
19 *Ibid., 86*
20 Ron George, "Poll Says Majority Favour Native Rights," *Regina Leader-Post* (1 December 1992).
21 David Roberts, "Listening for Ways to Heal Old Wounds," *Globe and Mail* (7 January 1994), A-4.
22 David Martin & Chris Adams, "Canadian Public Opinion Regarding Aboriginal Self-Government: Diverging Viewpoints as Found in National Survey Results," *The American Review of Canadian Studies* 30, no. 1 (2000): 87.
23 *Ibid.*
24 Rick Mofina, "Attitudes on Native Issues 'Hardening': Poll: Angus Reid Survey: More Canadians Dispute Legitimacy of Special Rights," *National Post* (5 July 2000), A-4.
25 See for example J. Anthony Long & Katherine Chiste, "Indian Governments and the *Canadian Charter of*

Rights and Freedoms," *American Indian Culture and Research Journal* 18, no. 2 (1994): 91-119; Colin H. Scott, "Customs, Traditions, and the Politics of Culture: *Aboriginal Self-Government in Canada*," in *Anthropology, Public Policy and Native Peoples in Canada,* eds. Noel Dyck & James B. Waldram (Montreal & Kingston: McGill-Queen's Press, 1993), 311-333; Brian Slattery, "The Paradoxes of National Self-Determination," *Osgoode Hall Law Journal* 32, no. 4 (1994): 703-733; and, Curtis Cook & Juan D. Lindau, "One Continent, Contrasting Styles: The Canadian Experience in North American Perspective," in Aboriginal Rights and Self-Government, eds. Curtis Cook & Juan D. Lindau (Montreal & Kingston: McGill-Queen's University Press, 2000), 3-36.

26 See Wells & Berry, "Attitudes Toward Aboriginal Self-Government."

27 See "In Depth: Aboriginal Canadians: B.C. treaty referendum," CBC News Online, www.cbc.ca/news/ background/aboriginals/bc_treaty_referendum.html.

28 Hylton (1999), 442-50.

29 Bradford Morse, "The Inherent Right of Self-Government," in *Aboriginal Self-Government in Canada: Current Trends and Issues,* 2nd Ed., ed. John H. Hylton (Saskatoon: Purich Publishing Ltd., 1999), 17; cf Bruce Clark, *Native Liberty, Crown Sovereignty: The Existing Aboriginal Right of Self-Government in Canada* (Montreal-Kingston: McGill-Queen's University Press, 1990).

30 See also James (Sákéj) Youngblood Henderson, "Aboriginal Jurisprudence and Rights," in *Advancing Aboriginal Claims: Visions/Strategies/Directions,* ed. Kerry Wilkins (Saskatoon: Purich Publishing, 2004), 67-89.

31 Brian Slattery, "First Nations and the Constitution: A Question of Trust," *Canadian Bar Review* (June 1992): 279.

32 Francis Paul Prucha, *American Indian Treaties: The History of a Political Anomaly* (Berkeley: University of California Press, 1994), 2.

33 RCAP, *For Seven Generations,* vol. 1, 678.

34 See Gabrielle A. Slowey, "Aboriginal Self-Government, Extinguishment of Title and the Canadian State: Effectively Removing the 'Other'?" *Native Studies Review* 13, no. 1 (2000): 1-17.

35 RCAP, *For Seven Generations,* vol. 2, 775.

36 Royal Commission on Aboriginal Peoples, *Partners in Confederation: Aboriginal Peoples, Self-Government, and the Constitution* (Ottawa: Royal Commission on Aboriginal Peoples, 1993), 51.

37 Sarah McGinnis, "Blood Tribe Calls for Urban Reserve: Federal Officials Warn Process is Lengthy," *Calgary Herald* (15 March 2006), B-8; also, Helen Buckley, *From Wooden Ploughs to Welfare: Why Indian Policy Failed in the Prairie Provinces* (Kingston & Montreal: McGill-Queen's University Press, 1992), 11.

38 Jonathan Kay, "Off the Reservation: The Reserve System is Canada's Worst Moral Failing. Let's Do the Right Thing and Get Rid of It," *National Post* (23 October 2007).

39 Hayden F. King, "Native Reserves Aren't the Problem," *National Post* (30 October 2007).

40 Assembly of First Nations, *Royal Commission on Aboriginal People at 10 Years,* 2.

41 Thomas Isaac, "Authority, Rights and an Economic Base: The Reality of Aboriginal Self-Government," *Native Studies Review* 7, no. 2 (1991): 69-74.

42 Royal Commission on Aboriginal Peoples, *Partners in Confederation,* 41.

43 Hylton (1999), 447.

44 *Ibid.,* 448.

FRANCES ABELE teaches in the School of Public Policy and Administration at Carleton University. She publishes in the areas of northern and Indigenous affairs, and has worked with Indigenous governments and organizations for the last three decades.

YVON ALLARD is an independent Aboriginal health consultant in Ottawa. As a member of the Manitoba Métis community, he has served as an advisor on health issues to regional and national Métis organizations.

COLETTE ARCAND is a fourth-year student majoring in Native Studies with a minor in Economics. Colette is a member of the Alexander First Nation in Alberta and a volunteer board member of the Friends of the Kipohtakaw Historical Foundation.

YALE BELANGER is Assistant Professor of Native American Studies at the University of Lethbridge where he divides his time as the department's history and politics specialist while also teaching in the First Nations Governance Program in the Faculty of Management. He is the author of *Gambling with the Future: The Evolution of Aboriginal Gaming in Canada* (Purich Publishing, 2006).

CATHERINE BELL is Professor of Law at the University of Alberta specializing in Aboriginal legal issues, property law, community based legal research, and dispute resolution. She has published extensively on Métis and First Nations legal issues including two books on the Métis settlements: *Alberta's Métis Settlement Legislation: An Overview of Ownership and Management of Settlement Lands* and *Contemporary Métis Justice: The Settlement Way.*

BRIAN CALLIOU is the program director for The Banff Centre's Aboriginal Leadership and Management. Brian is a member of the Sucker Creek First Nation in north central Alberta and holds memberships with the Canadian Bar Association, the Indigenous Bar Association, and the Legal Archives Society of Alberta.

ANGELA CAMERON is a Ph.D. candidate at the Faculty of Law, University of Victoria. Her areas of research and writing include: restorative justice, criminal law, intimate violence, reproductive technologies, property law, and feminist legal theory.

LARRY CHARTRAND is Associate Professor of Law at the University of Ottawa. His area of scholarship is in the field of Aboriginal rights and in particular, Métis rights. He obtained his B.ED. from the University of Alberta in 1986, his LL.B from York University in 1989, and his LL.M. from Queen's University in 2001. He was Director of the Aboriginal Governance Program and Professor of Politics at the University of Winnipeg from 2004–2007.

KEN COATES is Professor of History and Dean, Faculty of Arts, University of Waterloo. He specializes in the history of the Canadian North, Indigenous-newcomers relations and contemporary Aboriginal political issues. His most recent work is *A Global History of Indigenous Peoples: Struggle and Survival*.

JO-ANNE FISKE is Dean of Graduate Studies and professor of Women's Studies at the University of Lethbridge. She has worked with Aboriginal and First Nations communities on social policy, health policy, human rights, and homelessness.

AUGIE FLERAS is Associate Professor of sociology at the University of Waterloo. He is the author of numerous books, including *Social Problems in Canada* (Third Edition) and *Unequal Relations* (Third Edition; with Jean Elliott) and *Recalling Aotearoa* (with Paul Spoonley).

JIM FRIDERES is currently a professor of Sociology and the Director of the International Indigenous Studies program at the University of Calgary. He also holds the Chair of Ethnic Studies. He is the author of numerous articles and co-author with Rene Gadacz of *Aboriginal Peoples in Canada*, now in its 8th edition.

JOE GARCEA is a professor in the Department of Political Studies at the University of Saskatchewan, where he teaches local government, public adminis-tration, and public policy analysis. His areas of expertise include municipal and intergovernmental relations. He co-authored with F. Laurie Barron *Urban Indian Reserves: Forging New Relationships in Saskatchewan* (Purich Publishing, 1999).

AILSA HENDERSON is Assistant Professor in Political Science at the University of Toronto. The author of *Nunavut: Rethinking Political Culture* (UBC Press, 2007), she has published two books and more than twenty-five journal articles or book chapters on sub-state political culture in federal and multi-national states, and is the principal investigator of the Nunavut Social Attitudes Survey.

JAMES [SÁKÉJ] YOUNGBLOOD HENDERSON is the research director of the Native Law Centre of Canada and teaches Aboriginal law at the College of Law, University of Saskatchewan. He was awarded the Indigenous Peoples' Counsel (2005) and the National Aboriginal Achievement Award for Law and Justice (2006).

JOHN HYLTON has served as a chief executive, university educator, senior public servant, and consultant. He has served many commissions and inquiries in all parts of Canada, including the Royal Commission on Aboriginal Peoples and the Ipperwash Inquiry. He is currently active working with organizations to improve strategy, leadership, governance, and performance. John was the editor of the first two editions of *Aboriginal Self-Government in Canada* (Purich Publishing, 1994, 1999).

ROBERT ALEXANDER INNES is a Member of Cowessess First Nation and Assistant Professor in the Department of Native Studies at the University of Saskatchewan.

JOSEE LAVOIE is Assistant Professor in the Health Sciences Program at the University of Northern British Columbia who previously spent 10 years working for Indigenous controlled primary health care services in Nunavut and northern Saskatchewan.

ROGER MAAKA, NGATI KAHUNGUNU, is head of the Department of Native Studies at the University of Saskatchewan. He sits on the Waitangi Tribunal enquiry into the Indigenous Flora and Fauna and Intellectual Property claim. His research interests include urbanization and Indigenous peoples, Native Studies as an academic discipline, post-treaty settlement development, the construction of contemporary indigenous identities, and indigeneity as a global social movement.

W. R. MORRISON is Professor of History, University of Northern British Columbia. He works on aspects of northern Canada history and is currently working with Ken Coates on a survey history of major Canadian court cases.

BRADFORD W. MORSE is Professor of Law, University of Ottawa. He was Research Director to the Aboriginal Justice Inquiry of Manitoba 1988-91; Chief of Staff to Minister of INAC 1993-96; and legal advisor, consultant, and negotiator for many First Nations, national and regional Indigenous organizations, royal commissions, and governments in Canada, Australia, and New Zealand over the past 30 years.

VAL NAPOLEON is a member of the Saulteau First Nation in northeastern British Columbia and is of Cree and Dunnezah heritage. She worked as a community activist and consultant in northwestern B.C. for over twenty-five years. Since 2005, Val has been an assistant professor with the University of Alberta teaching in the Faculties of Law and Native Studies.

DAVID NEWHOUSE is Onondaga from the Six Nations of the Grand River community near Brantford, Ontario. He is the first Principal of the Peter Gzowski College at Trent University and former Chair of the Department of Native Studies. He is Associate Professor in the Department of Native Studies and the Business Administration Program.

JOHN O'NEIL is Dean of Health Sciences at Simon Fraser University. He has published more than 120 papers and reports on a variety of Aboriginal health issues, including self-government and health system development, cultural understandings of environmental health risks, and social determinants of health disparities.

TERRENCE ROSS PELLETIER is former Chief of Cowessess First Nation and served as the Treaty Land Entitlement Coordinator for Cowessess during the band's TLE process. He is currently pursuing a Masters in Educational Administration at the University of Saskatchewan.

MICHAEL PRINCE is Lansdowne Professor of Social Policy at the University of Victoria. Among his areas of research, he has collaborated with Frances Abele on numerous publications dealing with Aboriginal [Indigenous] government and Canadian federalism.

JEFF READING is a professor in the Faculty of Human and Social Development and a faculty associate with the Indigenous Governance Program at the University of Victoria. He is Fellow of the Canadian Academy of Health Sciences and his research has brought attention to issues such as disease prevention, tobacco use and misuse, and diabetes among Aboriginal people in Canada.

JEAN-PAUL RESTOULE is Assistant Professor of Aboriginal Education in the Department of Adult Education and Counselling Psychology at the Ontario Institute for Studies in Education of the University of Toronto. He is a member of the Dokis First Nation.

HAROLD ROBINSON is a member of the Métis Settlements General Council located in Edmonton, Alberta.

DAHTI SCOTT is currently studying at the University of Alberta where she is completing an undergraduate double major in Environmental Conservation Sciences and Native Studies. Dahti is a Tlicho Dene who grew up in the Northwest Territories.

GABRIELLE SLOWEY is an Assistant Professor in the Department of Political Science at York University (Toronto) where she teaches courses in Aboriginal Politics. Her research focuses on issues of self-government, land claims, and non-renewable resource development. Field sites include northern Alberta, Yukon, NWT, James Bay, and New Zealand.

Nations control over: Cowessess 253, 256; Maori 88; Métis 264-5, 273, 277, 380-1; Mi'kmaq 140; Nisga'a 53, 80, 110, 379

education *Acts*: in BC 56; *First Nations Education Act* 386, 384, 385-6; Kativik 380; Mi'kmaq 55, 384-5; Nunavut 382-3; Saskatchewan 300-1; various agreements 384-7

education of the public viii, ix, xiii, 3, 8, 12, 42, 79, 109, 128, 131, 222, 295-6, 381-2, 396, 403-4

elders ix, 117, 179, 235, 248, 253, 321, 323, 343, 359, 377, 383, 385; and justice 354, 357, 361, 362-3, 412; Inuit 55; Métis 269, 280

employment 39, 27, 51-2, 80, 195, 196, 198, 213, 216-17, 228, 231, 250, 272, 277-8, 310, 341, 343, 398

entitlement 9, 54, 78, 82, 91, 178, 189, 271, 310, 312-13, 316; land entitlement 57, 132, 298, 299, 301. *See also* Treaty Land Entitlement

ethnic government 158, 161; in Nunavut 222-5, 230, 232, 237

Ewing Commission 264

extinguishment. *See* Aboriginal title

federal government xv, 1, 10, 31, 44, 124, 125, 229, 230, 271, 384, 396, 406, 408; recent *Acts* 45-6, 48, 51, 55-6, 112, 122-4, 129, 207-9, 236, 255, 269-70, 382, 387, 401. *See also* Government of Canada

Federal Policy Statement on Indian self-government 2, 162

Federation of Métis Settlements (Alberta) xvii, 260, 265-6

Federation of Saskatchewan Indians (FSI) 2, 6, 7-8, 10, 14, 244, 245

Federation of Saskatchewan Indian Nations (FSIN) 246, 249, 257, 375

fee simple title 266-7, 270

fiduciary obligations of federal government 7, 12, 28, 40-1, 135, 158, 386; abuses of 30, 40, 58, 316-17; for health 188-9, 195

financing schemes xiv, xv-xvi, 12, 119, 158-60, 162-6, 212-13, 215, 223, 278, 375, 408; for education 162, 374, 376-7, 381, 385, 386; fiscal federalism 160, 162-5, 167; funding cuts to Aboriginal programs 411-12; for health 179-80, 183-4, 186, 187, 192, 193-5, 197; as necessary 12, 148, 158, 167, 213-14, 216, 221-2, 240; own-source revenue 159, 166, 333

First Nations and Inuit Health Branch (FNIHB) 183-5, 187, 191, 193, 194-5, 197

First Nations and Inuit Regional Health Surveys. *See* Regional Health Surveys

First Nations Governance Act 236, 406

First Nations Land Management Act 55, 255, 293, 315-16

First Nations people. *See* Aboriginal peoples

fiscal federalism. *See* financing schemes

foundational principles: of Métis 260, 281; of self-determination 75, 82-3; of self-government xi, xiv, 2, 6, 55, 69, 240, 350; of treaty interactions 20, 22, 73, 75, 92, 96

founding nations/ peoples 12, 16-17, 81, 127, 153, 410

Friendship Centres, National Association of 174, 195

gaming/ gambling 49, 62, 150, 343

gender equality xviii, 51, 232. *See also* women's issues

global: economy xviii, 137, 183, 277-8, 325, 332, 339; governance 77, 325; interdependence 70, 326, 328

globalization xvi, 95, 207, 214-15, 218

good governance processes and institutions 76, 134, 146, 256, 333, 335-6, 337-41

Government of Canada 4, 10, 40-1, 45-8, 51, 57, 60, 106, 107-12, 116, 121, 136, 141, 161, 187, 207, 212-13, 217-19. *See also* Federal government

Grand Council of the Crees 45, 212

grassroots efforts vii, ix, xi, xiii, xix, 2, 13, 229, 244, 376, 395

Guerin v. *The Queen* 40

Gwich'in First Nation 52, 112-13, 378; land claim settlement 57

"half breed": as historically used interchangeably with "Métis" 263-4

Harper, Stephen x, 59, 64, 94-5, 189, 399, 401

Harvard Project xvii, xviii, 240-2, 335-7, 339, 343 nation-building model 240-3, 335, 339, 343

Hawthorn-Tremblay Report xiii, 2, 3-5, 133, 140, 410

healing 93, 182-3, 366; ceremonies 180, 190, 356-8; of communities 173, 190, 192, 197, 408-10; of residential school legacy 174, 180, 191, 291; self-government as necessary for 333; traditional 174, 177, 178, 180-1, 188-92

health and health care xi, xv, xvi, 5, 10, 13, 39, 80, 173-99, 225, 398; *Canada Health Act* 192, 195; community-based 173, 177, 182, 184, 191, 194, 197, 411; community health services 183-5, 187, 191, 197, 198, 233; financing for

179-80, 183-4, 186, 187, 192, 193-5, 197;
holistics principles of 173-4, 178-9, 185, 190-3, 195, 197, 198; of the Inuit 174-175-8, 182-9, 190, 192-4, 196, 199; life expectancy 175, 410; medicine wheel 174, 185, 191; of the Métis 174, 175, 176, 177-8, 182, 185, 186-9, 195-7, 199; midwifery 182, 189-90; responsibility for 178, 179-80, 181-4, 185-6, 188-9, 192-7, 410, 411; self-government as healing xvi, 173, 181, 191, 197, 198-9, 333. *See also* chronic diseases; diabetes; infectious diseases; "medicine chest" clause; mental health; NIHB; traditional: medicine
Health Transfer Policy (HTP) 183-4, 196
holistic approach to community well-being xx, 173-4, 178-9, 185, 190-2, 196, 322, 323, 335, 343
honour of the Crown 22, 28, 29, 31, 87
House of Commons 4, 10, 136, 162
House of First Peoples 124, 136
human resources as necessary for development 33, 343, 363, 364, 365, 382; AHRDS 217, 267
human rights 71, 146, 326, 328; UN and international standards 59, 94, 146-7, 315, 316-7; violations of 71, 73, 94, 312
Hydro-Québec 211-12, 216

immigrant issues 73, 92, 152; policies 30; theories 32
Indian Act 9, 14, 31, 42, 44, 45-6, 53, 55-6, 58, 61, 80, 106, 110, 249, 250, 258, 333, 406-7; amendments of 225, 255, 312, 313, 317-18, 327, 389; band model 14, 31, 33, 46, 64, 125, 161, 200, 311, 315, 368; breaches of 245; determining "who is Indian" 310-11, 312-15, 318, 334; as discriminatory 42, 309-12, 313-18, 321, 328, 334; excluding Inuit 225-6; excluding Métis and non-status persons 42, 44, 192-3, 399, 405-6; and First Nations women 309-28, 406; and health 178, 180-1; as impetus for self-government 4, 15, 53, 61, 106, 111, 113, 115, 123, 133, 142, 178, 207, 209; 226, 294, 315-18; replaced by other legislation 47, 55, 61, 80, 108, 110, 111, 193, 209, 384-5, 386, 406; as violating human rights 42, 181-2, 192, 309-14, 316-17; section 6 312-13, 315; s.10 312; s.12 311-12, 318; s.73 180; s.88 31; and voting restrictions (s.77) 42, 192, 225-6, 310, 311, 316; and White Paper 181
Indian and Northern Affairs Canada (INAC) 46, 55, 61, 129, 140, 141, 187, 194, 210, 213, 250, 256, 288, 298, 312, 377, 385-6, 400, 403,

409; DIAND 9, 41, 106, 140, 164, 409
Indian Chiefs of Alberta vii, 5
Indian Claims Commission 6, 245
Indian Control of Indian Education xix, 373-4, 378, 380, 384, 390
Indian Government (FSI paper) 2, 7, 8
Indian peoples. *See* Aboriginal peoples
"Indian Policy" Statement 4, 120,
Indian Treaty Rights (FSI paper) 8
indigeneity, politics of 69-70, 73, 75, 81-2, 90, 92, 97
Indigenous peoples. *See* Aboriginal peoples; Maori
"indigenous ways of knowing" 124, 127. *See also* traditional: knowledge
individual rights 4, 12, 138, 309, 312, 317, 319, 325
infectious diseases 173, 175-6, 177, 179-80, 198
Inherent Rights Policy (IRP) xviii, 14-15, 44, 50, 137, 141, 160, 162, 374-5, 402, 406, 407-8
Institute of Aboriginal Peoples Health (IAPH) 207
integration 4, 73, 84, 124, 381; of Inuit 225-7, 232
intergovernmental relations 136, 162-4, 197, 207, 261, 304
International Covenant on Civil and Political Rights 60, 64, 71, 312
international law ix, 8, 44, 71, 81, 92, 94, 154, 312, 325, 326-7
Inuit peoples x, 3, 13, 15, 39, 44, 54, 61, 161; claims for 43, 44, 50-2, 56, 165, 208, 230-2; demographics 54, 175, 206, 222; and education 232-3, 379-80; as federal responsibility 40, 43-4, 225; and health 174-175-8, 182-9, 190, 192-4, 196, 199; and self-government 15, 39, 42, 456, 60, 117, 222-38; self-government models 108, 114, 130, 161, 223, 382-3; traditions 51, 190, 235-6
Inuit Qaujimajatuqangit (IQ) 234-6; as resistance 236
Inuit Tapariit Kanatami 174, 197, 383
Inuit Tapirisat of Canada (ITC) 127, 185-6, 227-30, 237
Inuktitut 55, 226, 232, 233, 235-7, 380, 383
Inuvialuit land settlement 52-3, 57, 112-13, 166, 182, 408; terms 52
Iqaluit 50-1, 232
isolation 79, 105, 118, 215, 287, 337, 408; needs of isolated communities 184, 192, 241; reserves 82, 106, 114

Nunatsiavut 54, 162, 163
Nunavik 118, 163, 182, 206, 380; regional government 54-5, 56, 114
Nunavut 50-2, 161; demographics 51-2, 54, 206, 222; consensus politics 232-5; ethnic government model 222-5, 230, 232, 237; governance xi, xvi, 108, 114, 130, 161, 382-3; Government of Nunavut (GN) 51-2, 166, 197, 235, 237; land claim settlement 50-1, 56, 233-8
Nunavut Act 382; s.23 (grants powers similar to provinces) 51
Nunavut Implementation Commission 51, 232, 235
Nunavut Land Claims Agreement Act 51, 161, 164, 222, 224-5, 228, 230-4, 237
Nunavut Political Accord 222, 224, 230-2, 237
Nunavut Tunngavik Inc (NTI) 164, 222, 224

Official Languages Act 153
Office of the Treaty Commissioner (OTC) 246, 247-8
off-reserve Aboriginal peoples 15, 42, 65, 108, 141, 159, 174, 194-5, 254, 257-8, 289; statistics 174-7, 292; and voting 42, 109, 192, 237, 254-5, 316
Ojibway peoples 62, 151-3
Oka (Kanesatake) 13, 56, 126, 403
Ontario First Nations 118, 149, 386-7
oral tradition 235, 249, 359, 361; treaty interpretations upheld 39, 189

Paix des Braves 207, 211-13, 214, 216-17, 218-19; terms of 212
Pamajewon v. The Queen 41, 62, 138, 150
Parliamentary Task Force on Indian Self-Government. *See* Penner Report
paternalistic biases in Aboriginal policies xv, 116, 120, 121, 225, 264, 379, 386
"peace and good order" clauses 23-6, 27, 28-30; as inter-national 30
Penner Report viii, 2, 9-11, 124, 209, 395, 411; Government of Canada response to 10-11
pluralism 32, 368; medical 189-90; political 73, 333
poverty 6, 33, 39, 76, 78, 82, 116, 215, 402, 409; and health 126, 141, 177, 193, 198-9, 222
prescription: law of 154-5
prisons: Aboriginal peoples over-represented in 39; to force assimilation 180
private sector 139; as model for economic development 215-16

program delivery 85, 90, 167, 406; Aboriginal controlled 10, 112, 125, 182, 218, 231, 265, 412; of education 374, 385, 388, 389; funding for 192, 211, 278
Progressive Conservative government ix-x, 11, 189, 399-401; and health 125, and Kelowna Accord 46, 399; and TLE 245-6, 401; and UN Declaration x, 59, 64, 94-5, 189, 399, 401
public attention to Aboriginal issues 4, 10, 42-3, 81-2, 94-6, 109, 115, 121, 133, 134, 137, 139, 396, 403-5, 409
public government models 11-12, 46, 52-3, 55, 108, 112, 119, 158, 160-1, 166, 197, 222-38, 373, 411; and education 380-4

Quebec 40, 41, 44-5, 106, 135, 182, 185, 206-19, 224-5, 237, 379-80, 398; Inuit in 54, 114, 117-8, 206-19

R. v. *Gladstone* 41
R. v. *Kelley* 283
R. v. *Marshall* 36n77, 41, 66n10
R. v. *Pamajewon* 41, 62, 138, 150
R. v. *Powley* 149, 154-5, 262, 280-2
R. v. *Sioui* 40, 41, 62
R. v. *Sparrow* 36n69, 40, 63, 186n4
R. v. *Van der Peet* 21-2, 41-2, 62
racism 33, 39, 85, 94, 142, 147, 174, 181, 310, 414
rangatiratanga (sovereignty/ Maori-driven models of self-determination) 82-7, 88, 89, 90
RCAP (Royal Commission on Aboriginal Peoples) vii, ix, 2, 13, 31, 62, 77-8, 124, 136, 405; Aboriginal response to 133-4, 141; cost of ix, 13, 126, 140, 141-2, 402; history of 13-14, 125-6, Report 127, 138-42, 162, 339, 396
Red Paper vii, 2, 5
Regional Health Surveys (RHS) 174, 176-7
religion 39, 134, 224, 312
reparations 76, 82, 85-6, 91, 93, 153, 240. *See also* restitution
Report on the Special Committee on Indian Self-government. *See* Penner Report
reserves 5, 31, 55-6, 82, 105-6, 166-7, 399-400; conditions on 3, 114, 174-8, 195, 409-10; surveying for 243-4, 246-7, 251-2, 298. *See also* off reserve Aboriginal peoples; satellite reserves; urban reserves
residential schools 39, 105, 180; and healing 174, 191, 291
resources: natural 10, 11, 42, 45, 49, 56, 64, 110, 111, 163, 166, 241, 337, 407; federal govern-

ment exploitation of 64; Métis resource
management 148-50, 155, 265, 272; oil, gas,
etc development 218, 265, 272-3; revenues
from xvii, 51, 54, 57, 114, 166; rights to 27,
45, 56, 74, 80, 93, 147, 166, 217, 274-5, 278-
9; surface and subsurface 7, 48, 51, 553, 208,
262, 267, 270, 272-4; sustainable resource
management 45, 88, 95, 184, 217, 272
restitution packages 76, 86, 87; policies 91, 93,
153. *See also* reparation
restorative justice 348-68; as local law *see* local
law; and self-government 349-50; values
365-7. *See also* Alexis First Nation
Romanow Report 186, 188
Royal Commission on Aboriginal Peoples. *See*
RCAP
Royal Proclamation, 1763 14, 129, 160, 405
Royal Proclamations: modern 35, 124, 129, 136-7
rule of law 26, 30, 128, 337, 360
"Rules of the Hunt" xv, 151-2, 155
rural municipalities and satellite reserves 247,
296, 299 301

Saskatchewan Association of Rural
Municipalities (SARM) 296
Saskatchewan First Nations 240-1, 245-6, 252,
275-6. *See also* Cowessess; satellite reserves
satellite reserves xviii-xix, 132, 287, 288-304; and
business 293, 295-6, 303; factors contributing
to creation of 292-4; and land claims 291,
292, 295, 298; lands converted to reserve status 247, 248-9, 296, 298, 291-2, 299, 301;
objections to 294, 295-7, 300; politics of creation 292-4; policies of creation 297-302;
proponents of 295, 303-4; statistics 288-92;
urban reserves 131-2, 240, 246, 250, 254
Sawridge Band v. *Canada* 313-15, 319
schools 232, 237; public schools 181, 376, 380-1;
schools on reserves 293-4, 384. *See also* residential schools
scrip 251-2; and Métis 263-4, 266
secession 70-1, 77, 118, 134, 135, 139
Sechelt Indian Band Self-government Act 1, 46,
55, 116, 378, 397
Sechelt First Nation 46, 57, 110, 378
segregation, policy of 44, 105, 287
self-determination 39, 60, 63, 92, 94, 125, 146-7,
231, 333-4, 376, 406; foundational principles
of 75, 82-3, 165; history of 71, 78-9, 146-7,
166, 182, 236 impact of 70-2, 79, 85-6, 96,
197, 215, 333, 349; Métis 146, 264; as self-
government ix, 1, 130, 227-30; vs state-deter-

mination 69-97; models of self vs state 69-
70, 72, 74-6, 97, 130, 159-62, 164-6, 182-3
self-financing 159
self-governance vs self-government 76-8, 217
self-government: according to traditional principles vii, xi, xii, 1, 14-15, 110, 117-8, 123-4, 128,
130; authority of xi, 10, 20, 26, 131-2; as
community control 116; in the Constitution
viii, 9, 10, 78, 80, 92, 106-7, 135, 404, 406;
foundational principles of xi, xiv, 2, 6, 8, 55,
69, 92, 240, 350; as healing 173, and health
173-87, 408; impact of 106, 119-20, 134; as
inherent right vii-viii, xii-xiii, 7-8, 14-15, 23-
5, 47, 48, 58, 60, 63, 74, 78, 92, 108, 133,
142, 207, 294, 333-4, 405 and constitutionally protected ix, 50, 197; and nationhood 13,
76-8; opposition to 118-19
and other governments xi, 60, 118-19, 129,
206-7, 218, 402; as political ideal 7, 94-7; as
pre-existing 20, 47, 60, 63, 334, 405; as self-
administration 116; as self-determination ix,
1, 92, 123, 130, 227, 229, 236, as a self-sustaining movement x; as treaties 107, vested
in treaties 20, 63, 188. *See also* American
perspectives on Aboriginal self-government;
self-government models
self-government agreements viii, xi, 50, 52-3, 55,
57, 64, 105, 107-8, 110, 115, 121, 141, 185, 189,
197, 333, 373, 396, 397, 401, 406
self-government legislated agreements 47-8, 60-
1, 108-9, 112, 113-14, 333, 334, 378, 387, 398,
403; and accords 51, 83, 105, 111-12, 116, 149,
222, 224, 230-2, 237, 317. *See also* the
Charlottetown; Kelowna; Meech Lake;
Métis Settlement; Nunavut Political; and
Transformative Change Accords, and the
JBNQA; NRTA; Northeastern Quebec;
Nunavut Land Claim; TLEFA; Westbank;
and Yukon *Agreements*
self-government models xii, xviii, 11, 53-5, 107-9,
117-18, 159, 160-2, 165, 397-9; adapted-feder-
alism model 160-1, 164-5; business model
333-4, 340-3; community-based model 124,
213; constructive engagement model 70, 90-
3, 97; co-sovereignty/ nation-to-nation
model xiv, 160-2, 164-5; Inuit models 108,
114, 130, 161, 382-3; need for various models
108, 113, 114, 167, 399, 405-6; RCAP models
13-14, 62, 128, 130-32, 134. *See also* de facto
self-government; Niga'a; public government
model; state-determination model
Selkirk First Nation (SFN) 48-50, 61
SFN Final Agreement 56

SFN Self-Government Agreement 48-50, 61; exclusive powers 48-9; local powers 49-50
Simon v. The Queen 41
social capital 7, 339, 343, 349, 367
social development of Aboriginal peoples 166, 173, 214, 222, 295, 339
socio-economic conditions vii, xiv, 3, 9, 39, 52, 59, 72, 84, 92, 105, 125, 249, 276, 396
social policy 162-3, 225, 274
social programs 5, 11, 12, 39, 90, 111, 192, 333. *See also* health; education; program delivery; welfare
sovereignty: of Crown 1, 7, 20-2, 23, 26, 41, 63, 69, 74, 79, 83, 88-9, 125, 145-7, 154-5, 311. *See also* Aboriginal sovereignty
spirituality 65, 81, 111, 123, 130, 178-9, 190, 196, 321-3, 340, 357-8, 368, 387; impact of colonialism on 322
starvation policy 252, 253, 258
state-determination model 70, 72-6, 77, 81-5, 87-8, 90-3,
sui generis: Aboriginal sovereignty 20-2, 28, 125; treaty governance 28-9, 32, 147-8
Supreme Court of Canada 6, 27-9, 135, 192, 225, 311-12, 316; Aboriginal member 136; affirming Aboriginal sovereignty 21-2, 40-2, 62-3, 138, 149-50, 406; and *Calder* 6, 43, 80, 227, 355; and the Métis 263, 280, 282-3; and treaty interpretation 31-2, 40, 41-2, 180, 189
surveys 233, 236, 403-5; Aboriginal Peoples Survey (APS) 174-5, 175; health 174-5, 177; TLE 243-4, 246-7, 251-2, 198
surveying for reserves 243-4, 246-7, 251-2, 298; DOFS formula 243-4, 251; Saskatchewan formula 245-6; equity formula 247

taxation: as Aboriginal jurisdiction 11, 43, 53, 56, 112, 152, 162-3, 223, 254, 262, 267, 275; exemptions 80, 114, 136, 165, 246, 247, 288, 409, and objections to exemptions 114, 295; municipal 247, 288, 295, 296-7, 298, 300-1; as revenue source 132, 166, 216, 254, 293; tax dollars to settle claims 248, 409
termination of special status for Indians, policy of viii, xx, 4-5, 11, 14-15, 47, 58, 80, 313; arguments against 27, 42
territorial integrity, principle of 71-2
third level/ third order of government 9, 12, 15, 48, 79, 81, 106, 110, 114, 115, 124-5, 133, 136, 138, 160, 161-2, 164, 165, 193
Tlicho First Nation 53, 56, 61, 162, 163, 166, 379
traditional: culture 1, 8, 15, 29, 46-7, 52-3, 64-5,
110, 124, 130-31, 134, 150-51, 215, 332, 334, 410-11; education 373-7, 381-2; healing ceremonies 180-1, 190, 351, 356-9, 412; knowledge 95, 142, 234-5, 321, 323, 325, 340, 343, 382, 412; government 46-7, 153, 410; law 51, 61, 62, 141, 153, 315; medicine 173-4, 177, 178-81, 182, 188-92, 198, 357-8; values 51, 117-118, 128, 131, 198, 279, 325, 332, 340
traditional lands 39, 41, 44-5, 112, 125, 128, 131, 146, 147, 159, 227, 282, 334, 336
traditional lifestyle 45, 86-7, 196, 206-7, 208, 210, 214-15, 217, 227-8, 341, 357; Métis 262, 264, 268, 270
transfer: of funds xvi, 164, 165, 193, 211; of land to Indians 4, 27, 31, 55, 80, 245, 260, 267, 270, 271, 274, 301; of responsibility to Aboriginals 6, 11, 45, 80, 90, 107, 108, 113, 116, 121, 140, 183-5, 189, 197, 210, 229, 266, 395; of responsibility to provinces 4, 185-6, 243; of sovereignty 83, 88. *See also* northern community transfer
transfer payments 51, 159, 163, 193, 333, 334
Transformative Change Accord 187
Transition Assessment and Planning (TAP) Project 262, 268-9, 276-8
treaties 8, 20-21, 24-5, 39-40, 43, 158, 162, 179, 197, 375-6; as consensual 20, 22-3, 27, 28, 31; Georgian 23, 30; Victorian 23-5, 30; to be interpreted in favour of First Nations 28, 29, 41, 66n10, 180, 189; not honoured 31, 86, 90, 148, 151, 188, 211, 212, 245; spirit of honoured 22, 28, 158, 404-5; as transnational law 20, 28, 31; underlying principles of 21, 23-5, 29, 30, 32, 37, 270. *See also* modern treaties; numbered treaties
treaty commissioner ix, 23-4, 25, 26, 179; Office of the Treaty Commissioner (OTC) 246-8
treaty federalism 20, 26, 27, 29, 31, 160
treaty governance xiii, 20-33
Treaty Land Entitlement (TLE) xvii, 57, 132, 240-1, 243-57; formula 244, 247
Treaty Land Entitlement Framework Agreement (TLEFA) 241, 248, 250, 253, 292, 293, 297-301, 302
Treaty Land Entitlement Implementation Act 300-1.
Treaty of Waitangi 82-3, 88; breaches of 86-7, 89; as foundational document 83
treaty rights 7, 8, 31, 162, 189; abrogated 40, 182; as sacred 22, 28; violated 31, 86, 87, 90, 148, 151, 188, 211, 212, 245
Trudeau, Pierre 4-5, 9, 43, 46, 80, 224, 407
Tsuu T'ina Nation (Alberta) 313

*Gambling with the Future: The Evolution
of Aboriginal Gaming in Canada*
by Yale D. Belanger
$31.00 • ISBN 978-1-895830-286

*Advancing Aboriginal Claims:
Visions/Strategies/Directions*
Kerry Wilkins, ed.
$38.00 • ISBN 978-1-895830-248

*A Breach of Duty: Fiduciary
Obligations and Aboriginal Peoples*
by James I. Reynolds
$38.00 • ISBN 978-1895830-255

*Aboriginal Law: Commentary,
Cases, and Materials*
by Thomas Isaac
$50.00 • ISBN 978-1-895830-231

*Reclaiming Aboriginal Justice,
Identity, and Community*
by Craig Proulx
$31.00 • ISBN 978-1-895830-217

*Who Are Canada's Aboriginal Peoples?
Recognition, Definition, and Jurisdiction*
Paul L.A.H. Chartrand, ed.
$37.00 • ISBN 978-1-895830-200

*An Overview of Aboriginal & Treaty
Rights and Compensation for their Breach*
by Robert Mainville
$27.00 • ISBN 978-1-895830-170

*Aboriginal and Treaty Rights
in the Maritimes: The Marshall
Decision and Beyond*
by Thomas Isaac
$33.00 • ISBN 978-1-895830-194

*Protecting Indigenous Knowledge
and Heritage: A Global Challenge*
by Marie Battiste
and James (Sa'ke'j)
Youngblood Henderson
$36.00 • ISBN 978-1-895830-125

*Urban Indian Reserves: Forging
new Relationships in Saskatchewan*
F. Laurie Barron
and Joseph Garcea, eds.
$36.50 • ISBN 978-1-895830-125

*Justice in Aboriginal Communities:
Sentencing Alternatives*
by Ross Gordon Green
$27.00 • ISBN 978-1-895830-101

*The Dynamics of Native Politics:
The Alberta Metis Experience*
by Joe Sawchuk
$26.00 • ISBN 978-1-895830-095

*Indigenous Peoples of the World:
Their Past, Present and Future*
by Brian Goehring
$15.50 • ISBN 978-1-892830-019

OTHER RELATED TITLES

Cree Narrative Memory:
From Treaties to Contemporary Times
by Neal McLeod
· $25.00 • ISBN 978-1-895830-316

Two Families:
Treaties and Government
by Harold Johnson
$20.00 • ISBN 978-1-895830-293

Treaty Promises, Indian Reality:
Life on a Reserve
by Harold LeRat
with Linda Ungar
$20.00 • ISBN 978-1-895830-262

The Cypress Hills:
An Island by Itself
by Walter Hildebrandt
and Brian Hubner
$25.00 • ISBN 978-1-895830-309

In Palliser's Triangle:
Living in the Grasslands 1850 – 1930
by Barry Potyondi
$18.50 • ISBN 978-1-895830-064

Visit our website for a full list of our titles.
Complete information, including Tables of Contents, can be found at:

WWW.PURICHPUBLISHING.COM